T0394443

Dutch and Contact Linguistics

IMPACT: Studies in Language, Culture and Society
ISSN 1385-7908

IMPACT publishes monographs, collective volumes, and text books on topics in sociolinguistics, anthropological linguistics, and applied linguistics that aim to advance thinking and understanding of the complex intersections of language, culture and society. The scope of the series is broad, with a goal to push traditional disciplinary boundaries through theoretical and methodological innovation. Explorations of new communicative contexts and practices are particularly welcome, as works that break new ground by making connections with other disciplines.

For an overview of all books published in this series, please see *benjamins.com/catalog/impact*

General Editor

Volume 55

Dutch and Contact Linguistics. The Dutch language outside the Low Countries
Edited by Christopher Joby and Nicoline van der Sijs

Dutch and Contact Linguistics

The Dutch language outside the Low Countries

Edited by

Christopher Joby
University of East Anglia

Nicoline van der Sijs
Institute for the Dutch Language

John Benjamins Publishing Company
Amsterdam / Philadelphia

The paper used in this publication meets the minimum requirements of the American National Standard for Information Sciences – Permanence of Paper for Printed Library Materials, ANSI Z39.48-1984.

DOI 10.1075/impact.55

Cataloging-in-Publication Data available from Library of Congress:
LCCN 2025012547 (PRINT) / 2025012548 (E-BOOK)

ISBN 978 90 272 2207 7 (HB)
ISBN 978 90 272 4480 2 (E-BOOK)

John Benjamins Publishing Company · https://benjamins.com

Table of contents

Introduction

Christopher Joby[1,2] & Nicoline van der Sijs[3]
[1] SOAS, University of London | [2] University of East Anglia | [3] Institute for the Dutch Language, Leiden

Introduction

"Dutch is not a world language" is a frequent refrain in discussions about European languages spoken in other parts of the world. More specifically, Peter Hans Nelde has written that "Dutch occupies a position between the major and minor languages of the world" (Nelde 1988: 112). There is of course much truth in these statements, for although speakers of Dutch sailed to the four corners of the earth from the late sixteenth century onwards, their language has not become a first or second language outside Europe in the manner of English, Spanish, Portuguese, and French. The reasons for this are complex and have to do with factors such as language policy and the use of other Languages of Wider Communication such as Portuguese before the arrival of the Dutch. Nevertheless, as Nelde continues, "although Dutch cannot function as an international means of communication because its speech community is too small, it cannot be overlooked in language-contact studies since it has long been involved in very intense language-contact situations" (Nelde 1988: 112). In other words, contact with Dutch has left its mark on many other languages in various ways and even led to the emergence of Dutch-based contact varieties. It is the story of this language contact and its consequences, above all in contact situations outside the Dutch-language area, that forms the basis of the present volume.

State of the subject: Contact linguistics in general

Simply put, contact linguistics is a branch of linguistics which studies language contact, which has been defined as "the situation in which languages [...] influence each other synchronically in shared socio-semiotic contexts" (Steiner 2008: 319). Although scholars have long studied the effects of language contact, in recent years there has been increasing scholarly interest in contact linguistics or contact studies because language contact was recognized as a major factor in lan-

https://doi.org/10.1075/impact.55.intro

guage change. An early work in this field was Uriel Weinreich's *Languages in Contact: Findings and Problems*, published in 1953 (Weinreich 1953). The renowned sociolinguist, William Labov, would later observe that Weinreich's study "remains the fundamental base for studies of multilingual communities and language shift". In 1988, Sarah Thomason and Terrence Kaufman published another landmark work in this field, *Language Contact, Creolization and Genetic Linguistics*. Thomason and Kaufman analyse contact-induced language change and propose a scale of 1–5 for measuring the effects of language contact (Thomason & Kaufman 1988: 74–76). This scale is still used by scholars of contact linguists today. Thomason has been one of the most important scholars in this field. In 2001, she published a state of the subject work *Language Contact – An Introduction* (Thomason 2001). Other important general works on language contact published since the turn of the millennium include Donald Winford's *An Introduction to Contact Linguistics* (Winford 2002); *The Handbook of Language Contact*, edited by Raymond Hickey (Hickey (ed.) 2010); and Lisa Lim and Umberto Ansaldo's *Languages in Contact* (Lim & Ansaldo 2015).

A range of linguistic phenomena arise from language contact. These include code switching, loanwords, grammatical and graphic interference, bilingualism, multilingualism, pidgins, creoles, language shift, and even language death, if all the speakers of one language shift to speaking another language. Afrikaans, for example, is thought to have emerged from contact between speakers of Dutch and speakers of other languages including Malay and Khoisan languages from the seventeenth century onwards (Carstens & Raidt 2019).

Some authors have published works which focus on only one or two of these contact phenomena. Mark Sebba published an extensive study of pidgins and creoles in 1997, whilst Joseph T. Farquharson and Bettina Migge published an edited volume, *Pidgins and Creoles: Critical Concepts in Linguistics*, in 2017 (Sebba 1997; Farquharson & Migge 2017). Articles in the *Journal of Pidgin and Creole Languages* add to our understanding of these outcomes of language contact. Loanwords are a popular theme in contact studies. In 2009, Martin Haspelmath & Uri Tadmor published *Loanwords in the World's Languages: A Comparative Handbook* (2009). As well as analysing loanwords in specific languages, this edited volume includes essays on issues relating to loanwords and loanword typology (Haspelmath 2009; Haspelmath & Tadmor 2009). Two important contributions to the study of another contact phenomenon, bilingualism, are René Appel and Pieter Muysken's *Language Contact and Bilingualism*, first published in 1987 and republished in 2005, and Carol Myers-Scotton's *Contact linguistics. Bilingual encounters and grammatical outcomes*, published in 2002 (Appel & Muysken 2005; Myers-Scotton 2002). Myers-Scotton examines what happens to the grammar of languages when bilingual speakers use both their languages in the same clause. This allows her to examine contact phenomena including lexical borrowing and codeswitching. A recent development in sociolinguistics including contact studies and intercultural communication research is the emergence of "translanguaging". One scholar who has contributed to this development is Li Wei (2017). As is often the case, when a new term or field of enquiry emerges, so too do different definitions. However, scholars agree that a distinctive feature of translanguaging is that it argues for a shift in focus from 'languages' as distinct standardised codes to individuals as agents engaged in creating language (Reynolds 2022: 141).

Other authors focus on language contact in well-defined geographical areas or between one language and others with which it has been in contact. Most of the contributions in an edited volume published in 2000 examine contact phenomena that emerged from contact situations in the USSR and its successor states (Gilbers *et al.* 2000). In 2003, Michael Clyne published a book on contact between English and languages spoken by immigrants in Anglophone countries (Clyne 2003). Clyne explores questions such as why some heritage languages survive longer than others. In 2011, Mark Irwin published his study of the phonological integration of foreign loanwords (*gairaigo*) from other languages into Japanese (Irwin 2011). A more recent example is an edited volume of essays on contact between Spanish and other languages edited by Luis A. Ortiz López (2020). Like the present volume, it analyses contact with several other languages, in this case including Catalan, English, and Quechua, and in a wide range of geographical areas in Spain and the Americas.

State of the subject: Dutch and contact linguistics

As for contact studies involving Dutch and other languages, both the editors of this volume have made contributions in the field, above all Nicoline van der Sijs. Indeed, if any one scholar can be credited with providing impetus to the field of Dutch and contact linguistics, it is Nicoline van der Sijs. She has published many articles and books which analyse the flows of loanwords from Dutch to other languages and vice versa. Three to mention are *Leenwoordenboek* [Loanword dictionary] (1996), *Geleend en uitgeleend: Nederlandse woorden in andere talen & andersom* [Borrowed and loaned out: Dutch words in other languages and vice versa] (1998), and *Nederlandse woorden wereldwijd* [Dutch words worldwide] (2010). Much of her work, however, remains in Dutch. So, one of the advantages of this volume is that it brings some of her work to scholars who do not read Dutch, both in her own contributions and those of other authors.

Thankfully, some of Van der Sijs's publications have been translated into English. One to mention is her book on Dutch as a contact language in North America. The Dutch edition, *Yankees, Cookies en Dollars: De Invloed van het Nederlands op de Noord-Amerikaanse Talen* [Yankees, Cookies and Dollars: The Influence of Dutch on North American Languages] was first published in 2009. The English translation of this was published in 2021 as *Cookies, coleslaw, and stoops: the influence of Dutch on the North American languages.* Finally, Van der Sijs has fully embraced the potential of the digital age and built databases with etymological and dialect information on Dutch including *Etymologiebank.nl* (https://etymologiebank.nl/) and the *Uitleenwoordenbank* (http://uitleenwoordenbank.ivdnt.org/).

Christopher Joby has published monographs on contact between Dutch and other languages, above all English, in early-modern Britain and between Dutch and Japanese and other languages spoken in Japan (1600–1900) (Joby 2015; 2020). He has also written a monograph on Dutch and Spanish missionary linguistics in seventeenth-century Taiwan published in 2025 (Joby 2025). Furthermore, he has published articles on contact between Dutch and other languages in Taiwan, Britain, Japan, and Indonesia. Other authors in the collection have also published important books and articles on language contact. For these, the reader is advised to consult the relevant contributions in this volume. To these we can add Part IV of a volume published in 2013 and edited by Frans Hinskens and Johan Taeldeman, which analyses the dynamics in varieties of Dutch resulting from language contact (Hinskens & Taeldeman 2013).

Contributions in this volume

Whilst all the contributions in this volume concern Dutch and contact linguistics, they are nevertheless marked by their diversity. A distinctive feature of the contributions is their geographical spread, reflecting the extent to which speakers of Dutch have reached the four corners of the earth. Several contributions examine contact between Dutch and other languages in Europe, including English, Polish, Czech, Hungarian, and Lithuanian, and to a lesser extent Latin, German, and French. Historical connections between the Dutch and southern Africa mean, perhaps inevitably, that several contributions examine contact with Afrikaans. Again, because of historical connections between the Dutch and Indonesia, the volume includes chapters on contact with languages spoken in the Indonesian archipelago. Dutch commercial relations with Japan mean that Japanese imported not only goods, but also loanwords from the Dutch, and created calques based on Dutch words, which were subsequently reloaned to other languages in East

Asia. As for the Americas, Dutch activities in the Caribbean inevitably resulted in contact with other languages, whilst emigration from Belgium to the US in the nineteenth century resulted in contact between Dutch and English in the American Mid-West, above all around the Great Lakes region. Finally, Martin Konvička brings us right up-to-date by analysing language contact not in a geographical space, but in cyberspace, on social media such as Twitter/X.

This geographical spread inevitably means that the contributions in this volume analyse languages with which Dutch had contact, which belong to many different language families and branches of those families and which are typologically diverse. Within Europe, Dutch has had contact with other Germanic languages, for example, English, Romance languages such as French and Latin, Slavic languages such as Polish and Czech, an East Baltic language, Lithuanian, and a Uralic language, Hungarian. Outside Europe, Dutch had contact with Portuguese in several geographical areas, such as the Indonesian archipelago, as the contributions of Reinier Salverda and Antoinette Schapper & Maria Zielenbach illustrate. Three of the contributions focus on contact between Dutch and Afrikaans. The comprehensive account of Dutch loanword borrowing presented by Van der Sijs in the opening chapter adds many more languages to this list. Joby's first contribution, on the other hand, illustrates that contact between Japanese and other languages in East Asia led to Dutch loanword borrowing in Taiwanese Austronesian or Formosan languages, an Austroasiatic language, Vietnamese, and possibly a Turkic language, Uygur.

Several contributions analyse contact between Dutch and the same language but focus on different contact phenomena. Two such languages are Polish and Afrikaans. Agata Kowalska-Szubert analyses Dutch loanwords in Polish, either directly, or via intermediate languages, whereas Paul Hulsenboom examines Dutch-Polish bilingualism in the seventeenth century. Two contributions, one by Adri Breed and Daniel Van Olmen, and the other by Maarten Bogaards and Roné Wierenga, compare specific grammatical features of Afrikaans and Dutch. By contrast, Gerhard van Huyssteen examines changes in Dutch *maledicta* adopted by Afrikaans.

As with Agata Kowalska-Szubert (Polish) and Kateřina Křížová's (Czech) chapter, several authors analyse Dutch loanwords in other languages. They nevertheless employ a range of methodologies to explore lexical interference. In the first chapter, Nicoline van der Sijs takes a statistical approach to examine the relative influence of Dutch on the lexis of other languages and indeed the relative extent to which languages in different continents have borrowed Dutch loanwords. By contrast, in her second contribution, Van der Sijs examines the sociolinguistic conditions, which may have influenced patterns of languages borrowing Dutch names for animals. In the second chapter, Christopher Joby analyses the effect of differences in phonemic sets, phonotactics, and morphology between Dutch and languages in East Asia on the form of Dutch loanwords adopted by these languages. Kowalska-Szubert and Křížová by contrast take a comparative approach by analysing why patterns of Dutch loanword borrowing by two languages that are linguistically and geographically close, Polish and Czech, are significantly different. The contributions on Dutch loanword borrowings also exhibit methodological diversity. Whereas Nicoline van der Sijs's first contribution and other contributions such as Roland Nagy's analysis of Dutch loanwords in Hungarian are quantitative analyses of lexical interference, Yasmin Crombez's study of language contact between Dutch and English in the United States adopts a largely qualitative approach to analysing the consequences of this contact using three Flemish-American newspapers published between 1890 and 1959. Specifically, she focusses on the discourse surrounding the use of Dutch and English in contact and conflict to discover the language beliefs propagated by the immigrant-language newspapers. Finally, whilst some contributions focus on contact between Dutch and one or two other languages, the first contributions of Van der Sijs and Joby, and the chapters by Roland Nagy, Antoinette Schapper & Maria Zielenbach, and Agata Kowalska-Szubert & Kateřina Křížová analyse the phenomenon that we describe as the "circulation of loanwords", i.e., the borrowing and re-borrowing of Dutch loanwords across several languages and the changes that these loanwords undergo.

In recent years, there has been increased academic interest in heritage languages. Several studies have analysed Dutch as a heritage language. In 1994, Kees de Bot and Michael Clyne examined the use of Dutch and English by Dutch immigrants in Australia (De Bot & Clyne 1994). Caroline Smits (1996) analysed the use of Dutch by immigrants who arrived in the American state of Iowa in the nineteenth century, whilst Madeleine Hulsen (2000) analysed language shift amongst three generations of Dutch migrants to New Zealand. In the present volume, Yasmin Crombez analyses extra-linguistic factors in language shift from Dutch to English amongst Flemish emigrants in the United States from the late nineteenth century onwards. Suzanne Aalberse and Robert Cloutier, by contrast, take a comparative approach by analysing linguistic variation in heritage Dutch in seven areas across the world.

Contact between speakers of Dutch and other languages resulted in the emergence of several creoles. One of these is Skepi, a now-extinct Dutch-lexified creole spoken along the Essequibo River, in what is today the Republic of Guyana. In their contribution, Bart Jacobs and Mikael Parkvall use historical records to analyse selected grammatical features of Skepi. Reinier Salverda, on the other hand, provides a diachronic analysis of data on a Portuguese-lexified creole, Tugu, and a Dutch-lexified creole, Petjoh, that emerged because of contact between

Dutch and other languages in Java. A *sprachbund* is a group of languages that share areal features because of geographical proximity and language contact. Scholars argue that Dutch is a core member of the Standard Average European (SAE) *sprachbund* (Haspelmath 1998: 271). In their contribution, Breed and Van Olmen test the theory that languages in the Standard Average European *sprachbund* can demonstrate SAE features outside Europe (Van der Auwera 2011: 299).

Individual and societal bilingualism and multilingualism often form the background to language contact. In some contributions in this volume, they are very much in the foreground. Paul Hulsenboom analyses individual and community bilingualism involving Dutch and Polish in the Dutch Republic and the Polish-Lithuanian Commonwealth. Reinier Salverda, on the other hand, offers a descriptive linguistic history of how Dutch functioned in the multilingual environment of Indonesia from c. 1600 onwards and outcomes of language contact in that environment. A recent development in sociolinguistics including contact studies and intercultural communication research is the emergence of "translanguaging", which describes a set of language practices of individual bilinguals and multilinguals. To date, most research on translanguaging has focused on contemporary language practices. In his second chapter, however, Joby offers a case study of translanguaging in a historical context. On a different note, Emma Hoebens offers a distinctive contribution by analysing Dutch call names amongst Mennonites of Dutch ancestry in Mennonite communities in Mexico.

Many outcomes of language contact occur because of contact between speakers of different languages. With translation, by contrast, we are dealing with written contact. Gina Kavaliūnaitė analyses how the language of a Lithuanian translation of the Bible was shaped by the language of the source text, the Dutch States Bible, first published in 1637. Many of the Dutch loanwords in Japanese were borrowed because of Japanese translations of Dutch scientific texts (Joby 2020). In his first contribution, Joby analyses how these were integrated into the Japanese phonotactic system and then borrowed by other languages written in Sinitic script including Sinitic varieties, such as Mandarin and Hokkien Chinese, Korean, and Vietnamese. He situates his study in a broader methodological context by employing a typology of outcomes of lexical interference developed by Martin Haspelmath and modified by the Formosanist, Rik De Busser (2018). Joby's contribution is also distinctive as it analyses Dutch lexical contact phenomena in writing systems other than the Roman alphabet, above all Sinitic script. Furthermore, Japanese is a pitch-accent language, whilst some of the other recipient languages are tonal.

Another co-ordinate in the volume is a temporal one. Although, of course, Dutch did have contact with other languages in the medieval period, it was in the early modern period, during the Age of European Expansion, that for the first time Dutch had contact with many new languages, both inside and outside Europe. Joby's second contribution analyses contact between Dutch and other languages in sixteenth and seventeenth-century Norwich. Antoinette Schapper and Maria Zielenbach examine Dutch loanword borrowing in languages in the eastern islands of the Indonesian archipelago, with which Dutch had contact from the beginning of the seventeenth century. Yasmin Crombez, on the other hand, focusses on language contact between Dutch-speaking Flemish emigrant communities and local populations in the United States from the late nineteenth century to the mid-twentieth century. Crombez in fact takes a diachronic approach to analysing this language contact. Likewise, Reinier Salverda takes a diachronic approach, analysing linguistic innovation over time in creoles spoken in Java. Other authors, such as Bogaards and Wieringa, take an essentially synchronic approach.

The study of language contact offers a way into thinking about reasons for population movements, and is therefore of interest to social, political, and economic historians. Much contact between Dutch and other languages resulted from the trading activities of the Dutch East India and West India Companies in the seventeenth and eighteenth centuries. However, this is not the whole story. As Joby observes in his second contribution, thousands of Dutch-speakers moved to Norwich in eastern England in the second half of the sixteenth century because of religious persecution and economic hardship. Likewise, Mennonite communities such as the one in Mexico that Emma Hoebens describes in her contribution on call names are descendants of Anabaptists from the sixteenth-century Netherlands. Religious tolerance in early modern Poland attracted migrants from the Low Countries. Furthermore, Dutch drainage workers and engineers migrated to and settled in Poland. Traces of the linguistic consequences of these population movements survive to the present day. On a different note, Paul Hulsenboom's analysis of Dutch-Polish bilingualism in the seventeenth century provides us with fresh perspectives on cultural and intellectual exchange between the Dutch Republic and the Polish-Lithuanian Commonwealth in this period. Something similar can be said of historical relations between Dutch and Hungarian polities in Roland Nagy's analysis of Dutch loanwords in Hungarian.

On a human level, the authors in this collection are at various stages of their academic careers. Whilst Yasmin Crombez, Martin Konvička, and Emma Hoebens are in the early stages of promising academic careers, other authors such as Nicoline van der Sijs, Reinier Salverda, and Adri Breed have built international reputations over long periods of time in their respective fields. The authors also have a range of nationalities. About a dozen authors are European: some from the Low Countries, and others from countries in Western, Central, Northern, and Eastern Europe. Several authors are from South Africa, and one is from Australia.

As far as possible, authors have attempted to place their studies and findings in broader research contexts. For example, Jacobs and Parkvall's analysis of Skepi allows them to contribute to an important debate in linguistics about whether creoles are genetic continuations of their lexifiers or nativised pidgins that defy classification along the family tree model. Work, however, remains to be done. This volume has intentionally focused on contact between Dutch and other languages *outside* the Dutch language area. Further work, possibly in the form of a second edited volume, could usefully be done on contact between Dutch and other languages *inside* and on the periphery of the Dutch language area. Another coordinate that requires further investigation is contact between Dutch and other languages in the Middle Ages. This, too, might be the subject of a future edited volume.

Concluding, this introduction has illustrated the diversity of the contributions and the richness of the theme of Dutch and Contact Linguistics, and placed it within the existing literature. Furthermore, it has hopefully whetted the reader's appetite for the main course of eighteen chapters on this theme and above all illustrates that although Dutch is not a world language, it cannot, as Peter Nelde rightly argued, be overlooked in language-contact studies.

References

Appel, René & Pieter Muysken. 2005. *Language Contact and Bilingualism.* Amsterdam: AUP [first ed. London: Edward Arnold, 1987].

doi Van der Auwera, Johan. 2011. "Standard Average European." In *The Languages and Linguistics of Europe: A Comprehensive Guide*, ed. by B. Kortmann, J. Van der Auwera, 291–306. Berlin: Mouton de Gruyter.

doi De Bot, Kees & Clyne, Michael. 1994. "A 16-Year Longitudinal Study of Language Attrition in Dutch immigrants in Australia," *Journal of Multilingual and Multicultural Development*, 15(1): 17–28.

Carstens, W.A.M., & E.H. Raidt. 2019. *Die Storie van Afrikaans uit Europa en van Afrika. Deel 2, Die Afrikageskiedenis van Afrikaans.* Eerste uitgawe, eerste druk. Pretoria: Protea Boekhuis.

doi Clyne, Michael. 2003. *Dynamics of language contact. English and immigrant languages. Cambridge approaches to language contact.* Cambridge: CUP.

De Busser, Rik. 2018. "An overview of linguistic mechanisms introducing a Christian conceptual universe into the Bunun language", *Ethnologia* 42: 5–38.

Farquharson, Joseph T. and Bettina Migge, ed. 2017. *Pidgins and Creoles: Critical Concepts in Linguistics*, I. London: Routledge.

doi Gilbers, Dicky et al.. 2000. *Languages in Contact.* Amsterdam: Rodopi.

doi Haspelmath, Martin. 1998. "How young is standard average European?" *Language Sciences*, 20(3): 271–287.

doi Haspelmath, Martin. 2009. "Lexical borrowing: Concepts and issues." In *Loanwords in the World's Languages: A Comparative Handbook*, ed. by Martin Haspelmath and Uri Tadmor, 35–54. Berlin: De Gruyter Mouton.

doi Haspelmath, Martin & Uri Tadmor. 2009. "The Loanword Typology Project and the World Loanword Database." In *Loanwords in the World's Languages: A Comparative Handbook*, ed. by Martin Haspelmath and Uri Tadmor, 1–34. Berlin: De Gruyter Mouton.

doi Hickey, Raymond (ed.). 2010. *The Handbook of Language Contact*. Malden, MA: Wiley-Blackwell.

Hinskens, Frans, & Johan Taeldeman. 2013. *Band 30: Language and Space: An International Handbook of Linguistic Variation: Dutch*. Berlin: De Gruyter Mouton.

Hulsen, Madeleine. 2000. *Language Loss and Language Processing: Three Generations of Dutch Migrants in New Zealand*. PhD thesis, RU Nijmegen.

doi Irwin, Mark. 2011. *Loanwords in Japanese*. Amsterdam: John Benjamins.

doi Joby, Christopher. 2015. *The Dutch Language in Britain (1550–1702)*. Leiden: Brill.

Joby, Christopher. 2020. *The Dutch Language in Japan (1600–1900)*. Leiden: Brill.

doi Joby, Christopher. 2025. *Christian Mission in Seventeenth-Century Taiwan*. Leiden: Brill.

Li, Wei. 2017. "Translanguaging as a Practical Theory of Language," *Applied Linguistics*, 39.1: 9–30.

doi Lim, Lisa & Umberto Ansaldo. 2015. *Languages in Contact*. Cambridge: CUP.

doi Myers-Scotton, Carol. 2002. *Contact linguistics. Bilingual encounters and grammatical outcomes*. Oxford: Oxford University Press.

doi Nelde, Peter Hans. 1988. "Dutch as a language of contact," *International Journal of the Sociology of Language*, 73: 111–9.

doi Ortiz López, Luis A., et al.. eds. 2020. *Hispanic Contact Linguistics: Theoretical, Methodological and Empirical Perspectives*. Amsterdam: John Benjamins Publishing Company.

Reynolds, Matthew. 2022. "Translanguaging Comparative Literature," *Recherche Littéraire / Literary Research, vol. 38, International Association for Comparative Literature*: 141–53.

doi Sebba, Mark. 1997. *Contact languages: pidgins and creoles*. New York: St. Martin's Press.

Smits, Caroline. 1996. *Disintegration of Inflection: The Case of Iowa Dutch*. The Hague: Holland Institute of Generative Linguistics.

doi Steiner, Erich. 2008. "Empirical studies of translations as a mode of language contact: 'Explicitness' of lexicogrammatical encoding as a relevant dimension." In *Language Contact and Contact Languages*, ed. by Peter Siemund & Noemi Kintana, 316–45. Amsterdam: John Benjamins.

Van der Sijs, Nicoline. 1996. *Leenwoordenboek*. The Hague: SDU Uitgevers.

Van der Sijs, Nicoline. 1998. *Geleend en uitgeleend: Nederlandse woorden in andere talen & andersom*. Amsterdam: Contact.

doi Van der Sijs, Nicoline. 2009. *Yankees, Cookies En Dollars: De Invloed van Het Nederlands Op de Noord-Amerikaanse Talen*. Amsterdam: AUP.

Van der Sijs, Nicoline. 2010. *Nederlandse woorden wereldwijd*. The Hague: SDU Uitgevers.

Van der Sijs, Nicoline. 2021. *Cookies, coleslaw, and stoops: the influence of Dutch on the North American languages*. Amsterdam: AUP.

Thomason, Sarah. 2001. *Language Contact – An Introduction*. Edinburgh: Edinburgh University Press

Thomason, Sarah & Terrence Kaufman. 1988. *Language Contact, Creolization and Genetic Linguistics*. Berkeley, CA: University of California Press.

Weinreich, Uriel. 1953. *Languages in Contact: Findings and Problems*. New York: Publications of the Linguistic circle of New York, No. 1.

Winford, Donald. 2002. *An Introduction to Contact Linguistics*. Oxford: Blackwell.

CHAPTER 1

The role of Dutch in the circulation of loanwords

Nicoline van der Sijs
Institute for the Dutch Language, Leiden

The speakers of Dutch have always been in contact with speakers of other languages. In olden times, immigrants moved to the Low Countries for their freedom, wealth and employment, and Dutch speakers maintained trade contacts with European countries and, after 1600, with countries in other continents. Some Dutch speakers settled abroad for some time. As a result, Dutch absorbed loanwords from many languages, and Dutch words were exported to other languages. It is self-evident that Dutch, being present on most continents, served as an intermediary language for loanwords: Dutch brought, for instance, Asian words to Europe, and Dutch spread French, Latin, English and German loanwords to other European languages, such as Russian, and to languages spoken on other continents. However, until now it has been unclear exactly what role Dutch played in the circulation of loanwords. In this chapter I shall address this question, based on some recently-compiled large databases.

Keywords: loanwords into Dutch, words imported from Dutch, migration, historical sociolinguistics

1. Introduction

The Dutch language area has no natural land boundaries: the territory changes without interruption into the German area in the east, and into the French area in the south. The main rivers (Rhine, Meuse) and the North Sea have from ancient times served as trade routes. The Low Countries have always been open to cultural and political influences from outside, and the inhabitants could not do without trade with other countries. The speakers of Dutch, then, have always been in contact with native speakers of other languages. As is well known, language contacts inevitably result in loanwords being adopted; the extent to which may vary, depending on all sorts of factors. This means that in some periods more words were borrowed than in others, or more words from a specific language.

https://doi.org/10.1075/impact.55.01sij

In this chapter I shall first describe broadly what language contacts there have been between Dutch and other languages in the course of time (Section 2). Next, in Sections 3 and 4, the loanwords into and from Dutch that resulted from those contacts will be discussed. Both sections begin with a description of the databases that have provided the information on the loanword data. I shall concentrate not so much on individual loanwords, but on general tendencies: from which languages did Dutch adopt most loanwords, and which languages borrowed most Dutch words? How extensive was the influx and the export of loanwords? In Section 5 a comparison is presented: the question will be addressed whether linguistic influence was mutual or one-way traffic. Some explanations for the general tendencies are given. In Section 6, I shall examine the role of Dutch as an intermediary language, and in Section 7 I shall draw some initial general conclusions on the role of Dutch in the transfer of loanwords.

2. Language contacts between Dutch and other languages

Which languages did the inhabitants of the Low Countries come into contact with over time? The language contacts within Europe are described in Section 2.1, while Section 2.2 is devoted to language contacts outside Europe. In each section, I will also briefly discuss the status of the various foreign languages, and the language skills of Dutch speakers. This is relevant because it is a well-established fact that bilinguals play an important role in the transfer of loanwords (Appel & Muysken 1987; Hickey 2013; Van Coetsem 2000).

2.1 Dutch language contacts in Europe

Which European languages did the inhabitants of the Low Countries come into contact with?

We can distinguish three layers: indigenous languages other than Dutch, neighbouring languages, and more distant languages.

The first layer consists of three languages: Frisian, Latin and Yiddish. Within the borders of the Netherlands traditionally not only Dutch dialects are spoken but also ***Frisian***. In the first centuries AD, Frisian was spoken in the coastal area between the Rhine in the west and the Ems and Weser in the east. But from the seventh century onwards, Dutch dialects spread into the Frisian-speaking area, which was increasingly reduced (see Munske (ed.) 2001). The influence of Dutch on Frisian became even stronger in the seventeenth century, when a written Standard Dutch language was developed. Currently, Frisian is spoken in the province of Friesland, in the far west of Groningen, and in Northwestern Germany. In addition, the Frisian substrate is still clearly present in many North Holland dialects. In the twenty-first century Frisian is recognized in Friesland as a second language and is taught at schools. In the Netherlands it is the native language of approximately 350,000 people, all of whom are bilingual Dutch and Frisian, and the number of speakers is steadily decreasing (Van der Sijs 2019a: 185–188).

Latin was spoken from 57 BC until the fifth century AD, when the south of the Low Countries was part of the Roman Empire. In the Middle Ages, Latin was, for the scholarly, literary and religious elite in Western Europe, a language in which they frequently communicated, both in speaking and in writing. In the sixteenth century, the position of Latin as the language of the church deteriorated, because the Protestants preferred their national languages. From the end of the sixteenth century, a growing number of literary and scientific works were written in the national language. But Latin remained the official language at universities and remained in use as the language of scholarship (Van der Sijs 2021: 34–36, Van der Sijs & Engelsman 2000, Van der Wal 1995: 36–38). Scholars were for a long time bilingual.

Yiddish was introduced in the Netherlands around 1620 by German Jews or Ashkenazim, having fled from persecutions in Germany. Most of them went to the Dutch Republic; not before the early part of the eighteenth century did a small number of Ashkenazim move to the Southern Netherlands. They were poor exiles, and their language was not very prestigious (Van der Sijs 2014: 127–128; Van der Sijs (ed.) 2005, Chapter 4). Jews in the Republic lived in a certain isolation. In 1796, under the French regime, Jews were given equal civil rights and were admitted to public schools. From 1857 onwards, they were obliged to attend public schools, which heralded the end of Yiddish as a spoken language in the Netherlands.

Of the neighbouring languages ***French*** had the longest and strongest influence on Dutch (Van der Sijs 2001: 213–215; Van der Sijs 2005: 162–226), partly because French was an important and prestigious language in the administrative domain, in trade and at court, and partly through personal contact with French speakers, especially in the Southern Netherlands, where many bilinguals lived. French influence has been evident since the thirteenth century. In 1482, the 'French school' was founded in the Netherlands, a commercial training course for the middle class where, among other things, French was taught as a foreign language. In the sixteenth and, especially, the seventeenth century, many Protestant refugees from France settled in the Dutch Republic, the more so when religious liberty in France was ended with the Revocation of the Edict of Nantes in 1685. In the Northern Netherlands, the position of French in the administrative domain deteriorated after 1582 – in that year, the States General decreed that the majority of the official documents should be written in Dutch instead of French. In the Southern Netherlands, French remained the main language used for official documents (De Vries et al. 2009: Chapter 11).

The influence of France did not only apply to the Low Countries but to the whole of Western Europe: for centuries France set the tone in all kinds of areas – in politics and military affairs, but also in art, music, food and clothing. From the fourteenth century until about 1800, French was the court language and the language of the highest circles in much of Europe. That changed in the Napoleonic era. In 1795, the troops of the French Republic annexed the Southern Netherlands and invaded the Northern Netherlands. In 1806, the Kingdom of Holland was formed under Louis Napoleon. This lasted until 1813. After that, the influence of France on Dutch society declined sharply throughout the nineteenth century (Assendelft 2023). When Belgium became a sovereign state in 1830, French had a firm position in society, but in the following years Dutch (or Flemish) gradually gained ground over French (Verheyden 2023).

From early on, there were intensive contacts with the neighbouring ***German*** language area; such contacts were facilitated by the fact that the dialects formed a continuum regardless of the boundary between the various states (Van der Sijs 2010: 62–64). The north and the east of the Netherlands attracted many German farm labourers who found work there temporarily or permanently, while in the seventeenth and eighteenth centuries many speakers of German came to the large Dutch cities, especially Amsterdam, to find work, or to take service in the Dutch East India Company or in the Dutch army. The inhabitants of the Republic doubtless heard many German dialects being spoken, but because these resembled Dutch dialects in many respects and the spoken language in this period showed great variation, it will perhaps not always have struck them as in any way remarkable (Van der Sijs 2021: 42–47). People did not yet distinguish sharply between Dutch and German. Some thought that Dutch had developed from German, while others regarded the two as variants, calling Dutch *Nederduits* 'Low Dutch', as opposed to *Hoogduits* 'High Dutch' for German. Because of the close relationship, the borrowing of German loanwords to replace French or Latin terms was encouraged (Van der Sijs 2021: 88–93).

Trade relations with Germany, too, always played a prominent role. In the Middle Ages, till the end of the sixteenth century, the Hanseatic League was a powerful organization, with merchants from present-day German, Dutch and Flemish towns and cities among its members. It dominated commerce in the North Sea and the Baltic Sea, carrying on trade with more northerly and eastern territories: the Scandinavian, Baltic, and Slavic countries, but also England. The central region from which the Hansa operated was Northern Germany and the Eastern Netherlands – the language of communication being the language spoken there, Saxon or ***Middle Low German***, a language that had a strong position in the Middle Ages (Van der Sijs 2006a: 36–38; Van der Sijs 2010: 97–99). Towards the end of the sixteenth century, the influence of the Hanseatic League dwindled, but the ties between the Republic and the Scandinavian countries remained strong: from 1521 on, groups of Dutch immigrants settled in Denmark. During his long rule of Denmark and Norway (1588–1648), King Christiaan IV was greatly impressed by the Dutch craftmanship, and he took in Dutch artisans, engineers, architects, and painters. When Gustav II Adolf became King of Sweden in 1611, he attracted Dutch contractors to help raise Sweden to a higher level. In 1621 Dutch architects built Gothenburg, and Dutch citizens became members of the city council. For a long time, Dutch was an official language of Gothenburg, next to Swedish (Van der Sijs 2006a: 72–74, 82–83, 93, 102; Van der Sijs 2010: 59–61, 102, 131–132).

Dutch speakers came into contact with ***English***, too, although that did not play an important role in Dutch society – unlike French, Latin or German. In the Middle Ages, a constant stream of North and South Netherlandic artisans travelled to England. They brought new industrial techniques to England and were thus able to earn a very comfortable living there. During the Dutch Revolt (1568–1648) many people from the Northern and Southern Netherlands fled to England, and English regiments were stationed in the Republic to help the Dutch in their fight against the Spaniards. But in the seventeenth century, too, three wars were fought against the English, followed in the eighteenth century by the Fourth Anglo-Dutch War (Joby 2015; Bense 1924).

Towards the end of the seventeenth century, close contacts developed with ***Russia*** as a result of Tsar Peter the Great's interest in the technological know-how of the Republic. He visited the Republic several times and took Dutch artisans, especially shipbuilders and architects, back with him to the newly-founded city of St. Petersburg (Van der Meulen 1909, 1959; Van der Sijs 2010: 111–112).

Already in the Middle Ages, the Dutch came into contact with ***Italian*** when Italian bankers settled in the Low Countries, introducing a new method of trading, of making payments by means of drafts, of money exchange and of the double or 'Italian' system of bookkeeping. Also, many Dutch artists – especially painters – travelled to Italy, the birthplace of the Renaissance, and, in the seventeenth century, of modern music and light opera (De Bruijn-van der Helm 1992, Francescato 1966, Van der Sijs 2001: 238–249).

There were of course contacts with ***Spanish*** during the Dutch Revolt, and also on the seas that Spanish, Portuguese and Dutch traders navigated on their way to other continents. The remaining European languages only played a marginal role, as witnessed by the relatively small number of loanwords in Dutch, mentioned in Table 1 of Section 3.

2.2 Dutch language contacts outside Europe

From the beginning of the seventeenth century the influence of the Republic expanded to other continents, in the wake of Spanish and Portuguese explorers such as Columbus and Vasco da Gama, who had travelled to America and Asia towards the end of the fifteenth century. In 1602, the East India Company (VOC) was founded for the trade with Asia, and in 1621, the West India Company (WIC) was set up for the transport of commodities and slaves from Africa to the Caribbean. For the slave trade, Dutch forts were built on the West Coast of Africa, especially in Ghana and the Ivory Coast. In India, Turkey and in Arab-speaking territories, factories were built, and with China, too, the Dutch were carrying on trade (see the contribution from Joby in this book).

Dutch traders settled all over Asia, notably on islands in the Indonesian archipelago, Sri Lanka (then called Ceylon), Taiwan (then Formosa) and on Deshima on the west coast of Japan. From these territories they expelled the Portuguese who had settled there before. The number of Dutchmen going to the territories was always small and they generally stayed there for a short while. Indonesia saw the birth of a few Dutch-based creole languages, or rather mixed languages: Petjoh with Malay, and Javindo with Javanese as the grammatical basis. But all this happened especially after 1800, because not until then did large groups of Dutch colonists settle in Indonesia for a longer period (Van der Sijs 2014: 127).

In 1609, the first settlers from the Low Countries landed on the American east coast, where they founded a Dutch province which they called New Netherland, with New Amsterdam as its capital. The colonists traded with Native American tribes and came into contact with various Amerindian languages. As early as 1664, the colony was taken over by the English. Still, this was not the end of the language contacts with the North American continent: the Dutch settlement held on to the Dutch language until well into the nineteenth century, and during the nineteenth and twentieth centuries a large number of new Dutch and Flemish immigrants settled in the US (Van der Sijs 2009a, and see the contribution from Crombez in this book).

In 1499, the islands of Aruba, Bonaire, Curaçao, Sint-Maarten, Sint-Eustatius and Saba (the Dutch Antilles) were conquered by Spain. There, the creole language Papiamentu developed. In 1634 the Dutch West India Company took over the islands. There is no consensus about the genesis of Papiamentu, however it is believed to be based on African languages, Portuguese, Spanish and, later, Dutch (Fouse 2002; Van der Sijs 2010: 104). In 1667, Holland took over Suriname from the English. Already during the English rule, the English-based creole language Sranan Tongo (literally 'Suriname language') had developed. Both on the Dutch

Antilles and in Suriname, Dutch was and still is the official language in administration and education.

For a while (1624–1654), Dutch colonists lived in a small area of Brazil, and for a longer time they occupied what is now called Guyana. Here, two creole languages developed based on Dutch: Berbice Dutch, which flourished between 1730 and 1830, and Skepi Dutch, spoken in the region of Essequibo (Iskepe) in the seventeenth and eighteenth centuries (Kouwenberg 1993, Robertson 1989, Van Rossem 2021). In 1800, Guyana passed over from Dutch into British ownership.

Around 1665, Dutch colonists settled on the Maagdeneilanden (called US Virgin Islands nowadays), but the islands were never Dutch. Yet, the creole language, Virgin Islands Dutch Creole (in the past called *Negerhollands* 'Negro Dutch'), was developed here, based especially on the Dutch dialect of the province of Zeeland. Virgin Islands Dutch Creole was spoken from around 1700. The last speaker died in 1987. All these Dutch-based creole languages have by now become extinct (Van Rossem 2017, Van Sluijs 2017, Van der Sijs 2005: 187–194, Van der Sijs 2014).

In 1652, the Dutch built a staging harbour in South Africa, which they used as a stopping place in their travels between the Indonesian Archipelago and the homeland. This post developed into a permanent settlement. Here, under the influence of the local languages, Dutch followed its own special development, resulting in what is now called a daughter language of Dutch, *Afrikaans* (Van den Toorn et al. 1997: Chapter 10).

The spread of Dutch came to a standstill around 1800. After the French invasion of the Dutch Republic, the Batavian Republic was founded in 1795, in fact as a vassal state of France, ruled by Napoleon. France was at war with Great Britain and involved the Republic in this war. The English took over the Dutch colonies on other continents one by one, for example Ceylon in 1796. The Peace of Amiens in 1802 stipulated that the Republic would regain all British-occupied colonies, except Ceylon. The following year, however, war between Great Britain and France resumed, and in 1803 the English took over the Dutch colony of Berbice along the river of the same name in present-day British Guiana. In 1811, Java became the last colony in the hands of Great Britain. In 1814, a treaty was concluded with Great Britain on the colonies, which provided, among other things, that the Netherlands retained the East Indies, but that Great Britain definitively took over the areas in Guyana (Essequibo, Berbice and Demerara), Ceylon and South Africa. The Netherlands regained Malabar in the East Indies (except Cochin), but in 1824 this was also transferred to the English.

In 1798 the Batavian Republic received its first constitution. This stipulated, among other things, that the assets of the Dutch East India Company would be transferred to the State, which formally marked the start of the colonial period. That period ended in 1954, when the Statute of the Kingdom of the Netherlands established that Suriname and the Dutch Antilles were given autonomous status within the Kingdom. Indonesia had become independent in 1949. In 1962, the Netherlands' last Asian possession, New Guinea (modern Papua), fell to Indonesia, despite resistance from the Dutch government. Dutch rule here was only short-lived (from 1828) and superficial.

Belgium, which became an independent state in 1830, also had a colony in the twentieth century, namely Congo in Africa (later Ruanda-Urundi was added). But here the administrative language was French, not Dutch or Flemish. Congo became independent in 1960.

Unlike English and French, Dutch was not adopted as an official language on other continents during the colonial period, except as an administrative language for (Dutch) civil servants. On the Dutch Antilles, Dutch became the official language of education in 1819, and in Suriname from 1876 onwards all children were compelled to learn Dutch. Indonesians were not admitted to Dutch schools until 1864 onwards, and then only the Indonesian elite. The Dutch government decided that education in Dutch for all Indonesian children was not in the interest of the Dutch, because through Dutch the Indonesian population gained access to Western knowledge, and this might give them ideas about autonomy. At the end of the colonial period, less than two percent of the Indonesian population knew Dutch. However, since the Indonesian Archipelago is densely populated, this still amounted to one and a half million people. This number far exceeds the whole population of Suriname and the Dutch Antilles together (Groeneboer 1993, 1998; Van der Sijs 2022).

South Africa was a special case: although it became part of the British Empire in 1814, Dutch remained an important everyday language. When the Union of South Africa was formed in 1910 as an independent state within the British Commonwealth, Dutch was declared an official language of the Union, next to and on an equal footing with English. From 1925 until 1961, Afrikaans was considered by law to be a variant of Dutch. The Constitution of 1961 declared English and Afrikaans as the official languages, and Afrikaans was deemed to include Dutch. In 1983 any mention of Dutch was removed.

The area where Dutch is spoken has shrunk considerably since the first half of the twentieth century, as seen from Maps 1 and 2, and as a result the Dutch influence on other languages has also diminished. Dutch is still fairly strong in South America and the Caribbean: it is the official language in the former Dutch Antilles, next to Papiamentu and English, and in Suriname, which became an independent republic in 1975. While the position of Dutch on the Antilles is very weak and only used in formal situations, in Suriname Dutch is the binding factor between the many languages spoken there, such as Sranan Tongo, Surinamese-Javanese, Saramaccan and Sarnami.

Map 1. Dutch settlements or factories in the seventeenth and eighteenth centuries (source: Van der Sijs (ed.) 2011: 76–77)

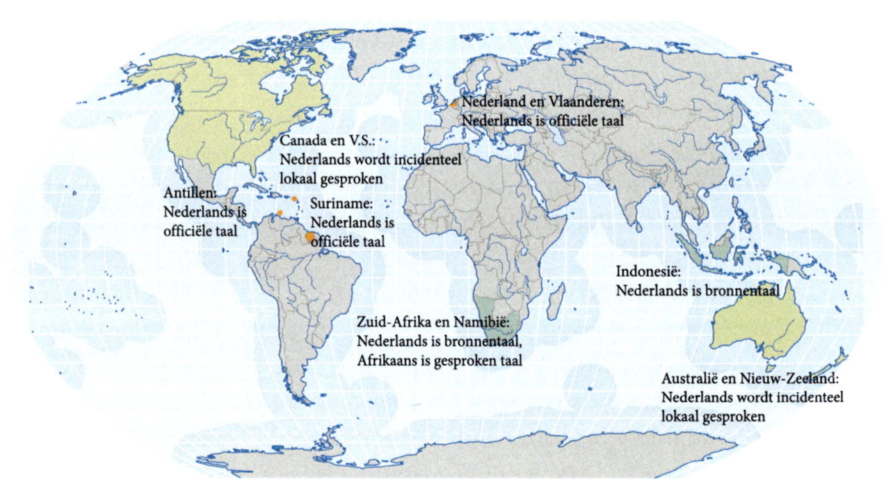

Map 2. The current position of Dutch in the world: in red areas, Dutch is an official language; in dark green areas, Dutch is an important archival language (historical sources, official documents, legal decisions, etc. are written in Dutch), and in light green areas, Dutch is occasionally spoken locally (source: Van der Sijs (ed.) 2011: 80–81)

3. Loanwords in Dutch

From which languages has Dutch borrowed words because of the language contacts mentioned in Section 2? And what (relative) numbers are we talking about? I have drawn the answers to these questions from several databases. In Section 3.1, I shall describe how these were put together, and what their methodological possibilities and restrictions are. In Section 3.2, the data from the databases will be presented.

3.1 The databases

In the past, I composed two substantial databases in which I indicated for each entry whether it was a native word or a loanword. The databases are the *Etymological Dictionary* with 31,038 entries (Van Veen & Van der Sijs 1997) and the *Chronological Dictionary* with 18,540 entries (Van der Sijs 2001).[1] For every loanword the source language is indicated.

In order to be able to establish the loanword imports, I have selected all loanwords from Van der Sijs (2001), totalling 10,746 entries. By loanwords, I mean those words that are adopted from a foreign language with little or no modification. Derivations or compounds from a loanword are left out. So although it is clear that *acetaat* ('acetate') and *automobiel* ('automobile, car') have a foreign origin, they are not counted as loanwords, since *acetaat* is formed after Latin *acetum* 'vinegar', and *automobiel* is a hybrid from Greek *autos* 'self' and Latin *mobilis* 'movable'. Furthermore, only the direct source languages are taken into consideration. So, the word *suiker* 'sugar' is considered a French loanword, although it ultimately has an Arabic or Persian source.

Both databases were compiled for etymological research purposes and therefore contain relatively few compounds and derivations. For loanword research this is not a problem. However, the databases contain a selection from the *modern* vocabulary of Dutch. Here we can see a methodological problem looming up: can we use the *modern* vocabulary to judge how extensive the influx of loanwords was in the past? Then we miss all the loanwords that have disappeared over time. This cannot be remedied in the current state of science. It is obvious that in the past

1. In Van der Sijs 2005, a detailed description is given of all languages that have influenced Dutch, but not in the form of a database; see also Van der Sijs 2009c. There are a few monographs on loanwords from separate languages in Dutch, such as Salverda de Grave 1906 (French); Van der Sijs & Engelsman 2000 (Latin), De Vooys 1936, 1956 (German and English). Two recent theses have investigated the occurrence and frequency of French loanwords in diachronic corpora (Assendelft 2023, Verheyden 2023).

more words were borrowed – words that have meanwhile disappeared from the Dutch language, for instance because social or technical innovations rendered the loanwords superfluous. The disappearance of loanwords (and of words in general) is a universal phenomenon, and there is no reason to suppose that loanwords from one language should disappear in larger numbers than loanwords from another language. It seems possible, therefore, and justified to make pronouncements from a modern point of view about influxes of loanwords in the past – there is bound to be some bias, but this, we assume, holds for all languages and will not distort the general picture.

3.2 The data from the database

In Table 1 we find a survey of loanwords per language, based on Van der Sijs (2001). Behind the absolute numbers per language is added the percentage that the loanwords of this particular language represent of the total number of loanwords from all languages.[2] The languages have been ordered in decreasing order of numbers of loanwords and are presented by continent.

Contacts with languages spoken within Europe have, by definition, been much older than those with other continents. This is reflected in the number of loanwords, which is by far the highest for European languages. However, there are marked differences. The languages from which most words have been borrowed are neighbouring languages of Dutch (with Latin as a second language in the Low Countries). All on its own at the top we find French, with loanwords such as *adres* 'address', *agent, aristocratie* 'aristocracy', *bajonet* 'bayonet', *ballet, balkon* 'balcony', *pensioen* 'pension', *terrine, trottoir* 'pavement'.

Latin's[3] second position is due to loanwords entering Dutch in the time of the Roman Empire (such as *kaas* 'cheese', *muur* 'wall' and *wijn* 'wine'), and the use of Latin as a religious and scientific language from the Middle Ages until the nineteenth century, providing loanwords such as *academie* 'academy', *centrum* 'centre', *collega* 'colleague', *foetus* 'fetus', *hernia, monnik* 'monk', *produceren* 'to produce', and *territorium* 'territory'. Furthermore, Latin words are still used to designate new scientific inventions (*transmittor, placebo*).

2. By way of a check, I compared the data from Van der Sijs 2001 with those from Van Veen & Van der Sijs 1997, containing 17,736 loanwords in Dutch (not counting their derivations). It appears that the relative percentages of loanwords tally with those given in Table 1, although absolute and relative numbers of course differ.

3. Sometimes it is difficult to ascertain whether a loanword is borrowed from French or Latin, then the most likely candidate is mentioned in the database.

Table 1. Languages that have supplied loanwords to Dutch, per continent

Language	Number of loanwords	% of all loanwords
EUROPE		
French	4605	42.8%
Latin	1906	17.7%
English (British and American)	1857	17.3%
(High and Low) German	1047	9.7%
Italian	360	3.3%
Spanish	169	1.6%
Yiddish	107	1.0%
Greek	80	0.7%
Russian	55	0.5%
Portuguese	53	0.5%
Scandinavian languages[a]	38	0.4%
Frisian	26	0.2%
MIDDLE EAST AND AFRICA		
Arabic	52	0.5%
Turkish	20	0.2%
Afrikaans	11	0.1%
ASIA AND OCEANIA		
Indonesian[b]	109	1.0%
Japanese	69	0.6%
Chinese[c]	22	0.2%
SOUTH AMERICA AND CARIBBEAN		
Sranan Tongo	8	0.1%
Papiamentu	4	0.1%
OTHER LANGUAGES[d]	166	1.5%
Total	**10,764**	**100%**

a. Nine loanwords from Danish, twelve from Norwegian, eleven from Old Norse and six from Swedish.

b. Under the term 'Indonesian loanwords' we understand words borrowed both from Malay and from Bahasa Indonesia – the variety of Malay that in 1928 was proclaimed the national language of Indonesia (embedded in the constitution in 1945).

c. Under 'Chinese' the loanwords from different varieties of Chinese such as Mandarin, Hokkien, or Hakka, are summarized.

d. Various languages with less than 5 loanwords, in or outside Europe, such as Polish, Finnish, Polynesian.

English holds the third position, but this position has only been achieved recently. In Van der Sijs (2001) I indicated for every entry when, as far as can be ascertained, it first appeared in Dutch. It turns out English owes its prominent third position to the large number of words that Dutch has borrowed from it in more recent times, such as *boycot, brainwave, cartoon, computer, facebook, paper* and *twitter*. This recent influence has been exerted both from the UK and the US, therefore I did not make a distinction between British and American English. In the Early and Late Modern Dutch period there were also regular contacts with British English, but these apparently did not result in large numbers of words being borrowed. This may be because in that period, English culture was being overshadowed by French, and perhaps also because of the political and economic competition between the Republic and the UK, which in the seventeenth and eighteenth centuries led to no fewer than four wars (cf. 2.1). Finally, it must be noted that the number of English loanwords reflects the situation at the beginning of the twenty-first century: since then, a substantial English loanwords has entered Dutch, but research has shown that forty percent of recent English loanwords have disappeared after about thirty years (Van der Sijs 2023).

German influence on Dutch brought loanwords such as *ambt* 'office', *argwaan* 'suspicion', *erts* 'ore', *kamermuziek* 'chamber music', *knakworst* 'frankfurter' and *overreden* 'to persuade'. However, the percentage of German loanwords is far below that of French. It is remarkable that the influence of these two neighbouring languages of Dutch varies so greatly. I presume that the difference is not as great as the figures suggest, but that the data are misrepresented: because of the close relationship between Dutch and German dialects it is often impossible, on the basis of sound or meaning, to decide whether a word spread via a German or a Dutch dialect. Wordlists in which German loanwords are specially marked as such often include words that at first sight would not have been recognized as German loanwords (*ezelsoor* – German *Eselsohr, leeshonger* – German *Lesehunger, voorwoord* – German *Vorwort*). These kinds of wordlists of German loanwords, however, do not date from before the nineteenth century (see *Etymologiebank*). Closer systematic investigation, into older sources as well, might well yield surprising results with regard to the German influence on Dutch and the other way round.

Italian takes fifth position with banking and music terms, followed by Spanish and Yiddish. The Spanish influx is especially due to relatively modern tourism and restaurants (such as *oregano, flamenco*). The contacts between Spanish and Dutch during the Dutch Revolt were not very intense: French was used as a diplomatic language between the upper Dutch and Spanish classes, so only a small number of Spanish loanwords entered Standard Dutch, often for products from the Americas (*tabak* 'tabacco', *tomaat* 'tomato'; Van der Sijs 2019b). More Spanish loanwords were absorbed in the Flemish dialects spoken in the southern provinces, that remained under Spanish reign until the eighteenth century (Van der Sijs 2018, 2019b).

Most Yiddish loanwords also penetrated into Dutch only in the nineteenth and twentieth centuries, usually via argot, providing words such as *gotspe* 'chutzpa', *heibel* 'row', *mazzel* 'good luck', *mesjogge* 'crazy', *pleite* 'away' and *sof* 'flop'. In trade contacts and in daily life, Yiddish words were preserved, when Yiddish as a spoken language disappeared in the course of the nineteenth century. In literary texts from Amsterdam, especially between 1850 and 1950, many more Yiddish words were in regular use, as appears from Van de Kamp and Van der Wijk (2006).

The influence of Greek, Russian, Portuguese, Scandinavian languages and Frisian is negligible. The same goes for the languages spoken in the Middle East, Africa, South America, and the Caribbean. Of the languages of the former Dutch colonies, most words were loaned from Indonesian, but the number of loanwords is still very small. Papiamentu and Sranan Tongo hardly played a role, and most loanwords from these languages, as from Japanese (*judo, bonsai*), date from the twentieth century. The much more extensive influence of Indonesian than of Papiamentu and Sranan Tongo must be because Indonesia had a much larger territory, with a much larger number of inhabitants, and was a much more important region economically. A great many more Dutch civil servants, consequently, lived there than on the Antilles and in Suriname. Most of the Indonesian loanwords, incidentally, were incorporated into Standard Dutch after 1800, i.e. in the colonial period, when the Dutch stayed longer in the same place and often married local women. Examples are *branie* 'daredevil', *loempia* 'pancake roll', *piekeren* 'worry', *pienter* 'smart', *rimboe* 'jungle' and *senang* 'pleasant'. Research has shown that in the past more Indonesian words were known in Dutch, but that their number has decreased with time (Rahman 1990 draws a comparison between the Indonesian loanwords in the Van Dale dictionary from 1924, i.e. the colonial days, and in Van Dale 1984, the post-colonial period; see also Mingaars *et al.* 2005).

4. Dutch export words

It is interesting to investigate whether the Dutch export of words has concerned the same languages as the import of words. In this section, too, I shall first describe the database I used (4.1), after which the data will be presented (4.2).

4.1 The database

The Dutch export words – Dutch words borrowed by other languages – have not been described as much as the words that were borrowed *into* Dutch,[4] but in 2010 I published the first survey. The book is based on a database that was filled, with the aid of a group of fifty trainees and volunteers, with as much data as we could find.[5] We gathered these data from etymological dictionaries and dictionaries of foreign words in other languages – through digital sources where possible, in practice largely by excerpting paper editions. In 2015, the database was also digitally published, with additional data, as *Uitleenwoordenbank*. Here also a survey is given of all the sources that were used for the compilation of the database.

The 2015 database comprises as many as 18,242 Dutch words that have been lent to one or more – often many more – other languages. In all, Dutch words have been borrowed into 138 languages, yielding 48,456 new words. This means that every Dutch word is borrowed by an average of 2.5 languages. Some languages, naturally, have only a handful of Dutch loanwords, e.g. Welsh, Icelandic, Swahili – among them also Dutch loanwords that have by now become obsolete and are no longer used in that foreign language. The vast majority of the export words are loanwords, but a small minority consists of loan translations or calques (French *pomme de terre* from Dutch *aardappel* 'potato', Japanese *bunshi* from Dutch *deelwoord* 'participle'), hybrids (Japanese *chō-chifusu* from Dutch *buiktyfus* 'typhoid') or semantic loans (Japanse *jōryū* from Dutch *distilleren* 'distil'). These types are found especially in Asiatic languages such as Japanese, Chinese, and Korean; see the contribution from Joby in this book. In the following I will include all borrowing types together under the heading export word.

The database is the first step to further and in-depth research. Now that we have collected all these data, we can try to establish the exact way a Dutch loanword has circulated to and through the different languages. In this way we can also ascertain lacunae: languages in which the Dutch loanword is not yet recorded, but which upon closer inspection turn out to have borrowed the Dutch word (maybe only in certain contexts, regions or periods). The greatest problem with

4. A few studies have appeared dealing with the Dutch influence on separate languages; the most comprehensive are: Bense 1939 (English), Hammerich 1945 (Danish), Joby 2015 (English), Joby 2020 (Japanese), Jones (ed.) 2007 (Indonesian), Van der Meulen 1909, 1959 (Russian), Sanasgala 1976 (Sinhala), Valkhoff 1931 (French), Vos 1980 (Japanese), De Vries 1988 (Indonesian). In Haspelmath & Tadmor 2009, the number of loanwords is described in a pre-arranged vocabulary of a large number of languages; some Dutch loanwords appear in this as well. For the dynamics of contact varieties of Dutch see part IV of Hinskens & Taeldeman 2013.

5. Van der Sijs 2010, in which the names of the collaborators are mentioned on pp. x-xii. First publications on the topic are Van der Sijs 1998, 2006b, 2009a and b.

the compilation of the database is that the material collection is dependent on the state of investigation of the languages that have adopted the Dutch words: the better a language has been described, the more is known about the history of a language, and the more extensive the etymological study of the vocabulary is, the more Dutch loanwords will emerge from the language. This means that we will obtain a distorted picture: in well-described, well-documented and well-investigated languages such as French and English proportionally more Dutch loanwords will emerge than in languages that have scarcely been investigated, such as native languages spoken in the Americas, the Caribbean area, and small islands in the Indonesian Archipelago.

4.2 The data from the database

In Tables 2–7 the languages that borrowed most Dutch words are listed, per continent in descending order. In this section only the first two columns of the tables – the languages that borrowed Dutch words and the number of words concerned – are discussed. In Section 6 the remaining columns will be examined. In the tables I have included the creole and pidgin languages based on Dutch, although strictly speaking we cannot speak of export words in these cases, because the vocabularies of these creoles were initially based on Dutch. This concerns the pidgin Delaware Jargon in North America, Virgin Islands Dutch Creole, Berbice Dutch and Skepi Dutch in South America and the Caribbean, and Petjoh and Javindo in Indonesia.

Table 2 shows the number of Dutch loanwords in European languages. No fewer than 40 European languages have, as far as we know, been influenced by Dutch. Most export words have been absorbed by Danish, Swedish and Norwegian, countries with which a lot of trade has traditionally been conducted, especially via the Hanseatic League (more on this in Section 6). The neighbouring languages Frisian, French, British-English and German take fourth, fifth, sixth and eighth position, while Russian (thanks to Peter the Great) takes seventh, and the vast majority of these loanwords were borrowed directly from Dutch.

The figures of the export words should not be taken absolutely, since, as mentioned in 4.1, they are also an indication of the information available. Thus, the large number of Dutch loanwords in French and English can be explained partly by the fact that these languages have been exhaustively described, historically and etymologically. Many of the Dutch loanwords in these languages have long been obsolete or have only been preserved in a dialect. Of the 1500-odd Dutch loanwords mentioned in the *OED*, only about five hundred are mentioned in the *ODEE* for Modern Standard English (*ODEE*, Van der Sijs 2009a: 10). Examples are *etch, gas, hanker, luck, spook*, from Dutch *etsen, gas, hunkeren, geluk* and *spook*. Of the 1600-odd French loanwords, for which the data are taken in part from the

Table 2. Languages having absorbed Dutch export words, in Europe

Language	Total number of Dutch loanwords (borrowed directly and indirectly)	Number of loanwords (probably) borrowed indirectly	Percentage indirectly borrowed (bold = 50% or more)	Number of these words which are loaned in Dutch	In percentage (bold = 50% or more)
Danish	2858	1731	**61%**	546	19%
Swedish	2187	1823	**83%**	400	18%
Norwegian	2109	1664	**79%**	411	19%
Frisian	1992	5	0%	26	1%
French	1657	72	4%	166	10%
British English	1498	508	34%	245	16%
Russian	1284	34	3%	218	17%
German	1247	287	23%	453	36%
Finnish	525	472	**90%**	164	31%
Polish	390	171	44%	92	24%
Ukrainian	333	328	**98%**	120	36%
Lithuanian	315	159	**50%**	86	27%
Estonian	243	154	**63%**	94	39%
Esperanto	231	223	**97%**	49	21%
Scottish	231	2	1%	35	15%
Azerbaijani	187	187	**100%**	65	35%
Latvian	175	98	**56%**	58	33%
Italian	164	118	**72%**	29	18%
Bulgarian	157	114	**73%**	40	25%
Maltese	123	121	**98%**	33	27%
Portuguese	117	89	**76%**	66	**56%**
Croatian	109	57	**52%**	35	32%
Czech	109	62	**57%**	6	6%
Belarusian	108	105	**97%**	45	42%
Spanish	103	68	**66%**	13	13%
Slovenian	101	59	**58%**	44	44%
Basque	100	97	**97%**	10	10%
Macedonian	98	53	**54%**	39	40%
Serbian	90	57	**63%**	12	13%

Table 2. *(continued)*

Language	Total number of Dutch loanwords (borrowed directly and indirectly)	Number of loanwords (probably) borrowed indirectly	Percentage indirectly borrowed (bold = 50% or more)	Number of these words which are loaned in Dutch	In percentage (bold = 50% or more)
Breton	76	63	**83%**	5	7%
Greek	71	56	**79%**	11	15%
Hungarian	57	45	**79%**	28	49%
Mainland North Frisian	55	1	2%	8	15%
Slovak	45	32	**71%**	21	47%
Eastern Yiddish	44	27	**61%**	11	25%
Romanian	17	10	**59%**	11	**65%**
Icelandic	8	2	25%	4	**50%**
Welsh	5	1	20%	0	0%
Irish	4	1	25%	1	25%
Gaelic	3	1	33%	0	0%

FEW, Modern Standard French as described in the *Petit Robert* (Robert 1983) has only about five hundred, such as *amarrer, bâbord, dune, hase, hareng, mannequin*, from Dutch *aanmeren* 'to moor', *bakboord* 'port side', *duin* 'dune', *haas* 'hare', *haring* 'herring', *manneke* 'little man, puppet'. Of the circa 1300 Russian words collected by Van der Meulen in 1909 and 1959, Vasmer (1953–1958) gives only 550 for Modern Russian, such as *apel'sin, bankrut, bur, brandspojt, kontora, magazin* from Dutch *appelsien* 'orange', *bankroet* 'bankrupt', *boor* 'brace', *brandspuit* 'fire engine', *kantoor* 'office', *magazijn* 'warehouse'.

As for Frisian, I presume the Dutch influence to be even greater than appears from the numbers, since new 'officialese' terms in Frisian are mainly based on their Dutch equivalents (such as *amtner, ambulânse, arrest, autoriteit, bankbiljet, beämte* from Dutch *ambtenaar* 'civil servant', *ambulance, arrest, autoriteit* 'authority', *bankbiljet* 'bank note' and *beambte* 'functionary'). However, we have only two sources with information on Dutch loans in Frisian: the *WFT*, which has added the qualification H = Hollandism to Dutch loanwords, and Århammar (2003). Here, too, we are faced, just as in the case of German (mentioned in 3.2), with the problem of the close relationship with Dutch, which complicates the issue of whether we are dealing with a loanword or a native word.

The influence of Dutch on the remaining languages is much more limited. It is clear from Table 2 that most Dutch export words were loaned directly into neighbouring languages, and also that the Hanseatic League has played a very important role.

How about the export words to other continents? From Table 3 it appears that the number of export words in languages spoken in the Middle East and North Africa is negligible.

Table 3. Languages having absorbed Dutch export words, in the Middle East and North Africa

Language	Total number of Dutch loanwords	(probably) borrowed indirectly	Percentage indirectly borrowed	Loaned in Dutch	In percentage
Arabic (MSA)	49	33	67%	9	18%
Turkish	41	33	80%	8	20%
Kurdish	40	31	78%	9	23%
Arabic (Egyptian)	29	26	90%	6	21%
Persian	19	19	100%	3	16%
Arabic (Iraqi)	8	6	75%	8	100%
Tamazight (Northern Morocco)	8	0	0%	1	13%
Arabic (Moroccan)	7	7	100%	2	29%
Arabic (Palestinian)	5	5	100%	2	40%
Tamazight (Algeria)	2	1	50%	0	0%
Tamazight (Central Morocco)	2	1	50%	0	0%
Arabic (classical)	1	1	100%	1	100%

In Sub-Saharan Africa the situation is quite different, as appears from Table 4. A relatively large number of Dutch words have entered South African English and languages that are native to South Africa. This is not surprising, since the Dutch presence in South Africa dates from 1652, and the Dutch language spoken here evolved into Afrikaans. Furthermore, some Dutch words were borrowed in

Table 4. Languages having absorbed Dutch export words, in Sub-Saharan Africa

Language	Total number of Dutch loanwords	(probably) borrowed indirectly	Percentage indirectly borrowed	Loaned in Dutch	In percentage
South African English	764	217	28%	121	16%
Southern Sotho	117	117	100%	19	16%
Northern Sotho	114	112	98%	66	58%
Zulu	101	101	100%	41	41%
Xhosa	94	94	100%	49	52%
Ga	56	28	50%	31	55%
Shona	50	49	98%	24	48%
Twi	24	16	67%	14	58%
Ewe	19	12	63%	12	63%
Lala	5	5	100%	1	20%
Sindebele	4	4	100%	0	0%
Akvambu	3	0	0%	1	33%
Swahili	2	0	0%	1	50%
Bemba	1	1	100%	0	0%
Fon	1	0	0%	0	0%
Lingala	1	0	0%	0	0%

Ghana (Akvambu, Ewe, Fon, Gã, Twi), where the Dutch built trading posts in the seventeenth century.

Table 5 shows that the Dutch influence in Asia and Oceania has been very extensive: the number of loanwords in Indonesian (Malay, later called Bahasa Indonesia) far exceeds that of any European language. As said before, the figures reflect the available information and are mostly based on the modern vocabulary of the languages mentioned. This explains, for instance, the difference in the numbers of Japanese loanwords in my database (428) and Joby's (577): Joby also includes Dutch export words that have by now disappeared from Japanese.

Table 6 shows that Dutch influence on South America and the Caribbean was also extensive, though less than in Asia.

Finally, in North America Dutch exerted influence on American English and on a number of native American languages; the situation is more or less comparable to that of Sub-Saharan Africa, see Table 7.

Table 5. Languages having absorbed Dutch export words, in Asia and Oceania

Language	Total number of Dutch loanwords	(probably) borrowed indirectly	Percentage indirectly borrowed	Loaned in Dutch	In percentage
Indonesian	5568	82	1%	4001	**72%**
Javanese	1262	11	1%	629	**50%**
Menadonese	1086	22	2%	578	**53%**
Madurese	737	46	6%	445	**60%**
Jakartan Malay	691	26	4%	337	49%
Ambon Malay	582	9	2%	234	40%
Kupang Malay	560	11	2%	231	41%
Makassar	470	28	6%	272	**58%**
Japanese	428	3	1%	209	49%
Sundanese	423	5	1%	245	**58%**
Petjoh	339	47	14%	105	31%
Buginese	318	11	3%	228	**72%**
Minangkabau	317	9	3%	219	**69%**
Ternatan Malay	285	4	1%	123	43%
Sinhala	233	48	21%	144	**62%**
Creole Portuguese (Ceylon)	158	0	0%	58	37%
Creole Portuguese (Batavia)	149	0	0%	78	**52%**
Muna	143	6	4%	77	**54%**
Acehnese	140	25	18%	98	**70%**
Keiese	123	4	3%	66	**54%**
Javindo	109	0	0%	38	35%
Chinese[a]	102	85	**83%**	20	20%
Sasak	91	5	5%	50	**55%**
Chinese Malay[b]	90	0	0%	35	39%
Balinese	88	0	0%	37	42%
Creole Portuguese (Malacca)	63	4	6%	23	37%

Table 5. *(continued)*

Language	Total number of Dutch loanwords	(probably) borrowed indirectly	Percentage indirectly borrowed	Loaned in Dutch	In percentage
Giman	58	0	0%	31	53%
Nias	52	0	0%	39	75%
Rotinese	52	3	6%	30	58%
Tamil	47	1	2%	22	47%
Korean	45	45	100%	31	69%
Iban	28	25	89%	23	82%
Letinese	25	0	0%	11	44%
Savu	25	2	8%	10	40%
Sahu	17	0	0%	2	12%
Alor Malay	10	0	0%	2	20%
Konkani	8	0	0%	2	25%
Polynesian	7	0	0%	1	14%
Dhivehi	4	0	0%	3	75%
Biak	3	0	0%	0	0%
Kannada	2	0	0%	1	50%
Malagasy	1	0	0%	0	0%

a. Dutch loanwords can be found in various Chinese varieties, see the contribution from Joby.
b. A Chinese-Malay creole language spoken around the large city of Surabaya in East Java, where a large Chinese population settled in the eighteenth century, and that is still spoken today.

We must conclude that the greatest influence of Dutch was exerted on the languages spoken in the erstwhile colonies – first and foremost the languages of Indonesia: not only the standard language Bahasa Indonesia (called 'Indonesian' in the database), but also on a variety of other indigenous languages: Javanese, Menadonese, Madurese, Jakartan Malay, Ambon Malay, Kupang Malay, Makassar, Sundanese, Buginese, Minangkabau, Ternatan Malay, Muna, Atjehnese and Keiese. Dutch loanwords in Bahasa Indonesia are, for example, *brutal, buncis, sitrun, komisi, operasi, sekrip*, from Dutch *brutaal* 'impudent', *boontjes* 'beans', *citroen* 'lemon', *commissie* 'commission', *operatie* 'operation' and *schrift* 'notebook'.

In Suriname, Dutch had a substantial impact not only on the colloquial language Sranan Tongo, but also on the languages Surinamese-Javanese, Sarnami, Aucan and Arowaks. Some Dutch words have been borrowed by all these languages, for instance *baas* 'boss', *doos* 'box', *kamer* 'room', *koekje* 'cookie', *kous* 'stocking' and *school*. Dutch also had some impact on other indigenous languages in Suriname, but since these languages have been so inadequately described lexi-

Table 6. Languages having absorbed Dutch export words, in South America and the Caribbean

Language	Total number of Dutch loanwords	(probably) borrowed indirectly	Percentage indirectly borrowed	Loaned in Dutch	In percentage
Virgin Islands Dutch Creole	3598	69	2%	595	17%
Sranan Tongo	2437	122	5%	717	29%
Papiamentu	2265	55	2%	719	32%
Surinamese-Javanese	853	261	31%	362	42%
Berbice Dutch	637	2	0%	112	18%
Saramaccan	344	188	**55%**	109	32%
Sarnami	290	15	5%	139	48%
Creole English (Virgin Islands)	276	224	**81%**	81	29%
Aucan	200	17	9%	73	37%
Skepi Dutch	179	1	1%	21	12%
Arawak	132	34	26%	63	48%
Karaib	54	50	**93%**	24	44%
Caribbean English	30	1	3%	9	30%
Tiriyó	25	8	32%	2	8%
Warau	8	0	0%	0	0%
Akawaio and Arekuna	5	5	**100%**	2	40%
Paramakan	4	4	**100%**	1	25%
Creole French (Martinique)	2	0	0%	1	**50%**

cographically, it is too early to make any pronouncements on the subject; further research is urgently required.

The fact that the languages that borrowed most Dutch words were all spoken in one-time Dutch settlements or colonies in Asia and North and South America, can be explained easily. Borrowing presupposes a knowledge of another language, and in these regions Dutch served as the language of communication in formal situations such as administration, and some of the Dutch and native people were bilingual.

Table 7. Languages having absorbed Dutch export words, in North America

Language	Total number of Dutch loanwords	(probably) borrowed indirectly	Percentage indirectly borrowed	Loaned in Dutch	In percentage
American English	259	18	7%	37	14%
Munsee Delaware	41	0	0%	16	39%
Unami Delaware	28	0	0%	9	32%
Mahican	22	4	18%	8	36%
Mohegan Pequot	14	2	14%	2	14%
Loup	13	0	0%	3	23%
Delaware Slang	3	0	0%	0	0%
Mohawk	3	0	0%	0	0%
Western Abnaki	1	0	0%	0	0%

It is interestingly to note here that the Dutch influence on other languages is not limited to loanwords. Also, Dutch suffixes have become productive in various languages. This applies, for example, to the suffix *mis-* in French, *-aar, -aard* and *her-* in Frisian, and *be-, bij-, ge-, ont-, -achtig, -baar, -heid, -in* and *-voudig* in Danish, Norwegian and Swedish (from Dutch or Middle Low German). In Indonesian neologisms can be formed with the Dutch postfixes *-atie, -centrisch, -isatie, -isch, -isme, -ist, -logie, -meter* and the prefixes *audio-, bio-, de-, intra-, macro-, micro-, neo-, post-, re-, semi-, sub-* and *super-* (Van der Sijs 2010:32, De Vries et al. 2009:105–114). Indonesian has loaned these international scientific suffxes from Dutch (see 6.2).

Even sounds and letters have been loaned from Dutch as part of the phonology and spelling of foreign languages. For example, the sounds *h* and *w* (later changed into *g(u)*) exist in French thanks to Dutch loanwords, cf. *haïr* 'hate', *heaume* 'helmet', *gage* 'pay' and *gant* 'mitten'. Due to the large influx of Dutch loanwords with *v* and Arabic and Dutch words with *f* and *z* in Indonesian, the letters *v, f* and *z* have become part of the Indonesian alphabet; originally these were unknown in Indonesian. The letters *v* and *z* are usually pronounced as *f* and *s* (or in colloquial speech *dj*), but *f* even entered Indonesian as a borrowed phoneme.

5. Dutch loanwords and Dutch export words compared

In order to find out the extent to which the influence of Dutch went both ways, I combined the languages that are mentioned in Table 1 with loanwords in Dutch as well as in Tables 2–7 with Dutch export words. The result is shown in Table 8.

Table 8. A comparison of the numbers of words borrowed by and from Dutch

Language	Number of loanwords in Dutch	Number of Dutch export words
EUROPE		
French	4605	1657
English (British and American)	1857	1757
(High and Low) German	1047	1247
Italian	360	164
Spanish	169	103
Yiddish	107	44
Greek	80	71
Russian	55	1284
Portuguese	53	117
Scandinavian languages	38	2385[a]
Frisian	26	1992
MIDDLE EAST AND AFRICA		
Arabic	52	58[b]
Turkish	20	41
ASIA AND OCEANIA		
Indonesian	109	5568
Japanese	69	428
Chinese	22	102
SOUTH AMERICA AND CARIBBEAN		
Sranan Tongo	8	2437
Papiamentu	4	2265
Total	**8,681**	**21,720**

a. I have taken the average of 2858 (Danish), 2187 (Swedish) and 2109 (Norwegian), since the loanwords were loaned in these languages at a time when they were not very much differentiated from each other.

b. I give here the number of different Dutch words, taken over in the various Arabic varieties (Algeria, Morocco, Palestine, etc.), since it mostly concerns the same loanwords.

It is only for English and German that we can say that the influence has worked both ways. For German the mutual influence can be explained by the fact that speakers of Dutch and German for centuries were in close contact with each other in the border regions. For English the situation is quite different, as mentioned in 4.2: Dutch export words in English date primarily from before 1800, while English loanwords entered Dutch especially after 1945.

For French, the influence was primarily from French to Dutch, even though a substantial number of Dutch words are found in the northern French dialects (as witnessed by the *FEW*, see 4.2); if we disregard these, the French supremacy is even greater. The same goes for Yiddish: the influence was primarily directed from Yiddish to Dutch.

For the Scandinavian languages, Russian, Frisian, Indonesian, Japanese, Chinese, Sranan Tongo and Papiamentu the opposite happened: those languages have had little impact on Dutch but were themselves thoroughly influenced by Dutch. For the remaining languages (such as Italian, Spanish, Greek, Portuguese) the numbers are too small to be able to draw firm conclusions: we can only establish that there has been (some) mutual influence between Dutch and these languages.

We can conclude that Dutch itself has been influenced especially by Western European languages, notably the neighbouring languages, and that the linguistic influence by the languages of the former Dutch colonies was small. Dutch, on the other hand, left its indelible mark on the languages of the former colonies and countries with which the Dutch carried on an intensive trade, such as Japan. This is not surprising since it was, after all, through Dutch mediation that these territories came into contact with Western European science, culture and engineering.

6. The circulation of loanwords

As is well known, loanwords are not bothered by boundaries between countries and languages: some loanwords wander from language to language. The last section of this chapter is devoted to the role of Dutch in the circulation of words through languages. In the loanword circulation chain, Dutch can either be the starting point, i.e. the donor language, or the intermediary language. Schematically:

1. donor language ***Dutch*** → intermediary language A → recipient language B (C, D, ...)
2. donor language A → intermediary language ***Dutch*** → recipient language B (C, D, ...)

The chains can of course be longer, with more than one language between the donor and recipient languages, but I leave out these cases, because the role of Dutch vis-à-vis the other languages in the chain is obscured here.

6.1 Dutch as starting point in a circulation chain

The role of Dutch as source language in a circulation chain can be gathered from the third and fourth columns in Tables 2–7. In these columns, the number and percentage of words is noted that were, as far as we know, loaned not directly from Dutch, but through some intermediary language. For instance, most Dutch export words entered Finnish through Swedish, while for Bulgarian Russian served as an intermediary language, and French functioned often as a conduit for Italian and Portuguese. In these columns also the words are included that may have been borrowed both from Dutch and from another language – thus, the Sinhala word *annāsi* 'pineapple' may have been borrowed either from Dutch *ananas* or from its Portuguese equivalent.

The tables show remarkable differences between the continents: the influence of Dutch on most European languages (28 of the 40 languages in question) has been indirect, with fifty per cent or more export words being mediated by another language. Only the Dutch export words in neighbouring languages were for the most part loaned directly. By contrast, most export words in Danish, Swedish, and Norwegian are loaned indirectly. In this case this means: loaned through Middle Low German or Dutch in the period of the Hanseatic League. For loanwords in this period, it is impossible to determine whether the influence came from the Eastern Netherlands or from Northern Germany: there was a great homogeneity among the dialects spoken in that area. Many of these loanwords are found in all three Scandinavian languages, often also in Finnish (through Swedish), and sometimes in the Baltic countries (Lithuanian, Estonian and Latvian), lower in the ranking of Table 2, as well. For instance, Dutch or Middle Low German *anker* is found as Danish *anker*, Norwegian *anker*, Swedish *ankar*, Finnish *ankkuri* (through Swedish), Estonian *ankur*, Latvian *enkurs* and Lithuanian *inkaras*.

The situation in the Middle East and North Africa, and in Sub-Saharan Africa is similar to that in Europe: most export words are loaned indirectly (in Sub-Saharan Africa Afrikaans served as an intermediary language).[6]

By contrast, the extensive Dutch influence in Asia and Oceania was mostly exerted directly, except on Chinese dialects and Korean (with Japanese as inter-

6. As to the Dutch words in South African English: these were partly loaned directly from Dutch and partly through Afrikaans, but the exact route is often difficult to decide on linguistic grounds.

mediary language, see the contribution from Joby), and on Iban (through Malay). In South America, the Caribbean and in North America, also, Dutch export words were almost exclusively borrowed directly, with the exception of some native Suriname languages (such as Saramaccan, Karaib), for which Sranan Tongo served as an intermediary language, and Creole English on the Virgin Islands, to which Dutch words were introduced via Virgin Islands Dutch Creole.

If we add up the numbers of the third and fourth columns of Tables 2–7, it appears that in 59 of the 138 languages fifty percent or more of the Dutch export words have been borrowed indirectly, through some intermediary language. This concerns 11,817 words of the 48,450 export words, i.e. 24 per cent. This is a very substantial number, and it proves that Dutch has played an important role in the transfer of loanwords as a source language.

An interesting subcategory is formed by those words that started in Dutch, were loaned by another language and then later were taken back by Dutch, in a new form or meaning. Schematically:

donor language ***Dutch*** → intermediary language A → recipient language ***Dutch***

In these cases as far as I know only French and English serve as intermediary languages, (except for Dutch *doek* 'cloth' > Sranan Tongo *duku* 'money' > Dutch (youth language) *doekoe*), and this reflects the long-lasting and extensive mutual influence between these languages and Dutch. The most well-known examples of words that were returned to sender are enumerated in Table 9.

Table 9. Examples of Dutch words that were returned to sender

Dutch source word	Intermediary word	Recipient Dutch word
baas	English *boss*	*boss*
bijwacht	French *bivouac*	*bivak*
blazen 'blow'	French *blasé*	*blasé* 'unimpressed'
boek 'book'	French *bouquiniste*	*bouquiniste* 'secondhand books seller'
bolwerk 'bulwark'	French *boulevard*	*boulevard* 'avenue'
brandewijn	English *brandy*	*brandy*
doop 'sauce'	English *dope*	*dope* 'drugs'
jacht	English *yacht*	*yacht*
jenever, genever	English *gin*	*gin*
jol	English *yawl*	*yawl*
kolf 'club'	English *golf*	*golf* 'game'
kreuner 'moaner'	English *crooner*	*crooner* 'singer'
kruiser	English *cruiser*	*cruiser*
landschap	English *landscape*	*landscape*

Table 9. *(continued)*

Dutch source word	Intermediary word	Recipient Dutch word
manneke 'little man'	French *mannequin*	*mannequin* 'model'
pak	French *paquet*	*pakket*
pekel 'brine'	English *pickles*	*pickles* 'vegetables in brine'
plak 'slice'	French *plaquette*	*plaket* 'plaquette'
rek	English *rack*	*rack*
schaats	English *skate*	*skate*
schets	English *sketch*	*sketch*
schipper	English *skipper*	*skipper*
schokken 'shake'	French *choquer*	*choqueren* 'shock'
schoonbrood 'white bread'	English *scone*	*scone* 'biscuitlike bread'
schop 'shovel'	English *scoop*	*scoop* 'news story'
snakken 'gasp'	English *snack*	*snack* 'light meal'
stapel 'staple, entrepôt'	French *étape*	*etappe* 'stage'
steken 'stab'	French *étiquette*	*etiquette* 'etiquette'
takel	English *tackle*	*tackle*
vouwstoel 'folding chair'	French *fauteuil*	*fauteuil* 'armchair'

6.2 Dutch as an intermediary language

To get to grips with the role of Dutch as an intermediary language, we turn to the fifth and sixth columns in Tables 2–7. Here, I state the number and percentage of export words that originally were loanwords in Dutch. For instance, Dutch borrowed *bankroet* 'bankrupt' from French *banqueroute*, and exported this word to Indonesian as *bangkrut*. The names for trade products from other continents went in the opposite direction: the Dutch imported products such as *bamboo, batik, soya, coffee* and *tea* with their native Asian or Turkish name to European countries and languages.

If we add up the numbers of the fifth and sixth columns of Tables 2–7, it appears that in 33 of the 138 languages fifty percent or more of the Dutch export words were loanwords. This concerns 16,393 of the 48,450 export words, i.e. 34 per cent.[7]

7. The loanwords in Dutch rely largely on Van Veen & Van der Sijs 1997, so probably the number of loanwords for which Dutch was an intermediary is still larger, since export words that are not mentioned in this dictionary, are not included in the numbers. However, this will not substantially change the general picture.

However, just as in 6.1 we see remarkable differences between the continents: in Europe, the Middle East and North Africa, in South America and the Caribbean, and in North America most export words are native Dutch, while in Asia and Oceania, and less so in Sub-Saharan Africa, most export words are loanwords in Dutch.

Especially striking is the difference between the former Dutch colonies: while in South America and the Caribbean most Dutch export words are native Dutch, in Asia and Oceania Dutch loanwords prevail. From 6.1 we learned that in both cases the Dutch export words were loaned directly without an intermediary language. How then can we explain the difference between the continents? To answer these questions we must look at the local situations.

Over the centuries, a common Western European science and culture had developed, resulting in a common vocabulary consisting largely of Latin and French loanwords. Furthermore, a common trade language was shaped, especially via the Hanseatic League. Innovations and new inventions were devised in various countries, and then adopted by other countries and languages, with their original name. In this way, several European languages adopted (native) Dutch words such as *bolwerk* 'bulwark', *gas* (in 1648 coined by the Flemish chemist J. van Helmont) and *polder*, and Dutch maritime terms such as *stuurboord* 'starboard', *boegspriet* 'bowsprit', *jacht* 'yacht' and *sloep* 'sloop'.

When the Dutch sailed across the oceans, they took with them all kind of practical utensils and foodstuff, resulting in Dutch export words as *pot, pan, pen, naald* 'needle', *oven*, and culinary terms such as *boontje* 'bean', *koek* 'cookie' and *brandewijn* 'brandy'. Again, most of these words are native Dutch.

It was only to Asia and Oceania (especially Japan and Indonesia) that the Dutch spread Western European science, culture, and engineering to a considerable extent, and they did this in the contemporary scientific jargon, which was based mostly on French and Latin loanwords. It is interesting to note here that Indonesian adopted almost twice as many Dutch export words as Sranan Tongo and Papiamentu, and that Dutch loanwords make up the difference. These scientific words even entered Indonesian after Indonesian independence in 1949. The reason for this was that the Indonesian elite continued to use Dutch after 1949, and they inevitably turned to Dutch when forming a new Indonesian scientific vocabulary. Thus, international scientific suffixes were loaned from Dutch and became productive in coining new Indonesian words (see 4.2). For instance, *-isatie* was used to form neologisms as *komputerisasi, kristenisasi* and *westernisasi*, which do not occur in Dutch (Van der Sijs 2010: 32). Indonesia thus developed a full-fledged scientific (juridical, medical, administrative) vocabulary, strongly relying on international words and morphemes that were adopted through Dutch. By contrast, only few scientific works have been and are being written in Sranan

Tongo and Papiamentu. For scientific purposes, English or Spanish are mostly preferred. This explains why the number of Dutch export words, and especially loanwords in Dutch, in Suriname and the Dutch Antilles is so much smaller than in Indonesia.

7. Conclusion

From the above, we can conclude that Dutch has always been very open to other languages: on the one hand, Dutch has adopted words from many languages – especially neighbouring ones, and on the other hand, Dutch has exported many words to languages spoken on all continents. Furthermore, Dutch has played a significant role in the circulation of words through languages and continents: 24 per cent of Dutch words were passed on by an intermediary language to a third language, while 34 per cent of the Dutch export words were former loanwords in Dutch, and thus transferred by Dutch. Of course, the exact numbers suggest a precision which we cannot really substantiate: the databases show all kinds of biases and lacunae, as mentioned in 3.1 and 4.1, and further research is necessary. However, I believe this has not distorted the general picture.

The Dutch influence on other languages is not limited to loanwords, but also includes loan translations, semantic loans, and even suffixes, sounds and letters. Evidently, the Dutch linguistic influence has made itself felt, throughout its history up to the nineteenth century, on all continents. Dutch clearly contributed to the international concert of languages. This is surprising, given the small size of the Low Countries.

References

Appel, René, and Pieter Muysken. 1987. *Language Contact and Bilingualism.* London and Baltimore, MD: Edward Arnold.

Århammar, Nils. 2003. "Oer inkelde ûndersiikstaken op it mêd fan it Westlauwersk Frysk." *Philologia Frisica 2002, Lêzingen fan it sechtjinde Frysk Filologekongres 11, 12 en 13 desimber* 2003, 203–234.

Assendelft, Brenda. 2023. *Verfransing onder de loep – Nederlands-Frans taalcontact (1500–1900) vanuit historisch-sociolinguïstisch perspectief.* PhD Leiden.

Bense, Johan Frederik. 1924. *The Anglo-Dutch Relations from the Earliest Times to the Death of William the Third.* Den Haag: Nijhoff.

Bense, Johan Frederik. 1939. *A Dictionary of the Low-Dutch Element in the English Vocabulary.* 's-Gravenhage: Nijhoff.

De Bruijn-van der Helm, José. 1992. *Merce, moneta e monte. Termini commerciali italiani attestati nei testi neerlandesi dei secoli XVI e XVII.* Utrecht: LEd.

De Vooys, C.G.N. 1936. "Nedersaksische en Hoogduitse invloeden op de Nederlandse woordvoorraad." *Mededeelingen der Koninklijke Akademie van Wetenschappen*, afd. Letterkunde, deel 81, serie A, 1: 1–39.

De Vooys, C.G.N. 1956. "Engelse invloed op het Nederlands." *Nieuwe Taalgids* 49: 3–9.

doi De Vries, Jan W. 1988. "Dutch Loanwords in Indonesian." *International Journal of the Sociology of Language* 73: 121–136.

De Vries, Jan W., Roland Willemyns, and Peter Burger. 2009. *Het verhaal van het Nederlands. Een geschiedenis van twaalf eeuwen*, adapted by Nicoline van der Sijs & Roland Willemyns. Amsterdam: Bert Bakker.

Etymologiebank: https://etymologiebank.nl/.

FEW = von Wartburg, Walther. 1928-. *Französisches etymologisches Wörterbuch. Eine Darstellung des galloromanischen Sprachschatzes.* Bd. 15–17: *Die germanischen Elemente.* Bonn/Basel: Klopp – Zbinden.

Fouse, Gary C. 2002. *The Story of Papiamentu: A Study in Slavery and Language.* New York: University Press of America.

Francescato, Giuseppe. 1966. "Contributi allo studio degli elementi italiani in olandese." *Studi di Filologia Italiana* 24: 443–607.

Groeneboer, K. 1993. *Weg tot het Westen. Het Nederlands voor Indië* 1600–1950. Leiden: KITLV Uitgeverij.

Groeneboer, K. 1998. *Westerse koloniale taalpolitiek in Azië: Het Nederlands, Portugees, Spaans, Engels en Frans in vergelijkend perspectief.* Amsterdam.

Hammerich, Louis Leonor. 1945. "Sproget." In *Holland Danmark*, ed. by Knud Fabricius, L.L. Hammerich, and Vilhelm Lorenzen, part 2, 327–356. Kopenhagen: Jespersen og Pios Forlag.

doi Haspelmath, Martin, and Uri Tadmor (eds). 2009. *Loanwords in the World's Languages: A Comparative Handbook.* Berlin: Mouton de Gruyter.

Hickey, Raymond (ed.). 2013. *The Handbook of Language Contact.* Oxford: OUP.

Hinskens, F.L.M.P., and J. Taeldeman (eds). 2013. *Language and space: Dutch.* De Gruyter Mouton.

doi Joby, Christopher. 2015. *The Dutch Language in Britain (1550–1702). A Social History of the Use of Dutch in Early Modern Britain.* Leiden: Brill.

Joby, Christopher. 2020. *The Dutch Language in Japan (1600–1900). A Cultural and Sociolinguistic Study of Dutch as a Contact Language in Tokugawa and Meiji Japan.* Leiden: Brill.

Jones, Russell (ed.). 2007. *Loan-words in Indonesian and Malay.* Leiden: Brill.

Kouwenberg, Silvia. 1993. *A grammar of Berbice Dutch Creole.* Berlin/New York: Mouton de Gruyter.

doi Mingaars, Peter, Jaap Heij, Maudy Smith, and Pim Posthumus. 2005. *Indisch Lexicon. Indische woorden in de Nederlandse literatuur.* Houten: Hes & De Graaf.

doi Munske, H.H. et al.. (eds). (2001). *Handbuch des Friesischen / Handbook of Frisian Studies.* Tübingen.

ODEE = Onions, C.T. (ed.). 1983. *The Oxford Dictionary of English Etymology.* Oxford: OUP.

OED = Simpson, J.A., and E.S.C. Weiner (eds). 1989. *Oxford English Dictionary*. Oxford: OUP.

Rahman, Syaifoel. 1990. "Lexicale beïnvloeding door Indonesische talen van het Nederlands." [Undergraduate paper Leiden]

Robert, Paul. 1993. *Le Petit Robert 1. Dictionnaire alphabétique et analogique de la langue française*. Paris.

Robertson, Ian E. (1989), "Berbice and Skepi Dutch." *Tijdschrift voor Nederlandsche Taal- en Letterkunde* 105: 3–21.

Salverda de Grave, J.J. 1906. *De Franse woorden in het Nederlands*. Amsterdam: Müller.

Sannasgala, Puñci Baṇḍāra. 1976. *A Study of Sinhala Vocables of Dutch Origin, with Appendices of Portuguese and Malay/Javanese Borrowings*. Colombo: Netherlands alumni association of Sri Lanka.

Uitleenwoordenbank: https://uitleenwoordenbank.ivdnt.org/. Based on Van der Sijs 2010.

Valkhoff, Marius. 1931. *Les mots français d'origine néerlandaise*. Amersfoort: Valkhoff & Cie.

Van Coetsem, Frans. 2000. *A general and unified theory of the transmission process in language contact*. Heidelberg: Carl Winter.

Van de Kamp, Justus, and Jacob van der Wijk. 2006. *Koosjer Nederlands. Joodse woorden in de Nederlandse taal*. Amsterdam: Contact.

doi Van den Toorn, M.C., W.J.J. Pijnenburg, J.A. van Leuvensteijn, and J.M. van der Horst (eds). 1997. *Geschiedenis van de Nederlandse taal*. Amsterdam: AUP.

Van der Meulen, Reinder. 1909. *De Hollandsche zee- en scheepstermen in het Russisch*. Amsterdam.

Van der Meulen, Reinder. 1959. *Nederlandse woorden in het Russisch (supplement op de Hollandsche zee- en scheepstermen in het Russisch)*. Amsterdam.

Van der Sijs, Nicoline. 1998. *Geleend en uitgeleend. Nederlandse woorden in andere talen en andersom*. Amsterdam/Antwerpen: Contact.

Van der Sijs, Nicoline, and Jaap Engelsman. 2000. *Nota bene. De invloed van het Latijn en Grieks op het Nederlands*. The Hague: SDU.

Van der Sijs, Nicoline. 2001. *Chronologisch woordenboek van het Nederlands. De ouderdom en herkomst van onze woorden en betekenissen*. Amsterdam: L.J. Veen.

Van der Sijs, Nicoline. 2005. *Van Dale Groot Leenwoordenboek. De invloed van andere talen op het Nederlands*. Utrecht/Antwerpen: Van Dale Lexicografie (First ed. 1996).

Van der Sijs, Nicoline (ed.). 2005. *Wereldnederlands. Oude en jonge variëteiten van het Nederlands*. The Hague: SDU.

Van der Sijs, Nicoline. 2006a. *Calendarium van de Nederlandse taal. De geschiedenis van het Nederlands in jaartallen*. The Hague: SDU.

Van der Sijs, Nicoline. 2006b. *Klein uitleenwoordenboek*. The Hague: SDU.

doi Van der Sijs, Nicoline. 2009a. *Cookies, coleslaw and stoops. The influence of Dutch on the North-American languages*. Amsterdam/Chicago: AUP.

Van der Sijs, Nicoline. 2009b. "Import en export van woorden: tijd voor een balans." *Tijdschrift voor Nederlandse Taal- en Letterkunde* 125: 194–200.

Van der Sijs, Nicoline. 2009c. "Loanwords in Dutch." In: Haspelmath and Tadmor (eds) 2009: 338–359.

Van der Sijs, Nicoline. 2010. *Nederlandse woorden wereldwijd*. The Hague: SDU.

Van der Sijs, Nicoline (ed.). 2011. *Dialectatlas van het Nederlands*. Amsterdam: Bert Bakker. Cartography: Geografiek.

Van der Sijs, Nicoline. 2014. "Systematisch onderzoek naar Nederlandse contactvariëteiten." *Taal & Tongval* 66: 117–142.

Van der Sijs, Nicoline. 2018. "Spaanse leenwoorden in de Nederlandse dialecten." In *Woorden om te bewaren – Huldeboek voor Jacques Van Keymeulen*, ed. by T. Colleman, J. De Caluwe et al.., 673–686. Gent.

Van der Sijs, Nicoline. 2019a. *15 eeuwen Nederlandse taal*. Gorredijk: Uitgeverij Sterck & De Vreese.

Van der Sijs, Nicoline. 2019b. "*Vlaming-Flamenco*: Spaans in het Nederlands, en andersom." *Onze Taal* 6: 9–11.

Van der Sijs, Nicoline. 2021. *Taalwetten maken en vinden: het ontstaan van het Standaardnederlands*. Gorredijk: Sterck & De Vreese.

Van der Sijs, Nicoline. 2022. "1602. De Nederlandse taal gaat overzee." In *Nog meer Wereldgeschiedenis van Nederland*, ed. by L. Heerma van Voss et al.., 183–188. Amsterdam.

Van der Sijs, Nicoline. 2023. "De overlevingsgraad van Engelse leenwoorden." *In termen van taal. Liber amicorum Frieda Steurs*, ed. by Piet van Sterkenburg, Roland de Bonth, and Kris Heylen: 286–296. Schiedam: Scriptum.

Van der Wal, Marijke J. 1995. *De moedertaal centraal. Standaardisatie-aspecten in de Nederlanden omstreeks* 1650. Den Haag: SDU.

Van Rossem, Cefas. 2017. *The Virgin Islands Dutch Creole Textual Heritage: Philological Perspectives on Authenticity and Audience Design*. Utrecht: LOT.

Van Rossem, Cefas. 2021. "Drie keer Nederlands Creools." In: *Wat gebeurt er in het Nederlands?! Over taal, frequentie en variatie*, ed. by N. van der Sijs, L. Fonteyn, and M. van der Meulen, 307–313. Gorredijk: Sterck & De Vreese.

Van Sluijs, Robbert. 2017. *Variation and change in Virgin Islands Dutch Creole*. Utrecht: LOT.

Van Veen, P.A.F., and Nicoline van der Sijs. 1997. *Etymologisch woordenboek. De herkomst van onze woorden*. Utrecht/Antwerpen: Van Dale Lexicografie.

Vasmer, Max. 1953–1958. *Russisches etymologisches Wörterbuch*. Heidelberg: Winter.

Verheyden, Charlotte. 2023. *"Ge moet zien dat gij uw vlaamsche taal niet vergeet". Een historisch-sociolinguïstisch onderzoek naar de invloed van het Frans op het Zuidelijke Nederland*. PhD Brussel.

Vos, Frits. 1980. *Van keurslijfjes en keesjes, bosschieters en lijfschutters: onze voorouders in Japan en Korea en het begin der Japanse en Koreaanse studiën in Nederland*. Leiden: Universitaire Pers.

WFT = Wurdboek fan de Fryske taal. 1984-. Leeuwarden: Fryske Akademy.

CHAPTER 2

The circulation of Dutch lexical phenomena in East Asia

Christopher Joby
SOAS, University of London | University of East Anglia

Between 1639 and 1853, the Dutch were the only Europeans permitted to trade with Japan. Japanese translated many Dutch books and thereby introduced Dutch words into Japanese in various forms known collectively as lexical contact phenomena. I begin by analysing words incorporated into Japanese and then analyse how contact between Japan and other societies in East Asia after the Meiji Restoration resulted in the re-loaning of Dutch lexical contact phenomena to other languages. These include Korean and Sinitic varieties. I also examine whether any of the loanwords coming from Dutch were adopted by other languages such as Vietnamese, Uygur, and Austronesian languages spoken in Taiwan via intermediary languages such as Mandarin Chinese. I pay special attention to changes that lexical contact phenomena underwent as they were borrowed and re-borrowed.

Keywords: Japanese, lexical contact phenomena, circulation of loanwords, loanwords, calques, Chinese, Sinitic varieties, Korean, Vietnamese, Formosan languages

1. Introduction

Between 1639 and 1853, the Dutch were the only Europeans allowed to trade with Japan.[1] Initially, this was a purely commercial relationship. However, Japanese soon realized that Dutch knowledge in fields of enquiry such as medicine and astronomy could be useful to them. They therefore imported many Dutch books and translated some 1000 of these into Japanese (Joby 2020: 255–308). In the process, they introduced Dutch words into Japanese as types of lexical contact phenomena including phonemic loanwords, calques, circumlocutions, and

1. Until 1799, Dutch interests in Japan were controlled by the Dutch East India Company (VOC). Thereafter, they were controlled by the Dutch state.

https://doi.org/10.1075/impact.55.02job

conceptual transfers. I begin this chapter by analysing which words were incorporated into Japanese including dialects of Japanese. I then analyse how contact between Japan and other societies in East Asia, above all from the Meiji Restoration (明治維新 *Meiji Ishin*) onwards, resulted in the re-loaning of Dutch lexical contact phenomena to other languages. These include varieties of another Japonic language, Ryukyuan, Sinitic varieties such as Standard Chinese or Mandarin and Hokkien, and Korean. This chapter will pay detailed attention to factors which influence the form and sound of Dutch loanwords in these languages. One factor is differences in the phonotactics of Japanese and the other languages. Another factor is that whereas Japanese is a pitch-accent language, some of the recipient languages are tonal. Loanwords borrowed by these languages may therefore appear and sound quite different from their correlates in Dutch.

I shall also examine whether any of the lexical contact phenomena that resulted from contact between Dutch and Japanese were adopted by other languages such as Austroasiatic languages spoken in southeast Asia and Austronesian languages spoken in Taiwan. Here, I shall need to address the question of which language such contact phenomena were adopted from. In the case of one Austroasiatic language, Vietnamese, it was most probably Standard Chinese, whilst for the Austronesian languages in Taiwan, it may have been Japanese or one of the Sinitic varieties spoken on the island: Mandarin, Hokkien, or Hakka.

In short, this contribution will argue that Dutch has influenced the lexis of languages with which it has historically had little contact, and that it has done so through various intermediary languages, above all Japanese which in some sense functioned as a vector for Dutch lexical contact phenomena in East Asia. It therefore aims to contribute further to our understanding of the nature and extent of the circulation of Dutch loanwords. More generally, it offers a way into thinking about the processes involved in the circulation of loanwords and how these processes influence the form and sound of lexical contact phenomena in recipient languages.

One scholar who has done much work on Dutch loanwords in other languages is the co-editor of this volume, Nicoline van der Sijs (e.g., 2006). She has also provided a useful summary of previous work on Dutch loanwords in Japanese (Van der Sijs 2010: 84–5). Two scholars who have analysed Dutch loanwords in Japanese in detail are Frits Vos (e.g., 2014) and Shizuka Saitō (1967). I have built on these scholars' work adding my own analysis of lexical contact phenomena in Japanese translations of Dutch texts in a monograph on the Dutch language in Tokugawa and Meiji Japan published in 2020 (Joby 2020). Some work has also been done on the re-loaning of Dutch lexical contact phenomena in Japanese to other languages in East Asia. Frits Vos and Koos Kuiper have analysed borrowing by Korean and Standard Chinese respectively, and I have done the same for

Taiwanese Hokkien (Vos 2000b; Kuiper 1993; Joby 2020: 377–8). Much work has been done on the borrowing of Japanese words in Austronesian languages in Taiwan during the Japanese colonial period (1895–1945). However, this work does not typically identify Dutch loanwords in Japanese separately. This contribution, by contrast, does so. Finally, to date, little work has been done on the borrowing of Dutch lexical contact phenomena by other languages spoken in East Asia via Japanese including Cantonese, Vietnamese, and Uygur.

2. Methodology

In my 2020 monograph, I group the lexical outcomes of contact with Dutch using a typology developed by Donald Winford (Winford 2003: 47; Joby 2020: 332). Whilst this typology is useful, it is somewhat complex and it is not always clear which category a loanword should belong to. In this contribution, therefore, I use a more straightforward typology developed by Martin Haspelmath and modified by the Formosanist Rik De Busser.

In his work on the translation of the Bible into the Taiwanese Austronesian language, Bunun, De Busser identifies at least four major formal strategies that are used to render novel Christian concepts in Bunun: (1) loanwords, (2) calques, (3) periphrasis, and (4) conceptual transfer (De Busser 2018: 15). These categories provide a useful means of analysing words borrowed by Japanese from Dutch and subsequently borrowed by other languages from Japanese:

1. Loanwords: A loanword is "a word that at some point in the history of a language entered its lexicon as a result of borrowing (or *transfer*, or *copying*)" (Haspelmath 2009: 36, quoted in De Busser 2018: 16). In this type of borrowing, the phonological form of a lexeme is transferred from a source language into a target language. The form that it adopts in the target language, or the extent to which it undergoes phonemic substitution, depends on several factors including the phonemic set of the target language, any other languages that may have adopted it before reaching the target language, and its phonotactic system.
2. Calques or loan translations: Martin Haspelmath and Uri Tadmor (2009: 14, quoted in De Busser 2018: 19) define these as 'complex form[s] that [were] created on the model of a complex form in a donor language and whose constituents correspond semantically to the donor language constituents'.
3. Periphrasis: Where the target language lacks a suitable word, translators often create a new, periphrastic phrase or circumlocution using elements of the target language. This can include the creation of new Sinitic characters.

4. Conceptual transfer: This is where 'no phonological or grammatical material is borrowed. Instead, a source concept is mapped onto an existing, often conceptually similar expression in the target language' (De Busser 2018: 21–2). In his typology of loanwords, Donald Winford calls these 'semantic loans'. They involve a shift in the semantics of existing words or phrases in the target language under the influence of a foreign word (Winford 2003: 43–5).

3. Dutch loanwords in Japanese

In broad terms, there are three layers of lexemes in Japanese. The first layer is the original Japanese or Yamato (大和) lexicon, which preceded the influence of Chinese from the first millennium A.D. onwards.[2] The second layer consists of words that were added to the Japanese lexicon because of the influence of Chinese. These are typically referred to as Sino-Japanese (S.-J.) morphemes and words. Third, since the sixteenth century contact with other, mainly Indo-European, languages has added a layer of lexemes to the Japanese lexicon called *gairaigo* (外来語) (lit. foreign or imported word). Initially, these were often written in Sinitic characters used phonetically called *ateji* (宛字). Nowadays, they are usually written in the *katakana* syllabary. The phonemic loanwords analysed in this section are *gairaigo*.

The starting point for the circulation of loanwords and other lexical contact phenomena is contact between Dutch and Japanese which took place in Japan between 1600 and 1900, intensively so between about 1750 and 1870. In my 2020 monograph, I list 577 Japanese words, mostly nouns, that are lexical outcomes of contact with Dutch (Joby 2020: 332).[3] In this chapter, I do not attempt to provide a comprehensive list of lexical outcomes of contact with Dutch. Rather, I focus on the processes that generate these lexical outcomes and the variables that determine their form and sound, above all differences in the phonotactic systems and phonemic sets of the two languages. To give but one example here, these differences explain why the Dutch word *blik* 'tin' was adopted as *buriki* in Japanese.

2. Yamato is an ancient word for Japan (日本 (*Nihon*) is Sino-Japanese).

3. This number is somewhat higher than the number given by Nicoline van der Sijs in her contribution in this volume. This illustrates well that the data presented by authors depend on the sources used.

3.1 Phonemic loanwords

I identified 315 Dutch phonemic loanwords in Japanese (Joby 2020: 332). This number is of a similar order to those given by Frits Vos and Nicoline van der Sijs (Vos 2014; van der Sijs 2006: 117). The question of precisely how these loanwords were adopted by Japanese is not always an easy one to answer. Many loanwords and other lexical outcomes of contact between Dutch and Japanese were adopted via translations of Dutch texts. However, these 'translations' were often not word-for-word translations of source texts but a compilation of written and oral sources. For example, medical texts might be based on one principal source text but integrate knowledge that Japanese translators had acquired from Dutch physicians through oral instruction (Joby 2020: 287–8, 305). On the other hand, Dutch words such as *bier* (beer) and *koffie* (coffee) probably entered Japanese through oral transmission as the Dutch introduced these new products to their hosts.

The sound of Dutch phonemic loanwords in Japanese differs from their sound in Dutch because of several factors. First, the basic phonotactic pattern in each language is quite different. The phonotactic pattern of Dutch syllables is (C)(C)(C)V(C)(C)(C)(C).[4] This reflects the fact that Dutch has many syllable-initial and syllable-final consonant clusters. By contrast, the basic phonotactic pattern of Japanese syllables is V(owel) or C(onsonant)V(owel) (Labrune 2012: 16). The word 'strychnine' exemplifies this difference well. The Dutch *strychnine* was integrated into Japanese as *sutorikinīne* (*katakana*: ストリキニーネ), with epenthetic 'u' and 'i' inserted in the word-initial consonant cluster to accord with the (C)V phonotactic pattern in Japanese. The second 'i' is a function of another process that occurs in loanword integration, which is perseverative replication, where the epenthetic vowel is the same as the one in the previous syllable. In this case, the second 'i' replicates the first (Irwin 2011: 111–2; Joby 2020: 333).

Second, the phonemic inventories of Dutch and Japanese differ in several respects. These differences mean that Dutch words borrowed by Japanese can undergo phonemic substitution. Frits Vos provides a detailed account of Japanese phonology and highlights the most important of these differences between the Dutch and Japanese phonemic inventories (Vos 2014: 160–1). One important difference is that whereas in most cases, the basic unit of phonemic analysis in Dutch is the letter, in Japanese it is the syllable, either a vowel or consonant-vowel. Table 1 provides examples of the consequences of these differences for phonemic

4. (C) and (V) refer to sounds rather than individual letters. For example, the word *schrijven* (to write) begins with four consonants but three phonemes, viz. [sxr]. A cluster of four consonantal phonemes in the coda is unusual, for example a small set of superlatives such as *benardst* (most precarious), and these forms are not borrowed by other languages.

loanword integration in Japanese in *katakana* and Latin transcription. In contrast to Dutch, Japanese syllables equate to or are divided into moras. In Latin transliterations of Japanese words, *Q* represents a moraic obstruent and *N* a moraic nasal (Irwin 2011: 72). The numbers in the first column of Table 1 and Tables 2 & 3 are unique indicators which I use in the rest of the chapter to link the Japanese borrowings from Dutch to correlates in other languages.

Third, contemporary modern Japanese (cMJ) is based on the Tokyo dialect, which is a pitch-accent dialect. Each mora in a word has a high or low pitch. A word may or may not possess an accent. The pitch pattern (combination of high and low pitched moras) is predictable if the position of the accent is known. *Gairaigo* including Dutch loanwords are typically accented, and in most cases the accent or stress of the donor word is retained in Japanese. For example, the accent in the Dutch word *kamfer* (camphor) is on the initial syllable. So too is the accent in the Japanese loanword *kaN-furu* (カンフル) (Irwin 2011: 126–30).

Table 1. Dutch loanword integration in Japanese

No.	Native Dutch sound system	Native Japanese sound system	Dutch	Example: Meaning	Japanese Latin transliteration & *katakana*
a1	/v/	no /v/ substituted by /h/	*vet*	fat	*heQto* [a] ヘット
a2	[fa] [fe] [fi]	no [fa] [fe] [fi] – substituted by [ha] etc.	*koffie*	coffee	*kōhī* コーヒー
a3	two alveolar liquids: /l/ and /r/ [b]	one liquid: /r/	*Latijn*	Latin	*raten* ラテン *ratengo* ラテン語
a4	[du] or [dɯ]	[zɯ]	*doek*	canvas	*zukku* ズック
a5	[di]	[ʑi] (word-internally and -initially); [dʑi] (word-initially)	*digitalis* (< Latin)	digitalis	*jigitarisu* ジギタリス
a6	[tu] or [tɯ] (unvoiced equivalent of [dɯ])	[tsɯ]	*Toengoes*	Tungus	*Tsungusu* ツングース
a7	[ti] (unvoiced equivalent of [di])	[tɕi]	*typhus*	typhus	*chifusu* チフス

Table 1. *(continued)*

No.	Native Dutch sound system	Native Japanese sound system	Dutch	Example: Meaning	Japanese Latin transliteration & *katakana*
a8	[si]	no [si]	*siroop*	syrup	*shiroQpu* シロップ
a9	[m] or [n][c]	moraic nasal	*pomp*	pump	*poNpu* ポンプ
a10	diphthong <ui> IPA: œy	no diphthongs:[d] two short vowels	*spuit*	syringe	*supoito* スポイト
a11	diphthong <ij> IPA: ɛi	no diphthongs: one short vowel	*satijn*	satin	*saten* サテン
a12i	velar fricative [x]	no velar fricative: voiced velar plosive [g]	*gom*	rubber	*gomu* ゴム
a12ia	velar fricative [x]	no velar fricative: voiced velar plosive [g]	*gas*	gas	*gasu* ガス
a12ii	velar fricative [x]	no velar fricative: unvoiced velar plosive [k]	*schop*	shovel	*sukoQpu* スコップ
a13	'ye' <je>	no 'ye': use 'ze'	*jenever* (also *genever*)	gin	*zeneifuru* ゼネイフル [e]
a14	*lu*/*ru*	*ryu* [rju] C(y)V[f]	*luchtsloep* (lit. 'air sloop')	airship	*ryukutosurōpu* リュクトスロープ
a15	word-final obstruent	moraic obstruent epenthesis	*kop*	cup	*koQpu* カップ [IPA: koppɯ]
a16		adaptation or clipping	*tinctuur*	tincture	*chinki* チンキ
a17	word-final consonant (non-obstruent)	phonotactic modification	*bier*	beer	*bīru* ビール [IPA: bi:rɯ]
a18	word-final consonant (non-obstruent)	phonotactic modification	*mes*	knife	*mesu* メス [IPA: mesɯ]

Table 1. *(continued)*

No.	Native Dutch sound system	Native Japanese sound system	Dutch	Example: Meaning	Japanese Latin transliteration & *katakana*
a19	consonant cluster (non-obstruent)	anticipatory replication (first 'a')	*glas*	glass	*garasu* ガラス [IPA: garasɯ]

a. Nowadays in loanwords, /v/ is typically rendered graphically as ⟨ b ⟩ and realized as [b]. However, in the Tokugawa period, the Dutch /v/ was rendered graphically as ⟨ h ⟩ or ⟨ w ⟩. So, the Dutch 'vet' ('fat') was incorporated as *hetto* (ヘット) in Japanese.
b. Both of these are realized in more than one way. In modern Dutch, the /r/ may be realised as an alveolar roll [r], as an alveolar flap [ɾ̥], as a uvular roll [ʀ], as a uvular fricative [χ] or as a uvular approximant [ʁ]. It may also be realized as a palatal approximant like [j] in postvocalic position (Booij 1995: 8).
c. This occurs where [m] or[n] are in a syllable-final position and not intervocalic.
d. Japanese only has five vowels, which are all monophthongs, viz. (IPA) /a, e, i, o, u/.
e. Nowadays *jin* ジン (< Eng.) is used.
f. Vos (2014: 161) lists other syllables which conform to the pattern C(y)V.

3.2 Calques

There are three types of calque:

1. those where only the structural-semantic template of the source construction is borrowed, but not the lexeme. In Japanese, the morphemes used to construct these calques are typically Sino-Japanese;
2. those which exhibit partial structural and material borrowing;
3. those which borrow both the structural template and the individual lexemes.

Japanese calques on Dutch words fall into several thematic categories. Amongst these are chemistry, anatomy and medicine, grammatical terms, and physics, mathematics, and astronomy.

In the first half of the nineteenth century, Udagawa Genshin, and his son, Udagawa Yōan, translated Dutch chemistry texts into Japanese and needed to coin calques for chemical elements, compounds, and processes, many of which lacked Japanese equivalents. Together they published *Ensei ihō meibutsukō* (遠西医方名物考 'Reflections on Far Western Medical Terminology', 1822) whilst Yōan later published the multi-volume *Seimi kaisō* ('Principles of Chemistry', 1837–49). The latter work above all introduced many phonemic loanwords and calques that are still used in cMJ.

An important work on anatomy and medicine which includes many calques on Dutch words is *Kaitai shinsho* (解体新書 'A New Treatise on Anatomy'), first published in 1774.[5] This was based on a Dutch translation of a German work by Johann Adam Kulmus. Japanese physicians who were trained in Chinese medicine had traditionally not practised anatomy. There were, therefore, no native terms for many parts of the body. *Kaitai shinsho* was in fact not translated into Japanese, but *kanbun* (漢文), a form of literary Sinitic used in Japan. The new terms that it introduced were, however, incorporated into the Japanese lexicon and many are still used in cMJ.

Several *rangakusha* or Dutch Studies scholars attempted to coin Japanese calques based on Dutch grammatical terms.[6] It was, however, Mitsukuri Genpo (1799–1863) whose calques form the basis of modern Japanese grammatical terminology. Genpo based these on terms in Matthijs Siegenbeek's Dutch grammar, *Grammatica of Nederduitsche Spraakkunst*, which he re-printed in 1842 with the Japanese title *Oranda bunten zenpen* (和蘭文典前篇 'Dutch grammar Part I'). Many of Genpo's terms were published in 1856 by Iizumi Shijō in *Oranda bunten jirui* (*zenpen*) (和蘭文典字類前編 'Dutch grammar and vocabulary (Part I)') and were later published with refinements by Nakagane Masahira in *Yamatogogaku tebikigusa* (大倭語学手引草 'Guide for the study of the Japanese language', 1871), and Ōtsuki Fumihiko in *Kō Nihon bunten* (広日本文典 'Comprehensive Japanese grammar', 1897). By this time, they had become the standard grammatical terms in Japanese (Vos 2000a).

An important text in the development of Japanese terminology for physics, mathematics, and astronomy was *Rekishō shinsho* (暦象新書 'New Writings on Calendrical Phenomena', 1798–1802), by the *rangakusha* Shizuki Tadao (1760–1806). He based his work on several Dutch sources, but primarily *Inleidinge tot de waare Natuur- en Sterrekunde* (1741) ('Introduction to the true Physics and Astronomy'), the Dutch translation of a Latin work by the Scottish natural philosopher, John Keill. Tadao introduced several calques which are still the standard terms in cMJ, such as *jū-ryoku* for 'gravity' (b16) (lit. 'heavy-force'). Table 2 illustrates how this and other Japanese calques were derived from Dutch words. It also indicates the type of calque based on the three-fold categorization mentioned above.

---

5. This was a collaborative effort, primarily involving Maeno Ryōtaku, a pupil of Aoki Kon'yō, who had an excellent knowledge of Dutch, Sugita Genpaku, who had been trained in Chinese medicine, and the physician and *rangakusha*, Nakagawa Jun'an.

6. *Rangakusha* 蘭学者 used to reference Japanese who studied Dutch learning was a new coinage. It means a person (sha 者) dedicated to *rangaku* Dutch Studies. The first morpheme *ran* derives from *Oranda*, the Portuguese word for Holland. *Gaku* is a Sino-Japanese morpheme for 'study/ies'.

Table 2. Examples of Japanese calques based on Dutch words

No.	Theme	Concept or object in English	Dutch word	Japanese calque	Type of calque
b1	chemistry	element	*grondstof/hoofdstof*[a] [principal + matter]	元素 *gen-so* [origin + element]	1
b2		oxygen	*zuurstof* [acid + matter]	酸素 *san-so*[b] [acid + element]	1
b3		sulphuric acid	*zwavelzuur* [sulphur + acid]	硫酸 *ryū-san* [sulphur + acid]	1
b4		soluble	*oplosbaar* [dissolve + able]	可溶 *ka-yō* [can + dissolve]	1
b5		Leyden or Leiden jar	*Leidse fles* [Leiden (adj.) + jar/ bottle]	ライデン瓶 *Raiden-bin* [Leiden + S.-J. *bin* 'jar']	2
b6	anatomy & medicine	appendix	*blindedarm* [blind i.e., closed + intestine]	盲腸 *mō-chō* [blind + intestine]	1
b7		retina	*netvlies* [net + membrane]	網膜 *mō-maku* [net + membrane]	1
b8		hydrophobia	*hydrophobie, watervrees* [water + fear]	恐水病 *kyō-sui-byō* [fear + water + illness]	1
b9		suppository	*zet-pil* [place (vb.) + pill]	座薬 *za-yaku* [seat + medicine]	1
b10		cornea	*hoorn-vlies* [horn + membrane]	角膜 *kaku-maku* [horn + membrane]	1
b11		nostrils	*neusvleugels* [nose + wings]	鼻翼 *bi-yoku* [nose + wings]	1

Table 2. *(continued)*

No.	Theme	Concept or object in English	Dutch word	Japanese calque	Type of calque
b12		vitreous humour	*glaslichaam* [glass + body]	ガラス体 *garasu-tai* [glass + body]	2
b13	grammar terms	noun	*naamwoord* [name + word]	名詞 *mei-shi* [name + word]	1
b14		pronoun	*voornaamwoord* [for + name + word]	代名詞 *dai-mei-shi* [stands for/substitutes + *mei-shi* noun]	1
b15		verb	*werkwoord* [work + word]	動詞 *dō-shi* [movement + word]	1
b16	physics, maths & astronomy	gravity	*zwaartekracht* [heaviness + force]	重力 *jū-ryoku* [heavy + force]	1
b17		horsepower	*paardenkracht* [horse + power]	馬力 *ba-riki* [horse + power]	1

a. I use modern spelling for Dutch words, although this often differs from the spelling in the source texts.
b. The morpheme *so*素 'element(ary)' occurs in the name of several elements and is still productive in Japanese.

3.3 Periphrasis

Periphrastic phrases or circumlocutions are new words or phrases that use elements of the target language. Most of the circumlocutions resulting from contact with Dutch denote scientific instruments or natural elements including parts of the body identified by Western scientific endeavour (see Table 3). Two exceptions are *sakoku* 鎖国 and *dōkō gōitsu* 同好合 both of which were coined by Shizuki Tadao to translate terms in texts on Japan by the German physician Engelbert Kaempfer (1651–1716). *Sakoku* comprises *sa* 'chain' and *koku* 'country'. Tadao coined it to render the Latin *regnum clausum* ('closed kingdom') into Japanese, a phrase used in an appendix to Kaempfer's history of Japan to refer to the country's policy of isolation (Joby 2020: 366–7). *Dōkō gōitsu* comprises *dōkō* 'friendly communion' and *gōitsu* 'unity', and so means 'unity of friendly communion'. Tadao coined it to render *gemenebest*, the Dutch for 'commonwealth', into Japanese (Mervart 2015: 27–28). The modern Japanese word for commonwealth is *renpō* 連邦. In one case, a new *kanji* or Sinitic character was created to render a Dutch word in Japanese. The character 腺 *sen* means 'gland' (Dutch *klier*) and is a combination of two meanings: 'spring (inside the human body)' and 'meat' (Kuiper 1993: 123).[7]

Table 3. Examples of periphrastic words and phrases derived from Dutch words

No.	Theme	Concept or object	Dutch word	Japanese circumlocution
c1	chemistry	oxide	*oxyde*	酸化 *san-ka* [acid + change]
c2		organic	*bewerktuigd*	有機 *yū-ki* [have + machine]
c3		inorganic	*onbewerktuigd*	無機 *mu-ki* [not have + machine]
c4		molecule	*molecule/* *molecuul*	分子 *bun-shi* [part + child]
c5	anatomy & medicine	clavicle	*sleutelbeen* [key +bone]	鎖骨 *sa-kotsu* [chain + bone]
c6		nerve	*zenuw*	神経 *shin-kei*[a] [spirit + meridian]
c7		gland	*klier*	腺 *sen*
c8	physics, maths & astronomy	telescope	*verrekijker,* *telescoop* [afar + viewer]	望遠鏡 *bōen-kyō* [far off + mirror]
c9		atmosphere	*atmosfeer*	大気 *dai-ki* [big + air]

7. For the character decomposition, see <https://www.mdbg.net/chinese/dictionary?cdqchc =%E8%85%BA> accessed 18 January 2025.

Table 3. *(continued)*

No.	Theme	Concept or object	Dutch word	Japanese circumlocution
c10		temperature	*temperatuur*	温度 *on-do* [warm + degree]
c11		sublimation	*sublimeren*	昇華 *shō-ka* [rise up + flower]
c12		conductor	*geleider* [conductor, guide]	導體 *dō-shi* [guide + body]
c13		Celsius	*Celsius*	摂氏 *Sesshi* [lit. Dr. Settsu]
c14	botany	(flower) style	*stijl*	花柱 *ka-chū* [flower + trunk/post]
c15		stigma (top of the pistil in a flower)	*stempel*	柱頭 *chū-tō* [trunk + head]
c16	miscellaneous	fibre	*vezel*	繊維 *sen-i* [cloth woven from tree fibres + fibrous tree]
c17		photography	*fotografie*	写真術 *sha-shin-jutsu* [copy + true + art/skill]
c18		closed country	*regnum clausum* (Latin)	鎖国 *sa-koku* [chained + kingdom]
c19	grammatical term	adjective	*bijvoeg(e)lijk naamwoord* [added [to] + noun]	形容詞 *kei-yō-shi* [form + appearance + word]

a. This word was coined by Sugita Genpaku to suggest that nerves were in some sense the meridian paths along which the *shin* or spirits that controlled the body passed.

3.4 Conceptual transfer

Japanese translators extended the meaning of several words already in existence to denote concepts and objects that were introduced by the Dutch. In *Rekishō shinsho*, Shizuki Tadao extended the meaning of 秒 *byō* (S.-J.), 分 *fun* (S.-J.) and 時 *toki* (Jap.) or *ji* (S.-J.) (d1, d2, d3) to allow Japanese to divide time in the Western manner. In Chinese, 秒 was used for various types of measures, but by the Song dynasty it was used to refer to a small angle. Tadao wrote that there were 60 秒 in one minute, and so 秒 came to mean 'second'. The character he used for 'minute' was 分, the core meaning of which is 'part'. He continued by observing that there were 60 分 to one hour, for which he used 時, the core meaning of which is 'time'. All three terms have retained these new meanings in cMJ. These Sinitic characters would eventually acquire these new meanings in Chinese and Korean. One other example of a conceptual transfer is *kaku* 格 (S.-J.). The core meaning of *kaku* is 'law' or 'method'. In older Dutch grammars, nouns have four cases (nominative, accusative, genitive, and dative). In *Oranda bunten jirui*, Iizumi Shijō used *kaku* to render 'grammatical case' (Dutch: *naamval*). It still has this meaning in cMJ.

Some Dutch loanwords were only adopted by dialects and did not become part of the lexicon of cMJ. Because the Dutch were based on Deshima, an artificial island in Nagasaki Bay, according to Koga Jūjirō (2000) the Nagasaki dialect adopted as some 1,520 words of Dutch origin. One item introduced by the Dutch which was adopted in different forms by different Japanese dialects was 'potato'. The modern Japanese word for 'potato' is *jaga-imo* じゃが芋. This is a periphrasis consisting of two elements: *jaga*, which is a clipped form of *Jaga(tara)*, a version of the toponym Jakarta, the port whence the Dutch brought potatoes to Japan, and *imo*, a native Japanese word for 'tuber' (Nakamura 2005: 190). Initially, Japanese used a phonemic loanword *aarudoapperen* ('potatoes'), from the Dutch *aardappel(en)*. Japanese dialects adopted clipped forms of the second part of this word. For example, *afura* has been used in Kawanobe County, Akita Prefecture, and Ojika County, Miyagi Prefecture; and *anpura* used in Akita Prefecture (Vos 2014: 176). Some dialects adopted hybrid forms. For example, *appura-imo* has been used in Ibaraki Prefecture, to the north of Tokyo, and *Oranda-imo* in and around Nagasaki and on the nearby Goto Islands (Tokugawa 1979: 69; Joby 2020: 322–3).

4. Dutch loanwords borrowed by other languages via Japanese

In the remainder of this chapter, I analyse how these lexical contact phenomena have been adopted by other languages spoken in East Asia.

4.1 Okinawan

Okinawan or Ryukyuan is a distinct language with several varieties spoken in the Ryukyu archipelago which extends to the southwest of Japan. It belongs to the Japonic language family, which includes Japanese.[8] It uses the Japanese writing system of Sinitic characters and syllabic *kana*. Some Dutch loanwords in Japanese have been borrowed by varieties of Okinawan with slight phonemic substitution. For example, in Miyako Okinawan, spoken on Miyako Island, Okinawa Prefecture, 'beer' has the IPA pronunciation *bi:ru:*, but in Okinoerabu, spoken on Okinoerabu Island in Kagoshima Prefecture, it is *bi:ru*, written in *katakana* (< Jap. ビール *bīru* 'beer' (a17)) (Karimata 2015: 135; Van der Lubbe & Tokunaga 2015: 372). One Dutch loanword adopted via standard Japanese by the Hatoma dialect, spoken on the small island of Hatoma in Okinawa Prefecture, is *kinīne* 'quinine' (< *Dutch kinine*) (Lawrence 2012: 865; Joby 2020: 344).

4.2 Mandarin and Cantonese Chinese

Although historically, Chinese culture has exerted great influence on Japanese culture, towards the end of the nineteenth century and in the first half of the twentieth century, because of rapid industrialisation, Japan exerted a greater influence on Chinese culture and language. Books translated from Dutch to Japanese and other Japanese books including Dutch loanwords were translated into Chinese. Furthermore, Chinese students went to study in Japan. One consequence was that Chinese borrowed many Dutch lexical contact phenomena from Japanese.[9] This process was facilitated by the fact that many of these contact phenomena, above all calques, were written in characters like those used in Chinese. Koos Kuiper has previously published his work on Dutch loanwords and other outcomes of lexical interference in Japanese which were subsequently borrowed by Chinese. He identified some ninety such words which he divided into six types (Kuiper 1993; Joby 2020: 375–7):

1. Phonemic loans. As noted above, previously loanwords in Japanese were often written in Sinitic characters called *ateji*, based not on meaning, but sound, and it was in this form that they were adopted by Chinese, with phonemic adaptation;

8. For a classification of varieties of Okinawan, see Curry (2004: 55).

9. Some authors refer to this language as Standard Chinese. Chinese terms include 國語 *Guóyǔ* (lit. national language), a term often used in Taiwan, and 普通話 *Pǔtōnghuà* (lit. common speech) (San 2007: 5).

2. Graphic loans. All outcomes of lexical interference because of contact between Japanese and Chinese are graphic loans, where it is the written form rather than the phonemic shape that is borrowed;
3. Hybrid words. These consist of native Japanese and loaned Dutch morphemes;
4. Loan-translations or calques 'in a strict sense'. These are words which were translated from Dutch to Japanese on a morpheme-by-morpheme basis;
5. Semantic loanwords. These are words that were drawn by Japanese translators of Dutch texts from Chinese classics and were subsequently re-borrowed by Chinese;
6. Induced new creations (cf. periphrasis). New coinages which are descriptive rather than having a morphemic connection to the foreign words that inspired them.

Chinese also adopted the new character 腺 'gland'.

Table 4 gives examples of each type of loanword in Standard Chinese or Mandarin. In contrast to cMJ, which is a pitch-accent language, Mandarin Chinese is a tonal language. It has four tones and a neutral tone. The tones are represented in the table in the *pinyin* transcription of the loanwords in Mandarin. The first tone is high and level, e.g., *ā*; the second tone rises *á*; the third tone falls and rises *ǎ*; and the fourth tone falls *à*. Furthermore, although all the loanwords are graphic loans (type 2), the phonemes used to pronounce the characters often differ significantly between the two languages. For example, 盲腸 'appendix' is pronounced *mōchō* in Japanese, but *máng-cháng* in Mandarin.

Cantonese Chinese has also borrowed loanwords from Dutch via Japanese, probably via Standard Chinese, although direct borrowing cannot be ruled out. Cantonese is spoken by over 80 million people in the southern province of Guangdong (廣東), in surrounding regions including Hong Kong and Macau, and by the extensive Cantonese and Hong Kong diasporas. The number of tones in Cantonese is subject to dialectal variation. Hong Kong Cantonese has six tones: 1. High-level; 2. High rising; 3. Mid-level; 4. Low falling; 5. Low rising; 6. Low-level. This affects how loanwords are integrated into Cantonese (Matthews & Yip 1994: 20–21).[10]

For example, Japanese borrowed the Dutch word for 'noun' *naamwoord* as the calque 名詞 *meishi* (b13). Chinese borrowed this as a graphic loanword, i.e., written as 名詞. In Mandarin *pinyin* this is written as *míngcí*, i.e., with two rising or second tones. In Cantonese, the word is also *mingci*, but with two fourth tones,

10. Some dialects of Cantonese have three entering tones for syllables ending in t, k, or p. However, in broad terms Cantonese has six tones.

represented in Cantonese *pinyin* as *ming4 ci4*. Whereas the second tone in Mandarin is rising, the fourth tone in Cantonese is low falling. There are also phonemic differences. For example, /ŋ/ <ng> can be word-initial in Cantonese, but not in Mandarin. This occurs in the Cantonese rendering of gas, *ngaa5 si1*, which contrasts with the Mandarin *wǎsī*.[11]

The case of Celsius is interesting. Japanese coined the calque 摂氏 *Sesshi* (c13) from the Dutch Celsius. The first element is a clipped form of Celsius and the second element is an honorific meaning Mr. or Dr. This was subsequently borrowed as a graphic loanword by Mandarin and Cantonese. Table 4 provides other examples of Dutch loanwords in Japanese which have been borrowed by Cantonese and Mandarin.

Table 4. Dutch loanwords in Mandarin Chinese borrowed via Japanese, and in Cantonese

Loan-word type	English meaning	Dutch	Jap. code	Japanese loanword	Mandarin graphic loanword with *pinyin*	Cantonese graphic loanword with *pinyin*
1.	gas	*gas*	a12ia	ガス *gasu*	瓦斯 *wǎsī*	瓦斯 *ngaa5 si1*
3.	Celsius	*Celsius*	c13	摂氏 *Sesshi* [lit. Dr. Settsu]	攝[a]氏 *Shèshì* [lit. Dr. Settsu]	攝氏 *sip3 si6* [lit. Dr. Settsu]
4.	element	*grondstof/ hoofdstof* [principal + matter]	b1	元素 *gen-so* [origin + element]	元素 *yuán-sù* [origin + element]	元素 *jyun4 sou3* [origin + element]
	sulphuric acid	*zwavelzuur* [sulphur + acid]	b3	硫酸 *ryū-san* [sulphur + acid]	硫酸 *liú-suān* [sulphur + acid]	硫酸 *lau4 syun1* [sulphur + acid]
	soluble	*oplosbaar* [dissolve + able]	b4	可溶 *ka-yō* [can + dissolve]	可溶 *kěróng* [can + dissolve]	可溶 *ho2 jung4* [can + dissolve]

11. Tone 5 is low rising and tone 1 high level. Nowadays, word-initial /ŋ/ is being replaced by a glottal stop in casual speech (Matthews & Yip 1994: 16, 21).

Table 4. *(continued)*

Loan-word type	English meaning	Dutch	Jap. code	Japanese loanword	Mandarin graphic loanword with *pinyin*	Cantonese graphic loanword with *pinyin*
	appendix	*blindedarm* [blind + intestine]	b6	盲腸 *mō-chō* [blind + intestine]	盲腸 *máng-cháng* [blind + intestine]	盲腸 *maang4 coeng2* [blind + intestine]
	retina	*netvlies* [net + membrane]	b7	網膜 *mo-maku* [net + membrane]	視網膜 *shì-wǎng-mó* [see + net + membrane]	視網膜 *si6 mong5 mok6* [see + net + membrane]
	suppository	*zetpil* [place + pill]	b9	座薬 *za-yaku* [seat + medicine]	座薬 *zuò-yào* [seat + medicine]	座薬 *zo6 joek6* [seat + medicine]
	noun	*naamwoord* [name + word]	b13	名詞 *mei-shi* [name + word]	名詞 *míng-cí* [name + word]	名詞 *ming4 ci4* [name + word]
	verb	*werkwoord* [work + word]	b15	動詞 *dō-shi* [movement + word]	動詞 *dòng-cí* [movement + word]	動詞 *dung6 ci4* [movement + word]
	horse-power	*paardenkracht* [horse + power]	b17	馬力 *ba-riki* [horse + power]	馬力 *mǎ-lì* [horse + power]	馬力 *maa5 lik6* [horse + power]
	organic	*bewerktuigd*	c2	有機 *yū-ki* [have + machine]	有機 *yǒu-jī* [have + machine]	有機 *jau5 gei1* [have + machine]
	inorganic	*onbewerktuigd*	c3	無機 *mu-ki* [not have+ machine]	無機 *wú-jī* [not have + machine]	無機 *mou4 gei1* [not have + machine]

Table 4. *(continued)*

Loan-word type	English meaning	Dutch	Jap. code	Japanese loanword	Mandarin graphic loanword with *pinyin*	Cantonese graphic loanword with *pinyin*
	molecule	*molecule/ molecuul*	c4	分子 *bun-shi* [part + child]	分子 *fēn-zǐ* [part + child]	分子 *fan1 zi2* [part + child]
	nerve	*zenuw*	c6	神経 *shin-kei* [spirit + meridian]	神経 *shén-jīng* [spirit + meridian]	神経 *san4 ging1* [spirit + meridian]
	atmosphere	*atmosfeer*	c9	大気 *dai-ki* [big + air]	大気 *dà-qì* [big + air]	大気 *daai6 hei3* [big + air]
	temperature	*temperatuur*	c10	温度 *on-do* [warm + degree]	溫度 *wēn-dù* [warm + degree]	溫度 *wan1 dou6* [warm + degree]
	conductor	*geleider* [conductor, guide]	c12	導體 *dō-shi* [guide + body]	導體 *dǎo-tǐ* [guide + body]	導體 *dou6 tai2* [guide + body]
	(flower) style	*stijl*	c14	花柱 *ka-chū* [flower + trunk/post]	花柱 *huā-zhù* [flower + trunk/post]	花柱 *faa1 cyu5* [flower + trunk/post]
	closed country	*regnum clausum*	c18	鎖国 *sa-koku* [chained + kingdom]	鎖国 *suǒ-guó* [chained + kingdom]	鎖国 *so2 gwok3* [chained + kingdom]
5.	cartilage	*kraakbeen* [crack-bone]		軟骨 *nan-kotsu* [flexible + bone][b]	软骨 *ruǎn-gǔ* [flexible + bone]	软骨 *jyun5 gwat1* [flexible + bone]
6.	clavicle	*sleutelbeen*	c5	鎖骨 *sa-kotsu* [chain + bone]	鎖骨 *suǒ-gǔ* [chain + bone]	鎖骨 *so2 gwat1* [chain + bone]

Table 4. *(continued)*

Loan-word type	English meaning	Dutch	Jap. code	Japanese loanword	Mandarin graphic loanword with *pinyin*	Cantonese graphic loanword with *pinyin*
	gland	*klier*	c7	腺 *sen*	腺 *xiàn*	腺 *sin*3
	fibre	*vezel*	c16	繊維 *sen-i* [cloth woven from tree fibres + fibrous tree]	纖維 *xiān-wéi* [cloth woven from tree fibres + fibrous tree]	纖維 *cim*1 *wai*4 [cloth woven from tree fibres + fibrous tree]

a. 摂 and 攝 are two forms of the same Sinitic character (*Shinjitai* (simplified) and Kyūjitai (traditional) respectively).
b. This term was first used by a Japanese author in *Kaitai shinsho* ('A New Treatise on Anatomy') (1774), written in *kanbun*, a mode of literary Sinitic used in Japan.

4.3 Other Sinitic varieties

A full survey of these loanwords in Sinitic varieties is beyond the scope of this contribution. I shall, however, give a few examples of lexical contact phenomena in other Sinitic varieties. Wu (吳語) is a group of Sinitic languages spoken in eastern China, which includes Shanghainese (上海話). One example of a loanword in Shanghainese is 'appendix' 盲腸 which is pronounced *maon*6 *zan*6, where the 'n' in *pinyin* is nasalized (IPA: mãzã).[12] Hakka (客家话) has several dialects and is spoken in southeast China and Taiwan as well as by the Hakka diaspora. It is therefore difficult to be certain of the donor language for loanwords. Furthermore, speakers of Hakka typically also speak Mandarin so may switch to Mandarin when discussing technical subjects such as medicine or physics. Further research therefore needs to be done on the Hakka borrowing of the loanwords analysed in this chapter.[13] Dialects of Hokkien or Southern Min (閩南語) are spoken in southeast China, Taiwan, and other countries such as Malaysia and Indonesia. After the First Sino-Japanese War (1894/5), Qing China ceded Taiwan to Japan.

12. < https://wugniu.com/search?char=%E7%9B%B2%E8%85%B8&table=shanghai> accessed 18 January 2025.

13. According to a Taiwanese Hakka informant, who speaks Hakka, Mandarin and English, she uses words such as 盲腸 (appendix), 温度 (temperature) and 神経 (nerve) but uses something close to Mandarin pronunciation.

Japanese became the official language of Taiwan and Taiwanese were obliged to learn Japanese at school. During the Japanese colonial period (1895–1945), Taiwanese Southern Min (TSM 臺灣閩南語) was the principal Sinitic language spoken in Taiwan. There was therefore intensive contact between Japanese and TSM which resulted in lexical borrowing by TSM. In 2011, the R.O.C. government made a list of 172 commonly-used Japanese words in TSM (Joby 2020: 377–8). These typically first entered Formosan Japanese, a variety of Japanese spoken in Taiwan during the Japanese colonial period, and then TSM. Whilst Japanese uses pitch, like other Sinitic varieties TSM uses tones. In fact, it has nine tones. Therefore, when a Dutch loanword was borrowed by Japanese each mora would be ascribed a high or low pitch. When that word was reborrowed by TSM, each syllable was ascribed a tone. Chang Yü-hung observes that there was a high degree of regularity in the relationship between Japanese pitch and TSM tone. One Dutch word that entered TSM in this manner was 'beer' (a17). In Japanese, this was borrowed as *bīru* (IPA: biːrɯ). Via Taiwanese Japanese it was borrowed by TSM as *bi²-lu³*, i.e., the first syllable has a second tone and the second syllable a third tone.[14] Another example is 'gas'. The Dutch word 'gas' was adopted by Japanese as *gasu* (IPA: gasɯ) (a12ia). It underwent two changes. The initial 'g' was hardened and a word-final 'u' (IPA: ɯ) was added to fit the Japanese phonotactic pattern of (V/C)V. This was adopted in TSM, via Formosan Japanese, as *ga¹-suh⁴* (Chang 1993: 111; Klöter 2005: 22).[15]

4.4 Taiwanese Austronesian languages

Japanese also had contact with speakers of Austronesian languages spoken by indigenous Austronesian people who have lived in Taiwan for some 5,000 years. Tables 5a and 5b give examples of Dutch loanwords and calques in Japanese which were borrowed by seven of these Taiwanese Austronesian languages, also called Formosan languages: Amis, Kanakanavu, Puyuma, Rukai (Labuan dialect), Saisiyat, Seediq (Toda dialect), and Tsou.[16] The available data is limited but a few trends emerge. Several of the languages borrowed the words for 'beer', 'gas', 'glass', and 'cup'.[17] Table 5a illustrates how these Formosan languages have adopted

14. There is not, however, universal agreement on the tones. Henning Klöter also gives *bi²-lu⁴*, based on Wu Shouli's Taiwanese-Mandarin dictionary published in 2000 (Klöter 2005: 193). This is transcribed in 'Modern Taiwanese Language' orthography as *bielux* or *bieluq*.

15. This is transcribed in 'Modern Taiwanese Language' orthography as *gafsuq*.

16. For more on language contact and Formosan languages, see Zeitoun and Goudin (2024).

17. Kavalan has borrowed Japanese *bīru* as bilu [βi.rú] (Lin 2023: 298). Mantauran Rukai has borrowed カップ [koQpu] < Dutch *kop* 'cup' as *kopo* (Zeitoun & Goudin 2024).

'beer' (a17) and 'gas' (a12ia). In some cases, phonemic substitution is minimal but in other cases it is significant. For example, central Amis has *filu* for beer (elsewhere in Amis *filo*) (< Jap. *bīru* (IPA: bi:rɯ) < Dutch *bier*). The shift from word-initial /b/ to /f/ in Amis arises from the lack of /b/ in the Amis phonemic set (Fey 1986).[18] Tsou also lacks /b/ in its native phonemic set, so it is replaced by a voiced labiodental fricative /v/ viz. *viiru* (Chen 2002: 93). The Japanese word *bīru* 'beer' ends in a short, open vowel (IPA: ɯ). By contrast, the form in Saisiyat, *biru'* [IPA: βiruʔ], ends in a glottal stop, which is phonemic (Kaybaybaw, Lim & Zeitoun 2020: 168–9). Furthermore, the word-initial voiced bilabial plosive /b/ shifts to a voiced bilabial fricative /β/. Puyuma lacks the high back unrounded vowel [IPA: ɯ]. In some cases, this is replaced by [u], e.g., IPA: *bi:rɯ* -> *biru*, but in other cases by schwa represented graphically with 'e', e.g. *gasu* -> *gase* (IPA: gasɯ -> gasə 'gas') (Lin 2015: 28–9). Amis has borrowed 'gas' as *kasu*. It has a velar nasal /ŋ/, but no voiced velar plosive /g/. It does, however, have an unvoiced velar plosive /k/, which probably explains the word-initial *k*.[19] Saisiyat also lacks a voiced velar plosive /g/ (Zeitoun *et al.* 2015: 15). It has therefore adopted 'gas' as *ngase* (IPA: ŋaθə), although via Hakka, which is spoken close to Saisiyat areas in northwest Taiwan, rather than directly from Japanese.

Table 5b provides details of other Japanese lexical contact phenomena in Formosan languages from or influenced by Dutch. As noted above, the meaning of 分 *fun* (d1) was extended in Japanese to denote 'minute'. This was borrowed as *hun* by Puyuma as it lacks /f/ (Lin 2015: 16). One Japanese calque on a Dutch word that has been borrowed by Toda Seediq is *byoying* 'hospital'. This derives from the Sino-Japanese 病院 *byō-in* (lit. 'illness' + 'public building') which is a calque on the Dutch *ziekenhuis* (sick people + house). The word-final moraic nasal /ɴ/ in Japanese is replaced by a velar nasal /ŋ/ in Toda Seediq. Also in Toda Seediq, *kopu* 'cup' (a15) has undergone degemination, or to put it another way the mora obstruent has been removed (< Jap. *koQpu*).

The Tsou word for 'potato', *zagaimo*, derives from the Japanese *jaga-imo* じゃが芋, mentioned above. The Tsou phonemic set lacks a voiced post-alveolar affricate [d͡ʒ], so the word-initial [d͡ʒ] in Japanese is replaced by [z] (Chen 2002: 16). Another Japanese loanword in Tsou is *kešigomu* 'eraser'. This derives from *keshi-gomu* 消しゴム, which is a hybrid calque derived from the Sino-Japanese *ke(shi)* 'to cancel' and the Dutch *gom* 'rubber'.

Finally, Yilan Creole emerged in northeast Taiwan because of contact between Japanese and another Formosan language, Atayal or Tayal. Most of its vocabulary derives from Japanese. Two examples of Dutch loanwords are *kopu* cup and

18. For the sound system of Amis, see the 'Linguistic Chart' in the front matter of Fey (1986).

19. For more on Japanese loanwords in Amis, see Chien (2018; 2019), Hsu (2003) and Ju (2022).

garas 'glass'. *Kopu* has undergone degemination, whilst *garas* has undergone vowel devoicing in the word-final position (Lin 2020).[20]

Table 5a. A comparative analysis of the borrowing of beer and gas by Formosan languages

	Japanese	Amis	Kan.	Puyuma	Labuan Rukai[a]	Saisiyat	Toda Seediq	Tsou
beer	ビール *bīru* IPA: bi:rɯ	*filo/ filu*	*piru*	*biru*	*bire* IPA: birə	*biru'* IPA: βiruʔ	*biru*	*viiru*
gas	ガス *gasu* IPA: gasɯ	*kasu*	*kasʉ*	*gase* IPA: gasə	*gase* IPA: gasə	*ngase*[b] IPA: ŋaθə	*gasu*	

a. I thank Elizabeth Zeitoun for this information.
b. This has been borrowed from Hakka, a Sinitic language spoken close to Saisiyat areas in northwest Taiwan.

Table 5b. Other Dutch loanwords in Formosan languages via Japanese

Formosan language and source	No.	Meaning in English	Japanese code	Dutch	Japanese loanword/ calque	Formosan word
Puyuma (Lin 2015)	1.	glass	a19	*glas*	ガラス *garasu* [IPA: garasɯ]	*garas*
	2.	rubber	a12i	*gom*	ゴム *gomu* [IPA: gomɯ]	*gumu*
	3.	minute	d2	*minuut*	分 *fun* [IPA: ɸɯn]	*hun*
Saisiyat	1.	cup	a15	*kop*	カップ *koQpu* [IPA: koppɯ]	*koppo'* [IPA: koppoʔ]

20. For more on Yilan Creole and on each of the Formosan languages mentioned in this chapter, see Li, Zeitoun & De Busser (2024).

Table 5b. *(continued)*

Formosan language and source	No.	Meaning in English	Japanese code	Dutch	Japanese loanword/ calque	Formosan word
Toda Seediq (Pai 2021)	1.	rubber	a12i	*gom*	ゴム *gomu* [IPA: gomɯ]	*gomu*
	2.	cup	a15	*kop*	カップ *koQpu*	*kopu*
	3.	hospital		*ziekenhuis* [ill + house]	病院 *byō-in* [illness + public building]	*byoying*
Tsou (Chen 2002)	1.	cup	a15	*kop*	カップ *koQpu*	*koppu* [a]
	2.	glass	a19	*glas*	ガラス *garasu*	*garasu*
	3.	eraser	a12i	*gom*	消しゴム *keshi-gomu*	*kešigomu*
	4.	potato		(*aardappel*)	じゃが芋 *jaga-imo*	*zagaimo*
Yilan Creole (Lin 2022)	1.	cup	a15	*kop*	カップ *koQpu*	*kopu*
	2.	glass	a19	*glas*	ガラス *garasu*	*garas*

a. Chen (2002) gives two renderings of 'cup' in Tsou, one aspirated *kopp^h^u* (p.145) and one non-aspirated *koppu* (p.108).

4.5 Korean

The origins of Korean are uncertain. One leading theory argues that it branched out several thousand years ago from Proto-Altaic (Chang 1996:1). Like Japanese, it has absorbed thousands of words from Chinese and more recently from Western languages. In the late nineteenth century, Korea came increasingly into the sphere of influence of the rapidly-modernizing Japan. Many Koreans went to study in Japan during this period. In 1910, Japan fully annexed Korea and colonized the country until the end of WWII. Because of this intensive contact, Korean borrowed many words from Japanese, including Dutch loanwords. Frits

Vos provides a detailed description of Dutch loanwords in Korean (Vos 2000b; 2014). Chiyuki Itō and colleagues analyse the adaptation into Korean of Japanese loanwords including Dutch loanwords in Japanese (Itō *et al.* 2006). More recently, I provided a summary of Vos's work and that of other scholars such as Sohn Ho-Min (Joby 2020; Sohn 1999). Here, I shall examine the processes involved in the borrowing of two types of Dutch loanword in Korean via Japanese: phonemic and graphic loanwords.

4.5.1 *Phonemic loanwords*

Vos (2000b) lists fifty-one phonemic loanwords in Korean which have entered the language via Japanese. Because of differences between the Japanese and Korean phonotactic systems and phonemic sets, the phonemic shape of the lexeme in Korean often differs from its equivalent in Japanese (Sohn 1999: 116). In contrast to the (C)V phonotactic pattern in Japanese, Korean has (C)(G)V(C), where (G) is a glide. One difference in the phonemic sets is that whereas Japanese has a word-initial /b/, Korean only has /b/ between sonorants (Itō *et al.* 2006: 75; Chang 1996: 15). So, *bīru* [IPA: biːrɯ] (< Dutch *bier* 'beer') (a17) was adopted by Korean with a word-initial [p] (Vos 2014: 180).[21] The word-final [*ɯ*] is often replaced by schwa in Korean. So, *mesu* [IPA: mesɯ] (< Dutch *mes* 'knife') (a18) in Japanese was adopted by Korean as *mesə*. This word has also undergone semantic shift, for it means 'knife' in Dutch, but 'scalpel' is Japanese and Korean.

4.5.2 *Graphic loanwords*

These loanwords were often borrowed from Dutch as calques or circumlocutions by Japanese. During the late nineteenth century and the Japanese colonial period in Korea, the use of Sinitic characters was still widespread. Therefore, these words were borrowed as graphic loanwords. Table 6 provides examples of these words. It gives the Dutch word, the code for lexical contact phenomena in Tables 1, 2 & 3 above, the Japanese calque or circumlocution and two versions of the loanword in Korean. The first uses Sinitic characters and the second uses *hangeul*, the official alphabetic writing system now used for Korean.[22] The Sinitic characters were read and pronounced in the Sino-Korean as opposed to the native Korean manner. Nevertheless, Sino-Korean pronunciation differs significantly from Sino-Japanese pronunciation because of the differences in the Korean and Japanese phonemic and phonotactic systems.[23] For example, 盲腸 is pronounced as *mōchō* in Japan-

21. The standard word for 'beer' in Korean is now the Sino-Korean *maekchu*. I use the McCune-Reischauer transliteration system.

22. *Hangeul* was invented in the fifteenth century, but usage only became widespread in the twentieth century.

23. For more on Korean phonetics and phonology, see Shin *et al.* (2013).

ese, but *maengjang* in Korean (b6). Another difference is that whereas Japanese has a word-initial /d/, Korean only has /d/ between sonorants. So, *dae-gi* 'atmosphere' in Japanese is pronounced *tae-gi* in Korean (Table 6, 10).

Table 6. Korean words borrowed as graphic loanwords from Japanese calques

No.	English meaning	Dutch	Jap. code	Japanese calque	Korean graphic loanword in Sinitic characters	Korean loanword in *hangeul*
1	element	*grondstof/ hoofdstof* [principal + matter]	b1	元素 *gen-so* [origin + element]	元素 *weon-so* [origin + element]	원소 *weon-so* [origin + element]
2	oxygen	*zuurstof* [acid + matter]	b2	酸素 *san-so* [acid + element]	酸素 *san-so* [acid + element]	산소 *san-so* [acid + element]
3	sulphuric acid	*zwavelzuur* [sulphur + acid]	b3	硫酸 *ryū-san* [sulphur + acid]	硫酸 *yu-san* [sulphur + acid]	유산 *yu-san* [sulphur + acid]
4	appendix	*blindedarm* [blind i.e., closed + intestine]	b6	盲腸 *mōchō* [blind + intestine]	盲腸 *maeng-jang* [blind + intestine]	맹장 *maeng-jang* [blind + intestine]
5	retina	*netvlies* [net + membrane]	b7	網膜 *mo-maku* [net + membrane]	網膜 *mang-mak* [net + membrane]	망막 *mang-mak* [net + membrane]
6.	hydrophobia	*hydrophobie, watervrees* [water + fear]	b8	恐水病 *kyō-sui-byō* [fear + water + illness]	恐水病 *gong-su-byeong* [fear + water + illness]	공수병 *gong-su-byeong* [fear + water + illness]
7.	noun	*naamwoord* [name + word]	b13	名詞 *mei-shi* [name + word]	名詞 *myŏng-sa* [name + word]	명사 *myŏng-sa* [name + word]

Table 6. *(continued)*

No.	English meaning	Dutch	Jap. code	Japanese calque	Korean graphic loanword in Sinitic characters	Korean loanword in *hangeul*
8.	verb	*werkwoord* [work + word]	b15	動詞 *dō-shi* [movement + word]	動詞 *tong-sa* [movement + word]	동사 *tong-sa* [movement + word]
9.	clavicle	*sleutelbeen*	c5	鎖骨 *sa-kotsu* [chain + bone]	鎖骨 *swae-gol* [chain + bone]	쇄골 *swae-gol* [chain + bone]
10.	atmosphere	*atmosfeer*	c9	大気 *dai-ki* [big + air]	大気 *tae-gi* [big + air]	대기 *tae-gi* [big + air]
11.	temperature	*temperatuur*	c10	温度 *on-do* [warm + degree]	温度 *on-do* [warm + degree]	온도 *on-do* [warm + degree]
12.	(flower) style	*stijl*	c14	花柱 *ka-chū* [flower + trunk/post]	花柱 *hwa-ju* [flower + trunk/post]	화주 *hwa-ju* [flower + trunk/post]

4.6 Vietnamese

Like Korean, Vietnamese has been influenced by Chinese for many centuries. Although Vietnam became part of French Indochina in the late nineteenth century, the Vietnamese language continued to be influenced by Chinese and borrow words from it.[24] As educated Vietnamese continued to use Sinitic characters, *Chữ Hán* for writing literary Chinese (*Hán văn*) and *Chữ Nôm*, a modified Sinitic script, to write Vietnamese, which has many Sino-Vietnamese words, loanwords from Chinese were graphic loanwords (Kornicki 2018: 63–4; Sinh 1993, 1996). These are now written in the Romanized Vietnamese script, *chữ Quốc ngữ*, originally developed by the Portuguese Jesuit missionary Francisco de

24. For more on loanwords in Vietnamese in general, see Alves (2009).

Pina (1585–1625).[25] The Sinitic characters in these Vietnamese words borrowed from Chinese are pronounced in the Sino-Vietnamese manner. However, Sino-Vietnamese pronunciation can differ significantly from the pronunciation of the same characters in Chinese. Whereas Standard Chinese has four tones, Vietnamese has six (with diacritical marks): 1. High (or mid) level (no mark); 2. Low falling (grave accent); 3. High (or mid) rising (acute accent); 4. Creaking-rising (glottalised) (tilde); 5. (Low) dipping-rising (hook above); and 6. Constricted (glottalised) (dot below) (Nguyễn 1997: 25–6).[26] For example, *trọng-lực* (Table 7, 5) has a sixth tone followed by a fifth tone. Furthermore, the Vietnamese phonemic set differs from that of Standard Chinese. Vietnamese, like Cantonese, but unlike Standard Chinese, has word-initial /ŋ/, realized graphically as <ng>. 'Element' 元素 (7, 1) is *nguyên tố* in Vietnamese, but *yuán-sù* in Standard Chinese. Table 7 gives examples of Dutch lexical borrowings in Vietnamese via Japanese and Chinese.

Table 7. Dutch loanwords in Vietnamese via Japanese and Chinese

No.	English meaning	Dutch word	Jap. code	Japanese calque	Chinese graphic loanword	Vietnamese graphic loanword & Romanized form (*chữ Quốc ngữ*)
1.	element	*grondstof/ hoofdstof* [principal + matter]	b1	元素 *gen-so* [origin + element]	元素 *yuán-sù* [origin + element]	元素 *nguyên tố* [origin + element]
2.	noun	*naamwoord* [name-word]	b13	名詞 *mei-shi* [name + word]	名詞 *myŏng-sa* [name + word]	名詞 *danh từ* [name + word]
3.	pronoun	*voornaamwoord* [stands for + name + word]	b14	代名詞 *dai-mei-shi* [stands for/ substitutes + noun]	代名詞 *dài-míng-cí* [stands for/ substitutes + noun]	代名詞 *đại danh từ* [stands for/substitutes + noun]

25. *Chữ Hán* means 'Chinese writing; *Chữ Nôm* means 'writing of the south' (Vietnam is south of China); and *chữ Quốc ngữ* means writing of the national language'.

26. Nguyễn (1997: 15–34) provides a detailed account of the Vietnamese sound system.

Table 7. *(continued)*

No.	English meaning	Dutch word	Jap. code	Japanese calque	Chinese graphic loanword	Vietnamese graphic loanword & Romanized form (*chữ Quốc ngữ*)
4.	verb	*werkwoord* [work + word]	b15	動詞 *dō-shi* [movement + word]	動詞 *dong-sa* [movement + word]	動詞 *động từ* [movement + word]
5.	gravity	*zwaartekracht* [heavy + force]	b16	重力 *jū-ryoku* [heavy + force]	重力 *zhòng-lì* [heavy + force]	重力 *trọng-lực* [heavy + force]
6.	horsepower	*paardenkracht* [horse + power]	b17	馬力 *ba-riki* [horse + power]	馬力 *mǎ-lì* [horse + power]	馬力 *mã lực* [horse + power]
7.	organic	*bewerktuigd*	c2	有機 *yū-ki* [have + machine]	有機 *yǒu-jī* [have + machine]	有機 *hữu cơ* [have + machine]
8.	inorganic	*onbewerktuigd*	c3	無機 *mu-ki* [not have + machine]	無機 *wú-jī* [not have + machine]	無機 *vô cơ* [not have + machine]
9.	molecule	*molecule/ moleculu*	c4	分子 *bun-shi* [part + child]	分子 *fēn-zǐ* [part + child]	分子 *phân tử* [part + child]
10.	nerve	*zenuw*	c6	神経 *shin-kei* [spirit + meridian]	神経 *shén-jīng* [spirit + meridian]	神経 *thần kinh* [spirit + canal]
11.	gland	*klier*	c7	腺 *sen*	腺 *xiàn*	腺 *tuyến*

4.7 Other languages

Other languages for which there is less evidence of borrowing of the lexical contact phenomena analysed in this chapter include Uygur, Tibetan, Ainu, Manchu, and Mongolian. Uygur is a Turkic language written in Arabic script spoken in the semi-autonomous province of Xinjiang (新疆) in northwest China. Given the influence of the Chinese state and Standard Chinese on the Uygur people and their language, several loanwords have probably been adopted by Uygur from Dutch via Japanese and Mandarin. Table 8 gives examples of likely Uygur calques on Chinese graphic loanwords of Japanese calques and circumlocutions from Dutch words.[27]

Tibetan is a Sino-Tibetan language spoken in the semi-autonomous province of Tibet in southwest China. Like Xinjiang, its language and culture have been subject to extensive Sinification. One probable loanword which can trace its origins back to Dutch via Standard Chinese and Japanese is the word for 'noun' མིང་ཚིག (ming tshig) (b13) cf. Standard Chinese 名詞 *míng-cí*.[28] Another possible candidate is the Tibetan word for 'adjective' རྒྱན་ཚིག (rgyan tshig). This may be derived from the second and third morphemes of the Mandarin Chinese word, 形容詞 *xíngróngcí*, which traces its origin via Japanese to the Dutch word for adjective, *bijvoeg(e)lijk naamwoord* (lit. added [to] noun) (c19) (Joby 2020:359). The Tibetan words are both loanwords that have undergone phonemic substitution.[29]

Ainu has historically been spoken on Hokkaido (formerly Ezo) and adjoining islands, but with the advance of Japanese, it is now an endangered language, which may no longer have any native speakers. It is generally agreed that Ainu is genetically unrelated to Japanese, but because of language contact it has adopted loanwords from its neighbour. Using Batchelor's 1905 English-Japanese-Ainu lexicon, although I have identified several loanwords from Portuguese via Japanese, I have not identified any Japanese loanwords in Ainu, which were borrowed from Dutch (Batchelor 1905; Joby 2020:380). On the other hand, Batchelor does not include entries for certain words that Japanese borrowed from Dutch, such as 'coffee' and 'potato'. Further investigation may reveal evidence for Ainu borrowing such loanwords.

27. A lack of written sources on Uygur make it difficult to confirm that these are definitely loanwords from Chinese, but this is most probable.

28. This replaces an earlier term transcribed as *dnos min* (Jäschke 1998:131). Jäschke's Tibetan lexicon was first published in the 1870s.

29. Given the small number of examples for Tibetan, I shall not address questions about tone in the language. Tibetan has two to four tones depending on the variety, although Lhasa Tibetan may lack tones (Kjellin 1977).

Table 8. Likely Uygur calques on Chinese graphic loanwords of Japanese calques and circumlocutions from Dutch

No.	English meaning	Dutch	Jap. code	Japanese calque	Chinese graphic loanword	Uygur calque in Arabic script & Roman transliteration[a]
1.	cornea	*hoorn-vlies* [horn + membrane]	b10	角膜 *kaku-maku* [horn + membrane]	角膜 *jiǎo-mó* [horn + membrane]	مۈڭگۈز پەردە *münggüz perde*[b] [horn + membrane]
2.	nostrils	*neus-vleugels* [nose + wings]	b11	鼻翼 *bi-yoku* [nose + wings]	鼻翼 *bí-yì* [nose + wings]	بۇرۇن قانىتى *burun qaniti* [nose + wings][c]
3.	appendix	*blindedarm* [blind + intestine]	b6	盲腸 *mō-chō* [blind + intestine]	盲腸 *máng-cháng* [blind + intestine]	سوقۇر ئۈچەي *soqur üchey* [blind + intestine][d]
4.	gravity	*zwaarte-kracht* [heaviness + force]	b16	重力 *jū-ryoku* [heavy + force]	重力 *zhòng-lì* [heavy + force]	ئېغىرلىق كۈچى *éghirliq küchi* [heaviness + force]
5.	conductor	*geleider* [conductor, guide]	c12	導體 *dō-shi* [guide + body]	導體 *dǎo-tǐ* [guide + body]	ئۆتكۈزگۈچ جىسىم *ötküzgüch jisim* [conductor + body]

a. Source: Uygur-Chinese dictionary: <http://www.uyghurche.com/chinese-uyghur> accessed 18 January 2025.
b. Schwarz (1992: 122) has *müñgüz pärdisi*. *-si* is a possessive affix.
c. Uygur also has بۇرۇن تۆشۈكى *burun töshügi* which literally means 'nose hole' (Schwarz 1992: 1031).
d. See also Schwarz (1992: 481).

Manchu is a Tungusic language, considered by some linguists to be a member of the Altaic language family. There are several ways in which the lexical contact phenomena under review could have been adopted by Manchu. It was one of the official languages of the Qing Empire, so may have adopted some of the words adopted by Chinese in the late nineteenth and early twentieth century. Manchu might also have adopted these loanwords directly from Japanese during the Japanese colonization of Manchuria (the Japanese called it Manchukuo or Manshū-koku 満州国) between 1932 and 1945. Finally, during this period a Japanese-based pidgin, *Kyowa-go* (協和語) was spoken in Manchukuo. This has now died out. Each of these cases offers the possibility of future research.[30]

Mongolian is a Mongolic language. Most of the Mongolian language area was in the Qing Empire, where Standard Chinese was one of the official languages.[31] After the fall of the Qing Empire in 1911, much of the language area was incorporated in the Mongolian People's Republic (est. 1924). However, part of it remained in the Inner Mongolia Autonomous Region in China, where Mandarin and Mongolian are the two official languages. One possible loanword from Dutch via Japanese and Mandarin is the word for 'noun' (b13) transliterated as *ner yge*, which literally means 'name word' (Lessing *et al.* 1960: 576).[32]

5. Conclusion

The aim of this contribution has been two-fold. First, it has attempted to show that the influence of Dutch on the lexis of languages in East Asia is significant and has occurred through borrowing of loanwords and other lexical contact phenomena such as calques. Second, this chapter has tried to offer a way into thinking about the processes involved in the circulation of loanwords and how these processes influence the form and sound of lexical contact phenomena in recipient languages.

I have focussed specifically on lexical contact phenomena which were borrowed by Japanese during the late Tokugawa period and then borrowed by other languages which had contact with Japanese in the late nineteenth and first half of the twentieth century. Some languages such as Korean and Formosan languages borrowed words directly from Japanese, whilst other languages such as Vietnamese borrowed them via intermediate languages.

Changes in the form and sound of loanwords as they pass from one language to another are driven by factors such as differences in phonemic sets, the number and type of tones, and the phonotactic systems of the donor and recipient languages. The examples of 'beer' and 'gas' in Formosan languages are instructive in this regard (Table 5a). The Dutch word for 'beer' (*bier*) has shifted to *biru'* (IPA: βiruʔ) in Saisiyat and *viiru* in Tsou. 'Gas' in Dutch has shifted to *kasu* in Amis and *ngase* (IPA: ŋaθə) in Saisiyat. Some lexical contact phenomena have gone through more than one borrowing process. For example, 'noun' was borrowed by Japanese

30. For loanwords in Manchu, see (Gruntov 2015).

31. There were some speakers of Mongolian in the Russian Empire and its successor states.

32. Several online sources give нэр үг (pronounced *ner üg*) as does a well-educated Mongolian informant of mine.

as a calque. It was then borrowed by Chinese as a graphic loanword, pronounced differently in Sinitic varieties. It was re-borrowed by Tibetan as a phonemic loanword. Its journey from Dutch to Tibetan has also taken it through several writing systems. Sinitic characters have played an important role in this story and their use by Sinitic language varieties, as well as Japanese, Korean, and Vietnamese has facilitated the spread of many of the lexical contact phenomena analysed in this chapter.

Work remains to be done. In the final section, I suggested that several lexical contact phenomena in languages such as Uygur, Tibetan, and Mongolian, which have had intensive contact with Sinitic varieties, can be traced back to Dutch. Further work may confirm these suggestions and reveal other such contact phenomena in these languages. Finally, this contribution adds something to our understanding of the circulation of loanwords. Typically, studies on this subject analyse the outcomes of contact between two languages, a donor and recipient language. I have tried to illustrate that loanwords can go through multiple phases changing their phonemic, morphemic, and graphic forms. Some might argue that the starting point for some of these words should not be Dutch, but languages such as Latin and its Indo-European predecessors and contemporaries. I agree. This merely adds to the notion that a study of the circulation of loanwords is vital to our understanding of how lexicons are formed and change over time. The Dutch word *naamwoord* 'noun' is a calque on the Latin *nomen*, from the (reconstructed) Proto Indo-European *$h_1$nómn̥* ('name'). It went from Dutch to Japanese to Chinese to Vietnamese, Tibetan, and possibly Mongolian. It did so because of specific historical events including the fact that the Dutch were the only Europeans who could trade with Japan for over two hundred years and the subsequent rise of Japan in the Meiji era. This illustrates well the interconnectedness of language and history and how shifts in language are shaped by historical events.

References

Alves, Mark J. 2009. "Loanwords in Vietnamese." In *Loanwords in the World's Languages: A Comparative Handbook*, ed. by Martin Haspelmath and Uri Tadmor, 617–637. Berlin: De Gruyter.

Batchelor, John. 1905. *An Ainu-English-Japanese Dictionary*, 2nd ed. Tokyo: The Methodist Publishing House.

Chang, Suk-jin. 1996. *Korean*. Amsterdam & Philadelphia: John Benjamins.

Chang, Yü-hung. 1993. "The assimilation of Japanese loanwords. In Taiwanese Hokkien." *The 3rd Symposium on Min Dialects 11–12 January* 1993: 107–22.

Chen, Yin-ling. 2002. *Tsou phonology: A study of its phonemes, syllable structure and loanwords*. MA thesis. Hsinchu: National Tsing Hua University.

Chien, Yuehchen. 2018. “Morphological consideration of Japanese loanwords in Taiwan with Amis as an example.” *Journal of Lexicography*, 15: 43–52.

Chien, Yuehchen. 2019. “Words that are not borrowed: Considering language contact between Japanese and Amis,” *Japanese Language Studies*, 36.12: 58–70.

Curry, Stewart A. 2004. *Small Linguistics: Phonological History and Lexical Loans in Nakajin Dialect Okinawan*. Dissertation: University of Hawai'i.

De Busser, Rik. 2018. “An overview of linguistic mechanisms introducing a Christian conceptual universe into the Bunun language.” *Ethnologia* 42: 5–38.

Fey, Virginia A. 1986. *Amis dictionary*. Taipei: The Bible Society.

Gruntov, Ilya. 2015. “Chinese Loanwords in Mongolic, Turkic and Manchu-Tungusic.” In *Encyclopedia of Chinese Language and Linguistics*, ed. by Rint Sybesma. Leiden: Brill (online).

doi Haspelmath, Martin. 2009. “Lexical borrowing: Concepts and issues.” In *Loanwords in the World's Languages: A Comparative Handbook*, ed. by Martin Haspelmath and Uri Tadmor, 35–54. Berlin: De Gruyter Mouton.

doi Haspelmath, Martin and Uri Tadmor (eds). 2009. “The Loanword Typology project and the World Loanword Database.” In *Loanwords in the World's Languages: A Comparative Handbook*, ed. by Martin Haspelmath and Uri Tadmor, 1–34. Berlin: De Gruyter Mouton.

Hsu, Wen-wen. 2003. *Japanese loanwords in Amis*. MA thesis. Hsinchu: National Tsing Hua University.

doi Irwin, Mark. 2011. *Loanwords in Japanese*. Amsterdam: John Benjamins.

Itō, Chiyuki, Yoonjung Kang & Michael Kenstowicz. 2006. “The Adaptation of Japanese Loanwords into Korean.” *MIT Working Papers in Linguistics* 52: 65–104.

Jäschke, H.A. 1998. *A Tibetan-English Dictionary*. Richmond: Curzon Press.

Joby, Christopher. 2020. *The Dutch Language in Japan (1600–1900)*. Leiden: Brill.

Ju, Jen-Jing. 2022. *Taiwanese Hokkien and Japanese loanwords in Amis*. MA thesis. Hualien: National Dong Hua University.

doi Karimata, Shigehisa. 2015. “Ryukyuan languages: A grammar overview.” In *Handbook of the Ryukyuan Languages: History, Structure, and Use*, ed. by Patrick Heinrich et al.., 113–140. Berlin: De Gruyter.

Kaybaybaw, Lalo a Tahesh, Hong-sui Lim, and Elizabeth Zeitoun. 2020. “A study of Japanese, Hakka and Taiwanese Southern Min loanwords in Saisiyat from a phonological perspective.” *Cahiers de Linguistique Orientale* 49.2: 168–216.

doi Kjellin, Olle. 1977. “Observations on consonant types and ‘tone’ in Tibetan.” *Journal of Phonetics* 5: 317–338.

Klöter, Henning. 2005. *Written Taiwanese*. Wiesbaden: Harrossowitz.

Koga, Jūjirō. 2000. *The Collected Words of Foreign Origin...The best book to trace the etymology of Japanese originated in Portuguese, Dutch, Latin, or Chinese*. Nagasaki: Nagasaki Konin University Comparative Culture Research Institute.

doi Kornicki, Peter. 2018. *Languages, scripts, and Chinese texts in East Asia*. Oxford: OUP.

Kuiper, Pieter Nicolaas (Koos). 1993. "Dutch loan-words and loan-translations in modern Chinese: an example of successful sinification by way of Japan." In *Words from the West, Western texts in Chinese literary context, Essays to honor Erik Zürcher on his sixty-fifth birthday*, ed. by L. Haft, 116–144. Leiden: CNWS Publications.

doi Labrune, Laurence. 2012. *The Phonology of Japanese*. Oxford: OUP.

Lawrence, Wayne P. 2012. "Southern Ryukyuan." In *The Languages of Japan and Korea*, ed. by Nicolas Tranter, 805–873. London & New York: Routledge.

doi Lessing, Ferdinand et al.. 1960. *Mongolian-English Dictionary*. Berkeley & Los Angeles: University of California Press.

Li, Paul Jen-kuei, Elizabeth Zeitoun and Rik De Busser (eds). 2024. *Handbook on Formosan languages: The indigenous languages of Taiwan*, 3 vols. Leiden: Brill.

Lin, Cheng-ming. 2015. *Loanwords in Nanwang Puyuma: An optimality theory analysis*. MA thesis. Taipei: National Taiwan Normal University.

Lin, Hui-shan. 2023. "Loanword adaptation of Japanese vowels in Kavalan." *Journal of Taiwanese Languages and Literature* 18(2): 273–322.

Lin, Kaidi. 2022. *A basic description of Yilan Creole phonology: with a special focus on the Aohua dialect*. MA Thesis. Kyushu: Kyushu University.

doi van der Lubbe, Gijs & Akiko Tokunaga. 2015. "Okinoerabu grammar." In *Handbook of the Ryukyuan Languages: History, Structure, and Use*, ed. by Patrick Heinrich et al.., 345–378. Berlin: De Gruyter.

Matthews, Stephen & Virginia Yip. 1994. *Cantonese: A Comprehensive Grammar*. London & New York: Routledge.

Mervart, David. 2015. "The Republic of Letters Comes to Nagasaki: Record of a Translator's Struggle." *Transcultural Studies* 2015.2: 8–35.

Nakamura, Ellen Gardner. 2005. *Practical Pursuits: Takano Choei, Takahashi Keisaku, and Western Medicine in Nineteenth-Century Japan*. Cambridge, MA: Harvard University Asia Center.

doi Nguyễn, Đình Hòa. 1997. *Vietnamese*. Amsterdam & Philadelphia: John Benjamins.

Pai, Tsang-hui. 2021. *A study of loanwords in Toda Seediq*. MA thesis. Kaohsiung: National Kaohsiung Normal University.

Saitō, Shizuka. 1967. 日本語に及ぼしたオランダ語の影響 *Nihongo ni oyoboshita Oranda-go no eikyo* [The Influence of Dutch on Japanese]. Tokyo: Shinozaki Shorin.

San, Duanmu. 2007. *The Phonology of Standard Chinese*. Oxford: OUP.

Schwarz, Henry G. 1992. *An Uyghur-English Dictionary*. Bellingham, WA: Center for East Asian Studies, Western Washington University.

Shin, Jiyoung, Jieun Kiaer & Jaeeun Cha. 2013. *The sounds of Korean*. Cambridge: CUP.

van der Sijs, Nicoline. 2006. *Calendarium van de Nederlandse Taal: De geschiedenis van het Nederlands in jaartallen* [Calendar of the Dutch language: the history of Dutch by year]. The Hague: SDU Uitgevers.

van der Sijs, Nicoline. 2010. *Nederlandse woorden wereldwijd* [*Dutch words worldwide*]. The Hague: SDU Uitgevers.

Sinh, Vinh. 1993. "Chinese characters as the medium for transmitting the vocabulary of modernization from Japan to Vietnam in Early 20th century." *Asian Pacific Quarterly* 25(1): 1–16.

Sinh, Vinh. 1996. “Chinese Characters as the Medium for Transmitting the Vocabulary of Modernization from Japan to Vietnam in Early Twentieth Century.” In *La Société civile en Asie de l’Est*, ed. by Charles Le Blanc, 313–332. Montreal: Centre d’étude de l’Asie de l’Est, Université de Montréal.

Sohn, Ho-Min. 1999. *The Korean language*. Cambridge: CUP.

Tokugawa, Munemasa. 1979. 日本の方言地図 *Nihon no hōgen chizu* [*Maps of Japanese dialects*]. Tokyo: Chūō kōronsha.

Vos, Frits. 2000a. “The Influence of Dutch Grammar on Japanese Language Research.” In *History of the Language Sciences*, ed. by Sylvain Auroux et al.., 102–104. Berlin: De Gruyter.

Vos, Frits. 2000b. “Latent Dutch in Modern Korean.” *Cahiers d’études coréennes* 7: 295–320.

Vos, Frits. 2014. “Dutch Influences on the Japanese Language.” *East Asian History* 29: 153–180 (first published in 1963: *Lingua* 12: 341–388).

Winford, Donald. 2003. *An Introduction to Contact Linguistics*. Oxford: Blackwell.

Zeitoun, Elizabeth, Tai-hwa Chu, and Lalo a tahesh kaybaybaw. 2015. *A Study of Saisiyat Morphology*. Honolulu: University of Hawai‘i Press.

Zeitoun, Elizabeth & Yoann Goudin. 2024. “Language contact.” In *Handbook on Formosan languages: The indigenous languages of Taiwan, 3 vols*, ed. by Paul Jen-kuei Li, Elizabeth Zeitoun and Rik De Busser, Chapter 35. Leiden: Brill.

CHAPTER 3

Dutch-Polish bilingualism in the seventeenth century

Places, communities, and mechanisms of language contact

Paul Hulsenboom
Radboud University

The seventeenth century was a period of thriving Dutch-Polish bilingualism. This chapter explores this understudied subject by examining how people in the United Provinces and the Polish-Lithuanian Commonwealth encountered and learned each other's languages, as well as by analysing places and communities in which Dutch-Polish bilingualism was particularly prevalent. It argues that, despite an apparent lack of relevant education infrastructures, Dutch-Polish bilingualism flourished in (1) Gdańsk, which attracted hundreds if not thousands of Netherlandish migrants, (2) Franeker, where numerous Calvinists from Poland-Lithuania came to study, (3) Leiden, which welcomed even more Polish students, including Socinians/Polish Brethren, and (4) Amsterdam, which became a home for several dozen Socinian families and hundreds of Jews from the Polish-Lithuanian Commonwealth. The main catalyst for Dutch-Polish bilingualism was migration, which was in turn fuelled by economic interests, intellectual pursuits, religious persecutions, and social relations. The chapter finishes by offering various future lines of inquiry.

Keywords: Dutch Republic, Polish-Lithuanian Commonwealth, early modern bilingualism/multilingualism/plurilingualism, language acquisition, migration, Amsterdam, Franeker, Gdańsk, Leiden, Calvinism, Polish Brethren, Ashkenazim

https://doi.org/10.1075/impact.55.03hul

1. Introduction

On 4 July 1654, the Amsterdam notary Henrick Schaeff (1599–1665) opened a mysterious tin box.[1] Schaeff, bookkeeper for the Dutch West-India Company, was busy listing all items once belonging to Annetgen Boeijens (d. 1654), which were bound for Brazil. The large, sealed box apparently needed careful inspection, for Schaeff opened it in the presence of three Dutch witnesses. He listed its contents as follows:

> handwritten letters in the Polish language, idem passports, travel letters, health letters, credentials, indulgence letters, Roman [i.e. papal] bulls, and many other similar religious records of the pilgrimage of one Paulus Vladislaus Meziinscki (sic), a Polish nobleman, both handwritten and printed.[2] (SA 5075, NA 1304: 71v)

The documents left Schaeff and the three witnesses unimpressed: they judged them to be of no value to Boeijens' inheritance, and promptly put them back inside the box. How the papers first came to be in Boeijens' possession, what happened to them afterwards, and who this "Meziinscki" (a misspelling of Mężyński) was, remains unclear. However, the case does offer a symbolic example of the Polish language's presence in seventeenth-century Amsterdam. In addition, it raises questions about Dutch-Polish bilingualism: how did Schaeff and the three witnesses recognize the documents' language and contents, and did Annetgen Boeijens possess the skill to read them?

Today, there are close to two hundred and fifty thousand registered Poles living in the Netherlands, many of whom learn Dutch and raise their children bilingually.[3] The same is undoubtedly true for Dutch immigrants in Poland, although their number is estimated at only fifteen hundred to two thousand.[4] Dutch-Polish bilingualism is hardly a modern phenomenon, however: it already blossomed during the seventeenth century, which witnessed a boom in Dutch-Polish relations. Whereas multiple aspects of these contacts have been examined in the past, particularly relating to commerce, culture, and religion (e.g. Bogucka

---

1. I would like to thank dr. Hanneke van Asperen, dr. Alisa van de Haar, and prof. dr. Marc van Oostendorp, as well as the editors of this volume, for their helpful comments on earlier versions of this chapter.

2. "gess. brieven inde Poolsche tale, idem pasporten, reysbrieven, gesondtbrieven, attestatien, afflaetbrieven, Roomsche bullen ende diergelicke veele andere religieuse bescheijden van de pelgrimasie van eenen Paulo Vladislao Meziinscki, Pools edelman, soo gess. als gedruckt." All translations are my own.

3. Data retrieved from the website of the *Centraal Bureau voor de Statistiek* on 23 February 2024.

4. Data received from the Dutch Embassy in Warsaw on 26 February 2024.

2011; Hulsenboom 2023c; Polkowski 2015; Thijssen 2003), linguistic interaction has remained virtually unstudied. Meanwhile, various researchers have devoted themselves to the multilingual character of the early modern Low Countries, for example by discussing matters of language acquisition, the status of different languages (especially Latin, French, German, English, Italian, and Spanish), and debates on the standardisation of the Netherlandish language known as Dutch, which mainly evolved from the dialect spoken in the province of Holland (e.g. Burke 2004:*passim*; Frijhoff 2017; Van de Haar 2019; Swiggers 2017; Van der Wal 1995). The *Rzeczpospolita* or Polish-Lithuanian Commonwealth constituted a highly multilingual space in its own right: while Polish was widely spoken throughout the Kingdom of Poland and amongst the elites of the Grand Duchy of Lithuania and the Commonwealth's Ukrainian territories, and like Dutch became increasingly standardised and applied in works of literature from the sixteenth century onwards, other commonly used languages included Latin, German, Ruthenian, and Yiddish (Walczak & Mielczarek 2017). Perhaps less obvious is the fact that numerous Dutch individuals in the seventeenth century knew Polish, just as large numbers of Poles knew Dutch. In other words: it was a period of thriving Dutch-Polish bilingualism.

In this chapter, I offer a first foray into the topic by asking how Polish and Dutch individuals came into contact with each other's languages, how they learned them, who knew both Dutch and Polish, where, and why. Just as today, seventeenth-century bilingualism could be both passive and active, and each individual scored differently on the scale of proficiency – something that is notoriously difficult to determine. Also, it should be clear that the term Dutch-Polish bilingualism does not exclude other languages: I use it to refer to people and places marked by a synthesis of Dutch and Polish, regardless of any other languages that might have been in play (resulting in multilingualism/plurilingualism). First, I consider the means and circumstances through which people in the United Provinces and the Polish-Lithuanian Commonwealth could encounter and learn Polish and Dutch respectively. Second, I discuss the places and communities in which Dutch-Polish bilingualism was particularly prevalent. My goal is to sketch a concise yet multifaceted outline of seventeenth-century Dutch-Polish bilingualism and to provide a variety of avenues for future research.

2. Getting acquainted

All Poles in seventeenth-century Amsterdam spoke Dutch fluently and flawlessly. That is to say, all fictional Poles. In the city's theatres, Dutch audiences could marvel at actors playing Polish characters in multiple plays, such as the vastly popular

Sigismundus, Prince van Poolen (*Sigismundus, Prince of Poland*), also known as *'t Leven is een droom* (*Life is a dream*), a translation of *La vida es sueño* by Pedro Calderón de la Barca (1600–1681). Despite being staged as Polish, the characters in these plays utter not a single word in their supposed native tongue. Instead, they speak Dutch as if they were born with it (Hulsenboom 2023c: 219–26). A fitting parallel can be found in a Polish satire from 1650, titled *Na ogołocone ściany w obronę* (*In defence of empty walls*), in which Maurits of Orange (1567–1625) shows himself fluent in Polish (Opaliński 2004: 65). Of course, these unlikely linguistic abilities fall under literary license, and contemporaries probably gave them hardly any thought. If not through these works of fiction, however, Dutch and Polish individuals did come into contact with each other's languages in real life, and had access to various means of learning them – although doing so was hardly a straightforward matter.

2.1 Dutch encounters with Polish

The seventeenth-century Dutch Republic produced numerous works in poetry and prose about Poland's history, its peoples, provinces, cities, and so forth (Hulsenboom 2023c: 183–361). Information about the Polish language was harder to come by, however. If offered, moreover, it was not necessarily accurate, let alone complete. In a brief Latin treatise published in Amsterdam in 1654, for example, historian Georgius Hornius (1620–1670) argued that the 'Sarmatian' or Polish language was identical to the Scythian tongue of the ancient Colchians (Boxhornius 1654: front matter, **r-v).[5] Perhaps the most extensive take on Polish can be found in one of the earliest works devoted solely to the Polish-Lithuanian Commonwealth produced on Dutch soil, written by Andreas Cellarius (ca. 1595–1665) and published in Amsterdam in 1659. Cellarius rejected the alleged Scythian pedigree of the Polish tongue, noted its Slavic heritage, and enumerated several other languages spoken in the *Rzeczpospolita*, including Latin (Cellarius 1659: 15–20).[6] Clearly, Cellarius was more nuanced and knowledgeable than Hornius, but he did tie in with a popular yet exaggerated narrative propagated by Polish and non-Polish authors alike, which held that even the common folk in Poland spoke Latin (Hulsenboom 2023c: 191–92). In short, Dutch readers with an academic interest in Polish would find little to their taste in the average local bookshop.

5. In the early modern period, Polish nobles presented themselves as the descendants of an ancient people called Sarmatians (or Sauromatians). Hence, Poles were regularly referred to as Sarmatians, and their language could be called Sarmatian as well.

6. In 1660, a Dutch translation of the Latin original was published in Amsterdam.

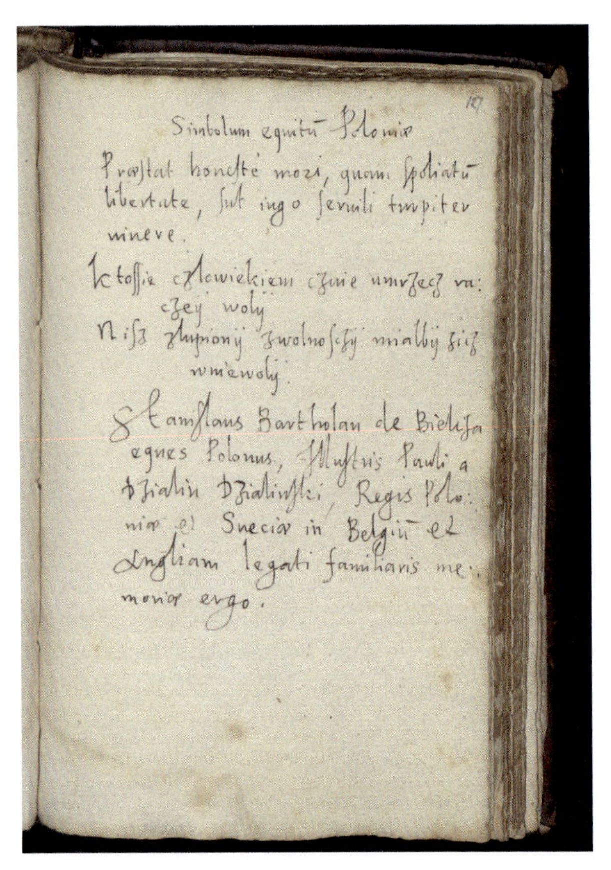

127

Simbolum equitu[m] Poloniae

Praestat honeste mori, quam spoliatu[m] libertate, sub iugo servili turpiter vivere.

Ktossie czlowiekiem czuie umrzecz ra:czeij wolij
Nisz zlupionij zwolnosczij mialbij zicz wniewolij.

Stanislaus Bartholan de Bielisza eques Polonus, Illustris Pauli a Dzialin Dzialinski, Regis Polo:niae et Sueciae in Belgiu[m] et Angliam legati familiaris me:moriae ergo.

Figure 1. Stanisław Bartolan, *Entry in Janus Dousa's album amicorum* (1597). Leiden University Library, BPL 1406: 127r

However, numerous Dutch individuals encountered Polish in their daily lives. They could hear Polish on the streets of their cities (see sections 3.2 to 3.4) or run into Polish words or texts. For instance, the nobleman and diplomatic secretary Stanisław Bartolan (d. 1618) in 1597 wrote a short Polish verse in the *album amicorum* of the famed humanist Jan van der Does, better known as Janus Dousa (1545–1604) (*Album amicorum* 1563–1597: 127r) (Figure 1). He also added a Latin motto with the same meaning, no doubt in order to help Van der Does understand his Polish contribution. Their brevity notwithstanding, the lines are not insignificant, as they may well be the oldest surviving Polish words written on Dutch soil.[7]

7. The verse reads: "Ktossie czlowiekiem czuie umrzecz raczeij wolij / Nisz zlupionij zwolnosczij mialbij zicz wniewolij": 'Whoever feels they are human, prefers to die / Rather than having to live in slavery, robbed of freedom'. The page carries the title "Simbolum equitu[m] Poloniae": 'A token of the Polish nobility'. See Gömöri 1987: 464–65.

In the seventeenth century, moreover, Dutch printing presses produced multiple Polish texts. For instance, congratulatory poems by Polish students were issued in Franeker from 1642 onwards (Postma 2014: *passim*). Similar poems may have appeared in other centres of higher education, especially Leiden, though they have yet to surface. Other works are of a religious nature. The Amsterdam-based printer Christoffel Cunradus (ca. 1615–1684) in 1660 published a Protestant Polish Bible (Figure 2), followed in 1679 by *Declaracia, Objasnienie abo Pokazanie o Swiadku Bozym, w człowieczych wewnętrzynych częściach*, a translation of *A Declaration of the Witnes (sic) of God, manifested in the inward parts* by the English Quaker William Ames (d. 1662). Johannes Crellius (d. 1722), furthermore, a Collegiant printer from Gdańsk (Danzig) who lived in Amsterdam, in 1686 published a Polish version of the New Testament. These books could of course be sent to Poland-Lithuania, but they probably also catered to local Polish-speaking communities, which I discuss in section 3.3.[8]

In addition, Polish words or phrases made their way into Dutch newspapers, which first started to appear in the early seventeenth century. For example, numerous reports mention certain administrative and military Polish titles (in various spellings), like "wojewoda" or "starosta" (e.g. *Amsterdamse Donderdaeghse Courant* 1687: no. 25v; *Tydinge uyt verscheyden Quartieren* 1645: no. 39r), as well as the "pospolite ruszenie" or mass mobilisation of armed forces, the meaning of which is sometimes explicated in Dutch (e.g. *Ordinaris Dingsdaeghse Courante* 1652: no. 32r; *Extraordinaire Haerlemse Donderdaeghse Courant* 1669: no. 25v). Another newspaper refers to the Polish gentry's (in)famous veto rights as "Nie Poz Walam", a misspelling of "nie pozwalam": 'I do not allow [it]' (*Amsterdamse Dingsdaegse Courant* 1698: no. 3v).[9] Some of these words and phrases entered local vocabularies. An eighteenth-century Dutch map of Poland, for instance, depicts the country's "Waywoodschappen", a term derived from "województwo": a province governed by a "wojewoda" (cf. Van Oostendorp & Van der Sijs 2019: 66).[10] Indeed, considering the fact that newspapers were produced and read all over the United Provinces, which had a comparatively high level of literacy (Van Groesen, 2016), bits and pieces of Polish undoubtedly reached many thousands of Dutch readers throughout the seventeenth and eighteenth centuries.[11]

8. Polish books were also published in the Southern Netherlands: in 1667, a collection of Catholic sermons by Kazimierz Jan Woysznarowicz was printed in Antwerp, entitled *Dom mądrości siedmiu kolumnami wsparty* (*The house of wisdom supported by seven columns*).

9. The so-called *liberum veto* allowed Polish nobles to thwart new legislation and disband meetings of the Sejm.

10. The map, titled *Nieuwe Kaart van t' (sic) Koninkryk Poolen verdeelt in zyn byzondere Waywoodschappen*, was produced in Amsterdam in 1733 by Isaak Tirion.

11. Another example is the word "pole", 'field', which features in every early modern work on Poland that discusses the origin of the country's name.

Figure 2. Anonymous, *Front page of the Biblia Święta* (Amsterdam 1660). Amsterdam University Library, OTM: O 84–20

Those who actually learned Polish were of course less numerous, although their number can only be estimated (see section 3.1). In fact, there was a remarkable scarcity or even absence of Polish language teachers and learning aids in the Dutch Republic. Even though the seventeenth-century Low Countries as a whole were home to scores of language instructors, there is as yet no evidence that any of them offered lessons in Polish (cf. Hulshof et al. 2015: 45–48). Similarly, the Low Countries produced a multitude of dictionaries, grammars, and dialogue books meant as learning materials, but none of these contained information about Polish. Instead, they reflected and stimulated a collective orientation towards other foreign languages, especially French, Italian, Spanish, German, and English (e.g. Van Els & Knops 1988; Hulshof et al. 2015: 42–45; Loonen 1990: 34–47). The only early modern dictionary combining Polish and Dutch was (probably) first produced in Basel in 1590, and the only conversation book which encompasses both languages was published in 1691 in Košice, in modern-day Slovakia (Calepino 1590; Prędota & Woronczak 2002; Warmer 1691). In short, the Dutch Republic lacked the basic infrastructure needed to learn Polish.

It follows that, even though works about Poland and its population were in demand and Poland's contribution to the seventeenth-century Dutch economy was crucial, people in the Northern Netherlands attached relatively little significance to knowledge of the Polish tongue. Hence, they excluded it from their contemporary canon of languages, which they limited to the western half of Europe: for example Czech, Hungarian, and Russian were treated with a similar disinterest. A Dutch pamphlet from 1649, which describes a dialogue between speakers of various European nationalities, rather symbolically stages only one individual from the continent's eastern half: a Pole introduced as Koenraed Popolski, who is allowed but a few short sentences (*Breeden-Raedt* 1649). This state of affairs suggests that Dutch and other 'Western' producers of sixteenth- and seventeenth-century language learning aids guided the mental parcelling of the continent, consciously or unconsciously determining which languages were 'in' and which were 'out', and thus contributing to the perceived rift between 'Western' and 'Eastern Europe' – concepts to which other scholars assign later dates (e.g. Adamovsky 2006; Kalmar 2022; Wolff 1994).

Still, foreigners could and did learn Polish. Since the beginning of the sixteenth century, numerous relevant handbooks were published in Cracow, Gdańsk, Vilnius, and other cities. An online inventory made by researchers from the University of Warsaw lists eighty-three orthographies, grammars, and other compendia from the sixteenth and seventeenth centuries combined, many of which had multiple editions.[12] They were usually written in Latin, Polish, or German, and often aimed specifically at non-Polish speakers. Indeed, in border

12. Data retrieved from *Dawne ortografie, gramatyki i podręczniki języka polskiego. Internetowe kompendium edukacyjne* on 1 March 2024.

regions like Prussia and Silesia, Polish had a high status and was widely used alongside German and other languages. In Gdańsk, which formed an integral part of the Kingdom of Poland together with the rest of Royal Prussia since 1466, Polish was taught in monastery and private schools alike, and the local *Gymnasium Academicum* added the language to the curriculum of its lower classes in 1589 (Jefimow 1970: 7–8). Similar institutions operated in Toruń (Thorn) and Elbląg (Elbing), in Royal Prussia, as well as in Königsberg in Ducal Prussia, a fiefdom of Poland until 1657. The same holds true for Silesian towns like Wrocław (Breslau) and Byczyna (Pitschen) (Dąbrowska 2012; 2019; Koelling 1892: 176–78).

Library inventories could indicate who in the United Provinces owned books about the Polish language, and which ones. For example, the statesman, writer, and polyglot Philips of Marnix, Lord of Saint-Aldegonde (1540–1598), possessed something listed as "Catechesis et Grammatica Polonica", 'Polish Catechism and Grammar' (*Catalogus Librorum* 1599: B4r), which he may have acquired during a diplomatic mission to Cracow in 1575 (Gerlo 1996). The entry could refer to two separate works, or possibly to a Polish catechism-cum-orthography by the Lutheran theologian Jan Seklucjan (Johannes Seclucianus, ca. 1510–1578), published in Königsberg in 1547 and 1549 – although this is not a work on grammar (Siess-Krzyszkowski 2024: 219–21). In any case, people from the United Provinces who wanted to learn Polish had roughly two options: procure the appropriate books and dedicate themselves to self-study, or travel east – Gdańsk being the obvious choice. My findings in section 3.1 suggest that the latter was the more common option.

2.2 Polish encounters with Dutch

The opposite situation was in many ways similar. Although the Dutch Republic features prominently in seventeenth-century Polish travelogues, poems, and other sources (Hulsenboom, 2023c: 25–180), they offer hardly any information on the Dutch language. To my knowledge, the only published Polish comments on the topic appear in a cosmography first printed in Cracow in 1609, which forms a translation of a work by the French philosopher Jean Bodin (1530–1596). Discussing the Low Countries, Bodin mentioned merely that the local tongue resembled German, and later contended that nearly all Dutch women read and wrote a variety of languages due to their commercial activities (Bodin 1609: 77, 80). More knowledge could theoretically be gained from foreign publications. In this case, too, library catalogues might reveal if and to what extent works on the Dutch language reached Polish readers.

Numerous Poles must have come into contact with the Dutch language, for example when they interacted with Dutch speakers in and around Gdańsk (see section 3.1), or when they encountered Dutch texts that circulated in Poland. King Jan III Sobieski (1629–1696), for instance, had several Dutch books in his royal library (*Katalog książek* 1879: 61). Most Dutch-language publications could be found in Gdańsk: they were included in the municipal library, which opened in 1596 (Dzienis 2016), owned by private individuals in the first decades of the following century (Pelus-Kaplan 2007: 366), and later sold by the hundreds by Gilles Janssonius van Waesberge (1646–1708), the scion of a successful book trading family from Amsterdam, who established a new branch in Gdańsk in 1679 (Pettegree 2021: 312). Up to the year 1700, his firm offered over 1,200 Dutch titles for sale, obviously catering to a substantial local readership (Der Weduwen 2022: 236). Newspapers and pamphlets from the United Provinces reached Poland as well (Hulsenboom 2023b; Hulsenboom 2023c: 134–35).

In addition, printers in Poland issued a number of Dutch-language publications themselves. Several Socinian books bear imprints from Raków, of which one appears to be genuine: the *Apologia* by Krzysztof Ostorodt (Christophorus Ostorodt, ca. 1560–1611) and Andrzej Wojdowski (Andreas Voidovius, 1565–1622), printed in February 1600 (*Bibliographia Sociniana* 2004: 29). Between 1608 and 1775, moreover, Gdańsk produced twenty-nine known Dutch price currents (lists of commodity prices and exchange rates, all but one dating from the seventeenth century), and a handful of religious works in Dutch (Der Weduwen 2022: 233, 237).[13] Also, Dutch poems were included in celebratory publications printed in Gdańsk until well into the eighteenth century (*Handbuch des personalen Gelegenheitsschrifttums* 2009: passim). Although its impact on the Polish language remains little-known, Dutch was certainly materially present in Poland.[14]

For all intents and purposes, however, the country lacked the basic conditions required to master Dutch, just as the United Provinces offered virtually no opportunities to learn Polish. As far as we know, the Polish-Lithuanian Commonwealth produced no Dutch learning materials, forcing any interested individuals to use foreign publications, such as the well-known conversation books by Noël de Berlaimont (d. 1531), first printed in Antwerp in 1527. A detailed study of household inven-

13. See the Universal Short Title Catalogue. A Dutch Bible from the late sixteenth century, which according to its imprint was published by Krijn Vermeulen in Gdańsk, is commonly ascribed to a Dutch printer (Valkema Blouw 2013: 83–84). By extension, the same presumably holds true for two Dutch pamphlets from the early seventeenth century, which carry a similar imprint.

14. For a concise overview of Dutch loanwords in Polish, see Van der Sijs 2010: 107–08. A work on Dutch loanwords in contemporary Polish, which argues that direct borrowings are rare, considers the history of the borrowing process only in passing (Kowalska-Szubert 2013). Polish and forms of (Low) German furthermore contributed to Wymysorys (also known as Vilamovian or Wilamowicean): a language with roots in the Middle Ages, used in the Silesian town of Wilamowice (Wicherkiewicz 2003). It is now almost extinct.

tories, for instance from Gdańsk, could tell much about the circulation of such books in Poland. Moreover, there is as yet hardly any evidence of Dutch language teachers in the *Rzeczpospolita*, although it is likely that at least some individuals taught Dutch in seventeenth-century Gdańsk and other Prussian towns: the Silesian poet Christian Hofman von Hofmanswaldau (1616–1679) apparently learned the language from Johann Mochinger (1603–1652) while he lived in Gdańsk between 1636 and 1638, before moving to Holland (Kiedroń 2007: 55). With the exception of Royal Prussia, it seems that the status of Dutch in Poland resembled that of Polish in the Northern Netherlands, that is to say it was comparatively low.

This is confirmed by sources pertaining to the educational practices of the Polish *szlachta*, i.e. the nobility. Making up some 6.6 to 9 per cent of the Commonwealth's total early modern population, nobles invested heavily in their (male) offsprings' upbringing, depending on their financial means. A crucial element was the *peregrinatio academica* to foreign universities, which first flourished during the sixteenth century and later evolved into a more general educational journey across European courts and academies, nowadays commonly known as the Grand Tour (e.g. Bömelburg 2005). To prepare for the task ahead, young itinerants received instructions written by their parents or guardians. Such texts make clear that learning foreign languages was one of the main goals of these journeys, especially German, French, and Italian (Żołądź-Strzelczyk 2020: 246–61).

However, they also reveal that mastering Dutch was not considered important, at least not amongst Catholic Poles. Indeed, the Catholic nobleman Aleksander Ługowski (1589–1650) in 1639 advised his son *not* to visit Louvain (Leuven) because of the language that he believed was spoken there: "gdyż to w Inderlandzie (sic) miasto jest i język bardzo gruby": 'for it is a city in the Netherlands, and the language is very coarse' (*Jasia Ługowskiego podróże* 1974: 95). The Catholic magnate Jakub Sobieski (1591–1646), father of the future king, was less harsh, but his comments resonate with a similar message: the Dutch language is insignificant. In the instructions he wrote for his brother and sons in 1620 and 1645 respectively, Sobieski stated simply that Dutch seemed a mixture of French, English, and German, which begs the question whether he perceived it as a language in its own right. Instead, he encouraged the learning of Latin, French, German, and Turkish (*Ojcowskie synom przestrogi* 2017: 168, 301–04, 315–17). As the international *lingua franca*, French was widely used in the Low Countries as well (e.g. Van de Haar 2019). To Ługowski, Sobieski, and others like them, therefore, there was no real need to know more about Dutch, especially if they had doubts about its status as a separate language. Still, my analyses in sections 3.2 to 3.4 demonstrate that many non-Catholic Poles did achieve Dutch-Polish bilingualism, particularly if they journeyed to or even settled in the Northern Netherlands themselves.

3. Locating bilingualism

In 1591, the aforementioned Philips of Marnix, Lord of Saint-Aldegonde, referred to Polish (and several other languages) to explain a choice he had made in his Dutch translation of Hebrew psalms (Van de Haar 2019: 227). As mentioned, he owned a book on the Polish language, and visited Cracow in 1575. A few decades later, around the year 1600, Joris (Georgius, 1574–1599) and Dirk (Theodorus, 1580–1663), sons of the abovementioned humanist Jan van der Does, both studied in Poland-Lithuania (Hulsenboom 2023c: 227–29). They probably picked up some of the local language: Joris possessed a Lutheran Polish Bible printed in Königsberg in 1574, with a handwritten dedicatory note in Polish by professor Filip Clüver, who came from Gdańsk (Philippus Cluverius, 1580–1622) (Thijssen 2003: 132). However, to what extent Philips, Joris, and Dirk actually mastered Polish remains unclear.

Other sources convincingly attest to instances of advanced Dutch-Polish bilingualism. One exceptional individual was Jaques or Jacob Joosten (b. ca. 1613), who wrote two Dutch travel journals and presented himself as a Pole working as an interpreter in Amsterdam (Ablonczyné-Nádor 2011: 133–34; Schoenaers et al. 2021: 223–25). To show off his linguistic prowess, Joosten began his books with poems in ten different languages, including Dutch and Polish – the latter having two versions, of which the second is notably better (Joosten 1649 & 1662: front matter, no page numbers).[15] Two other examples can be drawn from a Dutch travel journal published in Amsterdam in 1676 and later adapted into English, French, German, and Russian. It was composed by a ghostwriter on the basis of various publications and the recollections of Jan Struys (ca. 1629–1694), an adventurer who had travelled through for example Muscovy, Safavid Iran, and Batavia (Boterbloem 2008). While in the Caucasus in 1670, Struys allegedly met two people who were fluent in Dutch as well as Polish: a woman born of a Dutch father and a Polish mother, and a Polish nobleman who had lived in Amsterdam (Struys 1676: 244, 258).[16] In addition to such individuals, there were certain places

15. A German translation of Joosten's first Dutch journal, originally published in Amsterdam in 1649, was in 1652 issued in Lübeck and in Toruń, Royal Prussia.

16. According to Kees Boterbloem (2008: 102), a Dutch acquaintance of Struys named Lodewijk Faber (1648–1729) knew Polish, but I have not been able to verify this claim. The same applies to the alleged Dutch proficiency of the abovementioned Aleksander Ługowski, Wawrzyniec Zygmunt Rosen (Valerianus Sigismundus Rosen, b. ca. 1623), and Samuel Proski (1636-ca. 1710), mentioned by Andrzej Borowski (2007: 170). The only evidence concerning Ługowski seems to be his remark about Dutch being 'very coarse', which rather suggests that he hardly knew the language. Rosen may be the author of a short Dutch letter to Constantijn Huygens (1596–1687), but this attribution is uncertain (*De briefwisseling van Constantijn Huygens*

where Dutch-Polish bilingualism not only occurred incidentally, but even thrived amongst larger communities. In the following sections, I explore the most important cases in more or less chronological order.

3.1 Gdańsk: Netherlandish merchants and makers

Trade relations between the Low Countries and the Baltic reach back to the medieval Hanse. From ca. 1590 until at least the middle of the seventeenth century, however, Dutch merchants dominated Baltic commerce, which was especially profitable for the province of Holland and the regents of Amsterdam. Gdańsk was the main Baltic port, from which Dutch merchants imported vast amounts of grain and other bulk goods. Conversely, they sold luxury wares to local traders and Polish nobles (e.g. Bogucka 1973; Van Tielhof 2002: 43–50). In order to strengthen their commercial enterprises and manage their business interests in the Baltic, Dutch trading families often moved one or more members to Gdańsk. In other cases, these matters were arranged by unrelated Dutch factors who resided in Gdańsk either permanently or temporarily. Furthermore, the city was home to a Reformed Netherlandish Church (e.g. *Ecclesiae Londino-Batavae Archivum* 1897: 915, 920, 922, 926). According to Maria Bogucka, there were over three hundred Dutch Calvinists in Gdańsk in 1618, and seventy-five permanent Dutch residents by the end of the 1640s (1990: 22). Comparatively speaking, these numbers are remarkably low: in the mid-seventeenth century, Gdańsk had over seventy thousand inhabitants, most of whom were of German or Polish descent (Cieślak & Biernat 1995: 103). Registered immigrants must have constituted only part of the total Netherlandish population, however, and there can be little doubt that their numbers were substantial, possibly running into the thousands.

Likewise, their language was well-represented. The abovementioned material presence of Dutch texts evinces that many migrants continued to use their mother tongue. Concrete examples can be drawn from the Breyne (or Breine) family, who originally hailed from Antwerp, then moved to the Northern Netherlands, and in the early decades of the seventeenth century settled in Gdańsk: a reminder that Dutch-speaking immigrants came from various corners of the Low Countries. Jakob Breyne senior (early to mid-seventeenth century), who shipped Polish cochineal to Holland (Fleischer 2019: 116), corresponded in Dutch with the Amsterdam-based poet Joannes Six van Chandelier (1620–1695) (Six van Chandelier 1991: I, 286–87, 562–63). More telling is the fact that Jakob's grandson Johann Philipp Breyne (1680–1764) in the early eighteenth century still wrote let-

1915: 450). Albrecht Jan Zaborowski (ca. 1638–1711), possibly the first Pole to settle in Northern America, probably knew Dutch (Zabriskie 1963: 1–10).

ters in his ancestral language and received Dutch books from an acquaintance in Amsterdam (Noordegraaf 2007). No doubt, part of the reason why Netherlandish immigrants felt so at home in Gdańsk was that they could keep using their mother tongue, or else apply only slight changes.

The Baltic Sea area formed a highly multilingual space (*Networks, Poetics and Multilingual Society* 2025), where Low German functioned as a *lingua franca*, fuelling commerce. Anyone who spoke a version hereof, including the forms of Dutch used in the Low Countries, could readily communicate with other speakers (Kreslins 2003: 169). As well as being vital to trade, moreover, Dutch had a literary status. In particular, authors of Latin and German verse who worked in Gdańsk, such as Martin Opitz (1597–1639), Johannes Plavius (b. 1600), and Johann Peter Titz (Johannes Petrus Titius, 1619–1689), were heavily inspired by Dutch examples (Bornemann 1976; Schenkeveld-Van der Dussen and Schipperheijn 2003). Local citizens even transcribed Dutch poems into manuscripts of their own: a certain Eduard Bergman (or Bergmann) compiled multiple large volumes of poetry, which include epitaphs and other verses in the Dutch language, copied from foreign sources (Hulsenboom 2025). In short, Dutch was common in early modern Gdańsk, both on the streets and on paper.

If immigrants from the Low Countries could happily function using (a variant of) their own language, however, why would they go through the trouble of learning Polish? For a start, merchants sought to do business further inland as well, thereby cutting out the middlemen in Gdańsk and achieving better deals. Therefore, the city's authorities increasingly tried to curtail such contacts, to the point where Netherlandish merchants were forbidden to even converse with Polish noblemen, as was the case in 1638. If anything, however, measures like these indicate that such conversations were a regular occurrence, and it is questionable whether the authorities of Gdańsk could uphold their restrictions, considering how indispensable the Dutch had made themselves to the city's prosperity (Bogucka 1990: 24–25). Naturally, none of this proves that Netherlandish merchants spoke Polish, but there are strong indications that at least some of them did.

One such individual was Tamme Geijsbers (b. 1583), an aspiring merchant from Groningen who wrote a concise autobiography later in life. In early 1598, at only fourteen or fifteen years of age, he sailed to Gdańsk for the first time. Apparently convinced of the need to master Polish, he left his home once more in 1599, embarking on a venture which he later remembered briefly as "5 Martij bin ick in Polen gaen woonen om de sprake te leeren": 'on 5 March, I went to live in Poland in order to learn the language' (Geijsbers ca. 1636–1647: 2v) (Figure 3). Subsequent entries make clear that Tamme's Polish base of operations was Gdańsk: he regularly went there on matters of business, had family there, and even settled there himself between 1605 and 1611. To Tamme and other merchants, commerce proved a powerful incentive to learn Polish.

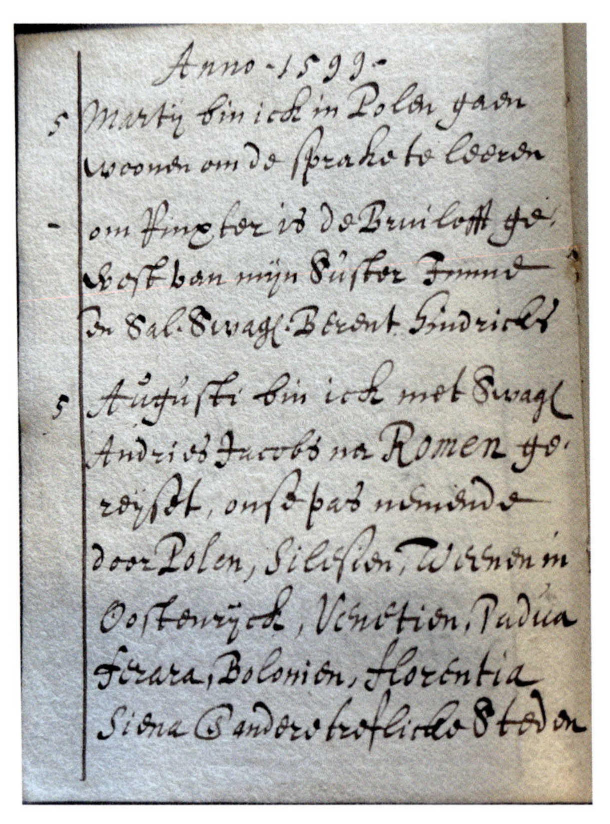

Figure 3. Tamme Geijsbers, *Page with comment about learning Polish in 1599* (ca. 1636–1647). Leiden University Library, LTK 2293: 2v

Furthermore, foreigners in Gdańsk often showed an interest in Polish culture. Household inventories of several dozen Dutch and other immigrants from the 1620s and 1630s reveal that they frequently owned pieces of Polish clothing, such as fur-lined and feathered caps, brightly-coloured robes, gloves, and boots. This suggests that they adapted to the *couleur locale* – or endeavoured to do so. Some inventories even list books in Polish (Pelus-Kaplan 2007: 367–68). Meanwhile, Eduard Bergman and other Gdańsk residents not only collected poems in Dutch, but in Polish as well. Indeed, their manuscript volumes also comprise Latin, German, French, Italian, and other compositions. These so-called *silvae rerum* are thus symbolic of the multilingual and cosmopolitan character of Gdańsk, where a combined command of Dutch and Polish, passive as well as active, was not uncommon.

Importantly, Netherlandish migrants also included people who could be called 'makers': numerous artists, artisans, architects, and engineers from the Low Countries made careers in Gdańsk and other cities across Poland-Lithuania. In several cases, it is likely that they picked up Polish. Examples include Anthonis van Obbergen (1543–1611) and Willem van den Blocke (1550–1628) from Mechelen, Willem Hondius from The Hague (ca. 1598-ca. 1652), Pieter Danckerts de Rij from Amsterdam (1605–1660), and Tilman (or Tylman/Tielman) van Gameren from Utrecht (1632–1706) (e.g. Grzybkowska 1995; Roding 1995; *Tilman van Gameren* 2002). Starting in the sixteenth century, moreover, scores of religious refugees from the Low Countries moved to Poland in search of a safe haven. The Mennonites, a moderate Anabaptist movement, took a prominent place, settling mostly in the Żuławy region near Gdańsk: by the mid-seventeenth century, there were about four thousand of them (Klassen 2016; Plett 1991: 113). There is little evidence that they mastered Polish, however. In fact, the Mennonites were slow to acclimatise to their new home, even holding church services in Dutch until well into the eighteenth century, when they switched to High German and Werder Platt or Plautdietsch (Klassen 2016: 161–75; Plett, 1991: 141–43, 160–71). Although some individuals did learn Polish (Plett 1991: 171–72), these were exceptions. However, Netherlandish colonists also settled in other parts of the country, such as Kuyavia, Greater Poland, and Mazovia (e.g. Szałygin 2004; 2008; Szmytka 2016). To what extent they immersed themselves in the local language remains to be researched.

3.2 Franeker: Polish-Lithuanian Calvinists

Dutch migration flows to Gdańsk and the rest of Poland-Lithuania were balanced by large-scale movements of people in the opposite direction, which are generally less well-known. Between 1601 and 1700, for example, 601 men and 145 women from Gdańsk married in Amsterdam (Hart 1976: 170).[17] Many of them must have had at least a basic command of Polish upon their arrival. Regarding Dutch-Polish bilingualism, however, more can currently be said about other social groups from Poland. The first concerns Calvinists who came to the United Provinces as students. The Northern Netherlands constituted a preeminent destination on the Polish *peregrinatio academica*, mentioned earlier. Travel diaries, letters, poems, *alba amicorum*, university entries, and other sources suggest that, from the late sixteenth century onwards, the number of educational Polish visits to the United Provinces ran into the thousands (Hulsenboom 2023a; 2023c: 25–92; Hulsenboom

17. In the years 1701–1800, the total numbers were only slightly lower: 671 grooms and 54 brides. Simon Hart also mentions seventy Polish sailors who married in Amsterdam between 1651 and 1665 (1976: 200). It is likely that most of them came from Gdańsk or other towns in Royal Prussia.

& Moss 2022). Most travellers were nobles of various denominations, including Catholics. However, it was mainly Protestants who matriculated at one or more of the renowned Dutch centres of learning, thereby coming into close contact with the Dutch language. One of the most popular universities was that of Franeker, in Frisia, founded in 1585: between 1613 and 1750, its academy received some two hundred Polish youths (Postma 2014), not counting other students from Royal Prussia, Lithuania, and Ruthenia, who often spoke Polish. While there are no indications that they mastered Frisian, their peregrinations did result in a modest yet prolonged presence of Dutch-Polish bilingual Calvinists.

Traces hereof first of all point to Jan Makowski from Łobżenica (Johannes Maccovius, 1588–1644), Jan Dymitr Gorajski (Johannes Demetrius à Gorai Goraisky, d. 1678), Mikołaj Arnold or Arnoldi from Leszno (Nicolaus Arnoldus, 1618–1680), and Szymon Karol Ogiński from Vilnius, Lithuania (ca. 1620–1694). All of them not only studied in Franeker, but also married Dutch women, thus entrenching themselves solidly in the local community. It stands to reason that this encouraged all four of them to learn Dutch. For example, two collections of poems published on the occasion of Arnold's second marriage in 1653 include Dutch verses addressed to the happy couple, implying that both bride and groom could read them (*Applausus Gratulatorius* 1653: no page numbers; *Venus ANAΔYOMENH*: 1653: A3ff.). Three years later, Arnold dedicated a Dutch book to his wife, citing the words he allegedly spoke upon holding their newborn son – in Dutch (Dyke 1656: *3r-v). Their spouses and children to some extent must have picked up Polish as well. This is especially plausible in the case of Ogiński's family. After his marriage to Titia Staackmans (b. after 1624) in 1645, the pair lived somewhere in Poland, before settling in Groningen in 1648. Following Staackmans' death in 1679, moreover, Ogiński moved back to Vilnius, where their daughter Sophia (after 1645-after 1698) joined him in 1686 (Broos 2015: 135; Broos 1974: 215–18). Much like today, mixed marriages must have stimulated Dutch-Polish bilingualism.[18]

In addition, the four men's Dutch proficiency levels were no doubt influenced by their professional endeavours. While Gorajski's and Ogiński's activities remain unknown, the careers of Makowski and Arnold can be reconstructed fairly accurately. Makowski matriculated in Franeker in October 1613 as the tutor of Jan Dymitr and Krystian (Christianus) Gorajski, obtained a doctoral degree less than

18. Ogiński and Staackmans had three children in total. Gorajski in 1622 married Everdina van Alberda (d. 1658), and the pair had a daughter. In 1626, Makowski married Antje Uylenburgh (ca. 1598–1633), a sister of Saskia Uylenburgh (1612–1642), who in 1634 wed Rembrandt (1606–1669). Arnold in 1645 married Remigia van (der) Nitzen (1611–1652). In 1653, he wed Anna Pybinga (1628–1700), with whom he had six children.

five months later, was named professor of theology in early 1615, and was twice elected rector (Kuyper Jr. 1899: 3–63; Kiedroń 2013). He used Latin to conduct his classes and write scholarly treatises, but his frequent interaction with his students – Makowski's drinking habits and nightly escapades made him rather popular – must have involved Dutch.

The case of Arnold (Figure 4) shows an even closer connection between his professional life and his command of the Dutch language. Arnold enrolled in Franeker in August 1641 (two months after Ogiński), and studied under Makowski. In 1645, the year of his first marriage, he became a minister in the Frisian town of Beetgum. According to himself, he was at that time "een beginnend Leerlingh (...) in de Nederduytsche Tale": 'a beginning student of the Dutch tongue' (Dyke 1669: front matter, no page numbers). In 1651, he was named professor of theology in Franeker, after which he became rector four times (Van Leeuwen 1851: 6–13). While he wrote numerous treatises in Latin, his command of Dutch was such that he managed to translate several English works by Thomas Taylor (1576–1632) and Jeremiah Dyke (1584–1639) – the book he dedicated to his second wife is an example. One of his reasons for doing so, he wrote, was to train himself in the English language (Taylor 1651: front matter, no page numbers), which he later taught to a Dutch student as well (Dyke 1664: front matter, no page numbers). Arnold continued to work as a minister, moreover, and gave public speeches in Dutch. He must have been very skilled and respected, for in 1664, he had the honour of giving a funerary oration for Prince Willem Frederik of Nassau-Dietz (1613–1664), which was then published in Leeuwarden (Arnold 1664). Arnold's systematic use of Dutch thus benefitted his career and probably resulted in an unusually high proficiency level.

Indeed, he even utilised his bilingual abilities to influence international relations. In 1656, after Sweden had invaded Poland, Arnold participated in a Dutch embassy to Polish territory. The mission was meant to mediate between the warring parties, and in so doing safeguard Dutch interests (Noordam 1940: esp. 19–53). Arnold was sent along as the embassy's minister, giving regular services in Dutch. However, he also employed his Polish proficiency. In an effort to convince the authorities of Gdańsk to ratify a treaty with the Dutch Republic, Arnold wrote a Polish poem over nine pages long, entitled *Satyr Belgo-Polonus* (*Dutch-Polish Satyr*), which survives in one of Eduard Bergman's manuscripts, kept in the Polish Academy of Sciences Library in Gdańsk. Although the text is unsigned, its title page states that it was written on 4 September 1656 aboard a ship near Gdańsk by "een Hollandisch Domine gebooren tot Polnisch Liß": 'a Dutch vicar, born in Polish Leszno' ([Arnold] 1656: 945r). This convincingly points to Arnold. Whether he wrote the poem of his own accord or acted on someone's

Figure 4. Jacob van Meurs after Pieter Schick, *Portrait of Mikołaj Arnold* (Amsterdam 1654). Rijksmuseum Amsterdam, RP-P-1907-3261

orders is unclear, but the title page does claim that the author had a patron: an unnamed admiral.[19]

Another question which requires consideration is: why did Arnold write the poem in Polish? In the preface to the text, he stated that he had heard that Latin was insufficiently known in Gdańsk. True or false, it does explain why Arnold refrained from using that language. Furthermore, his choice for Polish over German should be clarified as follows: first, Arnold probably considered his German to be inferior; second, he must have been convinced that many influential people in Gdańsk (including the German-speaking patriciate) could read Polish well enough to understand his verses; third, his use of Polish was critical to his rhetorical enterprise, which saw him tying in with a well-known poetical Polish genre (see below).

The preface itself, meanwhile, is in Dutch. It is addressed to one Jacques Wit, apparently of Dutch descent. Arnold asked him to publicise his "blauwe boexken" or 'blue booklet', i.e. pamphlet, which indicates that Wit was a printer. Furthermore, Arnold commented on his own knowledge of Polish and Dutch. I cite a passage from the original, followed by an English translation:

> Ghij moet niet quat nehmen, dat het Poolnisch is niet heel correct. Ick een hebbe het ten deel vergeten, ende doch het Hollandsch niet geleert perfect. *De omnibus aliquid, de toto nihil.* So Ghij mijn Poolnisch niet verstaen (sic), geat beij de groote boeckvercooper, hij sal u te recht helpen, ick weete niet waer sijn huijs ist, maerck ick hoore hij ist een goede kerel, eende heefft (sic) onse Scheeps Capiteins wel tractieret.
>
> You must not hold it against me, that my Polish is not entirely correct. I have partly forgotten it and not learned Dutch perfectly. *De omnibus aliquid, de toto nihil* [Something of everything, nothing in its entirety]. Should you not understand my Polish, go to the large bookseller, he will help you out – I do not know where his house is, but I hear he is a fine fellow, and he has treated our ships' captains well. ([Arnold] 1656: 945v)

Arnold clearly suspected that Wit could have difficulty reading (and thus typesetting) the Polish text, and believed a local 'large bookseller' might be of assistance. Regarding his own language proficiency, moreover, Arnold demonstrated a remarkable degree of self-awareness and modesty – although part of it may have been inspired by rhetorical convention. In any case, the spelling of certain words appears affected by German (for example "nehmen" and "Poolnisch"). To what extent this can be ascribed to Bergman remains uncertain. However, the preface

19. This may have been Jacob van Wassenaer Obdam (1610–1665), who at that time led a Dutch fleet anchored before Gdańsk. For detailed analyses of the context and the poem itself, see Hulsenboom 2023c: 119–24.

does provide an intimate view of Arnold's not-quite-native command of Dutch, suggesting that, talented though he was, he had help when composing his sermons and translations. Additionally, the statement that he had 'partly forgotten' the Polish language rings true: some researchers have dismissed the poem as 'primitive' and written in 'clumsy Polish' (Nowak-Dłużewski 1972: 185; Pelc 1965: 275). Because of this, and because the author has long remained unidentified and the preface unread, the poem has hardly received any scholarly attention.

However, the text constitutes an extraordinary source, which not only forms a tangible, up-close example of seventeenth-century Dutch-Polish bilingualism, but also reveals Arnold's personal experience thereof: he showed himself aware of his shortcomings, insecure even, since he knew 'nothing in its entirety'. Simultaneously, he presented himself as someone wielding both languages – and thus fostering a twofold, Dutch-Polish identity. This already shines through in the title, which on the one hand refers to the genre of 'satirical' Polish poems – named not after their humorous content, but after the mythological satyrs that often speak in them –, and on the other points to the author himself. Indeed, his double identity was exactly what allowed Arnold to take on the role of the outsider who stood at a distance to Polish society, but knew it well enough to comment on it – just as satyrs typically did in other 'satirical' Polish poems (Kochanowski 2018: 40–53, 64–71; Nowak-Dłużewski 1962; Pelc 1963). In other words: Arnold showed himself at home in both languages and both cultures. Even though there are no surviving printed copies of the text – which begs the question whether it was printed at all –, and although the proposed treaty between Gdańsk and the Dutch Republic did not materialise, the *Satyr Belgo-Polonus* shows how Arnold instrumentalised his bilingualism for diplomatic purposes, giving a valuable glimpse of his proficiency and personal identity in the process.

While it remains unclear exactly how Makowski, Gorajski, Arnold, and Ogiński learned Dutch, it is likely that they had lessons from their professors, even if university classes were conducted in Latin. Indeed, Makowski and Arnold probably acted as Dutch language tutors to other students from Poland-Lithuania, just as Arnold taught English to a Dutch pupil. If so, then the bilingual Dutch-Polish population of Franeker was decidedly more numerous, socially varied, and changeable, as students came and went. For instance, the Calvinist Polish nobleman Jan Nemorecki, who started his studies in Franeker in 1647, must have been able to read the Dutch document he signed five years later, declaring he would pay off his debts to his Frisian landlady, tailor, publisher, and others within a few years. This allowed him to return to Poland, but as a guarantee, he left behind a sizeable book collection, which could be sold if he failed to meet his obligation (Postma 2014: 164–68). Unfortunately, the contents of Nemorecki's library are unknown, but it may well have contained books in Dutch. In short, it seems that Franeker and its surroundings housed a relatively small yet vibrant community of Calvinist Dutch-Polish bilinguals during almost the entire seventeenth century, powered by its university.

What, then, of the other centres of learning in the Low Countries? The Dutch Republic boasted multiple academies for higher education, including in Amsterdam, Breda, Groningen, The Hague, Harderwijk, Leiden, Nijmegen, and Utrecht. Several of these were visited by young Polish students, especially Protestants, who would stay in the United Provinces for anything between several months and a few years. Similarly, Catholic Poles frequently enrolled at the university of Louvain, in the Southern Netherlands (Borowski 2007: 80–108). It is worth examining, therefore, how Franeker's situation corresponded to that in other university and academy towns. In the following section, I do so by probing the Polish Brethren's presence in Leiden and Amsterdam.

3.3 Leiden and Amsterdam: Polish Brethren

The Polish Brethren are known by many names, such as the Minor Church of Poland, Anti-Trinitarians, Arians, and Socinians, after the Italian exile Fausto Sozzini (Faustus Socinus, 1539–1604). They were the result of a split within the Polish Reformed Church, which occurred in the 1560s. The seventeenth century saw many of their young members studying in the United Provinces, such as Samuel Przypkowski (Samuel Przipcovius, ca. 1592–1670) and Jonasz Szlichtyng (Jonas Slichtingius, 1592–1661), who would become leading figures in their community. Przypkowski, Szlichtyng, and many others matriculated in Leiden, the oldest university in the Northern Netherlands, founded in 1575, which welcomed well over five hundred Polish students between 1586 and 1700 (Kiedroń 1992). Furthermore, Leiden employed at least one Polish-speaking professor, namely the aforementioned historian and geographer Filip Clüver from Gdańsk, although he only had a permanent position in Leiden for six years and travelled widely.[20] If and to what extent he taught Dutch to Polish students (and vice versa) is unknown.[21] Amsterdam, moreover, in 1632 gained an *Athenaeum Illustre*: an institute for higher education. Sources suggest that several members of the Polish Brethren learned Dutch while studying in Leiden and Amsterdam alike. In addition, numerous Socinians settled in Amsterdam.

20. Another Leiden professor who originally came from Poland was Filip Ferdynand (Philippus Ferdinandus, ca. 1555–1599), but he died during his trial period, shortly before the actual start of his appointment in 1600.

21. The fact that he donated a Lutheran Polish Bible to the abovementioned Joris van der Does may mean that he taught Polish to Joris, but this is conjecture.

To begin with, four poems relating to Polish students provide circumstantial evidence concerning their language proficiency. The first three are written in Dutch and were included in the *alba amicorum* of two Polish Brethren: Maciej Przypkowski (Mathias Przipcovius, 1626-after 1662), son of the aforementioned Samuel Przypkowski, and Szczęsny Morsztyn (Faustus Morstinus, ca. 1631–1687). Przypkowski registered as a student in Leiden in 1648, Morsztyn in 1654. Upon their return to Poland, in 1654 and 1656 respectively, Willem van Heemskerck (1613–1692) and Joachim Oudaen (1628–1692) each wrote a poem for Przypkowski, while Gerard Brandt (1626–1685) poetically saluted Morsztyn. The *alba* of the two Poles have apparently not survived, but the contributions made by their Dutch friends – Oudaen and Brandt are known to have had friendly dealings with the Socinians – were published in other collections (*Apollos Harp* 1658: 112; *Bloemkrans* 1659: 324–26; Brandt 1688: 474; Oudaen 1712: II, 154–55).[22] The fact that they were written in Dutch indicates that their authors trusted the addressees to understand the language. Importantly, moreover, the contributions are hardly the kind of short and simple mottos often found in *alba amicorum*: Brandt's poem has sixteen verses, Van Heemskerck's thirty-six, and Oudaen's forty. During their stays in the United Provinces, which lasted six and two years respectively, Przypkowski and Morsztyn most probably devoted themselves to the study of Dutch and mastered it to the point where they could read poetry.

The fourth poem reflects on this practice from a Polish perspective. It was written by the prolific Socinian poet Zbigniew Morsztyn (Zbigneus Morstinus, ca. 1628–1689) upon the death of Stefan Trembecki (ca. 1648–1664), a teenager of Socinian stock who had been sent to study in Amsterdam in 1663 (Krauze-Karpińska 2009: 132–33). Sadly, however, he succumbed to the plague one year later. According to Morsztyn, Trembecki had been a promising student with a great aptitude for learning languages, including Dutch:

> He used the Greek, Hebrew, Latin,
> German, and French languages as if they were
> Native to him, and he had already made great beginnings
> With Dutch, though he had little time. He first
> Disembarked on that [Dutch] shore and experienced a
> Kindness with which guests there are seldom welcomed.[23]
>
> (Trembecki 1910: I, 431–32)

22. Moreover, Oudaen translated several Latin letters by Samuel Przypkowski and Franciszek Morsztyn (Franciscus Morstinus, d. before 1726), and wrote a lengthy Dutch poem about them (Oudaen 1689: 147ff.; Oudaen 1712: I, 81–88).

23. "Języki przytym grecki, hebrejski, łaciński, / Niemiecki i francuski jako macierzyński / Umiał; i wielkie już niderlanskiego / Miał początki, choć za czas krotki, do ktorego / Brzegu najpierwej wysiadł i takiej ludzkości / Doznał, z jakową rzadko przyjmują tam gości."

As Morsztyn explained in the following few verses, the final comment refers to the fact that Trembecki's studies were not only financed by the Polish Brethren themselves, but also by Dutch sympathisers. Naturally, the poet's exuberant compliments cannot be taken at face value, but they do confirm that knowing Dutch and other languages was status-enhancing. Much like Maciej Przypkowski and Szczęsny Morsztyn before him, Stefan Trembecki presumably started learning Dutch during his stay in Holland. These Socinian students (and their parents or guardians) must have considered it worthwhile to invest in Dutch language acquisition because of their close ties with people in the Northern Netherlands.

Indeed, other sources indicate that such relations resulted in multiple cases of advanced Dutch-Polish bilingualism. Admittedly, extant correspondences between Polish Brethren and their Dutch contacts are written in Latin (e.g. Szczucki 1975). It is hard to draw conclusions from this, however, as the use of Latin was also a matter of convention. For example, the Silesian-Polish polymath Joachim Pastorius (1611–1681), who visited the United Provinces at least three times and became a professor at the *Gymnasium Academicum* in Gdańsk, wrote extensively in Latin, but a poem he composed on the Delft Thunderclap of 1654 suggests that he could read Dutch (Hulsenboom 2023b). Other sources are more explicit, however, and point to Polish Brethren who could write Dutch as well. A prime example is Krzysztof Arciszewski (also known as Christoffel Artichewsky, Artisoski, and other variants, 1592–1656), who wrote several Dutch reports in service of the West India Company (e.g. Urbański 1988; Warnsinck 1937). Moreover, the theologian Andrzej Wiszowaty (Andreas Wissowatius, 1608–1678) produced a Dutch commentary on a work on Tamil Hinduism by the missionary Abraham Rogiers or Rogerius (ca. 1609–1649), which was published in Leiden in 1651 (Noak 2014).[24] Conversely, it is likely that some Dutchmen who befriended Socinians picked up Polish. This applies especially to Samuel (1582–1641) and Johannes (1608–1679) van der Neer or Naeranus, who travelled through Poland extensively and lived in Gdańsk for some time (Visser 2011). Indeed, Wiszowaty in 1635 entered an eight-line Polish poem into Johannes' *album amicorum* ("*Album przyjaciół* Jana Naeranusa" 1989: 201), suggesting that the recipient could read it (Figure 5).

Meanwhile, many Polish Brethren decided to settle in the United Provinces, as they were faced with increased oppression in their homeland: in 1638, the Polish Sejm (Parliament) had the Socinian academy in Raków destroyed, and twenty years later, the Brethren were officially banned from the Polish-Lithuanian Commonwealth altogether. Even though the Dutch Reformed Church strongly opposed the Brethren's beliefs and acted to limit their numbers and influence

24. Gerard Brandt also composed a short Dutch epitaph for Wiszowaty (Brandt 1688: 428).

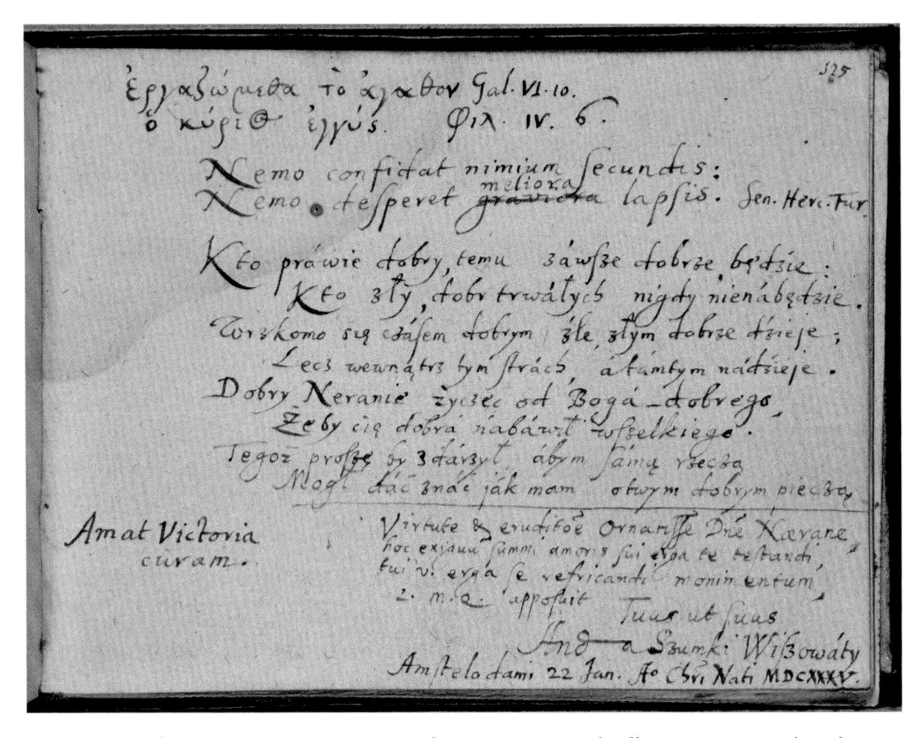
125

ἐργαζώμεθα τὸ ἀγαθὸν Gal. VI. 10.
ὁ κύριος ἐγγύς. Φιλ. IV. 6.

Nemo confidat nimium secundis:
Nemo desperet ~~graviora~~ meliora lapsis. Sen. Herc. Fur.

Kto prawie dobry, temu záwsze dobrze będzie:
Kto zły, dobr trwałych nigdy nienábędzie.
Wszkomo się czásem dobrym źle, złym dobrze dzieje;
Lecz wewnątrz tym strách, á tamtym nádzieje.
Dobry Neranie życzę od Bogá dobrego,
Żeby cię dobra nabáwił wszelkiego.
Tegoż proszę by sczarzył ábym sámą rzeczą
Mogł dáć znáć ják mam o twym dobrym pieczą.

Amat Victoria curam.

Virtute & eruditione Ornatisse Dne Naerane,
hoc exiguu summi amoris sui erga te testandi,
tui v. erga se refricandi monimentum,
... apposuit
Tuus ut suus
Andr. Szunk: Wiszowaty
Amstelodami 22 Jan. Ao Chri Nati MDCXXXV.

Figure 5. Andrzej Wiszowaty, *Entry in Johannes Naeranus's album amicorum* (1635). Koninklijke Bibliotheek, The Hague, 74 H 24: 125r

in the United Provinces, at least several dozen Socinian families found refuge in Holland after 1658 – mainly in Amsterdam, which formed a metropolis of some two hundred thousand inhabitants (Hart 1976: 118). Andrzej Wiszowaty and his family were amongst these migrants, settling in Amsterdam in 1666. They maintained close relations with other religious minorities, especially the Remonstrants, Mennonites, and Collegiants (Bem 2022; Lambour 1999; Quatrini 2021; Laskowska & Waszink 2025). Indeed, some of them even joined or married into their congregations, possibly raising their offspring bilingually. Furthermore, they engaged in publishing activities, the most notable result being the *Bibliotheca Fratrum Polonorum*: a series of works by Socinian theologians, issued in Amsterdam between 1668 and 1692. To conclude, the Polish Brethren's intensive personal and professional contacts with the United Provinces formed a stimulus to learn Dutch, and it is plausible that hundreds of Socinians during the second half of the seventeenth century had at least a passive knowledge of the language. Of necessity, the individuals and families who lived in Amsterdam must have achieved relative fluency in Polish and Dutch alike.

3.4 Amsterdam: 'Polish' Jews

That same period witnessed the establishment of a sizeable community in Amsterdam of Jewish refugees from the Polish-Lithuanian Commonwealth. Several decades before, the horrors of the Thirty Years War had already forced a thousand or more Ashkenazi Jews from the German lands to flee to Holland's principal trading centre. From there, some five hundred individuals during the 1630s migrated to Poland, a country with a strong Jewish presence. However, the Cossack Khmelnytsky Uprising against Poland in 1648, which included large-scale pogroms, as well as the subsequent Russian invasion of the Polish-Lithuanian Commonwealth in 1654, once again compelled numerous Ashkenazim to abandon their homes. Between the mid-1650s and mid-1660s in particular, many found a safe haven in Amsterdam, where they formed a separate Ashkenazi community in 1660. Although Jews from Lithuania outnumbered their Polish co-religionists, they were often treated simply as 'Poles'. In 1673, this Polish-Lithuanian group was forced to join the pre-existing local Ashkenazi community. It is estimated that the number of 'Polish' Jews in Amsterdam was at that time close to five hundred (Kaplan 2000: 78–107). Naturally, such Ashkenazi refugees also ended up in other cities.[25] Just as for the Socinians, however, Amsterdam was their main hub.

Letters and notary deeds allow for the identification of several Jews who knew Polish and Dutch, which must have been comparatively easy to learn if they spoke Yiddish. The most famous was Simon de Pool (also known as Szymon ben Menachem Nachum di Polonia, d. 1713), who arrived in Amsterdam in ca. 1650 and boasted an impressive linguistic skillset, including Dutch, Polish, German, Russian, Tatar, Latin, Hebrew, and Yiddish. Using this knowledge to make a living, De Pool established himself as a translator and in 1677 became the official factor in the United Provinces to King Jan III Sobieski (1629–1696), carrying out business on behalf of the Polish monarch and the Jewish community in Poland (Fuks, 1957). De Pool's precursor was one Moses Trajlowicz (or Trajtlowicz). According to a notary deed from 1676, he acted as factor to King Jan II Kazimierz Waza (1609–1672), King Michał Korybut Wiśniowiecki (1640–1673), and Prince Michał Kazimierz Radziwiłł (1635–1680). Trajlowicz himself translated this document from Polish to Dutch, after which the translation's accuracy was confirmed by a Polish nobleman named Jan Paweł Lubieniecki, who apparently had at least some knowledge of Dutch as well (SA 5075, NA 2249A: 546–49). Although both Simon de Pool and Moses Trajlowicz deserve more research, it is obvious that their knowledge of Dutch and Polish was a source of significant income – and hence, probably of pride.

25. For example, a disturbed Polish Jew was arrested in Haarlem in 1656 (Wallet 2024: 82).

Other Jews in the 1670s employed their bilingualism to translate official documents from Polish to Dutch, although it is as yet unclear how systematically they carried out these activities: a certain Joseph Lasarus and Jacob Abrahams in 1676 translated another Jew's last will and testament (SA 5075, NA 1180: 92r), and one Salomon Israels in 1678 did so with a trade agreement (SA 5075, NA 4087: 488). Another source which attests to Jewish Dutch-Polish bilingualism in late-seventeenth-century Amsterdam features in a newspaper report from April 1698, which describes a young runaway Jewish thief from Poland, who spoke "Hebreeus, Hoog- en Neerduyts, en Poolse Talen": 'the Hebrew, High and Low German, and Polish languages' (*Amsterdamse Donderdaegse Courant* 1698: no. 43v). Considering the large number of Ashkenazim who settled in Amsterdam, one can safely assume that these instances represent only the tip of the bilingual iceberg.

In fact, it is likely that the city during the final quarter of the seventeenth century was home to several hundred first- and second-generation Ashkenazi immigrants from Poland and Lithuania with an active knowledge of Dutch and Polish. Those with an unusually high proficiency level, like Simon de Pool, could use it to improve their economic position: a combined fluency in Polish and Dutch remained a relatively rare and thus potentially profitable asset. While the situation in other cities has yet to be researched, Amsterdam doubtless housed the largest community of Dutch-Polish bilingual Jews in the United Provinces.

4. Conclusion

After Henrick Schaeff in 1654 opened the mysterious tin box that had once belonged to Annetgen Boeijens, he quickly decided that the Polish papers he found inside had little value, and he probably soon forgot about them. Similarly, at first glance, the topic of seventeenth-century Dutch-Polish bilingualism may not seem particularly promising: neither the Dutch nor the Poles produced grammars, orthographies, dictionaries, colloquial books, or other learning aids about each other's languages. What is more, there is as yet no convincing evidence of Polish language teachers in the United Provinces, and only one mention of a Dutch language instructor in Poland, who lived in Gdańsk. Despite their commercial interdependence and other types of interaction, it seems as if the Dutch and Poles shared a linguistic indifference towards each other, and preferred to focus their attention on French, German, and other languages. On the whole, therefore, Polish had a comparatively low status in the Dutch Republic, and the same goes for Dutch in Poland – with the exception of Royal Prussia.

Still, both languages were present in both countries, where they circulated orally and in written form alike. Thousands of Polish and Dutch individuals encountered them on a regular basis, and many people learned one of the two as a second language. Specifically, Dutch-Polish bilingualism thrived in certain places and amongst certain communities. In chronological order, these were: (1) Gdańsk, which attracted hundreds if not thousands of Dutch merchants, artists, artisans, architects, engineers, and other Netherlandish migrants, many of whom settled in the city, (2) Franeker, where numerous Calvinists from Poland-Lithuania came to study, some of whom established families in Frisia or Groningen, (3) Leiden, which received even more Polish students, including Socinians/Polish Brethren, and (4) Amsterdam, which not only welcomed Socinian students, but also became a home for several dozen Socinian families and hundreds of Jews from the Polish-Lithuanian Commonwealth. In these places and amongst these communities, Dutch and Polish had a higher status than the lack of learning materials and teachers suggests. Considering the fact that Dutch-Polish bilingualism remained a prerogative of non-Catholic Poles, moreover, it follows that religious convictions were markers of interest in and knowledge of the Dutch tongue.

Even though some evidence is circumstantial (for example the Dutch poems addressed to Polish students), it is both numerically significant and backed up by sources which clearly attest to advanced instances of bilingualism, such as the Dutch texts found in Gdańsk or the notary deeds from Amsterdam. The *Satyr Belgo-Polonus* by Mikołaj Arnold provides an exceptional perspective on the practical and psychological facets of its author's linguistic abilities. Most testimonies concern young men, but they also hint at the bilingualism of their wives and children, as is the case with the Ogiński family. In most cases, however, it remains difficult to determine whether people had a passive or active command of both languages. Generally speaking, it must have been easier for Poles to master Dutch than the other way around, since many Poles knew German as well. Also, individuals who moved to Poland or the Dutch Republic and studied the local languages at a relatively young age were probably more proficient than those who did not migrate and/or were older at the time of learning.

Indeed, Dutch-Polish bilingualism was stimulated first and foremost by migration, which was spurred by several factors. To begin with, there were economic interests at play: Netherlandish migrants who acted in and around Gdańsk had better chances of making profitable deals if they spoke Polish. Moreover, for many Protestants from Poland-Lithuania, knowledge of both languages resulted from intellectual pursuits, specifically their studies in the United Provinces. On the other hand, many Jews and Socinians who settled in the Dutch Republic were basically religious refugees. The social relations involved in these migrations, particularly those of a friendly or romantic nature, provided a powerful stimulus to learn Dutch or Polish. The ensuing linguistic proficiencies in turn formed a type of capital that could yield financial gain, for example for Jews who earned a living as interpreters, translators, and factors. In short, the incentives that galvanised Dutch-Polish bilingualism differed, depending on specific historical contexts and communities.

Future research should move in various directions. Library catalogues and household inventories could identify more owners of Dutch and Polish books, and determine the focus of their collections. Newspaper advertisements, municipal records, and other sources might help to find Dutch and Polish language teachers who have thus far remained elusive. The bilingual communities that I have discussed in this chapter can be mapped in greater detail, and the role of languages (Dutch, Polish, and other) for people's personal and professional lives can be analysed further, for example with the aid of ego-documents. Other places and communities deserve scrutiny as well, such as immigrants from Gdańsk in Amsterdam and Dutch settlements across the Polish-Lithuanian Commonwealth. Also, scholars might examine the linguistic characteristics of the forms of Dutch and Polish used by migrants in this period, as well as the production and circulation of Polish texts in the United Provinces (particularly in centres of learning) and Dutch texts in Poland (mainly in Royal Prussia). Lastly, research into the mental mapping of the continent and the development of the concepts of 'Western' and 'Eastern Europe' should take into consideration the effects of early modern language learning materials. Similar to the tin box of Annetgen Boeijens, seventeenth-century Dutch-Polish bilingualism has emerged as an intriguing subject of study, one that has already unveiled many of its secrets and raised a wealth of new and exciting research questions in the process.

Bibliography

Manuscript sources

[*Album amicorum of Janus Dousa*]. 1563–1597. Leiden University Library, BPL 1406.

[Arnold, Mikołaj]. 1656. *Satyr Belgo-Polonus*. PAN Gdańsk Library, Rkps 1204.

Geijsbers, Tamme. ca. 1636–1647. *[Diary]*. Leiden University Library, LTK 2293.

SA (Amsterdam City Archives) 5075, NA (Notary Archives) 1180. 1676, not. Jan de Vos.

SA 5075, NA 1304. 1654, not. Henrick Schaeff.

SA 5075, NA 2249A. 1676, not. Adriaen Lock.

SA 5075, NA 4087. 1678, not. Dirck van der Groe.

Newspapers

Amsterdamse Dingsdaegse Courant. Amsterdam: Willem Arnold en de Weduwe Ossaan, 7 January 1698 (no. 3).

Amsterdamse Donderdaegse Courant. Amsterdam: Willem Arnold en de Weduwe Ossaan, 10 April 1698 (no. 43).

Amsterdamse Donderdaeghse Courant. Amsterdam: Casparus Commelin, 19 June 1687 (no. 25).

Extraordinaire Haerlemse Donderdaeghse Courant. Haarlem: Abraham Casteleyn, 20 June 1669 (no. 25).

Ordinaris Dingsdaeghse Courante. Amsterdam: Weduwe Joost Broersz., 6 August 1652 (no. 32).

Tydinge uyt verscheyden Quartieren. Amsterdam: Broer Jansz., 30 September 1645 (no. 39).

Other printed sources

"*Album przyjaciół Jana Naeranusa.*" 1989. Ed. by Katarzyna Kotońska. *Odrodzenie i Reformacja w Polsce* 34: 169–206.

Apollos Harp, Bestaande in Nederduytsche Mengelrymen. 1658. Amsterdam: Jan Hendriksz. en Jan Rieuwertsz.

Applausus Gratulatorius Secundis Nuptiis (...) D. Nicolai Arnoldi (...) Et (...) Annae Pybingae. 1653. Franeker: Idzardus Balck.

Arnold, Mikołaj. 1664. *Vorstelijke Rouw-Lijck-ende-Loff-Reeden, Ter geleegentheydt van 't Beklaagelijke Doods-Gerugt, Van den Doorlughtigsten Prince, ende Heere Wilhelm Frederik.* Leeuwarden: Claes Hansen.

Bloemkrans van Verscheiden Gedichten, Door eenige Liefhebbers der Poëzij bij een verzamelt. 1659. Amsterdam: Louwijs Spillebout.

Bodin, Jean. 1609. *Relatiae Powszechne. Abo Nowiny Pospolite: Iana Botera Benesiusa*, trans. by Paweł Łęczycki. Kraków: Mikołaj Lob.

Boxhornius, Marcus Zuerius. 1654. *Originum Gallicarum Liber.* Amsterdam: Joannes Janssonius.

Brandt, Gerardt. 1688. *Poëzy.* Amsterdam: Aart Dirksz. Ooszaan.

Breeden-Raedt aende Vereenichde Nederlandsche Provintien. 1649. Antwerpen: Francoys van Duynen.

De briefwisseling van Constantijn Huygens. Vol. 4: 1644–1649. 1915. Ed. by J.A. Worp. 's-Gravenhage: Martinus Nijhoff.

Catalogus Librorum Bibliothecae Nobilissimi Clarissimique viri piae memoriae D. Philippi Marnixii Sancto-Aldegondij. Catalogue Van de Boecken des Edelen wijtberoemden Heeren Saligher ghedachtenisse Philips van Marnix Heer van S[ain]te Aldegonde etc. 1599. Leiden: Christophorus Gujotius.

Calepino, Ambrogio. 1590. *Dictionarium undecim linguarum.* Basel: Sebastianus Henricpetri.

Cellarius, Andreas. 1659. *Regni Poloniae, Magnique Ducatus Lituaniae. Omniumque regionum juri Polonico Subjectorum. Novissima Descriptio.* Amsterdam: Aegidius Janssonius Valckenier.

Dyke, Jeremiah. 1656. *Een waerdigh Communicant, zynde Een uytmuntend tractaet van't waerdigh ontfangen des Heyligen Avondtmaels*, trans. by Mikołaj Arnold. Franeker: Johannes Arcerius.

Dyke, Jeremiah. 1664. *IV. Uitgeleesene Predikatien*, trans. by Mikołaj Arnold. Leeuwarden: Dominicus Lens.

Dyke, Jeremiah. 1669. *Een Waerdigh Communicant, Zijnde Een uytnemendt Tractaet van't waerdigh ontfanghen des Heylighen Avondtmaels*, trans. by Mikołaj Arnold. Amsterdam: Johannes van Someren.

Ecclesiae Londino-Batavae Archivum. Tomi Tertii Pars Prima. (…) Epistulae et Tractatus. 1897. Ed. by Joannes Henricus Hessels. Cambridge: Typis Academiae/Sumptibus Ecclesiae Londino-Batavae.

Jasia Ługowskiego podróże do szkół w cudzych krajach, 1639–1643. 1974. Ed. by Krystyna Muszyńska. Warszawa: Państwowy Instytut Wydawniczy.

Joosten, Jaques. 1649. *De Kleyne Wonderlijcke Werelt*. Amsterdam: Dirk Uittenbroek.

Joosten, Jaques. 1662. *De kleyne wonderlijcke Werelt*. Amsterdam: Marcus Willemsz. Doornick.

Katalog książek biblioteki Najjaśniejszego i najpotężniejszego króla Polskiego z Bożej łaski, Jana III, szczęśliwie panującego, spisany w 1689 roku. 1879. Kraków/Warszawa: Wł. L. Anczyc i Spółka.

Kochanowski, Jan. 2018. *Poematy okolicznościowe*. Ed. by Roman Krzywy. Warszawa: Wydawnictwo Naukowe Sub Lupa.

Ojcowskie synom przestrogi. Instrukcje rodzicielskie (XVI-XVII w.). 2017. Ed. by Dorota Żołądź-Strzelczyk and Małgorzata Kowalczyk. Wrocław: Wydawnictwo Chronicon.

Opaliński, Krzysztof. 2004. *Satyry*. Ed. by Jakub Niedźwiedź. Kraków: Universitas.

Oudaen, Joachim. 1689. *Bedenkelijke Toepassing, Op eenige Stukken, In de Openbaringe*. Rotterdam: Barent Bos.

Oudaen, Joachim. 1712. *Poëzy*. Amsterdam: Weduwe P. Arentz. en K. van der Sys.

Prędota, Stanisław, & Woronczak, Jerzy. 2002. *Christophorus Warmers Nederlandse en Poolse samenspraken van* 1691. Wrocław: Wydawnictwo Uniwersytetu Wrocławskiego.

Six van Chandelier, Joannes. 1991. *Gedichten*. Ed. by A. E. Jacobs. Assen: Van Gorcum.

Struys, Jan Jansz. 1676. *Drie aanmerkelijke en seer rampspoedige Reysen*. Amsterdam: Jacob van Meurs en Johannes van Someren.

Taylor, Thomas. 1651. *Des Pelgrims Belydenisse*. Franeker: Ids Albertsz.

Trembecki, Jakub Teodor. 1910. *Wirydarz Poetycki*. Ed. by Aleksander Brückner. Lviv: Towarzystwo dla Popierania Nauki Polskiej.

Venus ΑΝΑΔΥΟΜΕΝΗ, Sive Carmina Epithalamia, Scripta Honori (…) D. Nicolai Arnoldi, Poloni (…) Et (…) D. Annae van Pybinga. 1653. Franeker: Johannes Arcerius.

Warmer, Christophorus. 1691. *Gazophylacium Decem Linguarum Europaearum apertum*. Košice: Johannes Klein.

Secondary literature

Ablonczyné-Nádor, Zsuzsanna. 2011. *Ungarn. Das gesegneteste Land Europas. Das Ungarnbild der niederländischen Reisebeschreibungen (1555–1774): Vergleichende Analyse im Spiegel der rhetorisch-apodemischen Traditionen dargestellt an Werken der niederländischen, deutschen und englischen Reiseliteratur*. Frankfurt am Main: Peter Lang.

Adamovsky, Ezequiel. 2006. *Euro-Orientalism. Liberal Ideology and the Image of Russia in France (c. 1740–1880)*. Bern: Peter Lang.

Bem, Kazimierz. 2022. "Polish Brethren Refugees among the Amsterdam Remonstrants, ca. 1663-ca. 1736." *Journal of Unitarian Universalist Studies* 45: 48–88.

Bibliographia Sociniana. A Bibliographical Reference Tool for the Study of Dutch Socinianism and Antitrinitarianism. 2004. Ed. by Piet Visser, Philip Knijff, and Sibbe Jan Visser. Hilversum/Amsterdam: Verloren/Doopsgezinde Historische Kring.

doi Bogucka, Maria. 1973. "Amsterdam and the Baltic in the first half of the seventeenth century." *The Economic History Review (Second Series)* 26 (3): 433–447.

Bogucka, Maria. 1990. "Dutch merchants' activities in Gdansk (sic) in the first half of the seventeenth century." In *Baltic Affairs. Relations between the Netherlands and North-Eastern Europe, 1500–1800: Essays*, ed. by J. P. S. Lemmink and J. S. A. M. van Koningsbrugge, 19–32. Nijmegen: INOS.

Bogucka, Maria. 2011. "Reflections on Polish-Dutch Relations in the 16th and 17th Centuries." In *Poland and the Netherlands: A Case Study of European Relations*, ed. by Duco Hellema, Ryszard Żelichowski, and Bert van der Zwan, 1–26. Dordrecht: Republic of Letters Publishing.

Bornemann, Ulrich. 1976. *Anlehnung und Abgrenzung: Untersuchungen zur Rezeption der niederländischen Literatur in der deutschen Dichtungsreform des siebzehnten Jahrhunderts*. Assen/Amsterdam: Van Gorcum.

Borowski, Andrzej. 2007. *Iter Polono-Belgo-Ollandicum. Cultural and Literary Relationships between the Commonwealth of Poland and the Netherlands in the 16th and 17th Centuries.* Kraków: Księgarnia Akademicka.

doi Boterbloem, Kees. 2008. *The Fiction and Reality of Jan Struys. A Seventeenth-Century Dutch Globetrotter*. New York: Palgrave Macmillan.

Bömelburg, Hans-Jürgen. 2005. "Adelige Mobilität und Grand Tour im polnischen und litauischen Adel (1500–1700)." In *Grand Tour. Adeliges Reisen und Europäische Kultur vom 14. bis zum 18. Jahrhundert*, ed. by Rainder Babel and Werner Paravicini, 309–326. Ostfildern: Jan Thorbecke Verlag.

doi Broos, Ben. 2015. "Een vergeten leerling van Rembrandt: Jan Jansz. de Stomme." *Oud Holland* 128 (2–3): 125–138.

doi Broos, B. P. J. 1974. "Rembrandt's Portrait of a Pole and His Horse." *Simiolus: Netherlands Quarterly for the History of Art* 7 (4): 192–218.

doi Burke, Peter. 2004. *Languages and Communities in Early Modern Europe*. Cambridge: Cambridge University Press.

Cieślak, Emund, and Czesław Biernat. 1995. *History of Gdańsk*, trans. by Bożenna Blaim and Georgde M. Hyde. Gdańsk: Fundacja Biblioteki Gdańskiej.

Dąbrowska, Anna. 2012. "Kto, gdzie, kiedy i dlaczego uczył (się) dawniej języka polskiego jako obcego?" In *Oblicza polszczyzny*, ed. by Andrzej Markowski and Radosław Pawelec, 191–210. Warszawa: Narodowe Centrum Kultury.

doi Dąbrowska, Anna. 2019. "Teaching Polish as a Foreign Language within the History of the Polish Language." *Acta Universitatis Lodziensis. Kształcenie Polonistyczne Cudzoziemców* 26: 27–48.

Dzienis, Helena. 2016. "Gerhard Cimmermann i jego księgozbiór ofiarowany bibliotece Rady Miasta Gdańska." *Libri Gedanenses, Rocznik Biblioteki Gdańskiej* 33: 5–27.

van Els, Theo J.M., and Mathieu F. Knops. 1988. "The History of the Teaching of Foreign Languages in the Low Countries." *Historiographica Linguistica. International Journal for the History of the Language Sciences* 15 (1–2): 289–316.

Fleischer, Alette. 2019. "Breyne's Botany: (Re-)locating Nature and Knowledge in Danzig (circa 1660–1730)." In *Locations of Knowledge in Dutch Contexts*, ed. by Fokko Jan Dijksterhuis, Andreas Weber, and Huib Zuidervaart, 107–135. Leiden/Boston: Brill.

Frijhoff, Willem. 2017. "Multilingualism in the Dutch Golden Age. An Exploration." In *Multilingualism, Nationhood, and Cultural Identity*, ed. by Willem Frijhoff, Marie-Christine Kok Escalle, and Karène Sanchez-Summerer, 95–168. Amsterdam: Amsterdam University Press.

Fuks, L. 1957. "Simon de Pool – faktor króla Jana Sobieskiego w Holandii." *Biuletyn Żydowskiego Instytutu Historycznego* 21: 3–12.

Gerlo, Aloïs. 1996. "De reis van Marnix van Sint-Aldegonde naar Krakau in 1575. Status quaestionis." *Academiae Analecta. Mededelingen van de Koninklijke Academie voor Wetenschappen, Letteren en Schone Kunsten van België, Klasse der Letteren* 58 (1): 1–19.

van Groesen, Michiel. 2016. "Reading Newspapers in the Dutch Golden Age." *Media History* 22 (3–4): 334–352.

Grzybkowska, Teresa. 1995. "Niderlandyzm w sztuce gdańskiej." In *Niderlandyzm w sztuce polskiej*, ed. by Teresa Hrankowska, 93–111. Warszawa: Wydawnictwo Naukowe PWN.

Gömöri, George. 1987. "Some Polish Inscriptions in Alba Amicorum of the 16th – 18th Century." In *Sprach- und Kulturkontakte im Polnischen. Gesammelte Aufsätze für A. de Vincenz zum 65. Geburtstag*, ed. by Gerd Hentschel, Gustav Ineichen, and Alek Pohl, 463–472. München: Verlag Otto Sagner.

van de Haar, Alisa. 2019. *The Golden Mean of Languages. Forging Dutch and French in the Early Modern Low Countries (1540–1620)*. Leiden/Boston: Brill.

Handbuch des personalen Gelegenheitsschrifttums in europäischen Bibliotheken und Archiven. Vols. 23–26: Danzig. 2009. Ed. by Stefan Anders, Sabine Beckmann, and Klaus Garber. Hildesheim/Zürich/New York: Olms-Weidmann.

Hart, S. 1976. *Geschrift en Getal. Een keuze uit de demografisch-, economisch- en sociaal-historische studiën op grond van Amsterdamse en Zaanse archivalia*, 1600–1800. Dordrecht: Historische Vereniging Holland.

Hulsenboom, Paul. 2023a. "Books and Prints as Instruments of Early Modern Travel. How Polish visitors in the Dutch Republic used travel guides and other printed media in the seventeenth century." *Jaarboek voor Nederlandse Boekgeschiedenis/Yearbook for Dutch Book History* 30 (1): 126–157.

Hulsenboom, Paul. 2023b. "Early Modern Community Formation Across Northern Europe. How and why a poet in Poland engaged with the Delft Thunderclap of 1654." In *Dealing with Disasters from Early Modern to Modern Times. Cultural Responses to Catastrophes*, ed. by Hanneke van Asperen and Lotte Jensen, 61–81. Amsterdam: Amsterdam University Press.

Hulsenboom, Paul. 2023c. *Heretical Heroes and Savage Saviours. The Dutch and Poles in each other's imaginations during the long seventeenth century*. Alblasserdam: Ridderprint (PhD Thesis).

Hulsenboom, Paul. 2025. "Bloodstained Manuscripts. The Murder of the De Witt Brothers in Poland." In *The Dutch Disaster Year (1672) in European and Global Context. Foreign Impact, Representations and Aftermath*, ed. by Tony Claydon, Charles-Édouard Levillain, and Arthur der Weduwen (forthcoming). Amsterdam: Amsterdam University Press.

Hulsenboom, Paul, and Alan Moss. 2022. "Tracing the Sites of Learned Men. Places and Objects of Knowledge on the Dutch and Polish Grand Tour." In *Memory and Identity in the Learned World. Community Formation in the Early Modern World of Learning and Science*, ed. by Koen Scholten, Dirk van Miert, and Karl A. E. Enenkel, 257–306. Leiden/Boston: Brill.

Hulshof, Hans, Erik Kwakernaak, and Frans Wilhelm. 2015. *Geschiedenis van het talenonderwijs in Nederland. Onderwijs in de moderne talen van 1500 tot heden.* Groningen: Uitgeverij Passage.

Jefimow, Regina. 1970. *Z dziejów języka polskiego w Gdańsku. Stan wiedzy o polszczyźnie w XVII wieku.* Gdańsk: Wydawnictwo Morskie.

Kalmar, Ivan. 2022. *White But Not Quite. Central Europe's Illiberal Revolt.* Bristol: Bristol University Press.

Kaplan, Yosef. 2000. *An Alternative Path to Modernity. The Sephardi Diaspora in Western Europe.* Leiden/Boston/Köln: Brill.

Kiedroń, Stefan. 1992. "Poolse studenten in Leiden in de 16de en de 17de eeuw." *Acta Universitatis Wratislaviensis* 1356: Studia Neerlandica et Germanica: 189–204.

Kiedroń, Stefan. 2007. *Chrisian Hofman von Hofmanswaldau und seine 'niederländische Welt'.* Wrocław/Dresden: Oficyna Wydawnicza ATUT/Neisse Verlag.

Kiedroń, Stefan. 2013. "Jan Makowski (1588–1644). Polish Theologian in Frisian Franeker." *Odrodzenie i Reformacja w Polsce. Special Issue* 57: 205–224.

Klassen, Peter J. 2016. *Menonici w Polsce i Prusach w XVI-XIX w.*, trans. by Edyta Pawlikowska. Toruń: Muzeum Etnograficzne im. Marii Znamierowskiej-Prüfferowej w Toruniu.

Koelling, Hermann. 1892. *Geschichte der Stadt Pitschen.* Breslau: Grass, Barth und Comp.

Kowalska-Szubert, Agata. 2013. *Polder, lakmus en kordzik. Nederlandse lexicale ontleningen in het hedendaagse Pools.* Wrocław: Wydawnictwo Uniwersytetu Wrocławskiego.

Krauze-Karpińska, Joanna. 2009. *"Wirydarz poetycki" Jakuba Teodora Trembeckiego. Studium filologiczne.* Warszawa: Stowarzyszenie Pro Cultura Litteraria/Instytut Badań Literackich Polskiej Akademii Nauk – Wydawnictwo.

Kreslins, Janis. 2003. "Linguistic Landscapes in the Baltic." *Scandinavian Journal of History* 28 (3–4): 165–174.

Kuyper Jr., A. 1899. *Johannes Maccovius.* Leiden: D. Donner.

Lambour, R. C. 1999. "De familie en vrienden van Daniel Zwicker (1612–1678) in Amsterdam." *Doopsgezinde Bijdragen (nieuwe reeks)* 25: 113–166.

Laskowska, Anna Maria, and Jan Waszink. 2025. "Elusive toleration. The relations between Socinians and Remonstrants in the seventeenth century." *History of European Ideas* 51(4): 689–710.

van Leeuwen, J. 1851. *Het geslacht Arnoldi.* (n.p.)

Loonen, P. L. M. 1990. *For to Learne to Buye and Sell. Learning English in the Low Dutch Area between 1500 and 1800: A Critical Survey.* Groningen: Universiteitsbibliotheek (PhD Thesis).

doi *Networks, Poetics and Multilingual Society in the Early Modern Baltic Sea Region*. 2025. Ed. by Kati Kallio, Tuomas M. S. Lehtonen, Anu Lahtinen, and Ilkka Leskelä. Leiden/Boston: Brill.

doi Noak, Bettina. 2014. "Glossaries and Knowledge-Transfer: Andreas Wissowatius and Abraham Rogerius." In *Dynamics of Neo-Latin and the Vernacular. Language and Poetics, Translation and Transfer*, ed. by Tom Deneire, 251–265. Leiden/Boston: Brill.

Noordam, N. F. 1940. *De Republiek en de Noordse Oorlog* 1655–1660. Assen: Van Gorcum & Comp. N.V.

Noordegraaf, Jan. 2007. "Lambert ten Kate schrijft naar Dantsig. Brieven aan Johann Philipp Breyne." *De Achttiende Eeuw* 39: 96–101.

Nowak-Dłużewski, Juliusz. 1962. *Poemat satyrowy w literaturze polskiej w. XVI-XVII. Z dziejów inicjatywy artystycznej Jana Kochanowskiego*. Warszawa: Wydawnictwo Uniwersytetu Warszawskiego.

Nowak-Dłużewski, Juliusz. 1972. *Okolicznościowa poezja polityczna w Polsce. Dwaj młodsi Wazowie*. Warszawa: Instytut Wydawniczy Pax.

van Oostendorp, Marc, and Nicoline van der Sijs. 2019. '*Een mooie mengelmoes*.' *Meertaligheid in de Gouden Eeuw*. Amsterdam: Amsterdam University Press.

Pelc, Janusz. 1963. "Potomstwo "Satyra" Jana Kochanowskiego w poezji polskiej od XVI do połowy XVIII wieku." *Pamiętnik Literacki* 54 (4): 267–311.

Pelc, Janusz. 1965. *Jan Kochanowski w tradycjach literatury polskiej (od XVI do połowy XVIII w.)*. Warszawa: Państwowy Instytut Wydawniczy.

doi Pelus-Kaplan, Marie-Louise. 2007. "Les marchands étrangers à Dantzig dans la première moitié du XVIIe siècle." In *Commerce, voyage et expérience religieuse. XVIe-XVIIIe siècles*, ed. by Albrecht Burkardt, Gilles Bertrand, and Yves Krumenacker, 359–369. Rennes: Presses universitaires de Rennes.

doi Pettegree, Andrew. 2021. "The Dutch Baltic. The Dutch Book Trade and the Building of Libraries in the Baltic and Central Europe during the Dutch Golden Age." In *Book Trade Catalogues in Early Modern Europe*, ed. by Arthur der Weduwen, Andrew Pettegree, and Graeme Kemp, 286–316. Leiden/Boston: Brill.

Plett, Harvey. 1991. *Georg Hansen and the Danzig Flemish Mennonite Church: A Study in Continuity*. Winnipeg (PhD Thesis).

doi Polkowski, Marcin. 2015. "Rzeczpospolita a Niderlandy. Relacje literackie i kulturowe w dobie staropolskiej." In *Wśród krajów północy. Kultura Pierwszej Rzeczypospolitej wobec narodów germańskich, słowiańskich i naddunajskich: mapa spotkań, przestrzenie dialogu* ed. by Mirosława Hanusiewicz-Lavallee, 190–247. Warszawa: Wydawnictwa Uniwersytetu Warszawskiego.

Postma, Ferenc. 2014. *Studenci z Rzeczypospolitej we fryzyjskim uniwersytecie we Franeker (Spis nazwisk i bibliografia)*, trans. by Wojciech Rynduch-Walecki. Kraków: Collegium Columbinum.

doi Quatrini, Francesco. 2021. "Religious Tolerance and Freedom of Prophesying. Social and Intellectual Interrelations between the Polish Brethren and the Collegiants in Seventeenth-Century Amsterdam." *Church History and Religious Culture* 101 (2–3): 286–305.

Roding, Juliette. 1995. "Dutch architects and engineers in Danzig and the southern Baltic in the 16th and 17th centuries." In *The Baltic. Languages and Cultures in Interaction: Proceedings NOMES-Conference, 19–20 May, 1994*, ed. by J. J. van Baak, L. Honti, A. H. Huussen, and A. M. van der Hoeven, 223–235. Groningen: NOMES.

Schenkeveld-Van der Dussen, Maria A., and Dorthe Schipperheijn. 2003. "Johann Peter Titz als Übersetzungstheoretiker und Cats-Übersetzer." In *Niederländische Lyrik und ihre deutsche Rezeption in der Frühen Neuzeit*, ed. by Lothar Jordan, 193–205. Wiesbaden: Harrassowitz.

Schoenaers, Dirk, Theo Hermans, Inger Leemans, Cees Koster, and Ton Naaijkens. 2021. *Vertalen in de Nederlanden. Een cultuurgeschiedenis*. Amsterdam: Boom.

doi Siess-Krzyszkowski, Stanisław. 2024. "Polskie elementarze (podręczniki do nauki czytania) XVI i XVII w." *Z Badań nad Książką i Księgozbiorami Historycznymi* 18 (2): 215–235.

van der Sijs, Nicoline. 2010. *Nederlandse woorden wereldwijd*. Den Haag: Sdu Uitgevers.

doi Swiggers, Pierre. 2017. "Capitalizing Multilingual Competence. Language Learning and Teaching in the Early Modern Period." In *Multilingualism, Nationhood, and Cultural Identity*, ed. by Willem Frijhoff, Marie-Christine Kok Escalle, and Karène Sanchez-Summerer, 49–75. Amsterdam: Amsterdam University Press.

Szałygin, Jerzy. 2004. *Katalog zabytków osadnictwa holenderskiego na Mazowszu*. Warszawa: Wydawnictwo DiG.

Szałygin, Jerzy. 2008. *Katalog zabytków osadnictwa holenderskiego na ziemi łęczyckiej*. Warszawa: Wydawnictwo DiG.

Szczucki, Lech. 1975. "Z dziejów emigracji socyniańskiej w Holandii." *Odrodzenie i Reformacja w Polsce* 20: 201–209.

Szmytka, Rafał. 2016. "Osadnictwo Olęderskie na Żuławach w ujęciu historii środowiskowej. Perspektywy badawcze." *Historyka. Studia Metodologiczne* 46: 63–78.

Thijssen, Lucia. 2003. *Polska i Niderlandy: 1000 lat kontaktów*, trans. by Jerzy Koch, Bożena Czernecka, Alicja Dehue-Oczko, Anita Frank, Marzanna Jóźwiak-Kotynia, Barbara Kalla, and Jadwiga Tyszkiewicz-Pol. Zutphen: Walburg Pers.

van Tielhof, Milja. 2002. *The 'Mother of all Trades'. The Baltic Grain Trade in Amsterdam from the Late 16th to the Early 19th Century*. Leiden/Boston/Köln: Brill.

Tilman van Gameren 1632–1706. Een Nederlandse architect aan het hof in Polen. 2002. Ed. by Eymert-Jan Goossens and Koen Ottenheym. Amsterdam: Stichting Koninklijk Paleis Amsterdam.

Urbański, Edmund S. 1988. "The Military Adventures of Krzysztof Arciszewski in Seventeenth Century Brazil and Europe." *Polish American Studies* 45 (1): 63–73.

doi Valkema Blouw, Paul. 2013. "Mennonitica and Bibliographical Research." In *Dutch Typography in the Sixteenth Century. The Collected Works of Paul Valkema Blouw*, ed. by Ton Croiset van Uchelen and Paul Dijstelberge, 83–98. Leiden/Boston; Brill.

Visser, Sibbe Jan. 2011. *Samuel Naeranus (1582–1641) en Johannes Naeranus (1608–1679). Twee remonstrantse theologen op de bres voor godsdienstige verdraagzaamheid*. Hilversum: Verloren.

van der Wal, M. J. 1995. *De moedertaal centraal. Standaardisatie-aspecten in de Nederlanden omstreeks* 1650. Den Haag: Sdu Uitgevers.

doi Walczak, Bogdan, and Agnieszka Mielczarek. 2017. "Prolegomena historyczne – wielojęzyczność w Rzeczypospolitej Obojga Narodów." *Białostockie Archiwum Językowe* 17: 255–268.

Wallet, Bart. 2024. "Rembrandt's Other Jews: The Amsterdam Ashkenazim in the Seventeenth Century." In *Rembrandt Seen Through Jewish Eyes: The Artist's Meaning to Jews from His Time to Ours*, ed. by Mirjam Knotter and Gary Schwartz, 71–88. Amsterdam: Amsterdam University Press.

Warnsinck, J. C. M. 1937. *Christoffel Artichewsky. Poolsch krijgsoverste in dienst van de West-Indische Compagnie in Brazilië 1630–1639. Een proeve tot eerherstel.* 's-Gravenhage: Martinus Nijhoff.

doi der Weduwen, Arthur. 2022. "Exile, Expansion and Commerce: Dutch Printing outside the Low Countries in the Seventeenth and Eighteenth Centuries." In *The Book World in Early Modern Europe. Essays in Honour of Andrew Pettegree*. Vol. 2, ed. by Arthur der Weduwen and Malcolm Walsby, 211–240. Leiden/Boston: Brill.

doi Wicherkiewicz, Tomasz. 2003. *The Making of a Language. The Case of the Idiom of Wilamowice, Southern Poland.* Berlin/New York: Mouton de Gruyter.

Wolff, Larry. 1994. *Inventing Eastern Europe. The Map of Civilization on the Mind of the Enlightenment.* Stanford: Stanford University Press.

Zabriskie, George Olin. 1963. *The Zabriskie Family. A Three Hunded and one Year History of the descendants of Albrecht Zaborowskij (ca 1638–1711) of Bergen County, New Jersey.* Vol. 1. Salt Lake City: Publishers Press.

Żołądź-Strzelczyk, Dorota. 2020. *O przedsięwzięciu peregrynacyjej. Edukacyjne wojaże szlachty z Rzeczypospolitej w świetle instrukcji podróżnych.* Warszawa: Muzeum Pałacu Króla Jana III w Wilanowie.

Websites

Centraal Bureau voor de Statistiek: www.cbs.nl.

Dawne ortografie, gramatyki i podręczniki języka polskiego. Internetowe kompendium edukacyjne: www.gramatyki.uw.edu.pl.

Universal Short Title Catalogue: www.ustc.ac.uk.

CHAPTER 4

Comparison of Dutch loanwords in Polish and Czech

Agata Kowalska-Szubert & Kateřina Křížová
University of Wrocław | Palacký University, Olomouc

It is well known that Dutch loanwords can be found in various languages. The aim of this contribution is to give a brief characterization of Dutch loanwords in Polish and Czech and to compare their usage in these two West Slavic languages. According to the Dutch database *Uitleenwoordenbank* (Van der Sijs 2015), there are more than 380 Dutch loanwords in Polish and more than one hundred Dutch loanwords in Czech. Why do we find more of these words in Polish than in Czech? How did these words get from Dutch into these two languages? What sort of words are these actually and how have they been adapted? What role does language contact play here? It has been noted that the majority of Dutch loanwords in both Polish and Czech were borrowed through other languages. The Polish language, however, contains many more words related to shipbuilding and seafaring.

Keywords: borrowings, language contact, Czech, Polish, Dutch loanwords

Introduction

Although the area where Slavic languages are the official languages is not in close geographical proximity to the Dutch-language area, Dutch loanwords have found their way into Slavic languages. In this chapter, we focus on a comparison of Dutch loanwords in two West Slavic languages – Polish and Czech. These languages, which border each other, are close not only genetically but also typologically. However, the two languages differ significantly in the number of Dutch loanwords documented so far. According to the Dutch database *Uitleenwoordenbank* (Van der Sijs 2015), there are more than 380 Dutch loanwords in Polish and more than 100 Dutch loanwords in Czech. Why is this so? Are there any other differences regarding Dutch loanwords in these two Slavic languages? Which words of Dutch origin occur in both Polish and Czech?

https://doi.org/10.1075/impact.55.04kow

Dutch loanwords in Polish have already been made the subject of two monographs (Kowalska-Szubert 2013, Kowalska-Szubert 2021), but there are only a few studies on words of Dutch origin in Czech (Vandeputte & Krijtová 1993: 47–48, Křížová 2018). For this reason, the focus in some parts of our description is on Czech, which has been described less exhaustively in this respect. We aimed to identify the differences and similarities between Dutch loanwords in Polish and Czech. We paid attention to how words from Dutch were adopted into Polish and Czech, to their adaptations to the language systems of these two West Slavic languages as well as to the broader historical-cultural context.

1. Historical and cultural context

1.1 Contacts between the Low Countries and Poland

Over a thousand years of contact between the Low Countries and Poland (Thijssen 2003) are substantiated. What started with the export of grain and fish (including herring) from the Baltic Sea to Western Europe had various facets in subsequent times. The location of Polish territories played an important role in this. Unlike the Czech Republic, Poland has access to a sea – the Baltic Sea – which allowed participation in international maritime trade. There are a few cities in northern Poland, including Szczecin (whose German name is Stettin), Kołobrzeg (Kolberg) and Gdańsk (Danzig) that played a role as ports in the Hanseatic League. Cities with ports are visited by all kinds of people, both residents and sailors, who speak different languages. Moreover, the Dutch engaged in trade by sea, and put in at the Polish ports. The Polish territories are centrally located in Europe, so many overland trade routes ran through them. Thanks to international trade, Polish life became richer with many (hitherto) unknown goods, and this also had an impact on the language: the new products were mostly taken over with their native names. In this way, many names have entered Polish *via* Dutch, which can be illustrated, for example, by the word *kakadu* "cockatoo".

The Renaissance especially saw many new products (and words) from the Low Countries. There were two reasons for this. On the one hand, Poland had then become a haven for Protestants who had to flee their own country for religious reasons. With its religious diversity and openness to foreigners, they were then welcome in Poland. Water engineers were welcome and were invited to what are now Polish but were then Prussian territories as early as the 13th century and enjoyed all kinds of privileges. Moreover, this trend was reinforced in the 16th century: one of the most famous master builders who visited and provided Gdańsk and the surrounding areas with his work in the years 1577 and 1591 was

Simon Stevin. He was dispatched on behalf of the mayor of Delft, Jan de Groot (father of Hugo de Groot, co-founder of the Dutch legal system), to investigate the possibilities of deepening the harbour in Gdańsk (Thijssen 2003: 78).

Another reason was linked to the fact that the inhabitants of the Low Countries knew how to fight water levels like no other nation. The delta of the Vistula River was sometimes also called “Little Holland” (Mączak 1976) because of its location below sea level. What is more, this land was given this name because it was precisely Dutchmen (drain workers and engineers) who secured this area. The mounds that can still be found here and there date back to these times (16th century or earlier). The names of towns and villages called “Olendry”/“Olędry”/“Holendry”/ “Holędry” (or having one of these words in their names) still bear witness to the presence of the Dutch in Poland (Targowski 2016).

Poland lost its independence at the end of the 18th century. Its territories were divided between Prussia, Russia and Austria. Thus, in the areas inhabited by Polish speakers, German and Russian were the official languages respectively. This makes it difficult to point to direct contacts between Polish and Dutch. However, some borrowings undoubtedly originate from this period, mainly those that entered the Polish language via German or Russian.

In the history of direct contact, the Second World War is also important. Polish soldiers liberated parts of the Netherlands and settled in Dutch areas after the war and started families there. However, for political reasons, their contact with their homeland and their families in Poland was limited, so there is no evidence that the soldiers are the ones to whom we owe the borrowings of the mid-20th century.

Furthermore, since the opening of the European labour market, many Poles have recently left Poland and gone to work in the Netherlands while still considering Poland their country. Many of them stay in close contact with their relatives residing in Poland. Thus, they sometimes bring Dutch words with them. The era of the Internet also favours direct contact between people of different languages. Polish has become richer in the past decade with at least three substantiated new Dutch borrowings; we will return to this issue in the further parts of our contribution.

1.2 Contacts between the Low Countries and the Czech Republic

The Czech Republic lies in the heart of Europe; it has no access to the sea and has been in direct contact with the German-speaking world for centuries. Nevertheless, there are some interesting moments in the history of contact between the Low Countries and the Czech lands. According to historian H. Renner (2002), on whose study we rely in this chapter, Czech-Dutch relations also have a tradition of almost a thousand years.

Dutch and Flemish merchants were already working in the Czech lands in the Middle Ages, but direct business contacts had yet to be established. Cultural contacts were also quite sporadic at that time. Only after the founding of the University of Prague in 1348 did things change. During the humanist period, the works of Erasmus of Rotterdam, who corresponded with important Czech scholars, were very popular in Bohemia. A big boom in cultural relations occurred when the Holy Roman Emperor and King of Bohemia, Rudolf II (1552–1612), moved his imperial court from Vienna to Prague. Prague then became an important European centre; it gained the status of home not only to merchants but also to important artists and scholars from the Low Countries, such as the painter Bartholomeus Spranger, the engraver Aegidius Sadeler and the sculptor Adriaen de Vries. Thanks to its relative religious tolerance at this time, some Dutch Protestants who had fled the Netherlands at the beginning of the Eighty Years' War found refuge in Bohemia. "However, this emigration was very modest in scale, especially compared to flows of Czech exiles towards the Netherlands in the 17th, 18th and 20th centuries." (Renner 2002: 41)[1]

In 1618, a revolt against the Habsburgs broke out in Bohemia, and the Thirty Years' War began. At this time the Czech rebels received great financial and military support from the Protestant Netherlands. After the Battle of White Mountain (1620), the rebellion was suppressed. In the following years, at least a hundred thousand Protestants left Czech lands, many of whom found a new home in the Netherlands.[2] On the other hand, a large number of mercenaries from the Low Countries stayed in the Czech lands during the Thirty Years' War. The Czech word *flamender*, which refers to a person who often drinks alcohol and stays up late, is said to be a reminder of their way of life (Pokorný 1976: 139, Stěpanovová 1989).

After the end of the First World War the Czechoslovak Republic was established in 1918. In the period between the two world wars, official political relations between the Netherlands and the newly-formed Czechoslovakia were not very good, as noted by, for instance, H. Renner (2002: 48); however, economic contacts flourished. The Czech shoe company Bata successfully expanded into the Netherlands, while Dutch companies such as Philips and Unilever established their branches in Czechoslovakia. The popularity of the Netherlands in Czech areas was certainly also boosted by the travelogue *Obrázky z Holandska* [*Pictures from*

1. "Deze emigratie was echter zeer bescheiden van omvang, zeker vergeleken met stromen van Tsjechische bannelingen richting Nederland in de 17e, 18e en 20e eeuw."

2. Probably the most famous Czech exile of all time is the philosopher, pedagogue and theologian John Amos Comenius, who spent the last 14 years of his life in Amsterdam.

Holland, 1931], authored by renowned Czech writer Karel Čapek.[3] Interestingly, the title of the chapter, *Grachty a kanaaly* 'City Canals and Canals', contains two Dutch words with Czech plural endings.

The Second World War led to a reduction in mutual contacts. However, before the Second World War, the first wave of Czechoslovak emigrants arrived in the Netherlands. Another larger wave followed after the communist revolution in then Czechoslovakia in 1948. After this year, the paths of the Dutch and Czechs diverged completely as Czechoslovakia became part of communist Eastern Europe. The third large wave of Czechoslovak emigrants came to the Netherlands after the reform movement called "Prague Spring" ended in 1968 due to the military invasion by the Soviet Union and other Warsaw Pact countries. Contacts between Czechoslovakia and the Netherlands were then very limited until the Velvet Revolution in 1989. After 1989, Czech-Dutch relations flourished at all levels; cultural and economic cooperation developed, and a number of city ties between Dutch and Czech cities were established. This development continued after 1993 when the Czech Republic and Slovakia separated. It was also a period when people were free to travel abroad again, including to the Netherlands and Belgium, to learn, to obtain education, to visit family and friends, or to work. In the opposite direction, Dutch tourists and investors started flowing into the Czech Republic. Later, Dutch people also came to settle in the Czech Republic, and as a result, several so-called *nizozemské vesničky* ('Dutch villages')[4] were built, especially in southern and eastern Bohemia.[5]

2. Corpus of Dutch loan words

Our analysis was based mainly on the lists of Dutch loanwords in the *Uitleenwoordenbank* (Van der Sijs 2015). By comparing them, we were able to add some more Dutch loanwords to both the Czech and Polish lists. Examples of such words are given in Table 1 for Czech and in Table 2 for Polish.

---

3. Karel Čapek is also the author of the 1920 science-fiction play *R.U.R*, in which the word *robot* first appeared. This word was suggested to him by his brother Josef Čapek as a term for "a fictional humanoid". Later, it was adopted from Czech into a number of other languages, including Dutch.

4. "The term is a vernacular name for standardised recreational houses owned by the Dutch in Czech tourist areas. It is used in public discourse, predominantly by internet users, to assert strong criticism with this new form of tourism." (Horáková 2014: 11)

5. Further links between the Czech Republic and the Netherlands are also described in the publication *Tsjecholand* (Krijt & Goedhart 2008) and the publication *Samen op de 'laan van Europa'* (Goedhart *et al.* 2018).

Table 1. Dutch loanwords in Czech

Czech	Dutch	English
afrikánština/afrikaans	Afrikaans	Afrikaans
arminián	arminiaan	Arminian
bakelit	bakeliet	bakelite
boskoopské	(Boskoop)	"a type of apple tree from Boskoop in the Netherlands"
Búr(ové)	Boer(en)	Boer(s)
coleslaw	koolsla	coleslaw
fretka[a]	fret	ferret
garnát	garnaal	shrimp
harpuna	harpoen	harpoon
holandka	Holland(se)	"old Dutch breed of hens" or "a type of fired roof tile"
kadadu	kaketoe	cockatoo
kambuza	kombuis, kabuis	caboose ("kitchen on the boat")
klinker	klinker	clinker brick
lavírovat	laveren	to tack
plakát	plakkaat	poster
pumpa	pomp	pump
snoezelen	snoezelen	snoezelen ("controlled multisensory environment")
šlajsna (in slang)	sluis	sluice

a. According to Czech etymological and explanatory dictionaries (Holub & Lyer 1978: 163, Machek 1968: 146, Rejzek 2015: 196, ASCS 1998, SSJČ 1960-1971), the word *fretka* comes from German (*Frettchen*). The term did enter German from French *via* Dutch (*fret*) (Duden, DWDS).

We also took into account the words described in A. Kowalska-Szubert's publication (2021) or those that are clearly related to Dutch or Flemish reality, such as *kapsalon.* This word, originating in 2003 and meaning "snack of fries with meat, sauce, lettuce and melted cheese",[6] is starting to be used both in Polish and Czech. Our corpus was further supplemented with Dutch words that, according to J. Rakšányová (2008: 77–86), occur in Slovak and that are also of Dutch origin in

6. The original meaning of this Dutch word is "hairdressing salon". The fast food consisting of a lot of ingredients was first ordered by hairdresser Nathaniël Gomes, owner of hairdressing salon Tati in Rotterdam – see lemma *kapsalon* in the online dictionary *Woordenboek van Nieuwe Woorden* (WNW).

Table 2. Completed words for Polish

Polish	Dutch	English
bollandysta	bollandist	Bollandist
gracht	gracht	"a city-canal"
hotentot	Hottentot	Hotentot ("Khoekhoe")
olstro	holster	holster
jankes	Jan-Kees[a]	Yankee
sylwin	sylvien	sylvine; named after the Dutch physician and chemist François Sylvius (1614–1672)
terp	terp	terp
wrak	wrak	wreck

a. Van der Sijs (2010b: 49).

Czech, such as in Dutch *wafel,* in Slovak *vafle,* in Czech *vafle* (meaning 'waffle'), similar to the Polish word *wafel* (meaning 'wafer').[7]

The analysed group of Dutch loan words in Polish and Czech consisted mainly of common names (or appellative nouns), including appellativised toponyms (Cz: *afrikander, afrikán, barneveldka, brabantka, eidam, gouda, holand, holandka, holander/holender;* Pl: *arden, boskop, brukselka, fryz, gouda, mazdamer, holenderka*) and appellativised anthroponyms, often formed from the names of Dutch or Flemish persons (Cz: *bakelit, bintje, brajgl, deutzie, elzevir, jansenismus, lindan, sylvín;* Pl: *bakelit, bintje, elzewir, fokker, jansenizm, lindan, lobelia, stapelia, sylwin etc.*). Anthroponyms (*e.g.,* Cz: *Búr,* Pl: *Bur*) and names of languages (*e.g.,* Cz: *holandština, afrikánština* Pl: *holenderski, Afrikaans*) formed only a limited part of Czech and Polish corpus. Toponyms (*e.g.,* Pl: *Flandria, Holandia,* Cz: *Flandry, Holandsko*) were excluded from our study, unless other words have been derived from these toponyms or unless they have acquired a meaning in Polish or Czech that differs from the original geographic name.

In verifying the origin of the analysed words, we used mainly explanatory and etymological dictionaries of Czech (ASCS 1998, SSJČ 1960–1971, SSČ 2012, ASSČ 2017–2024, Machek 1968, Holub & Lyer 1978, and Rejzek 2001, 2015) and of Polish

7. Although Slovak and most Czech lexicons state that this word comes from German, German lexicons state that the German word *Waffel* is of Dutch origin (Duden, DWDS). The Dutch origin of the Czech word *vafle* is also mentioned in the latest Czech etymological dictionary by Rejzek (2015: 762).

(Zgółkowa 1994–2005, Bańkowski 2000, and Linde 1998, SJP, WSJP). However, when we found it necessary, we also referred to etymological and explanatory dictionaries of Dutch, German, English and Russian.[8] Nevertheless, it should be noted that the interpretations in different explanatory and etymological dictionaries of a given language often differ; likewise, the origin of certain words has not been precisely or sufficiently clarified yet.

These differences are especially true of Polish words that can have both Dutch and Low German[9] origins as well as of words that entered Polish *via* Russian or German. Polish etymologists are highly inconsistent here; sometimes, they only mention the language from which a given word was indeed adopted without dwelling on the fact that the word in question is also a derivation in the transit language (in this way, in a lot of maritime terms, Russian has been indicated as their origin). At times, they go deeper into it, mentioning the whole route the word followed to Polish. A good case in point is the word *doping*, which is indicated in many dictionaries (see, for example, Zgółkowa 1994–2005) as a borrowing from English, while Bańkowski (2000: 286) points to the Dutch origin of this word: "German, French, American-English *dope* [...]. This is a new slang word (derived) from the Anglo-American noun *dope* (since 1880) 'smear, lacquer, drug *etc.*', which is a fresh derivation from the Dutch *doop* 'sauce'."[10]

Another example is the Czech word *ančovička*, which is considered a Dutch loanword in the *Uitleenwoordenbank* database (Van der Sijs 2015). While older Czech etymological dictionaries do not mention this word at all (*cf.*, Machek 1968, Holub & Lyer 1978), the newer etymological dictionary of Czech (Rejzek 2001: 50) acknowledges a certain role of Dutch in the adoption of this word in Czech: "From German *Anchovis*, probably *via* Dutch or English, from French *anchois*, Spanish *anchoa*, probably of Basque origin."[11] According to the dictionary of foreign words ASCS (1998: 51), the word *ančovička* is of Basque origin and entered Czech *via* Spanish. The explanatory dictionary SSJČ mentions other forms of this word (*ančovka, anšovka*) as well, however it only gives its origin

8. *Etymologiebank* (Van der Sijs 2010a) for Dutch, online dictionaries *DUDEN* and *Digitale Wörterbuch der deutschen Sprache* (DWDS) for German and *Oxford English Dictionary* (OED) for English. We also used data from publications by Van der Meulen (1909, 1959) and *Wörterbuch der deutschen Lehnwörter in der polnischen Schrift- und Standardsprache* (WDLP).

9. Low German is a West Germanic language which is still spoken in northern Germany and the northeast of the Netherlands. The forms of words used in Low German closely resemble Dutch words. For more details about Low German see e.g. Stellmacher (2000).

10. "To nowe werbum żargonowe od szerzej używanego ang.-amer. sb. *dope* (od 1880) 'smar, lakier, narkotyk i in.', co świeżą pożyczką z hol. *dope* 'sos'."

11. "Z něm. *Anchovis*, a to asi niz. či angl. prostřednictvím, z fr. *anchois*, šp. *anchoa*, původu asi baskického."

as broadly from Romance languages. The interpretation of the most commonly-used form of the word *ančovička* in the accumulated online dictionary of the Czech language ASSČ is more accurate although, again, no Dutch origin is mentioned. According to the ASSČ, this word probably originated in Basque, from where it passed into the Romance languages and then through German into Czech. Consulting the DWDS, we learn that the word *Anchovis* comes from Basque and entered German *via* Dutch. Consistent with this view are the etymological explanations of the Dutch word *anchovis* in the database *Etymologiebank.nl* (see Van der Sijs 1998, De Vries 1971, Philippa *et al.* 2003–2009). Among other things, it is mentioned here that the Dutch word *anchovis* became the source for other languages, including German. Before that, however, the word had been partially changed in Dutch; the last syllable of the Spanish plural form *anchovas* was changed to *-vis*, meaning 'fish':

> *Ansjovis* hebben we overgenomen uit Spaans *anchoa*, ouder *anchova*. De oudste Nederlandse vorm, in 1518, luidde *anchiovis*. Door volksetymologie heeft het woord bij ons de uitgang *-vis* gekregen en in die vorm is het door het Duits overgenomen. [We adopted *anchovis* from Spanish *anchoa*, older *anchova*. The oldest Dutch form, in 1518, read *anchiovis*. By folk etymology, the word has gained the ending *-vis* and in that form it was adopted by German.] (Van der Sijs 1998: 25)

The form of the Dutch word *ansjovis* can still be "seen" in the Czech word *ančovička*. The German language certainly played the role of the intermediary language in this case. In Czech, the Czech diminutive suffix *-ička* was added to the spoken form of the German word *Anchovis* and fused with the word.

From the above examples, it is clear that not only direct borrowings were analysed, i.e., words taken directly from Dutch (Dutch → Pl/Cz), but also indirect borrowings, which were taken into Polish or Czech *via* another language (Dutch → A → Pl/Cz).[12] These can be words of Dutch origin (*e.g., baggeren, boei, makelaar, jacht*) as well as words that entered Dutch from other languages so that Dutch acted as one of the intermediary languages (A → Dutch → A → Pl/Cz). Furthermore, the existence of Czech and Polish words formed on the basis of a Dutch word/Dutch word compound but which do not occur in Dutch in the same meaning, such as *brukselka* ('Brussels sprout')[13] in Polish, will also be taken into account. We would now like to turn our attention to a more detailed description of the corpus of Dutch loan words in Polish and Czech.

---

12. Pl = Polish, Cz = Czech, A = other languages.

13. Named after the city of Brussels (in Polish *Bruksela*), near where the vegetable was grown. The Dutch equivalent is *spruitjes*, the Czech equivalent *růžičková kapusta* is also unrelated to the word Brussels (it is probably a calque from German *Rosenkohl)*.

3. Analysis of borrowing paths

There are two basic aspects of loanwords that can be examined. First, we can ask whether we are dealing with written or oral borrowing. This can be recognised by the form of the borrowing in the target language, especially when this borrowing is already somewhat embedded. How is the borrowed word written/pronounced? Where does the similarity lie, in the sound or in the written form? If the borrowed word is still pronounced in more or less the same way as is the case in Dutch or one of the possible intermediate languages but the spelling has been adapted to Polish/Czech spelling, we are probably dealing with an oral borrowing. If the loanword still resembles the Dutch word in terms of spelling, and its pronunciation has adapted to the Polish/Czech standard, we can assume that the word in question has been borrowed in writing. In the modern world, when we deal with the sound and the graphic image of a word in a foreign language at the same time *via* the Internet, it is no longer obvious which of the two paths has been followed, the oral or the written one.

Another question is whether a word was adopted directly from the language of origin or *via* another language. Because of the small amount of direct contact between Dutch and Czech/Polish, it can be assumed that indirect borrowings will predominate. In direct derivations, the borrowed word preserves the phonetic, graphic and/or morphological features of the source language. With indirect derivations these features are often influenced by the intermediate language. The main criterion in determining whether a borrowing is direct or indirect is an analysis of the form of the borrowed word (always assuming the same or nearly the same meaning in the source and target languages). Both its spelling and pronunciation are considered. If a borrowing is spelt/pronounced as in Dutch, there is a high probability that it is a direct borrowing. If it can be observed that a borrowing deviates from Dutch in form but resembles that of another language, it is a reason to assume that the borrowing in question comes from an intermediate language. In the following paragraphs of this chapter, based on an evaluation of data obtained from the various etymological and explanatory dictionaries mentioned in the previous chapter, we present examples of possible direct and indirect borrowings from Dutch in Polish and Czech.

3.1 Direct borrowings (Dutch → Pl/Cz)

Direct borrowings in Polish and Czech include primarily words: (1) that are identical or almost identical to Dutch words in graphical or sound terms and do not reflect the influence of another, intermediary language; and (2) for which Polish and Czech etymological dictionaries do not indicate the possibility of borrowing from another language (e.g. German, Low German, Russian, French, English).

Examples of such direct borrowings in Polish and Czech are given in Table 3.

Table 3. Direct borrowings in Polish and/or Czech

Dutch	Polish	Czech	English
afrikaan	–	afrikán	African marigold
bintje	bintje	bintje	bintje ("a potato variety")
bij de wind	bejdewind	–	by the wind
Fries	fryz	–	Friesian ("a horse breed from Friesland")
gracht	–	gracht	city-canal
halfwind	halfwind	–	half-wind
Hottentot	Hotentot	Hotentot, hotentot[a]	Hottentot
kapsalon	kapsalon	kapsalon	kapsalon ("a fast food")
keulenaar	–	keulnaar	"a long ship designed for use on the Rhine, around Cologne"
maatjesharing	matjas/matjes	matjes	pickled herring
polder	polder	polder	polder
texelaar	texel, teksel	–	texel ("a Dutch breed of sheep from the island of Texel")
terp	terp	terpa	terp
voordewind	fordewind	–	"running downwind"

a. Meaning "a person who is stupid or who speaks unintelligibly" (SSJČ), "according to older images of the Hottentots" (ASCS 1998: 298), i.e. the khoi-khoi people of Southern Africa.

It is obvious from the above examples that there are not many direct borrowings that can be found in both languages. Words in Polish are related to sailing or to the Dutch way of life, whereas others are names of animals that were most likely brought by immigrants and became popular in the Polish areas. Czech words are usually related to the Dutch way of life, shipbuilding, agriculture or the former Dutch colonies.

In some cases, however, we cannot claim definitively that the words were borrowed directly from Dutch because other languages also borrowed the same form of a given word, e.g. *kapsalon*. There is also a large group of borrowings in Polish, which are loaned from Dutch or Low German.[14] Table 4 lists examples of words that have the same or similar form and the same meaning in both Dutch and Low German, with their Polish and Czech equivalents. In such cases, we can conclude that these words are loaned from Saxon dialects, either spoken in the east of the Netherlands or in the west of Germany, and loaned because of trade contacts within the Hanseatic League.

Table 4. Words in both Dutch and Low German

Dutch	Low German	Polish	Czech	English
achterdek	achterdek	achterdek	–	quarterdeck
achterpiek	achterpiek	achterpik	–	afterpeak
achterstag	achterstag	achtersztag	–	backstay
bak	bak	bak	–	foredeck
baken	baken	bakan	–	forepeak
bakboord	bakboord	bakburta	–	port side
bakstag	bakstag	baksztag	–	running backstay
ballast	ballast	balast	- (balast)	ballast
blok	block	blok	- (blok)	block and tackle
boeireep	boeireep	bojrep	–	buoy line
bootshaak	bootshaken	bosak	–	boathook
bramsteng	bramsteng	bramstenga	–	topgallant mast
bras	brassc	bras	–	brace
dek	decke	dek	–	deck
fladder	vladder	flader	–	grain
fokkenra	fokreê	fokreja	–	jib boom
gaffel	gaffel(e)	gaf/gafel	–	gaff
gaffelval	gaffelval	gafelfał	–	gaff halyard
groot	grōt	grot	–	mainsail
grootmast	grōtmast	grotmaszt	–	mainmast
grootra	grōtree	grotreja	–	main yard

14. Low German and Saxon Dutch cannot be distinguished in the 16–18th century, so if a word is loaned in the period of the Hanseatic League, it will be loaned from the Saxon dialect spoken both in the Netherlands and North-Western Germany.

Table 4. *(continued)*

Dutch	Low German	Polish	Czech	English
handreling	handreling	handreling	–	handrail
kielwater	kielwāter	kilwater	–	wake
kieperen	keperen	kiprować	–	to steer
kluiver	klüwer	kliwer	–	jib
kluiverboom	klüwerbaum	kliwerbom	–	jib boom
kluiverval	klüwerfalle	kliwerfał	–	jib halyard
kok	kok	kok	–	cook
koebrug	kōbrugge	kubryk	–	crew quarter
lijzeil	lêseil	lizel	–	studding sail
mars	mars	mars	–	top
marszeil	marsseil	marsel	–	topsail
marsra	marsree	marsreja	–	topsail yard
negenoog	negen-ōg(e)	minóg	–	lamprey
net	net	neta	–	net
overstag	overstag	owersztag	–	tacking
piek	piek	pik	–	peak
piekval	piekfalle	pikfał	–	peak halyard
rak	rack	raks	–	rake
seizing	seising	sejzing	–	seizing
sloepbalk	slopebalk	szlupbelka	–	thwart
stagzeil	stagseil	sztaksel	–	staysail
storm	storm	sztorm	–	storm
stormfok	stormfok	sztormfok	–	storm jib
schipper	skipper	szyper	–	skipper
talreep	talrep	talrep	–	turnbuckle
topzeil	topsel	topsel	–	topsail
vaarwater	vārwāter	farwater	–	fairway
vlag	vlag(ge)	flaga	–	flag
vlaglijn	vlag + linie	flaglinka	–	flag halyard
vlagstok	vlagstok	flagsztok	–	flagstaff
vloot	vlote	flota	–	fleet
voorluik	forlûk	forluk	–	fore hatch
voorpiek	forpiek	forpik	–	forepeak
voorstag	forstag	forsztag	–	forestay

Table 4. *(continued)*

Dutch	Low German	Polish	Czech	English
want	wand	wanta	–	shroud
waterbakstag	waterbackstag	waterbaksztag	–	bakstag
waterlijn	waterlinie	waterlinia	–	waterline
waterstag	waterstag	watersztag	–	bobstay
werp	werp	werp	–	cast
wrak	wrack	wrak	- (vrak)	wreck

It is evident that this group of words is very poorly represented in Czech. Moreover, according to the Czech etymological dictionary (Rejzek 2015), the words in brackets entered Czech not directly from Dutch or Low German, but through German.

3.2 Indirect borrowings (Dutch → A → Pl/Cz)

In several cases, the mediation of another foreign language within our corpus is obvious. This means that linguists can still see the Dutch origin of a given word, but the form of the word in question differs from the original Dutch form.

The language that has contributed a lot to the transmission of Dutch words into other languages is undoubtedly German. There are two reasons for this. Firstly, German is precisely the language that has direct (border) contact with Dutch and with Polish and Czech. Secondly, Germany has had intense trade contact with Poland and the Czech Republic. In the past, some parts of Poland and the Czech Republic were also under German or Austrian control. German was then the official language in today's Polish areas for more than a century. The latter also applies to Russian, albeit in relation to a different part of present-day Poland.

These lively contacts especially between German and Polish/Czech, as well as between Russian and Polish/Czech, are reflected in the spectrum of Dutch borrowings in the two Slavic languages. The intensity and nature of these contacts justify the assumption that specific words entered Polish/Czech *via* this route. Likewise, the form functioning in Polish/Czech shows a greater morphological and/or phonetic resemblance to German/Russian than to the original Dutch form. This will be illustrated by several examples in the following paragraphs – see Table 5 and Table 6.

3.2.1 *German as an intermediary language*

The words in brackets exist in Czech or Polish, but there is no evidence that they were adopted *via* German (*e.g.*, the word *matjes* in Czech may be a direct loan word from Dutch, *cf.*, Rejzek 2015: 406). Polish, on the other hand, has the word

Table 5. Indirect borrowings via German[a]

Dutch	German	Polish	Czech	English
ansjovis	Anchovis	(anchois)	ančovička	anchovy
arminiaan, arminianen	Arminianen	arminianie	arminián	Arminian
baggermachine	Bagger	bagier	bagr	excavator, dredger
bakeliet	Bakelit	bakelit	bakelit	bakelite
barkas	Barkasse	barkas	barkasa	(longboat)
boei	Boje	boja	bóje	buoy
boeier	Bojer, Bujer	bojer	bojer	(type of yacht)
boombramzeil	Bombramsegel	bombramżagiel	–	beam canvas
bootshaak	Bootshaken	bosak	–	boathook
(de Schone van) Boskoop	Boskop/ Boskoop	bosko(o)p	Boskopské	'Belle de Boskoop apple' or 'Schone van Boskoop apple'
bramzeil	Bramsegel	bramżagiel	– (brámová plachta)	topgallant sail
doos	Dose	–	dóza	box
garnaal	Garnele, Garnat	garnela	garnát	shrimp
gulden	Gulden	gulden	gulden	guilder
hondenkooi	Hundekoje	hundekoja	–	"berth"
jansenisme	Jansenismus	jansenizm	jansenismus	Jansenism
keper	Köper	–	kepr	twill
kous	Kausch	kausza	–	thimble
klinker	Klinker	klinkier	klinker	clinker
kluis	Kluse	kluza	–	hawse
kooi	Koje	koja	kóje	"berth on board ship"
kraan	Kran	kran	–	crane
kof	Kufe	kufa	–	muzzle
laveren	lavieren	lawirować	lavírovat	to tack
lijklijn	Liekline	liklina	–	
lindaan	Lindan	lindan	lindan	lindane
lollard	Lollarde	lolard	– (lolard)	Lollard
lotterij	Lotterie	loteria	loterie	lottery

Table 5. *(continued)*

Dutch	German	Polish	Czech	English
ludolfiaans getal	Ludolfine	ludolfina	– (Ludolfovo číslo)	Ludolphian number
maat	Maat	mat	–	mate
maatjes(haring)	Maatjeshering	matiasy/ matiesy	– (matjes)	pickled herring
mennoniet	Mennonit	menonita	–	Mennonite
mops	Mops	mops	mops, mopsl, mopsík	pug
oorlogsschip	Orlogschiff	orlog	–	warship
piek	Piek	pik	–	peak
pruim	Priemchen	prymka	–	plum
pomp	Pumpe	(pompka)	pumpa	pump
spinozisme	Spinozismus	spinozyzm	–	Spinozism
spuigat	Speigatt	szpigat	–	scupper
stagzeil	Stagsegel	sztagżagiel	–	staysail
zuidwester	Südwester	zydwestka	–	southwester

a. In addition to Polish and Czech etymological dictionaries, we also used online dictionaries *Digitales Wörterbuch der deutschen Sprache* (DWDS) and *Wörterbuch der deutschen Lehnwörter in der polnischen Schrift- und Standardsprache* (WDLP).

anchois, that entered Polish *via* a different route. As can be seen from the form, it is not related to the element *-vis*, and this fact makes it clear that Dutch did not contribute to the Polish form in this case. Etymological dictionaries of Polish indicate *anchois* as a (borrowing) borrowing from French.

3.2.2 *Russian as an intermediary language*

The Czech etymological dictionaries indicate that the words *matróz* and *pinka* were adopted *via* Russian or German, while the word *kaper* was adopted only *via* German. The word *admirál* is not considered a possible loanword from Dutch in any of the available Czech sources. The word *kambuza* is mentioned only in ASCS (1998: 365) where it is considered a direct borrowing from Dutch. However, given the form of the word, we think the word was adopted into Czech *via* Russian, as it was in Polish. The Czech word *ústřice* (oyster) was apparently also adopted from Dutch (*oester*) *via* the Russian form *ústrica* (Rejzek 2015: 758). The Polish equivalent *ostryga*, however, is a direct derivation from Italian (Bańkowski 2000: 453). Another example of the Dutch loanword adopted *via* Russian is the

Table 6. Indirect borrowings via Russian[a]

Dutch	Russian	Polish	Czech
admiraal	admiral'	admirał	- (admirál)
aapzeil	apsel'	apsel	–
bak	bak	bak	–
bindsel	benzel', venzel'	bencel	–
boeireep	bujrep	bojrep	–
brander	brander	brander	–
braadspil	brašpil	braszpil	–
breefok	brifok	bryfok	–
gaffeltopzeil	gaftopsel'	gaftopsel	–
juffer	jufers	jufers	–
kabeltouw	kabel'tov	kabeltaw	–
kombuis	kambus, kambuz	kambuz	kambuza
kaper	kaper	kaper	- (kaper)
kielwater	kilvater	kilwater	–
kraan	kran	kran	–
lichter	lichter	lichtuga	–
lijzeil	lisel'	lizel	–
loods	locija	locja	–
leuver	ljuvers	luwers	–
marlijn	marlin	marlinka	–
marszeil	marsel'	marsel	–
matroos	matros	matros	- (matróz)
nagel	nagel'	nagiel	–
nachthuis	naktouz	naktuz	–
oester	ústrica	- (ostryga)	ústřice
peiling	peleng	peleng	–
pink	pinka	pinka	- (pinka)
rakkloot	raksklot	rak(s)klot	–
reis	rejs	rejs	–
roerpen	rulpen', rumpel'	rumpel	–
(het) ruim	trjum	(trym)	trum
steng	stenga	stenga	–

Table 6. *(continued)*

Dutch	Russian	Polish	Czech
stagzeil	štaksel	sztaksel	–
storm	štorm	sztorm	–
stuurman	šturman	szturman	–
trap	trap	trap	–
vanglijn	falen'	faleń	–
valreep	falrep	falrep	–
vlaggenstok	flagštok	flagsztok	–
val	fal	fał	–
vaarwater	farwater	farwater	–
werp	werp	werp	–
wimpel	vympel'	wimpel	–
zwabber	švabra	szwabra	–

a. In addition to Polish and Czech etymological dictionaries, we also used publications by Van der Meulen (1909, 1959).

obsolete Czech term *trum.*[15] Although the similarity between Russian and Czech in this case is unmistakable, the Polish form resembles the German one, namely *Trimm*. A special case is the name for a variety of tobacco grown in Russia called *machórka*. This Russian term is associated with the corruption of the name of the Dutch city of Amersfoort, from where tobacco was imported (see Van der Sijs 2010b: 179, Rejzek 2015: 394). Later, the word entered Czech and Polish from Russian (Pl *machorka*, Cz *machorka*).

3.2.3 *Borderline cases: Russian and German*

Table 7 presents cases where it cannot be determined through which language the loanword got into Polish based on the forms in the two most likely intermediary languages. In the case of Polish, it is particularly difficult to definitively determine whether a borrowing has come via German or Russian. As indicated in 3.2, German and Russian were the official languages in the Polish territories for over a century, and so both had an impact on Polish. It cannot be ruled out that borrowings were derived via both routes, albeit at the time in separate areas where Polish was also spoken.

15. The sound form of the Dutch word *ruim* (space) was adopted in Russian, including the definite article *het* – *'t ruim* (Van der Sijs 2010b: 91) and in the meaning "a cargo space in the ship's hold"; *cf.*, *ASCS* (1998: 784).

Table 7. Indirect borrowings via Russian or German

Dutch	German	Russian	Polish	Czech	English
actie	Aktie	ákcija	akcja	(akcie)	share
bakboord	Backbord	bakbórt	bakburta	–	portside
bramsteng	Bramstenge	bramstenga	bramstenga	–	topgallant mast
bocht	Bucht	buchta	buchta	–	bight
boegspriet	Bugspriet	búgšprit	bukszpryt	–	bowsprit
boord	Bord	bort	burta	–	board
dek	Deck	dek	dek	–	deck
duin	Düne	djuna	diuna	(duna)	dune
dok	Dock	dok	Dok	– (dok)	dock
vlag	Flagge	flag	flaga	–	flag
fok	Fock	fok	fok	–	jib
gaffel	Gaffel	gafel'	gaf/gafel	–	gaff
gas	Gas	gaz	gaz	–	gas
giek	Giek	gik	gik	–	gill
kabel	Kabel	kabel'	kabel	(kabel)	cable
kajuit	Kajüte	kajuta	kajuta	kajuta	cabin
kaper	Kaper	kaper	kaper	(kaper)	caper
kiel	Kiel	kil'	kil	–	keel
lak	Lack	lak	lak	–	sealing wax
lakmoes	Lackmus	lakmus	lakmus	(lakmus)	litmus
lijk	Liek	lik	lik	–	liek
makelaar	Makler	makler	makler	(makléř)	broker
makreel	Makrele	makrel'	makrela	(makrela)	mackerel
nok	Nock	nok	nok	–	nock
pardoen	Pardun, Pardune	pardún	parduna	parduna	pardun(e)
potas	Pottasche	potaš	potaż	(potaš)	potash
rabat	Rabatte	rabatka	rabata	–	rebate
reef	Reff, Reef	rif, ref	ref	–	reef
schellak	Schellack	šelak	szelak	(šelak)	shellac
schoener	Schoner	škuna	szkuner	–	schooner
stag	Stag	štag	sztag	–	stag
sluis	Schleuse	šljuz	śluza	(šlajsna)	sluice
toppenant	Toppenant	topenant	topenanta	–	topping lift
vracht	Fracht	fracht	fracht	–	freight

Czech etymological and explanatory dictionaries indicate that some of these Dutch words were adopted in Czech only *via* German (*akcie, kabel, kaper, lakmus, makléř, makrela, potaš, šelak, šlajsna*), or *via* English (*dok*), possibly *via* Germanic languages (*duna*). For the word *kajuta,* some sources mention Russian as an intermediary language (ASCS 1998:361, SSČ), while others only German (Rejzek 2015: 284). These examples illustrate different paths of Dutch loanwords to Czech than to Polish.

3.2.4 *English as an intermediary language*

Many cultures and languages, including Czech and Polish, have some words directly associated with English or American culture. However, they are Dutch in origin. Borrowed at the time because of the influence of Dutch on English, they became popular in English, and then they were adopted by other languages (and cultures). These words are spelled according to English, sometimes with only small modifications. Below in the Table 8 is an overview of such cases.

Table 8. Indirect borrowings via English

Dutch	English	Polish	Czech
baas	boss	boss	boss
brandewijn	brandy	brandy	brandy
daalder	dollar	dolar	dolar
hybrid based on doop	doping	doping	doping
jacht	yacht	jacht	jachta
Jan-Kees[a]	Yankee	jankes	yankee
jenever	gin	gin/dżin	gin
koolsla	coleslaw	colesław	coleslaw
korfbal	korfball	korfball	korfbal
trek	trekking (*trek* + suffix *-ing*)[b]	trekking	trekking

a. For detailed explanation see Van der Sijs (2009: 194–9). b. As explained in the OED dictionary.

3.2.5 *French as an intermediary language*

French used to be *the lingua franca* of Europe. In particular, this language had an impact on cultural life in many countries of Europe. Its reflection can also be found in the group of Dutch borrowings in Polish and Czech that entered these languages *via* French – see Table 9. The Dutch origin of these words has been verified against Polish/Czech dictionaries, including dictionaries of foreign words, where information on their Dutch source is also provided.

Table 9. Indirect borrowings via French

Dutch	French	Polish	Czech
berm	berme	berma	berma
hybrid based on boek [typography]	bouquinist	bukinista	bukinista
bolwerk	boulevard	bulwar	bulvár
elzevier	elzevier	elzewir	elzevir
manneken, mannekijn	mannequin	manekin	manekýn/manekýnka
plakkaat	placard	plakat	plakát
richel (regel)	rigole	–	rigol
vrijbuiter	flibustier	flibustier	flibustýr

In this group, we also find examples of originally Dutch words (*mannekijn, bolwerk*), which took on a different meaning in French (*mannequin, boulevard*)[16] and then both returned to Dutch (so-called reborrowing) and spread to other languages, including Czech and Polish (Cz: *manekýn/manekýnka, bulvár,* Pl: *manekin, bulwar*).[17]

3.3 Words borrowed through Dutch (A → Dutch → (A) → Pl/Cz)

Not all words in the corpus are Dutch in origin. There is a fairly large collection of words that had their origin elsewhere and for which Dutch acted as an intermediary language. Often this concerns words that Dutch borrowed from other continents, where the Dutch settled, or from which the Dutch imported products, especially in Asia and then loaned to other European languages. Below in the Table 10, we present examples of such borrowings described by Kowalska-Szubert (2021: 137).

Etymological dictionaries mention Dutch as one of the intermediary languages only for the Czech words *bambus, batika, kakadu, mops, orangutan, orkán.*

16. The original meaning of the Dutch word *mannekijn* is 'little male, doll'. Later, the word was used to refer to "wooden model, mannequin for showing off clothes", in French *mannequin.* Then the French word began to be used also in the meaning "someone presenting clothes at a fashion show". The meaning of the Dutch word *bolwerk* was 'bastion, fortification, bulwark', the meaning of the French word *boulevard* 'wide avenue, street'. For a detailed explanation see *Etymologiebank* (Van der Sijs 2010a).

17. Polish only has the word *manekin* in its original Dutch meaning "a figure/model in the shape of a human body". In Czech, on the other hand, the word *manekýn* is used mainly with the French meaning ("man wearing clothes during a fashion show"), with the feminine form *manekýnka.*

Table 10. Dutch as an intermediary language

Dutch	Polish	Czech	Other information
bamboe	bambus	bambus	< Malay; it may have spread through Dutch or Portuguese
batik	batik	batik, batika	< Malay; in many European languages in the same form
thee	herbata	–	a compound consisting of Latin *herba* and Chinese *ta*; probably brought to Poland under that name by Dutch merchants
kaketoe	kakadu	kakadu	< Indonesian (Malay)
kanarie(vogel)	kanarek	(kanárek)	the name comes from the Canary Islands; it entered European languages through Spanish or Dutch
mops	mops	mops	similar forms in many languages
orang-oetang	orangutan	orangutan	< Malay
orkaan	orkan	orkán	the Caribbean and one of the languages there
pompelmoes	pompela	–	a fruit growing on Java
rotan	ratan/rotang	(ratan)	country of origin: Indonesia; the name also from there

A special category encompasses the words which originate in form from another language but which Dutch has endowed with a new, previously non-existent meaning (A → Dutch_{m} → Pl/Cz). Although this category is small, its members are worth mentioning. Among the words that originate from Latin or Greek but have acquired the current meaning in the Low Countries are, *e.g.*, the Polish words *akcja* 'share' and *atlas* 'atlas' along with Czech words *akcie* and *atlas.*

3.4 Words with Dutch forms but meanings originating elsewhere

A reverse phenomenon can also be detected within the corpus. These are the words that are Dutch in form but have been given meanings in another language, e. g. Afrikaans – see Table 11. They are then borrowed, among others, in Polish and Czech.

Table 11. Words from Afrikaans

African	Dutch + meaning	Polish	Czech
Afrikaans	Afrikaans, "from Africa"	Afrikaans (language in South Africa)	afrikánština
Afrikaner	Afrikaner, "a human from South Africa"	Afrykaner	Afrikánec
apartheid	apart, "separation"	apartheid	apartheid
Boer	boer, "pitcher"	Bur	Búr
duiker	duiker, "diver"	dujker	–
kraal	kraal, "enclosed, restricted space for livestock"	kraal	kraal
rand	rand, "boundary or circumference of a surface"	rand	rand

3.5 Usage of Dutch geonyms

Quite a few terms, both in Polish and Czech, refer to Dutch/Flemish geonyms – see the examples in Table 12.

Table 12. Dutch geonyms

Polish	Czech	English
barnewelder/barnevelder	barneveldka	Barnevelder (a chicken breed from Barneveld)
boskop	Boskopské	the Belle de Boskoop (an apple variety)
–	brabantka	Brabant, a breed of chicken from Brabant
brukselka	–	Brussels sprout
edamski	eidam	Edam, Edam cheese
gouda	gouda	Gouda cheese
butelka lejdejska	Leidenská láhev	Leids bottle[a]
mazdamer	maasdam	Maasdam cheese

a. A Leyden jar, an early type of battery, invented in the mid-18th century by Pieter van Musschenbroek.

In this respect, the use of the words *holender* and *holenderka* is very interesting. In Polish, the term *holender* has the following meanings according the dictionary WSJP: (1) an object acquired in the Netherlands or associated with the Netherlands, (2) an arc circled on the ice by a skater during figure skating on ice, (3) curse. In the case of the third definition, it is certainly a corruption of the curse word *cholera*, and hence this meaning is etymologically unrelated to Dutch.

The term *holenderka* denotes the following (WSJP): (1) a cow with characteristic colours, in black and white patches, (2) a bicycle. An additional meaning not included in the WSJP but listed in Wikipedia refers to a roof tile.[18]

In Czech, the term *holandr/holendr* is also used in various meanings (*cf.*, ASCS, SSJČ): (1) a machine for grinding raw materials (rags) in paper production, (2) a machine for hulling barley in the production of groats, (3) a special type of fitting (disassembled threaded tube coupling with sliding nut).

Moreover, in Czech, there is the fixed phrase *pít jako holendr/holandr* (lit. 'to drink like a Hollander'), which means "to drink a lot of alcohol". According to M. Těšitelová (1963), this expression refers to the large consumption of water in machines for grinding groats, while the authors of the Czech idiomatic dictionary (Čermák *et al.* 1983: 115) relate this phrase to the consumption of water in machines for paper production. Other linguists share the view that the word *holendr/holandr* refers rather to the Dutch (*e.g.*, Procházka 1934, Holub & Lyer 1978: 181, Mokijenko 1973, Stěpanovová 1989). However, they disagree in further interpretation. Some see it as related to Bohemia-based Dutch carpenters' habit of drinking (Procházka 1934), while others view it as connected to the life of Dutch mercenaries in Bohemia during the Thirty Years' War (Stěpanovová 1989).

The term *holandka* can be found in Czech as the phrase meaning "a type of fired roof tile" or in the form *holanďanka/holandka* with the meaning "breed of hens".[19] The word *holand* is mentioned only in the dictionary ASCS (1998: 294) and has the following meaning: "very fine handmade paper (originally made in Holland)".

4. Adaptation of the Dutch loanwords

The assimilation of foreign words to the target language requires various adaptations. Below, we discuss the most common changes related to the pronunciation of the words (including their stress) and their spelling. Furthermore, we discuss morphological adaptations such as differences in genus, singular/multiple change and change of word type. The latter phenomenon occurs only in Polish; Czech remains faithful to the word types common in Dutch.

18. https://pl.wikipedia.org/wiki/Dach%C3%B3wka_holenderka; see also Zwolińska (1974).

19. The word *holandka,* meaning "type of roof tile" has not been included in Czech explanatory dictionaries, yet. The ASCS (1998: 294) gives only the meaning "old Dutch breed of chicken", which, however, is hardly used in contemporary Czech; instead, the variant "*holanďanka*" (literally "Dutchwoman") is sometimes used.

4.1 Adapted forms

4.1.1 *Phonetic, prosodic, and spelling changes*

The phonetic systems of Dutch, Polish and Czech are not identical. Both Slavic languages do not have, for example, Dutch diphthongs <*ij*> [ɛi] and <*ui*> [œy], whilst vowel length in Polish is not a distinctive feature. The letter <g> found in the Dutch alphabet corresponds to a different phoneme [ɣ] than the same letter in Polish and Czech [g].[20] This means that the target forms of the borrowings had to undergo modifications, both with regard to their pronunciation and their spelling.

The graphic form of the word *gulden* in Dutch, Czech and Polish is identical, but the words differ in pronunciation, viz., in Dutch [ˈxʏldə(n)],[21] in Czech [guldɛn], in Polish [guldɛn]. Polish does not have the word *gracht,* but Czech does; the pronunciation is then [xrɑxt] in Dutch and [grɑxt] in Czech, respectively. Incidentally, this is a typical sound adaptation that applies to both Czech and Polish: these languages do not use the [ɣ], and, therefore, replace it with an [x] in the case of oral derivations. The sound <g> is retained in written derivations; only the pronunciation then changes to [g].

In the case of other words, the spelling in Czech and/or Polish was adapted, while the Dutch pronunciation was more or less preserved, *cf.*, Dutch *lakmoes* – Cz *lakmus,* Pl *lakmus,* Dutch *Hottentot* – Cz *hotentot, Pl hotentot;* Dutch *passaat* – Cz *pasát,* Pl *passat;* Dutch *wrak* – Cz *vrak,* Pl *wrak.* Here, the Dutch spelling is changed but the pronunciation is as good as the same, which probably means these words are loaned orally, so Czech and Polish have applied their own native spellings, which led to the sounds in Czech and Polish taking on the graphic appearance peculiar to these languages.

Compared to the standard pronunciation of the Dutch word, the vowel length in Czech is in some cases shortened after the spelling is changed, *e.g.*, Dutch *lindaan* – Cz *lindan* or Dutch *bezaan* – Cz *bezan.* For Polish, vowel length is not a distinctive feature and, if necessary, all Dutch vowels have been shortened and written with a single vowel, *i.e.*, *lindan* and *bezan.*

When words are adopted into Czech *via* another language, the graphical, sound and/or morphological adaptations of Dutch words are very frequent. The borrowing of words from Dutch *via* German[22] can be demonstrated, for example,

---

20. For a contrastive description of the pronunciation of Dutch and Czech, see Kostelecká (2019).

21. Pronunciation of Dutch words taken from the electronic dictionary of the Dutch language available at www.woorden.org.

by the spelling and pronunciation of the original Dutch consonant group *sch*, which in these words is not pronounced as [sx] as in Dutch but as [ʃ] as in German. This is also reflected in the graphic form of Czech words, *e.g.*, Dutch *schellak* – Cz *šelak*, Dutch *schuit* – Cz *škuta*. In Polish, this process continues: not only words with the *sch* combination but many words that start with an *s* in Dutch are pronounced following the pronunciation of German, *i.e.*, with a [ʃ] and written down by means of the letter combination <sz>. The examples include *sztorm* 'storm', *sztag* 'stag', *szkuner* 'schoener'. The [s] in originally Dutch words is further sometimes replaced by a [ʒ] in Polish: compare the word pair *potas/potaż*. Sometimes, the voiceless [s] becomes the voiced [z]: Dutch *saling* is *zaling* in Polish.

Since Polish has no diphthongs, these also had to be adapted. Polish uses several possibilities for this; now let us demonstrate a few of the most typical cases: In Polish, the <ei>/<ij> become a combination of <ej>: *sejzing, rejs,* or they change into an <e>: *marsel* 'marching sail' or an <i>: *lizel* "line sail". The <ui> usually turns into a <u>: *kambuz* 'galley'; this is pretty much under the influence of Russian as an intermediate language. Furthermore, it becomes a <i/y> *kliwer* 'jib' or *prymka* 'plum', which may attest that such words were borrowed *via* German. The diphthong [au] is pronounced in Polish as [a^{w}]; it is also written in the following way: <aw>: *kabeltaw.*

The traces of Russian influences can also be seen in words that have a palatalisation of vowels that is absent in Dutch. A good case in point is *lugier* 'lugger".

As for the stress, in Polish, in most cases, it falls on the penultimate syllable. Often the same goes for the Dutch source words: *stapelia, kaper, rolmops etc.* However, there is also a group where a (regular) deviation occurs: in Dutch compounds, in many cases, the first syllable is stressed, even if it is not the penultimate one of the word in question, and Polish follows this example. Examples: *achterdek, watersztag.* Presumably, it emerges from the fact that the second part of the Dutch compound also functions independently in Polish and that Polish speakers intuitively sense that these forms actually consist of two words.

4.1.2 *Morphological changes*

Nouns entering the target language already have their morphological form. If it can be accommodated in a particular inflectional paradigm, as a rule reserved for a particular grammatical gender of the noun, the borrowing will, as it were, automatically take over this grammatical gender if necessary. During the adaptation of

22. This transition from [s] to [ʃ] is typical of borrowings from German. However, there are examples where the source language is Low German or Russian in which a similar change occurs.

Dutch loanwords to the morphological systems of Czech and Polish, a number of changes were made, which we will now illustrate with some examples.

1. *Difference in Gender*
   a. Neuter in Dutch and masculine in Polish/Czech
      Dutch *jansenism* – Cz *jansenismus*, Pl *jansenizm*; Dutch *lakmus* – Cz *lakmus*, Pl *lakmus;* Dutch *plakkaat* – Cz *plakát*, Pl *plakat;* Dutch *kantoor* – Pl kantor; Dutch *stuur* – Pl *ster etc.*
   b. Masculine/feminine[23] in Dutch and masculine in Polish/Czech
      Dutch *bezaan* – Pl *bezan*, Cz *bezan*; Dutch *potas* – Pl *potas/potaż*, Cz *potaš*; Dutch *stellage* – Pl *stelaż*
   c. Masculine/feminine in Dutch and feminine in Polish/Czech
      Dutch *makreel* – Pl *makrela*, Cz *makrela*; Dutch *barkas* – Pl *barkasa*, Cz *barkasa*; Dutch *boei* – Pl *boja*, Cz *bóje*; Dutch *fret* – Pl *fretka*, Cz *fretka*; Dutch *vlag* – Pl *flaga*
2. *Difference between the singular and the plural*
   In Czech, the Dutch loanword *matjes* is used in two forms – either with the original Dutch diminutive suffix *-je* and the plural ending *-s* (*matjes*), or in the modified form *mates (cf.*, ASCS 1998: 483). However, it is always a masculine form in the singular. The common plural form *matjesy/matjesi*[24] thus contains two plural endings – the Dutch *(-s)* and the Czech one *(-y/-i)*. In Polish, this word has the form in the singular *matjes/matjas*, and in the plural *matjesy/matjasy*, also showing two plural endings similarly to the Czech.
3. *Part of Speech / Part of Sentence Change*
   Polish has one word that has changed its word type. This is *bejdewind* "by the wind". This Polish word is a noun and serves as a hyponym related to the word *wind*, while in Dutch this is used as an adverb. No such forms are found in Czech.

4.1.3 *Morphological productivity of borrowings*

Nouns are most often adopted from Dutch into Czech while other word types are only rarely adopted (*e.g.*, the verb *baggeren*). However, other words (*i.e.*, word types) can also be formed from the copied words, *cf.*, *lakmus* → *lakmusový* (adjective), *batika* → *batikovaný* (adjective), *batikovat* (verb), *bóje* → *bójka* (noun, diminutive), *hotentot* → *hotentotský* (adjective), *hotentotština* (noun, the name of

23. Substantives with the definite article *het* are always neutral in Dutch. For words with the definite article *de*, Dutch often no longer distinguishes between feminine and masculine. Polish and Czech, however, still make this distinction.

24. In Czech, two forms are allowed in the nominative plural of this word – see IJP (2008–2024).

a language, meaning "unintelligible speech"), *vrak* → *vrakoviště* (noun meaning "scrapyard"), *autovrak* (composite), *zvrakovat* (verb), *zvrakovaný* (adjective).

Polish also has borrowed nouns that later became productive. What emerges is the following verbs: *holendrować* "to turn skating figures"; derived nouns: *frachtowiec* "freighter"; adjectives: *lakmusowy, rembrandtowski* and a compound word *bakier*, derived from *bak keren*, that can be used in the word combination *(na) bakier*, which means "at a rakish angle, at odds".

4.2 Unadapted/the most recent forms

Only a very small number of loanwords from Dutch are not adapted to the Polish or Czech language systems. Non-adapted words in Czech include:

aam, aak, kraal – here, the preservation of the original Dutch spelling (doubled *a* in a closed syllable) is easy to see; in Czech, the vocal length is indicated differently, namely by the use of an accent mark, the so-called comma (á).
bintje – the graphic form of the word with the Dutch diminutive suffix *-tje* is also at first sight strange for Czechs; moreover, without the knowledge of Dutch pronunciation rules, they are unlikely to pronounce this suffix correctly, *i.e.*, without palatalisation [tje].
snoezelen – this Dutch term, created by the fusion of two Dutch words, *snuffelen* 'sniffing, exploring' and *doezelen* 'resting, relaxing', retains its original spelling in both Czech and Polish. In professional Czech circles, this word is usually pronounced the same way as it is in Dutch [snu:zələn]. However, the pronunciation of this word has not yet been established in Czech, especially the pronunciation of the first syllable *snoe-* creates many problems. Some Czechs pronounce *snoe-* as two syllables [sno-ɛ], and some use the long Czech vocal <*é*> [ɛː] or German <*ö*> [ø] here. In Czech, this word is inflected as masculine and is used to mean "method, form of multisensory stimulation" or "space specially adapted for multisensory stimulation". As for Polish, the term is known almost exclusively to specialists who, however, pronounce it as a four-syllable word with the pronunciation of <o> and <e> as two separate sounds and with the emphasis, according to Polish rules, on the penultimate syllable. There is also a parallel Polish name for this therapeutic method, *i.e.*, "Sala Doświadczania Świata" (translatable as the World Experience Room), and it is used considerably more often.

Polish has also acquired two new Dutch words in recent years that are now in use across almost all of Poland. They are *kapsalon* (mentioned above) in the sense of 'a kind of fast food' and *woonerf* ('residential area'). The latter word is pronounced in a mixed English-Dutch way, namely as [u̯ũnɛrf].

5. Thematic division and recentness of loanwords

The next interesting aspect is the thematic classification of borrowings. Indeed, the study shows that borrowings are not entirely random after all. There are certain domains where Czech and Polish apparently needed Dutch words, as evidenced by the long lists of words within these domains. It is certainly not the intention to conclude that borrowing is always intentional, but rather to show that there are fields of meaning for which the Dutch vocabulary has been largely indispensable.

Words adopted directly or indirectly from Dutch into Czech and Polish relate mainly to the following domains:[25]

1. Sailing/fishing/sea
   Pl: *bezan* 'bezan', *boja* 'bouy', *flota* 'fleet', *fok* 'foresail', *jacht* 'yacht', *kajuta* 'cabin', *kaper* 'caper', *koja* 'berth', *raksa* 'raxa', *sztag* 'staysail', *sztorm* 'storm', *wimpel* 'wimpel' and many others
   Cz: *aak* (type of ship), *barkasa* (a tender), *bóje* 'bouy', *bojer* (type of yacht), *dok* 'dock', *jachta* 'yacht', *kajuta* 'cabin', *kaper* 'caper', *keulnaar* (type of ship), and many others
2. Inventions, sciences and technology
   Pl: *bagier* 'bagger', *bakelit* 'bakelite', *batik* 'batik', *fokker* 'fokker', *holenderka* (different meanings), *klinkier* 'clinker', *lakmus* 'litmus', *lindan* 'lindan', *manekin* 'dummy', *potas* 'kalium', *potaż* 'potash', *sylwin* 'sylvin', *szelak* 'shellac', *tombak* 'tombac'
   Cz: *bagr* 'bagger', *bakelit* 'bakelite', *batika* 'batik', *holendr/holandr* (a machine for paper production), *holandka* (a type of fired roof tile), *klinker* 'clinker', *lakmus* 'litmus', *lindan* 'lindan', *kepr* 'twill', *potaš* 'potash', *sylvín* 'sylvin', *šelak* 'shellac', *tombak* 'tombac'
3. Food and beverages
   Pl: *brandy* 'brandy', *brukselka* 'Brussels sprout', *colesław* 'coleslaw', *(ser) edamski* 'Edam cheese', *gouda* 'Gouda cheese', *makrela* 'mackerel', *matjesy/matjasy* 'pickled herring', *mazdamer* 'Maasdam cheese', *rolmops* 'rollmops'
   Cz: *ančovička* 'anchovy', *brandy* 'brandy', *coleslaw* 'coleslaw', *eidam* 'Edam cheese', *garnát* 'shrimp', *gouda* 'Gouda cheese', *maasdamer* 'Maasdam cheese', *makrela* 'mackerel', *matjesy/matjesi* 'pickled herring', *ústřice* 'oyster'
4. Titles/occupations
   Pl: *admirał* 'admiral', *boss* 'boss', *bosman* 'petty officer', *flibustier* 'flibustier', *makler* 'broker', *szyper* 'schipper'
   Cz: *boss* 'boss', *flibustýr* 'flibustier', *makléř* 'broker', *manekýn* 'model, mannequin'

25. This is not an exhaustive list.

5. Economy/trade
   Pl: *akcja* 'share', *dolar* 'dollar', *fracht* 'cargo', *gulden* 'guilder'.
   Cz: *akcie* 'share', *burza* 'stock exchange/market',[26] *dolar* 'dollar', *gulden* 'guilder'
6. Politics/religion/philosophy/society
   Pl: *apartheid* 'apartheid', *arminianin* 'Arminian', *beginka* 'Beguine', *hotentot* 'Hottentot', *jankes* 'Yankee', *jansenizm* 'Jansenism', *lollard* 'Lollard', *oranżysta* 'Orangist'
   Cz: *apartheid* 'apartheid', *arminián* 'Arminian', *bollandista* 'Bollandist', *hotentot* 'Hottentot', *jansenismus* 'Jansenism', *lollard* 'Lollard', *oranžista* 'Orangist', *yankee* 'Yankee'
7. Agriculture
   Pl: *arden* 'Ardennes'(a horse breed), *bintje* 'bintje' (a potato variety), *boskop* 'the Belle de Boskoop' (an apple variety), *fryz* 'Friesian' (a horse breed), *holenderka* (different meanings), *teksel* 'Texel' (a sheep breed), *rabata* 'plot'
   Cz: *afrikán* (flower Tagetes), *afrikander* (an African breed of cattle), *barneveldka* (a chicken breed), *bintje* ('bintje'; a potato variety), *Boskoopské* ('Belle de Boskoop'; an apple variety), *brabantka* (a breed of chicken), *deutzie* 'Deutzia'
8. Exotic animals or trading goods/things worth seeing
   Pl: *bambus* 'bamboo', *fretka* 'ferret', *kakadu* 'cockatoo', *kanarek* 'canary', *mops* 'pug', *orangutan* 'orang-utang', *ratan* 'rattan'
   Cz: *bambus* 'bamboo', *fretka* 'ferret', *kakadu* 'cockatoo', *mops/mopsík* 'pug', *orangutan* 'orang-utan'
9. Geography/geology/civil engineering
   Pl: *Afrykaner* 'Afrikaner', *atlas* 'atlas', *Bur* 'Boer', *diuna* 'dune', *kraal* 'corral', *polder* 'polder', *terp* 'terp'
   Cz: *Afrikánec* 'Afrikaner', *atlas* 'atlas', *Búr* 'Boer', *duna* 'dune', *gracht* (city canal), *kraal* 'corral', *polder* 'polder', *rigol* 'ditch', *terpa* 'terp'
10. Art
    Pl: *blik* "highlight', *elzewir* (font type), *karmin* 'carmine', *ochra* 'ochre', *plakat* 'poster'
    Cz: *elzevir* (font type), *plakát* 'poster'
11. Sports and games
    Pl: *korfball* 'korfball', *loteria* 'lottery'
    Cz: *korfbal* 'korfball', *loterie* 'lottery'

26. For a detailed explanation of the origin of this word (in Dutch *beurs*), which has not been adopted into Polish, see e.g. Holub & Lyer (1978: 103) or http://www.etymologiebank.nl/trefwoord/beurs2.

In general, far more shipbuilding and seafaring loanwords were recorded in Polish than in Czech. Czech explanatory and etymological dictionaries also mention no connection with Dutch for some words that are considered Dutch loanwords in Polish, *e.g.*, *admirál, blanket, kanár, kapoun, ratan,* and *terpentýn.*

On the other hand, the following Dutch loanwords can be found in Czech, but not in Polish: *aam* – Cz *aam, afrikaan* – Cz *afrikán, ansjovis* – Cz *ančovička, beurs* – Cz *burza, doos* – Cz *dóza, hongitocht* – Cz *hongitochten, keper* – Cz *kepr, oester* – Cz *ústřice, richel (regel)* – Cz *rigol.*

Moreover, we did not find the equivalents of the Czech words *burák, brajgl* or *flámovat* in Polish, either. The term *burák*, a synonym for Czech words *arašíd* or *arašídový ořech* (Dutch *pinda* Pl *orzech arachidowy, fistaszek,* meaning '*peanut*'), is a shortening of the expression *burský oříšek* ('Boer nut'), which is related to the Boers and the Boer Wars. Indeed, these nuts would have been imported into Bohemia to a greater extent at the time of the Boer Wars (Rejzek 2015: 106, ASSČ).

The Czech word *brajgl*, which explicitly refers to disorder or noise, is thought to have originated as a corruption of the surname of the Flemish painter Pieter Breughel, who painted "busy folk scenes" (Holub & Lyer 1978: 98).

The Czech word *flámovat,* meaning "to party and drink late into the night", is related to the aforementioned word *flamender*, which probably came into use as early as the Thirty Years' War as a designation for Flemish mercenaries who liked to drink. The term *flamendr* is based on the German word *Flamländer*, originally used to mean "inhabitant of Flanders", in Dutch *Vlaming*, in English *Flaming.* From the verb *flámovat,* the noun *flám* was then also formed with the meaning "a drinking spree/binge" (*cf.*, Rejzek 2015: 190).

Conclusion

We compared Dutch loanwords in Czech and Polish in terms of some features. The analysis showed that the Polish and Czech corpora of borrowings are essentially similar. What differs is the number of words in the corpora, clearly to the detriment of Czech. The Polish one contains many more words that have something to do with shipbuilding and seafaring, which is understandable since Poland, unlike the Czech Republic, has access to the sea. Otherwise, the corpora seem similar. As for the routes of borrowing, in both languages, more indirect than direct borrowings were found because these two West Slavic languages have not been in long-term direct contact with Dutch. In Polish, most borrowings came *via* German, Low German or Russian, whereas in Czech it was mainly *via* German. In a few cases, other languages (especially French and English) played the role of an intermediary language. Polish and Czech corpora of Dutch borrowings are also similar in the semantic fields of the borrowings and even with regard to the orthographic and phonetic adaptations the borrowings needed to become assimilated into Czech/Polish. Moreover, using two very recent examples, *i.e.*, *snoezelen* and *kapsalon*, we were able to observe that the assimilation processes of new borrowings in Polish and Czech are largely the same (the same pronunciation, and stress immediately adapted to the language norm). Our research needs a follow-up study in order to establish whether what has now been proven for Polish and Czech also applies to other Slavic languages.

References

ASCS = Petráčková, Věra, and Jiří Kraus. 1998. *Akademický slovník cizích slov*. Praha: Academia.

ASSČ = *Akademický slovník současné češtiny*. 2017–2024. Praha: Ústav pro jazyk český AV ČR. https://slovnikcestiny.cz

Bańkowski, Andrzej. 2000. *Etymologiczny słownik języka polskiego banden 1–2 (A-K and L-P)*. Warszawa: Wydawnictwo PWN.

Čermák, František et al.. 1983. *Slovník české frazeologie a idiomatiky. Přirovnání*. Praha: Academia.

"Dachówka holenderka." *Wikipedia*: https://pl.wikipedia.org/wiki/Dach%C3%B3wka_holenderka

De Vries, Jan. 1971. *Nederlands etymologisch woordenboek*. Leiden: Brill.

DUDEN = Dudenredaktion. *Duden online*. https://www.duden.de

DVD = Den Boon, Ton, and Ruud Hendrickx (eds). *Dikke Van Dale Online 2015 t/m 2022*. https://www.vandale.nl/

DWDS = *Digitales Wörterbuch der deutschen Sprache:* https://www.dwds.de

Goedhart, Pieter J., Jan C. Henneman, Kryštof Krijt, Rebecca Krijt, and Ivo Mostert. 2018. *Samen op de 'laan van Europa': 100 jaar Tsjechië & Slowakije in Nederland*. Amsterdam: Pegasus.

Holub, Josef, and Stanislav Lyer. 1978. *Stručný etymologický slovník jazyka českého se zvláštním zřetelem k slovům kulturním a cizím*. Praha: Státní pedagogické nakladatelství.

doi Horáková, Hana. 2014. "Multi-local research of modern rurality in the Czech Republic: epistemological and methodological challenges." *EUC Geographica* 49 (2): 7–19.

IJP = *Internetová jazyková příručka*. 2008–2024. Praha: Ústav pro jazyk český AV ČR. https://prirucka.ujc.cas.cz.

Kostelecká, Marta. 2019. *Konfrontační popis kultivované výslovnosti nizozemštiny a češtiny z pohledu českého mluvčího*. Brno: MUNI Press.

Kowalska-Szubert, Agata. 2013. *Polder, lakmus en kordzik. Nederlandse lexicale ontleningen in het hedendaagse Pools*. Wrocław: Wydawnictwo Uniwersytetu Wrocławskiego.

doi Kowalska-Szubert, Agata. 2021. *Dutch Loanwords in Contemporary Polish*. Wroclaw: Oficzna Wydawnicza ATUT.

Krijt, Kryštof, and Pieter J. Goedhart. 2008. *Tsjecholand: Over Tsjechen en Hollanders*. Den Haag: Koopman & Kraaijenbrink.

doi Křížová, Kateřina. 2018. "Bóje, eidam, polder aneb Příspěvek k popisu nizozemských lexikálních výpůjček v češtině." *Bohemica Olomucensia* 10 (1): 172–185.

Linde, Samuel Bogumił. 1998. *Słownik języka polskiego, banden I-VI*. Lwów 1854–1860, reprint Warszawa: Gutenberg Print.

Machek, Václav. 1968. *Etymologický slovník jazyka českého*. Praha: Academia.

Mączak, Antoni. 1976. "Rozwój społeczno-gospodarczy Prus Królewskich: wieś. Osadnictwo olęderskie." In *Historia Pomorza, tom II do roku 1815*, onder red. van G. Labuda, deel I (1464/66–1648/57). Poznań: Wydawnictwo Poznańskie.

Mokijenko, Valerij M. 1973. "Pije jako holendr – nebo jako Holendr?" *Naše řeč* 56 (2), 63–71.

OED = Simpson, J.A., and E.S.C. Weiner (eds). 1989. *Oxford English Dictionary*. Oxford: OUP. https://www.oed.com

Philippa, Marlies et al.. 2003–2009. *Etymologisch Woordenboek van het Nederlands*. Amsterdam: Amsterdam University Press.

Pokorný, Jindřich. 1976. *Zakopaný pes*. Praha: Albatros.

Procházka Antonín. 1934. "Haluzna - Naši - Krajánek." *Naše řeč* 18 (2), 45–48.

Rakšányiová, Jana. 2008. *Holandčina v sociokultúrnom kontexte*. Bratislava: Enigma.

Rejzek, Jiří. 2001. *Český etymologický slovník*. 1st ed. Voznice: Leda.

Rejzek, Jiří. 2015. *Český etymologický slovník*. 3rd ed. Voznice: Leda.

Renner, Hans. 2002. *Česká republika a Nizozemsko: Historie vzájemných vztahů . Tsjechië en Nederland: Historische raakvlakken*. Praha: Paseka.

SJP = *Słownik języka polskiego PWN*. www.sjp.pl

SSČ = *Slovník spisovné češtiny pro školu a veřejnost*. 2012. 4th ed. Praha: Academia.

SSJČ = *Slovník spisovného jazyka českého*. 1960–1971. Praha: Academia. http://ssjc.ujc.cas.cz

Stěpanovová, Ludmila. 1989. "K etymologii frazeologismů s vlastními jmény." *Naše řeč* 72 (1), 20–28.

Stellmacher, Dieter. 2000. *Niederdeutsche Sprache* . 2nd ed. Berlin: Weidler.

Targowski, Michał. 2016. "Osadnictwo olęderskie w Polsce – jego rozwój i specyfika." In *Olędrzy – osadnicy znad Wisły. Sąsiedzi bliscy i obcy*, red. by Andrzej Pabian, and Michał Targowski, 11–26. Toruń: Fundacja Ośrodek Inicjatyw Społecznych ANRO.

Těšitelová, Marie. 1963. "Slovník starých českých mlýnů." *Naše řeč* 46 (4), 186–193.

Thijssen, Lucia. 2003. *Polska i Niderlandy: 1000 lat kontaktów*. Zutphen: Walburg Pers.

Vandeputte, Omer, and Olga Krijtová. 1993. *Nizozemština: jazyk dvaceti miliónů Nizozemců a Vlámů*. Rekkem: Stichting Ons Erfdeel.

Van der Meulen, Reinder. 1909. *De Hollandse Zee- en Scheepstermen in het Russisch*. Amsterdam: KNAW.

Van der Meulen, Reinder. 1959. *Nederlandse woorden in het Russisch (supplement op de Hollandsche zee- en scheepstermen in het Russisch)*. Amsterdam: Noord-Hollandsche Uitgevers Maatschappij. Electronically accessible at http://www.dwc.knaw.nl/DL /publications/PU00010181.pdf.

Van der Sijs, Nicoline. 1998. *Geleend en uitgeleend. Nederlandse woorden in andere talen en andersom*. Amsterdam/Antwerpen: Contact.

Van der Sijs, Nicoline. 2009. *Cookies, Coleslaw and Stoops. The influence of Dutch on the North American Languages*. Den Haag: Sdu Uitgevers.

Van der Sijs, Nicoline. 2010a. *Etymologiebank*: http://etymologiebank.nl/

Van der Sijs, Nicoline. 2010b. *Nederlandse woorden wereldwijd*. The Hague: SDU.

Van der Sijs, Nicoline. 2015. *Uitleenwoordenbank:* http://uitleenwoordenbank.ivdnt.org/

WDLP = *Wörterbuch der deutschen Lehnwörter in der polnischen Schrift- und Standardsprache:* http://www.bis.uni-oldenburg.de/bis-verlag/wdlp/ab_A.html

WNW = *Woordenboek van Nieuwe Woorden*: https://neologismen.ivdnt.org/

Woorden.org: https://www.woorden.org/

WSJP = *Wielki słownik języka polskiego*: www.wsjp.pl

Zgółkowa, Halina et al.. 1994–2005. *Praktyczny słownik współczesnej polszczyzny*. Poznań: Wydawnictwo Kurpisz.

Zwolińska, Krystyna, and Zasław Malicki. 1974. *Mały słownik terminów plastycznych*. Warszawa: Wiedza Powszechna.

CHAPTER 5

Dutch loanwords in Hungarian

Roland Nagy
ELTE University, Budapest

This study investigates the influence of Dutch on the Hungarian lexicon, aiming to compile a comprehensive inventory of Dutch loanwords in Hungarian and explore the socio-cultural contexts of lexical borrowing. The research employs macrolevel data collection from various references, including the *Uitleenwoordenbank* (Van der Sijs 2015), Hungarian historical dictionaries and corpora; alongside microlevel analysis of individual etymologies, leading to several revisions of the sources. The study identifies 99 Hungarian words derived from 90 Dutch words across a period of nearly 800 years, with 10 potential direct loans. These borrowings correspond to periods of significant cultural and social contact, particularly the Peregrination of Hungarian students in the Netherlands (17th–18th centuries) and the Child Transport Action (early 20th century). Notable examples, such as *bischop(lé)* and *korfbal*, reflect these specific historical contexts. This study contributes to existing scholarship by uncovering new loanwords and potential direct borrowings, advancing our understanding of Dutch–Hungarian linguistic contact.

Keywords: lexical borrowing, historical sociolinguistics, Dutch loanwords, Dutch–Hungarian contact, etymology, Germanic studies

1. Introduction

1.1 Aims

Although numerous studies have been published recently on various aspects of the historical relations between the Low Countries and Hungary (e.g. Aalders, Pusztai, and Réthelyi 2020; Bozzay 2022; Perényi and Réthelyi 2023), limited attention has been paid to the linguistic dimensions of these interactions (Nagy and Réthelyi 2023). Most studies concentrated on cultural mediation and individual mediators, emphasizing language use and translation, with scant attention to lexical contact phenomena. In this study, I will examine the influence of Dutch on the Hungarian lexicon. My primary aim is to compile a comprehensive list of

https://doi.org/10.1075/impact.55.05nag

Dutch loanwords in the history of Hungarian in order to outline the general patterns of lexical contact between the two languages. Additionally, from a historical sociolinguistic perspective, my goal is to analyse potential correlations with sociocultural trends, such as the intensity of contact phenomena and lexical borrowing. In Section 1.2, I will outline the methodology. Section 1.3 will focus on some controversial etymological concepts central to the research. Section 1.4 will provide a brief overview of the historical sociolinguistic background of lexical transfer from Dutch into Hungarian. Section 2 will present the research results, and Section 3 will offer some general conclusions.

1.2 Methodology

The research began with two wordlists. During various lectures throughout the years focusing on the history of Dutch–Hungarian relations, I compiled a concise inventory of 47 Dutch loanwords in Hungarian based primarily on two Hungarian etymological dictionaries (Benkő 1967; Zaicz 2006). In late 2022, I received an additional list from Nicoline van der Sijs.[1] The list comprised a database of 57 Dutch loanwords in Hungarian, including many items previously published in her books and online database (Van der Sijs 2006; 2010; 2015). While 39 words were common to both lists, 17 items[2] were missing from mine and 8 from Van der Sijs's list. The discrepancies, along with the possibility of still unexplored words prompted me to attempt to create a comprehensive inventory.

Methodologically, the research was divided into two dimensions. At the macro level, the aim was to identify all potentially Dutch loanwords in the history of Hungarian in order to compile an exhaustive inventory. At the micro level, the etymology of each entry was scrutinized to identify and rectify potential inaccuracies.

The identification of potential Dutch loanwords began with a detailed analysis of the available Hungarian etymological and historical dictionaries (Szarvas and Simonyi 1890; Zolnai and Szamota 1902; Gombocz and Melich 1914; Bárczi 1994; TESz; EWUng; Tóthfalusi 2001; Zaicz 2006; 2021; ÚESzWeb). The findings, together with the loanwords from Van der Sijs's and my own list, were then cross-referenced with the major etymological and historical dictionaries of the relevant source languages: Dutch (etymological resources at *Etymologiebank.nl*, the historical dictionaries within the *Geïntegreerde Taalbank* (GTB)), German

1. I would like to express my gratitude to Nicoline van der Sijs for making her list available to me.

2. Van der Sijs's list also contained the word *kraker* 'squatter'. However, I omitted this word in the course of the research, because it was missing from the Hungarian Gigaword Corpus (HGC) and only occurred in other sources (ADT) as a quotation of the original Dutch word, and therefore cannot be considered a loanword, merely a part of the foreign language code.

(sources available through *Digitales Wörterbuch der deutschen Sprache* (DWDS); Kluge and Seebold 2011), French (resources available via the *Centre National de Ressources Textuelles et Lexicales* (CNRTL), including the *Trésor de La Langue Française informatisé* (TLFi); Wartburg and Carles 2019), English (OED; sources available at the *Online Etymology Dictionary*; Onions 1966), and Italian (LEI).

Subsequently, relevant Hungarian historical corpora (MTSZ; MGTSZ; TMK; ADT) and contemporary corpora (HGC; Oravecz, Váradi, and Sass 2014; ADT) were consulted to verify the actual usage, frequency, and contextual meanings of the loanwords. The results were systematically compiled into a database, which is summarised in Table 2. Methodological considerations regarding the categorization of loanwords (direct vs. indirect borrowing), the identification and role of the source language (ultimate vs. intermediate source) are discussed in the following sections (1.3, 1.4) and in Section 2.1.

Ultimately, I hope that the new data will contribute to etymological research, and in particular to the extensive work of Van der Sijs on the dissemination of Dutch loanwords across the world's languages, which remains a seminal reference in the field (Van der Sijs 2001; 1997; 1998; 2006; 2009; 2010; 2015).

1.3 Basic concepts

The first methodological question that needed to be answered at the beginning of the research is a seemingly simple one: Which Hungarian words have been borrowed from Dutch? Despite its apparent simplicity, this question is inherently complex. Although this chapter does not aim to comprehensively discuss every facet of this complexity, it is essential to underscore some fundamental aspects pertinent to this study.

First and foremost, it is crucial to establish a clear definition of the term *lexical borrowing*. In its broad sense, borrowing denotes the transfer of a word from one language or (dia)lect (referred to as the *source* or *donor* language) into another (referred to as the *recipient* or *borrowing* language) (Haspelmath and Tadmor 2009; Hock, 1991, chap. 14). Within the scope of this study, Dutch loanwords will be classified according to (1) the distance between the source and the recipient language (*direct* vs. *indirect* borrowings), and (2) the position of the donor language in the etymological lineage (*ultimate source* vs. *intermediary source*).

The first group is divided into two subgroups. First, it comprises words whose immediate donor language is Dutch, i.e. they were directly borrowed from Dutch, such as Hungarian (Hu)[3] *Bintje* 'Bintje, medium-sized potato variety'

3. Language names are hereafter abbreviated before examples: Hungarian=Hu, Dutch=Du. See also footnote a on p. 175.

[11][4] (see 2.2). Second, it contains words whose donor language is Dutch but have entered Hungarian through an intermediary language, typically German. For example, Hu *bulvár* 'boulevard; tabloid[5]', is directly derived from French *boulevard* 'rampart, promenade', which in turn is derived from Dutch (Du) *bolwerk* 'bastion' [15].

Loanwords can also be categorized according to the role of the donor language. Dutch being an Indo-European language, logically traces each of its words back to an older etymon along the genetic line Dutch < West-Germanic < Proto-Germanic < Indo-European. In this study, Dutch will be regarded as ultimate donor of a loanword in Hungarian, if the source word belongs to the inherited vocabulary of Dutch or is a result of internal word formation within Dutch. There are 39 such words that have been borrowed into Hungarian, e.g. Du *Holland* 'Holland' > Hu *holland* 'Dutch' [40A], which itself is a compound of Indo-European **kl̥əd-* > Proto-Germanic **hulta-* + Indo-European **londh/*landh* > Proto-Germanic **landa-* (Kluge and Seebold 2011, s.v. *Holland*, Holz, Land; EWN, s.v. *holland, hout, land*; Pokorny 1959, 546 f., 675). However, the majority of Dutch words discussed in this paper are loanwords themselves. Strictly speaking, therefore, Dutch is only an intermediary language through which (as well as through other languages) they have been transmitted into Hungarian. How can we justify labelling these as Dutch loanwords if they are themselves borrowings from another language? I will address this question below briefly.

The presumption underlying the question is rooted in the comparative historical linguistic tradition of the nineteenth century, where determining the ultimate origin of a word was crucial for understanding genetic relationships between languages and their linguistic evolution (Robins 1997, chap. 7). Ultimate origins – as far as they exist at all – can indeed help establish the basic vocabulary of a language, its genetically-related languages, their language family, the time of the separation of related languages, and the intensity and length of linguistic contact with other languages. However, the meticulous, form-oriented approach of the comparative method (now mostly known as genetic linguistics), particularly etymology, has long provided a flawed foundation for the popular notions that (1) determining the ultimate source of words is possible, and (2) the 'original' form and/or mean-

4. The numbers in square brackets following the examples correspond to their respective entry numbers in Table 2.

5. The meaning 'tabloid' was borrowed from German with words like *Boulevardzeitung* 'tabloid newspaper', *Boulevardstück* 'tabloid piece'. The original meaning 'wide road in the city' was metonymically linked to the 'casual lifestyle' associated with the popular boulevards of modern city centres. The original adjective *bulvár* was later nominalized in Hungarian (ÚESzWeb s.v. *bulvár*).

ing of a word in the ultimate source should be regarded as the true and actual one. The fallacy of this assumption is aptly summarized by Telegdi, an eminent Hungarian linguist of the 20th century, with the following sentence "Das ursprüngliche ist das eigentliche", i.e. 'the original one is the actual one' (cited by Nádasdy 1996). This search for the ultimate has not only given rise to etymological fallacies, for example, that the real meaning of Du *pupil* 'pupil' is 'little girl(-doll)', since it ultimately derives from the diminutive of Latin *pupa* 'little girl(-doll)', but has also contributed to the estrangement of etymology and modern linguistics (Malkiel 1975).

In this study, I adopt a hybrid approach to what constitutes a Dutch word with respect to lexical borrowing. This approach is rather similar to the one employed by Van der Sijs (2010; 2015). According to her perspective, the ultimate origin of a word is irrelevant with respect to its potential for being borrowed into another language (Van der Sijs 2010, 21). Instead, social factors, closely intertwined with political, economic, cultural, and technological ones, primarily determine whether words are transferred from one language to another, or whether a language can be considered a source from which a word disseminates. Therefore, these factors should be carefully considered alongside the formal linguistic ones when labelling Dutch a potential source of a loanword in Hungarian. For a better understanding of the historical social context of Dutch–Hungarian lexical contact I shall give an overview of the historical contacts of Hungarian with other languages and their historical background in 1.4.4.

In summary, from the historical sociolinguistic viewpoint of this study, all Hungarian words will be categorized as Dutch loanwords, whose ultimate or intermediary donor is Dutch, if they represent a distinguishable node in the etymological lineage. There are two primary sources of such nodes. Firstly, they may emerge from noticeable changes in the form or meaning of a word, e.g. Du *stellage* 'stand, showcase, rack' [83], which combines a Germanic stem (*stel(len)* 'place, set (v.)') with a suffix borrowed from French (*-age*) in a uniquely Dutch amalgamation. Secondly, they may result from identifiable cultural, technological innovations, or historical events, e.g. *orang-oetang* 'orang-utan' [66] was adopted from Malay during the Dutch colonisation of the Dutch East Indies.

Another methodological problem when labelling Dutch as a source language is that Dutch, as a West-Germanic language, shares a large portion of its vocabulary with closely related languages like Low German, Frisian and even High German and English. This means that in many cases the role of Dutch as a donor variety cannot be established with absolute certainty, e.g. Du *sleep* 'train of a dress' [81A] > Hu *slepp* 'train of a dress'. In Table 2, such dubious cases will be indicated with a (?) next to the source languages, and/or a slash '/' between the competing source languages. For example, Du *bolwerk* 'fortification' is regarded here as the (ultimate) source of Hu *bulvár* 'boulevard; tabloid' [15] based on the major historical and etymological dictionaries (see e.g. ÚESzWeb, s.v. *bulvár*; Kluge and Seebold 2011, s.v. *Bollwerk*, Boulvard; EWN, s.v. *boulevard*). Nonetheless, other historical sources suggest that the French term, which is the direct source of the Hungarian word, may have been borrowed from (High) German rather than from Dutch (TLFi, s.v. *boulevard*; Wartburg and Carles 2019, s.v. *bolwerc*). In this case, both languages will be provided as potential sources: Dutch/High German (Du/HG).

Finally, an inherent difficulty in etymology is that the further one delves into the past, the scarcer written sources will get. Therefore, we should be very cautious in drawing final conclusions concerning the etymology of a word. This is especially true for international words, like Du *pomp* 'pump' [76AB]. In this study, these will be marked as '*int.*'.

Calques, or loan translations, are complex words whose components are translated from the donor language into the recipient language. For example, Du *tuchthuis* 'correctional facility' (literally 'discipline house') [88] was translated into German as *Zuchthaus* in the 17th century, and it was also translated into Hungarian in the early 19th century as Hu *fegyház* 'correctional facility, prison' (literally 'discipline house', a compound of the back formation of Hu *fegyelem* 'discipline' and *ház* 'house'). In this study, calques will also be considered as Dutch loans, and will be labelled as '*calque*'. Further methodological details concerning the categorisation will be disclosed in Section 2.

In the following sections I will give a brief overview of the historical background of lexical borrowing into Hungarian. Section 1.4.1 will introduce the short history of Hungarian with special attention on lexical contact phenomena affecting the Hungarian lexicon (1.4.2.). In 1.4.4 I shall give an overview of the history of Dutch–Hungarian relations and linguistic contact.

1.4 Historical background

1.4.1 *Hungarian*

With roughly 15 million native speakers, Hungarian is the largest non-Indo-European language in Europe, as well as the largest Uralic, and Finno-Ugric language. It is distantly related to other members of the Finno-Ugric family, Finnish, Estonian, and more closely related to the lesser-known languages Mansi and Khanty, spoken in present day Russia, in the Khanty-Mansi Autonomous Okrug along the Ob River (Maticsák 2020). Unlike many Germanic, Slavic or Romance languages it has shared no mutual intelligibility with any of its relatives or other languages for about the past millennium. This linguistic isolation and the interaction with the different language groups has been given considerable attention in the linguistic literature of contact linguistics (e.g. Calabrese and Wetzels 2009; Haspelmath and Tadmor 2009; Rosenhouse and Kowner 2008 etc.).

Like other major European languages, the history of Hungarian is divided into major periods: Proto-Hungarian (1000 BC–896 AD), Old Hungarian (896–1526), Middle Hungarian (1526–1772), New Hungarian (1772–1920), and Contemporary Hungarian (1920–). The boundaries of these periods usually coincide with significant historical events, such as the settlement of the Hungarian tribes in 896 AD in the Carpathian basin. The fundamental grammatical changes that shaped Hungarian took place until the end of Old Hungarian period (e.g. the creation of a complex agglutinating morphology) (Kiss and Pusztai 2018). The later periods are dominated by phonological and lexical changes often motivated by contact with other languages. Until the end of the Old Hungarian period, Hungarian was primarily the language of informal communication, and a household language. Although the earliest Hungarian records date from the 11th century, longer written texts do not appear in larger numbers until the end of the late 15th, early 16th century (*NYELVEMLÉKEK | Magyar Nyelvemlékek*, n.d.). Along with most European languages, the first steps towards Hungarian as a modern language, suitable for all domains of life, were taken in the second half of the 16th century, also referred to as the 'golden age' of Hungarian (Pálffy and Evans 2021). Standardization intensified during the 18th and 19th centuries, and Hungarian acquired the status of an official language in 1844.

1.4.2 *Borrowing and contact with other languages*

From a contact linguistic perspective, the history of Hungarian can be further divided into seven periods (cf. Benkő 1978a; Gerstner 2015; Nádasdy 2020).

Hungarian tribes adopted a nomadic lifestyle after leaving the southern slopes of the Ural Mountains around 500 BC. Their journey into the Carpathian Basin until the 9th century exposed them to various cultures and languages. Early Hungarian borrowed from Iranian and Turkic dialects, including Alan and an ancient Chuvash variety. The number of Turkic loanwords predating the Hungarian settlement is about 300, contrasting with about 700 ancient etymons from the Finno-Ugric period, and about 70 from both the Uralic and the Ugric period (Benkő 1978b; Gerstner 2015; Kiss and Pusztai 2003).[6]

Interactions with Slavic groups intensified after the conquest of the Carpathian Basin. This led to a strong lexical influence from (Southern) Slavic varieties during the 10th and 11th centuries, continuing through direct contact with other

6. Indeed, the Hungarian language and culture have borrowed many elements from various Turkish tribes and dialects throughout their history, leading early linguists and historians to believe that Hungarian is related to Turkish. However, comparative historical linguistics has clearly refuted these ideas. Nevertheless, to this day there are many adherents to the theory of Turkic–Hungarian kinship. (for a summary see Maticsák 2020, chap. 4.5)

Table 1. Historical periods of Hungarian in relation to contact with other languages (languages with a significant linguistic impact are highlighted in bold)

Period	Approximate dates	Historical events marking the beginning and end of the period	Lexical influence
The nomadic period	500 A.D. – 895 A.D.	– Hungarian tribes leave their territories around the Ural – Hungarian tribes enter and settle in the Carpathian Basin	– **Old Turkic** – Iranian (Alan)
Independent Kingdom of Hungary	895–1526	– Hungarians settle in the Carpathian basin – Battle of Mohács (1526), where the Ottoman empire defeats the Hungarian king, leading to the partition of Hungary between the Ottoman Empire, the Habsburg monarchy, and the Principality of Transylvania	– **Slavic** – Latin – Turkish – Slavic
Partitioned Hungary	1526–1686	– Battle of Mohács (1526) – Siege and recapture of Buda by the Holy Leage from the Ottoman Empire, ending almost 150 years of Ottoman rule	– **German** – Turkish – Latin – Slavic
Habsburg rule of Hungary	1686–1920	– End of the Ottoman rule (1686) – End of the First World War and fall of the Austro-Hungarian Monarchy (1918), Treaty of Trianon (1920)[a]	– **German** – Latin – French (through German)
Independent Kingdom of Hungary	1920–1945	– Treaty of Trianon – End of the Second World War, leading to Soviet occupation	– German – French
Hungary under Soviet rule	1945–1989	– Soviet occupation of Hungary – Peaceful transition and disintegration of the East Bloc in the 1980s, proclamation of the Republic of Hungary (1989)	– Russian
Independent Republic of Hungary	1989 – present day	– Proclamation of the Republic of Hungary	– **English**

a. As a result of the Treaty of Trianon (1920) Hungary lost two-thirds of its territory, one-third of its Hungarian-speaking population, and approximately 90% of its population whose first language was not Hungarian.

neighbouring Slavic ethnic groups, like Slovak, Ukrainian, Serbian, Croatian, and Slovenian.

The impact of Latin, which served as the language of the church, law, historiography, and education in medieval Hungary, has fluctuated over the past millennium. Latin borrowings were facilitated by literacy. The Hungarian vernacular incorporates about 200 Latin loanwords (Gerstner 2015). A few Dutch words in Hungarian seem to have been borrowed through Latin religious sources or exhibit Latin features, Du *remonstrant* 'Remonstrant, follower of Jacobus Arminius' > (Latin?) > Hu *remonstráns* 'remonstrant' (1792) [78].

French–Hungarian relations were intensive during the 12th and 13th centuries due to dynastic ties. French noble families and knights, predominantly from Wallonia, frequented the Hungarian royal court. Monastic orders like the Benedictines, Cistercians, and Premonstratensians also settled in Hungary. During the 18th and 19th centuries, French became the second most popular foreign language often spoken alongside German by the Hungarian political, economic and cultural elite. Despite this, the number of direct borrowings from French remain limited, with most loanwords being internationalisms or transferred through German (Benkő 1978b).

1.4.3 *German influence*

The historical ties between German and Hungarian are crucial given German's role as an intermediary between Dutch and Hungarian. These linguistic connections trace back to the arrival of Hungarians in the Carpathian Basin (Mollay 1952). Cultural and linguistic exchange intensified during the early centuries of Hungary's Árpád dynasty, particularly with the adoption of Christianity and the establishment of the Kingdom of Hungary in 1001 under Stephen I. German (often Low-German) priests and knights settling in Hungary through dynastic ties were pivotal in this exchange. The German bourgeoisie played a central role in shaping medieval Hungarian cities and its economic life.

From the 12th century, German influence grew, especially with the influx of settlers into Hungary, including peasants migrating predominantly to Transylvania and the Szepes (Spiš) area (Protze 2006; Elst 2012). This period is characterized by a significant number of German loanwords, mainly concerning nobility, court life, and warfare. From the 16th century, German influence on Hungarian grew significantly for about three hundred years, surpassing any other linguistic or cultural influence. The political dominance of the House of Habsburgs extended over most of Hungary even during the Ottoman rule, and after the expulsion of the Turks, all Hungarian territories came under their control. The Holy Roman Empire created a direct border between the Low Countries and Hungary, and during the time of Austrian Netherlands (1715–1795) the southern parts of the Dutch language area and Hungary were part of the same empire. The prominence of German was further solidified during the 18th century with the influx of new German settlements for the reconstruction of the devastated areas. German became the lingua franca of the Habsburg Empire, declared as the exclusive official language in 1784 by Joseph II. Although his decree lasted only six years, it not only contributed to reducing the role of Latin as the language of administration and science, but also spurred the conscious development of the Hungarian standard language, which gradually acquired the status of an official language between 1790 and 1844. Despite its continuous decline during the 18th century, German retained its significance, particularly in Budapest and larger cities until World War I.

Approximately 400 loanwords in contemporary Hungarian vernacular originate from German, primarily from Middle Franconian and Bavarian-Austrian dialects (Benkő 1978b; Gerstner 2015; Mollay 1952).[7] German, alongside Latin, served as a cultural mediator between Western Europe and Hungary. Its geographical and linguistic continuum with Dutch made it the most significant intermediary language for loanwords from Western European languages, including Dutch (Kiss and Pusztai 2003, 190).

1.4.4 *Dutch–Hungarian cultural and linguistic contacts*

From the early days of Hungary's first ruling dynasty to contemporary times, Dutch and Hungarian speakers have engaged in interactions, occasionally involving broader groups during dynamic historical phases. While the lexical influence of Dutch on Hungarian is relatively modest compared to German or Slavic languages, it remains noteworthy. The scarcity of direct borrowings can mainly be ascribed to the limited scope and duration of direct interactions between the two linguistic communities, as well as the linguistic predominance of German as an intermediary language. In this section, I will briefly outline the major episodes in Dutch–Hungarian relations from their beginning to the present day.

Relations between the Low Countries and Hungary trace back to the 12th century. Although details from this early period are scarce, recent research indicates that during the reign of Géza II in the mid-12th century, a significant number of immigrants from the Low Countries settled in southeastern Hungary due to food shortages in their homeland (Pósán 2010; 2017). Among these settlers

7. While certain phonological criteria can help identify the specific German dialect from which a word was borrowed (e.g. Hungarian ***pór*** 'poor' (originally 'peasant') (1211) < Bavarian-Austrian German ***paur*** 'peasant' vs. Middle High German ***bûr*** 'peasant'), this is not always possible. Over a millennium of Hungarian-German language contact, several hundred German loanwords were borrowed from a wide variety of dialects and cultural contexts (Gerstner 2015).

were French-speaking Walloons and speakers of West Franconian dialects, as evidenced by the medieval placename *Borbánt*, derived from Du *Brabant* (Pósán 2017, 16; Elst 2012, 92).

In the early Middle Ages, trade networks linked the Low Countries, especially Flanders, with Hungary through established routes spanning Europe. Among the earliest records of such economic ties is a mention of Maastricht merchants traveling through Hungary around 1259 (Teszelszky 2012). These early trade connections seem to have facilitated the transfer of words like Hu *ganti/genti* (†) (1286) 'textile from Gent' [34] and Hu *dorni* (†) (1395) 'textile from Doornik' [23].

Throughout the later Middle Ages and particularly in the Early Modern era cultural ties intensified. Sigismund, Holy Roman Emperor and King of Hungary, welcomed several prominent Dutch scholars and clergy to Hungary during his reign (Bárány 2017). Mary of Hungary (1505–1558), Governor of the Habsburg Netherlands, wife of Louis II, is said to have learned Hungarian (Réthelyi 2010). Her personal secretary, Miklós Oláh (1493–1568) continued fostering cultural ties between the two regions upon his return to Hungary around 1542 (Köpeczi 1987). The first recorded Hungarian-Dutch diplomatic encounter occurred in 1606 between an envoy from the Hungarian monarch (Johannes Bocatius) and a Dutch envoy (Pieter van Brederode/Brederodius) (Teszelszky 2012).

Between the 17th and 18th centuries, Hungarian students' peregrination to the Netherlands marked a vibrant period in Dutch–Hungarian relations and language exchange. Over this approximately two-hundred-year period,[8] almost 3,000 Hungarian students attended Dutch universities in Leiden, Franeker, Harderwijk, Groningen, and Utrecht (Bozzay and Ladányi 2007; Ladányi 1987; varous chaptors in Pusztai Gábor and Bozzay Réka 2010).[9] Although Latin was the language of instruction, many students became proficient in Dutch, serving as cultural mediators upon their return. Notably, János Apáczai Csere (1625–1659), after studying extensively at Dutch universities (Franeker, Leiden, Utrecht and Harderwijk), published the most comprehensive scientific work of his time in Hungarian, the '*Hungarian Encyclopedia*'[10] in 1653 in Utrecht (Apáczai Csere 1653).[11] Miklós Misztótfalusi Kis (1650–1702) studied type-founding in Amsterdam

8. In fact, the peregrination of Hungarian students to Dutch universities started around 1575 and continued until the 1918, but the most significant period was during the 17th and 18th century, peaking in the mid-17th century (Bozzay and Ladányi 2007).

9. Catholic students from Hungary also studied in Flanders, but on a much smaller scale. During the 17th and 18th centuries only about 20 students are known to have attended the University of Leuven (Muzslay 2000)

10. With the exception of the Preface of the Encyclopedia and the concluding section containing Apáczai's treaties, which are in Latin, the majority of the book is written in Hungarian.

11. Apáczai married Aletta van der Maet, a Dutch bourgeois girl, with whom he moved to Hungary 1652 (Bellág 2010).

1680–1689 and published a Hungarian Bible in about 3500 copies (Haiman 1987; Jákó 1987). Students returning from the Netherlands often brought Dutch-language books back to Hungary, as did their Dutch wives (Csorba 2017).

It is impossible to quantify the full spectrum and extent of cultural exchange during this period. Nonetheless, it is evident that thousands of educated Hungarians acted as language mediators, facilitating the incorporation of Dutch words into Hungarian, mostly through German or Latin channels. Borrowed Dutch words from this period, possibly introduced by the peregrini, include Du *gomarist* 'Gomarist, follower of Francis Gomar' > Hu *gommarista* (†), *gomarista* 'Gomarist' (1626) [36] and Du *bisschop* > Hu *bischop (lé)* (†) 'bishop (drink); sweet alcoholic drink' [12].

During the 17th and 18th centuries, a shared anti-Habsburg sentiment and Protestant affiliations deepened political, diplomatic, and cultural bonds between (Eastern) Hungary and the Netherlands. A well-known symbol of these bonds was Admiral Michiel de Ruyter's liberation of 28 Hungarian Protestant preachers in 1676, previously expelled and enslaved by the Habsburg emperor (Pusztai 2017). Furthermore, Hungarian books were printed on Dutch presses, and alongside Latin works, several Dutch texts were translated into Hungarian (Eredics 2005). Notably, between 1645 and 1794, 10 Hungarian Bibles were published in the Netherlands, primarily based on Gáspár Károli's translation (Oláh 2017).[12] Recent research also highlights the intensive relations between the southern Low Countries and the Catholic regions of Hungary within the Habsburg Empire, an aspect often overlooked in literature (Monostori 2020).

In the early 19th century, Dutch–Hungarian cultural relations saw a decline, partly due to the Viennese government's prohibition on the education of Reformed students abroad in 1817 (Sivirsky 1987). Despite this, cultural ties persisted as the literary scene expanded and the press flourished. Travel accounts, press reports, and countless literary and scientific translations in both languages were produced by cultural mediators, such as Géza Antal and his wife Adéle Opzoomer (alias Wallis), who as bilinguals translated numerous important works into Hungarian (Gera and Nagy 2017; Sivirsky 1973).

A somewhat puzzling aspect of Dutch–Hungarian linguistic contact is the scarcity of language aids until the 20th century. Despite the significant presence of Hungarian students at Dutch universities, we can hardly find any glossaries[13] or

12. The substantial volume of Protestant publications in Hungarian was primarily attributable to the Van Alphen Fonds, which provided significant support for the dissemination of Protestant texts aimed at opposing the Habsburg recatholicization efforts (Bozzay 2022).

13. A notable exception is Christoph Warmer's booklet, published in Kassa (Košice, Kaschau) in 1691. The booklet features a brief grammatical description, conversations in everyday situations (e.g. 'at the inn', etc.), and a glossary in ten languages, including Dutch and Hungarian

language aids created by scholars, translators, or passionate bilinguals (Nagy and Réthelyi 2023). The absence of such resources could be attributed to the prevalence of intermediary languages like German, Latin and to some extent French, which served as primary mediators for Dutch loanwords entering Hungarian.

Between 1920 and 1930, the Child Transport Action sparked a significant shift. Following World War I and the Treaty of Trianon, Hungary's loss of territories (67%) and population (58%) pushed it to the edge of collapse. This led to widespread hardship, including a lack of public services, epidemics, and famine. In response, approximately 50,000 Hungarian children were sent to the Netherlands and Belgium as part of a humanitarian effort to aid their recovery (Aalders, Pusztai, and Réthelyi 2020; Perényi and Réthelyi 2023). Many quickly became fluent in Dutch and maintained the language even after their return through reading and correspondence with their host families. Prominent cultural mediators also participated in the Action as a child, including Antal Sivirsky, author of one of the first professional Duch–Hungarian, and a Hungarian–Dutch language book (Sivirsky 1957a; 1957b). This intensive social contact led to the creation of the first Dutch language resources in Hungary, from glossaries to professional language books (R. Nagy 2024a). Dutch–Hungarian relations saw a revival after World War II, with the reinitiation of the Child Transport Action in 1947–1948, again sending a few thousand children to the Netherlands and Belgium (Pusztai 2020). Also, during the Hungarian Revolution in 1956, some 3,500 Hungarian refugees arrived in the Netherlands and about twice as many in Belgium, many of whom settled in the Dutch-speaking areas. Throughout the latter half of the 20th century, the first professional Dutch dictionaries were published (R. Nagy 2024b). Despite the extensive interactions during the 20th century, only two words (*korfbal* [57] and *Bintje* [11]) seem to have been directly borrowed and integrated in the Hungarian lexicon.

In summary, Dutch–Hungarian cultural and linguistic contacts have been ongoing throughout history, marked by periods of intensive cultural and social interaction like the peregrination of Hungarian students to the Netherlands and the Child Transport Action. However, their direct impact on Hungarian vocabulary is less pronounced compared to major linguistic influences, like German. The borrowing of Dutch words generally occurred in two steps. (1) Borrowing into a language with a sufficiently intensive direct contact with Dutch, such as German or French. (2) The transfer of the original borrowing from the intermediary language into Hungarian with eventual adaptations.

(Warmer 1691; Szili 2016). It is an adaptation of Noël van Berlaimont's Dutch-French language aid, originally published in 1527 (Van der Sijs 2000; 2023).

2. Dutch words in Hungarian

2.1 General results

Table 2 summarizes the research findings in a succinct format. Column A lists the modern form of the Dutch source words. Column B outlines the etymology of the Dutch etymon using a shorthand, with alternative etymologies separated by a slash. Columns C and D provide the earliest Dutch forms alongside their meaning. The dates of the earliest attestations are sourced from the standard Dutch etymological works available at etymologiebank.nl, unless otherwise noted (*Etymologiebank.nl*). For controversial datings, the historical dictionaries in the *Geïntegreerd Taalbank* (GTB) were consulted. Column F categorizes the role of Dutch in the etymology of the Hungarian word into three options: (1) Dutch is the ultimate donor language (UD) of the Hungarian word where the Dutch word itself is not a loanword; (2) Dutch is an intermediary language (IM), if the word borrowed into Hungarian is itself a borrowing from another language; (3) it is uncertain (Unc.) whether the Hungarian word is derived from a Dutch or another source, such as Low German. Column G lists the intermediary language or languages between Dutch and Hungarian, with potential immediate source languages divided by a slash. This study does not attempt to reconstruct the precise sequence of intermediary languages. Columns H and I document the earliest and present-day Hungarian forms, respectively, with the earliest attestation in column J. The dates are based on standard Hungarian etymological and historical dictionaries (Szarvas and Simonyi 1890; Zolnai and Szamota 1902; Gombocz and Melich 1914; Bárczi 1994; TESz; EWUng; Tóthfalusi 2001; Zaicz 2006; 2021; ÚESzWeb), and historical corpora (MTSZ; MGTSZ; TMK; ADT). Revised attestations, such as Hu *dopping* 'doping' [25] (1905→1900) are underlined, with references provided in the footnotes. Columns K (still in use), L (technical or dialectal) and M (archaic) detail the contemporary distribution of the words in Hungarian. If a word is extinct, both K and M are marked 'Yes'. Column N represents the diffusion of the loanwords in modern Hungarian, expressed as frequency per million words in the Hungarian Gigaword Corpus (HGC).[14] Frequency was calculated based on the stem of each word in its relevant meaning, ensuring that derived and inflected forms, as well as compounds, were included in the analysis. Column O describes the meaning of the Hungarian form, and column P classifies the semantic fields, following the categorisation used by Van der Sijs's *Chronologisch woordenboek* and her other works (Van der Sijs 2001, chap. 1.2.6.; 2010; 2015; see also Hallig and Wartburg 1952).

---

14. The HGC comprises a representative selection of various registers, including journalism and transcribed spoken texts (Oravecz, Váradi, and Sass 2014), and contains 748,557,711 words in its latest version.

Table 2. Dutch loanwords in Hungarian[a]

Nr.	A	B	C	D	E	F	G	H	I	J	K	L	M	N	O	P[b]
	Present-day form in Dutch	Etymology	Earliest form of Dutch etymon	Relevant meaning in Dutch	Earliest record in Dutch	Position of Dutch in etymological lineage	Intermediary language(s)	Earliest form in Hungarian	Present-day form in Hungarian	Earliest attestation in Hungarian	Still in use	Technical/ Dialectal	Archaic	Frequency in HGC (per million words)	Relevant meaning in Hungarian	Semantic Field
1	*arminiaan (Arminius)*	Du<Lat	*arminiaan, (Arminius/J. Harmensen)*	Arminian *eponym*	1617	IM	G	*arminista*	*arminiánus*	1626[c]	Y	Y	N	0,028	remonstrant (follower of Jacobus Arminius)	8
2	*atlas*	Du<Gr	*attlas*	atlas (book)	1636	IM	G/Fr (int)	*atlás*	*atlasz*	1692	Y	N	N	3,639	atlas (book)	19
3	*bakeliet (Baekeland)*	Du	*bakeliet; (Baekeland)*	bakelite *eponym*	1908	UD	G/En (int)	*bakelit*	*bakelit*	1910	Y	Y	N	2,299	bakelite	19
4	*bagage*	Du<Fr	*baggaidge*	baggage	1470	IM	G	*pagasia/ bagasia*	*bagázs*	1644	Y	N	N	1,130	gang	9
5	*bamboe*	Du<Mal	*bambus*	bamboo	1598	IM	G/Fr (int)	*bambus-nád*	*bambusz*	1794	Y	N	N	2,479	bamboo	2
6	*Baptiste* (?)[d] (*batist* is a reborrowing through French)	Du/Fr	*Baptiste*	cambric *eponym*	13th c.	Unc.	G/Fr	*batis*	*batiszt*	1756	Y	N	N	0,297	cambric	9
7	*barnsteen* (?)	Du<LG	*bernsteen, barnsteen*	amber	1315	Unc.	G+Slav	*borostyán*	*borostyán*	1803	Y	N	N	2,680[e]	amber	1
8	*batik*	Du<Mal <Jav	*batik*	batik	1721	IM	G	*batik*	*batik*	1893	Y	N	N	0,620	batik	9
9	*baviaan*	Du<Fr	*babijn*	baboon	1450–1500	IM	G	*pávián*	*pávián*	1798	Y	N	N	1,066	baboon	3
10	*beurs*	Du<It (eponym)	*beurse*	stock exchange	1525	IM	G	*beurs*	*börze*	1793	Y	N	Y	10,579	stock exchange; in compouns: clearance, closeout, flee market	12
11	*bintje*	Du<Fri (<Lat)	*Bintje*	potato sort *eponym*	1910	IM	Du	*Bintje*	*Bintje*	1948[f]	Y	Y	N	0,003	Bintje (potato sort)	2

Table 2. *(continued)*

Nr.	A	B	C	D	E	F	G	H	I	J	K	L	M	N	O	P[b]
	Present-day form in Dutch	Etymology	Earliest form of Dutch etymon	Relevant meaning in Dutch	Earliest record in Dutch	Position of Dutch in etymological lineage	Intermediary language(s)	Earliest form in Hungarian	Present-day form in Hungarian	Earliest attestation in Hungarian	Still in use	Technical/ Dialectal	Archaic	Frequency in HGC (per million words)	Relevant meaning in Hungarian	Semantic Field
12	*bisschop(swijn)*	Du<Lat<Gr	*bisschop*	bishop (drink)	1778	IM	Du/En	*bischop (lé)*	(†)	1654 [g]	N	N	Y	0	bishop 'a certain alcoholic drink'	6
13	*boei*	Du/LG<Fr?	*boye*	floating object, buoy	1563	Unc.	G	*bója*	*bója*	1865	Y	N	N	1,196	buoy	11
14	*boer*	Du/Afr	*boer / buur*	farmer	1516 / 1280–87	UD	E/G/Afr	*boer*	*búr*	1842	Y	Y	N	1,719	Boer	8
15	*bolwerk*	Du(/HG)	*bolwerc*	fortification	1429	UD	Fr/G	*Boulevard*	*bulvár*	1824	Y	N	N	12,428	tabloid; boulevard	14
16	*Brabant*	Du/Cz	*Brabant drauant*	*toponym*; guardsman	1266–1267; 1515[h]	Unc.	G/Cz	*drabant*	*darabont, drabant*	1439	Y	Y	N	0,270	guardsman	14
17	*brik* (*brikett* is a reborrowing through French)	Du<Fr<Du	*bricke*	broken piece; brick	1282	IM	Fr/G/En (int)	*briquette*	*brikett*	1862 [i]	Y	Y	N	0,815	id	9
18	*Brugge*	Du	*Brugga*	*toponym*	840–875	UD	G?	*byrkös*	(†)	1522	N	Y	Y	0	textile made in Brugge	9
19	– (*cabaret* is a reborrowing through French)	Du<Fr(Pic)<Lat	*cambret*	pub	1360	IM	Fr/G (int)	*cabaret*	*kabaré*	1842 [j]	Y	N	N	7,847	cabaret	9
20	*chocolade*	Du<Sp<Nah	*chocolate/ choqolata*	chocolate	1644/ 1662	IM	G (int)	*csukorlaté/ csukaladi*	*csokoládé (csoki)*[k]	1699	Y	N	N	16,218 (19,158)	chocolate	6
21	*dek* (?)	Du (<meaning En)	*ouer-deck*	deck, covered area	1287	Unc.	En/G	*overdeck*	*dekk* (n.) *dekkol* (v.)[l]	1897 [m]	Y	Y	N	0,858	deck (of a ship); lie low	11
22	*dok*	Du/LG (<Lat?)	*docke*	harbour, dock	1525	Unc.	En/G	*dock*	*dokk*	1825	Y	Y	N	1,821	dock (n.) (for a ship) dock (v.)	11

Table 2. *(continued)*

Nr.	A	B	C	D	E	F	G	H	I	J	K	L	M	N	O	P[b]
	Present-day form in Dutch	Etymology	Earliest form of Dutch etymon	Relevant meaning in Dutch	Earliest record in Dutch	Position of Dutch in etymological lineage	Intermediary language(s)	Earliest form in Hungarian	Present-day form in Hungarian	Earliest attestation in Hungarian	Still in use	Technical/ Dialectal	Archaic	Frequency in HGC (per million words)	Relevant meaning in Hungarian	Semantic Field
23	*Doornik*	Du(<Kelt)	*dornetus, doarnetus*	*toponym*	1294–1295	UD	Lat/G	*dorni, darni, darnit*	(†)	1395/1405	N	Y	Y	0	textile made in Doornik (Tournai)	9
24	*doos*	Du	*dose*	box, chest	1361	UD	G	*dózni*	*dózni*	1932	N	N	Y	0,085	cigarett box	9
25	*doop(en)* (*doping* is a reborrowing through English)	Du	*dopen*	immerse; thick sauce	1240; 1623	UD	En/G (int)	*doping*	*dopping*	1900 [n]	Y	N	N	22,923	doping	22
26	*dribbel(en)*	Du/E	*dribbelen*	move with small steps	1384	Unc.	G/En	*dribliz* (v.), *dribli* (n.)	*dribliz* (v.), *dribli* (n.)	1899	Y	Y	Y	0,044	dribble (n./v.)	22
27	*duin*	Du<Kelt	*dunos*	dune	887	IM	G	*dűne(n)*	*dűne*	1830	Y	N	N	1,944	dune	1
28	*Edam(mer)*	Du	*Aedamme*	toponym	1725 [o]	UD	G	*edami (sajt)*	*e(i)dámi*	1814	Y	N	Y	0,135	Edam (cheese)	6
29	*stek(en)* (*etiket* is a reborrowing through French)	Fr/Du?	*stekan*	poke	1180	Unc.	G/Fr	*etiquette*	*etikett*	1787	Y	N	N	1,824	sticker, etiquette	9
30	*flint*	Du	*flint(e)*	flint; flintlock	1288/ 1594 [p]	UD	Du/G	*flinta*	*flinta*	1681	Y	Y	Y	0,115	flintlock	14
31	*floers*	Du<Fr?	*floers*	black transparent fabric	1336–39	Unc.	G/Fr	*flor*	*flór*	1704	N	Y	Y	0,013	lisle	9
32	*garnaal*	Du<(Lat?)	*gernaet*	shrimp	1514	Unc.	G	*garnát/ garnéla*	*garnéla*	1869 [q]	Y	Y	N	0,741	shrimp	3
33	*gas*	Du	*gas*	gas	1648	UD	G (int)	*gáz*	*gáz*	1789	Y	N	N	75,839	gas	19
34	*Gent*	Du	*Gent*	*toponym*	941	UD	Du/G	*ganti/genti*	(†)	1286/1344	N	N	Y	0	textile made in Gent	9

Table 2. *(continued)*

Nr.	A	B	C	D	E	F	G	H	I	J	K	L	M	N	O	P[b]
	Present-day form in Dutch	Etymology	Earliest form of Dutch etymon	Relevant meaning in Dutch	Earliest record in Dutch	Position of Dutch in etymological lineage	Intermediary language(s)	Earliest form in Hungarian	Present-day form in Hungarian	Earliest attestation in Hungarian	Still in use	Technical/ Dialectal	Archaic	Frequency in HGC (per million words)	Relevant meaning in Hungarian	Semantic Field
35	*kolf* (*golf* is a reborrowing through English)	Du	*kolf*	club, cudgel	1360	UD	En/G (int)	*golf*	*golf*	1829	Y	N	N	7,840	golf (game)	22
36	*gomarist (Gomaer)*	Du	*gomarist*	Gomarist *eponym*	1618	UD	G/Lat	*gommarista*	*gomarista*	1626 [r]	Y	Y	Y	0,011	Gomarist	8
37	*Gouda (kaas)*	Du	*Gouda*	Gouda cheese *toponym*	1811[s]	UD	G	*gouda-sajt*	*gouda-(sajt)*	1881 [t]	Y	N	N	0,045	Gouda (cheese)	6
38	*hanter(en)*	Du<Fr<ON	*hanter(en)*	make use of	1265–70	IM	G	*hontiroz*	*hantál/ hantázik* (v.) *hanta* (n.)	1782	Y	N	N	0,215	(talk) gibberish	9
39	*hap(pen)* (?)	Du/(L)G<Fr	*hap(pen)*	bite	1588	Unc.	G	*happol*	*(el)happol*	1881	Y	N	N	0,597	seize, snatch	4
40A	*Holland*	Du	*Holtlant*	Holland *toponym*	918–948	UD	Lat (int)	*holandus*	*holland*	1533	Y	N	N	77,152	Dutch; Holland	4
40B					918–948	UD	G	*hollandi (csavar/ anya)*	*hollandi (anya)*	1878 [u]	Y	Y	N	0,009	flare nut	13
41	*Hottentot*	Du<Kho	*khoikhoin*	Hottentot *ethnonym*	1652	IM	G (int)	*hottentóta*	*hottentotta*	1757	Y	Y	Y	0,223	Hottentot	4
42	*jacht*	Du	*jacht-schip*	fastmoving vessel	1528	UD	G (int)	*jagt*	*jacht*	1694	Y	N	N	2,666	yacht	11
43	*Jan, Jan Kees* (*jenki* is a reborrowing through English)	Du<Lat<Gr<Hebr	*Jan/Jan-Kees*	eponym	1254	UD	En/G	*Yankee*	*jenki*	1831	Y	Y	N	1,202	Yankee	4

Table 2. *(continued)*

Nr.	A	B	C	D	E	F	G	H	I	J	K	L	M	N	O	P[b]
	Present-day form in Dutch	Etymology	Earliest form of Dutch etymon	Relevant meaning in Dutch	Earliest record in Dutch	Position of Dutch in etymological lineage	Intermediary language(s)	Earliest form in Hungarian	Present-day form in Hungarian	Earliest attestation in Hungarian	Still in use	Technical/ Dialectal	Archaic	Frequency in HGC (per million words)	Relevant meaning in Hungarian	Semantic Field
44	*juwelier*	Du/LG<Fr	*juwelier jueel*	jeweller	1481/ 1265–1270	Unc.	Du/LG	*jubelir*	(†)	1625	N	N	Y	0	jeweller	12
45	*kabel*	Du<Fr	*cabel/câble*	cable	1285–1286	IM	G (int)	*kábel*	*kábel*	1867	Y	N	N	33,945	cable	9
46	*kabeljauw*	Du	*cabellauw(i)*	codfish	1163	UD	Du/G	*kábeljan* [v]	(†)	1783	N	Y	Y	0	codfish	3
47	*kajuit*	Du<Fr	*voorkayhute*	cabin	1455	IM	G (int)	*kájut*	*kajüt*	1789	Y	Y	N	0,381	cabin	11
48	*kaketoe*	Du<Mal	*kakketou*	cockatoo	1654	IM	G (int)	*kaketu*	*kakadu*	1693	Y	N	N	0,505	cockatoo	3
49	*kant*	Du<Fr (Pic?)<Lat	*cant*	side, edge	1221	IM	G	*kantni*	*kantni*	1859	Y	Y	N	0,020	edge (of a ski)	9
50	*katoen*	Du<Ar	*cotoen*	cotton	1272	IM	G (int)	*karton*	*karton*	1612	Y	Y	N	8,332	cotton	9
51	*kazuaris*	Du<Mal	*kazuar*	cassowary	(1597?) 1726 [w]	IM	G (int)	*kauzár* (sic!)[x]	*kazuár*	1628	Y	Y	N	0,148	cassowary	3
52	*kleed* (?)	Du/LG	*cleet*	clothe	1220–1240	Unc.	Du/LG	*kleder*	(†)	1625	N	N	Y	0	garb	9
53	*kleinood* (?)	Du/LG	*cleinode*	jewel, trinket	1240	Unc.	Du/LG	*cleinodia/ cleinod*	(†)	1619	N	N	Y	0	jewel, trinket	9
54	*klink(en)*	Du	*clink(en)/cling(en)*	cling; click	1285	UD	Fr (Pic)	*kelinch*	*kilincs*	1405	Y	N	N	6,752	door handle	9
55	*klomp(en)*	Du	*clompe*	clump; clogs	1377/1567[y]	UD	G	*klumpa*	*klumpa*	1847	Y	N	N	0,194	clogs	9
56	*koffer*	Du<Ofr<Lat<Gr	*cover*	chest	1285	IM	G	*kufer*	*koffer*	1757	Y	N	N	1,980	suitcase	9
57	*korfbal*	Du	*korfbal*	korfbal	1903	UD	Du/En (int)	*korfball*	*korfbal(l)*	1922 [z]	Y	N	N	0,279	korfball	22
58	*korvet*	Du<Fr<Du<Fr (Pic)	*korvet / corver*	herringboat	1445	IM	Fr/G/It (int)	*corvette*	*korvett*	1793 [aa]	N	Y	Y	0,391	corvet	11
59	*lakmoes*	Du	*lecmoes*	litmus	1252	UD	G (int)	*lakmus*	*lakmusz*	1788	Y	Y	N	0,378	lacmus	19
60	*laver(en)*	Du	*louer(en)*	navigate, zigzag	1328–1350	UD	G	*lavéroz*	*laviroz*	1706	Y	N	N	1,524	manoeuvre	11
61	*lever(en)*	Du<Fr<Lat	*lever(en)*	deliver	1249	IM	G	*liferál* (v.) *liferáns*, *liferántos* (n.)	*liferál* (v.) *liferáns* (n.)	1790	Y	Y	Y	0,035	deliver; supplier	13

Table 2. *(continued)*

Nr.	A	B	C	D	E	F	G	H	I	J	K	L	M	N	O	P[b]
	Present-day form in Dutch	Etymology	Earliest form of Dutch etymon	Relevant meaning in Dutch	Earliest record in Dutch	Position of Dutch in etymological lineage	Intermediary language(s)	Earliest form in Hungarian	Present-day form in Hungarian	Earliest attestation in Hungarian	Still in use	Technical/ Dialectal	Archaic	Frequency in HGC (per million words)	Relevant meaning in Hungarian	Semantic Field
62A	*lot(erij)*	Du<Fr<Du	*loterye/loting*	lottery, game of chance	1446/1363	UD	G/Fr (int)	*lottéria*	*lottéria*	1770	Y	N	Y	0,021	lottery	22
62B						UD	G (Bav) (int)	*lutri*	*lutri*	1787	Y	N	Y	0,741	lottery; chance	22
62C						UD	It (int)	*lotto*	*lottó*	1787	Y	N	N	7,934	lottery	22
63	*matroos*	Du	*maetroos*	sailor	1584	UD	G (int)	*matrosz*	*matróz*	1763	Y	N	N	4,372	sailor	11
64	*mennoniet*	Du	*mennoniet (Menno Simonsz)*	Mennonite *eponym*	1578	UD	En/Lat/G (int)	*mennonita*	*mennonita*	1793[bb]	Y	Y	N	0,160	mennonite	8
65	*mof*	Du<Fr	*mof(fel)*	muff	1540	IM	G	*muff*	*muff*	1833	Y	N	Y	0,386	muff (inf.: female genital)	9
66	*orang-oetan(g)*	Du<Mal	*orang (h)utan*	orangutan	1652	IM	G (int)	*urang utang*	*orangután*	1783	Y	Y	N	0,510	orangutan	3
67	*orkaan*	Du<Sp<Ta	*uracaen*	hurricane	1644	IM	G	*orkán*	*orkán*	1794	Y	N	N	1,759	hurricane	1
68A	*pak*	Du	*pac*	bundle, pack	1159–1164	UD	G	*pak(k)*	*pak(k)*	1787	Y	N	N	21,409	luggage, package	9
68B						UD	Fr/G	*pakéta*	*pakét(a)*	1656	Y	N	Y	0,020	pack, packet	9
68C						UD	G (Bav-Aust)	*pakli*	*pakli*	1765	Y	N	N	3,644	pack (of cards); packet	22
68D						UD	G+It	*paksaméta*	*paksaméta*	1799	Y	N	N	0,707	a bundle of documents	9
69	*palissander*	Du<Sp (<Guy)	*palissantenhout*	rosewood	1658	IM	G/Fr	*palissandre*	*paliszander*	1844	Y	Y	N	0,108	rosewood	2
70	*Papoea* (?)	En/Du<Mal	*papoea*	Papuan	1847	Unc.	En	*pápuán(us)*	*pápua*	1793[cc]	Y	Y	N	0,395	Papuan	4
71	*passaat*	Du<Port	*passage-wint*	trade wind	1596	IM	G	*passátszél*	*passzát(szél)*	1835	Y	Y	N	1,365	trade wind	1
72	*pastei*	Du<Fr	*pasteyde*	pâté	1240	IM	G	*pastetom*	*pástétom*	1601	Y	N	N	0,510	pâté	6
73A	*piek*	Du	*pike, piec(k)*	pike, lance	1275–1276	IM	Fr/It	*Pÿka*	*pika*	1546	Y	Y	N	0,166	pike, lance	14
73B				pointed object	1275–1276	IM	Fr	*pik*	*pikk*	1749	Y	N	N	0,486	spade (card)	22

Table 2. *(continued)*

Nr.	A Present-day form in Dutch	B Etymology	C Earliest form of Dutch etymon	D Relevant meaning in Dutch	E Earliest record in Dutch	F Position of Dutch in etymological lineage	G Intermediary language(s)	H Earliest form in Hungarian	I Present-day form in Hungarian	J Earliest attestation in Hungarian	K Still in use	L Technical/ Dialectal	M Archaic	N Frequency in HGC (per million words)	O Relevant meaning in Hungarian	P[b] Semantic Field
74	*plakkaat*	Du<Fr<Du	*plackaet*	poster	1414	UD	G	*placat*	*plakát*	1831	Y	N	N	27,120	poster	9
75	*polder*	Du	*polra/polre*	polder, drained land	1130–1161	UD	G	*polder*	*polder*	1816 [dd]	Y	Y	N	0,102	polder	1
76A	*pomp*	Du<G/Port/ Sp(<Lat?)	*pomp*	pump	1463	IM	G	*pumpol*	*pumpa*	1792	Y	N	N	8,156	pump	13
76B						IM	G	*pumpol*	*pumpol* [ee]	1866	Y	N	N	0,210	tap sb for money	9
77	*Poperinge* (*popeline* is a reborrowing through French)	Du	*Pupurninga*	*toponym*	844–864	UD	Fr/G	*puplin*	*puplin*	1841	Y	Y	N	0,065	poplin	9
78	*remonstrant*	Du<Lat	*remonstrant*	Remonstrant, follower of Jacobus Arminius	1536	IM	Lat/G	*remonstráns*	*remonstráns*	1792 [ff]	Y	Y	N	0,021	remonstrant, follower of Jacobus Arminius	8
79	*schok* (?)	Du/LG (<Fr?)	*schockelen/ schocken*	shake	1494/1562	Unc.	Fr/G/En (int)	*choc*	*sokk* (n.) *sokol* (v.)	1865	Y	N	N	16,414	shock	9
80	*schrappen/ schrapen* [gg]	Du/G	*sc(h)rapen sc(h)rappen sc(h)repen*	scratch, scrape	1367 1285 1350–1397	Unc.	G	*sarab(ol)*	*sarab(ol)* [hh]	1830	Y	Y	Y	0,147	hoe weed	9
81A	*sleep* (?)	Du/LG	*sleyp*	train (of a dress); retinue	1390–1410 [ii]	Unc.	G	*sleppes*	*slepp*	1789	Y	N	Y	0,580	train (of a dress); retinue	9
81B						Unc.	G	*sleifni*	*slejfni*	1885	N	N	Y	0,013	band, strip	9
82	*soja*	Du<Jap	*soya*	soy	1670	IM	G (int)	*Sója (bab)*	*szója*	1876	Y	N	N	1,352	soy	6
83	*stellage*	Du	*stallaghe*	stand, showcase, rack	1338	UD	G	*stellásy*	*stelázsi*	1774	Y	Y	Y	0,182	rack	16

Table 2. *(continued)*

Nr.	A	B	C	D	E	F	G	H	I	J	K	L	M	N	O	P[b]
	Present-day form in Dutch	Etymology	Earliest form of Dutch etymon	Relevant meaning in Dutch	Earliest record in Dutch	Position of Dutch in etymological lineage	Intermediary language(s)	Earliest form in Hungarian	Present-day form in Hungarian	Earliest attestation in Hungarian	Still in use	Technical/ Dialectal	Archaic	Frequency in HGC (per million words)	Relevant meaning in Hungarian	Semantic Field
84	*stilleven*	Du	*stilleven*	still life	1718–1721[jj]	UD	G (calque)	*csendélet*	*csendélet*	1832	Y	N	N	2,000	still life	16
85	*stofferen*	Du<Fr	*stofferen*	to dress	1430	IM	G	*stafíroz* (v.) *stafirung* (n.)	*stafíroz* (v.)[kk] *stafirung* (n.)	1766	Y	N	Y	1,248	(provide) dowry	9
86	*stokvis*	Du<(LG?)	*stocvisch*	stockfish	1388	Unc.	G (calque)	*toekehal*	*tőkehal*	1604	Y	Y	N	1,264	stockfish	6
87	*thee*	Du<Mal<Chin	*té, tee*	tea	1637	IM	G (int)	*thé*	*tea* (n.)	1664	Y	N	N	35,220	tea; drink tea	6
88	*tuchthuis*	Du<G	*tuchthuis*	correctional facility, prison	1602	IM	G (calque)	*fegyház*	*fegyház*	1808	Y	Y	N	6,378	correctional facility, prison	15
89	*tulp*	Du<Turk	*tulipa, tulp*	tulip	1581	IM	It/G (int)	*tulipa*	*tulipán*	1646	Y	N	N	3,529	tulip	2
90	*watten*	Du<Fr/Lat	*watten*	cotton wool	1655	IM	G	*vatta*	*vatta*	1828	Y	N	N	3,181	cotton wool	9

a. Abbreviations of languages in the table:
Afr=Afrikaans, **Ar**=Arabic, **Bav-Aust**=Bavarian-Austrian German, **Chin**=Chinese, **Cz**=Czech, **Du**=Dutch, E=English, **Fr**=French, **G**=German, **Gr**=Greek, **H**=Hungarian, **Hebr**=Hebrew, **It**=Italian, **Jap**=Japanese, **Kelt**=Keltic, **Kho**=Khoisan, **LG**=Low German, **Mal**=Malay, **Nah**=Nahuatl, **ON**=Old Norse **Pic**=Picard, **Port**=Portuguese, **Slav**=Slavic, **Sp**=Spanish, **Ta**=Taino, **Turk**=Turkish
b. Codes of semantic fields:

1 earth	7 time	13 work and industry	19 science
2 plant kingdom	8 religion	14 army	20 linguistics
3 animal kingdom	9 social life	15 government	21 communication
4 human world	10 mobility	16 art	22 sport and games
5 senses	11 maritime	17 literature	
6 consumption	12 trade	18 music	

c. (Káldi 1626)
d. The question mark (?) indicates words that are presumed to be of Dutch origin, but whose exact etymology remains unclear due to the possibility of another language as a potential source.
e. A total of 2,026 hits were recorded; no attempt was made to distinguish between the meanings 'ivy' and 'amber', so the results reflect the overall diffusion of the form *borostyán*.
f. (Cséry 1948)
g. (Miskolci C. 1654)
h. First record in the meaning 'guardsman'.
i. (Tóth 1862)
j. (Erdélyi 1842)
k. *Csoki* is an informal variant of *csokoládé*, formed through truncation and the addition of the diminutive suffix *-i*.
l. Informal Hu *dekkol* 'lie low, bide one's time' is a derivation of *dekk* with the denominal verbal suffix *-ol*. The meaning of the word has undergone metaphorical shift from 'remain under the deck' to 'lie low'.
m. (Cholnoky 1897)
n. ('Körültekintés' 1900)
o. First record as placename: 1342–1343
p. First record in the meaning 'flintlock' (WNT, s.v. *vlinte*)
q. (Kreisch 1869)
r. (Káldi 1626)
s. Fist record as placename: 1143
t. (Hauer 1881)
u. ('A Csőkarimák És Hollandi Csavarkötések (Flantschen Und Holländer-Verschraubungen) Biztosítása.' 1878)
v. Probably a printing error (*u* vs. *n*). Later forms show the regular spelling with *-u*.
w. The first source is from 1726, but according to the quotation the Dutch had brought the bird to Amsterdam in 1597 (WNT s.v. *kazuaris*).
x. The metathesis is probably a typo.
y. First record in the meaning 'clogs, wooden shoes'
z. (E. Nagy 1922)
aa. (D. Decsy 1793, 102)
bb. (Broughton and Mindszenti 1793)
cc. ('I. Némelly Nevezetes Emberekről Emlékeztetés, Betü-Rend-Szerént. II-Dik Betü-Rend' 1793)
dd. (Hübner 1816a, 327)
ee. Hu *pumpol* 'tap sb for money', originally 'pump (v.)' is a derivation of *pump* with the denominal verbal suffix *-ol*.
ff. (Mindszenti 1792, 152)
gg. All three forms are strikingly similar in form and meaning ('scratch, scrape'), and thus derive from the same (onomatopoeic) root, Gmc **skrapōn-*. The form with *-e-* seems to be the result of Ablaut (EWN, s.v. *schrapen*).
hh. Hu *sarabol* is a deriviation of *sarab* 'sharp tool for cutting weeds' with denominal verbal suffix *-ol*. The noun *sarab* may on the other hand may itself be a back-formation of German *schrabben* 'scrape'.
ii. MNW s.v. *beestelijc, beestelike*
jj. (Sijs 1998)
kk. The form *sta(f)fíroz* derives from an unattested nominal stem **sta(f)fír* with the Hungarian denominal verbal suffix *-oz*. This stem potentially originates from the noun *sta(f)fírung* with the removal of the German suffix *-ung* through back-formation.

Ninety Dutch lexemes have been borrowed into Hungarian throughout history. Since six of them were borrowed in more than one meaning and/or in different forms (*Holland* [40AB], *loterij* [62A-C], *pak* [68A-D], *piek* [73AB], *pomp* [76AB] and *sleep* [81AB]) there are in total 99 Hungarian words derived from them. The majority of Dutch loanwords is still in contemporary usage in Hungarian. Out of the 99 Hungarian words, 87 persist in modern Hungarian, while 12 have become extinct, such as Du *kleinood* 'jewel, trinket' > Hu *cleinod* (†) 'jewel, trinket' [53]. Thirty-nine words are exclusively used in technical language or non-standard varieties, such as Du *kant* 'side, edge' > Hu *kantni* 'edge (of a ski)' [49]. Twelve words, though still in use, are considered archaic, e.g. Du *stofferen* > Hu *staffiroz* (v.) and *staffirung* (n.)[15] '(provide) dowry' [85].

The frequency distribution of Dutch loanwords in contemporary Hungarian provides insights into the general historical sociolinguistic context of their integration. The five loanwords with the highest frequencies, such as Hu *holland* 'Dutch' [40A] (77.1520 per million words), Hu *gáz* 'gas' [33] (75.8390), and Hu *csokoládé* (and its informal variant Hu *csoki* 'chocolat') [20] (35.3760), Hu *tea* 'tea' [87] and Hu *kábel* 'cable' [45] are international words with widely recognized and frequently used meanings. In contrast, loanwords with the lowest frequency, such as hu *Bintje* 'Bintje (potato sort)' [11] (0.0030) and Hu *hollandi (csavar)* 'union connection' [40B] (0.009), Hu *gom(m)arista* 'Gomarist' [36] (0.011) are associated with more specialized contexts. Overall, the distribution underscores how frequency correlates with broader cultural and societal relevance.

Eight Dutch toponyms have been borrowed into Hungarian, namely: *Brabant, Brugge, Doornik, Edam, Gent, Gouda, Holland, Poperinge.* All these were genericized into common nouns through metonymy, whereby the product associated with the given place replaces the placename as reference. The dissemination of these words can be associated with the technological and economic (trade) influence of the Low Countries.

Four of the Hungarian words refer to textiles imported from Flanders during the golden age of the Flemish textile industry, with three of them being one of the oldest loanwords in the list: Hu *byrkös* (†) (1522) < Du *Brugge* [18], Hu *dorni* (†) (1395/1405) < Du *Doorinik* [23], *ganti/genti* (†) (1286) < Du *Gent* [34], all having the meaning of 'textile produced at the given place'. Hu *puplin* 'poplin' is a later borrowing from the 19th century (1841) originally derived from Du *Poperinge* [77].

Gouda and *Edam* became well-known in Europe for their cheese, and the names of both cities were transferred to their products, which were then bor-

15. The form *staffíroz* derives from an unattested nominal stem **staffír* with the Hungarian denominal verbal suffix *-oz*. This stem potentially originates from the noun *staffírung* with the removal of the German suffix *-ung* through back-formation.

rowed into Hungarian through German: Hu *e(i)dámi* (1814) < Du *Edam* [28], Hu *gouda* (1881) < Du *Gouda* [37].[16]

The Dutch toponym *Holland* 'Holland' was metonymically associated in German with several technical innovations, some of which were transferred into Hungarian. One such term, the 'union connection', used for connecting water pipes was borrowed into Hungarian as *hollandi (kötés)* [40B], but through ellipsis it lost its nominal element and is now used as a noun referring mostly to a 'flare nut'. Hu *darabont* 'guardsman' (1439) is most probably directly borrowed from German and is ultimately derived from the toponym *Brabant* [16] (Mollay 1982, 222 ff.; cf. Latin *brabantio* '(looting) mercenary' ÚESzWeb s.v. *darabont*).[17]

The table includes seven eponyms derived from personal names: *(Jacobus) Arminius* [1], *(Leo Hendrik) Baekeland* [3], *(Jean) Baptiste* [6], *Bintje* [11], *(François) Gomaer* [36], *Jan (Kees)* [43], *Menno (Simonsz)* [64]. Three religious terms were adopted during the 17th and 18th centuries, a period marked by flourishing Dutch–Hungarian relations. Hu *arminista* (†) 'Arminian' (1626) < Du *arminiaan* 'Arminian' [1] and Hu *gom(m)arista* (1626) 'Gomarist' < Du *gomarist* 'Gomarist' [36] were introduced in the lectures of György Káldy (1573–1634), a 17th century Hungarian Catholic Bible translator, in his Bible translation from 1626 (Káldi 1626); Hu *mennonita* 'Mennonite' (1793) < Du *mennoniet* 'Mennonite' [64] was first recorded in the Hungarian translation of Thomas Broughton's *An historical dictionary of all religions* by the reformed minister Sámuel Mindszenti (Broughton and Mindszenti 1793), indicating that the word was introduced in Hungarian through English. Hu *jenki* 'Yankee' (1831) [43], from the Dutch first names *Jan* and/or *Jan Kees* (Van der Sijs 2009) is an international loanword, borrowed through English and/or German. Hu *batiszt* (1756) [6] is probably derived from the name *Baptiste* of a weaver in Kamerijk during the 13th century (ÚESzWeb, s.v. *batiszt*; EWN, s.v. *batist*; Van der Sijs 2010, 25), although alternative derivations suggest it comes from Fr *battre* 'to bray' (Kluge and Seebold 2011, s.v. *Batist*; TLFi, s.v. *batiste*). Following Van der Sijs's approach, I have recorded the word as a potential Dutch loanword, denoted with a question mark.

Hungarian *bakelit* 'Bakelite' < Du *bakeliet* 'Bakelite' [3] represents a unique case. The new plastic sort is named after its inventor, Leo Hendrik Arthur Baekeland (1863–1944), who himself used the name *bakeliet* a year before the material

16. Although both words are derived from placenames, Hungarian *edami* (*sajt*) is a derived with the adjective-forming suffix *-i*, whereas *gouda* remains underived (cf. Hungarian *hágai* 'from/of the Hague'). One possible explanation is that *gouda* was interpreted as a common noun rather than a toponym.

17. An alternative derivation is from Czech *drabant* 'guardsman' (ÚESzWeb, s.v. *darabont*; EWN s.v. *trawant*).

was first marketed in 1909 in the U.S. (EWN, s.v. *bakeliet*; Van der Sijs 2010, 26, 190 f.). The name itself is derived from his family name and the suffix *-iet*, generally used for material names in chemistry. Through German, the word was already borrowed into Hungarian in 1910 and even an entire article was published on the possible uses of Bakelite in a professional journal (ÚESzWeb, s.v. *bakelit*; Pfeiffer and Péter 1910).

2.2 Direct vs. indirect loans and Dutch as ultimate vs. intermediary source

It is often impossible to determine with certainty from which language or (dia)lect a Dutch word has entered Hungarian. In other words, multiple competing languages come into play as potential direct sources of transmission. Figure 1 summarises the results concerning the intermediary languages between Dutch and Hungarian. The letter 'X' represents any of the intermediary languages mentioned in Table 2. Competing intermediary languages are separated by 'and/or', indicating that the transmission could have taken place separately or even in parallel.

The list contains 10 Hungarian words ('Dutch+Dutch and/or X') that could potentially be identified as direct borrowings from Dutch: *Bintje* 'Bintje (potato sort)' [11], *bischop (lé)* 'bishop (a certain alcoholic drink)' [12], *flinta* 'flintlock' [30], *ganti/genti* 'textiel from Gent' [34], *jubelir/jubiler* 'jeweller' [44], *kabeljan* (sic.) 'codfish' [46], *kleder* 'garb' [52], *cleinod(ia)* 'jewel, trinket' [53], *korfbal* 'korfball' [57] and *polder* 'polder' [75]. In the subsequent passages, I will delve into a more detailed analysis of these words.

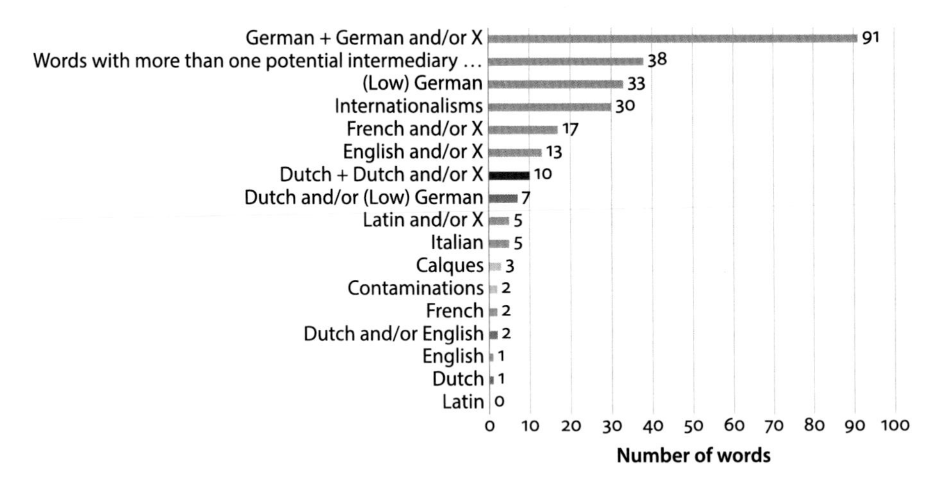

Figure 1. Dutch loanwords in Hungarian categorized by intermediary language plotted in descending order, including the number of calques and contaminations (X represents any of the intermediary languages in Table 2),

The potato variety *Bintje* was bred by the Frisian schoolmaster Kornelis Lieuwes de Vries in 1904 and named after one of his former students. It was first marketed in 1910 ('Bintje' 2023; EWN, s.v. *bintje*; Walker 1994). The name and the variety itself were directly imported from the Netherlands in 1948, when 500 wagons of Dutch *Bintje* potatoes were transported to Hungary in an effort to revive Hungarian agriculture, which had suffered severely from an epidemic (Cséry 1948). Linguistically, *Bintje* is remarkable as the only word in the list that is unquestionably borrowed directly from Dutch. In all other instances, German may have served as intermediary source. It may be coincidental, but it is worth noting that 1948 was the year when the last train carrying Hungarian children departed for the Netherlands as part of the revived Child Transport Action (Pusztai 2020). This suggests that Dutch–Hungarian relations, established during the earlier Child Transport Actions, remained rather strong even after World War II, until the communist takeover.

Hu *korfbal(l)* 'korfball' (1922) < Du *korfbal* 'korfball' [57] may also represent a case of direct borrowing. The original spelling of the first record with double *-ll* might reflect English influence, however, the word is first recorded in a letter of an 18-year-old Hungarian girl who was taken to Groningen to participate in the Child Transport Action (see 1.4.4). In her letter, published in a newspaper, she describes her holiday in the Netherlands, notably mentioning playing *korfball* (E. Nagy 1922).

Hu *polder* 'polder' < Du *polder* 'polder' [75] is first documented in a Hungarian lexicon of geographical names dating back to 1814 (Hübner 1816a, 327; 1816b, 138). The dictionary provides a description of a polder (*Beckmeir*) in Holland and another in Belgium (*Klundert*). Both entries refer distinctly to Dutch geographical names, indicating a direct adoption of the word *polder* in connection with these locations.

Given the context of the first record of the word in Hungarian, it seems likely that Du *bis(s)chop* 'bishop (alcoholic drink)' [12] was directly borrowed during the 17th century. Gáspár Miskolci Csulyak (Miskolci C. Caspar) was a Protestant student in Utrecht and later in Franeker, where he published a book (pamphlet) against Puritanism (Ágoston 2005). In his Hungarian pamphlet, he uses the word in the compound *bischop lé* (lit. 'bishop drink') with reference to a drink from which certain people had drunk more than enough to claim that the division within the Protestant Church of England had been caused by the episcopacy (Miskolci C. 1654).[18] This attestation is almost a hundred years before the first written record of the word with the relevant meaning in English (1738) (OED, s.v.

18. For more details on what exactly *bischop lé* could have been, see (Buchheister 1914, para. 55; Gombocz and Melich 1914, s.v. *bisop-lé*; Magyary-Kossa 1929, 186)

bishop) and more than a hundred years before it appears in Dutch sources (1768) (EWN, s.v. *bisschop*; WNT, s.v. *bisschop* II; NEW, s.v. *bisschop*). Although the word refers to an English context, it is very likely that, as opposed to the assumed German and/or English origin in etymological dictionaries, the word here is a direct borrowing from Dutch. This is supported by the early date of the record, with the Dutch spelling <sch> instead of <sh>. Miskolci studied in the Netherlands and published his book there, and also refers to his sources as "writings of trustworthy Belgian doctors" (Horváth 1978, 43).

There are six other cases where the immediate donor language from which the Hungarian word was borrowed may have been Dutch, or possibly a related Low German dialect: Hu *flinta* 'flintlock' (1681) < Du *flint(e)* 'flint' [30], from the 16th century also 'flintlock'; *ganti/genti* (†) 'textile from Gent' (1286) < Du *Gent* [34], Hu *jubelir* (†) (1625) 'jeweller' < Du *juwelier* 'jeweller' [44]; Hu *kábeljan* (†) (1783) 'codfish' < Du *kabeljauw* 'codfish' [46]; Hu *kléder* (†) (1625) 'garb' < Du *kleed* 'garment' [52]; Hu *cleinodia/cleinod* (†) (1619) 'jewel, trinket' < Du *kleinood* 'jewel, trinket' [53]. Except for *ganti/genti*, an early borrowing from a period when merchants from the Low Countries visited Hungary (see 1.4.4), the remaining five terms were adopted during the 17th and 18th centuries, the most intensive period of cultural exchange between the Low Countries and Hungary.

Hungarian sources argue that Hu *jubelir, jubil(l)er†* 'jeweller' [44] appearing in a Hungarian source from 1625, is a borrowing from German (TESz, s.v. *jubilér*; EWUng, s.v. *jubilér*; ÚESzWeb, s.v. *jublíér*). However, the context in which the word appears makes it possible that the word, along with two other words in the same text, were originally borrowed from Dutch or at least a closely related Low German dialect. The word appears several times among the accounting entries from the court of Gábor Bethlen (1580–1629), the Calvinist Prince of Transylvania, who led an anti-Habsburg insurrection between 1619–1626, a great supporter of Dutch-Hungarian relations, and a patron of the Hungarian peregrini (Kovács 2016; Radvánszky 1888). It seems that he often bought jewellery from different jewellers from Vienna and other parts of the Habsburg empire. One of the passages in which the words appear, refers to a "German" receipt of buying a *kopé*, some *cleinodia* from a *jubiller*[19] called Adrian Briers from Vienna (Horváth 1978, 15; Radvánszky 1888, 113). The Hungarian term for German in the text is *német* which at the time was a general term for Germanic dialects.[20] Based on the his-

19. The rough translation of the original text: „With this consideration Antal Csanádi brought from the jeweller Adrian Briers two German notes of a copy and a jewel/trinket which Briers had made of his own wife's things, and added his own stones and gold, the price of which Antal Csanádi gave him. Briers added [gold and stones] to the copy." [trans. RN] (Horváth 1978, 15)

torical context, the name of the goldsmith, and the word forms, it doesn't seem unlikely that all three words were from a Dutch or a closely related Low German dialect, cf. modern Du *kopie* 'copy', *kleinood* 'trinket, small jewel' and *juwelier* 'jeweller'. The ending *-ia* in *cleinodia* is considered in the Hungarian sources to be a Latin suffix, however it may as well be the adoption of the Dutch form *kleinodie* (MNW s.v. *cleinoot*; WNT s.v. *kleinood*).[21] Both *cleinodia* and *jubiller* have been recorded in the list of Dutch loanwords. However, *kopé* is of Latin origin, and the modern Hungarian form *kópia* goes back to the Latin form.

It is clear from Figure 1 that German was the most important intermediary language in the transfer of Dutch words into Hungarian. Ninety-one ('German + German and/or X') Hungarian words have been borrowed either exclusively ((Low) German = 33) through German or also through another intermediary language (91–33 = 58), which is unsurprising given the significant role German has played throughout the history of Hungarian (see 1.4.3). French was a potential intermediary language between Dutch and Hungarian in 17 cases ('French and/or X'). In two of these it seemed to have been the exclusive intermediary, Hu *kilincs* 'door handle' (<Fr *clinche* 'door handle') < Du *klinken* 'cling; click' [54], and Hu *pikk* 'spade (card)' (<Fr *pique* 'spade') Du *piek* 'pointed object' [73B]. English may have contributed to the borrowing in 13 cases ('English and/or X'), six of which are also international words. Latin, as well as Italian, may have been potential transmitters in five cases each.

Out of the 99 Hungarian borrowings, 38 were potentially transferred from Dutch through more than one intermediary language, of which 30 words were internationalisms. The list also includes three calques in the list (Hu *csendélet* 'still life' < Du *stilleven* 'still life' [84]; Hu *tőkehal* 'stock fish' < Du *stokvis* 'stock fish' [86]; Hu *fegyház* 'correctional facility' < Du *tuchthuis* 'correctional facility' [88]). There are also two contaminations, i.e. words in which two originally different forms are associated and gain a similar or the same form. Hu *borostyán* 'amber' < Du *barnsteen?* 'amber' [7] is a contamination with Hu *borostyán* 'ivy', derived from Serbo-Croatian (ÚESzWeb, s.v. *borostyán1*). The other contaminated form is Hu *paksaméta* 'bundle of documents' < Du *pak* 'bundle, pack' [68D], in which Hu *pakk* (< Du *pak*) [68A] was associated with the name of the Italian dance *passamezzo* (ÚESzWeb, s.v. *paksaméta2*).

Figure 2 represents the distribution of Dutch loanwords in Hungarian according to the position of Dutch in the etymological lineage of the word. In 38

20. cf. Hu *németalföld* 'the Low Countries', and as well as the historical use of E *Dutch*, Du *Duits*.

21. Du *kleinood* may itself be a borrowing from German, but their relationship is unclear. Als the mediaeval Latin form *clenodium* should be taken into consideration (cf. Kluge and Seebold 2011, s.v. *Kleinod*; EWN, s.v. *kleinood*)

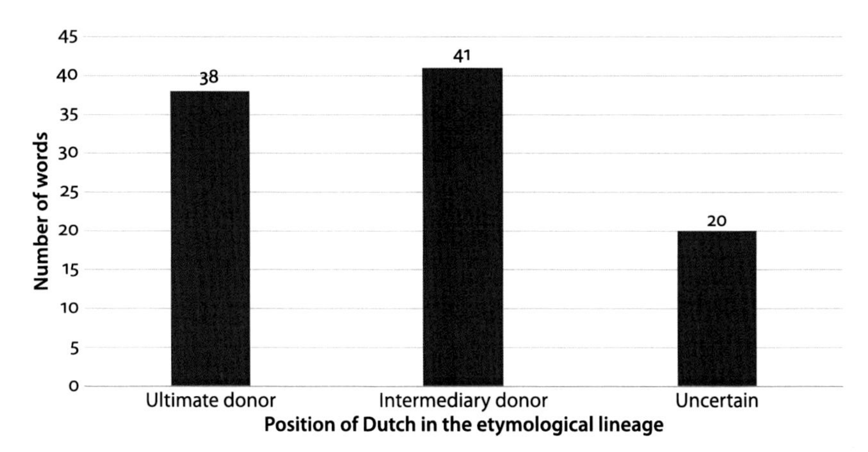

Figure 2. The position of Dutch in the etymological lineage as the source language for 99 loanwords in Hungarian

instances, Dutch served as the ultimate source language, i.e. as ultimate donor (UD, see 1.3) for the Hungarian words, e.g. Hu *matróz* 'sailor' < Du *matroos* 'sailor' [63]. Words whose origin cannot be traced back with absolute certainty to a source earlier than Dutch are also included in this group, such as the toponym *Doornik* [23]. Also, terms originally borrowed from Dutch to another language and later reborrowed into Dutch again are included in this group. Du *loterij* [62] is such an example, reborrowed from French *loterie* 'lottery' which itself is derived from Du *loot(ing)* 'game of chance' (EWN, s.v. *loterij*). In 41 instances the Dutch etymons themselves were loanwords, and Dutch served as an intermediary language (IM), such as in the case of Du *soja* [82], from Japanese.

In the remaining 20 cases, it is uncertain (Unc.) whether Dutch was indeed the ultimate donor language of the Hungarian words, as is the case with Du *batiste* [6], which has two competing etymologies (see in the previous section). Hu *borostyán(kő)* 'amber' [7] is another such example. The immediate donor language was German with a dialectal form *Bornstein* (ÚESzWeb s.v. *borostyán*). Additionally, the Hungarian form was associated with a much older word *borostyán* 'ivy'. Since the first attestations in both the Low German as the Middle Dutch sources are approximately from the same period, the late 13th–14th century, and since there was no sharp dividing line between Middle Low German and Middle Dutch we cannot definitively identify the original source variety (EWN, s.v. *barnsteen*; NEW; FEW; MNW, s.v. *brusten*). Other such examples include Hu *dokk* 'dock' [22] and Hu *(el)happol* 'seize, snatch' [39], which is a borrowing of German *happen* 'take a bite'. Due to its onomatopoeic nature, it remains uncertain whether it originated from Dutch or Low German. Further research is required to elucidate the etymological relations within this group of words.

2.3 Chronology and semantic fields

Figure 3 provides an overview of the chronological distribution of Dutch loanwords in Hungarian. The diagram is plotted at 50-year intervals. This shows the distribution of the data and is juxtaposed with Van der Sijs's data from the *Uitleenwoordenbank* (under the diagram) for comparison. The predominant influx of Dutch loanwords occurred between 1750 and 1850 (50), and especially during the second half of the 18th century (30), as evident from both diagrams. This period can be regarded as the peak of Dutch borrowings in Hungarian, coinciding with the Holy Roman Empire when Hungary and the Austrian Netherlands were under the same governance (1715–1795), the autumn of a still flourishing epoch of Hungarian Peregrination following the end of the Turkish rule in Hungary (1686). It marked a period of intensive cultural exchange, with German serving as a pivotal intermediary language. Of the 50 Dutch words borrowed during this period, 48 were transmitted (exclusively or in conjunction with another language) through German.[22] Another, albeit less prominent peak is discernible in the diagram during the 17th century, which can be associated with the time of the Hungarian golden age of peregrination in the Netherlands.

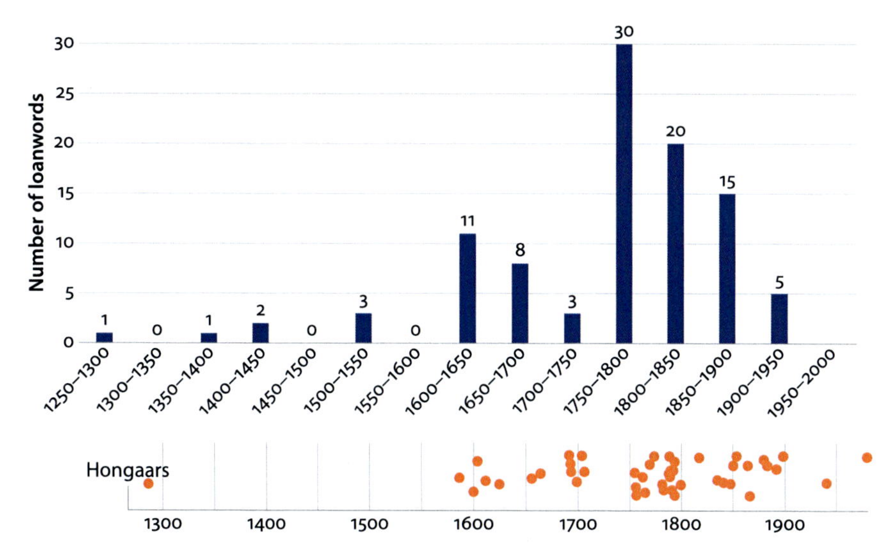

Figure 3. Chronological distribution of Dutch loanwords in Hungarian, plotted at 50-year intervals. Below: Distribution of 56 Dutch loanwords in Hungarian as recorded in the *Uitleenwoordenbank* (Van der Sijs, n.d.)

22. The two exeptions are Hu *lottó* (via Italian), *pápua* (via English, see 2.4).

Figure 4 presents an overview of the distribution of the semantic fields to which the borrowed words belong. Additionally, the data from the *Uitleenwoordenbank* are incorporated into the diagram to highlight the categories to which new items have been added.[23]

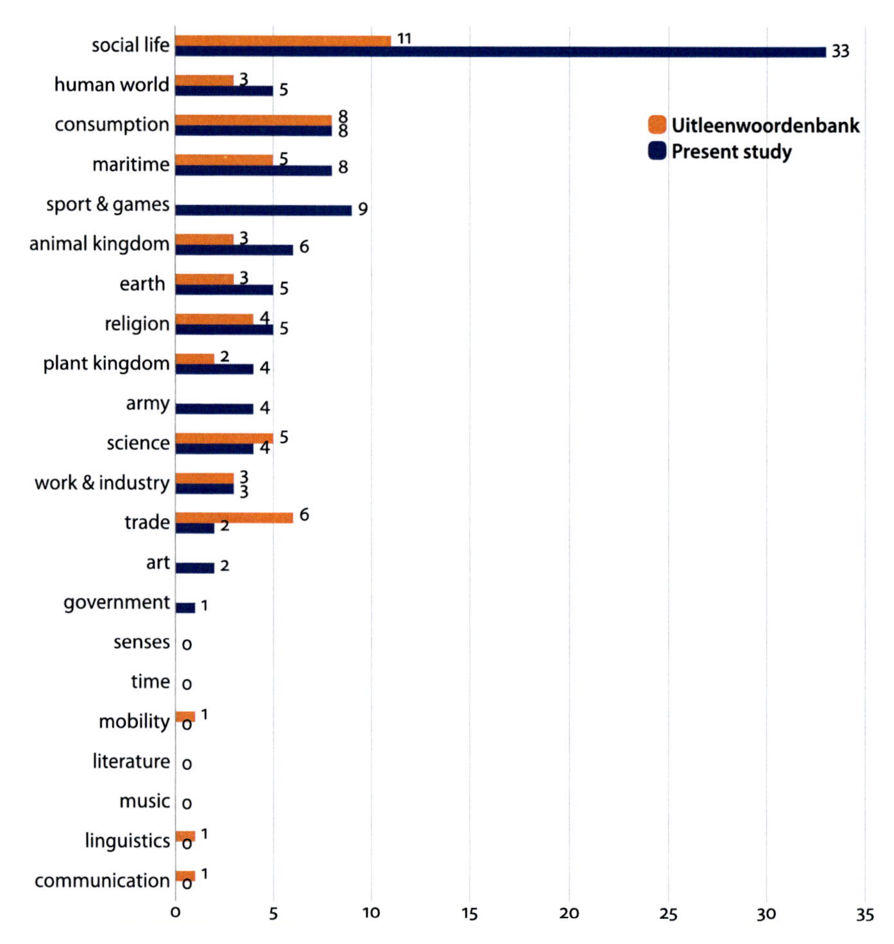

Figure 4. Distribution of Dutch loanwords in Hungarian by semantic fields in the present study and the *Uitleenwoordenbank* (cf. Van der Sijs 2001; 2010; 2015)

23. Semantic categorisation involves a degree of subjectivity, because words are not monosemic. Van der Sijs (Sijs, n.d.) categorizes Hu *batiszt* < Du *Baptist* as 'linguistic', possibly because it is an eponym. However, the 'original' meaning of the borrowed word is borrowed is 'cambric', which is a mass noun, and as such, belongs to the category 'social life'. This study does not address such variations in semantic categorisation.

The majority of the borrowings fall under the category of 'social life', encompassing everyday objects related to human existence (see Van der Sijs 2001, 76–78). Examples from this category include Hu *dózni* 'cigarette box' < Du *doos* 'box, chest' [24], Hu *muff* 'muff' < Du *mof* 'muff' [65]. The diagram indicates that many words, compared to Van der Sijs's research, have been added to this category, such as Hu *kantni* 'edge (of a ski)' < Du *kant* 'side, edge' [49] or Hu *cleinod/ cleinodia* (†) 'jewel, trinket' < Du *kleinood* 'jewel, trinket' [53]. Additionally, new loans have also been included in the maritime category, such as Hu *dekk* 'deck (of a ship)' < Du *(over)dek* 'covered area, deck' [21], and in 'sports and games', such as Hu *dopping* 'doping' < Du *doop* 'immersion; thick sauce' [25].

Overall, many words appear to reflect higher living standards, including various textiles (Hu *genti* [34], *byrkös* [18], *batiszt* [6], *puplin* [77] etc.), associated with export, as well as terms related to appearance and luxury items (Hu *cleinod(ia)* [53], *kleder* [52], *jubilér* [44] etc.), or sports and games (Hu *pikk* [73B], *dopping* [25], *korfball* [57]). This trend can be linked to the economic, cultural prestige and commercial power of the Low Countries, along with the prestige of the intermediary languages, like German and French, through which the Dutch words were assimilated into Hungarian.

2.4 Three additional case-studies

It is beyond the scope of this chapter to analyse each item in Table 2 in detail, or even those whose etymology is at some point controversial. The analysis presented here is therefore far from exhaustive. The cases I shall analyse here, are the ones that provided new additions to the data in the etymological dictionaries or were controversial.

The term *pápua* 'Papuan' [70] represents such a complex case. Van der Sijs (2010, 506) suggests that it is a potential source for G *Papua* and Hu *pápua.* The Hungarian word first appears in 1795 as *papuánusok* 'Papuans' (S. 1795),[24] while Dutch sources document it only half a decade later, in 1847 (GVD, s.v. *Papoea*; VDEW, s.v. *Papoea*). Surprisingly, the WNT offers no earlier evidence, despite the Dutch East India Company's control of much of the territory from the mid-16th century. Conversely, the OED traces the word *papua* back to 1601, supporting the hypothesis of an English, rather than a Dutch origin of the Hungarian word (OED, s.v. *papua*). This is further supported by the etymological *-n* in the earlier Hungarian attestations like *papuánusok* 'Papuans' and *papuáni* 'Papuan'. The

24. The first attestation given by the ÚESzWeb (ÚESzWeb, s.v. *pápua*) is from 1794, however this dating is not correct. The word *Pápua* refers to a certain mountain ('*Pápua hegyén*') in Africa, where Gelimer, the king of the Vandals (480–553) resided (M. 1794, 51).

English influence is also plausible given their presence in New Guinea from the 17th century competing with the Dutch.

Van der Sijs records Hu *tulipán* 'tulip' [89] as a potential borrowing from Dutch (Van der Sijs 2010, 664). While it is certainly true the Dutch Republic dominated tulip trade that during its Dutch Golden Age, tulips arrived in Hungary prior to their popularity in Western Europe, and certainly before the Tulip mania of the 16th century (Busbecq 2016; Krelage 1942, 17; EWN, s.v. *tulp*). Tulips appeared in Hungary also in the 16th century, coinciding with their emergence in Western Europe. Part of Hungary was under Turkish rule, and Hungary and the Ottoman Porte had intensive commercial ties, therefore oriental flowers, including tulips, adorned the horticultural gardens of the Hungarian nobility, and tulip bulbs were even exported to Western Europe (Hargita 1985; Takáts 1917). It is therefore not surprising that the first record of Hu *tulipán* is from 1587 (ÚESzWeb, s.v. *tulipán*). However, the relevance of the dating for Hungarian is disputable, since the citation is from a letter written in Latin to a Hungarian nobleman and general, Boldizsár Batthyány (1542–1590) in which he was asked by a certain János Honelius to send him a "tulipan" and some other flowers (Takáts 1917; Csefkó 1930; Hargita 1985). The earliest written record of *tulipán* as a Hungarian word, spelled as *tulipa*, is from 1646, found in a private letter referring to tulip bulbs as *tulipagyökér* (literally 'tulip root') (Takáts 1917). Although forms without *-n* are rare in Hungarian, the absence of the word-final *-n* in this case might indicate German or even Dutch influence, especially in view of the abundance of the 16th-century word forms *tulipa, tulpa* in Dutch (WNT, s.v. *tulp*), but the direct source of the Hungarian word remains unclear and needs to be clarified by further research.[25]

The geographical name Du *Holland* has been borrowed into Hungarian in two different phases, each with distinct meanings. The toponym, referring to the territory in the Low Countries, was borrowed from medieval Latin into Hungarian in its original form *Hol(l)andia* 'Holland' (1533) [40A] (contemporary Hu *Hollandia*) (Berrár and Károly 1984, 797). The adjective Hu *holandus* (†) 'Dutch' (1533) (contemporary Hu *holland*) was probably derived from Latin *Hollandus* 'Dutch person', although it may have been influenced by analogy with other Hungarian ethnonyms formed with the (pseudo-)Latin suffix *-us*, such as *dánus* (†) 'Danish', *gótus* (†) 'Goth' (Berrár and Károly 1984, 332; ÚESzWeb, s.v. *holland*).

During the first half of the 19th century, numerous industrial innovations, along with their terminology, were introduced in Hungary from Western Europe

25. The controversial etymology of the word has inspired alternative explanations of the origin of Hu *tulipán*, some of which try to trace the Hungarian word back to Finno-Ugric (Kacsoh 2013), others even to Sanskrit sources (Sándor 2018).

through German channels. Throughout the century, purists often expressed their concern over the widespread German influence on various technical jargons (e.g. Serli 1859). G *Holländer (Verschraubung)* 'union connection' (lit. 'Dutch joint') was also a commonly used term in Hungarian, however, it was later translated as *hollandi (csavar)* 'union connection' (1878) [40B] ('A Csőkarimák És Hollandi Csavarkötések (Flantschen Und Holländer-Verschraubungen) Biztosítása.' 1878). The adjectival form *hollandi* was derived with the suffix *-i* from the nominal stem *Holland*. While this form was replaced by contemporary standard form *holland* during the first half of the 20th century, it remained in use in the elliptic form *hollandi (anya)* 'flare nut'.[26]

3. Conclusion

The primary objective of this study was to present a comprehensive compilation of Dutch loanwords in Hungarian, while also elucidating the connections between lexical borrowing and socio-cultural trends within the historical framework of Dutch–Hungarian relations. Despite the limitations of direct and extensive social and cultural links, I have identified 99 Hungarian words that have been derived from 90 Dutch words. Among these there are also 10 potential direct loans from Dutch to Hungarian. Most of these borrowings correlate with periods of intensive direct cultural and social interaction between the Low Countries and Hungary.

Words such as Du *bisschop(swijn)* [12], *flint(e)* [30], *juwelier* [44], *kabeljauw* [46], *kleed* [52] and *kleinood* [53] were first recorded in Hungarian during the 17th and 18th centuries, characterized by extensive Dutch–Hungarian relations, partly due to the large number of Hungarian students studying at Dutch universities. Du *polder* was adopted into Hungarian in a scientific context with Dutch geographical names, just before Hungarian students were banned from going to Dutch universities (1817). Du *korfbal* entered the Hungarian lexicon in the 1920s, during the Child Transport Action, another notable period in the history of Dutch–Hungarian relations, when around 50,000 Hungarian children were sent to the Netherlands and Belgium for recuperation. *Bintje* stands out as the only word for which we have certainty of direct borrowing from Dutch. Its first recorded usage dates to the period following World War II, coinciding with the brief revival of the Child Transport Action, which facilitated renewed Dutch–Hungarian interactions.

---

26. The archaic form *hollandi* is also used in idiomatic expression, such as *mint a bolygó hollandi* 'like someone who can't find his/her way', literally 'like the Flying Dutchman'.

The findings of the research also serve as an addition to the *Uitleenwoordenbank* in several respects. Van der Sijs (2010, 137; 2015) catalogued 57 Dutch words borrowed into Hungarian. This study has expanded upon her findings by identifying several new words. Specifically, I have uncovered 90 Dutch words that have been borrowed into Hungarian, i.e. 35 new ones compared to the *Uitleenwoordenbank*. According to Van der Sijs's research 45 of the 57 words have been transmitted through intermediary languages, such as German. Here, I have identified 10 potential direct borrowings, of which Hu *Bintje* [11], *korfball* [57] and *polder* [75] are most probably identifiable as direct loans, although the latter two, being international loanwords, may have been influenced by English and, in the case of *polder*, German. In the remaining seven instances, except perhaps Hu *bischop (lé)* [12], other languages could have been intermediary sources.

The data presented in Table 2 also contributes to the extending of the existing knowledge base in several other respects. It provides a number of new data regarding the earliest attestations, the intermediary languages, and the role of Dutch as a donor language. Additionally, further investigation into the intermediary languages involved in lexical borrowing between Dutch and Hungarian could provide valuable insights into the dynamics of language contact in the region. Overall, this study sets a new stage for further exploration into Dutch–Hungarian linguistic contacts, enriching our understanding of the dissemination of Dutch words across the world's languages and cross-cultural influences on language development.

References

'A Csőkarimák És Hollandi Csavarkötések (Flantschen Und Holländer-Verschraubungen) Biztosítása.' 1878. *Pénzügyi Közlöny* 29 (August):501.

Aalders, Maarten J., Gábor Pusztai, and Orsolya Réthelyi, eds. 2020. *De Hongaarse Kindertreinen: Een Levende Brug Tussen Hongarije, Nederland En België Na de Eerste Wereldoorlog.* Hilversum: Uitgeverij Verloren BV.

ADT – Arcanum Digitális Tudománytár. n.d. Arcanum Adatbázis Kft. Accessed 10 March 2024. https://adt.arcanum.com/hu/discover/

Ágoston, István. 2005. 'Miskolczi Csulyak Gáspár Az Első Magyarnyelvű Állattankönyv Író'. *Collegium Doctorum, MAGYAR REFORMÁTUS TEOLÓGIA A Magyarországi Református Egyház Doktorok Kollégiumának Periodikája* 1 (1): 143–58.

Apáczai Csere, János. 1653. *Magyar encyclopaedia.* [Utrecht] Ultrajecti: Joannes a Waesberge.

Bárány, Attila. 2017. 'Attila Bárány: King Sigismund of Luxemburg and His Entourage in the Low Countries – Netherlandish Incomers in Hungary'. In *Németalföld Emlékei Magyarországon – Magyar – Holland Kapcsolatok*, edited by Attila Bárány, Gergely Tamás Fazakas, Gábor Pusztai, and Miklós Takács, 21–56. Loci Memoriae Hungaricae, V. Debrecen: Debreceni Egyetemi Kiadó.

Bárczi, Géza. 1994. *Magyar szófejtő szótár*. 2. kiadás. Budapest: Trezor Kiadó.

Bellág, Rózsa. 2010. 'Apáczai Csere János (1625–1659)'. *Református Szemle* 103 (2): 193–206.

Benkő, Loránd, ed. 1978a. *A Magyar Nyelv Története*. 2nd ed. Budapest: Tankönyvkiadó.

Benkő, Loránd, ed. 1978b. 'A magyar szókészlet eredet'. In *A Magyar Nyelv Története*, edited by Loránd Benkő, 2nd ed., 259–388. Budapest: Tankönyvkiadó.

Berrár, Jolán, and Sándor Károly. 1984. *Régi magyar glosszárium: szótárak, szójegyzékek és glosszák egyesített szótára*. Budapest: Akadémiai Kidaó.

'Bintje'. 2023. In *Wikipedia*. https://en.wikipedia.org/w/index.php?title=Bintje&oldid =1188108943#cite_note-Walker-1.

Bozzay Réka, and Ladányi Sándor. 2007. *Magyarországi diákok holland egyetemeken, 1595–1918 – Hongaase studenten aan Nederlandse universiteiten* 1595–1918. Eötvös Loránd Tudományegyetem Levéltára.

Bozzay, Réka. 2022. *Intézménytörténeti kapcsolatok Debrecen és Hollandia*. Debrecen: Tiszántúli Református Egyházkerület Közgyüjtményei.

Broughton, Thomas, and Sámuel Mindszenti. 1793. *Broughtonnak a' religióról való historiai lexicona ... magyar nyelvre fordította, és sok eredeti articulusoknak meg-bővítésekkel ... ki-botsátotta Mindszenti Sámuel*. Komárom: Wéber Simon Péter.

Buchheister, Georg Ottersbach. 1914. *Handbuch der Drogisten-Praxis Bd.2*. Hamburg: Verlag von Julius Springer.

Busbecq, Ogier Ghislain de. 2016. *The Life and Letters of Ogier Ghiselin de Busbecq, Vol. 1 (of 2)*. Edited by F.H. Blackburne (Francis Henry Blackburne) Daniell and Charles Thornton Forster. Project Gutenberg.

doi Calabrese, Andrea, and Leo Wetzels. 2009. *Loan Phonology*. Amsterdam; Philadelphia: John Benjamins Pub. Co..

Cholnoky, Jenő. 1897. 'Vegyes'. *Földrajzi Közlemények*, 124.

CNRTL – Centre National de Ressources Textuelles et Lexicales. n.d. *CNRTL: Centre National de Ressources Textuelles et Lexicales*. Accessed 1 March 2024. https://www.cnrtl .fr.

Csefkó, Gyula. 1930. 'A Tulipán Szó És Motívum Történetéhez'. Edited by István Bibó. *Népünk És Nyelvünk* 1:15–19.

Cséry, Dezső. 1948. 'Hollandiai "Injekció" a Fertőzött Magyar Krumplinak'. *Kis Újság*, 25 March 1948.

Csorba, Dávid. 2017. 'Seventeenth-Century Calvinist Relics from the Netherlands'. In *Németalföld Emlékei Magyarországon – Magyar – Holland Kapcsolatok*, edited by Attila Bárány, Gergely Tamás Fazakas, Gábor Pusztai, and Miklós Takács, 89–108. Loci Memoriae Hungaricae, V. Debrecen: Debreceni Egyetemi Kiadó.

D. Decsy, Sámuel. 1793. *A Félben Szakadott Magyar Kurirnak Folytatása*. Vol. Második darab. Bétsben: Schrambl Ferentz Antal.

DWDS – Digitales Wörterbuch der deutschen Sprache. n.d. *DWDS: Das digitale Wörterbuch der deutschen Sprache*. Accessed 1 March 2024. https://www.dwds.de.

Elst, Jean-Paul Van der. 2012. *De Lage Landen in Transsylvanië het aandeel van Nederlanders, Vlamingen en Walen in de koloniseering van Transsylvanië (11de-12de-13de eeuw)*. Merchtem: Jean-Paul Van der Elst.

Erdélyi, János. 1842. 'A' Költészetről. Boileau Tanköltemény e.' *A Kisfaludy-Társaság Évlapjai* 4:193.

Eredics, Péter. 2005. 'Ungarische Stundenten Und Ihre Übersetzungen Aus Dem Niederlendischen Ins Ungarische in Der Frühen Neuzeit.' In *Doktori Értekezés (PhD)*. Debrecen: Debreceni Egyetem.

'Etymologiebank.nl'. n.d. Accessed 1 March 2024. https://etymologiebank.nl/.

EWN – Philippa, Marlies, F. Debrabandere, Arend Quak, T.H. Schoonheim, and Nicoline van der Sijs, eds. 2003. *Etymologisch Woordenboek Van Het Nederlands*. 4 vols. Amsterdam: Amsterdam University Press. http://www.etymologie.nl/.

EWUng – Benkő, Loránd, Károly Gerstner, S.Antónia Hámori, Zaicz Gábor, Büky Béla, and Skripecz Sándor, eds. 1993. *Etymologisches Wörterbuch des Ungarischen*. Budapest: Akadémiai Kiadó.

FEW – Franck, Johannes. 1892. *Etymologisch Woordenboek Der Nederlandsche Taal*. 's-Gravenhage: Martinus Nijhoff.

Gera, Judit, and Roland Nagy, eds. 2017. *„Mert vesztett édenedbe visszavágyom". A magyar és a holland kultúra közvetítői a 19. század végén és a 20. század elején / 'Verloren Paradijs, mijn heerlijk Nederland' Hongaarse en Nederlandse cultuurbemiddelaars aan het eind van de 19de en het begin van de 20ste eeuw*. Néderlandisztikai füzetek, 8. Budapest: ELTE Néderlandisztika Tanszék, Németalföld – Magyarország Kulturális Transzfer Kutatóközpont.

doi Gerstner, Károly. 2015. 'A Magyar Nyelv Szókészlete'. In *Magyar Nyelv*, edited by Ferenc Kiefer, 306–34. Budapest: Akadémiai Kiadó.

Gombocz, Zoltán, and János Melich, eds. 1914. *Magyar etymologiai szótár: lexicon critico-etymologicum linguae Hungaricae*. Vol. 1–2. 2 vols. Budapest: Magyar Tudományos Akadémia.

GTB – 'De Geïntegreerde Taalbank' n.d. Instituut voor de Nederladse taal. Accessed 1 March 2024. https://gtb.ivdnt.org/search/.

GVD – Grote Van Dale. n.d. *Van Dale Online*. Van Dal Lexicografie. Accessed January 4, 2025. https://zoeken.vandale.nl/.

Haiman, György. 1987. 'Miklós Tótfalusi Kis, Designer of the Type "Janson"'. In *Nederlanders en Hongaren: Ontmoetingen tussen twee volken = The Dutch and Hungarians: Contacts between two peoples*, edited by István Heimlich, 44–47. Budapest: Magyar Könyvkiadók és Könyvterjesztők egyesülete.

Hallig, Rudolf, and Walther von Wartburg. 1952. *Begriffssystem als Grundlage für die Lexikographie: Versuch eines Ordnungsschemas*. Akademie-Verlag.

Hargita, P. 1985. 'Gardening in Hungary in the Days of the Turkish Rule, in the 16th Century'. *Acta Agronomica Academiae Scientiarum Hungaricae*, 34 (1–2): 207–15.

doi Haspelmath, Martin, and Uri Tadmor, eds. 2009. *Loanwords in the World's Languages: A Comparative Handbook*. Berlin, Germany: De Gruyter Mouton.

Hauer, Géza. 1881. 'Néhány Jelesebb Sajt-Faj Készítés-Módja'. *Földmivelési Érdekeink* 9 (6): 50–51.

HGC – Hungarian Gigaword Corpus. n.d. MTA Nyelvtudományi Intézet. Accessed 11 December 2024. https://mnsz2-ud.nytud.hu/#open

doi Hock, Hans Henrich. 1991. *Principles of Historical Linguistics*. 2nd rev. and updated ed. Berlin & New York: Mouton de Gruyter.

Horváth, Mária. 1978. *Német elemek a 17. század magyar nyelvében*. Budapest: Akad. Kiadó.

Hübner, János. 1816a. *Hübner János (Szerk.): Mostani És Régi Nemzeteket, Országokat, Tartományokat, Városokat, Emlékezetre Méltó Mezővárosokat, Helységeket, Folyókat, Tavakat, Tengereket, Öblöket, Fokokat, Szigeteket, Hegyeket, Erdőket, Barlangokat, Pénzeket, Mértékeket, 's t. e. f. Esmértető Lexikon*. Edited by Xav. Ferenc Sperl and György Fejér. Vol. 1. A-D. 5 vols. Pest: Trattner János Tamás.

Hübner, János. 1816b. *Hübner János (Szerk.): Mostani És Régi Nemzeteket, Országokat, Tartományokat, Városokat, Emlékezetre Méltó Mezővárosokat, Helységeket, Folyókat, Tavakat, Tengereket, Öblöket, Fokokat, Szigeteket, Hegyeket, Erdőket, Barlangokat, Pénzeket, Mértékeket, 's t. e. f. Esmértető Lexikon*. Edited by Xav. Ferenc Sperl and György Fejér. Vol. 2 I-O. 5 vols. Pest: Trattner János Tamás.

'I. Némelly Nevezetes Emberekről Emlékeztetés, Betü-Rend-Szerént. II-Dik Betü-Rend'. 1793. *Magyar Könyv-Ház* 6.

Jákó, Zsigmond. 1987. 'De Nederlandse jaren van Miklós Tótfalusi'. In *Nederlanders en Hongaren: Ontmoetingen tussen twee volken = The Dutch and Hungarians: Contacts between two peoples*, edited by István Heimlich, 48–57. Budapest: Magyar Könyvkiadók és Könyvterjesztők egyesülete.

Kacsoh, Bálint. 2013. 'Two Books by Two Sandors about the Origins of Hungarians'. *Hungarian Studies Review* XL (2): 191–204.

Káldi, György. 1626. *Szent Biblia az egész kereszténységben bé-vött régi deák bötűből, magyarra forditott a' Jésus-alatt vitézkedő társaság-béli nagy-szombati Káldi György Pap*. Nyomtatta Béchben: A' koloniai udvarban Formika Máte.

Kiss, Jenő, and Ferenc Pusztai, eds. 2003. *Magyar nyelvtörténet*. Budapest: Osiris.

Kiss, Jenő, and Ferenc Pusztai, eds. 2018. *A Magyar Nyelvtörténeti Kézikönyve*. A Magyar Nyelv Kézikönyvei, XXIX. Budapest: Tinta Kiadó.

Kluge, Friedrich, and Elmar Seebold. 2011. *Etymologisches Wörterbuch Der Deutschen Sprache*. 25., Durchgesehene und erw. Aufl. Berlin; Boston: De Gruyter.

Köpeczi, Béla. 1987. 'Enkele woorden over ons gemeenschappelijk verleden en onze culturele samenwerking'. In *Nederlanders en Hongaren: Ontmoetingen tussen twee volken = The Dutch and Hungarians: Contacts between two peoples*, edited by István Heimlich, 7–11. Budapest: Magyar Könyvkiadók és Könyvterjesztők egyesülete.

'Körültekintés'. 1900. *Vadász- És Versenylap* 44. (102): 617.

Kovács, Katalin Anita. 2016. 'Az Erdélyi Fejedelmi Udvar Hollandiai Diplomáciai És Ideológiai Kapcsolatai a 17. Században a Peregrináció Tükrében'. Doktori (PhD) értekezés, Budapest: Pázmány Péter Katolikus Egyetem Bölcsészettudományi Kar.

Kreisch, János. 1869. 'A Külföldi Aquariumok Különös Tekintettel a Pesten Fölállítandóra'. *Természettudományi Közlöny* 1 (1–9): 23.

Krelage, E. H. 1942. *Bloemenspeculatie in Nederland. de tulpomanie van 1636-'37 en de hyacintenhandel 1720-'36*. Amsterdam: s.n.

Ladányi, Sándor. 1987. 'Hongaarse studenten aan Nederlandse universiteiten'. In *Nederlanders en Hongaren: Ontmoetingen tussen twee volken = The Dutch and Hungarians: Contacts between two peoples*, edited by István Heimlich, 72–83. Budapest: Magyar Könyvkiadók és Könyvterjesztők egyesülete.

LEI – Lessico Etimologico Italiano. n.d. *LEI Digitale*. Istituto della Enciclopedia Italiana. Accessed 10 March 2024. https://online.lei-digitale.it/.

M., J. 1794. 'I. Némelly Nevezetes Emberekről Emlékeztetés, Betü-Rend-Szerént. II-Dik Betü-Rend'. *Magya Könyvház* 6:1–188.

Magyary-Kossa, Gyula. 1929. *Magyar orvosi emlékek: értekezések a magyar* orvostörténelem köréből. Budapest.

doi Malkiel, Yakov. 1975. 'Etymology and Modern Linguistics'. *Lingua* 36 (2): 101–20.

Maticsák, Sándor. 2020. *A magyar nyelv eredete és rokonsága*. Budapest: Gondolat.

MGTSZ – Magyar Generatív Történeti Szintaxis. n.d. MTA Nyelvtudományi Intézet. Accessed 10 March 2024 http://omagyarkorpusz.nytud.hu/hu-search.html.

Mindszenti, Sámuel. 1792. *Brougthonnak a' Religióról Való Históriai Lexicona A-C*. Komárom.

Miskolci C., Caspar. 1654. *Angliai Independentismus: Avagy Az Ecclésiai Fenyitékben, És a Külsö Isteni Tiszteletre Tartozó Jó Rendtártasokban, Minden Reformata Ecclesiaktól Különözö Fejetlen Lábság / Eggynehány Szava Hihető, Túdós, Belgiumi Doctoroknak Irasokbúl, Roevideden Öszve Szedegettetett, Es Magyar Nyelven Kibocsáttatott Miskolci C. Caspar Által*. Ultrajectum: Vásberg János.

MNW – Middelnederlands woordenboek. n.d. *De Geïntegreerde Taal-Bank*. Instituut voor de Nederlandse taal. Accessed 10 March 2024. https://gtb.ivdnt.org/

Mollay, Karl. 1952. 'Das Älteste Deutsche Lehngut Der Ungarischen Sprache'. *Acta Linguistica Academiae Scientiarum Hungaricae* 1 (2/4): 373–417.

Mollay, Károly. 1982. *Német-magyar nyelvi érintkezések a XVI. század végéig*. Nyelvészeti tanulmányok. Budapest: Akadémiai Kiadó.

Monostori Tibor. 2020. 'Egy félreértett kapcsolattörténet? Németalföld és Magyarország a 16–17. században'. *Ujkor.hu* (blog). 5 September 2020.

MTSZ – Magyar Történeti Szövegtár. n.d. MTA Nyelvtudományi Intézet. Accessed 10 March 2024. https://clara.nytud.hu/mtsz/run.cgi/first_form.

Muzslay, István. 2000. *Magyar Diákok a Leuveni Katolikus Egyetemen (1532–2000)*. Studia Theologica Budapestinensia 24. Budapest: Márton Áron Kiadó.

Nádasdy, Ádám. 1996. '„Das Ursprüngliche Ist Das Eigentliche" – Avagy Az Eredeti És a Tényleges'. Edited by Marianne Bakró-Nagy. *Nyelvtudományi Közlemények* 95 (1–2): 139–43.

Nádasdy, Ádám. 2020. *Milyen nyelv a magyar?* Budapest: Corvina.

Nagy, Etelka. 1922. 'Hollandiai Levél'. *Kecskeméti Közlöny*, 4 January 1922, 4/4. edition.

Nagy, Roland. 2024a. 'From First Aid to Professional Course Materials: The Development of Language Learning Tools at the Time of the Children's Trains'. In *(Hi)stories of Migration, Mobility, and Travel: Crossing Literary, Linguistic, and Historical Boundaries*, edited by Balázs Venkovits and Gábor Pusztai, 77-110. Debrecen: Debreceni Egyetemi Kiadó / Debrecen University Press.

Nagy, Roland. 2024b. 'Muzslay István holland szótára a holland – belga – magyar kapcsolatok és nyelvi segédeszközök történetének kontextusában'. In *Körüljárt, Jót Cselekedvén. Muzslay István SJ Útja Bajóttól Leuvenig*, edited by István Csonta. Agóra. Budapest: Jezsuita Kiadó.

doi Nagy, Roland, and Orsolya Réthelyi. 2023. 'Magyar Gyerekek Hollandiában, Ukrán Gyerekek Magyarországon. Nyelvi Közvetítés Humanitárius Gyermekakciókban 1922-Ben És 2022-Ben'. In *Nyelvi Közvetítés Fegyveres Konfliktusokban És Egyéb Válsághelyzetekben*, edited by Márta Seresi, Edina Robin, and Réka Eszenyi, 27–49. Budapest: ELTE BTK Fordító- és Tolmácsképző Tanszék.

NEW – De Vries, Jan. 1987. *Nederlands Etymologisch Woordenboek*. BRILL.

'*NYELVEMLÉKEK* | Magyar Nyelvemlékek'. n.d. Accessed 8 March 2024. https://nyelvemlekek.oszk.hu/tud/nyelvemlekek.

OED – Oxford English Dictionary. n.d. *OED Online*. Oxford University Press. Accessed 10 March 2024. https://www.oed.com/

Oláh, Róbert. 2017. '„...redux Ex Oris Hollandicis...": The Monuments of Netherlandish Bibliophile Culture and Intellect in the Great Library of the Tiszántúl Reformed Church District'. In *Németalföld Emlékei Magyarországon – Magyar – Holland Kapcsolatok*, edited by Attila Bárány, Gergely Tamás Fazakas, Gábor Pusztai, and Miklós Takács. Loci Memoriae Hungaricae, V. Debrecen: Debreceni Egyetemi Kiadó.

Onions, Charles. 1966. *The Oxford Dictionary of English Etymology*. Oxford: Clarendon.

Online Etymology Dictionary. n.d. *Online Etymology Dictionary*. Accessed 10 March 2024. https://www.etymonline.com/.

Oravecz, Csaba, Tamás Váradi, and Bálint Sass. 2014. 'The Hungarian Gigaword Corpus'. In *Proceedings of the Ninth International Conference on Language Resources and Evaluation (LREC'14)*, edited by Nicoletta Calzolari, Khalid Choukri, Thierry Declerck, Hrafn Loftsson, Bente Maegaard, Joseph Mariani, Asuncion Moreno, Jan Odijk, and Stelios Piperidis, 1719–23. Reykjavik, Iceland: European Language Resources Association (ELRA). https://aclanthology.org/L14-1536/.

doi Pálffy, Géza, and David Robert Evans. 2021. *Hungary between Two Empires, 1526–1711*. Studies in Hungarian History. Bloomington, Ind: Indiana University Press.

Perényi, Roland, and Orsolya Réthelyi, eds. 2023. *Destination: Hope: The International Chidren's Train Operation between the World Wars: Exhibition Catalogue*. Budapest: Budapest History Museum.

Pfeiffer Ignác, and Péter Jenő, eds. 1910. 'A "Bakelit" alkalmazása'. *Kazán- és Gépujság* 9 (18): 142.

Pokorny, Julius. 1959. *Indogermanisches Etymologisches Wörterbuch*. Bern: Francke.

Pósán, László. 2010. 'Németalföldi – magyar gazdasági kapcsolatok a középkorban'. In *Debrecentől Amszterdamig: Magyarország és Németalföld kapcsolata*, edited by Gábor Pusztai and Réka Bozzay, 13–23. Debrecen: Debreceni Egyetem Néderlandisztika Tanszék.

Pósán, László. 2017. 'Németalföldi Telepesek Az Árpád-Kori Magyarországon'. In *Németalföld Emlékei Magyarországon – Magyar – Holland Kapcsolatok*, edited by Attila Bárány, Gergely Tamás Fazakas, Gábor Pusztai, and Miklós Takács, 13–20. Loci Memoriae Hungaricae, V. Debrecen: Debreceni Egyetemi Kiadó.

doi Protze, Helmut. 2006. 'Die Zipser Sachsen im sprachgeographischen und sprachhistorischen Vergleich zu den Siebenbürger Sachsen'. *Zeitschrift für Siebenbürgische Landeskunde* 29 (2): 142–51.

Pusztai, Gábor. 2017. 'The Heritage of the Liberator: Michiel de Ruyter in Hungarian Memorabilia'. In *Németalföld Emlékei Magyarországon – Magyar – Holland Kapcsolatok*, edited by Attila Bárány, Gergely Tamás Fazakas, Gábor Pusztai, and Miklós Takács, 155–65. Loci Memoriae Hungaricae, V. Debrecen: Debreceni Egyetemi Kiadó.

Pusztai, Gábor. 2020. 'Tot Mislukking Gedoemd. Kinderacties Na 1945 in Hongarije'. In *De Hongaarse Kindertreinen: Een Levende Brug Tussen Hongarije, Nederland En België Na de Eerste Wereldoorlog*, edited by Maarten J. Aalders, Gábor Pusztai, and Orsolya Réthelyi, 165–99. Hilversum: Uitgeverij Verloren BV.

Pusztai Gábor and Bozzay Réka, eds. 2010. *Debrecentől Amszterdamig: Magyarország és Németalföld kapcsolata*. Debrecen: Debreceni Egyetem Néderlandisztika Tanszék.

Radvánszky, Béla. 1888. *Udvartartás és számadáskönyvek*. Házi történelmünk emlékei. Gyüjti Báró Radvánszky Béla. Kiadja a Magyar történelmi társulat. Elsö osztály. Budapest: Az Athenaeum R. Társ. bizománya.

Réthelyi, Orsolya. 2010. 'Habsburg Mária királyné, mint közvetítő a kultúrák között'. In *Debrecentől Amszterdamig: Magyarország és Németalföld kapcsolata*, edited by Gábor Pusztai and Réka Bozzay, 25–43. Debrecen: Debreceni Egyetem Néderlandisztika Tanszék.

Robins, Robert H. 1997. *A Short History of Linguistics*. 4. ed. Longman Linguistics Library. London: Longman.

doi Rosenhouse, Judith, and Rotem Kowner. 2008. *Globally Speaking: Motives for Adopting English Vocabulary in Other Languages*. Clevedon [UK]/Buffalo [N.Y.]: Multilingual Matters.

S. D.D. 1795. 'Polynésiának históriája.' *Magyar Almanák*, I – CXLIV.

Sándor, Frank. 2018. 'An Indic-Hungarian Reconstruction'. *International Journal of Sanskrit Research* 4 (1): 94–100.

Serli, Sándor. 1859. 'Kisérő Észrevételek s Egy Asztalos-Segéd Levele Parisból.' *Vasárnapi Ujság*, 20 November 1859, sec. Pályázati eredmény.

Sivirsky, Antal. 1957a. *Holland nyelvkönyv*. Amsterdam: Becht.

Sivirsky, Antal. 1957b. *Leergang Voor de Hongaarse Taal*. Amsterdam: Becht.

Sivirsky, Antal. 1973. *Magyarország a XIX. századi holland irodalom tükrében*. Irodalomtörténeti füzetek. Budapest: Akadémiai Kiadó.

Sivirsky, Antal. 1987. *Vijf eeuwen Hongaars-Nederlandse culturele betrekkingen*. Den Haag: Ministerie van Buitenlandse Zaken.

Szarvas, Gábor, and Zsigmond Simonyi. 1890. *Magyar Nyelvtörténeti Szótár a Legrégebbi Nyelvemlékektől a Nyelvújításig*. 3 vols. Budapest: Hornyánszky Viktor Akadémiai Könyvkereskedése.

Szili Katalin. 2016. 'Szívderítő utazás a 17. század végi beszélgetések világába (Warmer Kristóf tíznyelvű Gazophylacium-áról)'. *MAGYAR NYELV* 112 (3): 325–32.

Takáts, Sándor. 1917. 'Az Első Tulipánjaink'. In *Rajzok a Török Világból*, III:378–87. Budapest: Magyar Tudományos Akadémia.

Teszelszky, Kees. 2012. 'Hongaren, Bataven en Saksen. De rol van Hongaren en Hongarije in de ontwikkeling van een vroegmoderne nationale identiteit in de Nederlanden'. *Acta Neerlandica* 9:135–49.

TESz – Benkő, Loránd. 1967. *A magyar nyelv történeti-etimológiai szótára*. 4 vols. Budapest: Akadémiai Kiadó.

Teszelszky, K. 2012. Hongaren, Bataven en Saksen. De rol van Hongaren en Hongarije in de ontwikkeling van een vroegmoderne nationale identiteit in de Nederlanden. *Acta Neerlandica*, 9, 135–149.

TLFi – Trésor de La Langue Française informatisé. n.d. In *Centre National de Ressources Textuelles et Lexicales (CNRTL)*. Accessed 10 March 2024. https://www.cnrtl.fr/etymologie/

TMK – Történeti Magánéleti Korpusz. n.d. MTA Nyelvtudományi Intézet. Accessed 10 March 2024. https://tmk.nytud.hu/3/.

Tóth, Sándor. 1862. 'Különfélék'. *Pesti Napló*, 3 April 1862, 13. évf. 3643. sz. edition.

Tóthfalusi, István. 2001. *Magyar Etimológiai Nagyszótár*. Budapest: Arcanum Adatbázis.

ÚESzWeb – Gerstner, Károly, ed. 2011. *Új Magyar Etimológiai Szótár – Online Kiadás*. Budapest: MTA Nyelvtudományi Intézet/ELKH Nyelvtudományi Kutatóközpont.

Van der Sijs, Nicoline. 1997. *Nederlands in het buitenland, buitenlands in het Nederlands*. 's-Gravenhage: Nederlandse Taalunie.

Van der Sijs, Nicoline. 1998. *Geleend En Uitgeleend. Nederlandse Woorden in Andere Talen En Andersom*. Amsterdam/Antwerpen: L.J. Veen.

Van der Sijs, Nicoline. 2000. *'Wie komt daar aan op die olifant?': een zestiende-eeuws taalgidsje voor Nederland en Indië, inclusief het verhaal van de avontuurlijke gevangenschap van Frederik de Houtman in Indië*. Amsterdam: Veen.

Van der Sijs, Nicoline. 2001. *Chronologisch woordenboek: de ouderdom en herkomst van onze woorden en betekenissen*. 2nd ed. Amsterdam/Antwerpen: L.J. Veen.

Van der Sijs, Nicoline. 2006. *Klein Uitleenwoordenboek*. Den Haag: Sdu.

Van der Sijs, Nicoline. 2009. *Yankees, cookies en dollars: de invloed van het Nederlands op de Noord-Amerikaanse talen*. Amsterdam: Amsterdam University Press.

Van der Sijs, Nicoline. 2010. *Nederlandse Woorden Wereldwijd*. Den Haag: Sdu Uitgevers.

Van der Sijs, Nicoline. 2015. *Uitleenwoordenbank*. Instituut voor de Nederlandse Taal. https://uitleenwoordenbank.ivdnt.org/

Van der Sijs, Nicoline. 2023. 'Vijfhonderd jaar Nederlandse Wat & Hoe-gidsen'. *Instituut voor de Nederlandse Taal* (blog). 16 February 2023. https://ivdnt.org/actueel/columns/meertalig/vijfhonderd-jaar-nederlandse-wat-hoe-gidsen/

Van der Sijs, Nicoline, and Van Veen, P. A. F. 1997. *Etymologisch woordenboek. De herkomst van onze woorden*. Utrecht/Antwerpen: Van Dale Lexicografie.

VDEW – Van der Sijs, Nicoline, and Van Veen, P. A. F. 1997. *Etymologisch woordenboek. De herkomst van onze woorden*. Utrecht/Antwerpen: Van Dale Lexicografie.

Walker, Thomas S. 1994. 'Patterns and Implications of Varietal Change in Potatoes', Social Sciences Working Paper, 1994 (3).

Warmer, Christoph. 1691. *Gazophylacium Decem Lingvarum Europaearum Apertum, in Qvo Non Solum Pronunciationes, Declinationes & Conjugationes, Sed Etiam Diversi Dialogi in Sermone Germanico, Polonico, Bohemico, Belgico, Anglico, Latino, Gallico, Hispanico, Italico & Vngarico Reperiuntur*. Cassoviae [Kassa]: Johannes Klein.

Wartburg, Walther von, and Hélène Carles. 2019. *Französisches etymologisches Wörterbuch: eine Darstellung des galloromanischen Sprachschatzes: guide d'utilisation*. Bibliothèque de linguistique romane. Strasbourg: Editions de linguistique et de philologie.

WNT – Woordenboek der Nederlandsche Taal. n.d. *Geïntegreerde Taalbank (GTB)*. Instituut voor de Nederlandse Taal. http://gtb.inl.nl.

Zaicz Gábor. 2006. *Etimológiai szótár: magyar szavak és toldalékok eredete*. Budapest: Tinta könyvkiadó.

Zaicz, Gábor. 2021. *Etimológiai szótár: magyar szavak és toldalékok eredete*. 2. javított és bővített kiadás. A magyar nyelv kézikönyvei. Budapest: Tinta.

Zolnai, Gyula, and István. Szamota. 1902. *Magyar oklevél-szótár. Régi oklevelekben és egyéb iratokban magyar szók gyűjteménye. Legnagyobb részüket gyűjtötte Szamota I. ... szótárrá szerkesztette Zolnai Gy. (Lexicon vocabulorum hungaricorum, etc.).*

CHAPTER 6

Multilingual practices in the Dutch language exile community in early modern Norwich

Christopher Joby
University of East Anglia

In the sixteenth century, many people from the Low Countries whose first language was Dutch or French were forced to escape to Norwich in eastern England. The city therefore had three vernacular language communities. Latin was also used, so Norwich was a quadrilingual city. Because of language contact, multilingual practices emerged. This chapter analyses the practices involving Dutch and other languages. After analysing individual multilingualism, I examine whether translanguaging can offer any insights into these multilingual practices. I do so first by analysing four practices that arose in this multilingual environment, and then the practices of two multilingual members of the Dutch exile community. Here, I focus on a distinctive feature of translanguaging: the attention it pays to individual agency and identity formation in language use.

Keywords: multilingualism, Norwich, exiles, Dutch language community, translanguaging, code switching, John Cruso, proper names, toponyms, Latin

1. Introduction

In the mid-1500s, economic necessity and religious differences led to significant unrest in the Spanish Netherlands. In the wake of the Iconoclastic Fury (*Beeldenstorm*) of 1566, thousands of people, above all Calvinists, had to leave their homes in the Low Countries and seek refuge elsewhere (Joby 2024b). Many went to England where the Protestant queen, Elizabeth I, and her courtiers gave them a warm welcome. They settled in London and about twenty other towns in eastern England including Sandwich, Colchester, and Norwich (Joby 2015a: 57). Norwich was unusual for apart from London it was the only town with two exile language communities: Dutch and French. Three vernaculars were therefore spoken in Norwich. As Latin was also widely used, I have called Norwich a quadrilingual city in the early modern period (Joby 2015b: 78).

https://doi.org/10.1075/impact.55.06job

Whilst some members of the Dutch language community were monolingual, because of language contact others were multilingual. They engaged in practices that can be described as multilingual or multi-code i.e., they involved the use of more than one language. After providing a brief account of the history of the Dutch language community in Norwich, I analyse the language practices that emerged because of contact between Dutch and other languages. In particular, I explore whether a recent development within intercultural communication research, translanguaging, can offer any insights into multilinguals' language use in early modern Norwich. One definition of this concept asserts that it 'better captures multilingual language users' fluid and dynamic practices'; and points to the 'variety of cognitive, semiotic, and modal resources' which inextricably interact with 'language in its conventional sense of speech and writing'. Furthermore, it suggests that multilinguals go beyond culturally-defined language boundaries to the extent that these boundaries begin to evanesce (Li 2017: 18. Quoted in Reynolds 2022: 144). I explore this question by examining four practices that arose in this quadrilingual environment: the translation of Dutch textile trade terms into English, the use of personal names in Dutch and classical languages, the use of Dutch and other languages in administrative documents, and the rendering of Norwich toponyms in Dutch.

A distinctive feature of translanguaging is that it pays special attention to individual agency and how multilinguals use the full range of their language skills to form their identity. I therefore conclude by examining whether translanguaging can provide us with any insights into the language practices of two multilingual members of the Dutch exile community, Pieter Weynoet and John Cruso.

2. Historical background

In the mid-1560s, Norwich's economy was not in a good state. The fabric of the city had suffered badly from an uprising against land enclosures in 1549 known as Kett's Rebellion. Furthermore, a loss of demand for worsted cloth produced by the city's textile workers and a harsh winter in 1564/5 added to its distressed state. The mayor, Thomas Sotherton (in post June 1565–6), therefore suggested to the city council that it invite thirty 'Dutch masters' or skilled craftsmen along with up to ten members per household to Norwich to help revive its economy. The Duke of Norfolk was co-opted to ask Queen Elizabeth to issue letters patent allowing for this, which she did on 5 November 1565 (Joby 2024b). Events, however, overtook the civic leaders' plans, for the *Beeldenstorm* or Iconoclastic Fury of 1566 and subsequent Spanish reprisals led to the departure of thousands of Calvinists from the Spanish Netherlands, with many of them going to Norwich. When, eventually, in the summer of 1568, an official census of the exiles was taken, it was discovered that their number far exceeded that permitted by the letters patent: almost 1500 exiles, known locally as Strangers, spoke Dutch as a first language and 339 French (Meeres 2018: 27).[1] Norwich's population in 1565 was around 10,000, so they already made up some 15–20% of the population. About three-quarters of the Dutch-speaking Strangers in Norwich came from the Southern Netherlands, so they are often referred to as Flemish rather than Dutch. However, for the sake of simplicity in what follows I refer to both the language and the exile community as Dutch, although I use Flemish to refer specifically to the Flemish dialect of Dutch. Almost all the French-speaking Strangers came from the southern Spanish Netherlands and were typically called Walloons.

By 1569, the number of Strangers in Norwich had risen to 2,827 and by 1571 to almost 4,000. By 1578, they numbered around 7,000, or about 40% of Norwich's population. The ratio of Dutch to Walloons was about 3:1. Therefore by this time, there were some 5,000 exiles in Norwich, or almost one-third of the city's population, who belonged to the Dutch Stranger community. In 1578, however, there was a devastating plague in Norwich which killed many Strangers. By 1583, their number had reduced to 4,679 (Joby 2022: 36–9). The numbers in the Dutch exile community continued to decline as Strangers integrated into the local population or returned to the Low Countries, above all the Dutch Republic, where they could practise their Calvinist faith in relative safety. During the seventeenth century, Dutch continued to be used, although in a diminishing number of social domains, above all the home and church. By 1635, the Dutch exile church had 363 members but by 1677 this number had more than halved to about 170 members (Joby 2015a: 31). A few new members arrived from the Low Countries, but by now Dutch had largely become a heritage language in Norwich. Therefore, for about one hundred years, there was significant contact between Dutch and other languages in Norwich.

3. Multilingualism

As will already be clear, whilst there were three vernacular language communities in early modern Norwich, there was much individual multilingualism. Some Strangers were already multilingual when they arrived in Norwich. For example, Jan Ruytinck from Ghent was secretary to the Council of Flanders before being forced to leave Flanders because of his Calvinist beliefs (Decavele 1975: I, 105). In Norwich, he worked as a notary but also ran a school where he taught French

1. For the census, see MS, Norfolk Record Office (NRO), DN/DIS 10.

to local English children and boarders from Flanders (Hessels 1887–97: II, 593). He therefore probably knew Dutch, French, and Latin before leaving Flanders and acquired some English in Norwich. Using Latin, probably the most prestigious language in early modern Europe, was a means of accruing and exploiting symbolic power to use a term associated with Pierre Bourdieu (1979. Quoted in Zhu & Li 2020: 245). Its prestige allowed users such as Ruytinck and others such as Pieter Weynoet and John Cruso to assume a higher social position than those who could not use it. Furthermore, it allowed them to form a closed group, which included fellow Latinists, but excluded those not schooled in the language, including most women.

Although about three-quarters of the Strangers lived in two of the four Great Wards of Norwich: Over-the-Water and Wymer, there was no ghettoisation of them and there were therefore many opportunities for contact between speakers of Dutch and speakers of French and English (Meeres 2014: 151). The children of Dutch exiles probably played with Walloon and English-speaking children on the street and studied with them at school (Joby 2022: 53–73). Norwich had a thriving educational economy in which the free grammar school and private individuals including physicians and church ministers offered Latin tuition to children in all three language communities. One exercise that would have helped the multilingualism of these children was Latin composition and translating Latin texts into English. I analyse this and other translation practices in early modern Norwich in more detail in a chapter in another edited volume (Joby 2025).

Many Dutch exile adults joined the Stranger militia. Initially, there were separate Dutch and Walloon militias, but in the 1620s they combined into one Stranger militia company. The captain was John Cruso. In the early days of these militias, the members spoke Dutch or French, but during the seventeenth century there was a gradual shift to English. Most of the Strangers worked in the textile industry. Stranger merchants needed to deal with local wool merchants and the exiles needed to negotiate their privileges and restrictions on their trade with the civic authorities. Over time, as some Strangers gained their freedom, they could take on English apprentices (Meeres 2018: 48).

A Dutch exile who became a multilingual through language contact in Norwich was Vincentius Meusevoet. He was born in Eeklo in Flanders in around 1560. His first language was, therefore, the Flemish variety of Dutch. His family was Calvinist and so fled to Norwich later in the 1560s. Meusevoet grew up in Norwich where he learnt English and Latin, which allowed him to matriculate at Leiden University in 1586.[2] He remained in the Dutch Republic, where he

2. He is listed as 'Vincentius Reineri Aeclovensis Flander' (Vincent, son of Reynier, of Eeklo, Fleming), who matriculated at Leiden on 1 September 1586 (Du Rieu 1875: col. 20).

became a minister in the Dutch Reformed Church, but also a prodigious translator, translating at least thirty-five theological works from English to Dutch (Joby 2024a: 88–89).

Language contact did not always lead to multilingualism. In a case that came before the Politic Men in 1606, Robert Maier said that he had heard Noel Have call Everaert Wervekin's son, Isaac, a thief. In response, Everaert asked why his son was called a thief, but admitted that he did not understand well "de Walsche sprake", i.e., the Walloon dialect of French.[3] In some sense, this statement expresses Everaert's lack of symbolic power.

4. Translanguaging practices

In this environment of individual and societal multilingualism, various practices involving Dutch emerged that could be understood as translanguaging practices. Here, I shall analyse four of these: rendering Dutch textile trade terms into English, using personal names in Dutch and classical languages, using Dutch and other languages in administrative documents, and creating Dutch versions of Norwich toponyms. Most of the literature on translanguaging analyses contemporary language practices. Therefore, what follows offers a relatively rare analysis of translanguaging in a historical context.

4.1 Textile trade terms

In the early days of the Dutch exile community at least, exiles and local people moved between languages as they discussed the new textiles and techniques that the exiles introduced. In 1570, the governors of the Dutch Wool Hall or Bay Hall wrote a book of orders to regulate the Dutch exile textile industry. The civic authorities demanded that this set of regulations be translated into English.[4] This process added several terms to the English used in Norwich to denote the new practices and products that the Dutch weavers introduced and thereby generated a new trade jargon or technolect in Norwich English. These terms were used when a new book of orders comprising some 134 regulations was written in Eng-

3. MS British Library (BL), Add. MS 43862, fol. 10r. Dutch: "Robert Maier out ontrent 34 Jaren secht ghehoort te hebben dat Noel Haue heeft Eueraert Vervakens sone met name Isaac dief gheheten heeft waerop Evarart seyde waerom noemt ghy myn soone dief dan seyde dat hy de Walsche spracke niet wel en verstont".

4. The English translation is transcribed in MS, NRO, NCR 17d/9, fols 49r.-56v.

lish in 1577, which was translated into Dutch in 1581.[5] One example of a Dutch term that needed to be translated into English was *loyer*, which denoted an official who assayed the cloth and put a lead seal on it (*loyer* is also rendered in Dutch as *loder, looier*, a derivation from *lood*, the Dutch word for "lead"). This was rendered in English as "lower", "loier" and "loyer".[6] The related verb *loyen* (Late Modern Dutch *loden*, Southern Dutch *looien*) was in some cases simply inserted in the first English orders as *loyen*, but also shortened to *loy*. These English terms are not in the *Shorter Oxford English Dictionary* (OED) or the *English Dialect Dictionary* (EDD). A related Dutch term is *looikamer*, the room where cloth was checked and sealed by the *loyers*.[7] This generated the English term "loye chamber". Another Dutch term *nopteecken* (something like a manufacturer's mark) probably lacked a direct English equivalent. It was translated as "uptoken", a term not in the Shorter OED or the EDD. "Uptoken" was used again in the revised set of English orders and translated back into Dutch as *nopteecken* in 1581. These are examples of the creativity and innovation that emerge in language contact situations, qualities that are often deemed to be central to translanguaging practices (Li 2017: 15). Some of these trade-specific terms occur in texts written in textile towns in the Low Countries. *Nopteyken* appears in the 1572 Utrecht *Placaatboek* or book of ordinances (*Woordenboek der Nederlandsche Taal* henceforth *WNT*). A *persenaer* was an official who assessed the quality of cloth using a perch. This was translated into English as "persenar", "lower" or "judge". The Dutch term occurs in the 1641 edition of Jan Orlers' description of Leiden, *Beschrijvinge der stad Leyden* (*Woordenboek der Nederlandsche Taal (WNT)*). Like Norwich, Leiden had a significant textile industry which employed exiles from the Southern Netherlands including some who had previously lived in Norwich. Table 1 provides further examples of these terms. The textile workers in both Norwich and Leiden therefore formed communities of practice with a shared linguistic repertoire.

5. The English version is MS, NRO, NCR 17d/11, and the Dutch translation MS, NRO, NCR 17d/12. A transcription of the Dutch book, made in 1970–1974 by P.A. Harthoorn, is held at the NRO: MS 21539.

6. MS, NRO, NCR 17d/11, fol. 6r.

7. MS, NRO, NCR 17d/12, fol. 21r.

Table 1. Dutch and English terms that occur in the books of orders (NRO, NCR 17d/11 & 12)

No.	Dutch	English	WNT lemma	English meaning
1	plotwulle	pelt woolle	Not in the WNT	pelt wool
2	stockenaers[a]	prynters	stokkenaars	officials who measured the length of cloth with a stick and attached their mark or 'print' to it.
3	loycamer	loye chamber	looikamer.	the room where cloth was inspected and sealed by the 'loyers'
4	loyer	lower, loier, loyer	loder, looier	officials who inspected and sealed the cloth (lower is not in the shorter OED)
5	loyen[b]	loyen, to loy	looden, looien	To inspect and seal the cloth
6	hooghe loye	hye leades, hye seal howse		The section of the bay hall where cloth was sealed
7	neringe	baytrie	nering – this is a general word for industry, whilst baytrie specifically concerns bays	
8	mitloodt	measurer	meetloot (mitloodt may be dialectal)	measurer
9	pers	pearch/perch	pers	perch: a device over which cloth was stretched to check it for quality.
10	persenaer	persenar, lower, judge	persenaar[c]	The official who assesses the quality of cloth using a perch
11	cnape	servant	knaap	junior servant, who helped to ensure the smooth running of the Bay Hall.
12	nopteecken	uptoken	nopteken	a mark to indicate that a piece of cloth has been burled.
13	bijteecken	bye marke	bijteken	a mark placed next to something.

a. *Stok* means 'stick' in Dutch. The term *Stokkenaars* was also used for these officials in the bay hall in Leiden. WNT: 'stokkenaar: titel voor een dienaar van de baaihal te Leiden, die tot taak had stukken stof te stempelen'.
b. WNT: *looi* = 'inspection' (keuring) and 'approval' (goedkeuring).
c. WNT: Keurmeester van de pers der lakenen.

4.2 Proper names

Another aspect of translanguaging is the use of language to form identities (Li 2017: 18). Multilinguals often essentialise their identities in proper names. Some Strangers had more than one vernacular name. The Politic Men were a group of exiles elected annually to deal with matters such as guardianship of orphans, financial disputes, and minor offences in the exile community (Joby 2015a: 165). The minutes of their meetings were recorded by a clerk. For many years, Pieter Weynoet was the clerk to the Politic Men. In 1612, he was succeeded by a Dutch exile who often signed himself with a Latin version of his name, Johannes Coccelius. In a case heard in 1607, his vernacular Dutch name, Jan Cockeel, was used, and in a 1622 return of Strangers, an Anglicised version of his name, John Cokele (Moens 1888–9: II, 192).[8]

Proper names encode the multilingualism of another exile, Jan Cruso. He came from Hondschoote in Flanders and arrived in Norwich in the 1570s or early 1580s where he worked as a cloth merchant. His first language was the Flemish variety of Dutch. Jan Cruso is the form of his name in Dutch language records. As a Dutch church elder, he often worked with Walloon exile church leaders in Norwich and other towns in England. In the minutes of a synod of Dutch and Walloon churches in 1603, he is recorded as Jean Cruso, encoding his knowledge of French. He hints at a knowledge of Latin in the name of his third son, Aquila. In Latin, this means 'eagle'. *Aquilo(n)* was a name used by the Romans for the north wind. This choice of name may have been inspired by his family's move to Norwich, which means 'the northern settlement' (Joby 2022: 46, 31). If so, this is an example of a Dutch Stranger essentialising his learning in his offspring's name. As if to fulfil his father's wishes, Aquila became a noted classical scholar at Cambridge.

The ministers of Dutch exile churches also used more than one name to shape their identity. It was common at this time for men (it was almost always men) to follow the humanist practice of having a surname derived from a classical language as well as a vernacular surname. Some simply modified their vernacular name with a Latin suffix. The Norwich-born minister of the London Dutch church Simeon Ruytinck (d. 1621), son of Jan mentioned above, had the Latinised surname Ruytingius (Joby 2022: 112). Others used semantic equivalents in classical languages. An early leader of the London Dutch church had the Dutch name Marten de Cleyne. 'De Cleyne' means 'the small one'. He also used a surname Micron derived from the Greek word for small. The Colchester Dutch church minister, Theodore van den Bergh, had the Latinised name Theodorus Montanus, both versions of the surname meaning '(of the) mountain'.

8. MS, BL, Add. MS 43862, fol. 31r.

Norwich Dutch church ministers followed these practices. Johannes Elison was born in Norwich in 1581, matriculated at Leiden in 1598, and was appointed minister in Norwich in 1603. He served the Dutch exile church for thirty-six years before his death in 1639. He encoded his knowledge of Latin by using the Latinised version of his Christian name and, like Simeon Ruytinck, adding a Latin suffix to his surname, viz. Elisonius. This is the form of Elison's name that appears on a monumental inscription to him in Blackfriars' Hall, where the Dutch exile church met for worship. It is in three languages: Dutch, English, and Latin. These are probably the three languages that Elison used most frequently: Dutch to preach to his flock and correspond with leaders of other Dutch exile churches, English to work with colleagues in the Anglican Church, and Latin to read works of theology. The trilingual monument therefore in some sense memorialises Elison's linguistic identity.

Other ministers used semantic equivalents derived from Latin, Greek, and in one case, Hebrew. They often signed letters with these names from classical languages, in some sense adding prestige to a vernacular text and forming a bond with fellow humanists to whom the letters were addressed. Isbrand Balk had two Latin surnames, Balkius and Trabius. Trabius derives from the Latin *trabs* meaning 'beam' which is also the meaning of *balk* in Dutch. Michiel Panneel's surname means 'saddle'. He sometimes used a Latinised Greek semantic equivalent, Ephippius, as well as Pannelius. Herman de Strijcker was more commonly known as Hermannus Moded. A *strijker* in Dutch is someone who irons clothes, the probable occupation of his father. "Moded" was a free translation into Hebrew of his vernacular name (Brutel de la Rivière 1879: 147). His use of Hebrew suggests that he wanted to distinguish himself socially and intellectually as a *vir trilinguis*.[9] Anthonie Algoet used the Latin surname, Algotius. He also had a Dutch sobriquet: Antoon de Swaert (Antony the Black). This may have referenced the fact that he had been a Dominican friar before abjuring his Catholic faith. These are further examples of how multilinguals used their creativity to form their identities in early modern Norwich.

A final example involving personal names occurred in a case that came before the Politic Men on 18 November 1606. It was recorded in Dutch by Pieter Weynoet, so it was probably heard in Dutch. This involved two men called Jan Martin as plaintiff and defendant. To distinguish between them, the clerk named the plaintiff 'Jan Martin fait tout' i.e., 'Jan Martin does everything', and the defendant 'Jan Martin fait rien' or 'Jan Martin does nothing'. Perhaps these were commonly-used call names for the men.[10] Jan is a Dutch version of John whilst 'fait tout' and 'fait rien'

9. Literally, a trilingual man: the three languages here are Latin, Greek, and Hebrew.

10. MS, BL, Add. MS 43862, fol. 19r.

are French phrases. These are, then, bilingual personal names formed because of contact between Dutch and French in Norwich. Such names hint at what García & Lin (2017: 126. Quoted in Treffers-Daller 2024: 5) in their contribution to the translanguaging discourse describe as a softening of language boundaries.

4.3 Code switching between Dutch and other languages in administrative documents

Indeed, although the existence of language communities may suggest that there were rigid boundaries between these languages, members of each community frequently moved between languages and indeed language varieties, leading to the softening or weakening of boundaries between languages described by García & Lin and other authors within the translanguaging discourse. In fact, García & Lin (2017: 126. Quoted in Treffers-Daller 2024: 5) have identified two versions of translanguaging: a strong version whereby 'bilingual people do not speak languages but rather, use their repertoire of linguistic features selectively' and a weak version 'that supports national and state language boundaries and yet calls for softening these boundaries'. One multilingual practice often included within the gamut of translanguaging practices and which brings this discussion on language boundaries into sharp relief is code switching.

James Adams (2003: 19) defines code switching as "a full-blown switch from one language into another within one person's utterance or piece of writing", whilst Lisa Lim and Umberto Ansaldo (2015: 40–41) define it as "an alternation of languages within a conversation, usually at semantically or sociolinguistically meaningful junctures". These definitions affirm language boundaries. As Jeanine Dallers-Treffers (2024: 10) asserts, one problem that authors on translanguaging face by including code switching in the translanguaging repertoire is that whilst the code element in the term explicitly supports the separation of language boundaries, the translanguaging project attempts to move beyond these boundaries. However, Li Wei (2017: 19) offers a way forward here when he writes:

> Translanguaging has never intended to replace code-switching or any other term, although it challenges the code view of language. It does not deny the existence of named languages, but stresses that languages are historically, politically, and ideologically defined entities.

Code switching between Latin and the vernacular was common practice in early modern Europe for authors of official records. This practice was governed by a set of "unofficial" rules that determined which words were in Latin and which in the vernacular. One "rule" seems to have been switching to Latin to denote family relations. In baptismal records for Dutch children in Norwich, the author switches from Dutch to Latin for this purpose. Here, we can talk of a specific functional register with its own set of rules.[11] A typical example is the following (Rye 1907–1909: XII, 184):

> *Den 12 Octobris [1600], ghedoept. Barack Hechaert filius Joos et uxoris Marie. Testes clays van mersch, Susanna uxor Mateu ploijaert.*
> [12 October [1600], baptized. Barack Hechaert son of Joos and [his] wife Maria. Witnesses: Clays van Mersch, Susanna wife [of] Mateu Ploijaert]

The words for *filius* "son" and *uxor* "wife" are in Latin and *uxoris* and *Marie* are Latin genitive forms. The word for witnesses is the Latin *testes*, although sometimes the Dutch *getuigen* is used. A slightly different example is a baptismal record for 1604 (Rye 1907–1909: XII, 246):

> *1604. Abigael Degrant filia Tobyas et uxoris Janneken, geboren den 7 Julij in Xenodochio. Sponsores, Jan goybant, Pieter Gasebaer ende Jakemyne Cornelis*
> [1604. Abigael Degrant daughter of Tobyas and his wife Janneken, born on 7 July in *Xenodochium*. Godparents, Jan Goybant, Pieter Gasebaer and Jakemyne Cornelis]

Like the previous example, this entry gives familial relationships (*filia* and *uxor* daughter and wife respectively) in Latin. *Sponsores* [godparents] is also a Latin word, which was gradually integrated into Dutch. *Xenodochio* derives from the Greek *Ξενοδοχεῖον*. *Xenodochia* were established in the early Middle Ages to feed and house the poor, but also to provide for foreigners and pilgrims (Risse 1999: 82). Here, it is treated as a second-declension Latin neuter noun in the ablative case. One suggestion is that this refers to the building in Norwich now called Strangers' Hall, where Strangers are known to have rented rooms, although this is by no means certain (Meeres 2012: 128). Whilst on the one hand the sequence of Dutch, Latin, Dutch, Latin, Dutch, Latin/Greek, Latin, Dutch does not make the boundaries between the languages evanesce, it does perhaps point to the softening of these boundaries that García & Lin describe.

We see a similar pattern in one of the few monumental inscriptions in Dutch, to the wealthy merchant Franchoys van der Beke, which is in the parish church of St. Michael, Coslany:

11. Cf. Wright (2000: 151). Here, Laura Wright argues that the Latin used in late medieval accounts keeping Latin was not 'degenerate' but rather a functional register with its own internally-consistent grammar.

> *Hier licht begraven Franchoys van der Beke, fs. Huberts van Ypre wyt Vlandren Sterf af den XVIII dach May Anno Mccccclxxxvij.*
> [Here lies buried Franchoys van der Beke, son of Hubert from Ieper in Flanders. Died on the 18th day of May in the year 1587]

Here *fs.* stands for the Latin *filius* ('son'). *Huberts* is a Dutch genitive form of Hubert, Franchoys' father. Part of the date is in Latin. This mirrors the practice in ancient Rome of dating Greek texts in Latin to give them something of an official status (Joby 2014a: 224).

4.4 Toponyms

The fourth practice, the rendering of Norwich toponyms in Dutch, which in some sense is an attempt by Dutch language users to domesticate these English toponyms, also hints at the softening of boundaries between languages. Several examples occur in the minute-book of the Politic Men. In one case, a Stranger called Everaert had heard merchants talking in 'de platse van St. Joores op Tombland', i.e., the area of St. George's Tombland near Norwich Cathedral; "Joris" is the Dutch for 'George'. Similar Dutch versions occur in other texts. *St. Jooris a Colgate* and *St. Jooris a Coslaney* are two versions of the name of the church, St. George's Colegate; Colegate being the street and Coslany the district where the church was situated. In another case, Jacques le Rouge had overheard a conversation "int witte peert" i.e., a pub, one of many in Norwich, called "The White Horse".[12]

Children in the Dutch community were often baptised in local parish churches. The records give a Dutch version of the relevant church's name. In some cases, the Dutch equivalents are instantly recognisable. 'St. Pieters a mancraft' is St. Peter Mancroft in central Norwich and 'St. maertens at the oake' is 'St Martin at Oak' in the northwest of the city. Other names require a little further research. 'St. Michaels overtwarter' means 'St. Michael's Over-the-Water' and references St. Michael's Coslany in the Great Ward of Over-the-Water. 'S. Piet op de merck' is literally 'St. Peter's on the market'. This is another reference to St. Peter Mancroft, which is located adjacent to the market. *Merck* is a dialectal form, usually rendered *merkt*. There is an element of linguistic creativity and innovation here, something that authors on translanguaging often highlight (Reynolds 2022: 144; Kohl *et al.* 2020: i).

Finally, Dutch exiles wrote the name of their adopted hometown, 'Norwich', in different ways. In the late 1560s, many of the exiles who came from Ieper wrote

12. MS, BL, Add. MS 43862, fols 9v. & 15r. At one time there were no fewer than nine pubs with this name in Norwich (Sandred & Lindström 1989: 124).

letters to family and friends who remained in Flanders (Janssen 1857). In published transcriptions of some of these letters, this toponym occurs on eleven occasions, spelt differently in each case. Two features are of note in these variants. In some cases, there is a 't' at the end of the first syllable, in other cases not. Possible reasons for the insertion of a 't' are that the authors are basing their version on Dutch toponyms, such as Noordwijk in Holland, or they may be basing it on the etymology of the toponym, which is 'the northern settlement' (Noord [no:rt] is the Dutch for 'north'). The second noteworthy feature is the treatment of the word-final '-ch'. There is no phoneme /ʧ/ in the final position in modern Dutch (Booij 1995: 7). Some authors use the suffix *-wij(c)k*, possibly influenced by Dutch toponyms such as Katwijk and Noordwijk, e.g. *Noortwick* (letter 16). Other renderings are *Noortwichz* (1), *Noorduijts* (21), *Norewijs* (28) and *Norwits* (51). Other authors retain the word-final '-ch' (viz. *Noortwich* (2), and *Norwich* (7)), although we do not know whether they were successful in pronouncing the final phoneme as /ʧ/. Here, there is an element of improvisation and indeed creativity at work as Dutch authors struggle with an alien phoneme.

5. Individual case studies of translanguaging: Pieter Weynoet and John Cruso

I now turn to the language practices of two Dutch exile multilinguals: Pieter Weynoet and John Cruso. I explore whether placing these practices within the translanguaging discourse can deepen our understanding of them and therefore of how Weynoet and Cruso used language. For example, I examine whether the texts that they wrote point to their individual agency in using language to shape their identities. Furthermore, I analyse how they used language to accrue and exploit symbolic power, to return to Bourdieu's term. Finally, although they were both members of the Dutch exile community, I investigate whether their language practices in some sense challenge the notion of language community and lead to a softening of boundaries between languages, as authors in the translanguaging discourse assert (Reynolds 2022: 142–3).

5.1 Pieter Weynoet

Pieter Weynoet grew up in the Dutch exile community in Norwich. He was adopted by a bookbinder, Joos de Ram, who bequeathed him Latin and Dutch books (Forster 1967: 39). Weynoet matriculated at Corpus Christi College, Cambridge at Easter 1577.[13] After university, he returned to Norwich where for many years he worked as a notary and the clerk to the Politic Men (Dutch: *politicke mannen*). Weynoet often switches into Latin at the beginning and end of his entries in the minute-book of the Politic Men, adding prestige to the text and shaping his own identity.

In letters and the minute-book of the Politic Men, Weynoet demonstrates his multilingual skills by shifting with ease between the three vernaculars, Dutch, French, and English, as well as Latin. Entries in the minute-book are typically in Dutch or French, probably corresponding to the language in which cases were heard. Whereas the Dutch often exhibits dialectal features of Flemish, which was probably Weynoet's *vernaculus*, and an important part of his linguistic identity, his French does not, suggesting that he learnt that as a second or third language. A few entries are in English and several shorter entries in Latin. For example, if the Politic Men had no cases to hear, Weynoet would sometimes write the Latin phrase "nullus cucurrit" [nothing happened].[14] The use of Latin of course helped him to position himself as a man of learning.

Weynoet often engaged in code switching. In the main text, he switched between vernacular languages. At the end of an entry from 1610 concerning a work-related dispute between two men, he switches from English to Dutch: "could not do it. De mannen op alles ghelet hebbende ordonnenere den verwerer den herscher te gheven xij*s*..." [...The (politic) men, having examined everything, order the defendant to give the plaintiff 12*s*....]. One possible reason for switching is that the Dutch is a version of a fixed expression for recording the judgment of the Politic Men (Joby 2014a: 232–6).[15] Sometimes, Weynoet switches from Dutch to English to give an English commercial term: for example, "bill of seale" i.e., a bill of sale which transfers ownership from seller to buyer, and "deed of gyft", i.e., a deed of gift, which transfers part or all of a property from one person to another.[16]

In such cases, he may be simply mirroring switching in the spoken language, but this is not certain. We can be more certain about a case that came before the Politic Men in 1607. Here, Weynoet switches from Dutch to English to record

---

13. Weynoet is listed as Peter Ramus, the surname being the Latinised version of his stepfather's surname, De Ram (Venn & Venn 1922–7: III, 418).

14. For example, MS, BL, Add. MS 43862, fol. 45v. For two consecutive weeks in August 1607, no cases came before the men, so the clerk wrote in Dutch: "Desen dach en wasser niet te doen "(fol. 27v.).

15. MS, BL, Add. MS. 43862, fol. 81r.

16. MS, BL, Add. MS. 43862, fol. 30r. "...dat oock Bastiaen voor de selue schult oock heeft een **bill of seale** ghenomen van Elyseyus Claerbant"; "dat sy mogen sien wat dat daer voor een **bill ~~of~~ of saele** ofte **deed of gyft**".

that a widow claimed that the Governors of the Wool Hall and the bailiff were not simply "rogues", but "arrant rogues": "de gouveneurs ende den balliu *rooges* waeren Ja *arrant rooges*". She went onto assert that she was willing to confirm this under oath.[17]

Weynoet switched from Dutch to reference official positions in Norwich and Norfolk. The standard Dutch word for "mayor" was *burgemeester*. Another word, *meier*, was used in some places, above all Brabant, to reference an official charged with maintaining law and order. Both *meier* and the English word derive from the Latin *major* (*WNT*). In the minute-book, Weynoet uses the form "meyer", and occasionally "Mr. Meyer", which is suggestive of code switching.[18] Each year, in addition to the mayor, the Norwich aldermen elected two sheriffs from their number. In the minute-book for 1608, Weynoet refers to Mr. Hornset and Mr. Henry Ffasset as "Sherives".[19] The nearest Dutch equivalent was *schout* (*WNT*).

Often, at the start of an entry in Dutch, Weynoet gives the names of the plaintiff (x) and defendant (y) in the form "x tegen y", where *tegen* means "versus" in Dutch. However, quite often he uses the French equivalent *contre*. For example, an entry in Dutch in 1608 has the title "Jan Hooft heischer contre Clais Faes" [Jan Hooft plaintiff versus Clais Faes].[20] This may be a deliberate act of switching to French to add a certain prestige to the Dutch text. On the other hand, as proponents of translanguaging argue, it may be an example of Weynoet switching almost subconsciously between languages and thereby dissolving the rigid boundaries suggested by the three vernacular language communities (Reynolds 2022: 142–3). *Heischer* [plaintiff] in this example is a Flemish dialectal form. In other Dutch dialects the form is *eischer* (modern Dutch: *eiser*) (*WNT*). The word-initial "h" is added because some Flemish authors, in attempting to write "correctly", hypercorrect, and therefore prefix words beginning with vowels inappropriately with a prosthetic "h" (Willemyns 1979: 47; 2013: 73).

As was common practice in the early modern period, Weynoet used Latin for some titles and codas of entries in the minute-books. This imitated practice in antiquity, where authors often gave a Latin title to a Greek text to enhance the official status of the text (Adams 2003: 21–2). In 1612, an entry in French has the Latin title *Spiritus Sancti nobis adsit gratia* [The Grace of the Holy Spirit be present with us].[21] In some titles, however, he switches to Dutch for the date. In April 1608, he

17. MS, BL, Add. MS. 43862 fol. 33v. *arrant* is a variant of *errant* (*OED*). This collocation is still used in English.

18. MS, BL, Add. MS. 43862, fol. 16r.

19. MS, BL, Add. MS. 43862, fol. 38v.

20. MS, BL, Add. MS. 43862, fol. 40r.

21. MS, BL, Add. MS. 43862, fol. 122r.

begins the minute for one meeting with a Dutch date: "Den 12. Aprill 1608", i.e., 12 April 1608. However, he begins the following minute slightly differently: "Den 19. Aprillis 1608". "Aprillis" is a Latin genitive form: "of April".[22] As with the case of *contre*, rather than being a deliberate shift between languages, as authors on code switching often argue, it may rather point to an almost subconscious shift between Dutch and Latin, suggestive of the softening of the boundaries between languages proposed by advocates of translanguaging.

Giving a Latin coda to a vernacular text underlined Weynoet's social position as a well-educated man and in some sense essentialised his learning. In November 1584, he concluded an entry in French with the Latin words: *Actum die, mense, et anno ut supra* [Done on the day, month and year given above]. Another move to add to his social capital was his use of Ramus, a Latinised form of his adopted father's name, Joos de Ram. Under one entry in French, he signed himself in Latin *politicorum virorum scriba Pieter Weijnoet alias Ramus* [clerk of the Politic Men (viri politici), Pieter Weijnoet, also known as Ramus].[23]

In other codas, too, Weynoet positions himself as a learned man, shaping or affirming his multilingual identity. In 1593, in his capacity as clerk to the Politic Men, Weynoet wrote a document in Dutch concerning a case of adultery that had come before them. He then made a self-translation into French and sent both documents to the *coetus* of the three London exiles churches: Dutch, French, and Italian (Hessels 1887–97: III, i, 951–2). He added a coda in three languages, Dutch, French, and Latin:

> **Wt** Norwiche ce 16e Feburier 1592 [i.e., 1593] *stylo Anglię. Per me Petrum Weinoot alias Ramum pacificatorum apud Nordouicenses extraneorum scribam totius collegi[i] nomine.*
> [From Norwich 16 February 1592, English style. By me, Pieter Weinoot, alias Ramus, clerk, in the name of the whole college of foreigners [i.e., Strangers] who have found peace amongst the inhabitants of Norwich].

Most of the coda is in Latin (in italics). He gives the date in French (underlined by me). This had more prestige than Dutch, but less than Latin. It may be that only one word of this coda, *Wt* (from), is in Dutch, albeit the first word. This may be because he expected Dutch readers to be able to read the other languages, whilst few French and Italian speakers could read Dutch. It may also be because of the low prestige of Dutch compared with French and Latin. Interestingly, although he knew English he did not use it here. It is not clear which language he is using for the form *Norwiche*. This may be English or possibly a French form in which "ch"

22. MS, BL, Add. MS. 43862, fols 35r.-35v.

23. MS, NRO, MC 189/1, fol. 48v.

is pronounced /ʃ/. On the other hand, Weynoet may not view it as the property of one language or another. Rather, this may point again to the softening of boundaries between languages. Here, as well as using his alternative Latin name Ramus, he Latinises his first name as *Petrus*. Weynoet indicates that the date is *stylo Angliȩ*, i.e., in the English style. This is because England was still using the Julian calendar whereas the Dutch Republic had adopted the Gregorian calendar in 1592. He therefore needed to switch between not only languages but also timeframes. Such a coda could be understood as a "multilingual space". If, as I have suggested, the switching between languages points to a softening of boundaries between languages, we might even call it a "translingual space". The fact that Weynoet's text was a self-translation adds another dimension to his multilingual identity.

These examples illustrate that Weynoet often switched between the four most commonly-used languages in early modern Norwich. Furthermore, he often needed to translate between these languages as clerk to the Politic Men. His use of Latin helped to shape his linguistic identity and helped him to accrue social capital. Some cases of switching may, as Reynolds (2022: 146) suggests, cause the boundaries between languages to begin to evanesce.

5.2 John Cruso

As for John Cruso, both his parents came from Flanders, so like Weynoet his *vernaculus* was the Flemish variety of Dutch. He was baptised on 16 February 1593 in St. George's Colegate in Over-the-Water. He probably attended Norwich free grammar school, where he learnt Latin and possibly Greek. He could also improve his English as he was required to translate regularly between Latin and English. He would later translate two military works from French to English. He may have learnt French from his father who spoke the language, or a French teacher in the Walloon community, or from French-speakers in that community, or from a combination of these.

After several years in London, Cruso settled in the parish of St. Andrew's in Norwich, where he started a family and became a successful cloth merchant. He later moved to a large house in the wealthiest parish in Norwich, St. Peter Mancroft. He remained in the Dutch Stranger community becoming captain of the Dutch, and then the combined Dutch and Walloon, Stranger militia and an elder in the Dutch exile church. Such a pattern of upward mobility was not exceptional amongst the Strangers. However, what marks Cruso out above all is that he was a published author. He published five military works in English, including the two translations from French and one partial translation of a Dutch work on setting up camps on military campaigns by Simon Stevin (Joby 2022: 243–4). He also wrote English verse that remained unpublished and several Dutch verses.

Recent studies that problematise cultural differences indicate that identities are multiple and multilayered. Speakers or authors express their complex identities through language (Zhu & Li 2020: 238–9). Cruso does so by switching between vernacular languages, vernacular and classical languages, and dialect and standard language.[24] It is in his Dutch verses that Cruso engaged most actively in these different linguistic modes. They illustrate his agency as a creative user of language shaping his multilingual identity.

In 1622, Cruso published a short Dutch elegy on the Norwich-born minister of the London Dutch church, Simeon Ruytinck, who had died in the previous year. He gave the poem a Latin coda, which was one of the famous Roman poet, Horace's, *sententiae,* in some sense adding twice to the prestige of the vernacular poem.[25] He signed the verse "I.C. Norvic". "Norvic" is a shortened form of the Latin *Norvicensis*, by which Cruso identifies with his hometown. I.C. is Cruso's *onymat cryptique*, to use a phrase associated with the French literary theorist, Gérard Genette (Joby 2022: 107–8). He often used I.C. to sign his work. One possibility is that it allowed him to avoid associating himself with one language and one identity, although on the other hand it may have allowed him to embrace his multiple identities, or even to affirm his complex multilingual identity.[26] It could stand for the Latin Johannes Cruso, or the Dutch Jan Cruso or the English John Cruso. Alternatively, Cruso may be playing a game with his readers: some will know what the letters stand for, whilst others may have to do a little work with the hints that Cruso gives them to find out. Authors on translanguaging assert that this phenomenon involves a playful subversiveness, which we see at work here in Cruso's use of language (Zhu & Li 2020: 240, 242). On the other hand, as Jeanine Treffers-Daller (2024: 12) observes, literature outside the translanguaging discourse also references playfulness in language. Furthermore, it could be understood as an example of macaronics, a switching between linguistic modes that Peter Burke (2004: 133, 137) has aptly described as a form of clowning or "playful mixing".

24. In literary studies, the term "heterolingualism" is often used. This term, coined by Rainier Grutman (in French: 'hétérolinguisime') refers 'to the use of foreign languages or social, regional, and historical language varieties *in* literary texts'. It therefore "designates the *textual* insertion of speech differences in literature" (Meylaerts 2006: 4. Quoted in Sardin 2018: 4).

25. The *sententia* is from Horace, *Odes* (IV.8 line 28): "Dignum laude Virum Musa vetat mori" [The Muse will not let the Man worthy of praise perish]. A *sententia* is a generalising maxim encapsulating ethical wisdom (Joby 2022: 277).

26. One exception is a letter that he wrote in Dutch, but signed "Jo: Cruso" (i.e., Johannes) (Hessels 1887–97: III, i, 1285–6, letter 1793).

In 1642, Cruso published two Dutch verses; one was an elegy on Johannes Elison, whilst the other was an amplification of Psalm 8, in which Cruso, the church elder, reflected on the glory of God's creation. In the latter poem, Cruso both invents new Dutch compound words employing his creativity as a language user, and switches into Latin and Latinised Greek. One new compound word is *gelijck-voegentheyt*, which is a synonym for "symmetry". Whereas symmetry has Greek roots, *gelijck-voegentheyt* is formed with Dutch morphemes. Another new coinage is *graegh-gemaeghd* [greedy, lit. with a greedy stomach], which occurs in the phrase "graegh-gemaeghde Struys" [greedy ostrich] (Joby 2022: 230). One example of switching into Latin occurs in the phrase "Yeri koele stroom" [the Yare's cool stream]. *Yeri* is a genitive form of *Yerus*, a Latin name for the River Yare, which flows to the south of Norwich (Joby 2022: 227). The Yare has in fact had several Greek and Latin names. Ptolemy identified it as the *Γαρίεννον* (trans. *Gariennon*). In his chorography *Britannia* (1st ed. 1586), William Camden called it the *Gariensis*, whilst in a Latin verse on Norwich in the late sixteenth century, the diplomat Daniel Rogerius called it *Hierus*. This suggests that there was an element of freedom in the selection of Latin toponyms. Cruso's use of a Latin version of the river's name, correctly inflected, nevertheless, reminds the reader of his knowledge of this language. An example of Latinised Greek is *Chylus*. This comes from the Greek *χῦλός* (khūlós), which Cruso glosses as "een witte sap" [a white sap]. It is used by the Roman military author, Vegetius (*De Re Militari* [On the Art of War] 5: 37 & 65), whose work Cruso often cited in his own military books.

However, it is in his Dutch epigrams published in 1655 that we see Cruso's playfulness, which forms an intrinsic part of his multilingual identity, most clearly at work (Cruso 1655). Here, he steps over linguistic and social boundaries, highlighting the transgressive dimension of his use of language. In his epigrams, Cruso pokes fun at several characters, but they probably speak like Cruso. In this sense, he is "double-voicing", to use a term associated with Mikhail Bakhtin (e.g., Bakhtin 1963/1984). Here, "utterances (what has been articulated) carry with them 'tastes' of specific speakers and contexts, which can be re-articulated and recycled as well as being altered significantly and re-inscribed with new meanings" (Zhu & Li 2020: 236, 243). Another way of understanding "double-voicing" is that it presents the reader with two divergent discourses.

Like Weynoet, Cruso used Latin to add prestige to his vernacular texts. The title page includes two Latin quotations from the foremost Roman epigrammatist Martial. This helped to position and add prestige to the vernacular collection. Like other early modern epigrammatists, Cruso playfully worked at the interface of classical and vernacular languages, creating a new linguistic mode that fused these two types of language. He gave Latin titles to some of his Dutch epigrams, typically quotations from Roman and Neo-Latin authors including Horace, Virgil, Ovid, and Erasmus. As with the Latin coda to his 1622 elegy, this practice added prestige to his vernacular verses twice over (Joby 2022: 280, 283).

In several epigrams, Cruso presents the character *Monsieur*, a Dutchman who puffs himself up by trying to pass himself off as French. To emphasise his otherness, *Monsieur* is written in italics. On the one hand, this could be understood as code switching twice over: between languages and scripts. On the other hand, the shift in script could be viewed within the translanguaging discourse as a non-lingual practice: a graphic analogue of oral non-lingual practices such as intonation (Zhu & Li 2020: 242, 236).

In Epigram 179, Cruso presents Roemer, a Dutch soldier who has picked up some French whilst serving in France. He switches from Dutch to French to suggest playfully that Roemer has also adopted French manners: "'t Frans gereed'lick praat, / en draagt sich *A la Mod*" [speaks French with ease, / and comports himself *à la mode*] (lines 2b-3a). Cruso concludes that by adopting the French language and manners, switching cultures if you will, Roemer pretends to be "een groot Edelman" [a grand nobleman] (Joby 2022: 292, 344). Here, one might adapt the proverb recorded in Latin by Erasmus (*Adagia* 3.1.60) as "vestis virum facit" or "clothes make the man" to "lingua virum facit", i.e., "language makes man". Furthermore, one might add that "vir linguam facit", i.e., "man makes language". This points to the agency that authors on translanguaging emphasise as the language user creates language every day (Reynolds 2022: 144). Cruso's use of English marks him out as a social aspirer (Joby 2022: 158). One possibility is that he himself dropped some French in to his Dutch conversation to mark himself out as an educated man with social aspirations and that *Monsieur* represents one element of Cruso's complex social and linguistic identity: an example of Bakhtin's "double-voicing". Furthermore, by peppering his Dutch with French, he could build social capital within the Dutch Stranger community.

Epigram 84 concerns a Dutch-speaking courtier who drops French words into his Dutch or uses Dutch verbs derived from French to distinguish himself socially. He tells a peasant that his lord is too busy to see him:

> *Monsieur*, myn Heer is nu *Ge-occupeert*
> *Mafoy* 'k en durf hem niet *Importuneren*!
> Komt Mergen weer, en (so 't hem dan *Vaceert*)
> 'K sal myn *Devoir* doen u te *Depescheren*.
> [*Monsieur*, my Lord is now *occupé*
> By my *foi*, I dare not importune him!
> Come back tomorrow, and (if he is not occupied then)
> I shall do my *devoir* to dispatch you to him.]

The words in italics, marked as such in the printed version to emphasise their otherness, are either French words (Monsieur, Mafoy, devoir) or Dutch verbs derived from French ones (occuperen, importuneren, vaceren, depescheren).[27] French was a more prestigious language than Dutch, something of which Cruso, who had acute social antennae, knew well. He often switched from Dutch into more prestigious languages and so here may have been writing from his own experience as someone who used switching to distinguish himself socially. Such a shift would, however, mean that some speakers of Dutch would not understand what the courtier said. This leads to the punchline from the peasant:

> Ke (sey den Boer) wat moet ick nu betaalen.
> Van 't geen ghy secht in Duysch te doen vertaalen?
> [Well, (said the peasant), what do I have to pay
> To get what you say translated into Dutch?]

One concrete example of an exile switching between Dutch and French is Adriaan Walewein. In 1568, he wrote to a friend in Ieper, Gelein Everaert, to ensure that his younger brother was being looked after properly. He tells Gelein that it is high time that his brother learnt French, for he recognised its importance as a commercial language in southwest Flanders. He also recalls that he had taught him some Latin. He goes on to complain that some exiles were being called troublemakers (*uproermakers*), writing (Janssen 1857: 254):

> Maer waert te rechte gheinterpreteirt wie de uproermakers zijn, men zout vinden an huer teekenen ende ghwercken: *mes tout veint apoinct quil peult atendere.*
> [But if we want to correctly interpret who the troublemakers are, they would be found out by their signs and works: *but everything comes properly to those who wait*]

Walewein switches into French (in my italics) to give an apothegm, a common motivation for switching (Joby 2014a: 232–6). This could better be translated as "good things come to those who wait".

Returning to Cruso, going in the other direction, he uses Dutch dialects to mark the speech of those lower down the social order, exhibiting his playfulness as a user of language, and adding another layer to his complex multilingual identity. Furthermore, here again, he uses double-voicing, for the Dutch in his letters includes forms found in Flemish texts and he probably used these forms at home, at least in his younger days (Hessels 1887–97: III, i, 1285). In Epigram 169, a Fleming, Lieven, has travelled to Amsterdam, where the local people look down on him. In lines 3b-4a, Lieven addresses some of them, attempting to assert that he comes

27. *Vaceren* may be influenced by both the Latin *vacare* and the French *vaquer.*

from a family of a certain social standing: 'Myn Eere den Hontvangere / Va Ghent dat es myn Noom (secht hy)' [My Lord the Collector [of fines]/ Of Ghent, that is my uncle (he says)]. *Es* is a form of *is* [is] often found in Flemish texts including those written by Flemish exiles in Norwich (Willemyns 1979: 98–9). Just as Pieter Weynoet added a hypercorrect word-initial 'h' to *eischer*, so Cruso writes *hontvangere* instead of *ontvangere* [a collector of fines], which occurs in other forms of Dutch, to emphasise that Lieven comes from Flanders.[28] The use of dialectal forms by Lieven in some sense humorously undermines the claims that he is making about his social standing. The uncertainty over whether there is an 'h' before vowels led some Flemish authors to drop a word-initial 'h', an example of procope. This explains why Lieven says "Myn Eere" instead of "Myn Heere" [my Lord]. He drops the 'h' again in line 5, saying *uys* instead of *huys* [house] and in line 6, *ope* instead of *hope* [hope]. In line 12, we learn that Lieven comes from Cassel in the Flemish Westkwartier. This allows Cruso to conclude with a witty observation by a nobleman who had been listening to Lieven: "De Wijse (soomen leest) die quaamen uyt het Oosten" [The Wisemen (so one reads) came from the East].

In Epigram 160, Cruso switches from the emerging Standard Dutch to the Antwerp dialect, *Antwerps*, for comic effect. Here, a peasant, Iorden, must deliver a letter to a house next to the Antwerp Exchange. The Dutch for exchange is 'Beurs' (spelt 'Buers' here), but Iorden asks the way to the 'Buyel'. The reason for his confusion is that both "Beurs" and "Buyel" can mean "purse" or "wallet". However, of course, no-one can show him the way. Eventually, he meets a merchant, who tells him that he should ask for the 'Beurs', to which Iorden replies,

> S'Jaass (secht hy) wat sayn hier de luy vol spaytighayt!
> Een Buyel oft een Buers, wat isser onderscheyt?
> [Jesus (he says) how scornful the people here are!
> A purse or a bourse, what's the difference?]

S'jaass or *'Sjazus* [Jesus] is a common Antwerp curse. In *Antwerps*, the ij/ei diphthong sounds like aai or aij/ay, a feature that Cruso playfully exploits by writing *sayn* and *spaytighayt* instead of *zijn* [to be] and *spijtigheid* [scorn] in standard Dutch. *Buyel* is a southern dialectal form: *buidel* occurs elsewhere (*WNT*). Although dialectal forms point to social inferiority, Cruso's use of them marks him out as an insider in the Dutch or Flemish exile community, someone with sufficient knowledge of southern Dutch dialects not only to use them but exploit them for comic effect.

---

28. We may see the influence of Catullus here. In his *Carmen* 84, the subject Arrius adds an initial "h" to vowel-initial words to sound more Greek and therefore more educated calling himself Harrius and saying *hinsidias* instead of *insidias* [ambushes] and *Hionios* instead of *Ionios* [Ionian].

Cruso's Dutch contemporary Constantijn Huygens (1596–1687) playfully shifted between varieties of Dutch, too. He used the mutual incomprehensibility of *Haags Delflands*, a subdialect of *Hollands* spoken in and around The Hague, and *Antwerps* as the source of much humour in his play, *Trijntje Cornelis* (1653). Indeed, Huygens uses the same marked form aij for ij/ei employed by Cruso for the speech of the *Antwerpenaar* Francisco (note the Spanish name) (Act V, l. 57): "Per dio 't sal honde. Môij, en **waij zaijn** van ons stuck" (my bold) [By God, it will get nasty, Marie, and we'll get confused]. Other Dutch authors also mocked *Antwerps* or the broader regiolect, *Brabants*, of which *Antwerps* is a variety. The Amsterdam author Gerbrand Bredero (d. 1618) parodies the affected language of the *Antwerpenaar*, Jerolimo (again note the Spanish name), in his play set in Amsterdam, *Spaanschen Brabander* [Spanish Brabander] (1617). Again, this switching between varieties of the same language could be understood within the translanguaging discourse as playful subversiveness or as further examples of macaronics.

Authors on translanguaging draw attention not only to what is said, but also to the practice of not saying things, but leaving the reader in no doubt as to what is not being said. Matthew Reynolds gives an example from Charles Dickens' *Oliver Twist.* One of Fagin's boys, Charley Bates, is chatting about Oliver to the Artful Dodger. Charley says: "What a pity it is he isn't a prig!" The Artful Dodger then turns to Oliver to see whether he knows what a prig is. Oliver replies cautiously that he thinks he does know: "It's a th –; you're one, are you not?" (Reynolds 2022: 142–3). Similarly, in Epigram 30, Cruso leaves something unsaid, but also leaves the reader in no doubt what that is.

The epigram may have been inspired by an English version of a Latin epigram by Sir Thomas More. In his epigram, entitled *Medicinae ad Tollendos Foetores Anhelitus Provenientes a Cibis Quibusdam* [Remedies for taking away the foul breath that comes from eating certain foods], More writes that the remedy for covering up strong breath is eating onions. The remedy for covering up the onions is to eat garlic. He concludes by saying that if garlic does not remove the odour, then only one, scatological, solution remains: coprophagia (More 1963–97: III.ii (E254), 266–7):

> Spiritus at si post etiam grauis allia restat,
> Aut nihil, aut tantum tollere merda potest.
> [But if your breath remains offensive, even after garlic,
> Then either nothing or only shit can remove such a thing.]

The satirist Sir John Harington wrote an English epigram based on More's verse, which he published in his compendium on the flush toilet, *New Discourse of a Stale Subject, Called the Metamorphosis of Ajax*, in London in 1596. Two features of Harington's version, which are not in More's verse, also occur in Cruso's epigram. This suggests that Cruso used Harington's version rather than More's as his principal source. One is a reference in one version of his poem to tobacco, which had not reached Europe during More's lifetime.[29] The second is that in another version of his epigram, Harington replaces the reference to coprophagia with brackets (Kennedy 2016: 131; Hudson 1947: 71–2). Cruso includes the reference to tobacco and, like Harington, concludes his epigram with square brackets.[30] The final word in the first line of the final couplet is *ront* [round]. This allows the informed reader to deduce that the missing word is *stront* [stool]. In fact, in the British Library copy of Cruso's epigrams *Epigrammata*, *stront* has been written in the brackets in pen (Cruso 1655, Epigram 30; Joby 2022: 287–8).

Placing this example within the framework of translanguaging, it has something in common with the "translationality" or "that freer mode of re-writing which has the energy to mess with the standard forms" that Reynolds describes (Reynolds 2022: 143). Rather than giving a one-to-one equivalence of the Latin *merda*, which Reynolds calls "Translation Rigidly Conceived", Cruso uses []. The "silence" suggests something vulgar, something that cannot be said, but can like Dickens' "th—" be easily deduced. In another epigram based on one by More, number 28, Cruso again engages in "translationality". More's epigram concerns a girl whose nose is so large that her lover Tyndarus cannot kiss her on the lips. Her solution is to suggest very playfully that her lover kiss her where her nose does not get in the way. Cruso translates More's Latin epigram into Dutch but "translationalises" Tyndarus's name to "Cluchter" or "joker". This would be a suitable epithet for Cruso himself as a writer of Dutch epigrams (Joby 2022: 287–8).

Cruso does something similar with names in other epigrams, too. Epigram 185 is based on an epigram in the *Greek Anthology*, Epigram XI.104. It concerns a dwarf, Menestratus, who tries to ride an ant, but falls off. Cruso translates the Greek verse, possibly via a Neo-Latin model, into Dutch more or less literally, within the exigencies of metrical differences. However, he replaces Menestratus with Hansken. This could be translated into English as "Johnny". *-ken* is a Dutch diminutive suffix and encodes the dwarf's small stature (Joby 2022: 281). Epigram 214 is based on a Neo-Latin epigram by the Italian scholar and poet, Julius Caesar Scaliger. It concerns two sots, Loserus and Bibinus, and asks which one gets more drunk. At first, it seems that it is Loserus, for he gets drunk twice a day, whilst Bibinus only does so once. However, it turns out that Bibinus is always drunk, so he defeats Loserus in the inebriation stakes. In his Dutch version, Cruso replaces Loserus with Loy. This is a variant spelling of the Dutch word

29. Tobacco was first brought to Europe by the Spanish in the mid-sixteenth century.

30. In contrast to Harington who concludes his version with tobacco, Cruso begins with it, giving it as the initial reason for bad breath, 'Ghy drinckt Taback' [You smoke (lit. drink) tobacco].

lui, meaning "lazy". The name Bibinus is suggestive of *bibo*, the Latin "to drink". Cruso replaces Bibinus with *Suyper*. *Zuiper* in Modern Dutch means a toper. So, both names introduced by Cruso playfully embrace the theme of drinking (Joby 2022: 284–5). A final example occurs in Cruso's Epigram 120. It is based on the *Greek Anthology* Epigram XI.432 but may also owe something to another epigram by Sir Thomas More. The subject of the Greek version is *μῶρος* (transliteration: *mōros*) [fool]. Cruso "translationalises" this, to use Reynolds' term, as the Dutchman, Slechtaart, which in the seventeenth century meant "simpleton" (*WNT*). More wrote a couplet entitled *In Fatuum, E Graeco* [On a Fool. From the Greek], which was inspired by the same epigram from the *Anthology* (More 1963–97: III.ii (E106), 160–1). More's friend, Erasmus, famously used the fact that More's name sounds like the Greek *μῶρος* [stupid] in his work *Stultitiae Laus* [Praise of Folly, Gk: *Μωρίας ἐγκώμιον Mōrias enkōmion*]. This coincidence probably lay behind More's decision to name the fool Morio in his version of this epigram.

Concluding this section, the variety of language modes that Cruso uses in his verse is an expression of polyvocality or polyphony to use another term associated with Mikhail Bakhtin. It points to the complexity of Cruso's linguistic identity and indeed his own identity as a humorous, learned multilingual. Furthermore, his use of French and Latin indicate that he used language to build social capital. On the other hand, his use of Dutch dialects signal his position as an insider in the Dutch exile community in Norwich.

6. Conclusion

Although there was intensive contact between Dutch and other languages which resulted in a range of multilingual practices for some one hundred years in early modern Norwich, today there are very few vestiges of this contact. One possibility is that the word "plain" rather than "square" to indicate open areas in Norwich such as St. Andrews Plain comes from the Dutch word *plein*. However, this is not certain. Peter Trudgill has argued that a distinctive feature of the Norfolk dialect, zero-marking in the third-person singular present indicative, e.g., "he go" rather than "he goes", is a result of Dutch and French-speaking Strangers simplifying the verb conjugation when they learnt English. I, however, have raised questions about this suggestion by presenting examples of zero-marking in Norfolk texts written before the arrival of the Strangers in Norwich (Joby 2014b; 2016).

The aim of this chapter has been to analyse the multilingual practices that emerged because of contact between Dutch and three other languages in early modern Norwich: English, French, and Latin. The presence of three vernacular communities and of users of Latin was unusual in early modern England. This has afforded me a rare opportunity to use an English town as something like a laboratory to explore multilingual practices involving Dutch in a historical context. One limitation that I have encountered is the lack of evidence for the multilingual practices of women.[31] This is, of course, not to say that they did not engage in such practices, merely that the surviving documents were either written by men or include metalinguistic comment about men. Likewise, there is little evidence that natives who spoke English as a first language used Dutch. Nevertheless, the extant records have allowed me to provide a detailed account of multilingual practices involving Dutch in early modern Norwich.

A distinctive feature of this chapter has been its engagement with the literature on translanguaging. In her recent critique of the literature on translanguaging, Jeanine Treffers-Daller (2024) is right to assert that this concept has undergone semantic bleaching and that it currently lacks clear diagnostic criteria to specify which practices count as translanguaging and which do not. I acknowledge these concerns. However, rather than jettisoning the term and the related discourse, I have engaged with the literature on translanguaging to analyse whether this concept provides us with insights into the language practices that emerged from contact between Dutch and other languages in early modern Norwich, which I have described as a quadrilingual city.

First, I analysed practices that fall within definitions of translanguaging: shifts between Dutch and English in textile trade terminology; individuals' use of more than one proper name; code switching between Dutch and other languages in administrative documents; and the rendering of Norwich toponyms in Dutch. In each case, placing these multilingual practices within the translanguaging discourse has provided insights into these practices. For example, the use of more than one proper name, above all ones derived from Latin, Greek and Hebrew, allowed individuals to essentialise aspects of their identities and accrue social capital.

I then focused on the multilingual practices involving Dutch of two exiles, Pieter Weynoet and John Cruso. This, too, allowed me to engage with the aspect of the translanguaging discourse which focuses on individual agency and identity formation in the use or creation of language (Reynolds 2022: 144; Kohl *et al.* 2020: i). In the case of Weynoet, he used all three vernacular languages commonly

31. One possible case of a woman switching from Dutch to Latin is a letter written by Mayken, the wife of Clays Verbeke (Hessels 1887–97: III, i, 1052). She concludes with the date in Dutch and Latin: "Ady den 15en Augusti 1600 Stilo Anglię". In ancient Rome there is little evidence of women code switching. Indeed, Juvenal and Martial both castigated women for doing so (Adams 2003: 416). In the early modern period, the lack of opportunities for women to learn Latin was one reason why they switched language less than men. It is of course possible that Mayken received help from her husband, or merely copied the date from elsewhere, but we have no further information on her knowledge of languages.

spoken in early modern Norwich and translated between Dutch and French. Furthermore, he used Latin to position himself as a learned man. Some of the codas to his letters and minutes as clerk to the Politic Men raise questions about the relationship between code switching and intentionality. This, I have argued, may point in the direction of a softening of boundaries between languages, as advocates of translanguaging argue.

John Cruso, too, was a translator: from French and Dutch prose to English, and from Latin, and possibly Greek, verse, to Dutch. Like Weynoet, he wrote in Latin to position himself as a *vir eruditus.* One multilingual practice to which I paid special attention was his playful switching between Dutch and other languages and between standard and non-standard varieties of Dutch in his epigrams. This playfulness could be understood as macaronics. Alternatively, it could be viewed as an essential element of translanguaging which reflects Cruso's desire to express his complex multilingual identity (Zhu & Li 2020: 240). It allows him not only to demonstrate his knowledge of classical as well as vernacular languages, but also of non-standard varieties of Dutch including Flemish and *Antwerps.* By using these dialects, he expresses his identity as an insider in the Dutch exile community. By switching to French and drawing on a wide repertoire of Latin and Neo-Latin verse, he expresses another identity: that of a learned author who stands apart from, and implicitly above, the *hoi polloi* of the Dutch exile community. His extensive use of Latin alongside Dutch and French tells the reader that he was well-educated and can be understood as an attempt to build social capital, to return to Bourdieu's term. The scatological example in Cruso's verse points to the inclusion not only of the lingual but also the non-lingual in definitions of translanguaging

To conclude, whilst there is still work to be done on providing a close definition of translanguaging, the discourse that has emerged around this concept has, there can be little doubt, added energy to the study of multilingualism and multilingual practices. It draws attention to the use of different languages and shifts from one language to another to express identity and the language practices used to build social capital. Furthermore, it engages with questions concerning the ontology of language with some authors suggesting that practices described as translanguaging point to a softening of boundaries between languages and indeed social groups defined by language such as the language communities. I have explored these questions with reference to language users and communities in the early modern quadrilingual city of Norwich. In doing so, I have contributed not only to the current debate about the definition and the use of translanguaging, but also to the study of Dutch and contact linguistics.

Acknowledgement

I thank Nicoline van der Sijs for reading and commenting on an earlier version of this chapter.

References

doi Adams, James N. 2003. *Bilingualism and the Latin Language*. Cambridge: CUP.

Bakhtin, Mikhail. 1963/1984. *Problems of Dostoevsky's Poetics*, ed. and trans. by Caryl Emerson. Minneapolis: University of Minnesota Press.

Booij, Geert. 1995. *The Phonology of Dutch*. Oxford: Clarendon Press.

doi Bourdieu, Pierre. 1979. "Symbolic power." *Critique of Anthropology*, 4 (13–14): 77–85.

Brutel de la Rivière, Guilliam Johannes. 1879. *Het leven van Hermannus Moded* [*The life of Hermannus Moded*]. Haarlem: Erven F. Bohn.

doi Burke, Peter. 2004. *Languages and Communities in Early Modern Europe*. Cambridge: CUP.

Cruso, John. 1655. *EPIGRAMMATA: Ofte Winter-Avondts Tyt-korting*. Delft: Arnold Bon.

Decavele, Johan. 1975. *De Dageraad van de Reformatie in Vlaanderen (1520–1565)* [*The Dawn of the Reformation in Flanders*] (2 vols). Brussels: Paleis der Academiën.

Du Rieu, Willem. 1875. *Album studiosorum Academiae Lugduno Batavae MDLXXV-MDCCCLXXV* [*Album of students of Leiden University 1575–1875*]. The Hague: Martinus Nijhoff.

doi Forster, Leonard. 1967. *Janus Gruter's English Years*. London: OUP.

doi García, O., & Lin, A.M. 2017. "Translanguaging in bilingual education." In *Bilingual and multilingual education*, ed. by O. García, A.M. Lin & S. May, 117–130. Cham: Springer.

Hessels, J.H. 1887–97. *Ecclesiae Londino-Batavae archivum* [*Archive of the London Dutch Church*] (4 vols). Cambridge: Dutch Reformed Church.

doi Hudson, Hoyt H. 1947. *The Epigram in the English Renaissance*. Princeton: Princeton University Press.

Janssen, H.Q. 1857. "De Hervormde Vlugtelingen van Yperen in Engeland." [*The Reformed Exiles from Ieper in England*] In *Bijdragen tot de Oudheidkunde en Geschiedenis inzonderheid van Zeeuwsch-Vlaanderen*, ed. by H.Q. Janssen and J.H. van Dale, Tweede Deel, 211–304. Middelburg: J.C. & W. Altorffer.

Joby, Christopher. 2014a. *The Multilingualism of Constantijn Huygens (1596–1687)*. Amsterdam: AUP.

Joby, Christopher. 2014b. "Third-Person Singular Zero in the Norfolk Dialect: A Re-assessment." *Folia Linguistica Historica*, 35: 135–71.

doi Joby, Christopher. 2015a. *The Dutch Language in Britain (1550–1702)*. Leiden: Brill.

Joby, Christopher. 2015b. "The Use of Latin in Early Modern Norwich." *Neulateinisches Jahrbuch* 17: 47–78.

doi Joby, Christopher. 2016. "Third-Person Singular Zero in Norfolk English: An Addendum." *Folia Linguistica Historica*, 37: 33–60.

Joby, Christopher. 2022. *John Cruso of Norwich and Anglo-Dutch Literary Identity in the Seventeenth Century*. Cambridge: D.S. Brewer.

doi Joby, Christopher. 2024a. "The Norwich Exile Community and the Dutch Revolt." *History* 109 (384–385): 59–91.

doi Joby, Christopher. 2024b. "What does the birth of the Flemish and Walloon exile communities in Norwich tell us about local and national positions and practices adopted in response to large-scale migration from the Low Countries?" *Immigrants & Minorities*:

Joby, Christopher. 2025. "Translating in A Multilingual City. Norwich in the Early 17th Century." In *Polyglot Texts and Multilingualism in Early Modern Culture*. ed. by Adrian Izquierdo, 25–56. Leiden: Brill.

Kennedy, C.E. 2016. "Qualmish at the smell of leek." In *Disgust in Early Modern English Literature*, ed. by N.K. Eschenbaum and B. Correll, 124–142. London: Routledge.

doi Kohl, Katrin, Rajinder Dudrah, Andrew Gosler, Suzanne Graham, Martin Maiden, Wen-Chin Ouyang, and Matthew Reynolds (eds). 2020. *Creative Multilingualism: A Manifesto*. Cambridge: Open Book.

doi Li, Wei. 2017. "Translanguaging as a Practical Theory of Language." *Applied Linguistics*: 1–23.

doi Lim, Lisa and Umberto Ansaldo. 2015. *Languages in Contact*. Cambridge: CUP.

Meeres, Frank. 2012. *Strangers: A History of Norwich's Incomers*. Norwich: HEART.

doi Meeres, Frank. 2014. "Records Relating to the Strangers at the Norfolk Record Office." *Dutch Crossing*, 38(2): 132–53.

Meeres, Frank. 2018. *The Welcome Stranger: Dutch, Walloon and Huguenot Incomers to Norwich* 1550–1750. Norwich: Lasse Press.

doi Meylaerts, Reine (ed). 2006. *Heterolingualism in/and Translation*, Special issue of *Target* 18:1: 1–15.

Moens, W.J.C. 1888–9. *The Walloons and their Church at Norwich: Their History and Registers*. 1565–1832, 2 vols. Lymington: The Huguenot Society.

More, Thomas. 1963–97. *The Complete Works*, ed. by Clarence Miller et al.. 15 vols. New Haven & London: Yale University Press.

Reynolds, Matthew. 2022. "Translanguaging Comparative Literature." *Recherche Littéraire / Literary Research, vol. 38, International Association for Comparative Literature*: 141–53.

doi Risse, Guenter B. 1999. *Mending Bodies, Saving Souls: A History of Hospitals*. Oxford: OUP.

Rye, Walter. 1907–1909. *The Norwich Dutch Church: Register of Baptisms 1598–1619, in The East Anglian or Notes and Queries Vols.* 12–13. Norwich: Goose & Son.

Sandred, K.I. & B. Lindström. 1989. *The Place-Names of Norfolk. Part 1: The Place Names of the City of Norwich*. Nottingham: English Place-Name Society.

doi Sardin, Pascale. 2018. "Heterolingualism and interpretation in Atonement: Traduttore, traditore?" *'Études britanniques contemporaines* (55).

doi Treffers-Daller, Jeanine. 2024. "Translanguaging: What is it besides smoke and mirrors?" *Linguistic Approaches to Bilingualism*, pp. 1–16.

Venn, John & J.A. Venn. 1922–7. *Alumni Cantabrigienses: A Biographical List of All Known Students, Graduates and Holders of Office at the University of Cambridge, from the Earliest Times to 1900, Part I: From the Earliest Times to 1751*, 4 vols. Cambridge: CUP.

Willemyns, Roland. 1979. *Het niet-literaire Middelnederlands*. Assen: Van Gorcum.

Willemyns, Roland. 2013. *Dutch: Biography of a Language*. Oxford: OUP.

Wright, Laura. 2000. "Bills, Accounts, Inventories: Everyday Trilingual Activities in the Business World of Later Medieval England." In *Multilingualism in later medieval Britain*, ed. by D. Trotter, 149–156. Cambridge: D.S. Brewer.

doi Zhu Hua & Li Wei. 2020. "Translanguaging, identity, and migration." In *The Routledge Handbook of Language and Intercultural Communication*, 2nd ed., ed. by Jane Jackson, 234–48. London: Routledge.

CHAPTER 7

The Lithuanian translation of the *Statenbijbel* and how it was influenced by Dutch

Gina Kavaliūnaitė
Vilnius University

This chapter deals with the influence of the Dutch *Statenbijbel* and its language on a 17th-century Lithuanian Bible translation, the Chylinski Bible. In its language it differs from that of Chylinski's forerunner, the Lutheran Bretkūnas, and from Vilentas' *Gospels and Epistles,* which were used in Protestant churches. The difference was one of translation source as well as of dialect: Lutherans were active in Prussian Lithuania, whereas the Calvinists' centre was in the Grand Duchy of Lithuania (GDL). It was not until 2003 that research established that Chylinski's translation source was the *Statenbijbel*, and that many linguistic features of the Dutch translation shine through in the Lithuanian text. The influence of the *Statenbijbel* is manifest from the formal features of the text, and also from linguistic features. Besides bequeathing us a Lithuanian translation of the *Statenbijbel*, the Reformed Protestants of the GDL also started work on a Polish translation, which was never completed.

Keywords: Chylinski Bible, Dutch language influence, influence of the *Statenbijbel*

1. Introduction

This chapter deals with a little-known instance of the influence of the Dutch language abroad: a 17th-century Lithuanian Calvinist Bible translation that was based on a Dutch Bible, the so-called *Statenbijbel* or States Bible, and shows an unmistakable linguistic influence from Dutch. I shall briefly relate the circumstances in which this Dutch Bible, published in 1637, came to be the main source for a Lithuanian Bible translation and show in what ways the influence of the Dutch source and the Dutch language manifests itself.

https://doi.org/10.1075/impact.55.07kav

2. Lithuanians studying abroad in the 17th and 18th centuries

Between the late 16th and 18th centuries, many were the Lithuanians who went abroad to complete their education, as Lithuania had no university of its own. True, there was the Jesuit Academy founded in 1579, out of which Vilnius University would grow in time, but of course it was only for Roman Catholics. Protestants had to go abroad, and the universities of the Dutch Republic – Leiden, Utrecht and Franeker – were popular destinations for young Lithuanians who could afford a foreign education. Most of them were obviously sons of the privileged and affluent classes. In Leiden, the first Lithuanian matriculated in 1605. It was Joannes Mazginhieviz, on October 24, 1605 (Du Rieu, 1875:79). These Lithuanians included scions of the magnate families Radziwiłł, Zawisza, Hlebowicz, and Pac (Biržiška 1987:29). Sons of magnates sometimes brought their personal preachers and servants with them. On July 10, 1635, Andreas and Christophorus Mecinius and Nicolaus Krapha matriculated in Leiden with their personal preacher Johannes Petrigius and their servant Sigismundus Zaidlicius (Du Rieu, 1875:273). The *Album Studiosorum* of the Franeker Academy has many entries like *Melchior Johannes Bylewits, Nobilis Polonus* and *Boguslaus de Zbayns Zbayski, Nobilis Polonus* (matriculation numbers 5176 and 5348). But sons of less distinguished families also flocked to Franeker, such as *Samuel Reczynski, Polonus* (5279), or *Gideon Reczynski, Polonus* (5453). Most of them studied law, medicine or divinity. Some, such as Matthias Krasnowiecki (1636), Johannes Borzymowski (1637) and Gabriel Reczynski (1667), are on record as having defended disputations (Meijer 1972, Postma and van Sluis 1995). Some matriculated as *Polonus*, others as *Lituanus*, and Michael Mathischevisius matriculated in Leiden on November 27, 1635 as *Polonus Lituanus* (Du Rieu 1875:274). This should not surprise us, as in those days Poland and Lithuania were one state, the so-called Commonwealth of Two Nations. The Grand Duchy of Lithuania, which was part of the Commonwealth, was bilingual, with official documents usually written in Polish, the language that was also predominant among the gentry and the clergy, though many of them also spoke Lithuanian. The importance of Lithuanian increased as interconfessional competition gained strength and the need to spread religion among the Lithuanian-speaking common people was felt. Among the young people who turned to the Lithuanian language the one most worthy of being remembered was probably the prospective Bible translator Samuel Boguslaus Chylinski, who matriculated at Franeker University on May 5, 1654, initially as a Pole – *Polonus*. In later documents he figures as a Lithuanian – *Lituanus* (Chylinski 1659:7). Chylinski also emphasises his Lithuanian ethnicity on the title page of his New Testament manuscript, which states that the translation was made *užmariose, nog Samuelies Baguslawo Chylinska.* **Lietuwniko.** O *noklodu Diewo-*

Baymos karalistes Anglios, už karalawima Jo Milistos Karalaus KAROLO Antroia Karaliaus Anglios, Szkocios, Irlandios ir Francios ('overseas, by Samuel Boguslaus Chylinski **of Lithuania** [bold added for emphasis – GK], and published at the expense of the pious Kingdom of England during the reign of His Gracious Majesty Charles the Second, King of England, Scotland, Ireland and France'). Chylinski often signed the letters he wrote to his patrons as *Interpres Lituanus.*

Chylinski was, however, not of purely Lithuanian descent. His father Adrian Chylinski had come to Lithuania from the lands of the Polish Crown and found employment as court preacher to Christopher Radziwiłł, Hetman (Field Marshal) of the Grand Duchy and a fervent member of the Reformed Protestant Church. Adrian Chylinski became proficient in Lithuanian and was sent, in 1631, to the Lithuanian congregation of Raseiniai. Two years later he was transferred to Šventežeris in the district of Seiniai, where the future Bible translator would soon be born. His mother was descended from the gentry family Minwid (Minvydas), which greatly distinguished itself in the history of Lithuanian Protestantism: five of her close relatives rose to the rank of church superintendent (Lukšaitė 1971: 120–122). The young Samuel Boguslaus was trained at the leading Calvinist school, the Kėdainiai Gymnasium, where he was taught Latin, Greek, grammar, rhetoric and arithmetic, and also studied the Bible as well as the Polish and Latin Catechisms (Tworek 1970: 232–236). Plans entertained by the Radziwiłłs to transform the Kėdainiai Gymnasium into a university foundered as the Second Northern War broke out in 1655. A bursary from the Reformed Protestant Synod enabled Chylinski to go to Franeker for further study after completing the Gymnasium. When the war broke out, Chylinski found himself deprived of support from his home country and he went to England, where he arrived in 1657. He succeeded in securing the support of influential learned men including Robert Boyle, philosopher and chemist; John Wallis, Oxford professor of geometry; Samuel Hartlib, a prominent figure in the 'Republic of Letters'; and other scholars, several of whom were to become founding members of the Royal Society. In his desire to serve the Lithuanian Reformed community, Chylinski set out to translate the Bible into Lithuanian. Part of the Old Testament was printed in London in 1660 thanks to the support of influential benefactors. The printed part of the OT lacks a title page; the only extant copy is held by the British Library (shelfmark C 51.b.13). His work was also brought to the attention of King Charles II, and the King's Privy Council decreed a country-wide collection towards the printing of the Lithuanian Bible. Chylinski's endeavours to have a Lithuanian Bible printed are described in fair detail in a letter from John Wallis to Robert Boyle (a facsimile, with transcription and translation, can be found in Kavaliūnaitė 2015: doc. 44). In order to muster support for the collection, Chylinski published his brochure *An Account of the Translation of the Bible into the Lithvanian Tongve* (Chylinski 1659), in which he stressed the need for a Lithuanian Bible, briefly characterised the Lithuanian books already available to the faithful, and outlined his own translation project, which was to include the larger and shorter Westminster Catechisms, Theodore Haak's *Dutch and English Annotations* (1657) and a metrical Lithuanian version of the Psalms, to be sung to the English melodies. The booklet – the first advertising brochure in Lithuanian history – also contains recommendations from Christophorus Munsterus, Rector of the Franeker Academy, and G. Kaldenbach, Secretary and Librarian of the Academy – praising Chylinski as a gifted scholar and Bible translator.

Due to an unfavourable turn of circumstances – strife among the Lithuanian Reformed community, the plague that hit London in 1664 and 1665, and the fading influence of some of Chylinski's patrons after the Restoration of Charles II – the printing of the Lithuanian Bible was discontinued. Only three copies of the printed part of the Old Testament are known: 1. The Vilnius copy, the longest of the three, went as far as the 6th Psalm of David. Presumably, this was a copy Chylinski brought to Lithuania to have it approved by the Synod. In 1805, Jerzy Grużewski donated it to Vilnius University Library. When the Russians ordered the closure of Vilnius University in 1832 and divided its library collections among Russian universities, the Vilnius copy of the Chylinski Bible was taken to St Petersburg, and its subsequent fate is unknown. 2. The so-called Berlin copy, much shorter, was presumably purchased by the bibliophile Andreas Müller during a stay in London. After his death, it was held for some time by the Szczecin City Library, whence it was transferred to the Royal Library in Berlin. Trace of it was lost after World War II. 3. Only one copy of the printed part of the Old Testament as well as the manuscript of the New Testament are now extant, both held by the British Library in London (OT shelfmark C 51.b.13, NT shelfmark MS 41301). Vilnius University Library also holds photographs of the now lost Berlin copy, which was twice the length of the London copy (up to Job 6). It was photographed before getting lost and could thus be used for the facsimile edition of the Old Testament (Kavaliūnaitė 2008).

3. Chylinski's choice of translation source and translation method

From which language(s) did Chylinski translate? At the Franeker Academy, he had certainly been trained in Hebrew and Greek. As a cultivated person, educated at the Gymnasium of Kėdainiai, he was fluent in Latin. As a citizen of the Grand Duchy of Lithuania, he spoke both languages of the Polish-Lithuanian Commonwealth. Lithuanian was the language of the common people whom he wished to reach with his Bible translation, while Polish was the language of the privileged and educated classes, widely used not only by the gentry and the clergy of several denominations but also in official documents of the Lithuanian Reformed Church, such as the synodal records to which we owe much of what we know about Chylinski's life and deeds.

While Chylinski probably had quite a solid knowledge of the main Biblical languages, Hebrew and Greek, it is only natural that he should have looked for inspiration to the existing translations into the vernaculars. He was undoubtedly familiar with both Polish Calvinist Bible translations available in his days: the 1563 Brest Bible and the 1632 Danzig Bible. It was, however, the translation commissioned by the States General of the Dutch Republic, known as the *Statenvertaling* (States Translation) or *Statenbijbel* (States Bible), that made the deepest impression on him. First printed in 1637, a second edition was published in 1657 in which many inconsistencies in spelling were eliminated. This second edition was reprinted countless times until well into the 19th century. The *Statenbijbel* was widely respected for its faithfulness to the originals and famous for its elaborate annotations, known as the *Kanttekeningen*, an English translation of which was published in 1657 as *The Dutch Annotations Upon the Whole Bible* (Haak 1657). In his *Account of the Translation of the Bible into the Lithuanian Tongue*, Chylinski stressed the need to translate not only the Bible itself, but also the Annotations of the *Statenbijbel*: "Likewise they would do a thing very pleasing, both to God and good men, if they would compile Notes on the Bible, out of the most learned *English and Dutch Annotations*, (of which sort nothing hath as yet been done in several nations) or meerly by their joynt labor translate both of them" (Chylinski 1659: 5).

Although Chylinski does not state his sources, research (Kavaliūnaitė 2003, 2004) has shown that his translation is based mainly on the Dutch *Statenbijbel*. The printed part of his Old Testament does not contain a preface where he would have explained his choices, neither does he mention the Dutch Bible in his *Account*, which was, after all, meant for an English rather than Dutch public. Why he chose the *Statenbijbel* is, however, not a difficult guess. The authority of the Dutch divines at whose feet he sat at the Franeker Academy likely played a role, but it was probably the translation technique that was decisive in Chylinski's eyes. The Dutch translators followed the method of formal equivalence, as it is called by Eugene Nida, who contrasts this translation method with that of functional (or dynamic) equivalence (de Waard and Nida 1986: 40–42). The latter can best be illustrated with Luther's translation, which was intended to speak to a broad public. Luther wanted his translation to be understandable to people in the street, the market place and the household. In rendering complicated constructions of the originals, Luther did not shy away from freer interpretations, as he explains in his *Sendbrief vom Dolmetschen* ('An Open Letter on Translation'). Calvinists, who emphasised the importance of collective Bible study, valued literalness as a guarantee for a correct understanding of the Biblical text. Willem

Baudart and Johannes Bogerman, who were among the *Statenbijbel* translators, put it like this: "Wij zijn gebleven bij de oorspronckelicke woorden Godts, die in den Hebreuschen ende Chaldeuschen text staen, soo nae ende nauwe [...] als 't ons eenichsins mogelick geweest" ('We have stuck to God's original words as contained in the Hebrew and Chaldean texts as closely and narrowly as was at all possible'; cited from de Bruin 1993: 271). Whereas Lutheran translators strive for naturalness, Calvinist translators seek to reflect the structure of the original texts written in Hebrew and Greek (for more details cf. Kavaliūnaitė 2019a: 242–247, Kavaliūnaitė 2019b). This places the Dutch Bible in the same school of Bible translation to which the King James Bible also belongs, but the emphasis on faithfulness over naturalness was probably even stronger in the case of the Dutch Bible. In all cases where the renderings of the Dutch *Statenbijbel* stand out among those of translations with similar intentions by their particular closeness to the letter, Chylinski follows them, as we will see further on.

Before we move on to the influence of the *Statenbijbel*, and of the Dutch language, on Chylinski's translations, a few words should be said about the renown of the Dutch Calvinist Bible among Reformed Protestants in the Polish-Lithuanian Commonwealth in general. Chylinski was by no means alone in his high esteem for the Dutch Bible. It was gaining increased popularity abroad in the years that Chylinski spent in the Netherlands. In 1657 Haak published the Dutch Annotations in English; in 1669 a new edition of the Geneva Bible was printed with a French translation of the *Dutch annotations* (the Maresius Bible); editions of the Luther Bible printed in 1668 in Frankfurt, in 1715/6 in Minden and in 1729 in Basle by Paulus Tossanus contain *Glossen und Auslegungen* [Glosses and Explanations] based mostly on the annotations of the *Statenbijbel* (Jaakke 1996: 15–24; Jaakke 1997: 3–12; Bremmer 2015). The records from the meetings of the Lithuanian Reformed Synod held in Biržai, Belica and Župrany between 1692 and 1698 make repeated mention of plans to have the *Statenbijbel* translated into Polish. The Lithuanian Synod had obtained two copies of a *Statenbijbel* edition with the Annotations from the Netherlands, and the books of the Pentateuch were assigned for translation to the ministers Jan Jordan, Jan Paterson, Samuel Lutomirski and Daniel Mikołajewski. Subsequent synodal records also contain directions as to who is to translate the remaining books of the Old Testament. They furthermore state that the translators should confer among themselves in order to achieve uniformity in spelling, and that they should report to the Synod every year about advances made. Unfortunately, the work that was begun with such enthusiasm was never completed. In Canon 4 of the records from the 1698 synodal meeting of Župrany, we read the following: "Work on the Dutch Bible, which was distributed among several Brethren for translation into Polish, cannot be continued after the passing away of the Reverend Daniel Mikołajewski of blessed memory, Elder of the churches of the District of Samogitia and prime mover of this project; therefore the Brethren who hold the aforementioned Bible texts should return them to the Reverend Elder of the Vilnius District; such parts as they have already translated they should likewise hand in, to be kept for better times. Thus decided by the present Congregation" (Kavaliūnaitė 2015: docs. 96, 97, 98, 101). The subsequent fates of the manuscript translations are unknown. The archives of the Lithuanian Reformed churches were scattered and mostly destroyed during the following centuries of war and foreign occupation.

4. Research on the Chylinski Bible and its language

The printed part of the Chylinski Bible went as far as the Book of Psalms. In spite of the translator's efforts, the printing was never resumed, and the further parts of the Old Testament as well as the New Testament remained in manuscript. A fragment from his translation of the Lord's Prayer found its way into John Wilkins' *Essay Towards a Real Character and a Philosophical Language* (London 1668), which contained versions of this text in many languages. The Lithuanian version is provided with a note saying it is taken from a Lithuanian Bible printed in London in 1660. In actual fact Wilkins probably got the text in handwritten form from Chylinski himself or from some fellow of the Royal Society, as it contains copying mistakes pointing to handwriting. This inaccurate source reference was reproduced many times in 18th and 19th-century bibliographical works, and Chylinski's version of the Lord's Prayer can be found in many polyglots. The London Lithuanian Bible was a sought-after curiosity among bibliophiles, none of whom had actually seen it. After attempts to resume the printing had failed, the printed sheets of the Old Testament were handed over to the library of the Dutch Congregation in London, but no trace of them is extant. It was not until the final decade of the 19th century that three copies of the Old Testament emerged in London, Berlin and Vilnius, and by sheer accident the British Library acquired the New Testament from an antiquarian in the 1930s. Heinrich Reinhold has done extensive research on the Old Testament (Reinhold 1895; 1896). A transcription of the manuscript NT was published by Jan Otrębski and Czesław Kudzinowski (Kudzinowski, Otrębski 1958; Kudzinowski 1964; 1984). Finally, after the translation source of Chylinski's Bible had been established, Kavaliūnaitė published the editorial series *The Chylinski Bible*, containing facsimiles of the extant parts of the OT, higher-quality facsimiles of the NT manuscript and a collection of source texts relevant to the history of the Chylinski Bible (Kavaliūnaitė 2008; 2015; 2019).

Lithuanian is a language of relatively late attestation (the oldest books go back to the 16th century), and few Old Lithuanian texts have come down to us, so that a large text such as Chylinski's Bible is of great value. Modern linguistic research requires accurate transcriptions accessible in digital space. A digital version of the Chylinski Bible is under way. A Chylinski website developed by Vilnius University has been operational since 2019 (www.chylinskibible.flf.vu.lt). At the present stage, it contains the transcribed text of the Chylinski NT manuscript. Accurately rendering an old manuscript text always poses challenges. Chylinski's manuscript went through many stages of editing, the editors being concerned mainly with the language of the translation. The opening and closing pages of the manuscript moreover contain entries in various languages, some connected with the Bible translation while others allude to the circumstances of Chylinski's life and work, all this interspersed with occasional verse, riddles and the like. The palaeographer Rūta Čapaitė has concluded that at least three editors must have put their hands to the text apart from Chylinski himself. Who they were cannot be established (Čapaitė 2019: cxljv–clxxxvij). Various search functionalities were created for users' convenience: they can view different screen versions of the text reflecting successive editorial layers, and they can read first-hand and last-hand versions (the latter with additions from the website creators in places were the editorial process remained incomplete). Philologists and linguists will benefit from the version showing all successive text layers and corrections. A feature absent from other similar websites is that users can separately access different types of corrections (lexical, morphological, syntactic). The website offers direct, inverse and frequency-based lists of word-forms. Derived data sets are shown in the lower right screen section. Every word in the derived lists can be linked to a context (displayed in the lower left screen section) by pressing a reference to a Bible verse or manuscript line. Line or verse numbers in the left section lead in their turn, when clicked, to fragments of the manuscript facsimile. The website also covers the opening and closing pages of the manuscript with title pages and epigraph as well as sundry jottings in Lithuanian, Polish, Dutch, Latin, Hebrew, English and even Arabic. They range from work notes connected with the translation through short mini-glossaries to loose inscriptions. By selecting a language from a menu the user can generate a list of all entries in a given idiom.[1] A screen copy from the website is shown in Figure 1.

1. The website was developed in implementation of the project "Samuel Boguslaus Chylinski's New Testament. Research into the Manuscript, Facsimile and Interactive Digital Edition", financed by the Lithuanian Research Council, grant No. LIP-022/2016. The programmer of the website was Wolf-Dieter Syring (Buxtehude). Collaborators: Felix Thies (Frankfurt am Main, transcription and annotation), Bartłomiej Kowal (Warsaw, annotation), Valentinas Kulinič (Vilnius, annotation), Rūta Čapaitė (Vilnius, palaeographical advice); the project leader was Gina Kavaliūnaitė (Vilnius).

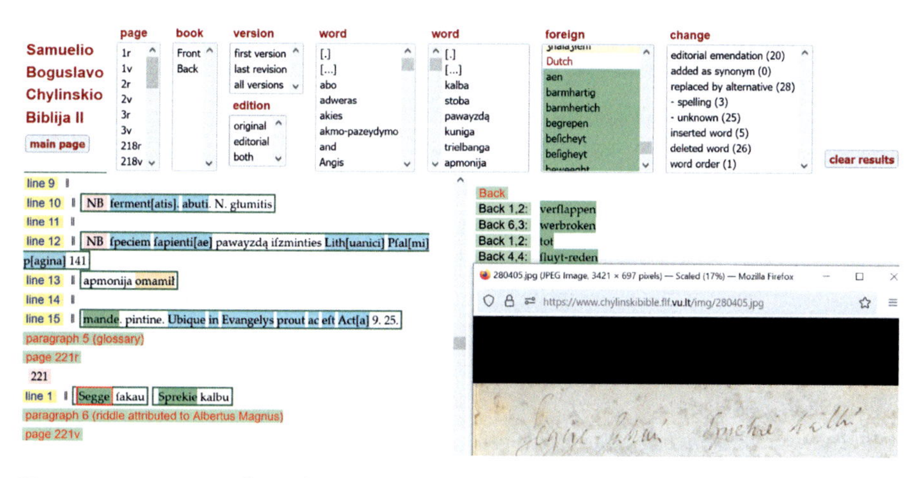

Figure 1. Screen copy from the website www.chylinskibible,flf.vu.lt showing a fragment of folios 220v–221r of the New Testament manuscript with sundry work notes. The user's search menus are indicated at the top of every column. The first column (*page*) enables a search according to page number, the second (*book*) enables choice between the opening and closing pages (in the New Testament text this column lists book and chapter numbers). The next two columns offer search facilities according to word form, with further choices between direct and inverse word-form lists. The penultimate column contains a list of non-Lithuanian words, with links to the places and contexts of their occurrence. The rightmost column shows a classification of editorial changes (this classification is relevant to the translation text rather than to the frame texts shown on this screen). The lower left screen section shows the manuscript text generated by searches in the three first search columns. The content of the lower right screen section is generated by searches in the direct and inverse word-form lists, the foreign word list or the list of editorial changes. The lowermost right screen section shows a fragment of the manuscript facsimile that can be accessed by clicking a verse or line number.

In the very near future, the website will be supplemented with the OT text. The whole text (OT and NT) will be completely lemmatised and morphologically annotated. Every verse of the Chylinski Bible will be paralleled with the corresponding place of the *Statenbijbel* and the Polish Danzig Bible. Every lemma will also be linked to the corresponding Dutch and Polish lemmas and their places of attestation in the texts, facilitating lexical research.

5. Textual influence of the Dutch Bible

The influence of the *Statenbijbel* on Chylinski's Bible is immediately obvious. His translation includes the book and chapter summaries contained in the *Statenbijbel*, compiled by the Dutch translators and absent from other Bible translations. A few places in Chylinski's translation show that he took the commentaries of the *Statenbijbel* into account, and we also find explicit references to them. So, for instance, one of the closing pages of the NT manuscript contains an entry referring to the Dutch annotations on the Book of Isaiah (Chylinski's translation of which is not extant): *Es. 59.19 hemistichion ultimum. Ateis nes kaypo siauras upelis, kuri pakiels Dwasia Wieszpaties uź kuniga. Dicitur hic Deum velle hostes suos et populi sui ulcisci et punire, vero eos adjuvare prosperareque volunt belgae Interpretes*[2] (ChNT: f. 220r). The annotion is not cited directly but paraphrased in Lithuanian and Latin, probably from memory. It is only natural to conjecture that Chylinski could also have used the Dutch text as the basis for his Lithuanian version of the Bible text itself. This is also suggested by the work notes left by Chylinski on the opening and closing pages of the New Testament manuscript. These notes are extremely heterogeneous in character, but part of them consists of Dutch words and their Lithuanian translation equivalents. The translator seems to have made these notes not because the meaning of the Dutch words was not clear to him but because he was concerned with their consistent rendering. In several places, he notes how semantically similar pairs of Dutch lexemes should be differentiated in the Lithuanian translation:

(1) ChNT MS 218r verston ismanit; begrepen suprast
verston 'understand'; *begrepen* 'comprehend'

(2) ChNT MS 221r segge sakau; sprekie kalbu
segge 'I say'; *sprekie* 'I speak'

(3) ChNT MS 218r Gal. 6.v.8. wertragen tingiet. Verslappen nustot
wertragen 'slack'; *verslappen* 'abate'

2. "Isaiah 59.19, final hemistich. For they will come as a narrow river, which the Spirit of the Lord will elevate as a priest. Here it is said that God will avenge Himself on His and His people's enemies and punish them, whereas the Belgic (i.e., Dutch, GK) translators say that He wants to assist and speed them." Chylinski seems to have misunderstood the wording of the Annotations here.

In most cases, it is easy to identify the Bible verses to which the notes refer:

(4) ChNT MS 224r *werbroken worden* susidauzyt Es. 8 v.15
StB Ende vele onder hen sullen struykelen / ende vallen / *ende verbroken worden*
'And many among them shall stumble, and fall, and be broken.'

(5) ChNT MS 220v Ecl. 5. v 13. *moejelich besticheyt* bingi rupestis
StB Ofte de rijckdom selfs vergaet door eene *moeijelicke besigheyt*
'But those riches perish by evil travail.'

These work notes are revealing in that they show that Chylinski must have translated the whole OT, though the extant printed part includes neither Isaiah nor Ecclesiastes. In between his work on the NT translation he must have been revising his OT text.

Other work notes deal with matters of grammar. There is one note on how to render the difference between the dative and the prepositional construction with *tot* with speech-act verbs:

(6) ChNT MS 218r hebbe ik u geschrewen raszau jumus
Ergo q[uan]do est tot u ad vos. Jusump
'so when it says *tot u, ad vos, jusump* [must be used]'

This means that the Dutch dative corresponds to a Lithuanian dative but the construction with *tot* ('to') must be rendered with the Lithuanian allative case. The allative was an Old Lithuanian case expressing direction but also the addressee of a speech act (for more details see Kavaliūnaitė 2003: 33–49). This concern with exact correspondences between Dutch and Lithuanian vocabulary items and constructions suggests that Chylinski was working with the Dutch text as the principal basis for his translation. The following example shows that in his translation he actually sticks to the correspondence stated above, and renders *tot* with the allative case:[3]

3. The following grammatical glosses are used: ACC = accusative, ALL = allative, a case denoting direction, GEN = genitive, ILL = illative, a case denoting motion inward, INE = inessive, a case denoting placement within, INF = infinitive, NEG = negation, PASS = passive, PL = plural, PRS = present, PST = past, PTCP = participle, Q = question marker, SBJV = subjunctive.

(7) Exod. 3.11

ChOT	Tare	tada	Mayźeszus	Diewop
	say.PST.3	then	Moses	God.ALL
StB	Doe syde Mose tot Godt			
KJV	And Moses said unto God			

This example also shows another thing: the forms of the Biblical proper names used by Chylinski are not taken over from the Dutch text. Instead, where the forms of proper names deviate from the original Hebrew or Greek forms Chylinski uses traditional Lithuanian forms based on the Polish ones: *Mayźeszus* is based on Polish *Mojżesz* (Moses), just as *Lukoszus* 'Luke' is based on Polish *Łukasz*, and *Judoszus* 'Judas' on Polish *Judasz*.

Of course, Chylinski took these traditional Polish-based forms from memory, and he didn't have to look at the Polish text in order to be reminded of them. However, his knowledge of Dutch was not perfect, as I will show below, and it would therefore also be natural to assume that he might from time to time have looked at the other, notably Polish, translations in order to gain a better understanding of the textual meaning. Providing irrefutable proof of this is hard, however. If we think, in particular, of Polish, we must keep in mind that this was one of his native languages, and Polish influences in his text may stem from his familiarity with the language rather than from reliance on the text. I will not pursue this point, concentrating instead on the influence of the Dutch text and, through the text, of the Dutch language. This influence can be proven beyond reasonable doubt not only for the book and chapter summaries, where it is only to be expected, but also for the Bible text. Two aspects are to be distinguished here, and to be discussed separately: the textual and the linguistic one. The influence of the Dutch text may be felt in certain interpretations of the Biblical text, certain formulations or constructions analogous to the Dutch ones, without the translation equivalent demonstrably diverging from what may be assumed to have been idiomatic Lithuanian expression. The other is the copying of structural properties of the Dutch language. Let us first look at the textual influences.

The first thing that strikes us is how Chylinski imitates the literal renderings of the *Statenbijbel* as opposed to the freer paraphrases offered by most other translations, including the Septuagint and the Vulgate. In the Authorised Version, the creation of Eve is announced in Genesis 2.18 with the words:

(8) KJV *It is not good that the man should be alone; I will make him an help meet for him.*

This is a relatively free translation. Let us compare a few authoritative texts:

(9) Sept ποιήσωμεν αὐτῷ βοηθὸν κατ᾽ αὐτόν
'a helpmate according to him',

(10) Vulg *faciamus ei adjutorium simile sibi*
'a helpmate similar to him'

The Hebrew text, however, has *kənegdô,* which literally means 'in front of him, opposite to him'. The Dutch translators render this literally, and Chylinski follows them:

(11) StB ick sal hem eene hulpe maken [die] als tegen hem over zy
ChOT [padarysiu jamuy pagiałbę]

kuriy	butu	kaypo	ties	ghi
which	be.SBJV.3	as	across	him.ACC

'as if opposite to him' or 'as if across from him'.

In other cases it is not necessarily the closeness of the Dutch translation to the original wordings that led Chylinski to follow the *Statenbijbel.* In some instances the *Statenbijbel* offers a divergent interpretation of a Hebrew sentence structure that sets it apart from all other translations both old and new. In such cases, Chylinski usually follows the Dutch translators. This can be seen in Genesis 11.6 where the building of the Tower of Babel is described. God observes the construction works and says, in the wordings of the King James Bible, the Septuagint and the Vulgate:

(12) KJV and now nothing will be restrained from them, which they have imagined to do
Sept καὶ νῦν οὐκ ἐκλείψει ἀπ᾽ αὐτῶν πάντα, ὅσα ἂν ἐπιθῶνται ποιεῖν
Vulg nec desistent a cogitationibus suis donec eas opere conpleant

The *Statenbijbel,* however, reads this as an interrogative sentence – a deliberative question in which God considers whether the time has not come for Him to put an end to this human endeavour. This interpretation is taken over by Chylinski:

(13) Gen. 11.6
StB Maer nu en soude hen niet afgesneden worden al wat sy bedacht hebben te maken?
ChOT

bet	dabarjen,	ne-butu=gu	jemus	wis	tey	nupjauta
but	now	NEG-be.SBJV=Q	them.DAT	all	that	cut.off.PTCP.PASS

[ką nukrowe padaryt]
'But should not everything they have imagined to do be cut short?'

In their wish to draw as much sense and guidance from the Biblical text as they possibly could, the authors of the *Statenbijbel* liked to etymologise, not always successfully in the light of more recent philological research. One of the Hebrew terms referring to the Holy of Holies, *dəbîr*, was associated by many Bible scholars with the verbal root *dbr* 'speak'. This interpretation, now generally considered incorrect, also underlies the Vulgate's rendering *oraculum*. Nowadays this word is explained as 'hindmost chamber, innermost room (of the Temple)' (Gesenius 1906: 184). In the *Statenbijbel* it is translated as *aenspraeckplaets*, 'place of address'. As explained in the Annotations (note on 1 Kings 6.5), the Holy of Holies is the place whence God addresses the High Priest and answers his prayers. Chylinski follows the *Statenbijbel* and translates this as *Kałbos-wieta* 'the place of speech'.

In the more literal Bible translations – the *Statenbijbel*, the King James Bible, the Polish Danzig Bible and others – words added by the translators for better comprehension of the text's meaning are printed in square brackets or in italics. Chylinski also uses italics for this purpose, e.g., Gen. 3.24; Gen. 6.16 etc. Such places are numerous. Interestingly, Chylinski also does this in his translations of the book and chapter summaries taken from the *Statenbijbel*, which must also, in Chylinski's eyes, have been imbued with high authority, something adding a particular value to the Bible text. If a learned word of Latin origin used in the Dutch text is judged to be in need of an explanatory gloss, this is added in italics:

(14) Lev., book summary
StB van de Levitische Ceremonien
ChOT ape Levitiszkias Ceremonias *aba budus*
about Levitic ceremony.ACC.PL or custom.ACC.PL
'about the Levitic ceremonies *or customs*'

(15) Lev., book summary
StB onder de wetten worden Historien in gevoeght
ChOT terp prowu idetos ira Historios *aba pasakos*
among laws inserted are histories or tales
'among the laws, histories *or tales* are inserted'

6. Lexical and grammatical influence of the Dutch Bible

Chylinski does not, in principle, borrow Dutch words used in the *Statenbijbel.* In a few places in the manuscript New Testament, he left untranslated Dutch words, but they were evidently meant to be replaced by suitable translation equivalents at a later stage. In Mark 12.1, Chylinski was not sure about the rendering of *toren* 'tower' (based on Chylinski's own rendering of Gen. 11.4, the word that escaped him could have been *turma* 'tower'):

(16) ChNT Zmogus nekuris [...] ir pabudawojo *toorn*
StB Een mensche [...] groef eenen wijnparsback / ende bouwde eenen *toren*
'A *certain* man planted a vineyard [..] and built a tower'

In a parallel passage in Matt. 21.33, Chylinski simply left a blank in the text:

(17) ChNT Buwo nekuris Gaspadorius, kursey uzsodyno Winnicźią, ir [...] pabudawojo teypag <...>
StB Daer was een heere des huys / die eenen wijngaert plantede [...] ende bouwde eenen *toren*
'There was a certain householder, who planted a vineyard, [...] and built a tower'

A few other places where Chylinski left untranslated Dutch words in the Lithuanian text:

(18) Tit. 2.15
ChNT Tey kalbek ir ragink ir bark su wisokiu *ernst*
StB Spreeckt dit / ende vermaent / ende bestraft met allen *ernst*
'These things speak, and exhort, and rebuke with all *authority*.'

(19) Tit. 3.8
ChNT ir noriu idand tus daykt[us] *ernstelich* stypryntumbey
StB ende dese dingen wil ick dat ghy *ernstelick* bevestight
'and these things I will that thou affirm *constantly*'

(20) 1 Tim. 4.2
ChNT turedami sązynę sawo <*toegeschrojs*> ikiepintą kaypo ikytusia gialazia
StB hebbende hare eygene conscientie [als] met eenen brandt-yser *toegeschroeyt*
'having their conscience *seared* with a hot iron'

(21) 1 Tim. 4.14
ChNT *En versuymt niet* <neapleisk> dowanos kuriy ira tawimpi
StB En *versuymt* de gave *niet* die in u is
'*neglect not* the gift that is in thee'

(22) Heb. 4.12
ChNT Zodis nes Diewo [...] pereÿt per skirimop dußios ir dwasios, ir mazgump sumezgimump, ir *mercks*
StB Want het woort Godts [...] gaet door tot de verdeelinge der siele ende des geests / ende der t' samenvoeghselen / ende des *merghs*
'For the word of God is quick [...] piercing even to the dividing asunder of soul and spirit, and of the joints and *marrow*'

By following the *Statenbijbel* Chylinski avoided difficult lexical choices. The Greek word σπλάγχνα 'inner organs, bowels' (literally rendered as *viscera* in the Vulgate) is used metaphorically for 'tenderness, compassion'. The Dutch translators avoid this bodily metaphor in passages referring to Christ. In such places, they use *innerlicke bewegingen*, which Chylinski renders literally as *widutiniai pajudinimai* 'inner motions':

(23) Phil. 1.8
ChNT didziej gieydziu jusu wisu su *widutynejs pajudynimejs* Jezusa CHristusa
StB hoe seer ick begeerigh ben na u alle / met *innerlicke bewegingen* Jesu Christi
(KJV) 'how greatly I long after you all in the bowels of Jesus Christ'.

In other cases, the Dutch translators have no problems with the literal rendering *ingewanden* 'bowels', and Chylinski follows them:

(24) Philem. 1.7
ChNT jog *widurej* Szwentuju ataußynti ira per tawe Brolau
StB dat de *ingewanden* der heyligen verquickt zijn geworden door u / broeder
'because the bowels of the saints are refreshed by thee, brother'

The influence of the Dutch lexicon in Chylinski's language is mainly structural. Dutch is a strongly compounding language, whereas compounds are relatively rare in Lithuanian, especially in the Lithuanian of Chylinski's time; in the modern language, compounding has become somewhat more productive in technical vocabulary, mainly under the influence of other languages like German. Authentic compounds, derived according to the rules of Lithuanian word formation, do occur but they are not modelled on Dutch; an example is *dydzźuwis* 'whale', probably modelled on Polish *wieloryb* (lit. 'great fish'):

(25) Gen. 1.21
ChOT Ir sutwere Diewas dydzius dydzźuwius
StB ende Godt schiep de groote Walvisschen
'and God created great whales'

Dutch compounds can usually not be matched with Lithuanian compounds, nor are there always derivatives or simple lexemes available as translation equivalents. The Lithuanian counterparts of Dutch compounds are often phrases with genitival modifiers; Chylinski then attempts to stay close to the Dutch text by connecting the genitival modifier to the head noun with a hyphen, as in

(26) Exod., book summary
StB uyt Egyptenland uyt den diensthuyse
ChOT isz namu-wergistes Egypto
from house[PL].GEN-bondage.GEN Egypt.GEN
'from the house of bondage of Egypt'

The number of such quasi-compounds inspired by Dutch in Chylinski's text is huge. Other examples include:

(27) 1 Sam. 4.16, uyt de slaghorden 'from the army'
isz kowos-redu
from battle.GEN-order.GEN.PL

(28) Luke 7.30 de Wetgeleerde 'lawyers'
Zokone-Mokiti law.INE-learned.NOM.PL
(lit. 'learned-in-the-Law', Latin *legis periti*)

(29) Rev. 14.2 donderslagh 'a clap of thunder' (Latin *tonitruum*)
perkuno-muszymo thunder.GEN-clap.GEN

The number of compounds is increased by the Dutch translators' search for accuracy. In the famous phrase *the great winepress of the wrath of God* from Rev. 14.19, the Dutch translators again go into greater detail, specifying it is actually the trough of the winepress that is meant, so they translate *in den grooten wijnpersback des toorns Godts,* which gives rise, in Chylinski's version, to the three-part compound *wino-prosos-kubilan* (lit. 'wine-press-trough').

Compound adjectives, like Dutch *veelverwig* 'many-coloured' do not have structural counterparts either. Genitival phrases, made into compounds by means of the hyphen, are mostly used in Chylinski's version:

(30) Gen. 37.3

StB	ende hy maeckte hem eenen veelverwigen rock				
ChOT	ir	padare	jamuy	tułu-forbu	jupą
	and	made	him	many.GEN.PL-colour.GEN	coat.ACC
	'and he made him a coat of many colours'				

Another feature of the Dutch lexicon is the ability to create substantivised adjectives functioning as distinct lexemes, like *het Alderheylichste* 'the Holy of Holies.' Lithuanian has this to a much lesser extent, so in some cases a head noun has to be added, again in italics (as the glosses show, Lithuanian has no articles):

(31) Deuteronomy Book Summary

StB	dat in het *Alderheylichste* wech te leggen			
ChOT	kad	iźdetu	ją	Szwęciausioń-*wietoń*
	that	put.away.SBJV	it	holiest.ILL-place.ILL

Grammatical influences of Dutch can also be found in Chylinski's language. The tense system of the Dutch verb occasionally presented Chylinski with a translation problem for which he had no adequate solution. Dutch has a tense form used, among other things, to express 'future in the past', that is, to refer to events situated in the future with regard to a reference point in the past. In the text of the Statenbijbel this is done with the aid of *zoude(n)*, the past tense form of the future tense auxiliary *zullen*. Lithuanian has no such tense and, as it has no sequence of tenses, can perfectly do without it: in a sentence like *I heard she would come* the 'future-in-the-past' form *would come* would now be rendered with a future tense. The function of the auxiliary *zoude(n)* was, however, not clear to Chylinski, who felt that it somehow had to be rendered with a corresponding Lithuanian modal verb. For this purpose he used *turėti* 'have to, be obliged to' in the past tense (reflecting the Dutch sequence of tenses, mainly in reported speech):

(32) Judg. 20.41

ChOT	regiejo	nes,	jog	*turejo*	ateyt	and ju	pikt.
	see.PST.3	for	that	have.to.PST.3	come.INF	on	them.GEN evil
StB	want sy sagen dat het quaet hen treffen *soude*						
	'for they saw that evil would come upon them'						

Another instance where a modal verb is added under the influence of Dutch is observed in subordinate clauses. In earlier Dutch, *mogen* 'may' was frequently used as a marker of sentential modality in complement clauses with verbs like 'request' or 'pray', as well as in purpose clauses. In such cases, the modal verb has no lexical meaning of its own. Chylinski was not aware of this and he mostly renders this *mogen* with *galėti* 'be able':

(33) John 1.22

ChNT	idand *galetumbime* atsakit tiemus kurie mus nusiunte
StB	op dat wy antwoorde geven *mogen* so that we answer give.INF may.PRS.1PL den genen die ons gesonden hebben
KJV	that we may give an answer to them that sent us.
Sept.	ἵνα ἀπόκρισιν δῶμεν τοῖς πέμψασιν ἡμᾶς

Some of the constructions that Chylinski translates literally were actually idioms in Dutch, so that a literal translation was not really called for. In Acts 17.3 the *Statenbijbel* uses the idiomatic expression *(iemand iets) voor ogen stellen* 'point out, demonstrate' (modern Dutch would have *iemand iets voor ogen houden*), and Chylinski copies this idiom in Lithuanian:

(34)

ChNT	Jzguldidamas [...] ir *po* *akis* *jems* → *ju* explaining and under eye.ACC.PL them.DAT their.GEN *ißstatydamas,* laying.out jog reykie buwo idand CHrist[us] kientetu ir kiełtus iß numirusiu
StB	[Deselve] openende / *ende voor* [*oogen*] *stellende* / dat de Christus moeste lijden ende opstaen uyt den dooden 'Opening and alleging, that Christ must needs have suffered, and risen again from the dead'

7. The further fates of Chylinski's Bible and his influence in Lithuania

Chylinski's activities in the Netherlands and England and his struggle for a Lithuanian Bible heightened the awareness of Lithuania and its language in Western Europe. However, his Bible translation, though its printing was begun with great promise (in his report to the synod, the delegate of the Lithuanian Reformed churches to England, Jan Krainski, mentions a print-run of 3000 copies), did not reach the Lithuanian readers and could therefore exert no influence on the Lithuanian tradition of Bible translation, or indeed on the Lithuanian language.

While in many other European countries, Bible translations helped shape the standard languages, in Lithuania no such role was played either by the Chylinski Bible or by more recent printed Bibles that gained wide distribution (such as the Quandt Bible, which was based on the Luther Bible and first printed in Königsberg in 1635). In spite of this, the Chylinski Bible remains a significant source for the history of the Lithuanian language and a testimony to Lithuania's multifarious cultural relations with other European countries.

Acknowledgement

I wish to thank the editors for the constructive comments on the first draft of my chapter, and my husband Axel Holvoet for his advice and his help with the English text.

Sources

ChNT	Chylinski's New Testament, quoted from: www.chylinskibible.flf.vu.lt.
ChOT	Chylinski's Old Testament, quoted from: Kavaliūnaitė (2008).
KJV	King James Version, quoted from: https://www.kingjamesbibleonline.org.
StB	States Bible, quoted from: https://www.dbnl.org/tekst/_sta001stat01_01/ (first edition 1637) and https://www.dbnl.org/tekst/_sta001stat02_01/ (second edition 1657).
Sept	The Septuagint, quoted from: Eberhard Nestle and Kurt Aland (eds.), *Novum Testamentum Graece*. Stuttgart: Deutsche Bibelgesellschaft, 1993.
V	The Vulgate, quoted from: Robert Weber and Roger Gryson (eds.), *Biblia Sacra iuxta Vulgatam versionem*. Stuttgart: Deutsche Bibelgesellschaft, 1994.

References

Biržiška, Vaclovas. 1987. *Lietuvos studentai užsienio universitetuose XIV–XVIII amžiais* [*Lithuanian students at foreign universities in the 14th–18th centuries*]. Chicago: Lituanistikos instituto leidykla.

Bremmer, Christiaan. 2015. *Deelhebben aan het geluk der Nederlanders. De internationale receptie van de Nederlandse Statenbijbel (1637): een casestudy naar een Duitse en Franse kanttekeningenbijbel* [*Sharing the good fortune of the Dutch. The international reception of the Dutch Statenbijbel: A case study of the German and French annotated Bibles*]. Master Thesis, Vrije Universiteit, Amsterdam.

Chylinski, Samuel B. 1659. *An Account of the Translation of the Bible into the Lithuanian Tongue [...]* Oxford: Printed by Hen[ry] Hall, Printer to the University.

Čapaitė, Rūta. 2019. Chylinski's New Testament in the context of the Latin cursive. In: Kavaliūnaitė, Gina (ed.). *Samuelio Boguslavo Chylinskio Biblija, vol. 2: Naujasis Testamentas Viešpaties mūsų Jėzaus Kristaus lietuvių kalba duotas Samuelio Boguslavo Chylinskio = Biblia Lithuanica Samueli Boguslai Chylinski. Tomus 2: Novum Testamentum Domini Nostri Jesu Christi Lthvanicâ Linguâ donatum a Samuelo Boguslao Chylinski*, Vilnius: Vilniaus universitetas.

de Bruin, C.C. 1993. *De Statenbijbel en zijn voorgangers. Nederlandse bijbelvertalingen vanaf Reformatie tot 1637*. Bewerkt door dr. F.M.G. Broeyer, Haarlem: Nederlands Bijbelgenootschap, Brussels: Belgisch Bijbelgenootschap.

de Waard, Jan and Eugene A. Nida. 1986: *From one Language to Another. Functional Equivalence in Bible Translating*. Nashwill – Camden – New York: Thomas Nelson Publishers.

du Rieu, W.N. (ed.). 1875. *Album studiosorum Academiae Lugduno-Batavae MDLXXV-MDCCCLXXV*. The Hague: Martinus Nijhoff.

Gesenius, Wilhelm. 1906. *A Hebrew and English Lexicon of the Old Testament based on the Lexicon by William Gesenius as translated by Edward Robinson*, ed. by Francis Brown. Boston-New York: Houghton Mifflin.

Haak, Theodore. 1657. *The Dutch Annotations upon the whole Bible* [...]. London: Printed by Henry Hills, for John Rotwell, Joshua Kirton, and Richard Tomlins.

Jaakke, Alfons. 1996. Ver over de grenzen. De invloed van de Statenvertaling in het buitenland II. *Met Andere Woorden* 15: 15–24.

Jaakke, Alfons. 1997. Ver over de grenzen. De invloed van de Statenvertaling in het buitenland III. *Met Andere Woorden* 16: 3–12.

Kavaliūnaitė, Gina. 2003. *Die Chylinskische Übersetzung des Neuen Testaments und ihr Verhältnis zu den Vorlagen*. Zusammenfassung der Doktordissertation, Vilnius.

Kavaliūnaitė, Gina. 2003. Postpozicinių vietininkų sistema Chylinskio Naujojo Testamento vertime [The system of postpositional cases in Chylinski's New Testament translation]. *Acta Linguistica Lithuanica* 49: 33–49.

doi Kavaliūnaitė, Gina 2004. Die Litauische Übersetzung der Statenbijbel. *Ons Geestelijk Erf* 78 (1): 99–114.

Kavaliūnaitė, Gina (ed.). 2008. *Samuelio Boguslavo Chylinskio Biblija. Senasis Testamentas, vol. 1: Lietuviško vertimo ir olandiško originalo faksimilės = Biblia Lithuanica Samueli Boguslai Chylinski, vol. 1: Vetus Testamentum Lithuanicâ Lingvâ donatum a Samuelo Boguslao Chylinski. Unâ cum texto belgico*, Vilnius: Lietuvių kalbos institutas.

Kavaliūnaitė, Gina (ed.). 2015. *Samuelio Boguslavo Chylinskio Biblija, vol. 3: Chylinskio Biblijos istorijos šaltiniai = Biblia Lithuanica Samueli Boguslai Chylinski. Tomus 3: Fontes ad Historiam Samueli Boguslai Chylinski Bibliae Lithuanicae Illustrandam*, Vilnius: Vilniaus universitetas.

Kavaliūnaitė, Gina (ed.). 2019a. *Samuelio Boguslavo Chylinskio Biblija, vol. 2: Naujasis Testamentas Viešpaties mūsų Jėzaus Kristaus lietuvių kalba duotas Samuelio Boguslavo Chylinskio = Biblia Lithuanica Samueli Boguslai Chylinski. Tomus 2: Novum Testamentum Domini Nostri Jesu Christi Lthvanicâ Linguâ donatum a Samuelo Boguslao Chylinski*, Vilnius: Vilniaus universitetas.

Kavaliūnaitė, Gina. 2019b. Calvinist Bibles in the Grand Duchy of Lithuania. In: *Word of God, Words of Men. Translations, Inspirations, Transmissions of the Bible in the Polish-Lithuanian Commonwealth in the Renaissance*, ed. by Joanna Pietrzak-Thébault [Refo 500 Academic Studies, Vol. 43]. Göttingen: Van den Hoeck & Ruprecht, 229–252.

Kudzinowski, Czesław. 1964: *Biblia litewska Chylińskiego. Nowy Testament.* 3, *Indeks* [*Chylinski's Lithuanian Bible Vol. 3. Index*], Poznań: Państwowe Wydawnictwo Naukowe.

Kudzinowski, Czesław. 1984: *Biblia litewska Chylińskiego. Nowy Testament.* 1, *Fotokopie* [*Chylinski's Lithuanian Bible Vol. 1. Photocopies*], Poznań: Wydawnictwo Naukowe UAM.

Kudzinowski, Czesław, and Jan Otrębski. 1958: *Biblia litewska Chylińskiego. Nowy Testament. 2, Tekst* [*Chylinski's Lithuanian Bible Vol. 2. Text*], Poznań: Zakład Narodowy im. Ossolińskich.

Lukšaitė, Ingė. 1971. Reformacijos veikėjai Lietuvoje ir lietuvių kalba XVII a. [Agents of the Lithuanian Reformation and the Lithuanian language in the 17th c.], *Lietuvos TSR Mokslų akademijos darbai*, A serija 1 (35): 111–125.

Meijer, Th. J. (ed.). 1972. *Album promotorum Academiae Franekerensis (1591–1811).* Franeker: T. Wever.

Postma, Ferenc, and Johan van Sluis. 1995. *Auditorium Academiae Franekerensis. Bibliographie der Reden, Disputationen und Gelegenheitsdruckwerke der Universität des Athenäums in Franeker 1585–1843.* Leeuwarden: Fryske Akademy.

Reinhold, Heinrich. 1895: Die sogenannte Chylinskische Bibelübersetzung. *Mitteilungen der Litauischen Literarischen Gesellschaft* Vol. IV, fasc. 2 (20): 105–163.

Reinhold, Heinrich. 1896: Die Bibelübersetzung von Chylinski. *Mitteilungen der Litauischen Literarischen Gesellschaft* Vol. IV, fasc. 3 (21): 207–273.

Tworek, Stanisław. 1970: Programy nauczania i prawa gimnazjum kalwińskiego w Kiejdanach z lat 1629 i 1685 [Curricula and house rules of the Kėdainiai Calvinist Gymnasium from 1629 and 1685], *Odrodzenie i Reformacja w Polsce* 15: 232–236.

Wilkins, John. 1668: *An Essay Towards a Real Character and a Philosophical Language* [...]., London: Printed for Samuel Gellibrand, and for John Martyn, Printer to the Royal Society.

CHAPTER 8

(Anti-)causativity in Dutch and Afrikaans

Uncovering subtle language shifts from contact influence

Adri Breed & Daniel Van Olmen
North-West University | Lancaster University

A Sprachbund refers to a region where languages, despite lacking common ancestry, exhibit similarities due to contact influence, as seen with Standard Average European (SAE). Colonialism spread European languages globally, resulting in creole languages and intercontinental varieties. Languages like Afrikaans, although geographically outside the SAE Sprachbund, may share features with SAE languages due to contact. This study examines how Afrikaans and Dutch express anticausative meanings, such as "the ice melts" versus "the sun is melting the ice." While both share SAE's anticausative feature, Afrikaans simplifies morphologically related pairs and favours analytical structures, likely due to language contact. Unlike Dutch, Afrikaans lacks reflexive anticausatives, instead using constructions like "the disease spreads," suggesting further contact influences. This study highlights language divergence within the Sprachbund and the impact of contact on language evolution.

Keywords: causative, anticausative, language contact, Sprachbund, extra-territorial, closely related language

1. The Standard Average European Sprachbund

A language area, also known as a "Sprachbund", is a geographical region where languages exhibit similarities due to contact influence, even if they are not related by ancestry. These similarities between not necessarily related languages indicate concurrent linguistic development or convergence and are a primary indicator of areal characteristics. The expectation is that a language located centrally within a Sprachbund area will show the most corresponding linguistic features with the rest of the languages in the language area, while a language located on the periphery of the Sprachbund area should show fewer of these features. In other words, a

https://doi.org/10.1075/impact.55.08bre

language that is geographically far from the Sprachbund should show less resemblance to the languages found within that area (see Joseph 2020: 882).

The study of Sprachbunds can be very useful, as (i) it can lead to insights about typological universals, (ii) this type of linguistic investigation leads to insights into language change processes that can be attributed to language contact, and (iii) the language-comparative approach associated with Sprachbund studies often leads to innovative and even unexpected insights into language-specific descriptions.

A number of Sprachbunds have already been identified, such as the Balkan Sprachbund (Friedman, 2006), the Mainland Southeast Asia Sprachbund (Sidwell & Jenny 2021), the Carpathian Sprachbund (Thomas 2007), and the Southern African Sprachbund (Maddieson 2003). Of specific relevance for this chapter, however, is the Standard Average European (SAE) Sprachbund (Haspelmath, 1998). This language area's core comprises German, French, Dutch, and the Northern Italian dialects. Surrounding this core are the remaining Germanic and Romance languages, along with Balkan, West, and South Slavic languages. Beyond these lie the peripheral languages, including Baltic, East Slavic, Balto-Finnic, and Hungarian, as well as potentially Basque, Maltese, Armenian, and Georgian (see Figure 1 below).

According to (Haspelmath, 2001), SAE languages share twelve Sprachbund features (see Table 1).

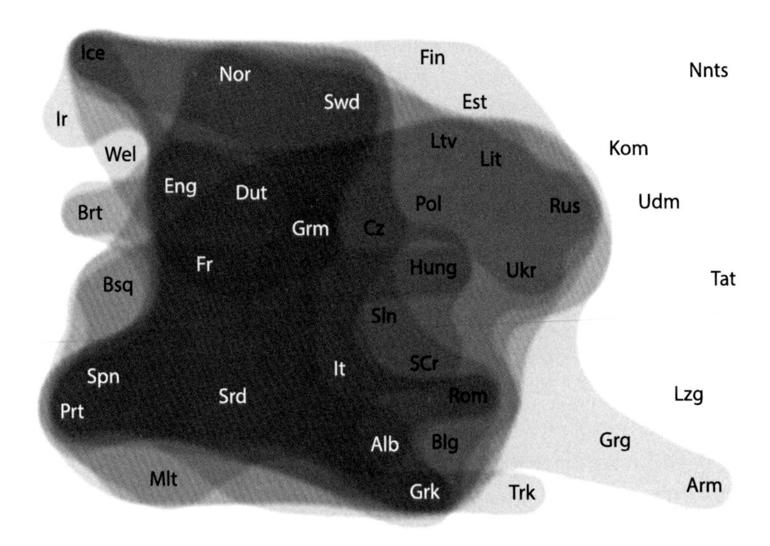

Figure 1. The SAE Sprachbund (Van Olmen & Breed, 2015: 230, based on Haspelmath 2001)

Several studies have already been conducted that investigate various aspects of the SAE Sprachbund (see, for example, Cysouw 2011; Irslinger 2013; Van Olmen & Auwera 2016). However, another addition to the more traditional investigation into SAE is what Van der Auwera (2011: 199) calls the "extra-territorial perspective" on this Sprachbund. As a result of colonisation, the languages of Europe spread across the world and influenced many indigenous languages to varying degrees. Van der Auwera (2011: 304) provides the example of Pipil, a language spoken in El Salvador, which has adopted at least eight SAE features from Spanish. He argues that this perspective should also be included in studies on SAE.

> If one is ready to say that Basque is a peripheral SAE language, then there is at least no linguistic reason to disqualify Pipil. [...] Of course, the locus of contact inference is not Europe and the (post)colonial social dynamics are different. Basically, the study of the SAE features of Pipil no longer concerns the areal typology of Europe, but it still concerns the areal typology of European languages.
> (Van der Auwera, 2011: 304)

Van Olmen & Breed (2015) expand the extra-territorial perspectives on SAE even further, by querying the fate of a Sprachbund language when it is moved or transplanted to a geographic area outside of the Sprachbund, while retaining the characteristics of the Sprachbund.

> What happens to a Sprachbund language when it is geographically removed from the language area? If a language that is a member of a language area and possesses the features of the language area shifts to a geographic area that is not part of the language area, will the language start to lose these features of the language area? Can such a language still be considered a member of the language area, even if it is no longer geographically close to the language area?
> (Van Olmen & Breed, 2015: 228, our translation)

They argue that, although the "geographic removal" of a language from a language area may seem like a strange concept, there are nevertheless several examples of this in the languages of the world. Many (if not most) creole languages, as well as intercontinental varieties (for example, American English), are examples of languages that have been geographically removed from their source language for various reasons. They further explain that a T1 language (e.g., French) can even be considered a core or central member of a Sprachbund (e.g., the Southern United States), despite the T2 language (e.g., Louisiana Creole) being geographically distant from the typical area associated with the T1 language within the Sprachbund. However, it is worth noting that despite this geographical separation, significant linguistic similarities may still exist between the T1 and T2 languages. Consequently, it is reasonable to expect that similar linguistic connections may also be present between the T2 language and other languages within the Sprachbund area.

To answer the question what happens to a Sprachbund language when it is geographically removed from the language area, Van Olmen & Breed (2015) compare Afrikaans[1] with Dutch in an exemplary manner, based on the Twelve Sprachbund Features of SAE. They find that Dutch, which – as mentioned – is a core language of SAE, exhibits all twelve of the SAE features, while Afrikaans shows ten out of the twelve features of SAE (see Table 1 below). Based on the number of features that correspond with the number of features shared by the languages found in the Sprachbund area, Afrikaans can in other words safely also be considered a Sprachbund language of SAE.

Table 1. SAE Features of Dutch and Afrikaans

SAE Feature		Du	Afr
Have both definite and indefinite articles		✓	✓
e.g. Dutch	***Het/ee'n*** *huis ('the/a house')*		
Afrikaans	***Die/'n*** *huis ('the/a house')*		
Use a perfect tense formed by the verb 'to have' plus a past participle		✓	✓
e.g. Dutch	*Ik* ***heb*** *gisteren een appel* ***gegeten*** *('Yesterday, I have eaten an apple')*		
Afrikaans	*Ek* ***het*** *gister'n appel* ***geëet*** *('Yesterday, I have eaten an apple')*		
The passive voice is formed by a participle and an intransitive 'copula-like' verb (such as 'to be' and 'to become'),		✓	✓
e.g. Dutch	*De auto* ***wordt*** *rood* ***gespoten*** *('the car is being painted red')*		
Afrikaans	*Die kar* ***word*** *rooi* ***geverf*** *('the car is being painted red')*		
Show anticausative prominence (see Section 3 for a discussion)		✓	✓
e.g. Dutch	*De ziekte verspreidt zich. ('the disease spreads')*		
Afrikaans	*Die mansjien verloor energie ('the machine loses energy')*		
Use nominative experiencers to express verbs of sensation, emotion, cognition, and perception		✓	✓
e.g. Dutch	***Ik*** *verheug mij over het goede nieuws ('I am delighted about the good news')*		
Afrikaans	***Ek*** *verheug my oor die goeie nuus ('I am delighted about the good news')*		

1. Afrikaans is a South African language that developed from the late 16th century in a South African colonial language contact situation. Based on the historical information regarding the development of Afrikaans, as well as the close linguistic relationship that exists between Dutch and Afrikaans, Van Olmen and Breed (2015: 230) consider Afrikaans a T2 language of 17th-century Dutch, and Contemporary Dutch and Standard Afrikaans as sister languages (also compare the following sources for the discussion of the development of Afrikaans as a possible creole, semi-creole or creoloid of 17th Century Dutch: Carstens & Raidt 2019; Coetzee 2009; De Ruyter 2004; Du Plessis 1994; Markey 1982; Nienaber 1953; Ponelis 1993; Raidt 1991; Roberge 2009; Du Ruyter & Kotze 2002; van der Wouden 2012; Van Rensburg 2012).

Table 1. *(continued)*

SAE Feature	**Du**	**Afr**
Use external possessors to express the relationship between a possessor and a possessum, *e.g. Dutch* *Ik heb* ***hem de keel*** *doorgesneden ('I cut his throat)* *Afrikaans* **Ek het hom die keel deurgesny (not a possbile Afrikaans construction)*	✓	±
Do not negate the verb form when a negative indefinite pronoun is used *e.g. Dutch* ***Niemand*** *komt ('nobody is coming')* *Afrikaans* ***Niemand*** *kom nie ('nobody is coming')*	✓	×
Use a particle in comparative constructions *e.g. Dutch* *Salomo was rijker* **dan** *David ('Solomon was richer than David')* *Afrikaans* *Salomo was ryker* **as** *David ('Solomon was richer than David')*	✓	✓
Base their constructions of equality on an adverbial clause construction *e.g. Dutch* *Hij is geen timmerman,* ***zoals*** *zijn vader ('He is not a carpenter, like his father')* *Afrikaans* *Sy is so vaal* ***soos*** *'n duifie. ('She is as pale as a dove')*	✓	✓
Use a relative clause that is characterised by (i) a post-nominal relative clause, (ii) an inflected relative pronoun, (iii) a relative pronoun that introduces the relative clause, and (iv) a relative pronoun that functions as a resumptive construction *e.g. Dutch* *Het schip,* ***dat*** *aangevaren was, bleek niet meer te herstellen ('The ship, which had been collided with, turned out to be irreparable')* *Afrikaans* *'n Aandeel* ***wat*** *nie diwidende oplewer nie, is 'n swak belegging ('A share that does not yield dividends is a poor investment.')*	✓	✓
Cannot omit the grammatically agreeing subject person *e.g. Dutch* ***Ik*** *werk ('I am working')* *Afrikaans* ***Ek*** *werk ('I am working')*	✓	✓
Use different pronouns to serve as intensifiers and reflexive pronouns. *e.g. Dutch* *De paus* ***zelf*** *gaf ons een lezing ('The pope himself gave us a lecture')* vs reflexive ***zichzelf*** *Afrikaans* *Die pous* ***self*** *het ons 'n oudiënsie gegee ('The pope himself gave us an audience')* vs reflexive ***homself***	✓	✓
Total	12	10

Although Afrikaans can still be considered a core language of SAE based on the number of features it exhibits, there has been a 'loss of SAE' features that occurred in Afrikaans after the T1 language (17th-century Dutch) developed into T2 (Contemporary Afrikaans) in a new language contact situation. This change can undoubtedly be attributed to language contact. For instance, while Dutch (typical for SAE languages) does not negate the verb when a negative indefinite pronoun is used in the clause (compare Example (1)), Afrikaans employs double negation (compare sentence Example (2)), meaning that verbs are indeed negated when a negative indefinite pronoun is used. The introduction of double negation constructions in Afrikaans is attributed by linguists such as Ponelis (1997) to language contact between Dutch and Creole Portuguese.

(1) *Dutch*
Niemand komt. Haspelmath (1998:1498)
nobody come
'Nobody is coming.'

(2) *Afrikaans*
Niemand kom ***nie.*** Van Olmen & Breed (2015:237)
nobody come PTCL.NEG
'Nobody is coming.'

Van Olmen & Breed's (2015) comparison underscores the importance of examining Sprachbund languages and their non-geographically related members from an extra-territorial perspective to gain deeper insights into the impact of language contact on the development of a language. This approach is crucial for better understanding how languages evolve in response to contact with others, particularly in scenarios where geographical proximity alone may not fully explain the linguistic dynamics at play.

The overarching goal of Sprachbund studies is to uncover commonalities across languages and identify and formulate the typological linguistic features of a group of languages. However, while not the primary focus of Sprachbund studies, the comparative and contrastive nature of this approach can also lead to the identification of specific linguistic traits unique to the individual languages under investigation. By comparing Afrikaans and Dutch, for instance, Van Olmen & Breed (2015:233–234) discern a potential variance in how (anti-)causativity is articulated differently in these two languages. Though this distinction may seem minor (and even irrelevant within the scope of Sprachbund studies), it prompts further investigation into the intricacies of language variation and language change that can be attributed to language contact. At first glance, it seems that both Afrikaans and Dutch exhibit the so-called SAE characteristic of "anticausative prominence," as the result of the analysis of this property in a language yielded positive results for both Afrikaans and Dutch. (Anti-)causativity is extensively discussed in Section 2.

From the perspective of Sprachbund studies, where the primary objective is to draw generalisations and typological deductions, it might suffice to conclude that Afrikaans and Dutch also align in terms of this SAE characteristic. However, due to the fact that Afrikaans and Dutch are closely related sister languages, and considering that 17th-century Dutch serves as the T1 in the language contact situation from which Afrikaans developed, and also noting that Afrikaans and Dutch predominantly use cognate verbs to express (anti-)causativity (as will be shown in Section 3 and 4), the difference in the divergence between the Afrikaans and Dutch verb pairs is striking. Despite sharing a significant linguistic heritage and using cognate verbs there are notable differences in the way these verb pairs are used in Afrikaans and Dutch. This divergence challenges the expectation of strict alignment between closely-related languages, highlighting the complexity and dynamic nature of language change, especially in the context of language contact and development.

In the remainder of this chapter, we investigate whether a language-comparative approach can yield deeper insights into the subtle language differences that emerge due to language contact, specifically on the (anti-)causative verb pairs of Afrikaans and Dutch. Thus, this chapter serves as an illustration of how seemingly minor discrepancies can offer rich avenues for understanding the intricacies of language change and divergence in language contact contexts. In this way we explore a specific, initially overlooked distinction between a Sprachbund language and its geographically distant sister language.

The chapter is structured as follows: In Section 2, we explain (anti-)causativity, detailing the different verb pair alternations found in languages. Section 3 introduces our research methodology, while Section 4 presents the results of our investigation and discusses our findings. Finally, Section 5 offers a summary and evaluation of our experiment.

2. Causative and anticausative verb pair alternations

The contrast in causative and anticausative meaning is illustrated in the sentence Example (3a) and (3b) below. In both sentences, the predicate revolves around the main verb *veranderen* 'to change'. However, in sentence 3a, a causative meaning is conveyed, as the subject, *Ik* 'I', is the agent effecting or causing the change of the object *de datum* 'the date'. On the other hand, sentence 3b expresses an anticausative meaning, as the subject, *dat beleid* 'that policy', is not an agentive subject; the policy change occurs involuntarily and spontaneously. The agent effecting the change of the policy is not realised in this anticausative example sentence.

(3) *Dutch*

a. *Ik* ***verander*** *de datum van tevoren in 7 maart.* CAUS (CHN)[2]
I change the date from before in 7 March
'I change the date from beforehand to March 7th.'

2. CHN refers to *Corpus Hedendaags Nederlands (https://chn.ivdnt.org/)*

b. *Maar dat beleid lijkt te* ***veranderen*** *de laatste jaren.*
but that policy seem PTCL.INF change the last years
'But that policy seems to be changing in recent years.' ANTIC (CHN, adapted)

2.1 Formal variations of CAUS/ANTIC verb pairs

The example presented in 3 is an example of a polysemous CAUS/ANTIC verb pair, where the same verb form is used to express both meaning contexts. However, the CAUS/ANTIC alternation does not necessarily have to be expressed by polysemous verbs. Haspelmath (1993) shows that for CAUS/ANTIC verb pair alternations, five possible formal variations can exist, namely (i) causative alternations, (ii) anti-causative alternations, (iii) equipollent alternations, (iv) suppletive alternations, and (v) labile alternations.

2.1.1 *Causative alternations (CA)*

In this verb pair alternation, the ANTIC verb is the basic verb of the verb pair, and the CAUS verb is derived. The derived CAUS verb can be marked with an affix, as in 4, an auxiliary verb, as in 5, or with a stem modification, as in 6.

(4) *Georgian*
a. *duy-s* Haspelmath (1993: 91–92)
cook.ANTIC
'cook' (as in 'the soup cooks')
b. ***a****-duy-****ebs***
cook.CAUS
'cook' (as in 'he cooks the soup')

(5) *French*
a. *fondre* Haspelmath (1993: 91–92)
melt.ANTIC
'melt' (as in 'the cheese melts')
b. ***faire*** *fondre*
melt.CAUS
'melt' (as in 'the microwave melts the cheese')

(6) *Arabic*
a. *darrasa* Haspelmath (1993: 91–92)
learn
b. *darrasa*
teach

2.1.2 *Anticausative alternation (AA)*

In this verb pair alternation, the CAUS verb is the base, and the ANTIC verb is derived. Similar to the causative alternation, the ANTIC verb can be marked with an affix, as in 7, an auxiliary verb, as in 8, or with a stem modification, as in 9.

(7) *Russian*

a. *katat'-**sja*** Haspelmath (1993: 91–92)
roll. ANTIC
'roll' (as in 'the dice roll')

b. ***katat'***
roll.CAUS
'roll' (as in 'she rolls the dice')

(8) *Lezgian*

a. *xkaž **x̂un*** Haspelmath (1993: 91–92)
rise

b. *xkažun*
raise

(9) *Hindi-Urdu*

a. ***khul**-naa* Haspelmath (1993: 91–92)
open.ANTIC
'open' (as in 'the door opens')

b. *khol-naa*
open.CAUS
'open' (as in 'I open the door')

2.1.3 *Equipollent alternations (EA)*

In this alternation, both verb pairs are derived from the same stem that describes the basic situation. This derivation occurs with affixes, as in 10, different non-finite verbs, as in 11, or with different stem modifications, as in 12.

(10) *Japanese*

a. *atum-**aru*** Haspelmath (1993: 91–92)
gather.ANTIC
'gather' (as in 'the leaves gather around the tree')

b. *atum-**eru***
gather.CAUS
'gather' (as in 'They are gathering leaves')

(11) *Hindi-Urdu*
a. *šuruu* ***honaa*** Haspelmath (1993: 91–92)
begin.ANTIC
'begin' (as in 'the meeting begins')
b. *šuruu* ***karnaa***
begin.CAUS
'begin' (as in 'the chair begins the meeting')

(12) *Lithuanian*
a. ***lūžti*** Haspelmath (1993: 91–92)
break.ANTIC
'break' (as in 'the vase breaks')
b. *lūažti*
break.CAUS
'break (as in 'she breaks the vase')

2.1.4 *Suppletive alternations (SA)*

In this alternation, the verbs in the verb pair have different stems, as in 13.

(13) *English*
a. *die*
b. *kill*

2.1.5 *Labile alternations (LA)*

In this alternation, the same verb is used in both CAUS and ANTIC interpretation, for Example (14).

(14) *Modern Greek*
a. *svíno* *Haspelmath (1993: 91–92)*
'go out'
b. *svíno*
'extinguish'

2.2 CAUS/ANTIC verb pairs in SAE, in Dutch and in Afrikaans

According to Haspelmath (1993: 102), most languages of the SAE Sprachbund show a preference for anticausative verbs: 'Languages that prefer anticausatives are spoken in Europe, and languages that prefer causatives are spoken elsewhere. The absence of causative morphology and the importance of anticausative derivations seem to be a European areal feature.' As already explained in Section 1, he further investigates this hypothesis in Haspelmath (2001: 1497–1498) by conducting an experiment comparing 31 situations (compare Table 2) that may be

Table 2. Causative/Anticausative situations (Haspelmath 1993: 97)

1.	'wake up'	12.	'change'	23.	'turn'
2.	'break'	13.	'melt'	24.	'roll'
3.	'burn'	14.	'be destroyed/destroy'	25.	'freeze'
4.	'die/kill'	15.	'get lost/lose'	26.	'dissolve'
5.	'open'	16.	'develop'	27.	'fill'
6.	'close'	17.	'connect'	28.	'improve'
7.	'begin'	18.	'boil'	29.	'dry'
8.	'learn'	19.	'rock'	30.	'split'
9.	'gather'	20.	'go out/put out'	31.	'stop'
10.	'spread'	21.	'rise/raise'		
11.	'sink'	22.	'finish'		

expressed using anticausative/anticausative verb pair alternations in 21 European languages.

It has also been mentioned that Van Olmen & Breed (2015) replicated this analysis for Afrikaans and Dutch to investigate the possibility of considering Afrikaans as an SAE language, based on the typical features inherent to SAE languages and its close relation to Dutch. They examined the same 31 verb pairs in Afrikaans and Dutch, finding that when the same test of 31 situations was conducted for Dutch, 10 of the situations used anticausative derivations (e.g.,15, while only two situations used causative derivations (e.g., 16). In contrast, for Afrikaans, when the same 31 types of situations were examined, only one example of anticausative derivation was found (e.g., 17), and no examples of causative derivation.

(15) *Dutch*
  a. *Ik verspreid een ziekte.* (*Van Olmen & Breed, 2015: 233*)
     'I spread a disease'
  b. *De ziekte verspreidt zich.*
     'The disease spreads itself'

(16) *Dutch*
  a. *De orkaan laat het schip zinken.* (*Van Olmen & Breed, 2015: 233*)
     'The hurricane is sinking the ship'
  b. *Het schip zinkt.*
     'The ship is sinking'

(17) *Afrikaans*
  a. *Die masjien verloor energie.* (*Van Olmen & Breed, 2015: 233*)
     'The machine loses energy'
  b. *Energie gaan verlore.*
     'Energy is being lost'

Due to the fact that Haspelmath only compares two of the five possible verb alternations with each other (and does not consider the three non-directed alternations), the conclusion was drawn that both Dutch and Afrikaans also exhibit this SAE characteristic of anticausative prominence. However, Van Olmen and Breed (2015: 234, our translation) already indicate the problem: "Although according to Haspelmath's criteria (i.e., by considering the ratio of causative to anticausative derivation), it can be said that Afrikaans has 100% (1/1) anticausative prominence, and therefore also has this SAE characteristic, the question can be asked whether the inference can be made with only one example of anticausative or causative derivation."

What was striking from Van Olmen and Breed's comparison of Afrikaans and Dutch anticausative/causative verb pairs is that the alternations differ between the two languages. This is surprising, considering Afrikaans and Dutch are closely related languages (with an estimated lexical similarity of 95%). One would expect that, given the high degree of agreement between the forms of these two languages, the specific group of verbs would also exhibit the same alternations, which is not the case.

There is, in other words, indeed, more to learn about the differences and similarities between the CAUS/ANTIC verb pairs in Afrikaans and Dutch, such as:

- If we examine a larger quantity of CAUS/ANTIC verb pairs, how significant are the differences or similarities between the alternations used in Afrikaans and Dutch?
- If we observe differences, can we begin to make deductions about the specific nature of these differences?
- Can we already identify what factors contribute to these differences in verb pair alternations?

3. Research method

To answer these questions, it was necessary, in other words, to compile a larger list of possible CAUS/ANTIC verb pairs from the outset than Haspelmath's (1993) 31 semantic verb pairs. To compile a more extensive list of CAUS/ANTIC verb pairs, we followed these steps:

Firstly, we included all the verbs that Haspelmath (1993) offers as typical verbs with ANTIC/CAUS meanings in our list. We consider this as the initial step, since these verbs can be regarded as the "prototypical" ANTIC/CAUS alternating verb pairs (as attested in Haspelmath's SAE studies, among others). It was therefore crucial that we also include these verbs in our comparison, also because the degree of membership of Afrikaans and Dutch in the SAE Sprachbund is relevant here.

As a second step, we consulted linguistic sources (e.g. Anyanwu 2013; Schäfer & Vivanco 2016, Heidinger & Huyghe 2024; Fernando 2013) that discuss the CAUS/ANTIC alternation to see if we could supplement Haspelmath's verb list. Based on this literature review, we added the following verbs to the list: 'bake', 'bend', 'darken', 'enlarge', 'fold', 'fry', 'light', 'multiply', 'pour', 'reduce', 'ring', 'ripen', 'snap', 'soften', 'spoil', 'stabilize', 'tear', 'tighten', 'transform', 'untie', 'wilt', and 'worsen'. This step was meaningful for us, as it supplements our list of possible typical or prototypical verbs with CAUS/ANTIC from other linguists' studies that extend beyond SAE studies.

Thirdly, we created a frequency list of Afrikaans and Dutch verbs and examined the first 200 verbs of each language to identify the most frequent potential CAUS/ANTIC verb pairs.[3] Although we did not further study the frequency of the verbs in this analysis, our aim was to identify the "typical" verb pairs in Afrikaans and Dutch, compare them, and locate suitable examples in corpora to compare the availability of the alternation in the two languages. For this comparison, we used corpora for each language, encompassing both written and edited standard language as well as language representative of both written and unedited conversational usage. Specifically, we employed the Afrikaans Language Commission Corpus (Taalkommisiekorpus 1.1, 2011) and the NWU Commentary Corpus 2.2. (CTexT 2023) for Afrikaans, and compiled comparable corpora[4] for these from

3. Based on the sources discussed in the second section of the papers, the verbs in the frequency list were evaluated based on their potential to exhibit the characteristics of the CAUS/ANTIC verb pair alternation, namely:

- Both the CAUS and the ANTIC verb of the pair describe the same fundamental situation.
- The situation described by the verb pair signifies a change of state or process.
- The CAUS verb in the pair is transitive.
- The ANTIC verb in the pair is intransitive.
- The subject of the sentence with the CAUS verb must be agentive.
- The subject of the sentence with the ANTIC verb may not be agentive (it may be a non-volitional agent).
- The change of state or process expressed by the intransitive verb must be presented as if it occurs spontaneously.
- The change of state or process expressed by the transitive verb must be presented as if it is caused by an agent.

4. The counterpart of the Taalkommissiekorpus consisted of the following components: "book", "e-magazines", "guides & manuals", "legal texts", "newspapers", "periodicals & magazines", "policy documents", "reports" and "written assignments", and the counterpart of the NWU Commentary corpus consisted of the following components: "discussion lists" and "tweets"

the components of the *Stevin Nederlandstalig Referentiecorpus* (SoNaR; Oostdijk, Reynaert, Hoste & Schuurman, 2011). Through this process, we incorporated the following verbs into the list of CAUS/ANTIC verb pairs: 'appear', 'beat', 'decrease', 'develop', 'disappear', 'fall', 'form', 'grow', 'happen', 'increase', 'lift up', 'loosen', 'move', 'play', 'pull', 'record', 'scoop', 'start', and 'turn around'.

The next and final step was to create typical and unobtrusive English CAUS/ANTIC example pairs for each of the 70 semantic verbs (compare, for example, sentence examples for the English CAUS/ANTIC verb pairs with the meaning 'loosen' and 'develop' in 18 and 19 below), and then use these English examples as a basis for translation into Afrikaans and Dutch.

(18) *English*
  a. *(CAUS) They are* ***loosening*** *the regulations.*
  b. *(ANTIC) The regulations are* ***loosening.***

(19) *English*
  a. *(CAUS) His teachers are* ***developing*** *his skills.*
  b. *(ANTIC) His skills are* ***developing.***

This step was crucial as we aimed to compare the Afrikaans and Dutch verb pairs directly. By employing English as an intermediary, we established a common ground for comparison beyond the two languages. Given the close relationship between English, Afrikaans, and Dutch, and the accessibility of English to the authors, it was feasible to use these English sentences as a basis to test for different alternations in Dutch and Afrikaans (compare 20 to 23 for the translations of the alternating Afrikaans and Dutch CAUS/ANTIC verb pairs with the meaning 'loosen' and 'reduce').

(20) a. *Afr (CAUS) Hulle* ***verslap*** *die regulasies.*
  b. *Du Ze* ***versoepelen*** *de regels.*
  'They are loosening the regulations'

(21) a. *Afr (ANTIC) Die regulasies* ***verslap.***
  b. *Du De regels* ***versoepelen.***
  'The regulations are loosening'

(22) a. *Afr (CAUS) Sy onderwysers* ***ontwikkel*** *sy vaardighede*
  b. *Du Zijn leraren* ***ontwikkelen*** *zijn vaardigheden.*
  'His teachers are developing his skills'

(23) a. *Afr (ANTIC) Sy vaardighede* ***ontwikkel.***
  b. *Du Zijn vaardigheden* ***ontwikkelen zich.***
  'His skills are developing'

To ensure the utmost accuracy and comparability in our translations, we've employed translation dictionaries[5] to identify the most typical translation of the main verb in the English sentence and to consider all potential translation equivalents. This approach enables us to determine if cognate verbs existed between Afrikaans and Dutch. In instances where we find cognate or semi-cognate verbs in the translation dictionaries, we've refrained from including suppletive forms, (because such forms would result in a proliferation of that category).

From the various translations in Afrikaans and Dutch, we were able to accomplish two key objectives: (i) determine the extent to which the CAUS/ANTIC verb pairs in Afrikaans and Dutch are cognates of each other, and (ii) identify the precise alternations used for each of the 70 verbs under comparison. These distinctions were crucial for examining the significance of the differences or similarities between the alternations used in Afrikaans and Dutch. Furthermore, they allowed us to draw deductions about the specific nature of these differences and to identify the factors contributing to variations in verb pair alternations.

4. Discussion of the results

The results of this comparison is summarised in Table 3 below, and visualised in Figure 2. We will use the following abbreviations for the five alternations: Causative alternation (CA), Anticausative alternation (AA), Equipollent Alternation (EA), Labile alternation (LA) and Suppletive alternation (SA). See again Section 2.1 for an explanation of the five types.

As outlined in the contextualisation of this chapter, the overarching objective is to explore the influence of language contact in Afrikaans and Dutch from an extra-territorial perspective on the SAE Sprachbund. The focus lies on discerning potential variances in how (anti-)causativity is articulated in Dutch and Afrikaans. While this distinction may seem minor within the scope of Sprachbund studies, it serves as a catalyst for further investigation into the intricacies of language variation and change attributable to language contact. This is achieved by examining a broader set of CAUS/ANTIC verb pairs to determine the significance of differences or similarities between Afrikaans and Dutch. Despite their close relationship, previous studies, notably Van Olmen & Breed (2015), suggest that Afrikaans could be considered a Standard Average European (SAE) language. However, it is argued that specific attention should be given to how Afrikaans and

5. For the Afrikaans translations, we used the *Pharos Afrikaans-Engels/English-Afrikaans Dictionary* (Pharos 2010), and for the Dutch translations, the *Van Dale Engels-Nederlands Online* (2024).

Table 3. Afrikaans and Dutch CAUS/ANTIC verb pair alternations

CAUS/ANTIC situations	Translation of verb		CA		AA		EA		LA		SA	
	Afr	Du	Afr	Du	Afr	Du	Afr	Du	Afr	Du	Afr	Du
'bake'	*bak*	*bakken*							✓	✓		
'pound'	*klop*	*kloppen*	✓	✓								
'begin'	*begin*	*beginnen*							✓	✓		
'bend'	*buig*	*buigen*							✓	✓		
'boil'	*kook*	*koken*							✓	✓		
'break'	*breek*	*breken*							✓	✓		
'burn'	*brand*	*(ver)branden*		✓					✓	✓		
'change'	*verander*	*veranderen*	✓						✓	✓		
'close'	*toemaak* *toegaan*	*dicht doen* *dicht gaan*					✓	✓				
'connect'	*koppel/verbind*	*koppelen/* *verbinden*							✓			✓
'destroy'	*vernietig*	*kapot maken* *kapot gaan*						✓				
'develop'	*ontwikkel*	*ontwikkelen*				✓			✓			
'die'	*doodmaak* *doodgaan*	*doodmaken/doden* *doodgaan*				✓	✓	✓				
'darken'	*verduister*	*verduisteren*							✓	✓		
'decrease'	*verminder*	*verminderen*							✓	✓		
'disappear'	*verdwyn*	*verdwijnen*	✓	✓								
'dissolve'	*oplos*	*oplossen*							✓	✓		
'dry'	*droogmaak* *droograak*	*drogen*					✓			✓		
'enlarge'	*vergroot*	*vergroten*	✓						✓			✓
'empty'	*leegmaak* *leegloop*	*leegmaken (legen)* *leeglopen (legen)*				✓	✓	✓				
'fall'	*val*	*vallen*	✓	✓								
'fill'	*volmaak / vul* *volraak / vul*	*vol doen / vullen* *vol raken / vullen*				✓	✓	✓	✓			
'finish'	*klaarmaak / eindig* *klaarraak / eindig*	*beëindigen*		✓					✓ ✓			
'flatten'	*afplat*	*afvlakken*	✓	✓					✓	✓		
'form'	*vorm*	*vormen*	✓			✓			✓			
'fold'	*vou*	*vouwen*				✓			✓			
'freeze'	*vries*	*bevriezen*							✓	✓		
'fry'	*braai*	*braden*							✓	✓		

Table 3. *(continued)*

CAUS/ANTIC situations	Translation of verb		CA		AA		EA		LA		SA	
	Afr	Du	Afr	Du	Afr	Du	Afr	Du	Afr	Du	Afr	Du
'gather'	*ophoop*	*hopen*	✓			✓						
'go out'	*uitdoof*	*uitdoen (doven)* *uitgaan (doven)*						✓	✓	✓		
'grow'	*kweek* *groei*	*kweken* *groeien*									✓	✓
'happen'	*gebeur*	*gebeuren*	✓	✓								
'improve'	*beter maak (verbeter)* *beter raak (verbeter)*	*verbeteren*					✓		✓	✓		
'increase'	*verhoog*	*verhogen*	✓	✓					✓	✓		
'lift up'	*oplig*	*optillen* *omhooggaan*						✓	✓			
'light'	*steek aan die brand* *slaan aan die brand*	*in brand steken* *in brand vliegen*					✓	✓				
'lock'	*sluit*	*sluiten*							✓	✓		
'lose'	*verloor* *raak weg*	*verliezen* *kwijtraken* *wegraken*								✓	✓ ✓	✓
'loosen'	*verslap*	*versoepelen*							✓	✓		
'melt'	*smelt*	*smelten*	✓	✓					✓			
'move'	*skuif*	*schuiven*							✓	✓		
'multiply'	*vermenigvuldig / meer maak* *vermenigvuldig / meer word*	*vermenigvuldigen*				✓	✓		✓			
'open'	*oopmaak* *oopgaan*	*openmaken (openen)* *opengaan (openen)*				✓	✓	✓				
'play'	*speel*	*spelen*							✓	✓		
'pour'	*ingooi* *inloop*	*ingieten* *instromen*									✓	✓
'pull'	*optrek*	*omhoog trekken*	✓						✓	✓		
'record'	*opneem*	*opnemen*							✓			
'reduce'	*verklein*	*verkleinen* *kleiner worden*							✓			✓
'rise'	*opwek* *opstaan*	*opwekken / verrijzen* *opstaan / doen verrijzen*		✓			✓	✓				

Table 3. *(continued)*

CAUS/ANTIC situations	Translation of verb		CA		AA		EA		LA		SA	
	Afr	Du	Afr	Du	Afr	Du	Afr	Du	Afr	Du	Afr	Du
'ring'	*lui*	*luiden*							✓	✓		
'ripen'	*rypmaak* *rypword*	*rijpen*		✓					✓			
'rock'	*wieg*	*schommelen*	✓						✓			
'roll'	*rol*	*rollen*							✓	✓		
'sink'	*sink*	*zinken*	✓	✓								
'snap'	*knak*	*knappen*							✓	✓		
'soften'	*sagmaak* *sagword*	*zacht maken* *zacht worden*					✓	✓				
'split'	*bars*	*splijten*	✓							✓		
'spoil'	*slegword*	*slecht worden* *(bederven)*	✓	✓						✓		
'spread'	*versprei*	*verspreiden*				✓			✓			
'stabilise'	*stabiliseer*	*stabiliseren*				✓			✓			
'stop'	*stop*	*stoppen*							✓	✓		
'tear'	*skeur*	*scheuren*							✓	✓		
'transform'	*transformeer*	*transformeren*							✓	✓		
'turn	*draai*	*draaien*							✓	✓		
'turn around'	*omdraai*	*omdraaien*							✓	✓		
'untie'	*losmaak/losraak* *losgaan*	*losgaan/losmaken* *losraken*					✓	✓				
'wake up'	*wakkermaak* *wakkerword*	*wakker maken* *wakker worden*					✓	✓				
'wilt'	*verlep/verwelk*	*verwelken*	✓	✓								
'worsen'	*erger maak /* *vererger* *erger word / vererger*	*erger maken /* *verergeren* *erger worden /* *verergeren*	✓				✓	✓	✓	✓		
Total			18	14	0	11	14	14	47	34	4	6

Dutch express causative and anticausative meanings, as earlier research indicates potential differences in this regard between the two languages. In this discussion section, we will therefore evaluate the significance of the differences or similarities between the alternations used in Afrikaans and Dutch by examining a larger quantity of CAUS/ANTIC verb pairs. If we observe differences, we can begin to make deductions about the specific nature of these differences and identify what factors contribute to these differences in verb pair alternations. This comprehen-

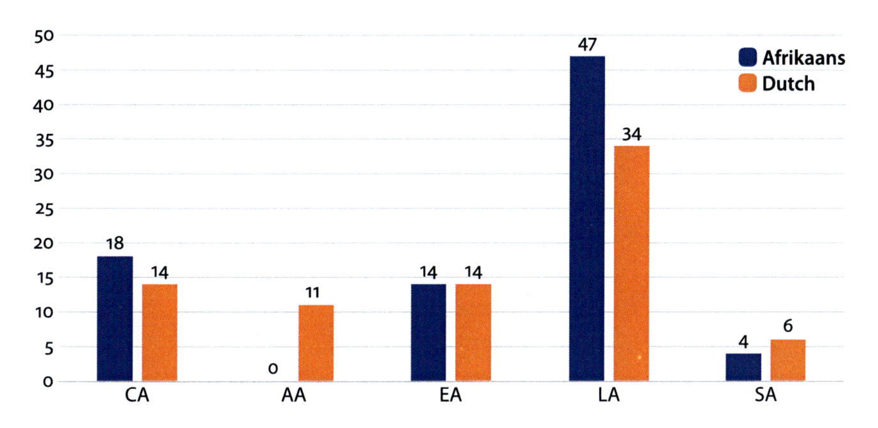

Figure 2. CAUS/ANTIC verb pair alternations in Afrikaans and Dutch

sive analysis will provide valuable insights into the influence of language contact on Afrikaans and Dutch within the SAE Sprachbund, shedding light on the intricacies of language variation and change attributable to this contact.

4.1 Cognateness of the Afrikaans and Dutch CAUS/ANTIC verb pairs

A first clue suggesting that language contact has influenced language evolution between Afrikaans and Dutch is to analyse the cognateness of the respective verb pairs in these two languages. We posit that Afrikaans and Contemporary Dutch share a common etymology (as discussed in part 1), stemming from 17th Century Dutch.[6] The geographical separation and distinct language contact environments in which 17th Century Dutch continued to evolve may have contributed to linguistic shifts between Afrikaans and Dutch. Beyond the anticipated spelling and pronunciation discrepancies, the degree of resemblance between Afrikaans and

6. One of the editors of the volume raised the question whether the main variety or varieties of 17th-century Dutch that gave rise to Afrikaans might explain some of the differences between the two present-day languages. Though potentially interesting, this question is difficult to answer, since there is still considerable debate among scholars about what those varieties and exact language influences were (see, for example, Raidt 1991: 154–199; Carstens & Raidt 2019: 22–36). Moreover, it would be wrong to assume that (Standard) Dutch had no further influence on Afrikaans after the 1600s. The Statenbijbel remained the translation used in Afrikaner churches for a long time (see du Plessis 1986: 37–50) and there were deliberate efforts to Dutchify Afrikaans when it was being encoded (Carstens & Raidt, 2019: 572–578). Finally, the processes that we will argue later on explain the differences between Afrikaans and Dutch (e.g. morphological simplification, contact with English) are fairly independent from whichever Dutch source variety or varieties Afrikaans may have developed.

Dutch CAUS/ANTIC verb pairs could offer insights into lexical alterations potentially caused by language contact. Compare the following examples:

(24) a. *Afr* (CAUS) *Hulle* ***verslap*** *die regulasies.*
b. *Du* *Ze* ***versoepelen*** *de regels.*
'They loosen the regulations'

(25) a. *Afr* (ANTIC) *Die regulasies* ***verslap.***
b. *Du* *De regels* ***versoepelen.***
'The regulations loosen'

(26) a. *Afr* (CAUS) *Die bakterieë laat die melk* ***sleg word.***
b. *Du* *De bacterieën doen de melk* ***slecht worden*** */ De bacterieën* ***bederven*** *de melk.*
'The bacteria are spoiling the milk'

(27) a. *Afr* (ANTIC) *Die melk* ***word sleg.***
b. *Du* *De melk* ***bederft*** */ De melk* ***wordt slecht.***
'The milk is spoiling'

(28) a. *Afr* (CAUS) *Ek* ***gooi*** *die water in die emmer.*
b. *Du* *Ik* ***giet*** *het water in de emmer.*
'I'm pouring the water into the bucket'

(29) a. *Afr* (ANTIC) *Die water* ***loop*** *in die emmer.*
b. *Du* *Het water* ***vloeit*** *in de emmer.*
'The water is pouring into the bucket'

(30) a. *Afr* (CAUS) *Ek* ***wieg*** *die stoel.*
b. *Du* *Ik* ***doe*** *de stoel* ***schommelen.***
'I am rocking the chair'

(31) a. *Afr* (ANTIC) *Die stoel* ***wieg.***
b. *Du* *De stoel* ***schommelt.***
'The chair is rocking'

(32) a. *Afr* (CAUS) *Ek* ***maak*** *my klere in die son* ***droog.***
b. *Du* *Ik* ***droog*** *mijn kleren in de zon.*
'I am drying my clothes in the sun'

(33) a. *Afr* (ANTIC) *My klere* ***raak*** *in die son* ***droog***
b. *Du* *Mijn kleren* ***drogen*** *in de zon*
'My clothes are drying in the sun'

We only lack cognates entirely for 10 of the 70 situations, namely for the situations 'split', 'rock', 'ripen', 'pour', 'loosen' (see Examples (24) and (25)), 'lift up', 'flatten', 'dry', 'be/get destroyed', and 'spoil' (see Examples (26) and (27)). There is, in other words, still a considerable lexical similarity between Dutch and Afrikaans. Among the other situations, there are still quite a few cases where there are differences between the cognates. Some observations emerge from the comparison. Firstly, there are instances of minor semantic shifts, such as differences in the specific contexts in which a verb can be applied, as seen in examples like *gieten/vloeien* (Du) / *ingooi/inloop* (Afr) (see Examples (28) and (29)) and *schommelen* (Du) / *wieg* (Afr) (see Examples (30) and (31)). However, these deviations are anticipated and have minimal relevance to the alternations under scrutiny. Secondly, in two cases, Afrikaans exhibits more analytical structures compared to Dutch, as is evident in the distinctions between *drogen* (Du) and *droog maak / raak* (Afr) (see Examples (32) and (33)). This disparity may be due to Afrikaans' stronger tendency towards analytical constructions than Dutch, using separate words rather than through inflectional changes.

Some of the situations for which we do have cognates are 'burn', 'close', 'die/kill', 'enlarge', 'fill', 'finish', 'go/put out', 'improve', 'ignite', 'lose', 'multiply', 'open', 'record', 'rise/raise', and 'empty'. Again, numerous insights emerge from the comparison:

(34) a. *Afr* (CAUS) *Ek* ***maak*** *die deur* ***toe.***
b. *Du* *Ik* ***doe*** *de deur* ***dicht.***
'I'm closing the door'

(35) a. *Afr* (ANTIC) *Die deur* ***gaan toe.***
b. *Du* *De deur* ***gaat dicht.***
'The door is closing'

(36) a. *Afr* (CAUS) *Die beleid* ***maak*** *die probleme* ***meer.***[7]
b. *Du* *Het beleid* ***vermenigvuldigt*** *de problemen.*
'The policy is multiplying the problems'

7. It is possible to use the non-analytical Afrikaans verb *vermenigvuldig* in this translation, i.e. *die beleid vermenigvuldig die probleme.* Moreover, in many other instances, it was possible to use an Afrikaans cognate verb (for example, *wek* instead of *wakker maak*). However, in all example sentences, we chose the most unobtrusive and frequent option for the translations (measured by speaker intuition, as well as the frequency of the construction in the two investigated corpora per language), and we base our discussion on these most frequent and default uses. They most clearly demonstrate the differences between the two languages and can therefore lead to deductions about language change. Thus, we are not truly concerned about whether a construction can indeed occur, but rather about the choices that speakers would typically make when expressing (anti)causative meaning.

(37) a. *Afr* (ANTIC) *Die probleme* ***word meer.***
b. *Du* *De problemen* ***vermenigvuldigen zich.***
'The problems are multiplying'

(38) a. *Du* (CAUS) *Ik* ***doof*** *de kaars* ***uit*** */ Ik* ***doe*** *de kaars* ***uit.***
'I'm putting out the candle'
b. (ANTIC) *De kaars* ***gaat uit*** */ De kaars* ***dooft uit.***
'The candle goes out'

(39) a. *Afr* (CAUS) *Ek* ***brand*** *die hout.*
b. *Du* *Ik* ***verbrand*** *het hout.*
'I am burning the wood'

(40) a. *Afr* (ANTIC) *Die hout* ***brand.***
b. *Du* *Het hout* ***brandt.***
'The wood is burning;

(41) a. *Afr* (CAUS) *Ek* ***eindig*** *die vergadering.*
b. *Du* *Ik* ***beëindig*** *de vergadering.*
'I'm ending the meeting'

(42) a. *Afr* (ANTIC) *Die vergadering* ***eindig***
b. *Du* *De vergadering* ***eindigt***
'The meeting is ending'

Firstly, Afrikaans consistently uses *maak* as the causative verb, as in *toemaak* (Afr), whereas Dutch often uses *doen* alongside *maak*, as in *toemaak* (Du) or *toedoen* (Du) (see 34 and 35). The reason behind this discrepancy between the two languages is not immediately apparent (but see Verhagen & Kemmer 1997 for a discussion of the use of *doen* vs *maken* as causative auxiliaries in Dutch). Secondly, Afrikaans tends to use more analytical methods for single verbs compared to Dutch, evident in pairs like *vermenigvuldigen* vs *meer maak/word* (see 36 and 37), although occasional exceptions exist, as seen in *uitdoen/uitgaan* vs *doof* (see 38). As for the choice between morphologically related verbs in Dutch causative alternation pairs, Afrikaans tends to feature only one of the verbs and employs it in a labile manner, without a discernible pattern, as demonstrated by *(ver)brand* as the causative verb in Dutch and labile one in Afrikaans (see Examples (39) and (40)) and *eindig(en)* as the anticausative verb in Dutch and labile one in Afrikaans (see Examples (41) and (42)). This suggests a form of simplification and a loss of morphological distinctions through prefixes in Afrikaans.

4.2 Specific CAUS/ANTIC alternations for each language

While there is agreement between most alternations, particularly those involving cognate verbs, significant differences nonetheless exist, indicating that further investigation into how Afrikaans and Dutch express causativity and anticausativity is warranted.

The frequencies with which the different alternations occur in the two languages are as follows:

*Afrikaans: labile > causative > equipollent > suppletive > **anticausative***
*Dutch: labile > causative > equipollent > **anticausative** > suppletive*

An important thing to note here is that suppletion was only added if there were no other alternative patterns, because otherwise there might be a risk of over-representing suppletion with intransitive and transitive verbs that have related meanings (e.g. *sterven* and *vermoorden*, while Dutch can, for instance, employ an equipollent alternation with *doodmaken* and *doodgaan*).

However, it is necessary to closely examine each of the five formal alternations to better delineate the difference between Afrikaans and Dutch in this regard.

4.2.1 *Causative alternations in Afrikaans and Dutch*

In the context of the causative alternation, there is no significant difference in frequency observed between Afrikaans and Dutch. However, a preference for *laat* in Afrikaans contrasts with Dutch's usage of *doen* and/or *laten*. Notably, Dutch occasionally employs a morphological alternation, as evidenced by pairs such as *eindigen* vs *beëindigen* (see Examples (41) and (42)) and *branden* vs *verbranden* (see Examples (39) and (40)). In contrast, Afrikaans has abandoned such distinctions in favour of a labile alternation, which appears to be influenced by either the causative verb *verbrand* or the anticausative verb *eindig*.

4.2.2 *Anticausative alternations in Afrikaans and Dutch*

The use of anticausative alternations presents a notable difference between Afrikaans and Dutch. While not particularly common in Dutch, the alternation is entirely absent from Afrikaans. In Dutch, the pattern often involves the anticausative variant featuring a reflexive pronoun. Conversely, Afrikaans typically employs a labile alternation, wherein the reflexive pronoun is omitted in the anticausative form (see Examples (43) and (44), and also again (37). This approach bears resemblance to English. However, it should be noted that Dutch is not entirely consistent in this aspect, as situations exist where both a labile pattern and an anticausative pattern are acceptable (such as (45)).

(43) a. *Afr* (CAUS) *Die reisigers* ***versprei*** *die siekte.*
b. *Du* *De reizigers* ***verspreiden*** *de ziekte.*
'The travellers are spreading the disease'

(44) a. *Afr* (ANTIC) *Die siekte* ***versprei.***
b. *Du* *De ziekte* ***verspreidt zich.***
'The disease is spreading'

(45) a. *Du* (ANTIC) *De toestand van de patiënt* ***stabiliseert zich*** /
De toestand van de patiënt ***stabiliseert.***
The patient's condition is stabilising.

4.2.3 *Equipollent alternations in Afrikaans and Dutch*

There is no substantial difference in frequency between Afrikaans and Dutch in this regard. However, investigating instances where the alternation occurs in one language but not the other remains intriguing. Afrikaans frequently employs this alternation in cases where it either prefers or lacks a clear counterpart to a Dutch verb, as seen in examples like *droograak/droogmaak* versus Dutch *drogen* or *ryp word/maak* versus *rijpen* (compare Examples (32) and (33)). This tendency may stem from Afrikaans' analytical nature, wherein separate verbs such as *maak*, *raak*, and *word* encode the causative and anticausative distinctions independently. The sole instance where Dutch arguably features a more analytical variant with no equivalent in Afrikaans is *uitdoen/uitgaan* 'put/go out' (see again (38)), although it is worth noting that *kapot maken/kapot gaan* (see (46)) likely doesn't qualify since Afrikaans, like English, appears unable to express this without resorting to a passive construction.

(46) a. *Du* (CAUS) *Dj's* ***maken*** *de muziekindustrie* ***kapot***
'DJs are destroying the music industry'
b. (ANTIC) *De muziekindustrie* ***gaat kapot.***
'The music industry is getting destroyed'

4.2.4 *Suppletive alternations in* Afrikaans *and Dutch*

Suppletive alternations are not commonly used in Afrikaans or Dutch (compare (47) and (48) below), but they were more prevalent in Dutch than in Afrikaans, with six instances in Dutch compared to four instances in Afrikaans.

(47) a. *Afr* (CAUS) *Ek* ***kweek*** *tamaties.*
b. *Du* *Ik* ***kweek*** *tomaten.*
'I am growing tomatoes'

(48) a. *Afr* (CAUS) *Die tamaties* ***groei.***
b. *Du* *De tomaten* ***groeien.***
'The tomatoes are growing'

4.2.5 *Labile alternations in Afrikaans and Dutch*

There is a clear difference here between Afrikaans and Dutch, with the former having more labile patterns than Dutch (compare Examples (49) and (50) below). We believe this difference is directly related to the variance in the anticausative alternation discussed above in 4.2.2, closely aligning with English, which also commonly employs the labile variation.

(49) a. *Afr* (CAUS) *Die beleid* ***vermenigvuldig*** *die probleme.*
b. *Du* *Het beleid* ***vermenigvuldigt*** *de problemen.*
'The policy is multiplying the problems'

(50) a. *Afr* (ANTIC) *Die probleme* ***vermenigvuldig.***
b. *Du* *De problemen* ***vermenigvuldigen zich.***
'The problems are multiplying'

4.3 Anticausative alternation prominence in Afrikaans and Dutch

In Section 2, we highlighted a notable difference in how Afrikaans and Dutch express anticausativity, a distinction that gained prominence after Van Olmen & Breed (2015) conducted a similar investigation to Haspelmath's (1993) study on the languages of the SAE. Haspelmath examined the ratio between anticausative alternation (AA) and causative alternation (CA) for each SAE language, analysing 31 verbs in each language. Van Olmen & Breed's study focused on the same 31 verb pairs in Afrikaans and Dutch. They found that in Dutch, 10 of the situations used anticausative derivations (see again Example (15)), while only two situations employed causative derivations (see again Example (16)). In contrast, for Afrikaans, when examining the same 31 types of situations, only one example of anticausative derivation was found (see again (17)), and no examples of causative derivation.

Upon repeating this test, both Dutch and Afrikaans continued to exhibit a preference for anticausative alternation. Out of the 70 verbs studied, Dutch utilised causative alternation in 17 cases and anticausative alternation in 11 cases. Afrikaans employed causative alternation 21 times, while anticausative alternation was absent in all Afrikaans verb pairs. Thus, while we can assert that Afrikaans also favours causative alternation over anticausative alternation, aligning with the SAE languages (including Dutch), it diverges from other SAE languages by completely lacking the use of causative alternations in the examined verb list. In our opinion, this difference is the clearest indication that Afrikaans has undergone changes influenced by languages outside the Sprachbund.

There is a distinction between Afrikaans and Dutch in regard to labile alternations, with Afrikaans exhibiting more labile patterns compared to Dutch. This difference is directly related to the variance observed in the anticausative alternation discussed previously, and it's also possible that it's influenced by Afrikaans's contact with English.

4.5 Conclusion

In the introduction of this chapter, we argued that the study of Sprachbunds can be highly beneficial for linguists, as it can yield insights into typological universals, language change processes attributed to language contact, and innovative insights into language-specific descriptions. While the overarching goal of Sprachbund studies is to uncover commonalities across languages and formulate typological linguistic features, the comparative nature of this research can also result in deductions specific to individual languages. This was the primary aim of our chapter – to examine an initially overlooked distinction between a Sprachbund language and its geographically distant sister language. Given previous research (see Van Olmen & Breed 2015) indicating potential differences in how Afrikaans and Dutch express causative and anticausative meanings, we chose this topic as the subject of our study. Our aim was to investigate whether a language-comparative approach could provide deeper insights into the subtle language differences arising from contact.

With our study, we aimed to address three main questions, namely (i) if we examine a larger quantity of CAUS/ANTIC verb pairs, how significant are the differences or similarities between the alternations used in Afrikaans and Dutch?; (ii) if differences are observed, can we begin to deduce the specific nature of these differences?; and (iii) can we identify factors contributing to these differences in verb pair alternations?

Based on our study, we believe that we were able to make several important findings regarding a specific language difference between the T1 (Dutch) and T2 (Afrikaans) languages of the SAE Sprachbund. Firstly, we observed that morphologically related causative-anticausative verb pairs in Dutch (e.g. ***beëindigen*** and *eindigen*) are replaced by a single verb in Afrikaans (e.g. *eindig*). This deviation in Afrikaans can be attributed to a general process of morphological simplification, which can be attributed to its entire historical development since the 17th century involving intense and constant contact with other languages. Secondly, single verbs in Dutch (e.g. *drogen*), whether or not they receive a reflexive in the anticausative, are regularly replaced by equipollent variants in Afrikaans (e.g. *droog maak/raak*), which are arguably more analytical. This tendency towards analytical structures in Afrikaans may again be linked to its history of contact with other languages. Lastly, the anticausative pattern with reflexives in Dutch (e.g. *(zich) verspreiden*)) has no counterpart in Afrikaans, which seems to prefer labile patterns here (e.g. *versprei*). This preference could be linked to contact influence from English, which also favours that pattern.

In conclusion, it is widely acknowledged that languages change over time due to language contact. Despite such change, languages can remain so closely related that it becomes challenging for linguists to pinpoint or determine precise differences between them. The study reported on in this chapter illustrated that even an examination of seemingly minor language differences between two languages is worthwhile to explore further, as it can provide insights into language change processes attributed to language contact and offer innovative perspectives on language-specific descriptions.

References

Anyanwu, Ogbonna. 2013. "Ibibio Causative and Anti-causative verb alternations." In *Selected Proceedings of the 43rd Annual Conference on African Linguistics*, ed. by Olanike Ola Orie and Karen W. Sanders, 106–114. Somerville: Cascadilla Proceedings Project.

Carstens, Wannie, and Edith Raidt. 2019. *Die storie van Afrikaans: uit Europa en van Afrika*. Pretoria: Protea Boekhuis.

Coetzee, Anna. 2009. "Pidgin-kreoolse retensies en taalvermenging". In *Afrikaans. Een drieluik*, ed. by Hans den Besten, Frans Hinskens and Jerzy Koch, 48–71. Amsterdam: Stichting Neerlandistiek VU.

Corpus Hedendaags Nederlands – CHN (Version 3.0) (October 2021) [Online Service]. Available at the Dutch Language Institute: http://hdl.handle.net/10032/tm-a2-s8. Consulted on 28 February 2024.

CTexT. 2023. NWU/Kommentaarkorpus 2.2. Potchefstroom: CTexT, Noordwes-Universiteit.

Cysouw, Michael. 2011. "Quantitative explorations of the world-wide distribution of rare characteristics, or: the exceptionality of north-western European languages." In *Exception in Language*, ed. by Horst Simon & Heike Wiese, 411–431. Berlin: Mouton de Gruyter.

Deumert, Anna. 2004. *Language standardization and language change: the dynamics of Cape Dutch*. Amsterdam: John Benjamins.

Du Plessis, Hans. 1994. Taalkontakvariasie in Afrikaans. In *Nuwe perspektiewe op die geskiedenis van Afrikaans*, ed by G. Olivier, A. Coetzee. Halfweghuis: Southern Book.

Du Plessis, Theo. 1986. *Afrikaans in Beweging*. Bloemfontein: Patmos.

Fernando, Mbiavanga. 2013. *The Causative and Anticausative Alternation in Kikongo (Kizombo)*. Stellenbosch: Stellenbosch University PhD dissertation.

doi Friedman, Victor. 2006. Balkans as a Linguistic Area. In *Encyclopedia of Language & Linguistics*, ed.by Keith Brown, 657–672. Amsterdam: Elsevier.

doi Haspelmath, Martin. 2001. The European linguistic area: Standard Average European. In *Language typology and language universals: an international handbook*, ed. by Martin Haspelmath, Ekkehard König, Wulf Oesterreicher, and Wolfgang Raible, 1492–1510. Berlin/New York: W. de Gruyter.

doi Haspelmath, Martin. 1993. More on the typology of inchoative/causative verb alternations. In *Causatives and Transitivity*, ed. by Bernard Comrie and Maria Polinsky, 87–121, Amsterdam: John Benjamins.

doi Haspelmath, Martin. 1998. How young is standard average European? *Language Sciences*, 20(3), 271–287.

doi Heidinger, Steffen, and Richard Huyghe. 2024. Semantic roles and the causative-anticausative alternation: Evidence from French change-of-state verbs. *Linguistics*, 62(1), 159–202.

doi Irslinger, Britta. 2013. Standard Average European and the Western Fringe – a Reconsideration. *Historische Sprachforschung*, 126, 33–88.

doi Joseph, Brian D. 2020. Language contact in the Balkans. In *The Handbook of Language Contact*, ed. by Raymond Hickey. 882–842. Newark: John Wiley & Sons.

Maddieson, Ian. 2003. The sounds of the Bantu languages". In *The Bantu languages*, ed. by Derek Nurse and Gérard Philippson, 15–41, Oxfordshire: Routledge.

Markey, Thomas. 1982. Afrikaans: creole or non-creole? *Zeitschrift für Dialektologie und Linguistik*, 49(2), 169–207.

Nienaber, Gabriël Stefanus. 1953. *Oor Afrikaans (2 ed.)*. Johannesburg: Afrikaanse Pers-Boekhandel.

doi Oostdijk, Nelleke, Martin Reynaert, Hoste, Veronique, and Ineke Schuurman. 2013. The construction of a 500-million-word reference corpus of contemporary written Dutch. In *Essential speech and language technology for Dutch: Results by the STEVIN programme*, ed. by Peter Spyns and Jan Odijs, 219–247. Dordrecht: Springer.

Pharos. 2010. *Afrikaans-Engels/English-Afrikaans Dictionary*. Cape Town: Pharos.

Ponelis, Fritz. 1993. *The development of Afrikaans*. Frankfurt am Main: P. Lang.

Ponelis, Fritz. 1997. Afrikaans. In *Geschiedenis van de Nederlandse taal*, ed. by J.M. van der Horst, J.A. van Leuvensteijn, W. Pijnenburg, M.C. van den Toorn, 597–598, Amsterdam: Amsterdam University Press.

Raidt, Edith. 1991. *Afrikaans en sy Europese verlede*. Kaapstad: Nasou.

Roberge, Paul. 2009. Afrikaans and creolization. In *Afrikaans. Een drieluik*, ed. by Hans den Besten, Frans Hinskens and Jerzy Koch, 209–223. Amsterdam: Stichting Neerlandistiek VU.

Schäfer, Florian, and Margot Vivanco. 2016. Anticausatives are weak scalar expressions, not reflexive expressions. *Glossa*, 1, 1–36.

doi Sidwell, Paul, and Mathias Jenny. 2021. The Languages and Linguistics of Mainland Southeast Asia. Berlin: De Gruyter.

doi Oostdijk, Nelleke, Martin Reynaert, Véronique Hoste & Ineke Schuurman. 2013. The construction of a 500-million-word reference corpus of contemporary written Dutch. In Peter Spyns & Jan Odijs (eds.), *Essential Speech and Language Technology for Dutch: Results by the STEVIN programme*. Dordrecht: Springer, 219–247.

Thomas, George. 2007. Exploring the Parameters of a Central European Sprachbund. Canadian Slavonic Papers/Revue Canadienne des Slavistes. *An Interdisciplinary Journal Devoted to Central and Eastern Europe (CSP) 2008 Mar-June*, 50(1–2), 123–153.

Van Dale. 2024. *Engels – Nederlands Online*. Amsterdam: Van Dale. https://www.vandale.nl

Van der Auwera, Johan. 2011. Standard Average European. In *The Languages and Linguistics of Europe: A Comprehensive Guide*, ed. by Bernd Kortmann & Johan Auwera, Berlin: de Gruyter Mouton.

Van der Wouden, Ton. (ed.) 2012. *Roots of Afrikaans: selected writings of Hans Den Besten*. Amsterdam: John Benjamins.

Van Olmen, Daniël & Auwera, Johan van der. 2016. Modality and mood in Standard Average European. In *Oxford Handbook of Modality and Mood*, ed. by Jan Nuyts, Johan van der Auwera, 1–26. Oxford: Oxford University Press

Van Olmen, Daniël, & Breed, Adri. 2015. Afrikaans as Standaard Gemiddelde Europees: Wanneer 'n lid uit sy taalarea beweeg. *Southern African Linguistics and Applied Language Studies*, 33(2), 227–246.

Van Rensburg, Christo. 2012. *So kry ons Afrikaans*. Pretoria: Lapa uitgewers.

Verhagen, Arie, and Suzanne Kemmer, S. (1997). Interaction and causation: Causative constructions in modern standard Dutch. *Journal of Pragmatics*, 27(1), 61–82.

CHAPTER 9

Aspectual cognate constructions in Afrikaans and Dutch

A language contact approach to prospective and ingressive aspect

Maarten Bogaards[1] & Roné Wierenga[2,3,4]
[1] Leiden University | [2] Ghent University | [3] North-West University | [4] Virtual Institute for Afrikaans

This chapter examines ingressive ('begin') and prospective ('about to') cognate constructions in Afrikaans and Dutch through the lens of language contact. We propose a theoretical account of the conceptual link between these aspectual viewpoints that generates predictions on their selectional restrictions. These predictions are tested using corpus data and interpreted within Diasystematic Construction Grammar: shared diachronic development aligns with equivalent selectional behavior (*diaconstructions*), diachronic divergence leads to distributional differences (*idioconstructions*). Our findings reveal a mix of diaconstructions and idioconstructions. For example, ingressive *gaan* 'go' distributes differently across Afrikaans and Dutch, whereas *begin(nen te)* 'begin (to)' patterns similarly. The results support a conceptual distinction between two types of prospective aspect and ingressive aspect, differentiated by respective restrictions on telicity and dynamicity.

Keywords: viewpoint aspect, language contact, ingressive aspect, prospective aspect, Diasystematic Construction Grammar, selection theory, corpus linguistics, Afrikaans, Dutch

1. Introduction

Afrikaans is a contact language originating from the 17th-century South African melting pot of Dutch, Khoekhoe, and Portuguese influences – to name just a few – and underwent a complex developmental trajectory (Van der Wouden 2012: 265). While geographically rooted on the African continent, it is linguisti-

https://doi.org/10.1075/impact.55.09bog

cally aligned with the West-Germanic family due to its historical development from 17th-century Dutch (Roberge 2024: 8).

The 19th-century British colonial period brought English to the forefront in South Africa. English became the dominant language of administration, education, and trade. This historical dominance had a profound and lasting influence on South African society and Afrikaans. Furthermore, in modern-day South Africa, English functions as a lingua franca between speakers of the country's 11 official languages (Carstens 2017: 195).[1] The influence of English on Afrikaans is widespread and evident across all linguistic levels. Codeswitching and codemixing between English and Afrikaans is very common and has resulted in several English expressions and vocabulary items being adopted into Afrikaans.

Both English and Dutch therefore constitute integral components of Afrikaans' grammatical diasystem. In this chapter, we utilize the historical background of language contact between Afrikaans and Dutch to investigate microvariation in the expression of two closely related types of viewpoint aspect: prospective ('about to') and ingressive ('begin') aspect. By taking a Diasystematic Construction Grammar (DCxG) approach (Höder 2018, 2019, i.a.), we explore how cognate constructions tied to these types of aspect have evolved and adapted across Afrikaans and Dutch.

In (1)–(2), we give examples of the types of construction that we are interested in.[2] At first glance, prospective (1) and ingressive devices (2) are very similar in Afrikaans and Dutch: (1a)–(1b) are both built around a phrase that translates to 'on the point to', and (2a)–(2b) both feature a non-main verb meaning 'begin'. However, closer inspection of a wider variety of prospective and ingressive expressions will reveal subtle differences between Afrikaans and Dutch.

(1) **Prospective aspect**

a. Die oond *is op die punt om te* ontplof. — Afrikaans
the oven is on the point COMP to explode
'The oven is about to explode.'

b. De oven *staat op het punt om te* ontploffen. — Dutch
the oven stands on the point COMP to explode
'The oven is about to explode.'

1. Sign language was instated as South Africa's twelfth official language in 2023. In addition to the official languages, a number of unofficial and lesser-known languages are spoken in South Africa, like N|uu, Nama, Damara and Isicamtho, to name just a few.

2. Examples (1a)–(2a) are from Wierenga (2023a: 349); (1b)–(2b) are our translations.

(2) **Ingressive aspect**

a. Ons *begin* onmiddellik eet. Afrikaans
we begin immediately eat
'We start eating immediately.'

b. We *beginnen* onmiddellijk *met* eten. Dutch
we begin immediately with eat
'We start eating immediately.'

Our focus on viewpoint aspect continues a research program – initiated in the past decade – exploring parallels between Afrikaans and Dutch aspectual constructions (Breed 2012, 2016; Breed & Brisard 2015; Breed et al. 2017; Breed et al. 2024; Bylund et al. 2013; Cavirani-Pots 2020; Geleyn & Colleman 2014; Wierenga & Breed 2021; Wierenga 2022). Studies in this tradition have concentrated mainly on progressive aspect. We build on this work by extending the scope to two lesser-studied types of viewpoint aspect.

Furthermore, there has been a recent upsurge in research interest on prospective and/or ingressive aspect in individual West-Germanic languages: English (Hill to appear), German (Fleischhauer & Gamerschlag 2019; Fleischhauer 2023), Afrikaans (Wierenga 2023a; Wierenga & Breed submitted) and Dutch (Andree & Oh 2024; Bogaards 2022, 2023a,b; Bogaards et al. 2022; Van Eynde to appear).[3] With the exception of one comparative corpus study (Bogaards & Fleischhauer 2024), these studies have been restricted to one language at a time. We contribute to this emergent line of inquiry in terms of both method – taking a DCxG perspective – and scope – examining microvariation in two West-Germanic languages with a history of language contact.

Finally, while it has been recognized that there is a conceptual connection between prospective and ingressive aspect (e.g., Dik 1997: 239; Michaelis 1998: 68; Kuteva et al. 2019: 862), this connection has not yet been made precise. Based on our fine-grained comparison of prospectivity and ingressivity in Afrikaans and Dutch, we examine the idea that there are at least two types of prospective aspect (Bogaards 2024), which vary in whether or not they embed the ingressive viewpoint in their conceptual representation. Our DCxG approach to microvariation in this conceptual space enables us to tease apart these closely related types of viewpoint aspect on clearly delineated empirical grounds.

This chapter is structured as follows. Section 2 introduces DCxG. Section 3 outlines our conceptual definitions of situation structure and viewpoint aspect, focusing in particular on prospective and ingressive aspect. We draw on selection-theoretical approaches (e.g., Koss et al. 2022) to clarify the potential conceptual

3. Recent work has also been done on ingressive aspect in French (Verroens 2018; Verroens & De Cuypere 2023; Verroens 2024).

relations between the two aspectual viewpoints (§ 3.1), identify Afrikaans and Dutch linguistic devices tied to these types of aspect (§ 3.2), and formulate specific hypotheses generated by our theoretical treatment of prospective/ingressive aspect (§ 3.3), to be tested in our corpus study. In Section 4, we describe the corpus assembly and annotation process. We present our corpus study in Section 5, subdivided into comparative analyses of specific cognate constructions in Afrikaans and Dutch: prospective *op (die/het punt)* (§ 5.1), ingressive non-main verbs (§ 5.2), and composite prospective expressions consisting of an ingressive device paired with a marker of temporal proximity or imminence (§ 5.3). Section 6 concludes and identifies open questions for future research.[4]

2. Diasystematic Construction Grammar

The relationship between prospective and ingressive aspect remains unexplored through a comparative analysis. The closely-linked Afrikaans and Dutch languages offer a distinctive chance to study the connection between these aspectual viewpoints, examining how they manifest in cognate constructions like *op die/het punt staan (om) te* (see (1)). The historical context of Afrikaans' development in relation to Dutch allow us to take a Diasystematic Construction Grammar (DCxG) approach.

Construction Grammar (CxG) – in line with its cognitive linguistic origins – is a comprehensive framework that links form and meaning. It views linguistic constructions as invariably comprising a form-meaning pair, regardless of the form's level of schematicity or the abstraction of the meaning (Van Rooy 2021: 111). This approach allows analysts to capture shifts in meaning over time, parallelling alternations in the structure of a construction. When both form and meaning undergo modifications, resulting in a novel form-meaning pair, this process is identified as constructionalization. Conversely, when changes occur in one aspect but not the other, Traugott & Trousdale (2013) categorize this as constructional change. The mechanisms behind constructional change have been extensively explored across various frameworks over an extended period. Croft (2000) proposes a relatively straightforward, integrated model that distinguishes between innovation, signifying the emergence of a new construction or modifications to an existing one, and propagation, the process through which the original change spreads within the broader speech community, eventually becoming an established norm. Croft (2000) aligns with Labov (2010) in this regard, as both

4. For readers unfamiliar with our use of technical terms such as (a)telic, dynamicity, and diaconstruction/idioconstruction, we include a Glossary at the end of this chapter.

emphasize linguistic elements and contact as pivotal factors in innovation, while underscoring the influence of social factors in the diffusion process.

Language contact contributes to innovation (Thomason 2001; Matras 2009). Diasystematic Construction Grammar (DCxG) – developed by Höder (2012, 2014, 2018, 2019) – focuses on constructions emerging from language contact, emphasizing the role of diachronic change. A key distinction is drawn in DCxG between *diaconstructions*, shared across languages, and *idioconstructions*, which are language-specific (Boas & Höder 2021). Speakers navigate diaconstructions and idioconstructions, catalyzing contact-induced changes (Höder 2019). Diaconstructions may evolve into idioconstructions and vice versa, influenced by social conventions and usage (Höder 2014). They embody shared structural elements across dialects or languages within a diasystem, reflecting multilingual speakers' acquisition and usage in contact communities. Schematic constructions are more abstract and generalizable, while less schematic ones are context-bound (Goldberg 2006), influencing acquisition and processing, particularly in multilingual environments like Afrikaans' diasystem.

Afrikaans emerged from a complex language contact situation in South Africa, influenced by Dutch, various African languages, Malay, and Portuguese (Van Rensburg 2015). This multilingual contact shaped Afrikaans, influenced by colonial history, slavery, apartheid, and language rights struggles (Roberge 2024). Afrikaans' cognate constructions with Dutch reflect its evolution from 17th-century Dutch, influenced by various languages, making it challenging to pinpoint specific influences.

Moreover, the scarcity of comprehensive corpus resources for Afrikaans complicates the exploration of these constructions. When cognate constructions operate similarly in both Afrikaans and Dutch, they may be considered part of the Afrikaans-Dutch diaconstructicon. However, instances where Afrikaans diverges from Dutch constructions likely signify the impact of language contact. Divergence suggests that a construction has transitioned into an idioconstruction, establishing itself as a distinctive language-specific norm within Afrikaans.

3. Prospective and ingressive aspect

3.1 Viewpoint aspect and the structure of situations

Prospective and ingressive aspect are subtypes of viewpoint aspect (in the sense of Smith 1997). We define viewpoint aspect as non-deictic perspective-taking on situation structure.[5] Take the situation denoted by the VP *write a poem*, which breaks down into distinct phases: onset, nucleus and offset (cessation or completion). Aspectual viewpoints pick out one of these phases.

For purposes of exposition, this section discusses English examples of the types of linguistic devices that we are interested in. English has verbs selecting present-participial complements – also called "aspectualizers" – dedicated to viewpoint aspect (cf. Brinton 1988 and references cited there): *start* profiles the onset (3a), *be* the nucleus (3b), *stop* cessation (3c) and *finish* completion (3d). Viewpoint aspect operates on situation structure in that the underlying situation denoted by the embedded VP *write a poem* stays the same throughout (3a)–(3d); only the phasal perspective changes.

(3) a. She *started* writing a poem. — Ingressive
b. She *was* writing a poem. — Progressive
c. She *stopped* writing a poem. — Egressive
d. She *finished* writing a poem. — Completive

The aspectual viewpoints are exemplified by (3) profile situation-internal phases. Viewpoint aspect may also operate on one of two situation-external phases (Dik 1997:§ 9.1.2; Michaelis 1998:§ 1.4.3): (i) the phase preceding the onset, in which case the embedded situation is presented as imminent; and (ii) the phase following cessation/completion. These are expressed in English by the constructions *be about to* (4a) and *have* + past participle (4b) (Comrie 1976:§ 3.3).

(4) a. She *is about to* write a poem. — Prospective
b. She *has written* a poem. — Retrospective

As a framework for our fine-grained comparison of specific subtypes of viewpoint aspect, we adopt a selection-theoretical approach (i.a., Breu 1994; Bickel 1996; Sasse 2002; Michaelis 2011; Koss et al. 2022; Bogaards & Fleischhauer 2024; Verroens 2024). On this approach, there is a direct operator-operandum relation between viewpoint aspect and situation structure. The main assumptions under-

5. We include 'non-deictic' in our definition to set viewpoint aspect apart from tense. Tense is deictic in that it temporally locates a situation relative to a reference point (e.g., the moment of speaking) – for instance, past tense (situation precedes reference point). Viewpoint aspect is non-deictic because no additional reference point is involved.

lying selection theories of aspect are that (i) situations are built out of a limited number of conceptual primitives; and (ii) viewpoint aspect operators are defined in terms of those same primitives, in the sense that they select or impose the building blocks constitutive of the structure of situations. Put another way, viewpoint aspect operators denote abstract situations that differ only from the denotation of VPs in that they are devoid of lexical root content; the VP *write a poem* maps 'poem writing' content to the situational building blocks (e.g., the onset of the 'poem writing'), whereas the non-main verb *begin* just makes reference to the building block itself (i.e., any onset).

What are the building blocks of situations? The present approach makes two primitive distinctions. The first is between phases ϕ – intervals extending over time – and bounds τ – which are punctual and may mark transitions between phases (Bickel 1996: 196). Second, phases ϕ are either stative ϕ_s (internally homogeneous) or dynamic ϕ_d (internally heterogeneous).[6] Using these building blocks, we can straightforwardly derive the standard taxonomy of situation types (Vendler 1967; Smith 1997, among many others), as shown in Table 1. States and Activities simply correspond to a single stative phase [ϕ_s] and dynamic phase [ϕ_d], respectively. Semelfactives are punctual events lacking a resultant state; we therefore model them using a single bound [τ].[7] Accomplishments and Achievements are composite structures incorporating the three simplex situation types. Accomplishments consist of a dynamic phase [ϕ_d] culminating in a resultant state [ϕ_s], the transition between them marked by a bound [τ]. Achievements lack duration, which is why they comprise only a transition [τ] followed by a resultant state [ϕ_s].

With these representations of situation structure in our toolkit, we can also model the conceptual makeup of aspectual viewpoints like the ingressive and prospective, as shown in Table 2.

6. This articulates the basic premise that the State-Event distinction is a primitive of situation structure, which is a widely-held assumption – also outside of selection theory (cf. Rothmayr 2009:§ 2.1-§ 2.3 and references cited there). For example, there are clear parallels between these selection-theoretical building blocks and Pustejovsky's (1991) decomposition of situations into states S (our ϕ_s), processes P (our ϕ_d) and transitions T (our τ), as well as Ramchand's (2019) primitive predicational types Pred$_s$ (our ϕ_s) and Pred$_d$ (our ϕ_d) which enter into 'lead to' relations representing change (bordered off by our τ).

7. We deviate from Michaelis (2011) on this point, who disallows standalone transitions – i.e., *[τ]. We conceptualize the primitive [τ] in a more general way, namely as a punctual bound rather than as a transition (in line with, e.g., Breu 1994 and Sasse 2002). This conceptual move extends the empirical coverage of our model so as to account for Semelfactives and their divergent linguistic behavior vis-à-vis Activities and Achievements.

Table 1. Situations derived from selection-theoretical building blocks

Situation type	Representation	Examples
State	$[\phi_s]$	*know, love, have money, be hungry*
Activity	$[\phi_d]$	*eat, push a cart, grow, rain*
Semelfactive	$[\tau]$	*knock, sneeze, blink, flash, tap*
Accomplishment	$[\phi_d\ \tau\ \phi_s]$	*eat a cookie, push off a cliff, dry*
Achievement	$[\tau\ \phi_s]$	*win, explode, collapse, realize*

Table 2. Aspectual viewpoints derived from selection-theoretical building blocks

Viewpoint aspect	Representation	Example
Ingressive	$[\tau\ \phi]$	*start* V-*ing*
Prospective	$[\phi_s]$ & IMM($[\tau\ \phi]$)	*be about to* V

Ingressive aspect profiles the initial bound of a situation. In the present terms, an initial bound is a transition into a phase – i.e., $[\tau\ \phi]$. This representation underspecifies the type of phase (stative or dynamic) because both states and non-states may be profiled ingressively. We illustrated ingressivity with a non-State in (3b); (5) gives an attested example of *start* profiling the onset of a State (*be hungry*).

(5) We *started being hungry* around 12 so we decided to make a stop somewhere along the road [...].
[https://montessorijourneyblog.wordpress.com/2019/09/07/mini-balkan-road-trip-part-6]

If (4a) holds, for instance, we can only say for certain that the subject has not started writing a poem yet. In addition to the pre-phase, which in our terms corresponds to $[\phi_s]$, the prospective viewpoint construes the onset of the situation itself as "imminent" (Van Rompaey et al. 2015; Kuteva et al. 2019). Following Bogaards & Fleischhauer (2024), we model this component using an imminence operator IMM() scoping over the embedded situation's onset.[8]

Of particular interest for our purposes is what is in the scope of IMM: $[\tau\ \phi]$. This is the construal of a predicate embedded under the prospective viewpoint, which can mean at least two things: either $[\tau\ \phi]$ is an input condition imposed

8. The IMM operator itself is beyond the scope of our chapter. For four different takes on what IMM does, we refer the reader to Kuteva et al.'s (2019) account in terms of futurity, Bogaards & Fleischhauer's (2024) proposal deriving IMM from alethic modality, work by Van Dooren (2024) combining root modality with tense/aspect, and Hill's (to appear) insertion of a non-modal perfective operator.

by the prospective viewpoint, or $[\tau\ \phi]$ is contributed by the prospective viewpoint as part of its construal. We'll come back to this issue in Section 3.3. For now, our analysis throws light on the affinities of prospective aspect with other viewpoints and situation structure. Limiting ourselves to the structures in Table 1, the denotation of the embedded predicate $[\tau\ \phi]$ is equivalent to the ingressive viewpoint $[\tau\ \phi]$, and is an abstraction over the structure of Achievements $[\tau\ \phi_s]$. This gives us a framework to understand the combinatory behavior of prospective constructions.

We can show how this works with English *be about to* in (6), in which the selection-theoretical representations are aligned with their corresponding linguistic devices. We expect the prospective viewpoint to be readily compatible with Achievements (e.g., *collapse*), as $[\tau\ \phi]$ can directly pick out the representation $[\tau\ \phi_s]$; (6a) confirms this expectation. According to the same logic, we expect to be able to insert the ingressive viewpoint $[\tau\ \phi]$ in between the prospective viewpoint and any compatible situation structure, which (6b) demonstrates with an embedded Activity (*rain*). With Accomplishments – i.e., $[\phi_d\ \tau\ \phi_s]$ – the prospective component $[\tau\ \phi]$ most straightforwardly maps to the resultant state transition $[\tau\ \phi_s]$, leading to an offset reading of *push the cart off the cliff* in (6c). However, an onset reading of the same predicate turns out to be possible too (6d). Contrary to (6c), in (6d) prospective $[\tau\ \phi]$ cannot pick out $[\tau\ ]$ from the underlying situation structure. This suggests that *be about to* incorporates the ingressive viewpoint $[\tau\ \phi]$.

(6) a. The building *is about to* *collapse.* — Achievement
$[[\phi_s]$ & IMM $([\tau\ \phi_s]\ )]$
b. It *is about to* *start raining.* — Ingressive[Activity]
$[[\phi_s]$ & IMM $([\tau\ \ [\phi_d]\ ])]$
c. She *is about to* *push the cart off the cliff.* — Accomplishment
$[[\phi_s]$ & IMM $([\tau\ \phi_s]\ )]$
Offset reading: 'She's already pushing the cart and now about to give it the final push sending it over the cliff.'
d. She *is about to* *push the cart off the cliff.* — Accomplishment
$[[\phi_s]$ & IMM $([\tau[\phi_d\ \tau\ \phi_s]\ ])]$
Onset reading: 'She's about to start pushing the cart with the intention of sending it over the cliff.'

The upshot of this subsection is that there is a potential embedding relation between the prospective and ingressive viewpoints such that the former embeds the latter. This seems to apply to English *be about to*. A conceivable alternative scenario is that the prospective does not incorporate ingressivity but merely imposes an input condition for situations of the type $[\tau\ \phi]$. One of our current objectives is to establish whether the relevant linguistic devices in Afrikaans and Dutch display this type of conceptual variability.

3.2 Ingressivity and prospectivity in Afrikaans and Dutch

Let's move on from our English-based exposition to prospective and ingressive devices in Afrikaans and Dutch. In recent research, we can find a range of expressions which encode these aspectual viewpoints in both Afrikaans (Breed 2016; Wierenga 2022, 2023a; Wierenga & Breed submitted) and Dutch (Andree & Oh 2024; Bogaards 2019, 2022, 2023a,b, 2024; Bogaards et al. 2022; Boogaart & Bogaards to appear; Kovač & Schoenmakers to appear).[9] Based on this body of work, we can distinguish three categories of ingressive and prospective expressions in Afrikaans and Dutch: ingressive non-main verbs, periphrastic prospective constructions, and what we shall call composite prospectives.

Leading off with ingressivity, both Afrikaans and Dutch have non-main verbs for this aspectual viewpoint, as shown in (7)–(8). Afrikaans has *gaan* 'go' and *begin* 'begin'. The former selects a bare infinitive (7a) whereas the latter may select either a bare infinitive (7b) or a long infinitive, with or without a complementizer (*om*) (7c).[10]

The Dutch picture is similar at first sight, with cognate verbs for *gaan* and *begin*: *gaan* and *beginnen*. Like in Afrikaans, *gaan* goes with a bare infinitive in Dutch (8a). *Beginnen* may combine with a long infinitive (8b), but not with the optional complementizer we saw in Afrikaans (e.g., **Hij begon om te helpen*), nor with a bare infinitive (e.g., **Hij begon helpen*). It can be paired with a complement not found in Afrikaans: an infinitive embedded in a constituent headed by the preposition *met* 'with' (8c). The infinitive in this type of *met*-phrase can be bare or long (i.e., *met te* + infinitive).[11]

---

9. Differences in terminology for the aspectual viewpoints exist among recent publications on Afrikaans and Dutch, as well as in the broader literature. This chapter adopts the terms used in the literature on the Dutch constructions: *ingressive* for 'begin'-type aspect and *prospective* for 'about to'-type aspect. Alternative terms for the former include *inchoative* (Van Olmen & Mortelmans 2009) and *inceptive* (Laca 2004); alternatives for the latter include *pre-inchoative* (Wierenga 2022), *proximative* (Kuteva et al. 2019, *proximate future* (Hill to appear) and *imminential* (Van Rompaey et al. 2015). We regard the labels within these two groups as synonyms here.

10. We omit *komen* 'come' and *loop* 'walk' because they still have a strong sense of spatial motion (which is less of an issue for *gaan* 'go', cf. Wierenga 2023a).

11. This observation was made independently by Kovač & Schoenmakers (to appear) and Boogaart & Bogaards (to appear).

(7) **Afrikaans ingressive non-main verbs**

a. Hy *gaan* help. — [*gaan* V_{inf}]
he go help

b. Hy *begin* help. — [*begin* V_{inf}]
he begin help

c. Hij *begin (om) te* help. — [*begin (om) te* V_{inf}]
he begin COMPL to help

(8) **Dutch ingressive non-main verbs**

a. Hij *ging* helpen. — [*gaan* V_{inf}]
he went help

b. Hij *begon te* helpen. — [*beginnen te* V_{inf}]
he begun to help

c. Hy *begon met (te)* helpen. — [*beginnen met (te)* V_{inf}]
he begun with to help

Moving to prospective aspect, both Afrikaans and Dutch have a construction built around the prepositional phrase *op die/het punt* 'on the point' which embeds some type of variable infinitive and combines with a matrix verb. In Afrikaans, the infinitival constituent is headed by *te* 'to' and an optional complementizer *om*, and the matrix verb is either *wees* 'be' or *staan* 'stand' (9a). Although both are possible, the combination with *wees* is more common.[12] There is also a prospective construction with the preposition *op* but without the sequence *die punt (om) te*, which appears to take only *staan* (not *wees*) as the matrix verb (9b).

The Dutch counterparts look basically identical, apart from the matrix verb in the construction *op het punt staan (om) te*, which can only be *staan* 'stand' (10a).[13] The pattern with *op* also exists in Dutch (10b). Dutch has one more prospective construction featuring *op het punt* not present in Afrikaans, where the embedded infinitival constituent is headed by the preposition *van* 'of' (10c).[14]

12. See Table 5 for empirical support of this claim.

13. The combination with *zijn* – e.g., ??*De oven is op het punt om te ontploffen* – is extremely marginal at best: Google searches (conducted on 2023/12/12) for "is op het punt om te" and "is op het punt te" yield 11 and 6 hits, respectively, as opposed to 392,000 and 266,000 hits for the same queries replacing *is* with *staat*. We'll therefore assume that the Dutch construction is formed only with *staan*, in contrast to the Afrikaans construction which exhibits variation.

14. Afrikaans does have a version of *op het punt van*, but the embedded element is restricted to nouns (e.g., *op die punt van bankrotskap* 'on the brink of bankruptcy'), which is also found in Dutch (e.g., *op het punt van faillissement* 'on the brink of bankruptcy'). Since we're limiting ourselves to verb-embedding constructions, these nominal patterns fall outside the present scope.

(9) **Afrikaans prospective *op (die punt)*-constructions**
a. Die oond *is/staan op die punt (om) te* ontplof.
the oven is/stand on the point COMPL to explode
[*op die punt wees/staan (om) te* V_{inf}]
b. Die oond *staan op* ontplof.
the oven stand on explode
'The oven is about to explode.' [*op* V_{inf} *staan*]

(10) **Dutch prospective *op (het punt)*-constructions**
a. De oven *staat op het punt (om) te* ontploffen.
the oven stands on the point COMPL to explode
[*op het punt staan (om) te* V_{inf}]
b. De oven *staat op* ontploffen.
the oven stands on explode [*op* V_{inf} *staan*]
c. De oven *staat op het punt van* ontploffen.
the oven stands on the point of explode
'The oven is about to explode.' [*op het punt van* V_{inf} *staan*]

The final category of prospective constructions in Afrikaans and Dutch distinguished here concerns combinations of an ingressive non-main verb and an adverb signaling temporal proximity or imminence (e.g., *net* 'just'). This type of combination is precisely what we'd expect given the idea – explored in § 3.1 – that prospective aspect is (or can be) a composite viewpoint made up of ingressivity and imminence. We therefore refer to these combinations as 'composite prospectivity'. In Afrikaans, the imminent adverbs *net* and *pas* 'just' may be combined with *gaan* (11) to get a meaning comprising the two components. The same goes for the Dutch adverbs *net* and *juist* 'just' (12).[15]

(11) **Afrikaans composite prospectivity: [*net/pas gaan* V_{inf}]**
Ek het *net/pas gaan* eet toe die klokkie lui.
I have just go eat when the doorbell ring
'I was just about to eat when the doorbell rang.'

15. There are at least two other options in Dutch with a volitional expression – *willen* 'want to' or *van plan zijn* 'intend to' – paired with *net/juist* (Bogaards 2023a), e.g., *Ik wil juist vertrekken* 'lit. I just want to leave' and *Ik ben net plan om te vertrekken* 'lit. I just intend to leave', both of which translate to 'I'm just about to leave'. Since we're focusing on the relationship of prospectivity to ingressivity rather than to volition, we set these expressions aside here. We refer the reader to Van Dooren (2024) for recent work on the relation between root modality (volition) and aspect/futurity in Dutch.

(12) **Dutch composite prospectivity: [*net/juist gaan* V_{inf}]**
Ik *ging net/juist* eten toen de deurbel ging.
I went just eat when the doorbell went
'I was just about to eat when the doorbell rang.'

This subsection has catalogued the Afrikaans and Dutch ingressive/prospective devices to be examined in our corpus study. The aim of the corpus study is to explore microvariation in the expression of ingressive and prospective aspect in the Afrikaans/Dutch diasystem: which cognates have remained stable, and which now display conceptual variation? To facilitate our exploration of these questions based on corpus data, we will now formulate a set of hypotheses.

3.3 Hypotheses and empirical scope

Our theoretical framework (§ 3.1) generates specific hypotheses which we will test on Afrikaans and Dutch corpus data. These hypotheses concern the situation structure of the predicates embedded in prospective and ingressive constructions. This is because our (selection-based) theory conceptualizes viewpoint and situation aspect as being in an operator-operandum relationship. So, aspectual viewpoints – in particular, competing definitions of those viewpoints – are differentiated by the predicates they select.

First, the framework makes a conceptual distinction between prospective aspect with an embedded ingressive viewpoint (13a) and without, in which case the prospective construction selects for Achievements (13b). In the former scenario, the ingressive component [τ ϕ] may either map to the corresponding structure from an embedded predicate (i.e., either an Achievement as in (6a) or the offset of an Accomplishment as in (6c)) or augment an embedded predicate lacking it (e.g., the onset of an Accomplishment as in (6d)). This generates the hypothesis that what is licensed by the *x*-slot may be inclined towards but not categorically restricted to telic predicates, see (13a). If, alternatively, the prospective viewpoint does not embed ingressive aspect, then we do expect categorical restrictions. This scenario generates the hypothesis that the *x*-slot is (nearly) exclusively constrained to telic predicates, as stated under (13b). In relation to language contact, the null hypothesis is that aspectual cognate constructions pattern the same way (13c): if cognate constructions derive from the same source structure, then at least one of them needs to have undergone change for them to distribute in different ways.

(13) **Hypotheses I: Prospective aspect**

a. $[\phi_s]$ & IMM($[\tau\ \phi(x)]$)
→ Expectation: The *x*-slot exhibits a possible affinity for telic predicates, but no categorical restriction.

b. $[\phi_s]$ & IMM(x), such that $x=[\tau\ \phi_s]$
→ Expectation: The *x*-slot is categorically restricted to telic predicates.

c. Null hypothesis: Prospective cognate constructions in Afrikaans and Dutch pattern alike, i.e., either both with (13a) or both with (13b).

Second, we conceptualized ingressivity as an abstraction over (stative and dynamic) onset transitions. However, more fine-grained subdistinctions have been proposed in the literature (e.g., Xiao & McEnery 2004 identify a separate category of onsets of dynamic situations, which they call 'inceptive'). This could be a point of microvariation between Afrikaans and Dutch. The relevant distinction is thus between the most general conceptualization of ingressive aspect shown in (14a) and a more specific one geared specifically to dynamic or stative situations (14b). The former leads us to expect no particular combinatorial tendencies, the latter does. Again, our null hypothesis is that aspectual cognates in Afrikaans and Dutch pattern identically (14c), for otherwise, language change needs to have occurred.

(14) **Hypotheses II: Ingressive aspect**

a. $[\tau\ \phi(x)]$
→ Expectation: The *x*-slot exhibits no particular combinatorial tendencies.

b. $[\tau\ \phi(x)]$, such that $x=[\tau\ \phi_s]$ or such that $x=[\phi_d]$
→ Expectation: The *x*-slot is restricted to either stative or dynamic predicates.

c. Null hypothesis: Ingressive cognate constructions in Afrikaans and Dutch pattern alike, i.e., either both with (14a) or both with (14b).

Last, we identified 'composite prospective' constructions which encode prospective meaning but are formally divisible into an ingressive non-main verb and an adverb signaling imminence. Using the notation employed in (13)–(14), the adverb (e.g., *net*) contributes the substructure $[[\phi_s]$ & IMM(...)] while the ingressive non-main verb (e.g., *gaan*) provides the (embedded) substructure $[\tau\ \phi]$, see (15a). Since this full structure equates to (13a) rather than (13b), we expect this type of construction to pattern in line with our first definition of prospectivity (13a).

(15) **Hypotheses III: Composite prospectivity**

a. $[\phi_s]$ & IMM($[\tau\ \phi(x)]$)
→ Expectation: Composite prospectivity patterns with prospective aspect with an embedded ingressive viewpoint (see (13a)).

b. Null hypothesis: Composite prospective cognate constructions in Afrikaans and Dutch pattern alike, viz., with (15a).

The hypotheses stated under (13)–(15) will be tested on corpus data instantiating several categories of prospective and ingressive constructions in Afrikaans and Dutch (§ 3.2). Table 3 demarcates the empirical scope of our study by reiterating the relevant constructions in the two languages. With our hypotheses and empirical scope in place, the next section reports on the corpus assembly and annotation process.

Table 3. Empirical scope of the corpus study

Aspectual viewpoint	**Afrikaans**	**Dutch**
Prospective	*op die punt wees/staan (om) te* V_{inf}	*op het punt staan (om) te* V_{inf}
	op V_{inf} *staan*	*op* V_{inf} *staan*
		op het punt van V_{inf} *staan*
Ingressive	*gaan* V_{inf}	*gaan* V_{inf}
	begin V_{inf}	*beginnen te* V_{inf}
	begin (om) te V_{inf}	*beginnen met (te)* V_{inf}
Composite prospective	*net/pas gaan* V_{inf}	*net/juist gaan* V_{inf}

4. Corpus assembly and annotation

Corpus data for the Dutch constructions were collected from the SoNaR corpus of contemporary written Dutch (Oostdijk et al. 2013).[16] We attempted to compile a cognate dataset for Afrikaans based on the Language Commission Corpus (*Taalkommissiekorpus 1.0*) but found fewer hits. We therefore queried VivA's comprehensive corpus portal along with the Afrikaans Wikipedia corpus. Ultimately, eleven Afrikaans corpora with a combined word count of 366,277,084 were queried. All CQL strings used to search the corpora are listed in the Appendix. Table 4 provides an overview of the corpora used to compile datasets for both languages.

We found a limited number of hits for the *op die punt staan*-construction in Afrikaans, compared to a much larger number (3,262 hits) in Dutch. We therefore decided on a random sample size of 300 for all constructions with more than 300 hits. There are several possible reasons why there were fewer Afrikaans than Dutch hits. First, in general, token size of Afrikaans corpora is far smaller than Dutch corpora. Second, a number of alternative constructions compete with *staan op die punt*

16. Part of the Dutch data was reused from previously compiled datasets (Bogaards & Fleischhauer 2024; Boogaart & Bogaards to appear).

Table 4. Overview of corpora

	Afrikaans	Dutch
Search engine	ViVA Corpus Portal	OpenSoNaR
Corpora used	Language Commission Corpus (*Taalkommissiekorpus 1.1*)	SoNaR Corpus of written Dutch
	Afrikaanse Leipzig Corpus 1.5	
	NCHLT-Afrikaanse Corpus 1.1	
	VivA Blog Corpus 1.0	
	VivA Speech Corpus 1.0	
	VivA/ATKV Teen Theater Corpus	
	VivA/FAK Corpus 1.0	
	VivA/Maroela Media Corpus 1.0	
	VivA/RSG News Corpus 1.0	
	VivA Publisher's Corpus 1.0	
	Wikipedia Afrikaans Corpus 1.6	
Corpus type	Combination of edited and unedited, spoken and written corpora	Combination of edited and unedited written corpora
Registers included	Formal and informal	Formal and informal
Genres included	Fiction and non-fiction	Fiction and non-fiction
Corpus size	366,277,084 words	appr. 500,000,000 words

(cf. Wierenga 2022 for an overview). Third, many hits for *op die punt staan* have a non-aspectual meaning. We give an example in (16): *staan* has its literal, spatial meaning of 'standing somewhere' and *die punt* indicates a physical location. The Afrikaans hits were therefore reviewed to rule out any instances of this type. This was not necessary for Dutch, as *op het punt staan* cannot be used in this way.

(16) Sy *staan op die punt van* die gang.
she stand on the point of the corridor
'She's standing at the end of the corridor.'

For Dutch *beginnen met (te)* and *gaan*, several types of noise had to be filtered out. First, *beginnen met (te)* allows a so-called "specificational" reading (Mourounas & Williamson 2019, cited in Kovač & Schoenmakers to appear:fn.15) where the embedded situation is identified as the first in a chain of situations. In (17), for instance, *begint met kiezen* does not designate the onset of 'choosing' as such, but construes 'choosing' as the first step in a process of 'eating well'. This falls outside of our definition of ingressive aspect.

(17) Er valt wat voor te zeggen dat goed eten *begint met* goed kiezen.
there falls something for to say that good eat begins with good choose
'There's something to say for the idea that eating well begins with choosing well.'

Second, both Afrikaans and Dutch *gaan* have uses other than marking ingressive aspect, most importantly as a future tense marker similar to English *be going to* (cf. Fehringer 2017 for Dutch; Wierenga 2023b for Afrikaans). The multi-functional character of *gaan* is reflected by very high token frequency in the Afrikaans and Dutch corpora (194,477 and 158,870 hits for the *gaan*-queries given in the Appendix). Examples of future *gaan* in Afrikaans and Dutch are given in (18a)–(18b).

(18) a. Ek hoor dat jou operasie bietjie later *gaan plaatsvind.*
I hear that your operation a.bit later go take.place
'I hear that your operation will take place a bit later.'
[Afrikaanse Leipzig Corpus 1.5]

b. Het blok had namelijk jaren aan haar achterban beloofd dat het zo'n wetsvoorstel nooit *ging goedkeuren.*
the Blok had namely years to her supporters promised that it such.a legislative.proposal never went approve
'After all, the (political party *Vlaams*) *Blok* had been promising their supporters for years that they were never going to pass such a bill.'
[SoNaR WR-P-E-A-0000014569]

To obtain a sample of 300 instances of Dutch ingressive *gaan*, we first limited the dataset to past tense forms (i.e., *ging* and *gingen*); for Afrikaans, both present and past tense forms were included because *gaan* is used in both tenses (i.e., *gaan* vs. *het gaan*). Then, we manually identified ingressive cases – in randomized order – until we reached 300. In order to establish ingressivity, we checked whether the verbal complex could be replaced by *begin* or *beginnen te* without changing the meaning. This distinguishes cases like (18b) (*#dat het zo'n wetsvoorstel nooit begon goed te keuren*) from cases like (19) (which can be paraphrased with *en begon ik me af te vragen waarom…*).[17]

17. We performed the same check for composite prospective *net/juist gaan*, but for all 357 hits; 165 of them were ingressive *gaan* according to this diagnostic.

(19) Maar geleidelijk aan kreeg ik meer verhalen van de andere kant te horen
but gradually on got I more stories from the other side to hear
en *ging* ik me afvragen waarom ik al die dingen niet wist.
and went I myself question why I all those things not know
'But, little by little, I got to hear more stories from the other side and I began to question why I was unaware of all those things.'
[SoNaR WR-P-P-H-0000174100]

For the remaining constructions, either no noise removal was necessary or noise was only incidental. For example, [*op* V_{inf} *staan*] included cases like *wat voor straf er op stelen staat* 'what the punishment is for stealing' (SoNaR WR-P-E-G-0000010817). These were removed manually. The final figures – post-noise removal – for the Afrikaans and Dutch corpus data are presented in Table 5.

Table 5. Overview of collected corpus data

Afrikaans		Dutch	
Construction	**Hits**	**Construction**	**Hits**
op die punt staan (om) te V_{inf}	69 (all)	*op het punt staan (om) te* V_{inf}	300 (sample)
op die punt wees (om) te V_{inf}	232 (all)	*op het punt van* V_{inf} *staan*	71 (all)
op V_{inf} *staan*	11 (all)	*op* V_{inf} *staan*	300 (sample)
gaan V_{inf}	300 (sample)	*gaan* V_{inf}	300 (sample)
begin V_{inf}	116 (all)	*beginnen te* V_{inf}	300 (sample)
begin (om) te V_{inf}	300 (sample)	*beginnen met (te)* V_{inf}	300 (sample)
net/pas gaan V_{inf}	16 (all)	*net/juist gaan* V_{inf}	165 (all)

The last stage of corpus preparation concerned the annotation of telicity and dynamicity. We coded these properties for the embedded V(P) in isolation, since our focus is on what each aspectual construction selects. We adopted standard diagnostics to classify predicates as telic or atelic, and as dynamic or stative (e.g., Vendler 1967; Dowty 1979).

For telicity we used the '*in* X *time*'-test (e.g., Afrikaans *binne vyftien minute* 'in fifteen minutes'). This type of adjunct probes for the offset of telic predicates; when adjoined to an atelic predicate, the result is either infelicitous or only an onset reading is possible. Take the Dutch corpus item (20a), for example. The embedded VP *geld wegen* 'weigh money' comes out as atelic because (20b) is infelicitous, or at best highly marked, with only an onset reading available.

(20) a. Dit is een schilderij van een vrouw die op het punt staat *geld* te
this is a painting of a woman that on the point stands money to
wegen. [SoNaR WR-P-P-B-0000000023]
weigh
'This painting depicts a woman who's about to weigh money.'
b. #Ze woog geld *in vijftien minuten.* → Atelic
she weighed money in fifteen minutes
(Marked reading: 'She started weighing money in (after) fifteen minutes.')

We used progressive *aan die* (Afrikaans) and *aan het* (Dutch) to distinguish between stative and dynamic predicates. Progressive aspect constructions, in general, impose a dynamic input condition (e.g., Boogaart 1999; Michaelis 2011). When combined with a state, the result is infelicitous, or the state is coerced into a marked activity reading, which can be paraphrased as 'perform actions indicative of the state' (e.g., *He's being annoying* ≈ 'he's doing annoying stuff'). As an example, consider Afrikaans *glo* 'believe' in (21a), which becomes infelicitous in (21b) and was therefore classified as stative.

(21) a. Hy het begin *glo* hulle dra vlooie.
he has begin believe they carry fleas
'He began to believe that they had fleas.'
b. #Hy was *aan die glo* dat hulle vlooie dra. → Stative
he was on the believe that they fleas carry
(Marked reading: 'He was believing that they had fleas.')

5. Results

This section explores the distribution of embedded predicates in Afrikaans and Dutch prospective (§ 5.1), ingressive (§ 5.2) and composite prospective (§ 5.3) cognate constructions. We inspect four standard corpus measures: number of tokens, types and hapaxes (hapax legomena, i.e., types occurring only once), and TTR (type/token ratio, i.e., the number of types divided by the number of tokens). Moreover, we follow Baayen & Lieber (1991) and Baayen (1993), among others, in taking as a measure of productivity "$\mathcal{P} = n_1/N$, where n_1 denotes the number of [...] hapax legomena and N the total number of tokens" (Baayen 1993: 181). Baayen & Lieber (1991) interpret $\mathcal{P}$ as a measure of the *degree of productivity*, augmented by the number of types as a measure of the *extent of use*. The synchronic concept of the extent of use is related to the diachronic process of grammaticalization, as increased type frequency "is a much-noted property of grammaticizing constructions" (Bybee 2003: 604, cited in Van Olmen & Mortelmans 2009: 362). Since the number of tokens varies strongly by construction in our data, we do not use types as such but rather TTR as a measure of grammaticalization. Taken together, this gives us two related yet independent general measures – TTR (grammaticalization) and $\mathcal{P}$ (productivity) – which we'll use to establish the status of these constructions in the Afrikaans/Dutch diasystem: as diaconstructions or idioconstructions. Finally, we investigate the relation between prospective and ingressive aspect by checking our hypotheses (§ 3.3) against our annotations for telicity (prospective) and dynamicity (ingressive).

5.1 Prospective constructions

Let's start by examining the corpus data for prospective constructions built around the preposition *op* 'on' and (in some cases) *die/het punt* 'the point'. Table 6 and Table 7 list the five most frequent infinitive types in these constructions in the Afrikaans and Dutch data. Some infinitives recur across both languages and constructions: *trou/trouwen* (4x), *vertrek/vertrekken* (4x), *gaan* (3x) and *word/worden* (2x). The most frequent infinitives are predominantly telic, with the exception of Afrikaans *maak* and *doen*, which can also be atelic. Finally, we observe that Dutch [*op* V_{inf} *staan*] combines with two highly frequent types (101x and 89x) with a steep decline towards the third most frequent type (18x), whilst the other constructions exhibit a more even distribution.

Table 6. Afrikaans prospective constructions: Most frequent infinitives

op die punt staan (om) te V_{inf}			***op die punt wees (om) te*** V_{inf}			***op*** V_{inf} ***staan***		
infinitive	**n**	**%**	**infinitive**	**n**	**%**	**infinitive**	**n**	**%**
trek 'cross'	3	4.3%	*vertrek* 'leave'	8	4.3%	*vertrek* 'leave'	7	63.6%
trou 'marry'	3	4.3%	*maak* 'make'	8	3.4%	*trou* 'marry'	3	27.3%
word 'become'	3	4.3%	*sterf* 'die'	7	3%	*vlug* 'flee'	1	9.1%
doodloop 'die out'	2	2.9%	*doen* 'do'	6	2.6%			
gaan 'go'	2	2.9%	*gaan* 'go'	6	2.6%			

Table 8 presents the general measures for these prospective constructions. There are stark contrasts within the Dutch data: [*op het punt staan (om) te* V_{inf}] measures higher than [*op* V_{inf} *staan*] on both TTR (61% vs. 12.3%) and $\mathcal{P}$ (45.7% vs. 6.7%), with [*op het punt van* V] 'in between' the two (40.8% and 18.3%). There is a similar contrast in Afrikaans between [*op die punt staan/wees (om) te* V_{inf}] on the one hand, and [*op* V_{inf} *staan*] on the other, where the former are more grammatical-

Table 7. Dutch prospective constructions: Most frequent infinitives

op het punt staan (om) te V_{inf}			*op* V_{inf} *staan*			*op het punt van* V_{inf} *staan*		
infinitive	**n**	**%**	**infinitive**	**n**	**%**	**infinitive**	**n**	**%**
vertrekken 'leave'	16	5.3%	*instorten* 'collapse'	101	33.7%	*beginnen* 'begin'	10	14.1%
gaan 'go'	13	4.3%	*springen* 'jump'	89	29.7%	*doorbreken* 'break through'	6	8.5%
worden 'become'	11	3.7%	*ontploffen* 'explode'	18	6%	*instorten* 'collapse'	4	5.6%
beginnen 'begin'	6	2%	*trouwen* 'marry'	12	4%	*vertrekken* 'leave'	6	8.5%
trouwen 'marry'	5	1.7%	*barsten* 'burst'	10	3.3%	*ontploffen* 'explode'	4	5.6%

ized and productive than the latter, according to these measures.[18] Across the two languages, Afrikaans [*op die punt wees (om) te* V_{inf}] and Dutch [*op het punt staan (om) te* V_{inf}] pattern remarkably similarly in terms of both TTR (63.8% vs. 61%) and $\mathcal{P}$ (47.4% vs. 45.7%). The [*op* V_{inf} *staan*] constructions in both languages pattern reasonably similarly, especially with respect to $\mathcal{P}$ (5.9% vs. 6.7%).

Table 8. Prospective constructions: General measures

	Afrikaans			**Dutch**		
	op die punt staan (om) te V_{inf}	*op die punt wees (om) te* V_{inf}	*op* V_{inf} *staan*	*op het punt staan (om) te* V_{inf}	*op* V_{inf} *staan*	*op het punt van* V_{inf} *staan*
tokens	72	232	11	300	300	71
types	55	148	3	183	37	29
hapaxes	42	110	1	137	20	13
TTR	76.4%	63.8%	27.3%	61%	12.3%	40.8%
$\mathcal{P}$	58.3%	47.4%	5.9%	45.7%	6.7%	18.3%

Table 9 reports on our annotations for telicity. We observe two groups: constructions which pattern (almost) exclusively with telic predicates, and constructions which exhibit an affinity for telicity but also regularly combine with atelic predi-

18. It should be noted that [*op* V_{inf} *staan*] has so few tokens in the Afrikaans corpus that the reported TTR and $\mathcal{P}$ are likely less reliable.

cates. The first group includes the cognates [*op* V_{inf} *staan*] and Dutch [*op het punt van* V_{inf} *staan*], which were all on the lower end of the grammaticalization and productivity measures in Table 8. The second group is formed by Afrikaans [*op die punt wees (om) te* V_{inf}] and Dutch [*op het punt staan (om) te* V_{inf}], which pattern almost identically once again (15.1% vs. 16.3% atelic predicates).

Table 9. Prospective constructions: Telicity

	Afrikaans			Dutch		
	op die punt staan (om) te V_{inf}	*op die punt wees (om) te* V_{inf}	*op* V_{inf} *staan*	*op het punt staan (om) te* V_{inf}	*op* V_{inf} *staan*	*op het punt van* V_{inf} *staan*
telic	72 (100%)	197 (84.9%)	11 (100%)	246 (82%)	294 (98%)	70 (98.6%)
atelic	0	35 (15.1%)	0	49 (16.3%)	4 (1.3%)	0 (0%)
unclear	0	0	0	5 (1.7%)	2 (0.7%)	1 (1.4%)

A surprising member of the first group is Afrikaans [*op die punt staan (om) te* V_{inf}], which patterns with the second group with respect to TTR and $\mathcal{P}$, but nonetheless licenses only telic predicates in our data.[19] We performed a χ^2-test which shows that the difference in association with (a)telicity between Afrikaans *op die punt staan* and Dutch *op het punt staan* is statistically significant ($\chi^2=12.4$, $df=1$, $p<0.005$, Cramér's $V=0.18$); the same goes for Afrikaans *op die punt staan* vs. *wees* ($\chi^2=10.84$, $df=1$, $p<0.005$, Cramér's $V=0.19$). In terms of DCxG, this leads us to conclude the following. There are two distinct *op die punt*-constructions in the synchronic system of Afrikaans, formally detectable by matrix verb (*staan* vs. *wees*). In the Afrikaans/Dutch diasystem, the cognate constructions [*op die/het punt staan (om) te* V_{inf}] qualify as idioconstructions: one of the two has moved away from the source structure. Conversely, Afrikaans [*op die punt wees (om) te* V_{inf}] and Dutch [*op het punt staan (om) te* V_{inf}] on the one hand, and both [*op* V_{inf} *staan*] cognates on the other, constitute two groups of diaconstructions. Although Dutch [*op het punt van*

19. We're unsure whether this distributional tendency reflects a categorical ban on atelic predicates in this construction; according to our intuitions, it's not impossible to replace *is* by *staan* in (22a). Still, the distribution in Table 9 requires an explanation. Moreover, even if we were to exclude [*op die punt staan (om) te* V_{inf}] from our account, the line of reasoning developed below would still apply to [*op (het punt van)* V_{inf} *staan*] vs. the other prospective constructions (e.g., (22b)).

V_{inf} staan] lacks a direct cognate in Afrikaans, we group it with the diaconstructions of the *op*-type, since it exhibits largely the same telicity distribution (0% atelic) in addition to relatively low TTR and $\mathcal{P}$.

One way to account for the different classes observed in our data is the theory of prospective/ingressive aspect laid out in Section 3. On this account, constructions of the type [*op* V_{inf} *staan*] impose a selectional restriction for the underlying structure [$\tau\ \phi_s$], whereas those of the type [*op het punt wees (om) te* V_{inf}] include the ingressive viewpoint [$\tau\ \phi$] in their conceptual representation. This explains why we encounter atelic cases such as (22a) with *wees* but not *staan* in Afrikaans, and why we consistently get an onset reading in such cases (e.g., 'start walking' in (22a)). It also correctly predicts that we can translate (22a) to Dutch with [*op het punt staan (om) te* V_{inf}] but not with [*op* V_{inf} *staan*] (22b).

(22) a. Hy *is* net *op die punt om* *te* loop toe sy om die hoek van die gebou verskyn. [*Taalkommissiekorpus*]
he is just on the point COMPL to walk when she around the corner of the building appear
'He's just about to walk [i.e., start walking] when she appears from around the corner of the building.'

b. Hij <**staat* net *op* lopen> <*staat* net *op het punt om* *te lopen*>.
he stands just on walk stands just on the point COMPL to walk
'He's just about to walk [i.e., start walking].'

Our findings are consistent with the idea that there are two types of prospective aspect (13a)–(13b). The null hypothesis (13c) – cognate constructions pattern similarly according to these types – is confirmed only for the *op*-type. For the *op die/het punt staan*-type, the null hypothesis must be rejected: these aspectual cognates have developed into idioconstructions. The two groups of synchronic diaconstructions pattern similarly, with the exception of general measures for Afrikaans [*op die punt staan (om) te* V_{inf}], which indicate higher grammaticalization and productivity than [*op die punt wees (om) te* V_{inf}] and [*op het punt staan (om) te* V_{inf}] (in contrast to the lower measures for [*op* V_{inf} *staan*] in both languages). This suggests that the type of prospectivity is independent of productivity and grammaticalization: development along these scales need not imply a particular change in conceptual representation. In fact, this constitutes additional evidence for the idea of subtypes of prospectivity, as it shows that the differences in distribution (regarding telicity) cannot be explained by the kind of 'loosening' of selectional restrictions that are traditionally associated with grammaticalization (e.g., Hopper 1991: 27–28).

5.2 Ingressive non-main verbs

Table 10 and Table 11 list the most frequent infinitives licensed by the ingressive non-main verbs in our data. Recurrent types spanning both languages include *werk/werken* (4x), *dink/denken* (2x) and *huil/huilen* (2x). Dutch [*beginnen te* V_{inf}] pairs frequently with the (telic) change-of-state copula *worden*, and [*gaan* V_{inf}] with the (stative) posture verbs *zitten* and *staan*; none of these is among the most frequent infinitives in Afrikaans.

Table 10. Afrikaans ingressive non-main verbs: Most frequent infinitives

begin (om) te V_{inf}			***begin*** V_{inf}			***gaan*** V_{inf}		
infinitive	**n**	**%**	**infinitive**	**n**	**%**	**infinitive**	**n**	**%**
dink 'think'	8	6.9%	*doen* 'do'	9	3%	*kyk* 'look	47	15.7%
kyk 'look'	5	4.3%	*wag* 'wait'	9	3%	*lees* 'read'	29	9.7%
werk 'work'	5	4.3%	*huil* 'cry'	8	2.7%	*speel* 'play'	18	6%
verseker 'assure'	5	4.3%	*werk* 'work'	6	2%	*werk* 'work'	16	5.3%
help 'help'	4	3.5%	*bly* 'remain'	6	2%	*eet* 'eat'	15	5%

Table 11. Dutch ingressive non-main verbs: Most frequent infinitives

beginnen te V_{inf}			***beginnen met (te)*** V_{inf}			***gaan*** V_{inf}		
infinitive	**n**	**%**	**infinitive**	**n**	**%**	**infinitive**	**n**	**%**
worden 'become'	14	4.7%	*schrijven* 'write'	25	8.3%	*zitten* 'sit'	33	11%
denken 'think'	8	2.7%	*voetballen* 'play soccer'	11	3.7%	*werken* 'work'	25	8.3%
maken 'make'	7	2.3%	*maken* 'make'	9	3%	*staan* 'stand'	12	4%
twijfelen 'doubt'	7	2.3%	*uitzenden* 'broadcast'	9	3%	*studeren* 'study'	11	3.7%
huilen 'cry'	6	2%	*tennissen* 'play tennis'	6	2%	*slapen* 'sleep'	10	3.3%

Proceeding to general measures, Table 12 shows one major point of variation between ingressive non-main verbs in terms of TTR and $\mathcal{P}$: Afrikaans *gaan* has lower values (29.3%/19.7%) than not only its Dutch cognate (48%/37.7%) but all ingressive non-main verbs in our sample, which range between 48.3%–66.4% TTR and 36.6%–50.9% $\mathcal{P}$. This is the first clue that Afrikaans and Dutch ingressive *gaan* have drifted apart.

We find further variation among our annotations for dynamicity in Table 13. Two categories emerge from these data: (i) constructions that pattern (almost) exclusively with dynamic situations (Afrikaans *gaan*; Dutch [*beginnen met (te)* V_{inf}]), and (ii) constructions which tend towards dynamic situations but also com-

Table 12. Ingressive non-main verbs: General measures

	Afrikaans				Dutch	
	begin V_{inf}	*begin (om) te* V_{inf}	*gaan* V_{inf}	*beginnen te* V_{inf}	*beginnen met (te)* V_{inf}	*gaan* V_{inf}
tokens	300	116	300	300	300	300
types	145	77	88	178	186	144
hapaxes	109	59	59	130	146	113
TTR	48.3%	66.4%	29.3%	59.3%	62%	48%
$\mathcal{P}$	36.3%	50.9%	19.7%	43.3%	48.7%	37.7%

monly license states (Afrikaans *begin*; Dutch *gaan* and [*beginnen te* V_{inf}]). While this is consistent with the idea that at least two types of ingressive aspect can be distinguished – with (i.e., (14b)) and without (i.e., (14a)) an input condition for the type of phase selected – our data reflect only one such input condition: [τ $\phi(x)$] such that $x = \phi_d$, not such that $x = \phi_s$, as none of the non-main verbs pattern exclusively with States. Based on the Afrikaans and Dutch ingressive non-main verbs, we therefore adopt (14a) and a more restrictive version of (14b) which includes only dynamic predicates.

Table 13. Ingressive non-main verbs: Dynamicity

	Afrikaans			Dutch		
	begin V_{inf}	*begin (om) te* V_{inf}	*gaan* V_{inf}	*beginnen te* V_{inf}	*beginnen met (te)* V_{inf}	*gaan* V_{inf}
dynamic	259 (86.3%)	104 (89.7%)	285 (95%)	250 (83.3%)	290 (96.7%)	201 (67%)
stative	41 (13.7%)	12 (10.3%)	15 (5%)	46 (15.3%)	4 (1.3%)	95 (31.7%)
unclear	0	0	0	4 (1.3%)	6 (2%)	4 (1.3%)

The distribution of dynamicity in Table 13 is not stable across cognate non-main verbs. The most striking contrast concerns [*gaan* V_{inf}], which is the most frequent State-selector in Dutch by far (31.7%) as opposed to taking far fewer States in the Afrikaans data (5%). The difference is statistically significant ($\chi^2 = 72.68$, $df = 1$, $p < 0.005$, Cramér's $V = 0.35$). This refutes our null hypothesis (14c) stating that ingressive cognate constructions pattern similarly with respect to dynamicity. In terms of DCxG, it thus seems that Afrikaans and Dutch *gaan* have developed into idioconstructions.

Dutch [*beginnen met (te)* V_{inf}] and Afrikaans [*begin (om) te* V_{inf}] pattern with Afrikaans *gaan*.[20] We can therefore distinguish between three classes: (i) constructions that never or rarely combine with States (viz., Afrikaans *gaan* and Dutch *beginnen met (te)*), (ii) those which regularly combine with States (viz., Dutch *gaan*), and (iii) an intermediate group (viz., Dutch [*beginnen te* V_{inf}] and Afrikaans [*begin* V_{inf}]). In the Afrikaans/Dutch diasystem, this means that there are idioconstructions of not only the *gaan*- but also the *begin*-type: Afrikaans [*begin* V_{inf}] and Dutch [*beginnen met (te)* V_{inf}]. Our theory of viewpoint aspect (§3) offers one way of understanding these differences: with *beginnen met (te)*, Dutch has developed a construction tied to ingressivity type 2 (i.e., the restrictive version of (14b)); in Afrikaans, *gaan* and – to a lesser extent – *begin (om) te* serve this function instead. Synchronically, this implies that Afrikaans *gaan* imposes a dynamic input condition that its Dutch cognate does not impose (cf. (14b)). This explains why Dutch *gaan* licenses stative predicates like *zich voelen* 'feel' (23a) – in contrast to Afrikaans, where *begin* but not *gaan* can do this job (23b).

(23) a. Mogelijk heeft die ertoe bijgedragen dat hij zich verbonden *ging*
possible has that thereto contributed that he himself connected went
voelen met taalminderheden [...]. [SoNaR WR-P-P-B-0000000364]
feel with language.minorities
'It's possible that they contributed to him starting to feel a connection with linguistic minorities.'

b. Hy het aan taalminderhede verbonde <#*gaan*> <*begin*> voel.
he has to language.minorities connected go begin feel
'He started to feel a connection to language minorities.'

5.3 Composite prospectivity

Composite prospectives are assembled from an ingressive non-main verb plus an imminent adverb. Our Afrikaans queries yielded a scarcity of instances of composite prospectivity, particularly when considering the overall frequency of *net* (453,566) and *pas* (45,997) in the corpora. Among all hits, *net* often conveys the

---

20. This is because – adopting a significance threshold of $p<0.005$ (Benjamin et al. 2018) – the differences between these constructions and Afrikaans *gaan* are not statistically significant: Dutch [*beginnen met (te)* V_{inf}] ($\chi^2=5.23$, $df=1$, $p>0.005$, Cramér's $V=0.09$) and Afrikaans [*begin (om) te* V_{inf}] ($\chi^2=3.94$, $df=1$, $p>0.005$, Cramér's $V=0.1$). Afrikaans [*begin* V_{inf}] ($\chi^2=13.31$, $df=1$, $p<0.005$, Cramér's $V=0.15$) and Dutch [*beginnen te* V_{inf}] ($\chi^2=18.02$, $df=1$, $p<0.005$, Cramér's $V=0.17$) do differ significantly from Afrikaans *gaan* in terms of dynamicity.

meaning of 'only', calling for future investigation into whether this sense predominates over the 'just' sense, potentially skewing the data. It also remains uncertain whether *net* 'just' competes with adverbs like *nou* 'now' or *nou net* 'just now' in such contexts. Speaking more generally, several other factors may account for the limited number of tokens. These include constraints related to corpus size and the represented genres/registers. It is also conceivable that composite prospectives have historically been infrequent or are declining in usage in Afrikaans. However, without further inquiry, definitive conclusions cannot be drawn here, and we are unable to test the null hypothesis (15b).

Given the limited number of Afrikaans tokens, we restrict our interpretation of the general measures in Table 14 to the Dutch construction, contrasting it with its non-composite prospective and ingressive counterparts (cf. §5.1–§5.2). The TTR and $\mathcal{P}$ of [*net/juist gaan* V_{inf}] (41.2%/26.1%) indicate lower grammaticalization and productivity than [*op het punt staan (om) te* V_{inf}] (61%/45.7%) and – to a lesser degree – ingressive *gaan* (48%/37.7%). These differences are not large enough to draw any conclusions.

Table 14. Composite prospectives: General measures

	Afrikaans	Dutch
	net/pas gaan V_{inf}	*net/juist gaan* V_{inf}
tokens	16	165
types	9	68
hapaxes	5	43
TTR	56.2%	41.2%
$\mathcal{P}$	31.3%	26.1%

Table 15 places our telicity annotations for [*net/juist gaan* V_{inf}] side by side with those for non-composite prospective [*op het punt staan (om) te* V] (taken from Table 9) and ingressive [*gaan* V_{inf}] (which were not yet reported). This shows that the composite prospective pattern is in between the two other constructions in terms of licensing telic predicates (82% > 51.5% > 7.3%). Two pairwise χ^2-tests indicate that both contrasts are statistically significant: [*op het punt staan (om) te* V_{inf}] vs. [*net/juist gaan* V_{inf}] ($\chi^2 = 35.15$, $df = 1$, $p < 0.005$), with small effect size (Cramér's $V = 0.28$); [*net/juist gaan* V_{inf}] vs. [*gaan* V_{inf}] ($\chi^2 = 134.85$, $df = 1$, $p < 0.005$), with large effect size (Cramér's $V = 0.55$).

This outcome is difficult to interpret, so we'll proceed with caution. On the one hand, the statistically significant contrast between non-composite and composite prospective constructions forces us to reject hypothesis (15a): the two con-

Table 15. Non-composite prospectivity, composite prospectivity and ingressivity in Dutch

	prospective	**composite**	**ingressive**
	op het punt staan (om) te V_{inf}	***net/juist gaan*** V_{inf}	***gaan*** V_{inf}
telic	246 (82%)	85 (51.5%)	22 (7.3%)
atelic	49 (16.3%)	63 (38.2%)	274 (91.3%)
unclear	5 (1.7%)	4 (1.3%)	4 (1.3%)

structions do not pattern identically, which is what we would expect if their underlying conceptual structures were identical. On the other hand, looking at effect size, the association between construction type and telicity is considerably weaker for non-composite and composite prospectivity than for the two uses of *gaan*. That is, composite-prospective *gaan* patterns more closely to non-composite prospective constructions than to ingressive *gaan*. This leaves open the possibility that the overt presence of *gaan* affects the outcome – in other words, that not only conceptual content, but also formal spell-out influences combinatorial behavior. This issue warrants further research. But, for now, our results are mixed: the theorized optional embedding relation between prospective and ingressive aspect lays out a way to explain the divergent distribution of Afrikaans and Dutch prospective constructions (§ 5.1), but this account is not directly corroborated by our composite prospective data.

5.4 Summary

Table 16 provides an overview of our findings in terms of DCxG: the cognates marked as idioconstructions and those marked as diaconstructions, as well as the empirical grounds these conclusions were based on (i.e., general measures and/or selectional tendencies regarding telicity/dynamicity). Our corpus data make the strongest case for Dutch/Afrikaans *gaan* as idioconstructions, and [*op die/het punt staan/wees (om) te* V_{inf}] as diaconstructions, as these constructions pattern highly (dis)similarly with respect to both sets of measures.

These groups of idioconstructions are consistent with the idea that there are at least two types of prospective aspect (one embedding ingressivity) and at least two types of ingressive aspect (one sensitive to dynamicity). The former finding was not corroborated by our composite prospective data, which did not pattern identically to the 'looser' prospective constructions, but instead exhibited a distribution in between that of the prospective and ingressive ones.

Table 16. Summary of findings

	Afrikaans	Dutch	Ground(s)
Idioconstructions	[*op die punt staan (om) te* V_{inf}]	[*op het punt staan (om) te* V_{inf}]	telicity
	[*gaan* V_{inf}]	[*gaan* V_{inf}]	TTR/$\mathcal{P}$; dynamicity
	[*begin* V_{inf}]	[*beginnen met (te)* V_{inf}]	dynamicity
Diaconstructions	[*op die punt wees (om) te* V_{inf}]	[*op het punt staan (om) te* V_{inf}]	TTR/$\mathcal{P}$; telicity
	[*op* V_{inf} *staan*]	[*op (het punt van)* V_{inf} *staan*]	telicity
	[*begin* V_{inf}]	[*beginnen te* V_{inf}]	dynamicity

6. Conclusion

This chapter introduced a theoretical framework proposing an embedding relation between prospective and ingressive aspect, suggesting that the former may integrate the latter. We also considered an alternative scenario where prospective aspect imposes an input condition for specific types of situations. Additionally, we conceptualized ingressivity as a broader abstraction over onset transitions and identified a category of 'composite prospective' constructions that convey prospective meaning while spelling out a distinct ingressive element. Our theoretical account generated three specific hypotheses with respect to the selectional behavior of viewpoint aspect constructions.

We tested these hypotheses by means of a corpus study, drawing on Diasystematic Construction Grammar (DCxG) as a framework for comparing Afrikaans/Dutch prospective *op (die/het punt) staan/wees*, ingressive non-main verbs, and composite prospective constructions. Our findings neither conclusively confirm nor refute our hypotheses regarding the embedding relation between prospective and ingressive aspect. The findings do support the proposed distinction between two types of prospective aspect and two types of ingressive aspect, differentiated by a restriction on – respectively – telicity and dynamicity. Our findings also allowed us to identify cognates that have developed into idioconstructions in the two languages (viz., *gaan* and *op die/het punt staan (om) te*), whereas others can be considered diaconstructions in the Afrikaans/Dutch diasystem.

We suggest that further research into the diachronic origin and development of these constructions could provide more insight into the influence of language contact, which we suggested could have resulted in the differences observed in the corpus data. Further research avenues include, first, closer inspection of the composite prospective constructions with *net/pas* in Afrikaans to determine why the tokens for these constructions are so limited. Second, the scope could be expanded to include periphrastic ingressive constructions consisting of the ingressive non-main verbs *gaan*, *slaan* and *raak/raken* paired with the constituent *aan die/het* (cf. Van Pottelberge 2004; Wierenga 2022), so as to further examine the relation between different types of viewpoint aspect. Finally, we found that ingressive *gaan* patterns particularly differently from the other ingressive constructions we investigated, which warrants further investigation into the diachronic trajectory and synchronic use of *gaan* in Afrikaans and Dutch.

Acknowledgement

The first author gratefully acknowledges funding from the Dutch Science Council (NWO), grant number PGW.20.013.

References

doi Andree, Milou & Heize Oh (2024). Je begint bijna te denken dat het een squib is! Betekenis en retorische functie van de cognitieve *bijna*-constructie. *Nederlandse Taalkunde* 29 (3), 401–412.

doi Baayen, Harald (1993). On frequency, transparency and productivity. In: *Yearbook of Morphology* 1992. Ed. by Geert Booij & Jaap van Marle. Dordrecht: Springer, 181–208.

doi Baayen, Harald & Rochelle Lieber (1991). Productivity and English derivation: A corpus-based study. *Linguistics* 29 (5), 801–843.

doi Benjamin, Daniel et al. (2018). Redefine statistical significance. *Nature Human Behaviour* 2, 6–10.

doi Bickel, Balthasar (1996). Aspect, mood, and time in Belhare: studies in the semantics-pragmatics interface of a Himalayan language. PhD thesis. Zürich: Universität Zürich.

doi Boas, Hans & Steffen Höder (2021). Widening the scope: Recent trends in constructional contact linguistics. In: *Constructions in Contact 2: Language change, multilingual practices, and additional language acquisition*. Ed. by Hans Boas & Steffen Höder. Amsterdam: John Benjamins, 1–13.

doi Bogaards, Maarten (2019). A Mandarin map for Dutch durativity: Parallel text analysis as a heuristic for investigating aspectuality. *Nederlandse Taalkunde* 24 (2), 157–193.

doi Bogaards, Maarten (2022). The discovery of aspect: A heuristic parallel corpus study of ingressive, continuative and resumptive viewpoint aspect. *Languages* 7 (3), 158.

doi Bogaards, Maarten (2023a). Prospectief aspect in het Nederlands: Over *op het punt staan* en gerelateerde constructies. *Nederlandse Taalkunde* 28 (1), 104–116.

doi Bogaards, Maarten (2023b). Top-down versus bottom-up approaches to aspect: The case of the Dutch prepositional progressive. *Journal of Germanic Linguistics* 35 (4), 311–338.

Bogaards, Maarten (2024). Aspectual coercion and verbal decomposition. In: *Proceedings of The 14th Generative Linguistics in The Old World in Asia (GLOW in Asia XIV)*. Ed. by Xiangyu Li, Zetao Xu, Yuqiao Du, Zhuo Chen, Chenghao Hu, Zhongyang Yu & Victor Junnan Pan. Hong Kong: The Chinese University of Hong Kong, 15–31. url: https://hdl.handle.net/1887/4092769.

doi Bogaards, Maarten, Ronny Boogaart & Sjef Barbiers (2022). The syntax of progressive and ingressive *aanhet*-constructions in Dutch. In: *Linguistics in the Netherlands* 2022. Ed. by Jorrig Vogels & Sterre Leufkens. Amsterdam: John Benjamins, 2–20.

doi Bogaards, Maarten & Jens Fleischhauer (2024). Prospective aspect constructions in West Germanic: A comparative corpus study of German and Dutch. *Leuvense Bijdragen* 104 (1), 5–37.

Boogaart, Ronny (1999). Aspect and temporal ordering. PhD thesis. Amsterdam: Vrije Universiteit.

Boogaart, Ronny & Maarten Bogaards (to appear). Aspect. In: *Elektronische Algemene Nederlandse Spraakkunst (e-ANS)*. Ed. by Maaike Beliën. 3rd edn. Leiden: Instituut voor de Nederlandse Taal. Chap. 30. url: https://e-ans.ivdnt.org/topics/pid/ans30lingtopic.

Breed, Adri (2012). Die grammatikalisering van aspek in Afrikaans: 'n Semantiese studie van perifrastiese progressiewe konstruksies. PhD thesis. Potchefstroom: Noordwes-Universiteit. url: https://repository.nwu.ac.za/handle/10394/11959.

doi Breed, Adri (2016). Aspek in Afrikaans: 'n Teoretiese beskrywing. *Tydskrif vir Geesteswetenskappe* 56 (1), 62–80.

doi Breed, Adri & Frank Brisard (2015). Postulêre werkwoorde as progressiewe merkers in Afrikaans en Nederlands. *Internationale Neerlandistiek* 53 (1), 3–28.

Breed, Adri, Frank Brisard & Astrid De Wit (2024). The progressive uses of BUSY in Dutch, Afrikaans and English. Paper presented at *A Germanic Sandwich* 9, Lancaster University, 11 April 2024. url: https://sites.google.com/view/germanicsandwich9/homepage /program.

doi Breed, Adri, Frank Brisard & Ben Verhoeven (2017). Periphrastic progressive constructions in Dutch and Afrikaans: A contrastive analysis. *Journal of Germanic Linguistics* 29 (4), 305–378.

doi Breu, Walter (1994). Interactions between lexical, temporal and aspectual meanings. *Studies in Language* 18 (1), 23–44.

Brinton, Laurel (1988). *The development of English aspectual systems: Aspectualizers and post-verbal particles*. Cambridge: Cambridge University Press.

doi Bybee, Joan (2003). Mechanisms of change in grammaticization: The role of frequency. In: *The Handbook of Historical Linguistics*. Ed. by Brian Joseph & Richard Janda. Malden, MA: Blackwell, 602–623.

doi Bylund, Emanuel, Panos Athanasopoulos & Marcelyn Oostendorp (2013). Motion event cognition and grammatical aspect: Evidence from Afrikaans. *Linguistics* 51 (5), 929–955.

doi Carstens, Wannie (2017). Meertaligheid en Afrikaans in Suid-Afrika: Die stand van sake. *Internationale Neerlandistiek* 55 (3), 191–207.

Cavirani-Pots, Cora (2020). Roots in Progress: Semi-lexicality in the Dutch and Afrikaans verbal domain. PhD thesis. Leuven: KU Leuven.

Comrie, Bernard (1976). *Aspect: An introduction to the study of verbal aspect and related problems.* Cambridge: Cambridge University Press.

Croft, William (2000). *Explaining language change: An evolutionary approach.* Harlow: Longman.

doi Dik, Simon (1997). *The Theory of Functional Grammar, Part 1: The Structure of the Clause.* Ed. by Kees Hengeveld. 2nd edn. Berlin: De Gruyter Mouton.

doi Dooren, Annemarie van (2024). Dutch *willen*'s steps towards a future marker. *Nota Bene* 1 (2), 261–275.

doi Dowty, David (1979). *Word meaning and Montague Grammar: The semantics of verbs and times in Generative Semantics and in Montague's PTQ.* Dordrecht: Springer.

doi Fehringer, Carol (2017). Internal constraints on the use of *gaan* versus *zullen* as future markers in spoken Dutch: A quantitative variationist approach. *Nederlandse Taalkunde* 22 (3), 359–387.

doi Fleischhauer, Jens (2023). Prospective aspect and current relevance: A case study of the German prospective '*stehen vor* NP' light verb construction. *Journal of Germanic Linguistics* 35 (4), 371–408.

doi Fleischhauer, Jens & Thomas Gamerschlag (2019). Deriving the meaning of light verb constructions: A frame account of German *stehen* 'stand'. In: *Yearbook of the German Cognitive Linguistics Association 7.* Ed. by Constanze Juchem-Grundmann, Michael Pleyer & Monika Pleyer. Berlin: De Gruyter Mouton, 137–156.

Geleyn, Tim & Timothy Colleman (2014). De progressieve constructies *bezig zijn* en *besig wees*: Een contrastief corpusonderzoek Nederlands-Afrikaans. *Tydskrif vir Geesteswetenskappe* 54 (1), 56–74. url: https://hdl.handle.net/10520/EJC151886.

doi Goldberg, Adele (2006). *Constructions at work: The nature of generalization in language.* Oxford: Oxford University Press.

Hill, Angelica (to appear). What about *about to?* A proposal for proximate future reference. In: *Proceedings of the 41st West Coast Conference on Formal Linguistics (WCCFL 41).* Somerville, MA: Cascadilla Press.

doi Höder, Steffen (2012). Multilingual constructions: A diasystematic approach to common structures. In: *Multilingual individuals and multilingual societies.* Ed. by Kurt Braunmüller & Christoph Gabriel. Amsterdam: John Benjamins, 241–258.

doi Höder, Steffen (2014). Constructing diasystems: Grammatical organisation in bilingual groups. In: *The Sociolinguistics of Grammar.* Ed. by Tor Åfarli & Brit Mæhlum. Amsterdam: John Benjamins, 137–152.

doi Höder, Steffen (2018). Grammar is community-specific: Background and basic concepts of Diasystematic Construction Grammar. In: *Constructions in contact: Constructional perspectives on contact phenomena in Germanic languages.* Ed. by Hans Boas & Steffen Höder. Amsterdam: John Benjamins, 37–70.

doi Höder, Steffen (2019). Phonological schematicity in multilingual constructions: A diasystematic perspective on lexical form. *Word Structure* 12 (3), 334–352.

doi Hopper, Paul (1991). On some principles of grammaticization. In: *Approaches to grammaticalization, Volume 1: Theoretical and methodological issues.* Ed. by Elizabeth Traugott & Bernd Heine. Amsterdam: John Benjamins, 17–35.

doi Koss, Tom, Astrid De Wit & Johan van der Auwera (2022). The aspectual meaning of non-aspectual constructions. *Languages* 7 (2), 143.

Kovač, Iva & Gert-Jan Schoenmakers (to appear). An experimental-syntactic take on long passive in Dutch: Unraveling the patterns underlying its (un)acceptability. *Syntactic Theory and Research.*

Kuteva, Tania, Bas Aarts, Gergana Popova & Anvita Abbi (2019). The grammar of 'non-realization'. *Studies in Language* 43 (4), 850–895.

Labov, William (2010). *Principles of linguistic change, Volume 3: Cognitive and cultural factors.* Hoboken, NJ: Wiley-Blackwell.

Laca, Brenda (2004). Romance "aspectual" periphrases: Eventuality modification versus "syntactic" aspect. In: *The Syntax of Time.* Ed. by Jacqueline Guéron & Jacqueline Lecarme. Cambridge, MA: MIT Press, 425–440.

Matras, Yaron (2009). *Language contact.* Cambridge: Cambridge University Press.

Michaelis, Laura (1998). *Aspectual grammar and past-time reference.* London: Routledge.

Michaelis, Laura (2011). Stative by construction. *Linguistics* 49 (6), 1359–1399.

Mourounas, Michael & Gregor Williamson (2019). Aspectual verbs and the (anti-)causative alternation: Deriving the raising/control ambiguity. Ms., University College London. url: https://www.researchgate.net/publication/331014899_Aspectual_verbs_and_the_anti-causative_alternation_Deriving_the_raisingcontrol_ambiguity.

Oostdijk, Nelleke, Martin Reynaert, Véronique Hoste & Ineke Schuurman (2013). The construction of a 500-million-word reference corpus of contemporary written Dutch. In: *Essential speech and language technology for Dutch: Results by the STEVIN-programme.* Ed. by Peter Spyns & Jan Odijk. Dordrecht: Springer, 219–247.

Pustejovsky, James (1991). The syntax of event structure. *Cognition* 41 (1–3), 47–81.

Ramchand, Gillian (2019). Event structure and verbal decomposition. In: *The Oxford handbook of event structure.* Ed. by Robert Truswell. Oxford: Oxford University Press, 314–341.

Rensburg, Christo van (2015). Oor die eerste 50 jaar se maak aan Standaardafrikaans. *Tydskrif vir Geesteswetenskappe* 55 (3), 319–342.

Roberge, Paul (2024). Afrikaans and creolization. In: *Afrikaans linguistics: Contemporary perspectives.* Ed. by Wannie Carstens & Nerina Bosman. Cape Town: SUN Media, 1–37.

Rothmayr, Antonia (2009). *The structure of stative verbs.* Amsterdam: John Benjamins.

Sasse, Hans-Jürgen (2002). Recent activity in the theory of aspect: Accomplishments, achievements, or just non-progressive state? *Linguistic Typology* 6 (2), 199–271.

Smith, Carlota (1997). *The parameter of aspect.* 2nd edn. Dordrecht: Kluwer.

Thomason, Sarah (2001). *Language contact: An introduction.* Edinburgh: Edinburgh University Press.

Traugott, Elizabeth & Graeme Trousdale (2013). *Constructionalization and constructional changes.* Oxford: Oxford University Press.

Van Eynde, Frank (to appear). On the infinitives that are introduced by aan het, op and uit. *Nederlandse Taalkunde* 30(1-2).

Van Olmen, Daniël & Tanja Mortelmans (2009). Movement futures in English and Dutch: A contrastive analysis of *be going to* and *gaan*. In: *Studies on English modality: In honour of Frank Palmer.* Ed. by Anastasios Tsangalidis & Roberta Facchinetti. Bern: Peter Lang, 357–386.

Van Pottelberge, Jeroen (2004). *Der am-Progressiv: Struktur und parallele Entwicklung in den kontinentalwestgermanischen Sprachen.* Tübingen: Gunter Narr. url: https://hdl.handle.net/1854/LU-294760.

doi Van Rompaey, Tinne, Kristin Davidse & Peter Petré (2015). Lexicalization and grammaticalization: The case of the verbo-nominal expressions *be on the/one's way/road. Functions of Language* 22 (2), 232–263.

doi Van Rooy, Bertus (2021). A Diasystematic Construction Grammar analysis of language change in the Afrikaans and English finite verb complement clause construction. In: *Constructions in Contact 2: Language change, multilingual practices, and additional language acquisition.* Ed. by Hans Boas & Steffen Höder. Amsterdam: John Benjamins, 109–137.

doi Vendler, Zeno (1967). *Linguistics in Philosophy.* Ithaca, NY: Cornell University Press.

doi Verroens, Filip (2018). La notion d'*inchoatif* en linguistique française. *Travaux de Linguistique* 76 (1), 91–111.

doi Verroens, Filip (2024). Zooming in on the semantics of French ingressives: A collostructional analysis. *Journal of French Language Studies* FirstView, 1–18.

doi Verroens, Filip & Ludovic De Cuypere (2023). French ingressives and (phasal) aspect: A frame-semantic corpus-based analysis. *Canadian Journal of Linguistics* 68 (3), 435–461.

Wierenga, Roné (2022). Inchoatiewe niehoofdwerkwoordskonstruksies in Afrikaans: 'n Korpusonderzoek. MA thesis. Potchefstroom: Noordwes-Universiteit. url: https://hdl.handle.net/10394/39517.

doi Wierenga, Roné (2023a). "Gaan loop speel!": Die inchoatiewe niehoofwerk-woorde *gaan* en *loop. Tydskrif vir Geesteswetenskappe* 63 (2), 346–363.

doi Wierenga, Roné (2023b). "Ek sal en jy gaan." The interaction between the modale auxiliaries *sal* and *gaan. Stellenbosch Papers in Linguistics* 66 (3), 25–46.

doi Wierenga, Roné & Adri Breed (2021). 'n Diachroniese benadering tot die ontwikkeling van die progressiewe perifrastiese konstruksies in Afrikaans en Nederlands: 'n Korpusondersoek. *Tydskrif vir Geesteswetenskappe* 61 (2), 588–619.

Wierenga, Roné & Adri Breed (submitted). Inchoativity: A theoretical description for inchoative auxiliary verb constructions in Afrikaans. Ms., Ghent University / North-West University.

doi Wouden, Ton van der, ed. (2012). *Roots of Afrikaans: Selected writings of Hans den Besten.* Amsterdam: John Benjamins.

doi Xiao, Richard & Tony McEnery (2004). *Aspect in Mandarin Chinese: A corpus-based study.* Amsterdam: John Benjamins.

Glossary

Atelic	Referring to an event that does not have an inherent, definite endpoint.
Telic	Referring to an event that has an inherent, definite endpoint.
Diaconstruction	A construction shared by two languages (resulting from, e.g., typological similarity or language contact).

Idioconstruction	A construction that is unique or specific to a particular language or linguistic variety.
Diasystem	The system of linguistic elements shared across different languages or linguistic varieties.
State (Stative)	Relating to a state of being or existence rather than an action or process.
Event (Dynamic)	Relating to situations that involve change or development as time passes.
Situation	Cover term for events and states.
Ingressive aspect	Viewpoint aspect indicating the beginning or onset of an event or state.
Prospective aspect	Aspect indicating an event or state that is expected to occur imminently.
Viewpoint aspect	The qualities of an event or state, such as whether it is ongoing, beginning, or imminent, without specifying the situation itself.

Appendix. Corpus queries

Appendix A. Afrikaans corpus queries

Construction	CQL query/queries
[*op die punt staan (om) te* V_{inf}]	"op" "die" "punt" [lemma="staan" & pos="WW.pv.*"] [pos!="LET.*"]{0,9} "te" [pos="WW.inf.*"]
	[lemma="staan"&pos="WW.pv.*"] [pos!="LET.*"]{0,6} "op" "die" "punt" [pos!="LET.*"]{0,9} "te" [pos="WW.inf.*"]
[*op die punt wees (om) te* V_{inf}]	"op" "die" "punt" [lemma="wees"&pos="WW.pv.*"] [pos!="LET.*"]{0,9} "te" [pos="WW.inf.*"]
	[lemma="wees"&pos="WW.pv.*"] [pos!="LET.*"]{0,6} "op" "die" "punt" [pos!="LET.*"]{0,9} "te" [pos="WW.inf.*"]
[*op* V_{inf} *staan*]	[pos!="LET.*"] "op" [pos="WW.inf.*"] [lemma="staan" & pos="WW.pv.*"]
	[lemma="staan" & pos="WW.pv.*"] "op" [pos="WW.inf.*"]
[*begin* V_{inf}]	["begin" & pos="WW.pv.*"][word!="aan" & pos!="LET.*"]{0,1} [pos!""LET.*""]{0,1} [pos="WW.inf.*"]
[*begin (om) te* V_{inf}]	[lemma="begin" & pos="WW.*"][word="om"& pos="VZ.*"]{0,1} [word!="te" & pos!="LET.*"]{0,4}[word="te" & pos="VZ.*"] [pos="WW.inf.*"]
[*gaan* V_{inf}]	["gaan"&pos="WW.pv.*"][word!="aan"&pos!="LET.*"]{0,1}[pos!="LET.*"]{0,1} [pos="WW.inf.*"]
[*net/juist gaan* V_{inf}]	(manually extracted from hits for [gaan Vinf], see query above)

Appendix B. Dutch corpus queries

Construction	CQL query/queries
[*op het punt staan (om) te* V_{inf}]	“op” “het” “punt” [lemma=“staan” & pos=“WW.pv.*”] [pos!=“LET.*”]{0,9} “te” [pos=“WW.inf.*”]
	[lemma=“staan” & pos=“WW.pv.*”] [pos!=“LET.*”]{0,6} “op” “het” “punt” [pos!=“LET.*”]{0,9} “te” [pos=“WW.inf.*”]
	“op” “het” “punt” [lemma=“hebben”] [lemma=“staan” & pos=“WW.vd.*”] [pos!=“LET.*”]{0,8} “te” [pos=“WW.inf.*”]
	“op” “het” “punt” [lemma=“staan” & pos=“WW.vd.*”] [lemma=“hebben”] [pos!=“LET.*”]{0,8} “te” [pos=“WW.inf.*”]
	[lemma=“hebben”] [pos!=“LET.*”]{0,8} “op” “het” “punt” [lemma=“staan” & pos=“WW.vd.*”] [pos!=“LET.*”]{0,9} “te” [pos=“WW.inf.*”]
[*op het punt van* V_{inf} *staan*]	[lemma=“staan” & pos=“WW.pv.*”] [pos!=“LET.*”]{0,4} “op” “het” “punt” “van” [pos=“WW.inf.*”]
	“op” “het” “punt” “van” [pos=“WW.inf.*”] [lemma=“staan” & pos=“WW.*”]
	“op” “het” “punt” [lemma=“staan” & pos=“WW.*”] “van” [pos=“WW.inf.*”]
[*op* V_{inf} *staan*]	[pos!=“LET.*”] “op” [pos=“WW.inf.*”] [lemma=“staan” & pos=“WW.pv.*”]
	[lemma=“staan” & pos=“WW.pv.*”] “op” [pos=“WW.inf.*”]
[*beginnen te* V_{inf}]	[lemma=“beginnen” & pos=“WW.pv.*”] [word!=“met”]{0,3} “te” [pos=“WW.inf.*”]
[*beginnen met (te)* V_{inf}]	[lemma=“beginnen” & pos=“WW.pv.*”] “met” [pos!=“WW.inf.*”]{0,3} [pos=“WW.inf.*”]
[*gaan* V_{inf}]	[lemma=“gaan” & pos=“WW.pv.*”] [word!=“aan” & pos!=“LET.*”]{0,1} [pos=“WW.inf.*”]
[*net/juist gaan* V_{inf}]	[lemma=“gaan” & pos=“WW.pv.*”] [“net”|“juist”] [pos!=“LET.*”]{0,4} [pos=“WW.inf.*”]
	[“net”|“juist”] [pos!=“LET.*”]{0,1} [lemma=“gaan” & pos=“WW.pv.*”] [pos=“WW.inf.*”]

CHAPTER 10

Dutch taboo words adrift

Gerhard B. van Huyssteen
Centre for Text Technology (CTexT) | North-West University

In this chapter, it is investigated to what extent Dutch influenced other languages' maledicticons, i.e., taboo-language usage such as swearwords, insults, euphemisms and dysphemisms, impolite language, etc. (collectively called maledicta). The focus here is how borrowing of especially lexical maledicta motivates language change. The description is set against a general background of what we know about lexical semantic change, specifically also from a maledictological perspective. Subsequently, the chapter summarises our current knowledge about the spreading of Dutch maledicta, before delving into the analysis of a dataset extracted from Van der Sijs' *Nederlandse woorden wereldwijd* (NWWW 2010). The chapter closes with suggestions for future work.

Keywords: colonial language, euphemism, impolite language, language contact, lexical semantic change, maledicta, taboo language, tabooness, xphemism

1. Introduction

That words and their meanings are naturally unstable and subject to change is a well-established and largely undisputed fact in modern-day linguistics. It is also generally accepted that language evolution (a.k.a. language change, or constructional change) happens over time due to a combination of internal and external factors (Bybee 2015: ch. 11). Internal factors include the adaptability of linguistic structure (such as pronunciation, grammar, or vocabulary), and cognitive processes of speakers acting as an "invisible hand" mechanism (Keller 1994). External factors involve social interactions (e.g., through trade, conquest, migration, and globalization), cultural influences (such as technological innovations, shifts in political power, and social attitudes related to the Zeitgeist), and most importantly, contact with other languages (Gramley 2012). The latter leads to, inter alia, analogical changes in phonetic traits and phonological patterns (e.g., changes in words stress), changes in morphological and syntactic constructions,

https://doi.org/10.1075/impact.55.10huy

changes in lexical meaning, and borrowing of lexical constructions (i.e., words, phrases, idioms, etc.).

One area of the constructicon[1] that is of special interest in the study of constructionalisation and constructional change (specifically lexical semantic change) is the maledicticon: the area containing information on taboo-language usage, such as swearwords, "bad words", "dirty language", insults, euphemisms and dysphemisms, impolite language, hate speech, etc. (collectively referred to as maledicta).[2] Given the socio-cognitive need for variation of expression, the maledicticon seems to be especially susceptible to change, with "exclamations and expletives alternating and replacing each other over time" (Van der Sijs 2002: 524–526). Orthophemisms, euphemisms, and dysphemisms (collectively referred to as xphemisms – see Allan and Burridge (1991)) "motivate language change by promoting new expressions, or new meanings for old expressions, and causing some existing vocabulary to be abandoned" (Allan 2016: 22).

In addition, maledicta are borrowed generously between languages (Andersen 2014) in language contact situations. For example, Van der Sijs (2002: 524–526) shows that about half of the 45 Dutch maledicta that she studied, were loanwords or derivations of such loans. The general explanation for this phenomenon is that loan maledicta make the expression of negative emotions and attitudes more acceptable for conversational participants (Van Sterkenburg 2001: 77), since swearing in one's first language is "perceived to have a stronger emotional resonance" (Dewaele 2012: 595).

However, despite "... the volatile nature of the vocabulary surrounding taboos ..." (Burridge and Benczes 2019: 183) being a glaringly obvious study object for historical linguistics, "... it has been only relatively recently that the effects of taboo on language development have made an appearance in the mainstream linguistics literature ... [Until recently], [d]iscussions of taboo, even within historical linguistic textbooks, focused on remote examples involving ancient naming rituals and taboos on dangerous animals." (Burridge and Benczes 2019: 198). This sentiment is echoed by several other scholars, among them Burridge (2012: 88)

1. Within constructionist theories, the term "constructicon" is used to refer to the inventory of conventional linguistic units in a given linguistic system that is available to construct larger expressions, whether "morphological" (roughly, "word"-based) or "syntactic" (roughly, supra-"word" or phrase-based). It therefore includes morphemes, words, multiword items, and schemas with open (underspecified) slots for constructing complex units. See Diessel (2023) for a short, recent introduction.

2. For the term "maledictum" (PL "maledicta" or "maledictums") see, among others, Aman (1996, 1979), Drößiger (2018), Harjung (2000: 284). "Maledicticon" is proposed here as a blend of "maledictum" and "constructicon", similar to the latter's formation as a blend of "construction" and "lexicon".

(who refers to it as "a striking example of scholarly squeamishness"), Van der Sijs (2002: 524–526), and Zenner et al. (2017: 107).

This lack of historical perspectives on the maledicticon is even more true for relatively understudied languages, and within the context of this book, for minority, indigenous languages that were heavily influenced and reshaped by a dominant, intrusive language. While these language contact situations and resulting phenomena might be extensively described, the same cannot be said about maledictological phenomena. For example, the development of Afrikaans – through contact primarily between Khoekhoegowab of the indigenous people, Malayo-Portuguese of the enslaved people, and first Dutch and later English of the colonising people – has been described and debated locally and internationally in a vast literature. In contrast, only one publication to date has been devoted to the historical development of maledicta in Afrikaans, viz. *Vloeken in Afrikaans* [*Swearing in Afrikaans*] (Van der Sijs 2007). As is the case for most other similar language situations, research is usually limited to a few cursory remarks in a few scholarly publications (e.g., Donaldson 1991: 281–282 on the influence of English on the Afrikaans maledicticon), or otherwise to (selected) entries in etymological dictionaries.

The aim of this chapter is to sketch a first, broad picture of the influence of Dutch on the maledicticons of language with which it came into contact with. The description will firstly be set against a general background of what we know about lexical semantic change (Section 2), before zooming in on what we know about lexical semantic change from a maledictological perspective (Section 3). In Section 4 the focus is specifically on what we know about the development and spreading of specifically Dutch maledicta, before delving into the analysis of a dataset extracted from Van der Sijs' *Nederlandse woorden wereldwijd* (NWWW 2010). The chapter closes with a discussion of the results, conclusions, and ideas for future work, in Section 5.

2. Words adrift: What do we know?

In the general field of language change, the literature is vast yet yields a relatively modest corpus of universally-recognized principles and theories. In the context of this chapter, several key theses and observations relevant to the study of lexical semantic change in general are highlighted, mainly based on literature from computational linguistics (e.g., Schlechtweg et al. 2020; Tahmasebi et al. 2021), construction grammar (e.g., Traugott and Trousdale 2013), and maledictology (e.g., Burridge 2012; Burridge and Benczes 2019). The specific aim is to provide a foundation for understanding how and why languages evolve over time.

1.1 Thesis 1.1 – The perpetual motion of language change: All languages are always changing

It is a fundamental linguistic principle that all languages are in a perpetual state of evolution, with words undergoing constant transformation, emergence, and disappearance. Van de Velde (2023) points out that while most words remain extant (with approximately 80% surviving over a span of 350 years), a significant minority do fade into obsolescence. This phenomenon is succinctly captured by Burridge and Benczes (2019: 186), who note that "words disappear;[3] new ones are created (or borrowed); meanings too are in a constant state of flux." Such borrowed words are called loanwords and are defined here simply as words that were "copied" (e.g., though adoption or adaptation) by speakers from one language (the donor language/languoid) into another language (the recipient language). Note that even if a loanword from the donor language is fully integrated in, and adapted for the recipient language, it remains in its essence a loanword, because a loanword never ceases to be a loanword.[4]

1.2 Thesis 1.2 – Internal and external forces as drivers of language change: Language evolution is propelled by a combination of internal and external factors

- *Internal factors* are those dynamic mechanisms and characteristics of a language that prompt evolution, such as shifts in pronunciation, grammatical structures, and vocabulary that occur organically over time.
- *External factors* entail influences external to the language itself, including social, political, and technological changes. These external changes could not only change languages structurally (e.g., adding vocabulary), but also pragmatically (e.g., certain linguistic features could become markers of social identity or prestige). Computational models, as discussed by Hamilton et al. (2016a), have further refined our understanding of these dynamics, distinguishing between "global shifts in a word's distributional semantics" versus "local changes to a word's nearest semantic neighbours."

3. Regarding disappearing words, Van de Velde (2023) observes that over a period of 350 years, only one out of five words disappears: Most words that appear as lemmas in the *Woordenboek der Nederlandse Taal* survived. Only 1 out of 5 words became extinct ... After 350 years, the chance of survival is about 80% ..." [my translation].

4. https://wold.clld.org/terms#loanword

1.3 Thesis 1.3 – Evolutionary patterns: Patterns of language change are predictable

Deo (2015: 180) posits that functional and meaning changes in language follow unidirectional diachronic trajectories, also known as grammaticalization paths or clines. This notion aligns with the broader understanding of how languages evolve, adhering to patterns that can be traced and predicted. Yet, as she points out: "We have little precise understanding, though, of why and how this happens. We know even less about its implications for our models of grammar, communication, and cognition" (Deo 2015: 179)

1.4 Thesis 1.4 – Sapir's Drift: Changes in language families evolve in parallel ways

The phenomenon of genetically related languages independently undergoing similar linguistic changes long after their separation, is known as Sapir's Drift (Yanovich 2016). This concept reflects the deep-rooted tendencies within language families to evolve in parallel ways.

1.5 Thesis 1.5 – The Regularity Hypothesis: Phonetic changes are predictable, barring non-phonetic factors

Burridge and Benczes (2019) articulate the regularity hypothesis, emphasizing the predictable nature of sound changes in a language, barring the influence of non-phonetic factors (e.g., analogisation). This hypothesis also underscores the systematic nature of linguistic change that is grounded in cognitive and/or physiological processes.

1.6 Thesis 1.6 – The role of cognitive processes: Analogisation and neoanalysis are central to language change

The cognitive processes of analogisation and neoanalysis (Traugott and Trousdale 2013) involve drawing comparisons and establishing links between elements based on observed similarities (Burridge 2012; Fischer 2019), as well as re-analyses of the form and/or meaning of constructions (Noël 2016). These processes are central not only to changes in grammar, but also to the innovative and creative development of metaphors, metonymies, understatements, hyperboles, etc. in language.

1.7 Thesis 1.7 – The law of conformity, and the law of innovation: Low-frequency words, and polysemous words tend to change faster over time

Based on the axiom that "[w]ords gain senses [i.e., become more polysemous] over time as they semantically drift" (Hamilton et al. 2016b: 1489; [my addition]), they introduce the laws of conformity and innovation, which describe the dynamics of word frequency and polysemy in linguistic change.

- *The law of conformity*: "Rates of semantic change scale with a negative power of word frequency" (Hamilton et al. 2016b: 1490), or in other words: high-frequency words tend to change slower over time. Van de Velde (2023) concurs when he demonstrates that higher-frequency words have a better chance to survive that lower-frequency words.
- *The law of innovation*: "After controlling for frequency, polysemous words have significantly higher rates of semantic change" (Hamilton et al. 2016b: 1490), or in other words: polysemous words tend to change faster over time.

1.8 Thesis 1.8 – Survival traits: Short words, nouns and verbs, and uniquely-sounding words tend to change slower over time

In addition to the above two laws, Van de Velde (2023) provides further insights into the survival probabilities of linguistic elements, noting that:

- shorter words are more likely to persist over time than longer ones;[5]
- nouns and verbs have higher survival rates than adjectives; and
- uniquely-sounding words – i.e., "words with a greater weighted difference to other words" (Van de Velde 2023; [my translation]) – are more likely to persist than those with similar phonetic profiles, suggesting that distinctiveness plays a key role in the longevity of words.

Despite the large literature on lexical semantic change, "many core questions about semantic change remain unanswered" (Hamilton et al. 2016b). One of these questions relates to lexical semantic change of taboo words.

5. He notes that "more frequent words are also shorter; therefore, length and frequency might not be totally separate variables" (Van de Velde 2023 [my translation]). The same uncertainty applies to polysemous words, as Hamilton et al. (2016) point out: "... polysemy is strongly correlated with frequency – high frequency words have more senses [...] – so understanding how polysemy relates to semantic change requires controlling for word frequency ..."

3. Taboo words adrift: What do we know?

Like in the previous section, several key axioms and observations relevant to the study of lexical semantic change in taboo constructions are extracted here – mainly based on maledictological literature. The specific aim is to summarise what we know about the evolution of taboo constructions over time.

2.1 Thesis 2.1 – The naturalist hypothesis: Taboo concepts give rise to constructions with negative valence

Allan (2001) hypothesises that the negative valence of maledicta arises from the distaste in taboo concepts in a particular community. These naturalist beliefs are then transferred to the expressions they represent. Pienaar (1945 [1965]) lists numerous examples of this kind of (religious) belief in the supernatural power of language, and specifically of mentioning certain taboos out loud. As Burridge and Benczes (2019: 180) state: "Speakers make a link here between sound and sense, as if the form of the expression somehow communicates the essential nature of what it represents."

Valence of words – whether negative/pejorative, or positive/ameliorative – is therefore directly linked to social changes (Borkowska and Kleparski 2007). While what is considered taboo might differ from one era to the next, "the sheer fact of taboo does not" McWhorter (2021: 5). To illustrate this, Beelen and Van der Sijs (2022) conclude that the absence of Dutch words related to homosexuality in their corpus of texts in the period 1583–1796, could be ascribed to the notion that homosexuality was probably considered too ghastly for words (quite literally!). Based on this changing world-view and norms over the ages, McWhorter (2021: 8) claims that profanity – at least in English – has known three main eras (also see Van der Sijs 2002: 53):

a. When the worst you could say was about religion (e.g., *damn* or *hell*);
b. When the worst you could say was about the body (e.g., *fuck* or *shit*); and
c. When the worst you could say was about groups of people (e.g., the n-word or *faggot*).[6]

6. McWhorter (2021) does not delineate these three generalised eras according to specific dates. One could though roughly say a. = pre-Renaissance (when the (Roman Catholic) church and beliefs in the gods reigned supreme); b. = post-Renaissance (when humans, and their bodies and minds came to the fore); and c. = post-structuralist (with specifically the world wars and the sexual revolution as important markers). In addition, one should of course recognise that these eras represent a broad, Anglocentric perspective. As Christopher Joby rightly pointed out in an earlier version of this chapter, these generalisations don't necessarily hold true for non-

2.2 Thesis 2.2 – Volatility of the maledicticon: Some maledicta are prone to change

Related to the naturalist hypothesis and the negative valency of maledicta, Burridge and Benczes (2019: 186) point out that "taboo words and their meanings are culturally potent, and this makes them prone to rapid and unpredictable changes." Swearwords are not stable – they compete over time constantly with each other, due to factors such as euphemisation (see below), the need for variation, and changing language trends (Van der Sijs 2002: 524–526). Burridge and Benczes (2019: 194, 198) continue to note that "arbitrariness also falls away because speakers create very real connections between the sound of a taboo word and what it refers to, thus questioning the overall pervasiveness of the symbolic thesis." For example, Allan and Burridge (2006: 243) claim that there are more than 1,000 English expressions for [PENIS], 1,200 for [VULVA/VAGINA], 800 for [HUMAN COPULATION], and 2,000 expressions for [SEXUALLY UNRESTRAINED WOMAN].[7]

As is the nature of slang and informal, expressive language, it is especially euphemisms – and even more specifically so-called attention-seeking euphemisms (Burridge and Benczes 2019: 189) – that are more likely to be ephemeral. As McWhorter (2016) summarises: "euphemism tends to require regular renewal. This is because thought changes more slowly than we can change the words for it, and has a way of catching up with our new coinages." When euphemisms do survive, it is because conventionality confers pragmatic stealth and mindlessness-inducing qualities (Burridge and Benczes 2019: 189). (Also see thesis 2.4 below regarding the X-phemism mill.)

2.3 Thesis 2.3 – Stability of the maledicticon: Some maledicta are resistant to change

The counter side of this volatility is that some maledicta are extremely stable, which can be ascribed to their high emotional arousal value: "taboo words are always more stimulating [emotionally arousing] than non-taboo words and people remember them better than neutral words" (Burridge and Benczes 2019: 181). This not only relates to language learning (e.g., Dewaele 2012, 2015, 2016, 2018b, 2018a; Harris et al. 2003), but also to children acquiring language (e.g., T.B. Jay 1992, 2000; K.L. Jay and Jay 2013; T.B. Jay 2019). Van Sterkenburg (2001: 70) also argues that

Anglophonic cultures and societies, e.g., in Islamic societies where "the worst you could say" is still "about religion".

7. It is not clear whether their counts are synchronically or diachronically based.

words with a high emotional arousal value are more fit to be used as swearwords than words with a lower arousal value. Specifically with regard to language change, Burridge and Benczes (2019: 181) note that the "attention-grabbing nature of these words … can extend across languages [so that] [s]peakers today share with their ancestors a profound awareness of the close relationship … between word and meaning and this remains a powerful motive for language change."

The stability (i.e., hardiness and longevity) of some maledicta remains an anomaly: some words simply survive over many decades or even centuries, often with the same tabooness and senses (e.g., *fuck, shag, screw* for [TO HAVE SEXUAL INTERCOURSE]). As Burridge and Benczes (2019: 192) summarise: "Certain turns of phrase seem to capture people's imagination and manage to survive, but the puzzle is still how they retain their effectiveness over so many years. The shelf life of these durable '- phemisms' remains a mystery."

2.4 Thesis 2.4 – The Allan-Burridge law of semantic change: Bad connotations drive out good

Based on the well-known Gresham's law in economics ("Bad money drives out good"), Allan and Burridge (1991: 22ff; 2006: 243) claim that bad connotations drive out good (the Allan-Burridge law of semantic change). Not only are words more likely to take on negative overtones than they are favourable ones (Burridge and Benczes 2019: 188; Burridge 2012: 78), but maledicta can even dominate and contaminate other (similar-sounding) words (Burridge and Benczes 2019: 181).

This axiom is the foundation of the well-known so-called X-phemism mill: "… euphemistic expressions become sullied by the disagreeable concepts they designate. As the negative associations reassert themselves, they undermine the euphemistic quality of the word, and the next generation of speakers grows up learning the word either as the direct term (orthophemism) or an offensive term (dysphemism)" (Burridge and Benczes 2019: 189). Such X-phemistic recycling underlies the rapid turnover of maledicta in severely taboo domains, such as constructions in the sexual domain (see Section 2.2 above).

2.5 Thesis 2.5 – Generally observed euphemisation strategies

Burridge (2006) and Burridge and Benczes (2019: 186–188) list various strategies (i.e., internal forces) of euphemisation, including:

- *Masking*
  - Orthographical disguises, including asterisks, long dashes, suspension points or symbols (e.g., *c**t, c – t, c…t, c*!t*)

- Antithetical disguises, like circumlocution through periphrases (e.g., *the miraculous pitcher* for [PENIS]), or renaming (e.g., *Ou Niek* for [SATAN] (Pienaar 1945 [1965]: 79)).

- *Evaluative word-formation* [8]
  - Phonological distortions, e.g., rhyming (*Berkeley Hunt*; which are often end-clipped and abbreviated to *berk*), backslang (*cunt* > *tenuc/teenuc*), Pig Latin (*cunt* > *untcay*), or other phonetic disguises (*regina* instead of *vagina*)
  - Shortenings, like clippings (*pud* for *pudendum*), abbreviations (*the n-word*), acronyms (*OMG* for *oh my God*), and omissions (e.g., *I need to go [to the toilet]*)
  - Blending, e.g., *God's truth* > *strewth*
  - Reduplication, e.g., *jeepers creepers*
  - Affixation, e.g., using the DIM suffix in Afrikaans (*poep·ie* < *poep* 'fart')

- *Semantic change in existing words* [9]
  - (Inter)subjectification involves "the development of markers that encode the Speaker's (or Writer's) attention to the cognitive stances and social identities of the Addressee" (Traugott 2012: 9), and is often involved in the development of euphemisms (Traugott 2017); also see Traugott (2010); López-Couso (2010).
  - Metaphorisation (e.g., *meat muffin* for [VULVA/VAGINA])
  - Metonymisation (e.g., *groin* for [PENIS]); note that it is quite common that terms for [BUTTOCKS] and [GENITALIA] could be used interchangeably due to whole-for-part metonymies of the so-called "unmentionables" (e.g., *prat, tail, fanny, bottom, bum, twat*)
  - Hyperbole (e.g., *to be in hell* for *to have trouble*)
  - Understatement (e.g., *anatomically correct doll* for *doll with a vagina*)
  - Elevation (e.g., *the deed* for *sexual intercourse*)
  - Litotes (e.g., *unwell* for *sick*; *unpretty* for *ugly*; *unintelligent* for *stupid*)

- *External lexical borrowing* (e.g., *faeces* borrowed from Latin, instead of *shit*)
- *External pragmatic borrowing* (e.g., numerous languages borrowed *fuck* as "a non-propositional expletive marker to intensify a message and express attitudes such as hostility, aggression, annoyance and nuances thereof"

8. Burridge and Benczes (2019) refer to these mechanisms as "remodelling"; Allan (2016) also uses "remodelling" as superordinate for all formal changes to a word (and "figurative language" for all semantic changes to a word).

9. Also see Burridge (2012); she discusses metaphors, metonymies, understatements and hyperboles as forms of analogisation.

(Andersen 2014: 25); also see Zenner et al. (2017: 133) who maintain that "swearwords are less likely to be borrowed if they belong to the sexuality and physiology category, or if they are deemed to be very offensive in the receptor language." They also claim that "short and frequent swearwords are more likely to be borrowed" (Zenner et al. 2017: 131).
- *Internal borrowing* (i.e., borrowing from sublanguages, such as euphemisms from technical jargon – e.g., *luetic disease* instead of *syphilis*)

Lastly, many scholars remark on the methodological difficulty to study maledicta. For example, Van der Sijs (2002: 41; 2007: 317–318) notes that maledicta, similar to informal words in general, have most often simply not been recorded in writing. This makes accurate dating of such words extremely difficult, and we should therefore assume that maledicta are much older than the dates recorded in, for example, dictionaries. Similarly, since lexicographic practice changes with time (Burridge and Benczes 2019: 184), we cannot simply assume that a word or sense did not exist in a certain period because it does not appear in a dictionary from that period. This will be aptly illustrated in the following section, where the focus is on our understanding of changes in the Dutch maledicticon.

4. Dutch taboo words adrift: What do we know?

Compared to other Germanic languages - English excluded - Dutch and German arguably have the largest collections of maledictiological research and maledictionaria (i.e., dictionaries of taboo languages) and bodies of maledictiological research of any of the other Germanic languages. Notwithstanding, publications on the diachronic development of maledicta in these two languages remain limited to entries in etymological dictionaries, mentioning in passing in studies on (cultural) history, and a few linguistic publications. Regarding the latter for Dutch, these are – to the best of my knowledge – limited to the following: Beelen and Van der Sijs (2022); De Baere (1940); De Blécourt (1992); De Jager and Leendertz Wz. (1878); Fabry and Engelbrecht (2021); Frohn (2006); Hallema (1946); Hindriks and Van Hofwegen (2014); Leuker (1992); Loosjes (1814); Ruette (2018); Van der Sijs (2021); Van Sterkenburg (1993, 2001, 2007, 2008, 2011, 2019); Willems (1834).

While some research on the diachronic development of Dutch maledicta exists, nothing – bar two publications – exists on the influence of Dutch on the maledicticons of other languages. The first of these two publications is the abovementioned (see Section 1) article on swearing in Afrikaans by Van der Sijs (2007). In this article, she hypothesises that Afrikaans would have borrowed maledicta abundantly from other languages, specifically African (Ntu)[10] languages and English, and that only a minority of Afrikaans maledicta would be traceable back to Dutch (Van der Sijs 2007: 317). After studying roughly three hundred Afrikaans maledicta – mainly from dictionary material, but also some lists from the internet – she concludes that her hypothesis is to be rejected. Her main findings regarding the development of Afrikaans maledicta within the language contact situation in South Africa, which stand to be corroborated with other Afrikaans data, or to be investigated for other, similar language contact situations, are the following (Van der Sijs 2007: 324):

1. Most Afrikaans maledicta can be traced back directly to Dutch. However, many of these have been modified or deformed differently than in Dutch. For example, Afrikaans deformations (i.e., minced oaths) like *jissie* (< AFR/ENG/NDL *Jesus*), *jirre* (< AFR/NDL *Here* 'Lord'), and *gots* (< AFR/ENG/NDL *God*) were not inherited from Dutch. As Van der Sijs (2007: 326) puts it: "Dutch and Afrikaans have each gone their own way over time, but they both build on the existing Dutch word-stock" [my translation]. She ascribes this to a basic tenet in maledictological studies: Speakers are continuously looking for new ways to express emotive or evaluative content, and/or to name taboos (see Thesis 2.4 above, as well as Pinker 2008).
2. Influence from English is minimal, with only a small stock of loanwords (e.g., *demmit* (< *damn it*), *fok* (< *fuck*), and *shit* (id.)) that have been borrowed by many other languages worldwide.
3. Loan maledicta from African languages (e.g., Zulu, Xhosa, or Tswana) are as good as non-existent.

The second publication that indicates rather comprehensively how Dutch words, including maledicta, have been borrowed by other languages is Van der Sijs' comprehensive inventory *Nederlandse woorden wereldwijd* (NWWW 2010). While a broad-ranging, meticulous endeavour was undertaken to compile the database for this book (see NWWW 2010: 5–7), the quality and scope of materials largely depend on lexicographic and other written material for each of the languages considered: "The description of the Dutch loan words depends by definition on the state of research for each individual language" (NWWW 2010: 7; [my translation]). When looking at maledicta in NWWW, one should in addition consider

10. Traditionally, Ntu languages were called Bantu languages – the largest African language family – and include among others the Nguni languages (like Zulu and Xhosa) and Sotho-Tswana languages (like Northern and Southern Sotho) spoken in South Africa. Note that the southern African languages of the Khoe, Kx'a and Taa-!Kwi language families are not considered Ntu languages.

that dictionary material for many of these languages (especially smaller languages) represent only mainstream, standardised texts, thereby potentially missing peripheral areas of the constructicon, such as maledicta. See in this regard also the last paragraph of Section 3.

Despite these caveats, NWWW is a rich source for finding Dutch maledicta borrowed and changed by other languages. For example, the entry for the lemma **hondsvot** in (1) illustrates that *hondsvot* has three senses in Dutch, but only the usage as a swearword was borrowed into Finnish and English (either directly from Dutch, or otherwise from Low German or German respectively). The English *houndsfoot*, however, is now obsolete (indicated with the † symbol). Norwegian borrowed the word either from Dutch or Low German, but has developed a completely new sense ('backseat of a sledge'). The Danish loanword – either from Dutch or German – also has this sense, and yet another new one ('noose at the end of a rope') that is probably an extension from one of the Dutch senses. In addition, the swearword usage is also attested in Danish.

(1) **hondsvot** 'scheldwoord; onbeduidend voorwerp; oog voor het derdepart onder aan een katrol' → Engels † *houndsfoot* 'scheldwoord' (uit Nl of Duits); Deens *hundsvot* 'scheldwoord; oog of strop aan het einde van een touw; achterzitje op een slee' (uit Nl of Duits); Noors *hundsvott* 'achterzitje op een slee' (uit Nl of Nederduits); Fins *hunsvotti* 'scheldwoord' (uit Nl of Nederduits).
[Translation:] **hondsvot** 'swearword; insignificant object; eye for the third part at the bottom of a pulley' → English † *houndsfoot* 'swearword' (from Dutch or German); Danish *hundsvot* 'swearword; eye or noose at the end of a rope; backseat of a sledge' (from Dutch or German); Norwegian *hundsvott* 'backseat of a sledge' (from Dutch or Low German); Finnish *hunsvotti* 'swearword' (from Dutch or Low German).

4.1 Dataset

The scope of NWWW is wide and general: it contains 17,560 Dutch words (lemmas) that have been found in 138 other languages or language varieties. Van der Sijs calculates that each Dutch word occurs on average in 2.6 other languages, for a total of 46,310 loanwords (NWWW 2010: 133). Because of its documented and systematic methodology, it is possible to use its data for comparative purposes, while always keeping the limitations mentioned above in mind (the last paragraph of Section 3) when considering maledicta.

Through iterative searching in the NWWW, all entries (lemma, tag, and/or definition) with words starting with or containing the search terms in (2) were extracted. These entries serve as the basis for a dataset of maledicta in languages that were influenced directly or indirectly by Dutch.

(2) taboe|vloek|scheld|eufemis|slang|plat|vulgair|drek|uitwerpsel|seks|mannelijk|vrouwelijk|masturb|menstru|testikel|testis|scrotum|prostit|duivel

Relevant cases were subsequently parsed so that information about a loanword in a specific language could be treated as a single record. For example, the **hondsvot** entry in (1) above, resulted in four separate records: one for each of the borrowing languages. If a Dutch lemma is defined as a maledictum (like **hondsvot**, whose first sense is 'swearword'), all subentries (i.e., for each language in that entry) were included as separate records, so that one can see how Dutch maledicta developed in other language.

Conversely, if a Dutch lemma is not defined as a maledictum, only those subentries for languages where maledicta developed from the Dutch word, were included. Consider for example the entry for **aas** in (3). In Dutch, *aas* refers, among others, to 'bait', or more generally to 'food' or 'prey (for large animals and birds)' (VDO 2021). In Virgin Islands Dutch Creole,[11] Berbice Creole Dutch, and Papiamentu, this sense was borrowed with the word; these three languages are therefore not considered part of the data, since neither the Dutch word, nor the loanwords have taboo senses. However, the Swedish loanword developed a new, taboo sense ('swearword as villain or sod'), and the Dutch/Swedish part of the entry is therefore kept as a record in the dataset.

(3) **aas** 'lokspijs, voedsel' → Zweeds *as* 'kadaver, scheldwoord als schoft of secreet' (uit Nl of Nederduits); Negerhollands *aes*; Berbice-Nederlands *asi*; Papiaments *as* (ouder: *aas, haas*) 'lokspijs'.
[Translation:] **aas** 'bait, food' → Swedish *as* 'cadaver, swearword as villain or sod' (from Dutch or Low German); Virgin Islands Dutch Creole *aes*; Berbice Creole Dutch *asi*; Papiamentu *as* (older: *aas, haas*) 'bait'.

From a total of 176 lemmas, 384 records were extracted in this manner. This means that each Dutch word occurs as a loanword on average in 2.2 languages, which is proportionally comparable to the above-mentioned 2.6 languages for NWWW as a whole. However, while NWWW covers a total of 138 languages (NWWW 2010: 133), the loan maledicta were only found in 66 different languages and/or language varieties. These languages can geographically be grouped as either continental (e.g., English, Frisian, or Danish, through direct or indirect contact situations), or colonial. The colonial group can be broadly divided into the Caribbean (e.g., Sranan Tongo, or Papiamentu), Southern Africa (e.g., South African English, or Southern Sotho), and Southeast Asia (e.g., Indonesian, or Petjo). On the map in Figure 1 this geographical division is illustrated in colour: the darker the colour, the more

11. The extinct language "Negerhollands" (NWWW 2010: 99–101) is referred to as "Virgin Islands Dutch Creole" in the remainder of this chapter, unless it is quoted from another source.

entries in NWWW that refer to a language spoken in that country/region. It is unsurprising that most of the maledicta relate to languages spoken in Indonesia, followed by Suriname and the ABC islands (Aruba, Bonaire, and Curaçao). It is however important to note that loanwords in Afrikaans are not included in NWWW; the records reflected on the map relate to South African English and Ntu languages in the region, which have all inherited the words via Afrikaans.

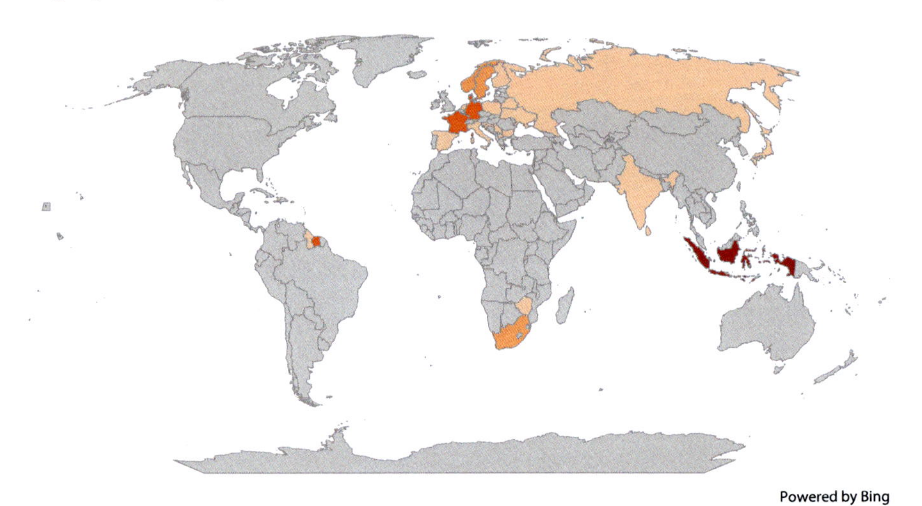

Figure 1. Geographical distribution of languages mentioned in NWWW entries

Based only on the information provided in each lexicographic entry in NWWW, these records were annotated using the following attributes and values (or combinations of values):

- Attribute: *meaning*, with values (see Table 2 for examples):
  - = or ≈ (same or somewhat similar meaning/usage)
  - < (narrowing)
  - > (broadening)
  - *new* (new meaning/usage)
- Attribute: *tabooness*, with values (see Table 3 for examples):[12]
  - = or ≈ (same or somewhat similar tabooness)
  - + (amelioration)
  - – (pejoration)

12. We solely relied on information provided in NWWW. If no mention was made of a change in tabooness, it was assumed to be the same as in the Dutch word with the same sense.

- Attribute: *part-of-speech / grammatical function*, with values:
  - N (noun)
  - V (verb)
  - ADJ (adjective)
  - ADV (adverb)
  - INTERJ (interjection)
  - N.PR-N (conversion of proper noun to noun)
  - N-INTERJ (conversion of noun to interjection)
  - N-V (conversion of noun to verb)
  - ADJ-N (conversion of adjective to noun)
- Attributes: *Loanword Typology* (LWT) *code, meaning,* and *semantic field* from the World Loanword Database (Haspelmath and Tadmor 2009)
- Attribute: *semantic subfield*, with values:
  - ANIMAL
  - ANTAGONIST[13]
  - BODY PART
  - CRIMINALITY
  - DISEASE
  - EXCRETION
  - NATURE
  - NEG (expression of negative valence, or negative state)
  - OUTSIDER
  - RELIGION
  - SEX

The data was annotated by the author, and the dataset was subsequently quality-checked by a colleague who is also specialising in Afrikaans and Dutch linguistics. The dataset is freely available at https://gerhard.pro/publications/vanhuyssteen 2025a/.

13. The difference between **protagonist/antagonist** and **ingrouper/outgrouper** (Brewer 2016) has mostly to do with agency. An antagonist is commonly seen as an opponent who opposes or attacks you (i.e., with agency), while an outgrouper is merely a member of another social category, an outgroup (i.e., without agency necessarily as part of its construal). Oftentimes epithets can be used to describe both antagonists and outgroupers – simply depending on the context.

4.2 Results

While languages in Southeast Asia are collectively mentioned most in the entries in NWWW (see Figure 1), the individual languages mentioned most are English (32), Sranan Tongo (an English-based creole language spoken in Suriname) (31), and Danish (31) (see Table 1). If we add up all English varieties and creoles, (i.e., English, Sranan Tongo, South African English (11), English Creole from the Virgin Islands (7), Caribbean English (1), and "English dialect" (1)), it emerges that English and its international varieties spoken in South Africa and the Dutch Caribbean (i.e., in the historic Dutch West Indies) rake up almost the same number of mentions (82) as languages in Indonesia (83) (i.e., in the historic Dutch East Indies – see Figure 1). This picture is, of course, skewed by the fact that Afrikaans is not included in NWWW.

Table 1. Top 20 borrowing languages in dataset

	Borrowing language	N
1	English	32
2	Sranan Tongo	31
3	Danish	31
4	Papiamentu	21
5	Frisian	20
6	Virgin Islands Dutch Creole	18
7	Norwegian	17
8	French dialect	16
9	Swedish	15
10	Indonesian	12
11	South African English	11
12	Manado Malay	11
13	French	10
14	Petjo	10
15	German	10
16	Javanese	8
17	Russian	8
18	Berbice Creole Dutch	7
19	English Creole (Virgin Islands)	7
20	Ambonese Malay	7

In terms of meaning changes (see Table 2), it seems that the majority of records in NWWW has the same (39%), or roughly the same (7%) meaning, with another small cluster having the same meaning, plus a broadened meaning (11%). More cases of narrowing can be observed (90), compared to broadening (48). The remaining records contain new senses (23), or combinations of these values.

Table 2. Meaning change in NWWW

Value	Example: Dutch	Example: Borrowing language	N	%
=	**verdomme** 'minced oath'	Indonesian *perdom*	149	39%
<	**jongens** 'young men; servants'	Madurese *jongos, jungos* 'male servant'	90	23%
>	**meeuw** 'type of bird'	Danish † *mæfik* 'type of bird; abusive term for woman'	48	13%
=>	**vink** 'songbird'	Danish *finke* 'songbird; abusive term for young woman'	43	11%
≈	**verrek** 'curse'	Indonesian *perék!* 'curse: go to hell!'	25	7%
new	**hooi** 'dried grass'	Indonesian *indehoj, indehoy* 'to have (forbidden) sex'	23	6%
=; new	**geboorte** 'birth'	Frisian *geboarte* 'birth; female genitalia; penis'	4	1%
<; new	**donder** 'sound of lightning; devil; beating'	Frisian *donder* 'skilful person; devil; body'	1	0%
<>	**zwabber** 'mop; (obsolete) pervert, hedonist'	Russian *švábra* 'ship's mop; impure, lowly person; woman, girl, untidy or tall, skinny woman; wife; prostitute'	1	0%
Total			384	100%

The same cannot be said about the tabooness of these words. Only 25% of the words underwent pejoration, while 11% amelioration. In the remaining records, 47% is the same, 15% roughly the same, and 2% some combination of these four main values – see Table 3.

Regarding the grammatical function (i.e., part-of-speech) of the loanwords, it emerges that it is predominantly nouns that are being borrowed and used as nouns (75%), followed by verbs (8%), interjections (8%), and adjectives (2%). Cases of conversion are scarce, with the most frequent four cases of noun-verb conversion (e.g., the noun *hooi* in Dutch is used as a verb in Betawi and Indone-

Table 3. Changes in tabooness in NWWW

Value	Example: Dutch	Example: Borrowing language	N	%
=	**pielemans** 'penis'	Sranan Tongo *pileman*	179	47%
–	**makelaar** 'broker, middleman'	Bulgarian *makro* 'pimp'	95	25%
≈	**dikzak** 'fat person'	Frisian *diksek* 'term of abuse: fat person'	59	15%
+	**guit** 'scoundrel'	Norwegian *gutt* 'boy'	42	11%
=/-	**buffel** 'type of animal'	Danish *bøffel* 'type of animal; term of abuse for crude, clumsy person'	4	1%
≈/-	**poes** 'female cat'	English *puss* 'proper name for a cat, rabbit, and tiger; nickname for woman; (vulgar) female genitalia'	2	1%
=/+/-	**drol** 'turd'	French *drouille* 'excretion, diarrhoea; mud; prostitute'	1	0%
=/+	**stront** 'shit'	French *étron* 'turd; (obsolete) object of lesser value'	1	0%
–/+	**zwabber** 'mop; (obsolete) pervert, hedonist'	Russian *švábra* 'ship's mop; impure, lowly person; woman, girl, untidy or tall, skinny woman; wife; prostitute'	1	0%
Total			**384**	**100%**

sian – see Table 2), and three cases of proper noun-noun conversion (e.g., the Dutch proper name *Joost* is used as a noun *yosi* 'devil' in Sranan Tongo).

Table 5 presents the semantic subfields (in capital letters), together with the LWT meanings resorted under those subfields. Meanings between square brackets are meanings not included verbatim in the LWT (e.g., 'shit' does not appear in the LWT, but only 'to shit'). Meanings in parentheses indicate cases where the meaning is:

- either an approximation (e.g., Frisian *bearput* means 'cesspool', which is closest to (the toilet) in the LWT);
- or polysemous, and the first taboo sense was chosen for purposes of annotation (e.g., Russian *švábra* (see Table 3) is polysemous, and since the first taboo sense listed in NWWW is 'impure, lowly person', it is annotated as (the enemy)).

Unsurprisingly, the semantic fields of the loanwords are dominated by words referring to ANTAGONIST and OUTSIDER (combined 29%); SEX and BODY PARTS (combined 24%); EXCRETION (24%); and words expressing NEGA-

Table 4. POS categories in NWWW

Value	N	%
N	288	75%
V	32	8%
INTERJ	29	8%
ADJ	8	2%
N; INTERJ	5	1%
N; ADJ	5	1%
N > V change	4	1%
N.PR > N change	3	1%
INTERJ; ADJ	3	1%
ADJ; ADV	2	1%
N; V; INTERJ	1	0%
N > INTERJ change	1	0%
ADJ > N change	1	0%
N; V	1	0%
ADV	1	0%
Total	384	100%

TIVE VALENCE[14] (11). While it might be surprising to see that only 5% of loanwords comes from the RELIGION domain, this picture is probably skewed by the fact that many of the RELIGION (i.e., blasphemous) words have been defined in NWWW in a way that make them more fitting for the domain NEGATIVE VALENCE. For example, Dutch *verdomme* is merely defined as 'minced oath', without any indication that it relates to *godverdomme*, which originates from a religious-based oath 'God could curse me (if I don't speak the truth)' (Van Sterkenburg 2001: 341–344).

14. These are words that have simply been defined as 'curse' (e.g., *godverdorie*), 'minced oath' (e.g., *verdomme*), 'exclamation' (e.g., *godehere*), 'swearword' (e.g., *vervloekt*), etc. in NWWW.

Table 5. Semantic fields in NWWW

Semantic subfields and LWT meanings	N	%
EXCRETION	**82**	**24%**
[shit]	37	11%
the toilet	25	7%
to shit	14	4%
the nasal mucus	2	1%
(the toilet)	2	1%
to strike or hit or beat	1	0%
to piss	1	0%
ANTAGONIST	**53**	**16%**
(the enemy)	52	16%
[the homosexual]	1	0%
SEX	**47**	**14%**
the prostitute	16	5%
to have sex	10	3%
[the pimp]	10	3%
(to have sex)	4	1%
the adultery	3	1%
[the fornicator]	2	1%
(the adultery)	1	0%
[to have homosexual sex]	1	0%
OUTSIDER	**44**	**13%**
(the servant)	35	10%
(the enemy)	6	2%
[the homosexual]	3	1%
NEG	**37**	**11%**
(the anger)	36	11%
surprised or astonished	1	0%
BODY PARTS	**35**	**10%**
the vulva	12	4%
the penis	10	3%
the testicles	5	1%
the mouth	3	1%
[the underpants]	1	0%
(the womb)	1	0%

Table 5. *(continued)*

Semantic subfields and LWT meanings	N	%
the womb	1	0%
(the penis)	1	0%
the penis/vulva	1	0%
RELIGION	**17**	**5%**
the demon	15	4%
the god	2	1%
CRIMINALITY	**13**	**4%**
the thief	9	3%
(the thief)	2	1%
the rape	2	1%
DISEASE	**3**	**1%**
the disease	3	1%
NATURE	**2**	**1%**
the thunder	1	0%
the storm	1	0%
ANIMAL	**2**	**1%**
female	2	1%
Grand Total	**335**	**100%**

5. Discussion and conclusions

In this chapter, it was investigated to what extent Dutch influenced the maledicticons of a large variety of languages with which its speakers had contact. When considering the results based on data extracted from Van der Sijs' NWWW (2010), we could deliberate to what extent they support or contradict the general theses about language change (see 1.1 to 1.8 in Section 2), or the more specific theses about the evolution of maledicta (see 2.1 to 2.4 in Section 3). To this end, we could conclude the following:

- In terms of meaning changes, the data aptly illustrates the opposing stability vs. volatility forces that are expressed in thesis 2.2 and 2.3. Some maledicta are unstable and change rapidly (43% combined), while others are extremely stable (57% combined). No new evidence transpired from our dataset to explain this phenomenon.

- Regarding the tabooness of maledicta, the Allan-Burridge law of semantic change (thesis 2.4) predicts that "bad" connotations drive out the "good". However, only 25% of the words in our dataset underwent pejoration, while 62% remained (roughly) the same. The data therefore seems to be more supportive of the stable nature of some maledicta (thesis 2.3). Of course, one cannot take our data as counterproof for the Allan-Burridge law, given the limitations of this data discussed above. However, it does raise the question whether the Allan-Burridge law should really be considered a law, or merely as a general tendency. More data from more languages is needed to come to any decisive conclusion.
- The parts-of-speech of the loanwords conform at least in one sense to one of the survival traits listed in thesis 1.8, namely that nouns used as nouns (75%) have higher survival rates than other part-of-speech categories. Unlike the prediction in thesis 1.8, verbs borrowed and used as verbs only account for 8% of the cases, similar to interjections. This finding uncovers a potential new hypothesis to be explored: Nominal maledicta are best suited for loaning in language contact situations.
- As part of thesis 2.5, it was mentioned that "swearwords are less likely to be borrowed if they belong to the sexuality and physiology category" (Zenner et al. 2017: 133). This part of the thesis simply does not hold when considering the Dutch data. Almost half of the data relates to SEX, BODY PARTS, and EXCRETION. While this might be the result of skewed data, it does beg for further investigation, especially by looking into the maledicticons of one specific language to see how many loanwords are from these semantic domains – i.e., to prove or disprove Zenner et al. (2017)'s claim.

In addition to the above suggestions for future research, many other research questions could stem from the theses in Section 2 and 3. For example:

- From thesis 1.2: Based on the approach of Hamilton et al. (2016a), how do the global shifts in the distributional semantics of a Dutch word like *poes* ('female cat') compare to the local changes in its nearest semantic neighbours? For example, what is the effect of English *puss(y)* ('female genitalia') on the usage of *poes* in Dutch and other languages (like Afrikaans)?
- From thesis 1.4: Do maledicta support the tendencies of Sapir's Drift, or are there too many other pragmatic factors that influence the evolution of maledicta?
- From thesis 1.6: Are the processes of analogisation and neoanalysis only at work in the minds of monolingual people, or to what extent does it play a role in bilingual people? For example, how did Dutch *asbak* ('ashtray') became

ba'ak ('female genitalia') in the Bahasa Prokem variety of Indonesian? Why only in Bahasa Prokem, and not in other varieties, or in other languages?
- From thesis 1.7 and 1.8: What is the role of the following traits in the survival and/or change of loan maledicta:
  - frequency;
  - polysemy;
  - word length;
  - parts-of-speech; and
  - uniqueness?
- From thesis 2.1: What can we learn from the evolution of words that refers to highly taboo or contentious concepts that are often considered too ghastly to mention (e.g., homosexuality in the past, or transsexuality, abortion, or euthanasia in the present)? Are people using only orthophemisms to refer to such sensitive matters? How are they treated nowadays for example in standup-comedy texts, or in pop music lyrics?
- From thesis 2.1: Do the three time periods identified by McWhorter (2021: 8) hold true?
- From thesis 2.2 and 2.3: What kind of data or evidence would be required to resolve and/or model the volatility vs. stability contradiction? For example, it is claimed on the one hand that attention-seeking euphemisms are ephemeral, but on the other hand that the attention-grabbing nature of maledicta could be a motivation for stability.
- From thesis 2.4: If bad connotations drive out good, why do some euphemisms survive? Is there sufficient counter-evidence for the euphemism-orthophemism-dysphemism cline?
- From thesis 2.5: What is the nature and scope of various euphemisation strategies, also across languages and language families? And if there are euphemisation strategies, what about dysphemisation strategies?

6. Ethical matters

Ethical clearance for the research project was obtained through the Language Matters Ethics Committee of the North-West University (ethics number: NWU-00632-19-A7).

References

Allan, Keith. 2001. *Natural Language Semantics*. Oxford: Blackwell.

doi Allan, Keith. 2016. "Pragmatics in language change and lexical creativity." *Springerplus* 5 (1–342): 1–23.. https://www.ncbi.nlm.nih.gov/pubmed/27066361.

Allan, Keith, and Kate Burridge. 1991. *Euphemism and Dysphemism: Language Used as Shield and Weapon*. New York/Oxford: Oxford University Press.

doi Allan, Keith, and Kate Burridge. 2006. *Forbidden words: Taboo and the censoring of language*. Cambridge: Cambridge University Press.

Aman, Reinhold. (ed.) 1979. *Maledicta: The International Journal of Verbal Aggression*. Waukesha: Maledicta Press.

Aman, Reinhold. 1996. *Opus Maledictorum: A Book of Bad Words*. New York: Marlowe & Co.

doi Andersen, Gisle. 2014. "Pragmatic borrowing." *Journal of Pragmatics* 67: 17–33.

Beelen, Hans, and Nicoline VAN DER SIJS. 2022. ""Injurieuse expressien". Scheldwoorden in Amsterdamse notarisakten 1583–1796." *Alle Amsterdamse Akten, Jaarboek Amstelodamum* 2022: 166–181.

Borkowska, Paulina, and Grzegorz A. Kleparski. 2007. "It befalls words to fall down: Pejoration as a type of semantic change." *Studia anglica Resoviensia* 4 (47/2007): 33–50. http://www.univ.rzeszow.pl/file/1294/sar_v4_03.pdf.

doi Brewer, Marilynn B. 2016. "Intergroup Discrimination: Ingroup Love or Outgroup Hate?." In *The Cambridge Handbook of the Psychology of Prejudice*, edited by Chris G. Sibley and Fiona Kate Barlow, In Cambridge Handbooks in Psychology, 90-110. Cambridge: Cambridge University Press.

doi Burridge, Kate. 2006. "Taboo, Euphemism, and Political Correctness." In *Encyclopedia of Language & Linguistics (Second Edition)*, edited by Keith Brown, 455–462. Oxford: Elsevier.

doi Burridge, Kate. 2012. "Euphemism and Language Change: The Sixth and Seventh Ages." *Lexis* (7).

Burridge, Kate, and Reka Agnes Benczes. 2019. "Taboo as a driver of language change." In *The Oxford Handbook of Taboo Words and Language*, edited by Keith Allan, 180–199. Oxford: Oxford University Press.

Bybee, Joan. 2015. *Language Change. Cambridge Textbooks in Linguistics*. Cambridge: Cambridge University Press.

De Baere, C. 1940. *Krachtpatsers in de Nederlandsche volkstaal. Een verzameling oudere en jongere bastaardvloeken*. Antwerpen: De Nederlandsche Boekhandel.

De Blécourt, Willem 1992. "'Schelm, hoer en kenaille': Schelden in achttiende-eeuws Kolderveen." *Volkskundig Bulletin* 18 (3): 389–414. https://www.meertens.knaw.nl/meertenspublicaties/pdf/vb/201_VB_1992_18.3.pdf.

De Jager, H., and P. Leendertz Wz. 1878. "Vloeken door onze vaderen gebruikt." *De Navorscher* 28: 175–189. http://www.heraldry-wiki.com/arms/literature/journals/Navorscher/28_1878.PDF.

doi Deo, Ashwini. 2015. "Diachronic Semantics." *Annual Review of Linguistics* 1 (1): 179–197.. https://www.annualreviews.org/doi/abs/10.1146/annurev-linguist-030514-125100.

Dewaele, Jean-Marc. 2012. ""Christ fucking shit merde!" Language Preferences for Swearing Among Maximally Proficient Multilinguals." *Sociolinguistic Studies* 4 (3).

Dewaele, Jean-Marc. 2015. "British 'Bollocks' versus American 'Jerk': Do native British English speakers swear more – or differently – compared to American English speakers?" *Applied Linguistics Review* 6 (3).

Dewaele, Jean-Marc. 2016. "Thirty shades of offensiveness: L1 and LX English users' understanding, perception and self-reported use of negative emotion-laden words." *Journal of Pragmatics* 94: 112–127.

Dewaele, Jean-Marc. 2018a. ""Cunt": On the perception and handling of verbal dynamite by L1 and LX users of English." *Multilingua* 37: 53–81. . https://api.semanticscholar.org/CorpusID:54086158.

Dewaele, Jean-Marc. 2018b. "Glimpses of semantic restructuring of English emotion-laden words of American English L1 users residing outside the USA." *Linguistic Approaches to Bilingualism* 8 (3): 320–342.

Diessel, Holger. 2023. *The Constructicon: Taxonomies and Networks.* Cambridge: Cambridge University Press.

Donaldson, Bruce C. 1991. *The influence of English on Afrikaans: A case study of linguistic change in a language contact situation.* Pretoria: Academica.

Drößiger, Hans-Henry. 2018. "Schimpfwörter und Beschimpfungen: Thesen zur Terminologie und zum Forschungsstand in der Sprachforschung." *Žmogus ir žodis* 19 (3): 23–37.

Fabry, Jan, and Wilken Engelbrecht. 2021. "Vandaag heeft hij weer een pesthumeur, wat een klerelijer is dat toch! Over de historische invloed van pandemieën op Nederlandse verwensingen." *Roczniki Humanistyczne* 69 (5 Zeszyt specjalny): 43–53.

Fischer, Olga. 2019. Analogy in Language and Linguistics. In *Oxfor Bibliographies Online.* https://www.oxfordbibliographies.com/: Oxford University Press.

Frohn, Helen. 2006. "'Geen duivel kan een mens meer plagen als zy doen': Schimp en smaad aan het adres van de regenten." PhD, Utrecht University. https://www.bondtegenvloeken.nl/kenniscentrum-taal/onderzoeken.

Gramley, Stephan. 2012. *The History of English: An Introduction.* New York: Routledge.

Hallema, A. 1946. *Scheld-, schimp- en spotnamen: Voorheen en thans.* Naarden: N.V. Uitgevers – Mij. A. Rutgers.

Hamilton, William L., Jure Leskovec, and Dan Jurafsky. 2016a. "Cultural Shift or Linguistic Drift? Comparing Two Computational Measures of Semantic Change." *Proceedings of the 2016 Conference on Empirical Methods in Natural Language Processing*, Austin, Texas, November 1–5. pp. 2116–2121.

Hamilton, William L., Jure Leskovec, and Dan Jurafsky. 2016b. "Diachronic Word Embeddings Reveal Statistical Laws of Semantic Change." *Proceedings of the 54th Annual Meeting of the Association for Computational Linguistics* (Volume 1: Long Papers), Berlin, Germany, August. pp. 1489-1501.

Harjung, J. Dominik. 2000. *Lexikon der Sprachkunst: Die rhetorischen Stilformen, mit über 1000 Beispielen.* München: Beck.

Harris, Catherine L., Ayse Ayçiçeği, and Jean Berko Gleason. 2003. "Taboo words and reprimands elicit greater autonomic reactivity in a first language than in a second language." *Applied Psycholinguistics* 24 (4): 561–579.

Haspelmath, Martin, and Uri Tadmor. 2009. *World Loanword Database*. Leipzig: Max Planck Institute for Evolutionary Anthropology.

Hindriks, Inge, and Rosalie Van Hofwegen. 2014. *"Godverdomme, ik zie een haai!" A Diachronic Research on Swearing Habits in a Dutch Reality TV-show*.

doi Jay, Kristin L., and Timothy B. Jay. 2013. "A Child's Garden of Curses: A Gender, Historical, and Age-Related Evaluation of the Taboo Lexicon." *The American Journal of Psychology* 126 (4): 459–475.

doi Jay, Timothy B. 1992. *Cursing in America: A psycholinguistic study of dirty language in the courts, in the movies, in the schoolyards and on the streets*. Amsterdam: John Benjamins.

Jay, Timothy B. 2000. *Why we curse: A neuro-psycho-social theory of speech*. Amsterdam: John Benjamins.

Jay, Timothy B. 2019. "Taboo language awareness in early childhood." In *The Oxford Handbook of Taboo Words and Language*, edited by Keith Allan, 96–107. Oxford: Oxford University Press.

Keller, Rudi. 1994. *On Language Change: The Invisible Hand in Language*. London: Routledge.

Leuker, Maria-Theresia. 1992. "Schelmen, hoeren, eerdieven en lastertongen Smaad en belediging in zeventiende-eeuwse kluchten en blijspelen." *Volkskundig Bulletin* 18 (3): 314–339. https://www.meertens.knaw.nl/meertenspublicaties/pdf/vb/198_VB_1992_18.3.pdf.

Loosjes, Adriaan Pietersz. 1814. *Drie schuitpraatjes (Over het vloeken; Over het bangmaken der kinderen; Over het liegen)*. Amsterdam: Cornelis de Vries, Hendrik van Munster en zoon en Johannes van der Hey.

doi López-Couso, María José. 2010. "Subjectification and intersubjectification." In *Historical Pragmatics*, edited by Andreas H. Jucker and Irma Taavitsainen, 127–164. Berlin: De Gruyter Mouton.

McWhorter, John H. 2016. "Euphemise this." *Aeon* (blog).

McWhorter, John H. 2021. *Nine nasty words: English in the gutter: then, now, and forever*. Kindle ed. New York: Penguin.

doi Noël, Dirk. 2016. "For a radically usage-based diachronic construction grammar." *Belgian Journal of Linguistics* 30: 39–53.

NWWW. 2010. In *Nederlandse woorden wereldwijd*, edited by Nicoline Van der Sijs. Den Haag: Sdu Uitgevers.

Pienaar, P. de V. 1945 [1965]. "Spraaktaboe en eufemismes in Afrikaans [Speech taboo and euphemisms in Afrikaans]." *Tydskrif vir Volkskunde en Volkstaal* 2 (11): 44–52.

Pinker, Steven. 2008. *The Seven Words You Can't Say On Television*. Kindle ed. London: Penguin.

doi Ruette, Tom. 2018. "Why do the Dutch swear with diseases?" In *Linguistic Taboo Revisited: Novel Insights from Cognitive Perspectives*, edited by Andrea Pizarro Pedraza, In Cognitive Linguistics Research [CLR], 225–244. Berlin: De Gruyter Mouton.

Schlechtweg, Dominik, Barbara McGillivray, Simon Hengchen, Haim Dubossarsky, and Nina Tahmasebi. 2020. "SemEval-2020 Task 1: Unsupervised Lexical Semantic Change Detection." Proceedings of the Fourteenth Workshop on Semantic Evaluation, Barcelona (online), 8 December.

Tahmasebi, Nina, Lars Borin, Adam Jatowt, Yang Xu, and Simon Hengchen. (eds.). 2021. *Computational approaches to semantic change*. Berlin: Language Science Press.

doi Traugott, Elizabeth Closs. 2010. "(Inter)subjectivity and (inter)subjectification: A reassessment." In *Subjectification, Intersubjectification and Grammaticalization*, edited by Davidse Kristin, Vandelanotte Lieven and Cuyckens Hubert, 29–74. Berlin, New York: De Gruyter Mouton.

doi Traugott, Elizabeth Closs. 2012. "Intersubjectification and clause periphery." *English Text Construction* 5: 7–28.

doi Traugott, Elizabeth Closs. 2017. Semantic Change. In *Oxford Research Encyclopedia of Linguistics*, edited by Mark Aronoff. Oxford: Oxford University Press.

doi Traugott, Elizabeth Closs, and Graeme Trousdale. 2013. *Constructionalization and constructional changes*. Oxford: Oxford University Press.

Van de Velde, Freek. 2023. "Zwindende woorden." Invited talk.

Van der Sijs, Nicoline. 2002. *Chronologisch woordenboek. De ouderdom en herkomst van onze woorden en betekenissen*. 2e ed. Amsterdam: Veen.

Van der Sijs, Nicoline. 2007. "Vloeken in het Afrikaans [Swearing in Afrikaans]." In *Leven met woorden. Opstellen aangeboden aan Piet van Sterkenburg bij zijn afscheid als directeur van het Instituut voor Nederlandse Lexicologie en als hoogleraar Lexicologie aan de Universiteit Leiden*, edited by Fons Moerdijk, Ariane Van Santen and Rob Tempelaars, 317–326. Leiden: Instituut voor Nederlandse Lexicologie / Koninklijke Brill Leiden.

Van der Sijs, Nicoline. 2021. "Etymologica: moe(de)rneuker." *Neerlandistiek: Online tijdschrift voor taal- en letterkunde* (17 May). https://neerlandistiek.nl/2021/05/etymologica-moederneuker/.

Van Sterkenburg, Piet G.J. 1993. "Veranderingen in de lexicale onderwereld van het Nederlands: vloeken." In *Zin dat het heeft. Een liber amicorum voor Jan van Bakel*, edited by Bas Van Bakel, Peter-Arno Coppen and Piet Rolf. Nijmegen: Coppen.

Van Sterkenburg, Piet G.J. 2001. *Vloeken. Een cultuurbepaalde reactie op woede, irritatie en frustratie*. 2e ed. Den Haag: Sdu Uitgevers.

Van Sterkenburg, Piet G.J. 2007. *Woorden van en voor emotie*. Leiden: Universiteit Leiden.

Van Sterkenburg, Piet G.J. 2008. *Krachttermen*. Schiedam: Scriptum.

Van Sterkenburg, Piet G.J. 2011. "Blasphemous swearing in Dutch." *Sociolinguistica* 25: 41–50.

Van Sterkenburg, Piet G.J. 2019. *Rot lekker zelf op: Over politiek incorrect en ander ongepast taalgebruik*. Schiedam: Scriptum.

VDO. 2021. In *Van Dale Online*. Utrecht: Van Dale Uitgevers.

Willems, J.F. 1834. "Over eenige oude Nederlandsche vloeken, eeden en uitroepingen." *Nederduitsche Letteroefeningen*: 218–230.

Yanovich, Igor. 2016. "Genetic Drift Explains Sapir's "drift" In Semantic Change." The Evolution of Language: Proceedings of the 11th International Conference (EVOLANGX11), New Orleans.

Zenner, Eline, Tom Ruette, and Emma Devriendt. 2017. "The borrowability of English swearwords: An exploration of Belgian Dutch and Netherlandic Dutch tweets." In *Advances in Swearing Research: New languages and new contexts*, edited by Kristy Beers Fägersten and Karyn Stapleton, 107–136. Amsterdam: John Benjamins.

CHAPTER 11

Rethinking language contact in the Malay archipelago

Reinier Salverda
University College London

This contribution on language contact in the Malay archipelago starts from the discovery around 1520 of Malay by Pigafetta and its ensuing contact with Portuguese. A century later, Dutch was added to the mix by De Houtman in his Malay-Dutch guide of 1603. Exploring such contacts I'll take my cue from the Dutch linguist Gonda and his 1941 survey of Indonesian multilingualism and its diversity. In the *Capita Selecta* that follow – covering both the Dutch VOC period (1602–1799) and the Dutch Kingdom (1816–1950) – I'll be pursuing such questions as: What about early Malay scholars like Werndly and their achievements in grammar, dictionary making and bible translation?, How did Radermacher's *New Vocabulary* (1780) revolutionize the study of contemporary trilingualism?, What new discoveries on the mixed Malayo-Portuguese formerly spoken in Batavia did Schuchardt add in his *Creole Studies* (1890)?, What insights have these and other linguists contributed on Dutch-Indonesian language mixing and its varieties?

Keywords: multilingualism, *lingua franca* , language contact and mixing, Dutch and its Indies varieties, Portuguese and Portuguese-based creoles (Tugu), and Malay pioneers: Pigafetta, De Houtman, Werndly, Mohr, Radermacher, De Hollander, Schuchardt, Van Ginneken, Gonda, Van den Toorn, Tjalie Robinson, Teeuw, De Vries

1. Early language contact – Pigafetta and the discovery of Malay

When in 1596 the Dutch first came to the East Indies, many others had already preceded them, in search of the fabled spices of the Moluccas. From time immemorial, Hindus, Arabs, Ottomans, Gujarati, Chinese and so many others from all over Asia, had all been coming to the Spice Islands for trade, bringing with them new inventions, religions and ideas, new skills, practices, knowledge, culture and beliefs, and also their languages, such as Sanskrit, Persian, Hindi, Gujarati, Chinese and Javanese. In the process, the archipelago became a vast

https://doi.org/10.1075/impact.55.11sal

multilingual and multicultural area, at the cross-roads between India, Persia, the Middle East and Africa to the west, and Indo-China, Japan and China to the east (cf. Cribb 2000).[1] In due course, many words from those languages have found their way into the archipelago, and have since been preserved in etymological dictionaries such as Jones's *Loanwords in Indonesian and in Malay* (2007)[2] – the culmination, really, of a long tradition of earlier multilingual dictionaries, such as the colonial Anglo-Indian *Hobson-Jobson* (1886)[3] and the scholarly work in Dutch East Indies colonial lexicography, *Uit Oost en West* ('From East and West', 1893)[4] by Veth and others.

It is this issue – the diversity of language and languages in the Malay archipelago, first addressed by the Dutch scholar Jan Gonda in his inspirational essay of 1941[5] – that will be the central theme of my contribution. For on arrival in that immense archipelago, its linguistic diversity was by no means a simple and easy matter. How could one possibly succeed in trade, diplomacy and communication when confronted by so many different languages, and so many obstacles to communication? This was the problem that the Dutch VOC-commander Frederick de Houtman set out to deal with in 1603 in his *Spraeck ende woord-boeck.*[6]

But first things first: how had those two *lingua francas* – Malay and Portuguese – come to dominate trade and contact all over the archipelago? For the first, Malay, we have a key document which we owe to the Italian nobleman Antonio Pigafetta (1491–1534), who early in the 16th century accompanied the explorer Ferdinand Magellan on his first Circumnavigation (1519–1521). When sailing through the Moluccas, Pigafetta collected a useful vocabulary of some 450 words of Malay.[7] As Bausani (1972) tells us, Pigafetta acquired those words

1. Robert Cribb (ed.) (2000). *Historical Atlas of Indonesia*, Richmond: Curson, 29–72.

2. Russel Jones (ed.) (2007). *Loan-words in Indonesian and Malay*. Leiden: KITLV Press.

3. Henry Yule & A.C. Burrell (eds.) (1886 [1996]). *Hobson-Jobson. The Anglo-Indian dictionary*. Ware: Wordsworth (new ed. 1996).

4. P.J. Veth et al. (eds.) (1889). *Uit Oost en West. Verklaring van 1000 woorden uit Nederlands-Indië* (new ed. Nicoline van der Sijs, 2003).

5. Jan Gonda (1941), 'De verscheidenheid van inheemsche talen en letterkunde' [On the Diversity of Indonesian Languages and Cultures]. In W.H. van Helsdingen & H. Hoogenberk (eds.), *Daar wèrd wat groots verricht ... Nederlandsch Indië in de XXste eeuw*. Amsterdam: Elsevier, 150–170.

6. Frederick de Houtman (1603), *Spraeck ende woord-boeck, in de Maleysche ende Madagaskarsche talen*. Amsterdam: Cloppenburgh (see also p. 350 n. 26).

7. Jan Gonda (1938), 'Pigafetta's Vocabularium'. *Bijdragen Taal-, Land- en Volkenkunde* [*BTLV*] 97:101–124. Also: Antonio Pigafetta, *Magellan's Voyage*. Transl. & edited by R.A. Skelton (1969). New York: Dover; and A. Bausani (1972). *L'Indonesia nella Relazione di Viaggio di Antonio Pigafetta*. Djakarta: Centro Cultura: 14–21.

from the Malay-speaking sailors, pilots, traders and slaves he encountered in the harbours of the Moluccas, in Ternate and Malacca (probably also with some help from the Portuguese traders he encountered there). In the *Journal* he kept, Pigafetta wrote these down, with their Italian translation, and thus brought home to Europe not just a very important *lingua franca*, but actually also a first vital key to understanding both the Malay language and its world.

Meanwhile, in the course of the next century, the Portuguese set out to conquer the archipelago, chasing away their rivals and enemies, and spreading their own seaborne empire[8] from one end of the archipelago to the other – from Malacca in the west via Ternate and Tidore in the Moluccas, to Flores and Timor in the east. From those strategic strongholds, through conquest and conversion, by settlement and slavery, they spread not just their trade and power, but also their Catholic religion and the Portuguese language which they maintained – often bastardized, pidginized and creolised in the process – as the spoken contact language on many of the archipelago's islands – and today still in East Timor[9] – which testify to the tenacity and the longevity of their oral cultures and communities.

Having seen Pigafetta's collection of Malay words, it is worth noting how, two hundred years later, in Jonathan Swift's immortal satire *Gulliver's Travels* (1726), the same problem of language contact still vexed his hero, *Gulliver*, when he landed on the island of Lilliput, south-west of the Sunda Straits in Indonesia. As Gulliver explains, when he and the Emperor of Lilliput could "neither of us understand a syllable", he tried the King's advisers "and spoke to them in as many languages as I had the least smattering of, which were High and Low-Dutch, Latin, French, Spanish, Italian and lingua franca; but all to no purpose".[10] But, as we learn from the Anglo-Indian dictionary, *Hobson-Jobson* (1996: xviii), Gulliver's eyes (and ears) were opened by two of his contemporaries. First, Captain Alexander Hamilton, in the *Preface* to his *A New Account of the East Indies* (1727), explained that:

> Along the Sea-coasts the *Portuguese* have left a Vestige of their Language, tho' much corrupted, yet it is the Language that most *Europeans* learn first to qualify them for a general Converse with one another, as well with the different inhabitants of *India*.

8. Charles R. Boxer (1969). *The Portuguese Seaborne Empire*. London: Hutchinson. And Boxer (1965) *The Dutch Seaborne Empire*. London: Hutchinson.

9. J. Clancy Clements (2009). *The Linguistic Legacy of Spanish and Portuguese*. Cambridge University Press.

10. Jonathan Swift, *Gulliver's Travels* (1726). New ed: Everyman Library, 1991: 26.

To which Charles Lockyer, in his *An Account of the Trade in India* (London, 1711) added:

> This they (the *Portuguese*) may justly boast, they have established a kind of *Lingua Franca* in all the Sea Ports in *India*, of great use to other *Europeans*, who would find it difficult in many places to be well understood without it.

As we see, beyond Pigafetta's collecting and describing of Malay words, there was a further key into Gulliver's problem which was common practice throughout the eastern seas and harbours, viz. to make use of intermediaries – pilots, translators and linguists – who knew Portuguese.[11] Now, while speaking Portuguese, these intermediaries were not necessarily Portuguese themselves,[12] as we know from the so-called Black Portuguese and others in Batavia (see below notes 49, 94). Their knowledge of Portuguese made them useful as interpreters and pilots on European ships, witness a letter of 1695 from Cape Town, South-Africa, about a three-men black chain gang, all speaking Malay, Dutch and Portuguese, who were sent along as pilots on three ships heading to Batavia – one of whom, named Aje of Clompong, was experienced in 11 languages: "Maleyers, Lampioenders, Biema, Sambauwe [Soembawa], Tambora, Tacy, Sauger, Macassaars, Javaans, Portugees, Duytsch", while his friend, Mongodua from Macassar, had eight languages, and the third, Jongman from Baly, had five.[13]

2. Questions and focus – Gonda (1941) and the diversity of languages

My focus in this contribution is on multilingualism and the worldwide diversity of languages, specifically on language contact between Dutch and Malay in the East. Such contact has been the basic situation throughout the Dutch presence in the Malay archipelago from 1600 onwards. For the history of the Dutch language in Indonesia during the colonial era, we benefit immensely from the study by Kees Groeneboer, *Gateway to the West.*[14] Thanks to his research we now know

11. The word 'Linguist' (first recorded in 1700 in *Hobson-Jobson*) originally came from Portuguese 'lingoa', an old term for 'interpreter' (first recorded in 1554).

12. Ivor Lewis (1997). *Sahibs, Nabobs and Boxwallahs.* Delhi: Oxford University Press, s.v. 'Linguist' (154) and 'Topaz' (238), in Anglo-Indian, "A dark-skinned half-caste of Portuguese descent, whose occupation might be soldier, ship's scavenger, bath-attendant or interpreter, depending on circumstances".

13. Hesseling, D.C. (1923^2). *Het Afrikaans. Bijdrage tot de geschiedenis der Nederlandse taal in Zuid-Afrika.* Leiden: Brill, 34–35.

that the Dutch language policy of the Dutch East India Company (VOC) has only been a limited success: the two *lingua francas*, Malay and Portuguese, with their far larger numbers and social weight, were too widely used for the Dutch to be able to change this. Other scholars have come to similar conclusions and explanations: the Dutch didn't really have a *mission civilisatrice* (Bouquet 1939); and the efforts they made for their own language were always too little and too late (Willemyns 2023).[15] As a consequence – unlike all other colonizing powers from Europe, and despite being a global trading power themselves – the language of the Dutch has never reached the status of world language. In 1945, the arrival of Indonesian Independence then brought "The triumph of bahasa Indonesia", as the sociologist De Swaan[16] put it.

What matters here is to recognise that the issue of language which occupied Gulliver is still with us today, witness the online *Ethnologue* database and its 7,164 languages worldwide, of which 704 in Indonesia alone. To me, this is one of the central challenges for us linguists: How are we ever to deal with such immense linguistic diversity?

In my earlier studies I focused on contacts between Dutch and Indonesian.[17] More generally, I then moved to three different but comparable situations of language contact – (i) Dutch in Indonesia (Salverda 1994, 2013 and 2018a); (ii) contemporary multilingualism in London and worldwide (Salverda 2006, 2018b); and (iii) the Frisian minority language in the Netherlands and Europe (Salverda

14. Kees Groeneboer (1998). *Gateway to the West. The Dutch Language in Colonial Indonesia 160–1950. A History of Language Policy.* Amsterdam: Amsterdam University Press. And Groeneboer (2013). 'A Comparison of Colonial Language Policy in Asia', In H. Brand (ed.), *De tienduizend dingen. Feestbundel Reinier Salverda.* Ljouwert: Fryske Akademy, 347–359.

15. G.H. Bousquet (1939) *La Politique Musulmane et Coloniale des Pays-Bas.* Paris: Centre d'Étude de Politique Étrangère. And: R. Willemyns (2023). 'Why Colonial Dutch Failed to Become a Global Lingua Franca'. In: Aneta Pavlova (ed.), *Multilingualism and History.* Cambridge: CUP, 138–152.

16. De Swaan, Abram (2001). *Words of the World. The Global Language System.* Cambridge: Polity, 81–95.

17. Reinier Salverda (1994). 'Between Dutch and Indonesian: Some Observations on Indo-Dutch in Pre-War Batavia'. In: Liberty P. Sihombing et al. (eds). *Bahasawan Cendekia. Seuntai Karangan untuk Anton M. Moeliono.* Jakarta: Fakultas Sastra Universitas Indonesia, PT Intermasa, 356–380. Also: Salverda (2013). 'Between Dutch and Indonesian: Colonial Dutch in time and space'. In: F. Hinskens & J. Taeldeman (eds.)(2013). *Dutch. An International Handbook of Language Variation.* Berlin: De Gruyter Mouton, 800–821; And: Salverda (2018a), 'Saussure in Indonesia: Translation and Reception', In: J. Joseph & E. Velmezova (eds.), 'Traductions du Cours de linguistique générale de Ferdinand de Saussure. Lausanne: *Cahiers de l'ILSL*, 55, 99–114

2016).[18] In all three I have been exploring how these cases may teach us what really matters when studying multilingualism – questions such as: What human abilities can we muster in such contact? What skills do we, as language users, have available for this, skills such as practiced, for example, by today's *Médécins Sans Frontières*: good listening; asking for help when hearing something we don't understand; trying to guess what a speaker might mean; using hands, feet, sounds and mimics to get some mutual understanding going; learning and sharing a new language; developing practical translation skills; acquiring one or more *lingua francas* and build bridges with other people, especially in the ever-more interconnected world of today.

In neighbouring fields of language study, meanwhile, my colleagues Nicoline van der Sijs and Christopher Joby have been pursuing comparable questions – Van der Sijs specialising in the global dissemination of loanwords, including the worldwide spread of Dutch words in contact with other languages (Van der Sijs 2005, 2010 and 2013);[19] while Joby has been investigating the history of Dutch words, first in early modern history in contact with English speakers in Great Britain; then later with the Japanese during centuries of trade and exchange between the two nations; and today also in contact with Indonesian languages (Joby 2021, 2022).[20]

From these various perspectives it makes sense to join forces and move towards a contact linguistic study of the history of Dutch in Indonesia in relation to other such cases of Dutch in multilingual contact settings – as was commonplace everywhere throughout the global network of the Dutch East India Company, the world's first multinational trading company (VOC, 1602–1799)[21] and the

---

18. For (i) Salverda 1994, 2013, 2018a, see note 17 above. For (ii) Salverda 2006 and 2018b: (2006) 'Multilingual London and its Literatures', in: *Opticon 1826* (UCL), vol. i: 1, 1–15; Salverda (2018b), 'Empires and their languages', 60–64. In: Jens Braarvig & Markham J. Geller (eds.), *Studies in Multilingualism, Lingua Franca and Lingua Sacra*. Berlin: Max Planck Research Library for the History and Development of Knowledge vol. 10, p. 25–90. And for (iii) Salverda 2016: 'Linguistic justice and Endangered languages', in: *Acta Universitatis Sapientiae/ European and Regional Studies* 9, 39–47 [De Gruyter, Berlin]. See also note 114 below.

19. Nicoline Van der Sijs (2005). *Wereldnederlands*. Den Haag: Sdu Uitgevers; Van der Sijs (2010). *Nederlandse woorden wereldwijd*. Den Haag: Sdu Uitgevers; Van der Sijs (2013). 'Sluitdagen en afpakschuur: de Indisch-Nederlandse woordenschat', in: Hanno Brand et al. (eds.). *De tienduizend dingen. Feestbundel voor Reinier Salverda* Ljouwert: Fryske Akademy, 389–402.

20. Christopher Joby (2021). *The Dutch language in Japan*. Leiden: Brill; and Joby (2022). 'Taalcontact tussen Het Nederlands en andere talen in de Indonesische archipel', in: *Internationale Neerlandistiek* vol. 60 nr. 3 (dec), 255–277 (Amsterdam University Press).

21. Nicholas Ostler (2005). 'Dutch Interlopers'. In Ostler, *Empires of the World*. London: HarperCollins, 395–403.

many languages that were used, alongside and in contact with Dutch, spoken in its harbours, markets and trading stations all round the world, from New York, Cape Town, Curaçao, Nagasaki, Paramaribo, Amsterdam and Batavia (now: Jakarta), to St Petersburg, Istanbul, China, Taiwan, India, Jeddah, Sri Lanka and Bombay (now: Mumbai).

For our investigation here we take our starting point from Diderot's dictum, "*Il faut commencer par le commencement*" – we have to begin at the beginning. For me, as a linguist, this means we start at the central challenge of linguistic diversity. The basic fact here is the existence of those 7,164 very different languages. So many languages in the world, but so few states[22] – and so, inevitably (or rather, necessarily), language contact is the basic living reality of humankind everywhere. And thanks to the language abilities of our species, we are not confined to using just our own individual language. Goethe (1747–1832) rightly held that if one knows only one language, one actually knows nothing. Think too of Von Humboldt (1767–1835), who – in preparation for his language studies, especially his *Über die Kawi-Sprache auf der Insel Java* (Berlin, 1836)[23] – first immersed himself in studying the grammars and dictionaries of at least a hundred different languages, as a necessary precondition for understanding what language really is and how it operates. This is also what Saussure (1857–1913) was looking for; what he (but not his editors, Bally and Sechehaye) put before us, as the central task of our field, viz: that linguistics is the study not just of *langue* in the singular, but necessarily in the plural, of *both* language *and* languages.[24]

Turning now to the diversity of languages in the Malay archipelago, no modern linguist, to my mind, has addressed this issue with more clarity than the Dutch Sanskrit scholar, Jan Gonda (1905–1991). In a series of stunning articles early in his scholarly career, Gonda first presented, in 1937, an in-depth discussion of the inaugural lecture, given in 1737, in Latin, in the University of Lingen, Prussia, by the first-ever Professor of Malay Studies in Europe, the Swiss Malay grammarian and Bible translator, George Henrik Werndly (1693–1744).[25] Then, in 1938,

---

22. *Ethnologue: Languages of the World*, SIL International online database 2024, 7168 languages. Cf. Li Wei (2008). 'Research Perspectives on Bilingualism and Multilingualism', in Li Wei & Melissa G. Moyer (eds.), *The Blackwell Guide to Research Methods in Bilingualism and Multilingualism*. Oxford: Blackwell, p. 3: 193 countries versus 6000 languages.

23. Wilhelm von Humboldt (1988). *On Language. The Diversity of Human Language-Structure and Its Influence on the Mental Development of Mankind*. With an introduction by Hans Aarsleff. Translated by Peter Heath. Cambridge: Cambridge University Press.

24. For Salverda 2018, see note 17 above; and secondly: Salverda (2025), 'Foreword: Saussure in Search of Language. In: John Joseph (ed.), *The Bloomsbury Handbook of Saussure*. London: Bloomsbury, xx-xxxvii.

Gonda published a thorough analysis and annotation of Pigafetta's first European list of Malay words of 1520.[26] Next, in 1940, Gonda continued with his critical review of Dutch achievements in the study of languages of the Malay archipelago, in particular during the 17th and 18th centuries.[27] And in 1941, in his eye-opening survey of the very many languages, literatures and cultures in use in the Malay archipelago, Gonda addressed head-on the central given of the immense and colourful diversity of those languages.[28] With these key contributions – all four in Dutch – he has left us some solid starting points for our own new investigation of Indonesian-Dutch language contact.

He himself, meanwhile, just kept going forward as a scholar. Early in 1947 he published an impressively documented, 370-page scholarly anthology – an absolute first of its kind – of some forty works of literature from all over the archipelago, translated into Dutch from Malay, Balinese, Arabic, Sundanese, Nias, Toradja, Bare'e, Dayak, Acehnese, Batak, Makassarese, Bugis, Tontemboan, Javanese and Old-Javanese. In 1951–53 this was followed in the Amsterdam journal *Lingua* by his two groundbreaking scholarly articles on the linguistic study of Indonesian from the perspective of general linguistics. And in 1952 the International Academy of Indian Culture in New Delhi published Gonda's authoritative study of *Sanskrit in Indonesia* (reprinted in 1973 and 1998).

To me the real key into Gonda's work is his brilliant survey of 1941, written in the Netherlands under German occupation, in which he gave central place to the investigation of the diversity of languages and culture in the archipelago; not just the larger languages, such as Javanese and Sundanese, but many others too, all brought together under the umbrella of the widely dispersed *lingua franca*, Malay, which was spoken in all the harbours and markets on all the coasts and islands of the archipelago. This largely concerned the study of Indonesian languages, but the interesting thing about Gonda was how he framed his presentation between two key points of modern linguistics which, at the time, were still far beyond the horizon and almost unknown to his Dutch readership.

25. Gonda (1937). 'De inaugurele rede van Werndly (17 December 1737)'. *Indische Gids* 59 (2), 1067–1076.

26. Gonda (1938). 'Pigafetta's Vocabularium van het "Molukken-Maleis"'. *BTLV* 97 (1), 101–12.4. Gonda here expressed his regret over the lack of scholarly attention among Dutch linguists to Hugo Schuchardt study, *Kreolische Studien* IX. *Ueber das Malaioportugiesisch von Batavia und Tugu*. In Sitzungsberichte d. Wien. Akad. 122, IX (1890), 1–256. See also: *Hugo Schuchardt Archiv*: https://schuchardt.uni-graz.at/.

27. Gonda (1940). 'Taalbeschouwing en Taalbeoefening'. *BTLV* 99 (1), 1–63.

28. Gonda (1941). 'De verscheidenheid van inheemsche talen en letterkunde'. In: Helsdingen (ed.), *Daar wèrd wat groots verricht.*, 150–170.

The first of these was his observation concerning the position of Batavia, the colonial capital of the Dutch East Indies, as a linguistic enclave on the island of Java, between the Sundanese in the west and the Javanese in the east – an enclave housing very many different languages, and where many people also spoke so-called Batavia Malay. The point about this is the extensive language mixing that could be witnessed at the time in Batavia, as in the following spontaneous utterance:

> *Sturm und Drang*-periode ini terkenal sebagai zaman "losbandig" dalam ilmoe kesoesasteraannja.
> [= The *Sturm und Drang*-movement is known as a dissolute period in literary studies] (Gonda 1941:159)

To Dutch ears this mishmash would have been a most uncommon utterance at the time, because of its combination into one single, everyday, mixed sentence, of words from no fewer than five different languages: German [*Sturm und Drang*]; Arabic [*ilmoe* (studies); *zaman* (period)]; Dutch [*losbandig* (dissolute)]; Malay [*terkenal sebagai* (known as)]; and Sanskrit [*kesoesasteraan* (literature)].

Gonda's second observation is his remark about the modernising efforts and multilingual cultural policies of the Dutch colonial government in the East Indies, as implemented by the *Kantoor voor de Volkslectuur* (Office for Popular Reading Matter/ *Balai Pustaka*), a Government Service established in 1911, which had been working to bring books, journals, novels, educational materials and all kinds of other reading matter, in many different genres, in Dutch as well as a number of the largest Indonesian languages, via its vast library network, to readers in the far corners of the Dutch empire – an area, in European terms stretching from the west of Ireland to beyond the Ural mountains in the east. At the time Gonda wrote this, the vast activities of the *Kantoor voor de Volkslectuur* were hardly known in the Netherlands;[29] today we are better informed thanks to Jedamski, McGlynn, Fitzpatrick and Kuitert.[30]

29. See: D.A. Rinkes (1921). 'Volkslectuur', in: D.G. Stibbe & E.M. Uhlenbeck (red.). *Encyclopaedie van Nederlandsch-Indië.* 's-Gravenhage: Nijhoff/Leiden: Brill. dl. 4 (1921), 610–612.

30. See: Doris Jedamski (1992), *Die Institution Literatur und der Prozess ihrer Kolonisation.* Münster. Also: John McGlynn (ed.). *Indonesian Heritage: Language and Literature.* Singapore: Archipelago Press (1998: 86–87); E. Fitzpatrick (2000). 'Balai Pustaka in the Dutch East Indies: Colonizing a Literature'. In: S. Sherry & Paul St George (eds.). *Changing the Terms: Translating in the Postcolonial.* Ottawa: Presses Universitaires de l'Université d'Ottawa, 113–127; and Lisa Kuitert (2020). *Met een drukpers de oceaan over. Koloniale boekcultuur in Nederlands-Indië, 1816–1920.* Amsterdam: Prometheus.

3. Dictionaries and Bible translations – Dutch, Malay and Portuguese during the VOC-period (1602–1799)

Back to the beginning now. Not long before the foundation of the Dutch East India Company (VOC), Frederick de Houtman (1571–1627), commander of one of the ships on the second voyage to the East Indies, was captured and held prisoner for two years by the Sultan of Aceh in northern Sumatra. There he studied the Malay language and wrote his *Spraeck ende woord-boeck: Inde Maleysche ende Madagaskarsche talen* – the first Dutch guide for learning Malay, published in Amsterdam in 1603.[31] This was a book of words and conversations in Malay and the related Malagasy spoken on Madagascar, produced on the model of an earlier European guide for contact and trade, the bilingual French-Dutch *Vocabularium* (1527) by the Antwerp French teacher, Noel de Berlaimont (?-1531), which in Europe grew into an eight-language guide, in Latin, French, Flemish, German, Spanish, Italian, English and Portuguese, under the title of *Colloquia et Dictionariolum Octo Linguarum* (1656).[32] Many times reprinted, it continued to be widely used well into the 18th century. Out in the East, De Houtman's Malay and Malagasy version – with its helpful words, dialogues and instructions for how to negotiate, to make deals, agree contracts and sort out all kinds of business – offered a clear and practical instrument for the Dutch merchants of the VOC operating in the Malay world.

Now, while the Portuguese had been making every effort to convert their native subjects to their Catholic religion, teach them the Portuguese language, and subject them to their King, the VOC had quite different priorities, the first of which was the Company's trade, profits and power. The Dutch, above all, were merchants – and only then also, skippers, explorers, soldiers, writers, administrators, lawyers, botanists and planters, and not to forget, church ministers, theologians and teachers. The emerging Dutch empire in the east was strategically run from Amsterdam – its general endeavour, its governance and expansion; its trade and commerce; its conquests, fleet and armies; its administration, archives, bookkeeping, law, order, justice and urban development; its harbours, churches, fortresses, warehouses and palaces. All this was done, on land, at sea, in every con-

31. It was reprinted in 1673, 1680 and 1708. A modern French edition – *'Le Spraeck ende woordboek'* – was published in 1970 by the indonesianist Denys Lombard in Paris. A recent Dutch version by Van der Sijs came out in 2000: *Wie komt daar aan op die olifant?* Amsterdam/ Antwerpen: Veen.

32. Scholarly edition: *Colloquia, Et Dictionariolum Octo Linguarum, Latinae, Gallicae, Belgicae, Teutonicae, Hispanicae, Italicae, Anglicae, Portugalicae*, ed. by Riccardo Rizza. Viareggio-Lucca: Mauro Baroni, 1996.

tinent, like their enemies the Portuguese, with the support of a vast multilingual force of mostly slave labour.[33] But always, from its foundation through to the middle of the 20th century, the language used by the VOC for its wide-ranging strategic and commercial operations and also its vast knowledge-industry concerning Indonesia continued to be Dutch until the end.[34]

So, when faced with the presence in the archipelago of those rivals and their languages, what did those 17th & 18th century Dutchmen do?

For many VOC-men – curiosity-driven like Pigafetta and De Houtman – their first contacts often led to the collection of further new language data from the world in which they moved. Thus, Isaac Commelin, in his *Begin ende Voortgangh van de Vereenighde Nederlandsche geoctroieerde Oost-Indische Compagnie* (Amsterdam, 1646), included a very early *Vocabulaer* (word list) of Dutch, Malay and Javanese words, collected on Ternate island during Van Neck and Van Waerwijck's second Voyage (1598–1600) to the East Indies (cf. Gonda 1940: 44). The same key multilingual interest we also find in the works of the great German biologist Georg Everhardus Rumphius (1627–1702), who for the plants included in his Moluccan *Herbal* (*Het Ambonsch Kruid-boek*, 1741–1753, 7 vols) ensured that "Each entry described the plant or tree in details, followed by its name in various languages, always including its Dutch, Latin, Malay, and Ambonese names, and Rumphius often provided Javanese, Hindostani, Portuguese, or Chinese nomenclature."[35]

33. Around 1780, Batavia counted some 150,000 slaves plus very many uncounted domestic slaves, against 10,000 whites. See: Abbé Raynal 1780, *Histoire des deux Indes*. Anthony Strugnell et al. (eds.), Ferney-Voltaire: Centre International d'Étude du xviiie siècle, 2010, vol 1, 222. See also R. Salverda (2022). 'On Reading the *Histoire des deux Indes* (1780) by Raynal and Diderot'. In *Diciottesimo Secolo* vol 7, 89. Cf. R. Salverda (2008). 'Slavery and Abolition: East Indies', in: Prem Poddar et al. (eds), *A Historical Companion to Postcolonial Literatures – Continental Europe and its Empires*. Edinburgh: Edinburgh University Press, 2008, 390–391. But see also the different numbers and percentages of speakers of Dutch, Malay, Portuguese and Chinese in Batavia between 1680 and 1795, in Groeneboer (1998), *Gateway*, 314–315; in L. Blussé (1986), *Strange Company. Chinese settlers, mestizo women and the Dutch in VOC Batavia*, Dordrecht: Foris, 83–84; and in Jean Gelman Taylor (1983). *The Social World of Batavia*. University of Wisconsin Press, Index s.v. Dutch, Malay and Portuguese. Within their colonies, the Dutch always were an all-powerful minority, see Reggie Baay (2015 [2021^4]). *Daar werd wat gruwelijks verricht. Slavernij in Nederlands-Indië*. Amsterdam: Athenaeum-Polak & Van Gennep.

34. R. Salverda (1989a). 'Nederlands als wetenschappelijke bronnentaal voor Indonesische Studiën in Indonesië'. In: Kees Groeneboer (ed.), *Studi Belanda di Indonesia/Nederlandse Studiën in Indonesië*. Jakarta: Djambatan, 401–409. Cf. W.Ph. Coolhaas/G.J. Schutte (1980^2). *A Critical Survey of Studies on Dutch Colonial History*. The Hague: Nijhoff.

35. E.M. Beekman (ed.) (1999). *The Ambonese Curiosity Cabinet, Georgius Everhardus Rumphius*. New Haven/London: Yale, lxxxi.

The VOC also engaged in very different pursuits. One of its official duties, assigned to it in its second charter of 1623, was to spread the word of God, specifically the 'Reformed public religion', in foreign parts. In 1629, the Gospel according to Matthew became the first New Testament book to be translated into Malay, by the Dutch VOC merchant Albert Corneliszn Ruyll, which he published in Enkhuizen.[36] As early as 1611 and 1612, Ruyll had already published in Amsterdam two little books for Moluccan boys learning their ABC and morals via the Dutch language.[37] Yet, in the eyes of the Dutch Church this was not going to work, and so, for their bible translations they decided not to use Dutch but instead the two *lingua francas*, Malay and Portuguese. Their religious anchor, meanwhile, was to remain the Dutch Protestant States Bible, which in 1637 had been officially and exclusively proclaimed throughout the Dutch Republic by its highest authority, the States-General. From then on, therefore, it fell to the learned men and church ministers in Batavia who had studied theology and knew the biblical languages, to validate not just the correctness of their dictionaries but also the Protestant purity of their translations.

A century on, and in the early 1700s this long-running project culminated in the publication of two massive dictionaries. The first, the *Maleische Woordboek Sameling*, or *Collectanea Malaica vocabularia*, in Dutch, Latin and Malay, was published in 1707–08 in Batavia by the printer Andreas Lambertus Loderus, in two large volumes, together containing five large Dutch dictionaries, all previously published in Batavia, the cumulative fruit of the previous century's dictionary makers. Its first volume (1707) holds the Malay *Vocabularium* by Wiltens and Danckaerts (1623); corrected and improved (with the help of Jan van Hasel and Albert Ruyll) by Heurnius in 1650; together with the Latin-Malay and Malay-Latin Dictionary by David Haex (Rome, 1631). Its second volume (1708) contains De Houtman's language guide of 1603, followed by C. Wiltens' *Dictionary*, as corrected and improved by Frederik Gueynier in 1677 and then again by Petrus van der Vorm in 1708.[38]

The other dictionary was the voluminous *Tésouro dos vocábulos das dúas línguas, Portuguéza, e Bélgica/ Woordenschat der twee Taalen, Portugeesch en Neder-*

36. J.L. Swellengrebel (1974). *In Leijdeckers voetspoor. Anderhalve eeuw bijbelvertaling en taalkunde in de Indonesische talen.* 's-Gravenhage: Nijhoff, vol. I (1820–1900): 11.

37. Kees Groeneboer (1998). *Gateway*, 30–31.

38. J.J. de Hollander (1893). *Handleiding bij de beoefening der Maleische taal en letterkunde.* Breda: Van Broese, 332 sub 4, 333 sub 8. Also: A. Teeuw (1961 [2013]). *A Critical Survey of Studies on Malay and Bahasa Indonesia.* The Hague: Nijhoff [Springer].

duitsch, produced in Batavia by Abraham Alewyn & Joannes Collé, and published in 1714 in Amsterdam on the orders of the Amsterdam Chamber of the VOC.[39]

Why those two big dictionaries? Why indeed? Traditionally, the Dutch used to keep their trading secrets in their own language. As Coolhaas (1980^2: 27) put it: "The Directors of the Company felt that it was extremely important not to divulge their business secrets". But of course, for their negotiations, trade and communication with the Portuguese and the Malays they needed good quality language tools. All the more so when it now came to the Sacred Scriptures: de Houtman's simple everyday spoken Malay would not do; a higher standard would be needed, in line with a key socio-cultural value widely held in the Dutch Republic: the Renaissance ideal of elevating and purifying the Dutch language.[40] The point was made explicit in Alewyn's 'Dedication' of his *Tesouro/ Woordenschat* (1714) to the VOC Director of the Amsterdam Chamber, in his complaint about the 'broken Portuguese' which he encountered everywhere in Batavia. As he writes:

> whereas from the Pulpit God's word is preached here [in Batavia] in good Portuguese, in daily intercourse everywhere one hears 'broken Portuguese' spoken, which is mixed up with lots of broken and bastard Malay and Dutch words picked up from the streets – as a consequence of which it is impossible to acquire proper pure Portuguese. (Alewyn & Collé 1714, *Opdragt*, p. 3–4)[41]

Alewyn and Collé had managed to acquire a large trilingual dictionary by the learned Portuguese Jesuit Benedictus Pereira (1536–1610), in Latin, Portuguese and Castilian, published posthumously in 1674 in Evora, followed by its English translation of 1701 by Alexander Justice in London.[42] Working with these two dictionaries, the standard which Collé and Alewyn now managed to achieve was "that in stead of speaking broken Portuguese and street Dutch" they managed to bring themselves up to "a pure and regular language" (p. 7).

Once those five standard dictionaries had been completed, what followed in the first half of the 18th century was a battle over the proper language and the right norm for translating the Sacred Scriptures of the States Bible. Here Alewyn

39. Abraham Alewyn & Joannes Collé, *Tesouro/Woordenschat*. Te Amsterdam, By Pieter van den Berge, op de Heylige Weg, in de Groene Berg, 1714, 933 pp. Short Title Catalogue Netherlands.

40. L. Van den Branden (1967). *Het streven naar verheerlijking, zuivering en opbouw van het Nederlands in de 16de eeuw*. Gent: Koninklijke Vlaamse Academie voor Taal- en Letterkunde.

41. But see also: G. Huet (1909). 'La communauté portugaise de Batavia', In *Revista Lusitania* 12, 3: 149–170.

42. Alexander Justice (1701). *A Compleat Account of the Portugueze Language. Being a Copious Dictionary of English with Portugueze, and Portugueze with English*. London: R. Janeway, 1701, 440 pp.

and others, like the churchmen and the VOC, were firmly of the view that biblical Dutch, the language of the official Dutch State Bible of 1637, was a *lingua sacra*,[43] and thus necessitated a high standard and an elevated style of language for its translation into High Malay and Pure Portuguese.

For its Malay translation, a new start was made by the Batavia minister, Melchior Leijdecker (1645–1701), who in 1691 was given the task of producing a full translation in High Malay.[44] The opposite view was to translate the Bible as accessibly as possible, hence into the language of the people – just as Saint Jerome had done around 400 in his *Biblia Sacra Vulgata*. This proposal was put forward by the Dutch colonial historian François Valentyn (1666–1727) in his *Deure der Waarheid* (Door of Truth, 1698). Yet it was Valentyn who lost, despite his long-running lobby and his production of two Malay translations, one in Low and one in High Malay.[45] The winner became the Swiss Malay scholar and bible translator, George Hendrik Werndly (1694–1744) – not so much for his position on the High/Low controversy, but rather because he had better Malay and also a better scholarly insight into the stylistic variation and grammatical structure of Malay. From 1722 Werndly worked in Batavia as secretary of the commission of revision. He then took the results to Amsterdam, where he oversaw the printing (in Roman script, on the orders of the VOC) of the Malay New Testament in 1731, and his full Malay Bible in 1733.[46] Staying on in Amsterdam, where he studied the work of the great Dutch linguist, Lambert ten Kate (1674–1731),[47] Werndly then in 1736 pub-

43. R. Salverda (2018). 'Empires and their Languages: Reflections on the History and the Linguistics of Lingua Franca and Lingua Sacra'. In: J. Braarvig & M.J. Geller (eds.). *Studies in Multilingualism, Lingua Franca and Lingua Sacra*. Berlin: Max Planck Institute for the History of Science, 13–18, 47.

44. Swellengrebel (1974), *In Leijdeckers voetspoor*, vol. 1: 13.

45. Siegfried Huigen (2023). *Shaping A Dutch East Indies: François Valentyn's VOC Empire*. Leiden: Brill: 79. But see: Christopher Joby (2025, to appear, *Internationale Neerlandistiek*), 'Nederlands en het ontstaan van de Maleise grammaticale traditie', with special focus on the little known but important Dutch malaicus Johannes Roman (d. 1658, from 1647 reverend in Batavia) and his *Grondt ofte Kort Bericht van de Maleysche tale* (Amsterdam: Paulus Matthysz, 1674, 1689^2) – mentioned neither in Huigen (2023) nor in Swellengrebel (1974–1978).

46. Swellengrebel (1974), *In Leijdeckers voetspoor*, vol. 1: 18–19.

47. Lourens de Vries (2018). 'Newton goes East: Natural Philosophy in the First Malay Grammar (1736) and the First Malay Bible (1733)'. In *The Bible Translator* vol. 69 (2), 214–232. Cf. Waruno Mahdi (2018). 'The First standard grammar of Malay: George Werndli's 1736 Maleische Spraakkunst'. In *Wacana. Journal of Humanities of Indonesia* vol. 19 (2), 257–290. Also, Reinier Salverda (2001). 'Newtonian Linguistics: The Contribution of Lambert ten Kate (1674–1731) to the Study of Language.' In Maire C. Davies et al. (eds.). *Proper Words in Proper Places. Studies in Lexicology and Lexicography in Honour of William Jervis Jones*. Stuttgart: Heinz, 115–132.

lished his own *Maleische Spraakkunst*[48] and in 1737 in Lingen, Prussia, became the first professor of Malay in Europe.

Work on the Portuguese translation began around 1645, by the Portuguese Protestant João Ferreira d'Almeida (born in Lisbon, died Batavia 1691). From 1656 onwards, he was a minister of the Reformed Portuguese Church in Batavia, the Church of the Black Portuguese and *Mardijkers* – Indian slaves captured at Malacca, but freed by the Dutch on condition they converted to Protestantism and took Dutch names.[49] Almeida's Portuguese New Testament was first published in Amsterdam in 1681, then also in Batavia in 1693, both on behalf of the VOC. By 1694 his Old Testament was ready in manuscript, but it took decades before the text could be corrected and revised. Chief revisor was the learned Johan Maurits Mohr (1716–1775) – eminent scholar, astronomer, volcanologist, theologian, president of the Batavia College for the training of church ministers, and for many years pastor of its Portuguese church – in which capacity he became revisor[50] and had to check whether and how the translations were correctly adapted from the Protestant Authorized version of the Dutch State Bible of 1637. In his Prefaces, in Dutch, Mohr reported his findings – not only on Almeida's three Portuguese Bibles of 1747, 1753 and 1773, all three in Batavia; but also on the Malay Bible of 1758, which was now published in Batavia too, this time in Arabic characters.

Thus, towards the end of the VOC era, both the Malay and the Portuguese Bible had at long last been translated and published by the Dutch – the outcome of the VOC's official, Calvinist language policy, after a long process of studying the other two languages and making dictionaries; assiduously working also to improve the quality of their translations; and in the end, after solid theological revision, publishing, as their crowning achievement, those Protestant Bibles in Malay and Portuguese.

48. Jan Gonda (1940). 'Taalbeschouwing en Taalbeoefening'. In: *BTLV* 99 (1): 15–34.

49. Adolf Heuken (1982). *Historical Sites of Jakarta*. Jakarta: Cipta Loka Caraka, 71. *Mardijker* from *merdeka* (free). Cf. note 94.

50. J.P.M. Groot (2009). *Van de Grote Rivier naar het Koningsplein: Het Bataviaasch Genootschap van Kunsten en wetenschappen*. Leiden PhD, 21. And also P.J. Veth (1885). 'Joan Mauritz Mohr (1716–1775)'. In *De Gids* 49 (1885), 55–87.

4. The *New Vocabulary* of 1780 – trilingual Batavia in a new key

In 1780, a new language guide was anonymously published in Batavia under the title of *Nieuwe Woordenschat*, or New Vocabulary (NW-1780).[51] Its contents were presented in three juxtaposed columns, each of which listed words and expressions from one of the three main languages spoken in Batavian society: Dutch, Malay and Portuguese.[52] Of particular interest is that those language data themselves here took centre stage, underlining the promise in its subtitle that this would deliver a 'Languages Made Easy' to Dutch newcomers in Batavia, who – by working from the Dutch column in this *Vocabulary* – could learn without difficulty both the Malay and Portuguese in the other two columns. Beyond this, however, the book offers almost no linguistic terminology; it just presents the data as they were and leaves it to the reader to figure out what and how to do with them. On first inspection then, NW-1780 was a book of colloquial usage made accessible in the simplest way possible, by systematic juxtaposition, observation, comparison, putting the data directly before the reader's eyes on the assumption that those data, while different in language and form, were actually the same in meaning and translation.

With those endless columns of words, however, the book does not look much like a guide for teaching or learning languages. It is neither a dictionary, nor is presentation alphabetical; and it appears to touch on just about anything. Each topic is handled on its own, covering the words and expressions from the three languages on the particular topic under discussion. Overall order is not very rigid. Subheadings, if present, are helpful in the three languages that are used to cover successive the lexical fields at issue – such as: *Days of the Week*, and *Months of the Year* (p.7); *Of Numbers* (p.8); *Moneys* (p.9); *Precious stones* (p.11); *Of Colours*, and *Measures and Weights* (p.12); *Writing Utensils* and related topics of modernity such as a writing room or study (p.13) – followed, further on, by headings such as: *Things relating to a House* (p.18); *Clothing of Native Women and Girls* (p.42); *Creams and Oils* (p.44); *Fragrant Herbs*, and *Male Native Clothing* (p.46).

In other parts, organisation looks more haphazard. Without any subheading we encounter a long list of *Trees* (p.52–57), followed by a section – this time with a heading – on *Trees with fruits from which to press oils* (p.57–61); then, without heading again, by another list of *Trees, including Fragrant trees* (p.65–67). On a different principle, we next find three short dictionaries, each in strict alpha-

51. *Nieuwe Woordenschat uyt het Nederduitsch in het gemeene Maleidsch en Portugeesch* zeer gemakkelyk voor die eerst op Batavia komen. Te Batavia, By Lodewyck Dominicus, Stadsdrukker op de Tygers-Gragt, aan de West-Zyde, 1780 [STCD].

52. Groeneboer (1998), *Gateway*: 25–27, 43 and 62.

betical order and properly headed – first, *Animals* (from *Aap* (monkey) to *Zwyn* (swine, p.72–81)); then *Plants* (from *Aardakers* (Jerusalem artichoke) to *Zwaluwwortel* (swallow root, p.82–97)); and *Minerals* (from *Agaat* (Agate) to *Zwavel* (Sulphur, p.97–100). Together, these last three lists amount to 43 pages of encyclopedic information. Finally, the book turns to actual language use, in a chapter headed (this time in Dutch only) *Common Sayings* (p.100–111), presenting all kinds of expressions, question-and-answers, conversations and further examples of practical language use. The book then comes to a rather sudden end, on a piece of explicit grammar, headed *Declinatio* (p.111–115); followed by the *Tenses and Moods* of the single Dutch regular verb '*werken*' (to work), from '*Ik werke doe of make wat*' (= 'I work, do or make something', p.116) all the way to '*Zy zullen gewerkt hebben*' (= 'They will have worked', p.121), juxtaposed to their equivalents in Malay, '*boewat*' or '*kirja*' and in Portuguese '*faay*'.

All of this is useful and practical. The book is a wide-ranging collection of everyday information on all kinds of everything – a vademecum, really, of heavenly bodies, the weather, seasons, the landscape, insults, professions, kinship terms, household utensils, body parts, feelings, illnesses, foods, fruits, flowers, working the land, finery, marriage, the house, gardens, calendars, numbers, calculations, arithmetic, and so on.

So one wonders, what is this? It looks as if this could be somebody's little book of language notes on their everyday activities, written down to keep track of and memorize the colloquial usages they were picking up along the way. But whose notebook could this be?

My guess is that NW-1780 is a collection of notes put together over many years by someone like J.C.M. Radermacher (1741–1783), founder in 1778 of the Batavian Society (Bataviaasch Genootschap), the first western learned society established in Asia. As we know from Zuiderweg (1991) and Groot (2008), Radermacher was the Society's driving force – a high-ranking and very well-connected colonial official, Councillor Extraordinary of the Council of the Indies, stepson-in-law to governor-general Reinier de Klerk (1710–1780). He was also Chief Merchant of the VOC, Administrator of Batavia City, and Commissioner of the Uplands; Freemason and founder of the first Masonic Lodge "La Choisie" in 1762 in Batavia, while also keeping order and justice as a Judge, a Bailiff, and Colonel of the city's Militia, but equally a practical Enlightenment man who gave Batavia its first city lights.[53]

53. Groot 2009, *Van de Grote Rivier naar het Koningsplein*, 52; Adrienne Zuiderweg (1991). 'Jacobus Cornelis Mattheus Radermacher (1741–1783), een notabele wetenschapper te Batavia'. In *Indische Letteren* vol. 6, 161–174 [DBNL]; also: Jean Gelman Taylor (1983), *Social World of Batavia*, 85–86; and *Encyclopaedie van Nederlandsch Oost-Indië*. 's-Gravenhage/Leiden: Nijhoff/Brill, vol. 3 (1919), 531–532.

He also was a well-travelled botanist and natural scientist who had done extensive research on the trees of Java, which he published in 1780–1782 in Batavia in three volumes under his own name, as the *Naamlyst der planten, die gevonden worden op het eiland Java* [Names of the Plants found on the island of Java]. Using at least five different languages – Latin, Malay, Dutch, Javanese and French – this *Naamlijst* brings together the world's botanic terminology from the West (Linnaeus) as well as the East (Rumphius), using the same grid-like format we also find in NW-1780 in its list of *Trees* (pp. 61–67) and its dictionary of *Plants* (pp. 82–97).

Beyond this, in Radermacher's further publications between 1780 and 1786 in the *Verhandelingen* [Transactions] of the Batavian Society,[54] we find the same interest in Indonesian language data collection on his travels – specifically of Malay, Banjarese, Biadjoos, Makassarese, Boni and Balinese – which he published, alongside his own Nederduytsch, again in the same grid-like juxtaposition. On this evidence we conclude that Radermacher was definitely involved in the production of the anonymous NW-1780, though he may well have had other collaborators, colleagues and servants helping him out, in particular for the data in Malay and Portuguese.

By 1780 Radermacher had already spent more than twenty years in Batavia, in an impressive career, rising from second administrator in 1758 to Councillor Extraordinary of the Council of the Indies in its governing centre in the Kasteel of Batavia. There he was in an excellent position to get the official decree of 15 May 1778[55] passed, which issued the combined order both to reprint the Portuguese *Tesouro/Woordschat* (1714) by Alewyn and Collé, and to publish the NW-1780, calling this "een handleiding in de Nederduitsche spraakkunst (a manual of Dutch grammar) in *Nederduitsch*, *Maleidsch* and *Portugeesch*". This is the only official document we have concerning the *Nieuwe Woordenschat* of 1780; it establishes a direct link between those two word books through their title of *Woordenschat*; and their common focus on the Portuguese language as spoken in the streets of Batavia.

---

54. *Verhandelingen Bataviaasch Genootschap* (online at Harvard University, Hathi Trust Digital Collection): (i) Radermacher's 'Register der Geslagten van de drie Ryken der Natuur, in het Maleidsch, Hollandsch en Latyn', vol 1 (1779), 87–112; (ii) his 'Beschryving van het Eiland Borneo', vol. 2 (1780), 107–148); and (iii) his 'Korte Beschryving van het Eiland Celebes', vol. 4 (1786), 199–286.

55. J.A. Van der Chijs (ed.). Register op de Generale Resolutien van het Kasteel te Batavia, 1632-1805, vol. III (1806), 270. Cf. Hugo Schuchardt (1890), *Kreolische Studien IX*, esp p. 18. Also: *Bibliothèque de M. l'Abbé P. Favre* (1888–1889). Reprint: Paris: Maisonneuve & Larose, 1974. See also: Denys Lombard, 'En mémoire de l'Abbé P. Favre', In: *Archipel* 12 (1976), 3–8.

Taking a closer look now into NW-1780 and its trilingual contents, we note how the book offers its readers all kinds of entry points to its language data. As we open the book, its initial chapters start by presenting simple bits from the three languages. Its first page opens with a series of seven pairs of short, contrasting adjectives from everyday spoken Dutch – *groot/klein, hoog/laag, lang/kort, vol/leeg, heet/koud, vet/mager, wyd/nauw* [big/small, high/low, long/short, full/empty, fat/thin, hot/cold, wide/narrow] – triggering our interest in these common distinctions in Dutch; suggesting some mnemotechnic activity being applied to these antonyms, not least when trying to acquire the equivalent expressions in the adjacent columns, while we readers are learning how to say things in Malay and Portuguese which we already know in Dutch. An effective trilingual first lesson, from which we can work our way (or ways) towards mastering the language data of the other two columns.

The next page continues with a further twelve antonymic pairs of adjectives, then moves on to a second series of common words in everyday Dutch, this time nine Verbs (not antonymic; and not using terms like 'adjective' or 'verb' or predicate) – *geeven, zeggen, leeren, schryven, vraagen, antwoorden, leenen, zenden* and *belooven* [give, say, learn, write, ask, answer, borrow, send and promise]. The adjacent Malay column presents their translational equivalents, written differently from today perhaps, but when read out aloud clearly the same words (or rather, their verbal roots, without inflectional adornments) as spoken in today's basic Malay – *kassi* [to give], *kata* [to say], *adjar* [to learn or teach], *toelies* [to write], *tanja* [to ask], *menjawoet* [to reply], *pinjang* [to borrow], *kieriem* [to send] and *berjanjie* [to promise] – which, like those Dutch words, are today still written almost exactly as back then in NW-1780.[56] As for the Portuguese words in the third column, these may look slightly different from today, but with a little effort and a Portuguese pocket dictionary they are easily identifiable as Portuguese words as spoken in Batavia back then. The systematic NW-1780 presentation in adjacent columns of these translation equivalents clearly provides its readers with a helpful language learning device.

Following on after these first three pages of single words – adjectives, verbs, then adverbs – we encounter on p. 5 the first question in the book, an everyday one – *Waar woont gy?* [Where do you live?], with its answer – *Hier dichte by* [Here close by] – which together constitute a simple oral dialogue (as in a Catechism), a first key step into further language learning. Woven into the text, we encounter a succession of further such patterns – first, single Dutch nouns in iso-

---

56. See J.M. Echols & H. Shadily (1979), *An Indonesian-English Dictionary*. Second Edition. Ithaca: Cornell University Press, s.v. *kasi, kata, adjar, tulis, tanja, djawab, pindjam, kirim, djandji.*

lation, like *Een schrijfvertrek* (A writing room; p. 13); then, a noun-verb group like *Medicynen gebruiken* (taking medicines, p. 37); and on p. 49 our first basic sentence pattern, *Hy koopt een thuyn* (He buys a garden), followed by a further list of such simple descriptive sentences, all on the same pattern, all to do with marriage: *Hy zoekt een vrouw, Hy trouwt, Hij houd feest, Hy danst, Hy noodigt gasten, Hy springt* [He finds a woman, He marries, He holds a party, He dances, He invites guests, He jumps, p. 50]. The next step then is learning how to make these basic sentences longer by extension, as in: *De bruydegom staat op.// En reddert de boel* [The bridegroom rises//and clears up the mess]; and *Hy gaat na het land// van zyn schoonvader* [He goes to the garden/of his father-in-law (p. 51)].

After passing through the *Trees* section, we then get to read a five-page narrative (from p. 60–65), which expands the above-mentioned bridegroom-and-father-in-law fragment into a five-page tale about a man walking along a tree-lined road, past a well, to a grave near a tall Waringin tree, where an old man awaits who tells him that this is the grave of his relatives, and asks him to swear that he will bury him there as his wife's father (which he does, after having asked for forgiveness); they then embrace, pray and weep, after which the man comes to a place of beautiful flowers and many a Cambodia tree (frangipani), the traditional sign of a Malay graveyard[57] (p. 60–65).

The book offers a succession of such types of data, each in the three different languages – going from simple words, to word groups, then small sentences, which can be developed into longer sentences; and how these can be joined into larger narratives (including dialogues, tales, questions and answers) until we come to the final section of the book, on spoken conversations in the three languages, headed, in Dutch only: 'Gemeene Spreekwyzen' (= *Common Sayings*), which features wishes, greetings, exchanges and question-answer pairs like: 'What are you looking for?', 'How much?', 'Bring me some other food', 'Is it true?', 'What is new?' 'Have some patience', 'I will hit you', 'Where do you live?' (giving lots of Batavia addresses), etcetera. All this in its customary trilingual presentation, and without any linguistic terminology, yet all the way applying a systematic method to the data and clearly serving the purpose of what the book was called in 1778: a *spraakkunst* (grammar) of those three languages.

The real innovation here was that NW-1780 with its grid-like presentation offered a linguistic tool for doing a systematic analysis of Batavia's trilingualism, on the basis of real data of spoken language, and nothing else: no terminology, no description, no theory – solely by displaying the plain facts of those three lan-

57. Anthony Burgess (1981³). *Language Maid Plane (Made Plain). Revised edition.* Glasgow: Fontana/ Collins (ch. 7 'Malay', 186–187) discusses one of the loveliest of the traditional *pantuns*, known everywhere in South-east Asia", sings of love and death, longing and the Cambodia tree.

guages in juxtaposition. Thus, its enlightened maker(s) produced an ingenious language learning instrument geared to making structural analyses *avant la lettre*, which its readers/learners could do by themselves, just using their own minds and wits – in effect, *doing* linguistics rather than talking about it.

The new language learning methods involved in this approach – i.e. learning by doing; using concrete language data and examples in translation; while starting from what they already know from their own mother tongue – were originally developed by the Czech philosopher and pedagogue Jan Amos Comenius [1592–1670], in particular in his *Janua Linguarum* (Deure off Portaal der Taalen, 1638; Door of Languages) and *Vestibulum* (1658). In Amsterdam, where Comenius lived from 1656 until his death, his ideas, books and learning methods were well known in VOC circles. Those ideas may also have been behind the realization, a century later in Batavia in the circle around Radermacher, "that Dutch could only be taught to the Indigenous people by means of Portuguese and Malay" (Groeneboer 1989, *Gateway*, 43).

With its modern approach and enlightened organisation, the *Nieuwe Woordenschat* of 1780 was far ahead of its time. In the end, however, the new book was almost totally forgotten; by its second edition of 1802 its Portuguese section had already disappeared, and it took well over a century for the original edition to be rediscovered by Schuchardt in 1890, who teased out from the Malay and Portuguese data it contained, what further discoveries and yet unthought-of new findings could on this basis be made in linguistics, in creolistics and in contact linguistics.

5. Unity and diversity – One language, and many others as well

Before we come to Schuchardt, however, we will first take a look at two more general though contrasting developments after 1800 in the domain of language, viz. (i) the growing trend in the archipelago towards unity of language, and (ii) the growing numbers of languages that were being discovered and described.

5.1 Towards a united Indonesian language

When after the London Treaty of 1814 the Kingdom of the Netherlands was given back its Indonesian colonies, the Dutch soon took a line quite different from the British in India. In India, colonial men were expected to be rulers and gentlemen of Empire, with a proper English military or classical education from a good school. The Dutch, on the other hand, wanted their colonial administrators to be well trained in law, business, administration and to have a command of indigenous languages, preferably Malay and Javanese. Around the middle of the 19th century, this then also became the standard for training their native administrators – whereas all through that period hardly anyone ever mentioned the importance of the Dutch language.[58]

Even more remarkable, when the British in 1835, following Lord Macaulay's English Education Act, decided that Education in India should be in English, and not in Sanskrit or Arabic, the Dutch, instead, frowned upon the idea that their own language should be propagated among the native population. This would be far too costly for the government; learning Dutch might also give the Indonesian natives the wrong ideas; they might become arrogant and find working beneath their dignity; and it might well lead to the same "bastardization' of the Dutch language which occurred in the Black English spoken in Surinam".[59] As a consequence, the idea "of introducing Dutch as a general medium of communication, of replacing the lingua franca Malay with Dutch, was permanently abandoned in 1864".[60]

1864 thus became a pivotal moment for the future of the two languages: Dutch was to remain the preserve of Europeans, alongside a pragmatic acceptance of Malay as a general language of administration. From here on, a long-drawn-out process began of standardization and regulation of Malay, under the direction of the Dutch, which culminated in Van Ophuysen's official government *Wordlist* for the spelling of Malay in Latin characters (1901), and his authoritative standard *Malay Grammar* (1910).[61]

On the Indonesian side this development was met by a growing desire for a good school education for their children, in Dutch as well as in Malay. This led in 1918, in the new *People's Council* (Volksraad) in Batavia, to the recognition of Malay as a co-official language. Then next, in 1928, the Second Indonesian Youth Conference adopted their epoch-making Pledge of "One people, one country, one language: Indonesian".[62] In 1945 this was followed by the Proclamation of Indonesian Independence and its declaration of Malay as Indonesian, the language of

58. Groeneboer (1998). *Gateway*, 72–77.

59. Groeneboer (1998). *Gateway*, 119.

60. Groeneboer (1998). *Gateway*, 122 and 297.

61. Ophuijsen's Wordlist (1900) and his Malay Grammar (1910): both in Dutch. As for the real *mission civilisatrice* of the Dutch, we might suggest – with the Abbé Raynal in his *Histoire des deux Indes* (1780, vol. 1, 2–3) – the role of the Dutch as the Phoenicians of the East, on account of their introduction of Latin script for Malay in 1901, together with their earlier decision to print their Malay and Portuguese bible translations in the 18th century in Latin characters too. Cf. Salverda (2022), 'On Reading Raynal', *Diciottesimo Secolo*, 88.

62. Groeneboer (1998). *Gateway*, 261–266.

the new Republic: *Bahasa negara ialah bahasa Indonesia* [The language of our country is the Indonesian language].[63] This now became the sole vehicle for the new Republic, and this political triumph of Bahasa Indonesia as the new national language[64] heralded the end of the Dutch East Indies when the Indonesians in 1950, straight after Independence, abolished Dutch as its language of education.[65] Instead, the new Republic invested heavily in its new national language, and by around 1980 "the speech of educated Indonesians in the capital city of Jakarta and other big towns had generally become the accepted model of the language which people in the provinces try to imitate".[66]

5.2 Discovering and describing the other languages in the archipelago

Alongside the rise to prominence of Indonesian, there was, during the 19th and 20th centuries, a different but no less important development in the field of languages. To begin with, there was the disappearance from the Dutch East Indies of Portuguese, which was no longer included in the second and third editions of the *Nieuwe Woordenschat* (1802, 1815); and linked to this its replacement by Malay as the general *lingua franca*, especially in Batavia, whose population changed too: in 1815, on a total of some 47.000 inhabitants, Batavia now counted 2.000 Europeans; 11.000 Chinese; 300 Arabs and 100 Moors; 18.500 Natives; and 14.000 slaves – and so too did their *Betawi Malay* language, which acquired features of Balinese, Javanese, Sundanese, Chinese, Arab, Portuguese, Dutch and English.[67] As Raffles noted in his *History of Java* (1817: 358–363): Batavia speech was now a "jargon of Dutch, Portuguese, Chinese, Javanese and Maláyu".[68]

Other languages too began to attract interest, for example Javanese. Of special importance has been the herculean *Dictionary of Javanese* by C.F. Winter (1799–1859) and J.A. Wilkens (1813–1888), their joint 26 folio volumes (1851–1859),

63. Groeneboer (1998). *Gateway*, 283–284, 291. See also: Khaidir Anwar (1980). *Indonesian. The Development and Use of A National Language.* Yogyakarta: Gadjah Mada University Press, 12, 50; and James Sneddon (2003). *The Indonesian Language. Its history and role in modern society.* Sydney: UNSW Press, 113.

64. Benedict Anderson (1983 [1991²]), *Imagined Communities. Reflections on the Origin and Spread of Nationalism*, London/New York: *Verso*, 120–121, 132, 177–178.

65. See: S. Dardjowidjojo (1978), *Sentence Patterns of Indonesian*, Hawaii, 3-5, 291; Salverda (2009), 'Doing Justice', 154, 167; Sneddon (2003). *Indonesian language*, 113.

66. Anwar (1980), *Indonesian*, 185.

67. Muhadjir (1981). *Morphology of Jakarta Dialect, Affixation and Reduplication.* Jakarta: Seri Nusa, 1–7. Hans Kähler (1966). *Wörterverzeichnuis des Omong Djakarta.* Berlin: Dietrich Reimer. And L. Castles (1967). 'The ethnic profile of Djakarta', in: *Indonesia* 1: 153–204.

68. Thomas Stamford Raffles (1817). *The History of Java.* London: John Murray, 358–363.

followed by the 43 of Wilkens alone, all held today in Leiden University Library. In the Netherlands, meanwhile, a new Dutch Bible Society (NBG) was established in 1814, giving a new impulse to its bible translation activities, especially after these translators were upgraded to 'language officials' and became part of the colonial service. Looking back from the 1970s on their achievements, the Dutch historian Swellengrebel[69] lists a total of 52 indigenous languages, each with at least one (Protestant) bible book translated. These were all documented on a map (in Swellengrebel 1970, vol. 2:341) with an annotated Language List running from Alfurese to South-Toradja (p.297–309), and a series of chapters on the NBG's chief translators and the languages they had been working on.

As time went by, more and more languages began to be reported. In the 1850s, it was Darwin's fellow evolutionist, Alfred Russell Wallace [1823–1913], who like a second Radermacher, spent eight years doing field research in the Moluccas, gathering many more language data than Pigafetta, which he then published in his *The Malay Archipelago* (1869) – in two tables: one of nine words in 59 Indonesian languages, from Malay and Javanese to Solor and Bajau (Sea Gypsies); and the other of 117 words in 33 languages, from Malay to Mysol and Baju; all neatly arranged in adjacent columns for comparative purposes.[70]

In 1875, similarly, the East Indies archivist J.A. van der Chijs [1802–1882], in his first essay in colonial bibliography, his *Proeve eener Nederlandsch-Indische Bibliografie* (Essay in Dutch East-Indies bibliography)[71] listed some twenty languages, from Alfurese, Buginese, Chinese, Dayak, Formosan, Japanese, Letti, Madurese, Makassarese to Malay, and a further nine with an ancient indigenous script, Balinese, Batak, Dayak, Javanese, Madurese, Nias, Sangirese Sundanese and Tu'undulu.

In their footsteps, as the Netherlands East Indies expanded further, we find growing numbers of 'language officials', especially during the first half of the 20th century – not just in the Dutch Bible Society or the *Kantoor voor de Volkslectuur*, but also in the Archaeological Service, in the Royal Batavian Society of Arts and Sciences, the new University Faculties of Arts and Law in Batavia, the Government Bureau for Native Affairs, and many other such departments of the Dutch colonial administration.[72] Alongside this, there was the vast multilingual docu-

69. Swellengrebel (ed.). *In Leijdeckers voetspoor*. 's-Gravenhage: Nijhoff 2 vols, 1974–1978.

70. Alfred Russell Wallace (1869). *The Malay Archipelago*. New York: Dover: 468–493.

71. J.A. Van der Chijs (1875). *Proeve eener Nederlandsch-Indische Bibliografie, 1659–1870* [Essay in Dutch East-Indies bibliography], in: *Verhandelingen* van het Bataviaasch Genootschap, Batavia: Bruining & Wijt, vol. 37, 320–323.

72. A. Teeuw (1973). 'Taalambtenaren, taalafgevaardigden en Indonesische taalwetenschap', in: *Forum der letteren* 14 nr. 3, 163–180.

mentation on traditional indigenous laws and anthropology, brought together in some 39 volumes covering all areas of the Malay archipelago, by the Leiden scholar Cornelis van Vollenhoven [1874–1933] in his magnum opus *Het adatrecht van Nederlandsch-Indië* [Adat law of the Dutch East Indies], 3 vols, 1918–1933 (today online in Delpher).[73]

Not long afterwards, in the *Atlas of the Tropical Netherlands* of 1938, a first map of the languages of Indonesia was published by the Dutch translator and Indonesianist S.J. Esser (1900–1944).[74] This comprehensive map of all known indigenous languages in Indonesia presented some 200 languages in all, divided into three different groups: first the Papua languages; then also the North Halmahera family (Ternatan, Tidorese), both groups at the time still largely unknown; and then, thirdly, the vast main group of Malayo-Polynesian languages [today: 'Austronesian languages'], which covered the whole archipelago with its 17 often large subgroupings containing at least 94 languages and some 10 dialects with their names, from Acehnese in the far west to Yotafa-Sarmi near the north-eastern coast of West Papua.

Today, well into the 21st century, we know very much more about the languages of Indonesia. There is a most informative array of detailed maps and language data available in Robert Cribb's *Historical Atlas of Indonesia* (2000), which presents "over two hundred Austronesian languages and over 150 Papuan (Melanesian) languages".[75] In 2007, Christopher Moseley's *Encyclopedia of the World's Endangered Languages* gave detailed information on the very many Austronesian and Papuan languages in Indonesia and widely dispersed in the surrounding oceans.[76] In 2008 the Indonesian national language centre, Pusat Bahasa Jakarta, published its *Atlas of Languages and Language Maps*[77] for a total

73. R. Salverda (2009). 'Doing Justice in a Plural Society: A Postcolonial Perspective on Dutch Law and Other Legal Traditions in the Indonesian Archipelago, 1600-Present', in: *Dutch Crossing* 33 no. 2, 153–171, esp.154, 167. Cf. Salverda (1989), 'Nederlands als wetenschappelijke bronnentaal', 401–407.

74. *Atlas van Tropisch Nederlands.* Batavia: Topografische Dienst Nederlandsch-Indië/KNAG, Blad 9 en 9B: 'TALEN door S.J. Esser'. On Esser, cf. Swellengrebel 1978. *In Leijdecker's voetspoor*, vol. II, 71–75.

75. Robert Cribb (2000). *Historical Atlas of Indonesia.* Surrey: Curzon, ch. 2, 29–72. Also: Stephen A. Wurm, Sarmi-Yotafa languages', in: Chris Mosley (ed.) (2007). *Encyclopedia of the World's Endangered Languages.* London: Routledge, 567. For 'Yotafa-Sarmi': Cribb (2000), map 35.

76. Chr. Moseley (2007). *Encyclopedia*, 420–435 [Austronesian & Papuan languages, 438–442].

77. H. Dendy Sugono (ed.)(2008). *Bahasa dan Peta Bahasa di Indonesia* [Languages and Language Maps in Indonesia]. Jakarta: Pusat Bahasa/Departemen Pendidikan Nasional.

of 690 languages; and today on the *SIL Global/Etnologue* website the count for 'Languages of Indonesia' stands at 704 languages.[78]

In line with this we note also the increasing international cooperation between Indonesian and other linguists in research projects and handbooks, of which I here name the following five: Adelaar & Himmelman (2005), *The Austronesian languages of Asia and Madagascar*; Ansaldo & Meyerhoff (2020), *The Routledge Handbook of Pidgins and Creole Languages*; Gil & Schaffer (2020), *Austronesian Undressed: How and Why Languages become Isolating*; Michaelis et al. (eds.) (2013), *The Atlas of Pidgin and Creole Language Structures* (4 vols); and Subhan Zein (2020), *Language Policy in Superdiverse Indonesia.*[79]

6. Language contact, *Sprachmischung* and Creolistics

6.1 Hugo Schuchardt and the Portuguese Creole of Batavia and Tugu (1890)

In the 1880s a new chapter in linguistics began when Hugo Schuchardt (1842–1927) turned to the study of pidgins and creoles. At the time just forty years old, he had already made a brilliant career with his major publications: *Der Vokalismus des Vulgärlateins* (his PhD, 1866–67, 3 vols); his *Phonétique comparée* (1874); his *Basque studies* (from 1880 onwards); his *Schlawo-Deutsch und Schlawo-Italienisch* (1884–1886); his earlier *Kreolische Studien* (from 1882); and his critical attack of 1885 on the Sound Laws of the dominant school in linguistics, the *Neogrammarians* (Junggrammatiker). He was not only a leading romanist and latinist, a philologist, phonetician and historical linguist, but also a freethinking iconoclast,[80] and an excellent scholar of many languages, Latin, Portuguese, Hungarian, Slavonic, Basque, Malay, Esperanto and Lingua franca. Today his

78. Stephen A. Wurm, 'Shortcomings in present knowledge, and current work', in Moseley (2007). *Encyclopedia*, 454–461. Cf. the well-documented Wikipedia report, *Languages of Indonesia* (2023), consulted June 2024. And also: *SIL Global* (August, 2024).

79. Alexander Adelaar & Nikolaus Himmelman (2005). *The Austronesian languages of Asia and Madagascar.* London: Routledge; Umberto Ansaldo & Miriam Meyerhoff (2020). *The Routledge Handbook of Pidgins and Creole Languages.* Abingdon: Routledge; David Gil & Antoinette Schaffer (2020). *Austronesian Undressed: How and Why Languages become Isolating.* Amsterdam: Benjamins; Susanne Maria Michaelis et al. (eds.) (2013). *The Atlas of Pidgin and Creole Language Structures.* Oxford: Oxford University Press; and Subhan Zein (2020). *Language Policy in Superdiverse Indonesia.* New York/London: Routledge.

80. Raf van Rooy (2020). 'Schuchardt the Iconoclast', in: Van Rooy, *Language or Dialect. The History of a Conceptual Pair.* Oxford: Oxford University Press, 231–243.

many publications are available online at the Hugo Schuchardt Archiv in the University of Graz, Austria.[81]

His interest in creoles grew from his knowledge of Portuguese and his wideranging correspondence with scholars and missionaries in Portuguese-speaking areas all around the world. On that basis he produced his solid 255-page monograph, *Ueber das Malaioportugiesische von Batavia und Tugu* (1890), a thorough investigation of the Portuguese-based creole language that used to be spoken in the 17th and 18th centuries in Batavia, the capital of the Dutch colonial empire in the Malay archipelago (today, Jakarta, Indonesia). In the book's opening chapter he presented the earliest creole text which he could find, a dialogue in a mix of Malay-Portuguese and German, set in Batavia, between two soldiers, a Swedish old hand and a Dutch newcomer, written by a philosophical German gardner, George Meister, who from 1677 to 1687 had spent time in the East, mostly in Batavia, and then in 1692 published his tale in Dresden, Germany.

Batavia became a key focus of Schuchardt's investigation of the question, How this Portuguese creole might have changed under the influence of its Malay speakers. This was the fundamental question to be investigated in linguistics, that of Language Mixing, or *Sprachmischung*: "Of all the problems with which we are concerned in linguistics today, none is of greater significance, really, than that of language mixing".[82] Dismissing the purist tenet, "There is no mixed language" of Max Müller (1823–1900), Schuchardt took the opposite view: "There is no completely unmixed language".[83] The key source on which he based his new investigation was the trilingual *Nieuwe Woordenschat* (New Vocabulary, NW-1780, cf, Schuchardt 1890: 18), which as we saw in Section 4, was originally published in 1780 in Batavia in Dutch, Malay and Portuguese. As Schuchardt observed: "the Tugu dialect presents us with one of the most peculiar examples of language mixing",[84] which makes it an excellent example for studying the Malay influence on this 18th-century Portuguese creole.

Schuchardt's book is a difficult and complex book, hard to read on account of the five languages he used: German, Dutch, French, Malay and Portuguese. Equally challenging were its contents – its many densely written pages of Malay

81. Hugo Schuchardt Archiv, https://gams.uni-graz.at.

82. *Schuchardt-Brevier, Ein Vademecum der allgemeinen Sprachwissenschaft*, Ed. Leo Spitzer. Darmstadt, WBG, 1976² [1928², 1922], III 'Sprachmischung': 150–163.

83. *Schuchardt-Brevier* 1976: 153 – against Max Müller: "es gibt keine Mischsprache", Schuchardt held: "es gibt keine völlig ungemischte Sprache". Originally from: Schuchardt (1883), 'Schlawodeutsches und Schlawo – italienisch: 1'.

84. "der tugusche Dialekt bietet uns eines dir merkwürdigsten Beispiele von Sprachmischung dar" (Schuchardt 1890: 23).

and Portuguese data; its detailed discussions of the grammar and vocabulary of Malay and Portuguese; discussed in heavy-going academic German; with extensive expert annotations in its various languages; and with detailed and precise references to the many sources he consulted, including the expert publications of the best Dutch Indonesianists he could find, scholars such as Van der Tuuk, Van de Wall, Kern, Klinkert, Mansvelt, Pijnappel, Roorda van Eysinga, Homan, van der Meulen and many others.[85]

On the basis of these sources and data Schuchardt discussed many original issues – questions unheard of in the time of Radermacher – on key points such as: (1) What about the study of Batavia Malay: what kind of language was this, was it a creole, a pidgin, a mixed language?;[86] (2) How was Portuguese impacted by the *Inner Form* of Malay?;[87] (3) How did Malay Creole syntax work, and what about its use of special words (creole markers) like *ada, sama* and *dengan*?;[88] (4) Could there perhaps be a Dutch Creole – or were there any?;[89] and (5) the question provoked by Max Müller: how could genetically unrelated languages possibly be mixed?

Given its level of difficulty, the book was for a long time more a work of praise than of thorough study. So it was a major step forwards when Philippe Maurer in 2011 published his thoroughly annotated systematic reconstruction in English of Schuchardt's study. But note how – just as Schuchardt selected only the Malay and Portuguese data from the *Nieuwe Woordenschat* (but not its Dutch materials) – so too in 2011 Maurer significantly shortened Schuchardt's book, by focussing only on the data and leaving out his key discussions of notes 87 to 90 above, to which we will come back in Chapter 7 below.

Isabella Matauschek (2014) has made a justified criticism of Maurer's reduction.[90] Even so, Maurer's reconstruction deserves great praise for the detailed, six-line annotations [in Portuguese, Creole, Malay, Dutch, German and English] which he produced for each of Schuchardt's 524 mixed Malayo-Portuguese utter-

85. For details see Teeuw (1961). *A critical survey of studies on Malay and Bahasa Indonesia.* 's-Gravenhage: Nijhoff [Reprint: Dordrecht, Springer 2013]. Also: J.J. de Hollander (1893, 6th ed.). *Handleiding bij de beoefening der Maleische taal- en letterkunde.* Breda, ch. 8.

86. Schuchardt (1890). *Kreolisch IX*, 154–173 – Batavia Malay

87. Schuchardt (1890), *Kreolisch IX*, 182–193 – The term *Inner Form* refers to Humboldt 1836.

88. Schuchardt (1890) *Kreolisch IX*, 193–247 – creole particles like *ada, sama*' (228–230), and *dengan* (235).

89. Schuchardt (1890). *Kreolisch IX*, 148 – Dutch? Here Schuchardt gives data from 1882 collected by Mr Metzger, Indies literature, texts by Annie Foore, IJzerman, Van Rees and Multatuli.

90. Isabella Matauschek (2014). 'Malay – Latin of the Pacific: Hugo Schuchardt's pursuit of language mixing and creole languages in the Malay world', in: *Indonesia and the Malay World* vol. 42, nr. 123, pp. 246–266 [Routledge/Taylor & Francis].

ances [and his link to Radermacher's data of 1780], which Maurer presents in his Texts chapter (Maurer 2011: 127–194); and also for the annotated lexical items in his Word Lists (Maurer 2011: 195–304), especially their creole etymologies, which Maurer drew from a wide range of etymological dictionaries, in Dutch, Malay, Javanese, Papia Kristang creole, Indo-Portuguese, Portuguese, Old Portuguese.

Here, as an example of Schuchardt's Malay-Portuguese data, we start from Maurer's sentence number 1 (2011: 128), as follows:

NW-1780:49	Ile freta ung pedas chang.	Ile kompra ung orta	na su kontenti
Spelling 1780:	Ille frëtta oen pedas tjang.	Ille kompra oeng orta.	Na soe konteentie
Ling. gloss:	3SG hire ART piece land.	3SG buy ART plot	LOCPOSS pleasure
Holl. 1780:	Hy huurt een stuk lands.	Hy koopt een thuyn.	Na zyn genoegen
Mal. 1780:	Dia sëwa sapotong tana.	Dia blie satoe koboong.	Dalam soekanja
German:	Er pachtet ein Stück Land.	Er kauft ein Garten.	Nach sein Vergnügen
English:	He hired a piece of land.	He bought a plot for planting as pleased	

This first example of Maurer's edition corresponds to Schuchardt's numbers 520–523 (1890: 105–106) and to Radermacher's data numbers 7 to 5 in *Nieuwe Woordenschat* (1780: 49 from below). However, this doesn't yet show how Malay and Portuguese interact. For this we need Maurer's next example, nr 2, where Malay/Javanese *luku* (plow) has clearly made its way into Portuguese; and nr 3, Malay *kandang* (stable) and 4, Malay *betel* (siri), which both had been borrowed and inserted into Portuguese already.

An important general outcome of Maurer's analysis are his impressive statistics and percentages of language elements occurring in the two corpora he has produced – a solid basis, which enables his readers to check every one of his sentences, words and annotations, and so, step-by-step, to verify his analysis of Schuchardt's creolisations (see Maurer p. 195):

i. first, in the Batavia corpus: 72,5% of Portuguese words; 3% Indo-Portuguese; 12% Malay; 7,5% Dutch; 1% other; and 4% unknown –
ii. secondly, in the Tugu Corpus, with broadly similar outcomes: 75% Portuguese words; 3% Indo-Portuguese; some 10% Malay, and 6% Dutch.

6.2 Schuchardt's impact on Dutch and Creole linguistics

Looking back, we can now trace the impact which Schuchardt has had on subsequent developments in Dutch and Creole linguistics.

First, from 1890 up to the second world war we find a series of Dutch scholars who were deeply interested in Schuchardt's writings on creoles – Veth; Prick van Wely; Van Ginneken; Hesseling; De Geus & Van Dam and Gonda – with their combined expertise in Dutch colonial lexicography, sociolinguistics, history of language, language teaching and general linguistics[91] – who took Schuchardt's ideas further in their own publications on creole languages in the (former) Dutch colonies. In striking contrast we also note how the Dutch Indonesianists mentioned above (p.370), with whom Schuchardt himself had sought such extensive and lively debates in his monograph of 1890, by and large did not reciprocate. Their interest, instead, was in Dutch colonial language policy, with its central focus on the standardization, regularization and practical educational build-up of Malay as the archipelago's language of general intercourse. They were not much interested in Schuchardt's pursuit of mixed Malayo-Portuguese, which was dying out anyway. And let us not forget the longstanding Dutch attitude against language mixing and 'broken language', which dated as far back as Alewyn's *Tesouro* of 1714.

It took a long time until scholarly interest in Schuchardt's ideas and writings revived and took off again in 1971 with the classic *Pidginization and Creolization of Languages*, edited by Dell Hymes, followed by the young Dutch creolist scholars Meijer and Muysken (1977) and many others such as Hall, Bickerton, Holm (1988–89) and Clancey Clements (2009).[92] As a result, today Creolistics is a thriving internationalised field of study in modern linguistics, with a strong new focus on Schuchardt's creole writings, boosted by Maurer's new edition of 2011 of Schuchardt's *Batavia and Tugu Creole*, and supported by the formidable open

91. P.J. Veth (2003 [1889]), *Uit Oost en West*. Ed. Nicoline van der Sijs. Amsterdam/Antwerpen: Veen; F.P.H. Prick van Wely (1906). *Nederlands taal in 't Verre Oosten*. Semarang: Van Dorp; and (1910) *Viertalig aanvullend Hulpwoordenboek*. Weltevreden: Visser; J.J. van Ginneken (1913). 'Het Oost-Indisch'. In *Handboek Nederlandsche Taal*. Den Bosch: Malmberg; D.C. Hesseling (1923), *Het Afrikaans*. Leiden: Brill; and (1979) 'How did Creoles originate?'. In T.L Markey & P.T. Robergé (eds.) (1979). *On the Origin and Formation of Creoles*. Ann Arbor: Karoma; A. De Geus & J.J.M. Van Dam (1935). *"Indische fouten"*. Batavia/Bandoeng: Visser.

92. Dell Hymes (ed.) (1971). *Pidginization and Creolization of Languages*. Cambridge: Cambridge University Press. Ian Hancock (1971), 'A Map and List of Pidgin and Creole Languages, in: Hymes (ed.), *Pidginization*, 509–523. Guus Meijer & Pieter Muysken (1977). 'On the Beginning of Pidginization and Creole Studies: Schuchardt and Hesseling', in: Albert Valdman (ed). *Pidgin and Creole Linguistics*. Bloomington: Indiana University Press, 21–45. John Holm (1988–89). *Pidgins and Creoles*, Cambridge: Cambridge University Press, 2 vols, J. Clancey Clements (2009). *The Linguistic Legacy of Spanish and Portuguese*. Cambridge: Cambridge University Press.

access website of the Hugo Schuchardt Archive in Graz, Austria. Of central importance here is Schuchardt's point of 1890: his solid finding that in language contact the Portuguese language of Batavia and Tugu could effectively be mixed with the genetically totally unrelated Malay. Confirmed again in 2011 by Maurer, this point has since received further independent further confirmation from Saad's Leiden PhD of 2020, who demonstrated how, in language contact on the Indonesian island of Alor, two unrelated languages – the Austronesian language, Alor Malay, and the Papuan language, Abui – could be mixed too, and brought about a simplification in the minority language Abui. The same point – the historic mixing in language contact between Portuguese, Malay and the Papia Kristang Creoles of Malacca, Macau, Batavia and Tugu – was demonstrated too by Laub in his SOAS PhD of 2022, *A Comparison of Portuguese-lexified Creoles of South-East Asia: Kristang, Makista, Batavia and Tugu.*[93]

As for the language of Tugu, finally, we note that this too is a project *de longue durée*. It may be relevant here to note that, from 1661 onwards, the Tugu community – consisting originally of 23 Black Portuguese *Mardijker* families, of Portuguese-speaking Bengali and Coromandel men with their Buginese women (says Schuchardt 1890: 21)[94] – had their own land and freedom; with their own Protestant church, which from 1678 was led by the Dutch reverend and bible translator, Melchior Leijdekker; and a cultural identity of their own as an increasingly mixed community. After Indonesian Independence in 1949, many Tugunese left for Dutch New Guinea; from where they moved in 1962 to the Netherlands; then again in 1963 in a group of 170 to the Slootwijk plantation in Surinam; but since this did not really work out, by 1967 they were readmitted to Holland by the Dutch government (Baay 2015: 270–272). In Indonesia, meanwhile, the Tugu narrative was one of slow extinction: Jacob Quiko, the last full speaker of Tugu Portuguese, died in 1978, leaving behind a 700-wordlist of Tugu vocabulary. The last church service in Portuguese was held in 1984, and the language has now been almost totally replaced by Bahasa Indonesia. However, even today there are still some cultural maintenance activities going on, around what keeps surviving of Tugu vocabulary (cf. França da Pinto 1985; Tadmor 2004; and Suratminto 2019); and of Tugu culture, with its Portuguese and Morisco singing

93. Saad (2020). *Variation and Change in Abui*. PhD Leiden University. And Robert W. Laub (2022). *A Comparison of Portuguese-lexified Creoles of South-East Asia: Kristang, Makista, Batavia and Tugu*. London: SOAS PhD.

94. Adolf Heuken s.j. (1982). *Historical Sites of Jakarta*. Jakarta: Cipta Loka Caraka, esp. ch. iv: 'The Church of the Black Portuguese' (69–84), & ch. V: 'Tugu' (85–92). Also: J.R. van Driessen (1989). *Jakarta/Batavia*. De Bilt: Cantecleer, s.v. 'Portugese Buitenkerk' (186–195) & 'Tugu' (306–309).

and its thriving Krontjong music (Grooss 1972; Mutsaers 2012).[95] We are looking here at a life span of the Tugu language going on for some 350 years, and it is not quite over yet.

7. Varieties of mixing in Indies Dutch

In his book *on Malayoportugiesisch* (1890: 148–150), Schuchardt asked the question [see Section 6.1 above, p. 380 nr. (4)]: Is there, can there actually be something like a Creole Dutch?

In answer, from his correspondent, Dr Metzger, he received some interesting Dutch data, labelled as *Kreolenhholländisch* (p. 148), taken from the field of contemporary Dutch East Indies colonial literature, in texts by Van Rees, the journal *De Gids* 1882, Van Höevell 1851, Annie Foore (=mw IJzerman) and Multatuli. Upon inspection, however, Schuchardt concluded that: yes, possibly, while Dutch people had made some effort, they only managed a few individual and ridiculous distortions, but failed to produce a true '*kreolische Mundart*' (148). This then was as far as Schuchardt would go: the data might suggest the possibility of a Creole Dutch, but no more than that.

So he left the question open. But it was a fair one, so it did come back, and over the next twenty years, a number of Dutch linguists took to it, both in Batavia (Prick van Wely 1906, 1910, with the help of Kern 1910) and in the Netherlands (Te Winkel 1904, Van Ginneken 1913, Hesseling 1899, 1923). In what follows we will now, first, in 7.1, discuss those early Dutch views on variation in *Indies Dutch* and then, next in 7.2, explore their continuation about mixing, creole and Indies Dutch between the wars.

95. Reggie Baay (2015). *Daar werd wat gruwelijks verricht. Slavernij in Nederlands-Indië*. Amsterdam: Athenaeum- Polak & Van Gennep, 270–273; Antonio d'Oliveira Pinto da França, (1985). *Portuguese Influence in Indonesia*. Lisbon: Calouste Gulbenkian Foundation [Vocabulary, 72–86]. Uri Tadmor (2004). 'Kreol Portugis Batavia: Riwayat Hidup dan Matinya Sebuah Bahasa', in: Katharina Endriati Sukamto (ed.)(2004). *Menabur Benih, Menuai Kasih*. Jakarta: Universitas Katolik, Indonesia Atmajaya/ Yayasan Obor Indonesia, 405–420. Lilie Suratminto (2019). 'Cultural maintenance based on the vocabulary of the extinct language of Tugu Creole', in: Christina T. Suprihatin et al (eds.). *Weg tot het Oosten. Afscheidsbundel voor Kees Groeneboer*. Depok: Universitas Indonesia, Program Studi Belanda, 161–195 [Tugu vocabulary, 167–186]. Rosalie Grooss (1972). De *Krontjong Guitaar*. 's-Gravenhage: Uitgeverij Tong Tong [in: DBNL] And Lutgard Mutsaers (2012). 'Tjalies muzikale missie: De revival van krontjong als Indo-genre', in: *Indische Letteren* vol. 27 (2012), 56–72 [a;so DBNL].

7.1 Mixing between Dutch and Indonesian: Before the first world war

Early in the twentieth century, before the first world war, two leading Dutch linguists gave different assessments of the use of Dutch and Malay in the colonies. Around 1904, the Amsterdam Professor of Dutch, Te Winkel, observed:

> In the Dutch East Indies, in contact with the population of the various islands, the Europeans mostly spoke a very simple Malay, also called Low Malay, which has spread across all islands as a kind of common spoken language, without, however, being a civilised tongue, and which has incorporated many elements, especially from Portuguese, Dutch and Arabic.
> (Te Winkel 1904: 357; my translation, rs)[96]

Not much later, in 1913, but on a slightly different note, the up-and-coming young linguist Van Ginneken noted how the Dutch speech of the Europeans in the East Indies, in contrast to the lower class, less educated and mixed-race Indos, was characterised by:

> an often very clear and neatly articulated, rather formal, polite, and dated Dutch, laced through with lots of Malay and Dutch colonial words coined in the Dutch East Indies, and sounding clearly different from native Dutch as spoken in Holland. (Van Ginneken 1913: 306; my translation, rs)[97]

In a way, the two statements above sound like the end points of a spectrum.[98] Te Winkel's dictum concerns 'a very simple Malay', a commonly used contact variety, but not a civilised tongue, bordering on Low Malay, mixed with Portuguese, Dutch and Arabic elements, used by Europeans in contact with the natives on the Indonesian islands. Van Ginneken's observation, in contrast, is not about Malay, but about a variety of Dutch which goes under the name of '*Indisch Nederlands*'

96. J. Te Winkel (1904). *Inleiding tot de geschiedenis der Nederlandsche Taal.* Culemborg: Blom & Olivierse, 357. Cf. Ian F. Hancock (1971). 'A Map and List of Pidgin and Creole Languages', in: Dell Hymes (ed.), *Pidginization and Creolization of Languages.* Cambridge: Cambridge University Press, 509–524, esp. 522 nr. 67: *Pasá or Bazaar Malay* – "a pidginized variety of High Malay, in long and widespread use in Malaysia and Indonesia".

97. J.J. van Ginkel (1913). 'Het Oost-indisch'. Ch. 12, in: *Handboek der Nederlandsche Taal.* Vol. 1. *De sociologische structuur der Nederlandsche taal.* Nijmegen: Malmberg, 300–324 [plus also ch. 7 'Afrikaans', 206–212, and ch. 11. Ceylonese', 296–299].

98. Another difference concerned their views of Schuchardt. Te Winkel was a *Neogrammarian* while Van Ginneken was a more Italian-minded *Neolinguist.* Te Winkel was not much taken with Schuchardt's 1885 critique of the Sound Laws of the *Neogrammarians,* while Van Ginneken in his great sociological *Handbook* of all known varieties of Dutch of 1913 included a comprehensive, Schuchard-inspired presentation of creole variation in the Dutch colonies.

[or 'Indies Dutch'[99]] as spoken by the so-called 'Indies' community in the Dutch East Indies.

Both varieties were neither pure Dutch nor proper Malay; they are just mixed. But they are different in how they are mixed: in pronunciation, in education, in civility and politeness, in degree of mixedness. Both varieties contain Dutch and Malay elements, but 'Low Malay' often also has Portuguese and Arabic elements, which 'Indies Dutch' usually does not. Here we touch on Bourdieu's views[100] concerning the small but socially significant distinctions in operation between different usages, expressions and styles in speech. This is how 'Low Malay' and 'Indies Dutch' may mark different forms of usage – though, for all their differences, both do fall under the wide umbrella of colonial Dutch.

Another important contribution came from the lexical studies, inspired by Schuchardt, of Indies Dutch by Prick van Wely (1906, 1910), in which he presented lots of *slang* about Indo-speakers, like the many pejorative labels in use in the colonies to denote the mixed-race people known as Indos, from *Indo* through *Indiër, Indische, halfbloed, kleurling, blauwe, liplap, Kreool, mestiese, nonna, sinjo, petjoek, serani* and *Eurasian* (Prick 1906: 112–117).[101] The word "Indo" itself, meanwhile, in whatever language, in Dutch, Indies Dutch, Indo Dutch or in Indonesian, always had (and still has) the same meaning, i.e. of 'mixed, descent', 'Eurasian', 'métis', 'someone with mixed Indies/ Indonesian descent", to denote the intermediate category in colonial society, the 'Sinjo's & Nonna's'[102] of the Dutch East Indies.

Here, Prick's colleague Kern (1910: 310) brought further clarification when he explained how the term *creole* in the Netherlands East Indies at the time was used only in the general sense of "children born in the colony from Dutch native parents". Back then, this was the correct meaning, to label children born in the Indies from native Dutch parents as *creoles*; even Couperus – 'himself an Indisch boy' – used this correctly in his novel *De Stille Kracht* [The Hidden Force, 1900] about Van Helderen. As Kern added, it was a mistake made by recently arrived *totoks*

99. J.W. De Vries (2005). 'Indisch Nederlands', in: Nicoline van der Sijs (ed.) *Wereldnederlands*, The Hague: Sdu, 59–78. See further again below, (see notes 112, 113, 115 and 116).

100. Pierre Bourdieu (1982). *Ce que parler veut dire. L'économie des échanges linguistiques.* Paris: Fayard.

101. See Teeuw 1990, Cress 1998 and Van der Sijs 2010. Note that not even half of Prick's labels for Indos are included in Sijs *Wereldwijd* 2010.

102. From Portugese: *Senhor & Lady*, cf. Van Ginneken 1900, 'De taal der Sinjo's', 300–306. Also: Prick van Wely (1906), 62; Prick van Wely (1910). *Viertalig aanvullend Hulpwoordenboek voor Groot-Nederland*, including: (i) Prick, 'Lexicografisch gedeelte', 124: 'Kreool' = 'native'; and (ii) Kern (1910). 'Etymologisch gedeelte', 310, 'creool' = 'criollo'. See also: *Encyclopaedie Nederlandsch Oost-Indië*, Leiden, vol. 1, 1917: 542.

[white European colonials in the East Indies] to believe, in error, that a 'creole' is not *pur sang*. Nevertheless, over the past century there has been a confusing semantic shift in the word 'creole' in Dutch, from meaning 'unmixed white person born in the colonies' to 'mixed-race colonial' today, as we see in 'creool' = 'Iemand van gemengd bloed' (Van der Sijs (2010), *Nederlandse woorden wereldwijd*, 262). To further disentangle this confusion we, there is also the helpful advice given by Cress in his study *Petjoh* (1998: 233–239, 155, 185) on the lexical field 'Indisch', 'Indo', '(Indo-)Europeaan', 'Indonesiër', and 'Inlander' (Native).

7.2 Before the Second World War: Kijdsmeir and others on Indo Dutch

Social distinctions in colonial society allow us to draw a portrait of *Indisch*-speaking society in the 1930s and its use of Dutch and Malay in contact in the former Dutch East Indies. At the top there would be *Totok* Dutch – i.e. pure Dutch, as spoken by the Dutch from Holland, which back then was the unquestioned dominant social standard and norm for educated, cultivated usage in the Dutch East Indies by Europeans. At the bottom, amongst Native Indonesians, there was Malay as the most widely used medium for spoken interaction and communication throughout the archipelago, which at the same time was recognised officially as administrative and school language, but often also often looked-down-upon and denigrated. In between, under the umbrella of Indies Dutch, there were the in-between speakers, the Indos, speaking all kinds of Dutch variants and mixes with a colonial flavour – not only dialects of Indo-Dutch as spoken by Indo people, but beyond that also *Petjoh* and other heavily mixed varieties of local usage like *Javindo* and *Cindo*. Or simply labelled *Tjampoeran* see notes *Campuran* (note 115) and *Petjoh* (note 116).

It is those various kinds of Indies Dutch which were used in exchanges and conversations, ranging from the lowest illiterate creole speech to the most cultivated expressions of politeness for use in civil conversation. As a whole their language was mixed, impacted in pronunciation, vocabulary and grammar by the influence of Malay and perhaps other languages too. Often labelled as the speech of the lower class, mixed-race Indo people in their kampongs spoke "a curious mish-mash of the mother's Malay, Javanese or some other tongue mixed with the father's Dutch".[103]

---

103. Reinier Salverda (1994), 'Indisch Nederlands in het Batavia van de jaren dertig: De roman *Goena-Goena* van Caesar Kijdsmeir', in: *Indische letteren* 1994 nr. 1, 29–43. Or, as Van der Sijs (2010: 37–38) put it: "In Indonesia there were a few Dutch creole languages, or rather mixed languages: Petjoh with Malay as grammatical base, and Javindo with Javanese, and then its vocabulary largely based on Dutch. These were mixed languages, and not a variant of Dutch such as

The language of the Indos, that was the language of Tjalie Robinson. It was not the language of the school and the teachers. In their *Guide of correct usage for Indo's and Indies people*, De Geus & Van Dam (*Indische fouten,* 1935: 3–4) emphasised that they would "stay within the boundaries of "Indo-Nederlands" as spoken in civilised Indies circles ('Indische kringen')". As a consequence they explicitly excluded the vulgar speech of the *'patjoeq'* from Kemajoran (Batavia/Jakarta), the 'njo' (= 'sinjo') from Karangbidara (Semarang) and Krambangan' (Surabaya). As we can see, the old taboo against 'broken Portuguese' – first encountered in 1714 in Alewyn's preface to his Portuguese Dictionary – was still alive and well in Dutch-speaking Batavia in 1935.

The lowest rung in Indo-society was at the very edge between the Europeans and the kampung; that's where people fought, where it was not safe at night (Koks 1931: 232).[104] Those who lived there were the Indo-paupers, trying to survive not by agriculture, but by small-time crime, as thieves, spies, robbers and racketeers, violence and counter-violence. They had a culture totally their own, between those of the Europeans and that of the Natives, with their own language and music, their own Stamboel-theatre with their Batavian language and clowns, and their own Krontjong-muziek – "real mestizo music, which neither a Native nor a European can perform" (p. 241), and note, "about krontjong and stamboel-muziek there is no literatuur" (241).

In the 1930s, many educational efforts were made to smarten up how those Indos spoke, directed from the Dutch colonial schoolsystem by G.J Nieuwenhuis (1930). *Het Nederlandsch in Indië. Een bronnenboek voor het onderwijs in de nieuwe richting.* Groningen/Den Haag/Weltevreden: Wolters. At the same time, the Indos were at the receiving end of negative attitudes, derogatory comments, taboos on their substandard Indo-Dutch language, and explicitly negative campaigns against their mixed Indo-Dutch and Petjoh.[105]

Indies Dutch. Indies Dutch is a variant of Dutch, and not a creole language. It's not a separate language, and it only lives in the Netherlands where most of its speakers live.

104. Cf. J.Th. Koks (1931), *De Indo.* Amsterdam: H.J. Paris, esp. ch. 'De Paupers', 230–242.

105. See: Groeneboer, *Gateway* 1998, 183–188: on Indo-Dutch, Petjoh and Robinson.

7.3 After the second world war: Tjalie Robinson, M.C. van den Toorn, Jan de Vries

(1) *Tjalie Robinson* (1949; 1976)

When Kees Groeneboer, in his monograph, *Gateway to the East* (1998:188), came to the contribution of Tjalie Robinson (1911–1974), he started from the *Petjoh* which Robinson spoke, and from the story, 'Anak Betawie' which he wrote about this in 1949 in the literary-cultural journal in Indonesia, *Oriëntatie* 27 (Dec. 1949:7–16).[106] Two things stand out here. First of all, Robinson revealed what he spoke was "a characteristic type of Batavia street dialect, consisting of words from Malay, Sundanese, Chinese, Dutch, English and Unknown" (Robinson 1949:8). Secondly, at this precise moment, he spoke of what he expected when looking forward to the future of his fellow Batavians: "Perhaps they'll say something different, but even that shall be typically Batavian" (in: *Oriëntatie* 1988:122). In a way, this was his credo as a man of languages and of the future, and he has always remained true to those ideas.

In 1952, coming out of the Indies-speaking community as the Indo-Dutch writer and cultural activist he was, Tjalie Robinson demonstrated how in his writing and storytelling he was exploring different varieties of style and language – first, in his novels *Tjies* (1955) and *Tjoek* (1960), written in Indies Dutch (almost standard but not quite) under the pseudonym of Vincent Mahieu; then, secondly, in his little book of *Ik en Bentiet* (1976), writing under his original pen-name of *Tjalie* (< Charlie) his very non-standard, highly informal and witty dialogues in the much looked-down-upon *Petjoh* dialect of the Djakarta streets where he grew up; and thirdly, in his lifelong *Piekerans* columns, written in an informal spoken Dutch laced with many Malay words and expressions, as the Jakarta *Flâneur* he was, in stories that are full of his life and memories – and all three brimming with Indies language, humor, creativity and a growing sense of identity, freedom and the in-between, which he celebrated at the annual *Pasar Malam* and *Tong Tong* Festivals in The Hague, which started in 1960 and is still continuing today.[107]

---

106. Reprinted in: Peter van Zonneveld (ed)(1988), *Oriëntatie. Literair-cultureel tijdschrift in Indonesië* (1947–1953). Schoorl: Conserve 1988, 120–133.

107. Bert Paasman et al. (eds.) (1994), *Tjalie Robinson, de stem van Indisch Nederlands.* Den Haag: Stichting Tong Tong. On *Petjoh* see Miel de Gruiter 'Javindo', and Hadewych van Rheeden, 'Petjo: the Mixed Language of the Indos in Batavia', 223–237, both in Bakker & Mous (1994), *Mixed Languages*, resp. 151–159, and 223–237. Also: Jeroen Dewulf (2007), 'Framing a Deterritorialized, Hybrid Alternative to Nationalist Essentialism in the Postcolonial Era: Tjalie Robinson and the Diasporic 'Indo' Community", in: *Diaspora: A Journal of Transnational Studies* vol. 16 nr.1 /2, 1–28. And Edy Seriese (2023). 'Retour Jakarta: Tjalie Robinson als Java-Mens', in: *Armada Tijdschrift voor Wereldliteratuur*, 2023: 9–10.

To him, all was language. He used *Petjoh* in his *Piekerans van een straatslijper*, and in his *Ik en Bentiet* in his journal *Tong-Tong* (column, 1959–1966), and played about in his opening piece on Petjo en Super-Dutch (cf. Groeneboer 1998: 187) about "Super-Dutch" which he heard

> in Holland, on a busy Saturday train, between the hum of many languages and dialects, suddenly, a conversation, in an unusually well-modulated, grammatically correct and stylish Dutch, which strikes a note of perfection between all the clear and direct dialects and jargons of Amsterdam, Zaandam, Rotterdam and Hague.

This is how he satirised the very rare, perfect Dutch which in Indonesia was spoken by Indo's as the most important means if one wanted to get ahead in society. For, to get rid of that Petjo, the average Indo simply had to acquire that Super-Nederlands, so that's why this is spoken by "Indo's, teachers, officials, officers, and especially women, as typical speakers of this stilted, hypercorrect language" (Robinson, 'Ik en Bentiet', 1976, 5). [Though that has never kept any Indo-speakers from mixing languages as they pleased]. This is how all his life he continued the satire and to debunk it too as seriously as he could.[108]

(2) *M.C. van den Toorn* (1957)

In 1957 in the Netherlands, well after the end of the colonial era, the Dutch linguist Van den Toorn gave a strong integrative push forward to the topic of language diversity and contact.

> Indies Dutch', as he put it, 'was a collective term for what actually was a range of sociolects, social usages within a range of widely differing regional, social, historical, structural, stylistical and individual variation. Those sociolects could range from almost incomprehensible spoken creole on a mixed Dutch and Indonesian basis to neatly spoken and almost standard Dutch, carefully articulated, often more careful even than Dutch as spoken by born Dutchmen.[109]

Developing this further, Van den Toorn emphasised how Indies Dutch thrives on all sorts of distinctions, which could be marked, for example, by the use of a particular speech sound, an intonation pattern, a stylistic device, the use of special

---

108. Jeroen Dewulf (2007).'Framing a Deterritorialized, Hybrid Alternative to Nationalistic Essentialism in the Postcolonial Era: Tjalie Robinson and the Diasporic Eurasian "Indo" Community', in: *Diaspora: A Journal of Transnational Studies*, vol. 16 nr,. 1/ 2, 1–28.

109. M.C. van den Toorn (1957). 'De taal van de Indische Nederlanders', in: *De Nieuwe taalgids* 50, 218–229; and Van den Toorn (1995), 'Couperus en het Indisch-Nederlands', in: *De Nieuwe Taalgids* 88 nr. 1,1.

words, meanings and constructions, or loanwords, code switching and language mixing. This made 'Indisch' *the* label for variation and diversity, and the umbrella concept which it still is today.[110]

(3) *Jan de Vries* (2005)

Of special importance among the many publications on Dutch and Indonesian by J.W. de Vries is his 'De Depokkers: geschiedenis, sociale structuur en taalgebruik van een geïsoleerde gemeenschap', in: *BTLV* vol. 132 nr. 2/3, 228–248.

This was the first time he used the common Indonesian term for 'mixed': '*campuran*' ('mixed', 'confused') (in: De Vries, 1976), *Depokkers*, 241–248) as the common label for the spoken variety known as Melayu-Jakarta, which actually meant 'neither Bahasa Indonesia, nor Dutch'. Its meaning may not have been very clear, but its use was: the term was regularly used in contact with house servants and market sellers, but remained otherwise unspecified and uninvestigated.[111]

Many other publications followed, such as his (1988) 'Dutch loanwords in Indonesian', in: *International Journal of the Sociology of Languages* 73, 121–136; and also: Cor van Bree & J.W. de Vries (1977). 'Netherlands', in: Hans Goebl et al. (eds)(1997). *Kontaktlinguistik* etc. Berlin/New York: Walter de Gruyter, vol. 2, 1143–1152.

His final publication on 'Indisch Nederlands', in: Van der Sijs (2005), *Wereldnederlands*, 59–78, contains his detailed findings on *Petjoh* (Vries 2005: 74–77), its vocabulary, its speech sounds, melody and stress patterns, its morphological and grammatical characteristics, of which he said:

> Petjoh has a vocabulary that is largely borrowed from Dutch. Its pronunciation is unmistakeably Malay. But since its grammar in large part come from Malay, Petjoh may rightly be considered a mixed language, and not a variant of Dutch or of Indies-Dutch.[112]

7.4 *Nicoline van der Sijs* (2010)

What else is there to say about variation between speakers of Indies Dutch? What significant differences do we encounter here; and how do these matter?

---

110. 'Indisch' was the inclusive title of the Leiden journal *Indische Letteren* (from 1986). See the editorial note on 'Indisch', in Edy Seriese (1992), 'Indische Letteren als Mestiezenliteratuur', *Indische Letteren* 7.

111. Cress (1998). *Petjoh*. Amsterdam: 15–32. Cf. also his essay in this book, on 'Background and characteristics of Petjoh and Indies Dutch'.

112. Cf. De Vries 2005:75–76; and see further below in Section 7.3.2. sub (1) Petjoh, below.

Thanks to Van der Sijs's study of Dutch loanwords all over the world in her *Nederlandse woorden wereldwijd* [The Hague: Sdu Uitgevers, 2010], today we are much better informed, and with lots more detail, for example, of the history of Dutch loanwords in Indonesia, in her survey of Indonesian on pages, 79–83.

Over the centuries, both Java and the Moluccas were the longest, most strategically placed and most continuously occupied locations of language contact in the archipelago – and so that is also where we find the most numerous Dutch loanwords. On Java, we thus find the four mixed languages – Petjoh, Javindo, Chinese-Malay and Jakarta Malay. In the Moluccas too: Alor-Malay, Ambon-Maleis, Kupang-Malay and Ternatan-Malay.

Beyond this, there are more than twenty other Indonesian languages holding significant numbers of Dutch loan words, in alphabetical order: Aceh, Alor, Ambon, Bali, Biak, Buginese, Gimán, Iban, Java, Kei, Leti, Kupang, Madura, Manado, Minangkabau, Muna, Nias, Roti, Sahu, Sasak, Savu, Sundanese and Ternatan Malay. More than 14 Indonesian languages, listed on Table 3 (pp. 140–141) hold at least a hundred Dutch loan words each. Thus, across the archipelago as a whole, there is a vast lexical imprint of Dutch in Indonesia, in an asymmetric distribution: against the 109 Indonesian words that have ended as loans in the Dutch language, the Indonesian language has incorporated a grand total of 5569 loanwords from Dutch.[113]

There are also clear patterns of contact and dissemination here of the number of Dutch loanwords incorporated in Indonesian languages, in decreasing order: Javanese (1262), Manado (1086), Madurese (737), Jakarta Malay (691), Ambon-Malay (582), Kupang-Malay (560), Makassarese (470), Sundanese (423), Petjoh (340), Buginese (318), Minangkabau (317), Ternatan Malay (285), Muna (143), Aceh (140) and Kei (123).

But that's not all. What is particularly interesting in the large and very useful 'Alphabetic Lexicon' by Van der Sijs (2010: 170–723), is that from the wide range of Variation in the Dutch lexical entries listed, we learn not just how these Dutch words were disseminated across the archipelago, but also how they were differently adapted to the many archipelagic languages they came into contact with, as in the following Dutch words:

> *Aandeel* [share, 163] > *andél, andil* (Indonesian) – *andèl* (Ambon Malay) – *andhil* (Javanese) – *ândelé* (Macassarese) – *handel, andel* (Menadonese – *anden* (Minangkabau)

113. Note: A comparable total of 5400 Dutch loanwords in Indonesian was confirmed by Grijns et al. (1983), *European loan words*, xi; and J.W. De Vries (1988), 'Loanwords', 121]. But see also Sneddon 2003: 165–166.

Ontslag [dismissal, 489] > *ontslag* (dismissal, Indonesian) – *ons, ontslag* (Ambon Malay) – *onslah* (Jakarta Malay, Javanese, Sundanese) – *ontslak* (Kupang Malay, Menadonese, Ternatan Malay) – *onsla, onslah* (Madurese) – *onsalá* (Makassarese)
Radijs [radice, 539] > *radés* (Indonian) – *radès* (Ambon-Malay, Menadonese) – *radies* [Creole-Portuguese (Batavia)]
Straf [punishment, 616] > *setrap, strap* (punishment, Indonesian) – *seterap, setrap* (Jakarta Malay) – *setrap* (Javanese) – *strap* (Kupang Malay) – *sěttrap* (Madurese) – *nisitará, sitarapang, sitará, sitarap* (Makassarese) – *sětrap* (Sundanese)
Voorloper [precursor, 682 > *pelopor* (Indonesian: pioneer, forefighter during the war of independence) – *plopor* (Javanese) – *pelopper, pelopper, plopper ploppor* (Petjoh).

Continuing about words now, note that in the list of lexical fields, in Van der Sijs 2010, Table 2 (p.152 paragraph 4.2), there is no mention of the term Law (Recht), even though in Indonesia so very many Dutch, Indo-Dutch and also Indonesian legal terms have been coined, and are often still in common use, even if by now many have become outdated or forgotten in the Netherlands. In Van der Sijs, *Nederlandse woorden wereldwijd* (2010), fortunately, a lot of Dutch legal terminology in Indonesia has been preserved, such as: *boei, boedel, breidel, concordantie, ekstremis, executie, haatzaai, landraad, inlander, vonnis.* But just as many have not, see: *exorbitante rechten* (extraordinary powers), *handschoentje* (marriage by proxy, with a little glove), *plopper* (pioneer, frontline), *rijstchristenen* (rice Christians), *voorkinderen* (children from earlier relationship), *vrijwillige onderwerping* (free choice to submit to Dutch law).[114]

Turning to other legal terms, Van der Sijs (2010) records how e.g. *wét* (law) has been preserved in at least six languages – Indonesian, Jakarta Malay, Javanese, Madurese, Menadonese and Sundanese (Van der Sijs 2010: 700), in contrast to *haatzaai* (fomenting hatred) which is only recorded in the Indonesian standard language. As for its definition, *haatzaai* (on pp.29 and 334), is listed as a Dutch-Indonesian legal term "for publications that would displease the colonial government". More research on such findings would be interesting, as I found in my 2009 'Doing Justice in a Plural Society' (*Dutch Crossing* 33 no. 2, 2009, 153–171): historically, those articles, with their draconian punishments (seven years!), were often used against Indonesian nationalists, for whom they were "amongst the most offensive and repressive elements of the colonial legal system" (p.165).

114. See: Reinier Salverda (2009). 'Doing Justice in a Plural Society: A Postcolonial Perspective on Dutch Law and Other Legal Traditions in the Indonesian Archipelago, 1600-Present,'in: *Dutch Crossing* vol. 33 No. 2, October, 2009, 153–171.

7.4.2 *Of the four mixed languages*

Of the four mixed languages under discussion here, the common point is their same basic structure – *Petjoh* has Malay grammar with Dutch words – *Javindo* has Javanese grammar with Dutch words – *Peranakan* has Javanese grammar with Malay lexicon – *Melaju Sini* (*Moluks Maleis*) has a simplified structural basis of Malay and a vocabulary largely borrowed from Dutch.

In recent language contact research Donald Winford (2013), 'Social factors in contact languages', in: Bakker & Matras (eds.) 2013, *Contact languages*, 363–416, we find *Petjo, Javindo* and *Chindo* all three described as *mixed languages* (p. 375). The same analysis we find also in [De Vries 2005; Van der Sijs 2010]. It also applies in the Moluccas, e.g. to Alor-Malay, Ambon-Malay, Kupang-Malay and Ternatan-Malay. All are rated 'mixed', since they have the same overall structure. The term *mixed language* gives a much more precise linguistic term than the term 'creole';[115] it also does much more justice to Schuchardt's original *Sprachmischung* (language mixing).

(i) **Petjoh** – a heavily mixed oral variety of Malay-Dutch in use in Batavia and Jakarta, deeply impacted by Malay, Javanese and other languages as well; an informal street language used between friends, and far more heavily mixed than Indisch Dutch and Indo-Dutch. Much looked down upon in colonial days, *Petjoh* later, in the Netherlands today, in a postcolonial reversal, is being upgraded to an expression of cultural Indo-identity, sometimes even used as a literary medium. *Petjoh* see De Vries (2005: 67–76) [wel veel maleise woorden, maar woordenschat grotendeels nederlands. Uitspraak onmiskenbaar Maleis, ook grammatica is Maleis. Daarom geen Nederlands maar een andere taal 74] Petjoh dus met recht een mengtaal en niet een variant van het NederLands of van Indisch Nederlands (p. 75–76). Verschil in woordenschat: For Jakarta Maleis Nicoline van der Sijs p. 84. Dan p. 140–141: 691 Dutch loan words. For Petjoh, Van der Sijs (2010: 106) lists almost 380 Dutch loan words.

115. *mixed, creole, campuran* – Petjo, Javindo and Cindo are all included in Winford's contribution as 'mixed language', p. 375 – not as creole languages. The same too in Angela Bartens' contribution 'Creole languages', in: Bakker & Matras (2013), 65–158. *Campuran* (mixing) was common also in Cress (1998: 32), in his label of *Lingua tjampoer* [mixed language]. Cf also De Vries 1976 and 2005.

Data: Hadewych van Rheeden (1994: 226)
Petjo: *'Kleren* njang di-*wassen door die frouw'*
English: The clothes that are washed by that woman[116]

(ii) **Javindo** – Dutch-Javanese mixed language spoken in Semarang, Central Java: 'a language which was structurally Javanese with as many Dutch words as possible'. Its speakers in Indonesia used to identify themselves as 'Indo-European', that is, 'neither Dutch nor Indonesian'. Derogatory labels, both in Dutch: *'Krom Hollands'* [*crooked* or *broken*]; in Javanese: *Krōjo.*

Data: De Gruiter (1994: 153)
Javindo: *Als ken-niet,* ja di-*ken-ken-a,* wong *so muulek* kok *sommen*-nja
English: If it is not possible, try to get them done, for the sums are very difficult[117]

(iii) **Peranakan (Cindo, Singkeh, Njo)** – Mixed variety spoken by people of Chinese descent in the Netherlands East Indies, speakers of Dutch-Malay-Hokkien, on Java since the 17th century. Van der Sijs (2010: 58) lists a total of 90 Dutch Peranakan loanwords. In family terms: the grammatical frame comes from the mother; while the lexicon is from the father. In social terms, Peranakan was often seen as a vulgar, un-civilised, un-educated mishmash of Betawi dialect or Javindo or other back street varieties (see *Indische fouten*, 1935: 4, below). In the eyes of Hoogervorst (2017: 398), Peranakan is marked by a 'pluriformity in stylistic registers' – it is 'neither 'Chinese Malay, 'Bazaar Malay', 'Betawi Malay' nor 'Java Malay'. In fact, it 'constitutes four different sociolinguistic phenomena: (i) a contact variety in flux; (ii) a language of translated books; (iii) an ethnolinguistic repertoire; and (iv) a popular stereotype'

116. Ref. Petjoh: see Tjalie Robinson (1976). 'Ik en Bentiet', 5–11 & Rosalie Grooss (1976), 'De verstoten taal', 12–16. Also: J.W. de Vries (1997). 'Verbal morphology in Javindo and Pecok', in: Cecilia Odé & W. Stokhof (eds.), *Proceedings 7th International Conference of Austronesian Linguistics* [ICALL], Amsterdam: Rodopi, 351–359. And: De Vries 2005 *Wereldnederlands.* Hadewych van Rheeden, H. (1994), 'Petjo: the mixed language of the Indos in Batavia', in: Bakker, P. & M. Mous (eds.), *Mixed languages. 15 Case Studies in Language Intertwining*, Amsterdam: IFOTT, 223–237. Reinier Salverda (1997), 'Mengsyntaxis: Tjalie Robinsons Piekerans in contactlinguistisch perspectief', in: 'Wim de Geest (ed.), *Plurilingua.* Bonn: Dümmler, 97–105. Richard Cress (1998), *Petjoh*, Amsterdam. Dewulf (2007) notes the at once global diasporic and deeply local and rooted character of Petjoh, in the Netherlands just as much as in Australia and the United States.

117. Ref. Javindo: **see** Miel de Gruiter (1994). 'Javindo, A Contact-Language in Pre-War Semarang', in: Bakker, P. & M. Mous, *Mixed languages*, 151–159.

Data: Hoogervorst (2017: 398)
Peranakan: 'Apakah ia soedah masoek sekola' – '*Soeta, soeta* masoek haktong lay-tauwhoen pitglap, say ia pikit mau *kilim* Nanking' – 'Apakah ia bisa naek *fiets*?' – 'Ho, *lia* wisa pekang *piet* toelit-an tjintjio soei bauwboet sitkali'
English: 'Does he already go to school? – '*Yes, yes,* he already goes to school and in another year he will graduate, I'm thinking to *send* him to Nanking' – 'Can he ride a *bicycle*?' – 'Right, *he* knows how to handle the writing *pen* in a nice way, very nicely'.[118]

(iv) **Melaju sini/Moluccan Malay** – Maluku today is an active field of international linguistic research. Since Indonesian Independence, different labels mark the various kinds of Moluccan Malay, which together constitute a diasporic creole language, spoken by small Malay communities, scattered all over the Indonesian archipelago and beyond, and since 1950 also in the Netherlands.
The language area is broadly divided into: (i) Moluccan Malay and Ambon Malay, spread from Ternate via North Maluku to West Papua (Paauw 2013); and (ii) Melaju Sini and Moluks Maleis in the Netherlands (Tahitu 1989 and Tahitu & Lasomer 2001). Melaju Sini as spoken in the Netherlands has a mixed structure: a simplified structural basis of Malay; with a vocabulary largely borrowed from Dutch. Its spelling is the old Dutch colonial one, not the modern Indonesian one.

Data Melaju Sini: Tahitu & Lasomer 2001: 158
Informal Malay: *aku panggil kue* Ambon and Tangsi Malay
Formal Malay *beta memanggil engkau* Standard and Church Malay
English: I call you[119]

(v) **Further mixed languages?** – Language always continues, it seems, and so too, it seems, do mixing languages here.

118. Ref. Peranakan: see Kay Ikranegara (1980). *Melayu Betawi Grammar.* Jakarta: Seri Nusa vol. 9. Also: Dédé Oetomo (1984). *The Chinese in Pasuruan.* Ithaca: NY: Cornell University. Felicity Meakins (2013), 'Mixed languages', in: Bakker & Matras (eds.), *Contact languages* p. 159–229, mentions Cindo, 161: Chindo – Indonesia – Peranakan Chinese – Malay lexicon with Javanese grammar. And Nicoline Van der Sijs (2010). *Nederlandse woorden wereldwijd,* 58). In hun *Indische fouten,* De Geus & Van Dam (1935: 4) mention without further details the "njo" van Karangbidara (Semarang) and Krambangan (Soerabaya).

119. Refs Maluku, see: Scott Paauw (2013). 'Ambon Malay', in: Michaelis (ed.) (2013), *Atlas of Pidgin and Creole Language Structure,* vol 1, 94–104. Also: Bert Tahitu & Xaf Lasomer (2001).'Moluks Maleis', in: Guus Extra & Jan Jaap de Ruiter (eds.), *Babylon aan de Noordzee. Nieuwe talen in Nederland.* Amsterdam: Bulaaq: 153–174. And: Van Bree & De Vries, 'Netherlands', in: Goebl (1997). *Kontaktlinguistik,* vol: 2, 1143–1152.

Steurtjestaal – Language in the Indo-orphanage for Dutch mixed children in Semarang, from Indonesian mothers and Dutch fathers, all orphans speaking some form of Malay (cf. Hadewych van Rheeden (1998). 'The role of functional categories in language contact and change', ref. in: Bakker & Matras 2013, 261).

Frisian-Malay mixed language used by Frisian soldiers during their war with Indonesia, 1945–1948. Bastardized Malay loanwords and lexical roots (Nom, Adj, V en Adv) in spoken Dutch/Frisian structural context, like *kembali* (again), *panas* (hot), *perloe* (need), *pigi* (gone), *sobat* (friend), *wang* (money) etcetera.

Data: *Even de barang wegpikoelen, ja*
English: Just taking away the luggage, OK?[120]

7.4.3 *Betawi – Batavia – Jakarta*

When considering the question of Batavia Malay, several questions arise. What about its name, what about its many names: Betawi, Batavia Malay, Jakarta Malay, Indonesian? What kind of language is this? Is it a mixed language, or a multi-ethnolect, as Jacomine Nortier & Margreet Dorlein have suggested, in their 'Multi-ethnolects: Kebabnorsk, Perketdansk, Verlan, Kanakensprache, Straattaal, etc' (in: Bakker & Matras, (2013), *Contact languages* (2013), 229–271? One answer to questions such as these would be that of James Sneddon (2003):

> In many ways, especially in its grammatical elaboration and incorporation of affixes from both Sankrit and European languages, Indonesian has moved far away from its Malay roots. Since the name 'Indonesian' was proclaimed in 1928, the language has undergone development at a speed experienced by few other languages in history, changing more than it did in the preceding 500 years.[121]

Following Sneddon's line, we may capture this process of change in the following series of five shifts in the modern history of Malay:

1. Local Betawi Malay had been called a '*brabbeltaal*' (mishmash) by Van der Tuuk in 1867, on account of the desperately low quality of its linguistic analysis and description.[122]

---

120. Ref: T. Kingma (ed.)(1948). *Friesland was hier. De lotgevallen van 1-9-R.I Bataljon Friesland 1945–1948*. Leeuwarden: Van der Weij, esp. 225–226

121. Sneddon 2003: 212.

122. Cf. Groeneboer (2002). *Een vorst onder de taalgeleerden: Herman Neubronner van der Tuuk*, Leiden: KITLV, 483–484 – see: Letter Van der Tuuk, nr 175 (1867): 'brabbeltaal, brabbel-Maleisch', p. 617, 618.

2. After Independence, growing immigration from Java reduced Anak Betawi-speakers of Betawi Malay to 5,5% of Jakarta population (cf. Grijns 1991), and brought a shift to Jakarta Malay,[123] growing influence of Jakarta as the national capital, with Indonesian the national language.
3. A further shift followed towards Jakarta multilingualism, when Kähler 1966[124] identified the *lingua franca* of Batavia as a multilingual *'omong'*: a Malay dialect with elements from Balinese, Javanese, Sundanese, Arabic, Portuguese, Dutch and English; and also increasing plurality of terms: *Omong* (Kähler 1966), *Jakarta Dialekt* (Muhadjir 1981), *Jakarta Malay* (Grijns 1991) and *Betawi Malay* (Roosman 2006).
4. The next shift went towards Colloquial Jakartan Indonesian, which led to the status of a prestige variety for informal Indonesian (Sneddon 2003: 215): Indonesian became THE language of modernisation (p. 209) and promotes increase in urbanisation.
5. Today, the rise of informal Jakarta Indonesian (Sneddon 153–156), growing immigration, and also concern about the decline of regional languages – Javanese, Sundanese, Madurese, Minangkabau, Buginese, Batak, Balinese, Banjarese (Table p. 203, 208–209) – all now move us towards to the Superdiversity of languages in Indonesia (Zein 2022).

8. Revisiting Gonda and Schuchardt

Coming to the end of these *Capita Selecta* on Language Contact in the Malay Archipelago, we first sum up our findings – from Gonda's pioneering scholarly insights on the diversity, contact and mixing of languages; via Pigafetta's discovery of Malay in 1520; Gulliver and Hobson/Jobson on the key position long held by Portuguese; then De Houtman's Dutch language guide of 1603 for learning Malay and Malagasy, adopting the European language learning model of Antwerp's Noël de Berlaimont (1527); via the production by Dutch scholars in Batavia of dictionaries and Bible translations into Malay and Portuguese; then next, Radermacher's enlightened, innovative, Comenius-inspired trilingual *Nieuwe Woordenschat* (1780) in Batavia; leading to the extraordinary creole discoveries by Schuchardt (1890) and continued by creolists of today such as Maurer (2011), Saad (2022) and Laub (2022); noting also the long-standing cooperation of linguists on Dutch and Malay, leading to the eventual triumph of Bahasa Indonesia in 1945, the ongoing investigation of very many other languages in contact across the arch-

123. James Sneddon (2003). *The Indonesian language*, 154–155.

124. Hans Kähler (1966). *Wörterverzeichnis des Omong Djakarta*. Berlin: Reimer

ipelago; culminating today in Turchia and Djuhari's *Indonesian Slang* (2011) full of contemporary multilingual orality, and a pioneering study such as *Language Policy in Superdiverse Indonesia* (2020) by Subhan Zein.[125] In this vast domain of language contact developments, there are many interesting and important topics calling for further investigation by linguists of the Universitas Indonesia in Jakarta-Depok with their expertise in the field of Dutch as a source language in its Studi Belanda section.[126]

Here we return to Gonda (1941) and his observation that the colonial capital of Batavia was a coastal enclave on Java, between and outside the far larger Sundanese and Javanese language areas. Batavia, with its immense multilingualism, was the colonial capital and at the same time a city where, in contact with many other idioms, people spoke *Bataviaasch-Maleisch* [Batavia Malay], with all the mixing, switching, shifting, language play and further such processes characteristic of everyday contact between (mostly oral) varieties.

From here on, Gonda developed his point concerning the diversity of languages and cultures in the Indonesian archipelago. It is this diversity which down the centuries has kept those languages growing, rejuvenating, enriching, playing and spreading while incorporating what they could from other languages such as Sanskrit, Arabic, Chinese, Dutch, English, French, Portuguese and many more (cf. Jones 2007).

Back then, Gonda rightly regretted the lack of thorough scholarly attention in the Netherlands to Schuchardt's *Malayoportuguese* (1890). Today, when we revisit Gonda, we note how for the study of Batavia/Jakarta Malay we have some very good starting points in the works of Chaer (1982), Muhadjir (1981, 2000), Grijns (1991) and Roosman (2006);[127] as well as a solid basis in the contact studies by Adelaar (1996), Steinhauer (2005) and Zein (2022), for the central prob-

125. Christopher Turchia & Lely Djuhari (2011), *Indonesian Slang: Colloquial Indonesian At Work*. Tuttle Publishing, Vermont. See also: Edwin Paul Wieringa (2012), 'Jakarta in een postmodern Indonesisch stripverhaal over een mislukte detective', in: *Rozenberg Quarterly*. And the film trilogy of twelve years of family life in Jakarta, by Leonard Retel Helmich (1959–2023), *De stand van de zon* (2001), *De stand van de maan* (2004), en *De stand van de sterren* (2010).

126. See Achmad Sunjayadi, acting head Studi Belanda Universitas Indonesia (2024). 'Two papers on the future of Dutch in Indonesia', in: *Neerlandistiek*, 4 October & 12 November 2024, at: https://neerlandistiek.nl. And his online interview, 25 September 2024, with the *Nederlandse Taalunie*, at: https://taalunie.org.actueel. See also: R. Salverda (1989a). 'Nederlands als wetenschappelijke bronnentaal voor Indonesische Studiën in Indonesië', in: Kees Groeneboer (ed.), *Studi Belanda di Indonesia/Nederlandse Studiën in Indonesië*. Jakarta: Djambatan, 401–409.

127. Chaer 1982, *Kamus Dialek Jakarta*; Grijns 1991, *Jakarta Malay*; Muhadjir 2000, *Bahasa betawi*; and Roosman 2006, *Phonetic Experiments on Betawi Malay and Toba Batak*.

lem which Gonda put before us – that of contact between languages all over the Malay archipelago.[128]

As De Vries (2005) noted, *Petjoh* is vanishing and my be all but gone today. However, it is language which always continues. The language spoken in Jakarta in the 1980s was already very different from that of the 1940s; and today, the language of the early 21st century – with its street lingo, orality, postmodern exeriments and language play – is quite different again from that of the 1980s. Language never dies, it renews itself continuously. In the history of languages there never is a fixed day which we can point to and say: Today, Latin is at its end, and from here on, French will now begin (Saussure 2002: 152–156; cf. Richter 1995: 109–119).[129] On the contrary, new shoots of spoken language will always sprout, take off and renew themselves. When we look back to the creole beginnings of Dutch-Indonesian language contact – which Schuchard was able to trace back to the oldest creole text by Meister, dating from 1692, but possibly from 1677 – we reckon that today Malay Portuguese Creole already has a documented history of some 350 years – despite (or perhaps thanks to) the many complaints which such creoles attracted, that they were not proper languages, but a 'mishmash' or just garbage, without standards, rules or grammar.

In language contact, variety really is the spice of life. Thus, Werndly (1736), following Ten Kate (1723), spoke of different 'styles' in Malay. Raffles (1817) observed that during his rule over Batavia, people there spoke "a jargon of five different languages, Dutch, Portuguese, Chinese, Javan and Maláyu" (in his *History of Java,* 1817: 358–363). Almost a century later, Prick van Wely (1906) used a similar term, 'slang', which reminds us of what Eric Partridge once said: "*Jargon* is often misused to mean slang or cant or even pidgin English" (1948: 117). In 1949, Tjalie Robinson heard a mix of Malay, Sundanese, Chinese, Dutch, English and Unknown in the streets of Jakarta. In 1966, Kähler, in his *Wörterverzeichnis des Omong Djakarta.* Berlin, spoke of the '*omong*' (talk) of Jakarta: a complex multilingual mix of nine languages, composed of a Malay dialect with elements from Balinese, Javanese, Sundanese, Chinese, Arabic, Portuguese, Dutch and English (cf. Muhadjir 1981: 1).

128. Adelaar 1996, *Contact languages in Indonesia.* Steinhauer 2005, *Colonial history and language policy in insular Southeast Asia.* And Zein 2020, *Language Policy in Superdiverse Indonesia.*

129. Simon Bouquet & Rudolph Engler (eds.), *Écrits de linguistique générale par Ferdinand de Saussure,* Paris: Gallimard, 2002, 152-156. Cf. Á quelle époque a-t-on cessé de parler Latin en Gaule? Á propos d'une question mal posée', in M. Richter (1995), *Studies in Medieval Language and Culture,* Dublin: Four Courts Press, 109-119.

Today, Winford (2013) speaks of 'mixed languages', and Hoogervorst (2017) of a 'pluriformity of stylistic registers'. The same can be said of modern Indonesian today, especially in Jakarta, with its rampant slang and colloquialisms everywhere in that superdiverse capital of languages, where we constantly encounter contact phenomena in everyday interaction as spoken between Indonesians and speakers of many other contributing languages – such as Javanese, Sundanese, Chinese, Arabic, Hokkien, Acehnese, Batak, Betawi, Dutch (Belanda), Balinese, Hindi, Tetum, Prokem, Portuguese, Petjoh, and so many others. And just as in Raffles's time, the colloquial Indonesian of Jakarta today is a multilingual *Slang* characterised by "the vast ethnic mix and breadth of linguistic influences in Indonesia" (Trochia & Djuhari 2011: 6).[130]

In these cases, behind their various terms what we have before us are contact processes of mostly spoken language. Language is not a thing or an object; it is a form or a way of behaviour – never static but dynamic and always moving. This is what Schuchardt has taught us about creoles. It is also the view which Roman Jakobson held of linguistics in general – that it is "*an inquiry into the structuration, restructuration and destructuration of language*".[131]

Terms such as *jargon* (1817), *slang* (2011) or *mixed* (2013) are quite suitable for capturing the fluid and plural features of Malay and its creole contact variations. They also fit in well with Schuchardt's ultimate scholarly aims – what he was really after with his critique both of the *Neogrammarian* Sound Laws (in 1885), and of Saussure's *Cours* (in 1917) – i.e. his expectation that one day, in our Digital Age, in a fusion of philology, lexicology and linguistics, each and every single word or feature of any individual language will eventually have its own particular grammar and rules.

In his vast descriptive explorations of the *MalayoPortuguese of Batavia and Tugu* (1890), there is much that justifies such terms as 'jargon', 'slang' or 'mixed', or for that matter, 'translanguaging', the new concept recently coined by Ofelia García & Li Wei in their book *Translanguaging* (2014).[132] Using terms such as these,

130. Cf. Torchia & Djuhari (2011), *Indonesian Slang: Colloquial Indonesian at work*. Singapore: Tuttle. Cf. Salverda (2006). 'Multilingual London and its Literatures', in:*Opticon 1826*, 1, 1–15. Also: Muhadjir (1981). *Morphology of Jakarta Dialect, Affixation and Reduplication*. Translated by Kay Ikranegara. Seri Nusa, Universitas Atma Jaya, vol. 11, 117 pp.

131. Roman Jakobson & Linda Waugh (1979), *The Sound Shape of Language*, Sussex: Harvester Press, 237.

132. Benny H. Hoed (2011). *Semiotika & Dinamika Sosial Budaya: Ferdinand de Saussure, Roland Barthes, Julia Kristeva, Jacques Derrida, Charles Sanders Peirce, Marcel Danesi & Paul Perron*. Depok: Komunitas Bambu. Also: Ofelia Garcia & Li Wei (2014). *Translanguaging: Language, Bilingualism and Education*. Basingstoke: Palgrave Macmillan. And see: Fiona English

the key point, to me, is to do with the oral life of language. Speakers are always moving forward, from alpha to omega and da capo again; and their speaking is the core element of the longevity and the *longue durée* of language.

This, in the end, is the great significance of Schuchardt's pioneering studies in Creole studies, in particular of Batavian Creole and of Tugu Malay-Portuguese: his discovery of the intricate processes of language contact and change, including pidginization, creolization, language mixing, shifting, attrition as well as survival – and what this can teach us and continues to teach us about the languages we speak.

The future of Indonesian, of Dutch, and of so many other languages, will always be a matter of the oral, the colloquial and the interactive, of the new, creative and social, of the mixed, fluid and slangy – and it is this that will keep evolving through the interactions of our minds, ears and mouths, and the never-ending conversations we are pursuing in contact. Ad infinitum. Or, as Schuchardt himself would say: '*Allotria*'.[133]

& Tim Marr (2015 [2023^2]. *Why Do Linguistics? Reflective Linguistics and the Study of Language.* London: Bloomsbury.

133. Hugo Schuchardt (1925), 'Der Individualismus in der Sprachforschung'. In: Leo Spitzer (ed.), *Hugo Schuchardt-Brevier. Ein vademecum der allgemeinen Sprachwissenschaft*, Darmstadt: Wissenschaftliche Buchgesellschaft, 1976^2, 422, 435 & 436 – *Allotria*, 'trifle, butterfly, child's play'.

CHAPTER 12

Dutch loanwords in Ternate and their circulation in the Moluccas

Antoinette Schapper[1,2] & Maria Zielenbach[1]
[1] Vrije Universiteit Amsterdam | [2] Lacito-CNRS

This chapter examines the appearance of Dutch loanwords in Ternate, a Papuan language spoken on a small volcanic island in the North Moluccas that was at the centre of the clove trade at the time of European arrival in the region. The Dutch maintained a near continuous presence in Ternate from 1606 and although communities of Dutch speakers here were at all times small, a number of loanwords bear witness to their presence and influence. We catalogue the Dutch loanwords that are peculiar to Ternate, and their dispersal into other languages of the region in order to create a picture of the dynamics and chronology of lexical borrowing from Dutch in eastern Indonesia. We argue that loanwords from Dutch indicate that Ternate was an important contact language in the early period of the Dutch presence in the Moluccas, a fact that is easily overlooked given the subsequent dominance of Malay.

1. Introduction

Dutch speakers first arrived in the islands of today's Indonesia at the end of the 16th century; they remained in significant numbers as part of the apparatus of the colonial Dutch state until the middle of the 20th century. Grown out of western Malay varieties in wide use during the colonial period, Indonesian, the national language of Indonesia, bears a significant lexical mark from these centuries of contact: over 5,000 Dutch loanwords have been noted by scholars (Jones 2007). Through Indonesian and/or its Malay antecedents, Dutch words have come to be found in many of the hundreds of indigenous languages of Indonesia.

Given the long presence of the Dutch in the Indonesian archipelago, it is reasonable to assume that Dutch speakers had many and varied contacts with indigenous peoples and their languages across Indonesia. Yet, because much of the loanword analysis to-date has centred on etymologies in Indonesian and its westerly predecessors (e.g., Gonda 1952, Madhava Sharma 1985, Jones 2007), still today

https://doi.org/10.1075/impact.55.12sch

very little is known about Dutch loans in the many other languages of Indonesia (van den Berg 1995). The undoubtably varied local processes of contact with and borrowing from Dutch, particularly in the early modern period before Malay standardisation began, have been altogether neglected by scholars. Van der Sijs's (2010) loanword dictionary *Nederlandse woorden wereldwijd* is the first work to attempt a catalogue of Dutch loans in a wide range of Indonesian languages. The complexity and enormity of the documentation task that van der Sijs takes upon herself means that the pathways by which Dutch words have entered the different languages is for the most part not handled. She writes: "There is still much to be learned through tracing the precise pathways that a Dutch word has followed before it ended up in another language [...] there is still a lot of additional research to be done in this area." (van der Sijs 2010: 13).[1]

In this chapter, we draw attention to the various lexical marks left across eastern Indonesia by scattered groups of Dutch speakers over the long course of the Dutch presence in the region. We show that the many unique Dutch loanwords found in eastern Indonesia have entered and circulated by different routes. In particular we argue that a major source for Dutch loanwords in the Moluccas is through Ternate, a language spoken on a small volcanic island in the Moluccas that was at the centre of the global clove trade at the time of European arrival.[2] The historical political power of Ternate is reflected today in loanwords emanating out from Ternate into other indigenous languages and local varieties of Malay spoken throughout the Moluccas, in northeast Sulawesi, as well as through Halmahera and Raja Ampat to the Bird's Head of New Guinea and Cenderawasih Bay. Among these are Dutch loans that came to have a wide circulation in eastern Indonesia through their borrowing into Ternate. The Dutch maintained a near continuous presence in Ternate from 1606 when Fort Oranje was constructed near the main harbour. Although communities of Dutch speakers on Ternate were at all times small, a body of loanwords bear witness to their presence and influence. We catalogue the Dutch loanwords that are peculiar to Ternate, and chart their dispersal into other languages of the region in order to create a picture of the dynamics and chronology of lexical borrowing from Dutch.

1. Original: "In het achterhalen van de exacte wegen die een Nederlands woord gevolgd heeft voordat het in een andere taal terechtgekomen is, valt nog een wereld te winnen [...] er valt op dit terrein nog veel aanvullend onderzoek te doen"

2. Ternate is the indigenous language of the island of Ternate, but it is only spoken by a minority of the people who live there today. The Ternate language should not to be confused with Ternate Malay (also sometimes referred to as North Moluccan Malay), which is a form of the Malay language that first emerged on Ternate and is now widely spoken in the region (Litamahuputty 2012).

A major point of emphasis throughout this chapter is that Malay varieties, although undoubtedly important for the linguistic history of Indonesia as a whole, are not the only conduit, let alone necessarily the most important one, by which loanwords have historically been transmitted in much of eastern Indonesia. The dominant narrative of what Collins (2003a: xxiv) calls the 'ancient and persistent role of Malay in Maluku [the Moluccas]' has been largely accepted by linguists working in the area without examination. According to this quietly assumed account, when loans from Ternate, Javanese, Portuguese or Dutch, for instance, are encountered, Malay is almost always the vehicle of transmission. The possibility that lexical influence from Ternate—and Dutch loans in it—spread independent of Malay has not been considered. We show that Dutch loanwords that are not attested in Malay circulated in the Moluccas, and that Ternate was very likely the means by which many achieved a wider dispersal. This chapter thus contributes to a growing body of linguistic research showing that Malay was of relatively limited importance in much of the Moluccas and adjacent regions where Europeans settled potentially even into the 20th century.

This chapter is structured as follows. Section 2 briefly overviews the language situation across the Moluccas and the broader eastern Indonesian area. Section 3 gives a taste of the kinds of small-scale contact events between Dutch speakers and local peoples across eastern Indonesia that have led to borrowing from Dutch. Section 4 reviews the historical importance of Ternate as a lingua franca and shows that the language had a broad lexical influence throughout the Moluccas. In Section 5 we show that Ternate has a set of distinctive Dutch loans, many of which have been further borrowed into local languages. Dutch loans into Ternate also appear to have been borrowed into local varieties of Malay, but we argue that Malay varieties do not look to have had a central role in dispersing these loans. We suggest that Dutch loans into eastern Malay varieties were probably largely distinct in time and trajectory to Dutch loans that were dispersed through Ternate. Section 6 concludes.

2. Language situation in the Moluccas and surrounds

Once known as the Spice Islands because of the nutmeg, mace, and cloves that naturally occurred there, the Moluccas encompasses multiple island groups in the eastern part of Indonesia. They extend from Halmahera in the north, through Buru and Seram, to Aru and Tanimbar in the east, stopping just short of Timor at the Southwest Maluku Island group, containing Kisar, Leti among others. Together with the Bird's Head of New Guinea, Bomberai peninsula, Cenderawasih Bay as well as the island of Timor and its satellites, the area is referred to as "Eastern Indonesia" (Map 1).

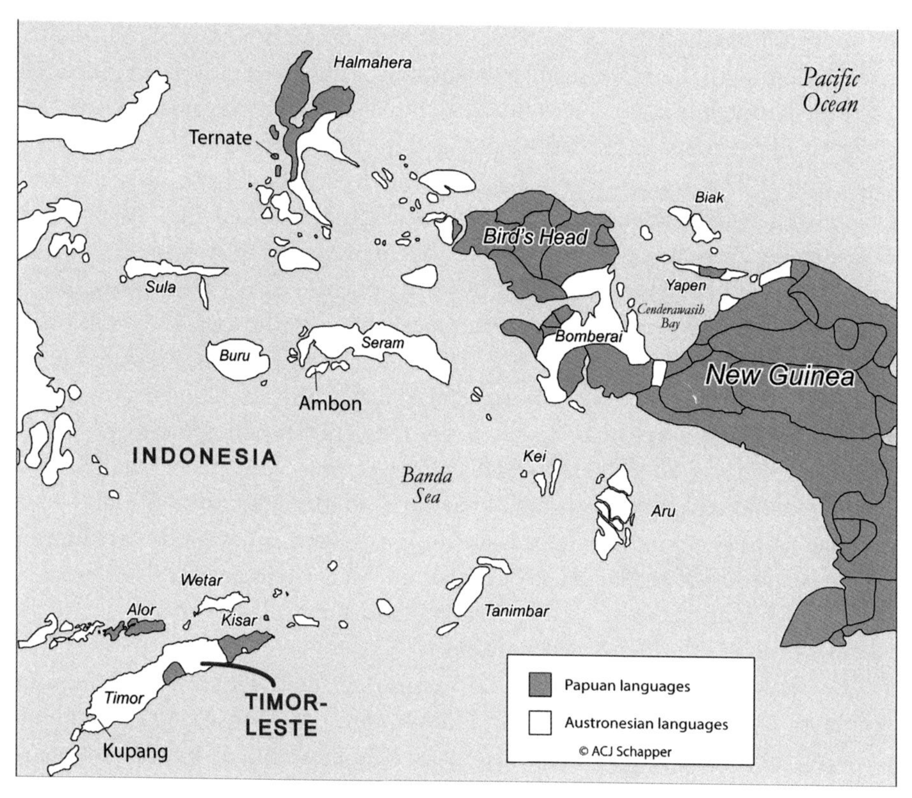

Map 1. Eastern Indonesian linguistic divisions

Eastern Indonesia is characterised by an extraordinarily rich linguistic profile. The precise number of languages in the region is unknown, but it is thought to be upwards of 200 distinct languages. Languages in the region are typically divided into two broad types. The first are those languages belonging to the Austronesian language family, and the second are Papuan languages. The label "Papuan" has a negative denomination in that it refers to languages that *do not* belong to the Austronesian language family. Papuan languages belong to multiple different language families. Most important for our discussion is the North Halmahera family, encompassing around a dozen languages on Halmahera Island and some small satellite islands in what are today known as the North Moluccas.

While enormously diverse, the languages of eastern Indonesia are severely endangered. A large number are rapidly becoming obsolescent, with often only the oldest community members still having fluency in the indigenous languages.

Language shift is occurring primarily towards local varieties of vehicular Malay (see, e.g., Florey & Ewing 2010). Malay is an Austronesian language, but not one that is indigenous to eastern Indonesia. The homeland of the Malays is thought to be in the coastal areas of east and southeast Sumatra and offshore islands, later spreading to the Malay Peninsula and to coastal areas of Borneo (Sneddon 2003: 7). Through the activities of traders, the Malay language came to be understood in many parts of the Indonesian archipelago already by the time of the 16th century (Adelaar & Prentice 1996). Under the Dutch, use of Malay was encouraged and local varieties of Malay became established in urban centres across eastern Indonesia slowly over the course of the last few hundred years, at the expense of indigenous languages (Collins 2003b). From these centres, use of Malay expanded, gradually crowding out local languages further. Today, we often speak of Malay varieties such as *Ambonese Malay*, *Kupang Malay*, *Manado Malay* and *Ternate Malay*.[3] These are all named after major urban settlements in eastern Indonesia where Europeans were based, but they are typically spoken over wider regions with local adjustments and flavourings. Since independence, Indonesian—the national language of Indonesia and a standardised form of Malay—has also had an impact on the linguistic situation in eastern Indonesia on account of its status and role as the language of education, media, and government. Broadly speaking, Indonesian exists in a diglossic relationship to local varieties of Malay, where it occupies the high-status position.

Before Malay—in its different local variants—came to its present position of dominance, the islands of eastern Indonesia were criss-crossed by overlapping networks of smaller regional lingua francas. Numerous lingua francas are mentioned in the literature of the region, and a few examples will suffice for our purposes. On the islands of Alor and Pantar to the north of Timor, Alorese was reportedly used as the language of wider communication in coastal regions at least until the 1970s until it was superseded by Malay in more recent times (Stokhof 1975: 8). From at least the early 18th century, the Geser language was used widely in trade by groups in the large maritime area east of Seram extending from the coastal regions to the Bomberai peninsula of New Guinea to the islands of southern Maluku (Donohue 1996). In the area around the Bird's Head of New Guinea, Malay knowledge seems to have been unusual before the 20th century. Instead, Biak acted as the lingua franca throughout Raja Ampat and along the top of the Bird's Head to the north coast of Yapen island, while Wamesa was the language

3. By contrast, the term "Papuan Malay" is a cover label encompassing multiple vehicular varieties of Malay that are spoken in the western half of New Guinea, with each having a different set of influences. Most existing discussions of Papuan Malay deal with the closely connected varieties spoken in Northwest New Guinea (see, e.g., Gil 2023).

of intergroup interaction across the southern sweep of Yapen island and Cenderawasih Bay (Schapper and van Schie forthcoming). The most influential lingua franca of the pre-Malay period was Ternate, the Papuan language that stands at the centre of this chapter. Its importance in the linguistic history of the Moluccas is sketched in Section 4.

3. Microcosms of contact

Loanwords directly from Dutch, rather than mediated through Malay, can be found springing up like mushrooms across the map of eastern Indonesia. These loans are the result of highly localised contact events between indigenous groups and small groups of Dutch speakers stationed as soldiers, administrators or missionaries in remote locations. Loanwords of this type can be distinguished from loans that have been circulated by vehicular Malays on the basis of their distinctive phonological and semantic patterns and their highly circumscribed geographical distributions. In the settings where they are found, they are limited in number and often are restricted to very particular semantic domains. Since it is essential to differentiate these loan events from those that led to a wider circulation of Dutch loans in eastern Indonesia, it is useful to have a broad picture of such microcosms of contact and the kinds of loanwords that evidence them.

At the smallest end of the contact scale we have Inanwatan, a small language spoken on the south coast of the Bird's Head of New Guinea. Included in a rich vocabulary of swear words and curses of diverse origins are two Dutch loans: *fodome* < Dutch *verdomme* 'damn' and *kloset* < Dutch *klootzak* 'asshole' (Lourens de Vries pers. comm.). Neither of these words are known to be present in any Malays or other languages of the region. According to de Vries (1998), the oldest Inanwatan speakers he worked with recalled these words being used by Dutch soldiers and police who would pass through the Inawantan settlement. It shows that even the most fleeting contacts with Dutch speakers in relatively recent times can have left their mark on indigenous languages.

Outside of major towns, local Dutch administrators and patrols seem to have frequently been the source of loanwords into indigenous languages. However, for much of eastern Indonesia, this contact only began in the early twentieth century when the Dutch colonial administration abandoned its long-standing "ethical" policy of non-intervention in the outer regions of the Indonesian archipelago (see, e.g., Locher-Scholten 1981 on this). On the islands of Alor and Pantar, the easternmost group of the Solor archipelago, for instance, contact with speakers of Dutch only began after 1910 when a *controleur* post was established there and military patrols began crisscrossing the islands to pacify the unruly locals

(Rodemeier 2006: 80). The majority of Dutch loanwords that are known in the languages of Alor and Pantar seem to have come by way of the Malay variety spoken in Kupang, where a Dutch fort had been established in the 17th century and a sizeable number of distinct Dutch loans are documented (Steinhauer 1983, Jacob & Grimes 2003). Nonetheless, there are several loanwords attested in the indigenous languages of Alor and Pantar that do not seem to have been mediated by Kupang Malay, either because the particular form is not attested in Kupang Malay or, where it is attested, because the form or meaning is not compatible with a Kupang Malay or any other Malay source. These include:

(1) Nedebang *herandis* 'forced labour', Teiwa *herandiis* 'forced labour, do something ordered by the government', Western Pantar *randis* 'cooperate' < Dutch *herendienst.*[4]
Teiwa *diis* 'service, service, work (e g., in the military, government)', Reta *dis* 'service, duty, service, duty', Kamang *diisi* 'forced labour, service' < Dutch *dienst* (cf. Malay *dinas*).
Teiwa *harnat* 'grenade' < Dutch *granaat.* (cf. Malay *granat*; loaning not via Malay is suggested by the adaption of Dutch *g* [ɣ] with Teiwa *h* [h]. Malay borrowings with *g* are maintained as *g* in Teiwa).
Teiwa *tehel* 'tile', Alorese *tehel* 'floor' < Dutch *tegel* (cf. Malay *tegel*).
Teiwa *feer* 'fastener, zipper' < Dutch *veer.*
Teiwa *weker* 'chalice used in church' < Dutch *beker* (cf. Malay *beker*; loaning not via Malay is suggested by the adaption of Dutch *b* with Teiwa *w*. Malay borrowings with *b* are maintained as *b* in Teiwa).
Blagar *kang*, Reta *kaang* 'jar, stone bottle' < Dutch *kan.*
Blagar *opas* 'policeman' < Dutch *oppas* (cf. Kupang Malay *opas* 'servant, slave, errand boy', this is an older meaning of the word that is retained in Kupang Malay, and the difference with the Blagar meaning indicates a separate borrowing event. The meaning 'policeman' was typical of the late colonial period and in evidence elsewhere, e.g., Ambonese Malay *opas* 'police during the colonial period').

Not all loans directly from Dutch are from the last phases of the colonial presence in Indonesia. During the VOC period, the Dutch established forts in places of major importance for trade, either as centres for trade or as places from which trading lanes could be overseen. These posts typically became the significant cities of eastern Indonesia, such as Ambon and Kupang, where local Malay varieties with distinctive Dutch influences became established (Paauw 2009: 18–28). Small VOC forts on far-flung islands monitoring the flow of indigenous trade,

4. Taxation was extracted through forced labour and in Alor enabled the construction of a regional centre at Kalabahi (Nieuwenkamp 1922: 71).

however, did not usually dislodge indigenous languages. One particularly notable case is represented by the fort established in 1668 on Kisar in southwest Maluku (Hägerdal 2019). The handful of Dutch-speaking soldiers that manned the fort took local wives and from there issued a population of Eurasian children that maintained a distinct identity until recent times. Members of the Dutch authorities repeatedly expressed concern for the children's welfare and at different times ministers and teachers were dispatched to Kisar to ensure a Dutch, Christian education for them (van Engelenhoven 2016). This distinctive history has left its mark in the form of loanwords from Dutch that are present in the languages of Kisar, Meher and Oirata. In some cases, it appears that Dutch loans made originally on Kisar Island have spread through borrowing into nearby languages such as Leti, Luang, Wetan and Fataluku. These include:

(2) Meher *domin* 'pastor', Oirata *domin* 'pastor' < Dutch *dominee* (cf. Malay *domine,* the lack of a final vowel indicates that Malay was not the immediate source for the Meher and Oirata forms).
Oirata *emer* 'pail, bucket', Wetan *emre* 'pail, bucket' < Dutch *emmer* (cf. Malay *ember* 'bucket' with the intrusive bilabial stop. The fact that this is not found in the forms here indicates a distinct borrowing event. Meher has *ember* today, a recent borrowing from Malay replacing an earlier direct borrowing, such as still attested in Oirata and Wetan).
Meher *kaki* 'diarrhoea' < Dutch *kakje.*
Meher *kukis* 'bread, cookies', Oirata *kokis* 'bread', Luang *kuksi* 'cookie, bread, cake' < Dutch *koekjes.* (Loans of *koekjes* are widespread in eastern Indonesia. The extension of the loan to bread is peculiar to the Kisar area and suggests a separate borrowing event. If this form had been borrowed at a later time from Ambonese Malay *kukis* 'cake', we would not expect the additional 'bread' meaning to be shared across the languages here).
Meher *leter* 'letter' < Dutch *letter.*
Oirata *hāk pai* [crochet do] 'do crochet-work, embroider', Luang *n-haka* 'crochet' < Dutch *haken.*
Meher *meser* 'teacher', Oirata *meser* 'teacher, physician, midwife', Leti *mèsra* 'master, teacher' < Dutch *meester.*
Meher *morso* 'dirty' < Dutch *morsig.* (This etymology is from van Engelenhoven 2016).
Meher *poroti,* Leti *protu* 'bread' < Dutch *broodje.*
Meher *pusi,* Fataluku *posi* 'cat' < Dutch *poesje.* (cf. Ambonese Malay *pus* < Dutch *poes*).
Oirata *opasa* 'spy', Leti *òpsa* 'kind of supervising function within a clan', Wetan *opse* 'spy, policeman' < Dutch *oppas* (The meaning 'spy' is distinctive to the loans in the Kisar area and suggests a separate borrowing event from loans of

oppas elsewhere, which is either 'servant' as in Kupang Malay or 'policeman' as in Ambonese Malay).
Oirata *pēl* 'bow (the weapon)' < Dutch *pijl.*
Oirata *pōt* 'boat' < Dutch *boot.*
Meher *soldata,* Oirata *solrata* 'soldier', Leti *sòldata* 'soldier', Wetan *soltata* 'soldier' < Dutch *soldaat.*

Missionaries in eastern Indonesia were often Dutch speakers and Dutch loanwords often cluster around places where missions were established. In Halmahera, for instance, a mission was set up in 1869 at Duma on Lake Galela where a small community lived in relative isolation from the surrounding non-Christians (Hueting 1930). The Dutch missionaries at Duma are the most likely source of several distinctive loans in the Galela language. These include:

(3) Galela *anisi* 'gin, alcoholic drink' < Dutch *anijs.*
Galela *bibeli* 'bible' < Dutch *bijbel.*
Galela *ʤeneweri* 'juniper' < Dutch *jenever.*
Galela *keperi* 'cotton twill' < Dutch *keper(stof).*

The contact events that occasioned many loans from Dutch are rarely identifiable with any precision within the eastern Indonesian area. And because none of the languages has a continuous documentary record, the moment of borrowing can never be retrieved. An example of borrowing where the contact with Dutch speakers that lead to borrowing is equivocal is the appearance of loans of Dutch *komkommer* 'cucumber' in eastern Indonesia. We observe that this word is borrowed into one language in Halmahera, Pagu, and a cluster of languages in the region of Seram Laut between Banda and New Guinea (Map 2). This distribution must reflect minimally two independent borrowing events, one in Halmahera and one in Seram Laut, which is known as a zone of intense contact and exchange (Ellen 2003). The contact situations that led to the loans are in both cases mysterious. The Pagu form is attested in a Holle list collected in the 1930s; it is possible that an individual missionary spread the Dutch word among the Pagu. The forms in the Seram Laut area may have spread from Banda where a sizeable Dutch-speaking population was housed to run the nutmeg plantations following the 1621 massacre of the Bandanese (Loth 1995). Alternatively, they may have spread from the first Dutch settlement on New Guinea in the area of Triton Bay on the south coast, near to where Koiwai is spoken. Only in place for a short time, between 1828–1836, the post was staffed with a handful of Dutch soldiers and officials tasked with monitoring trading activities (Huizinga 2004). Whilst both are plausible sources, nothing is known about the time at which the loans entered the languages and so it is by no means certain when or how the loaning of *komkommer* occurred. Regardless of the precise borrowing event and its timing, the distri-

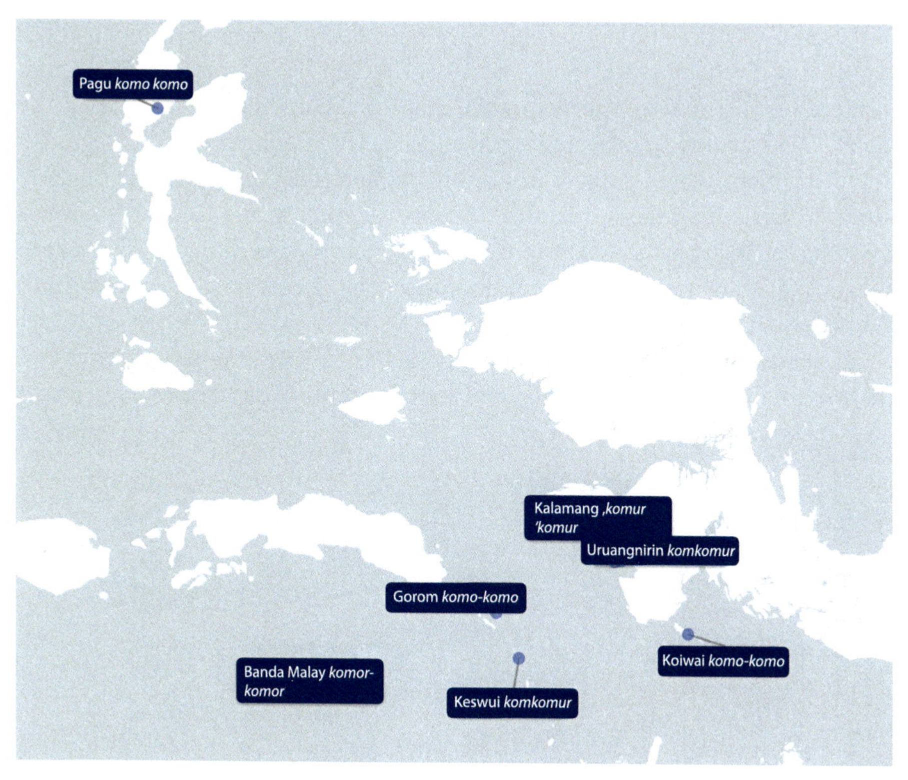

Map 2. Loans of Dutch *komkommer* in eastern Indonesia.

bution of this word in the Banda Sea indicates that highly influential traders from Geser and Gorom were almost certainly responsible for spreading this word in the Seram Laut region.

Rarely are loanwords from Dutch unique in Indonesia; the same words tend to be borrowed over and over. This poses challenges for understanding the precise nature of loaning events from Dutch. Where attested in multiple places in eastern Indonesia, it is often difficult to determine whether a loan has been borrowed repeatedly or is the result of spread through vehicular Malays. Take, for instance, the recurrent appearance of the Dutch loan *papa* 'father' in eastern Indonesia. On first glance it might be thought that the form diffused via local Malays such as Kupang Malay and Ternate Malay, which both attest loans of *papa*. The form is stable and so phonological adaptions that might give us clues about the circulation in the region are lacking. However, its geographical distribution is striking and this might offer some vital clues into its borrowing and the mode of its circulation. In Map 3 we see that loans of *papa* are highly circumscribed, clustering in small areas around key settlements (named on map) where Dutch is known to have had particular influence. And although it has been loaned into local Malays in these places, these do not seem to have been decisive in its spread; we might expect that if vehicular Malays played a large role in the spread of this loan that instances of it would appear across the map of eastern Indonesia. Instead, the highly clustered appearance indicates that it might rather be proximity to groups of Dutch (men) that is decisive in loaning of *papa*. This scenario is particularly useful in explaining the appearance of loans of *papa* in the languages around Kisar; a scenario in which *papa* spread through local Malay varieties for instance fails to explain why *papa* is borrowed into local languages on and around Kisar, but not elsewhere in the southern Moluccas.

In short, Dutch loans in eastern Indonesia have varied, complex histories that are often difficult to unpick the different strands of. What is clear, however, is that

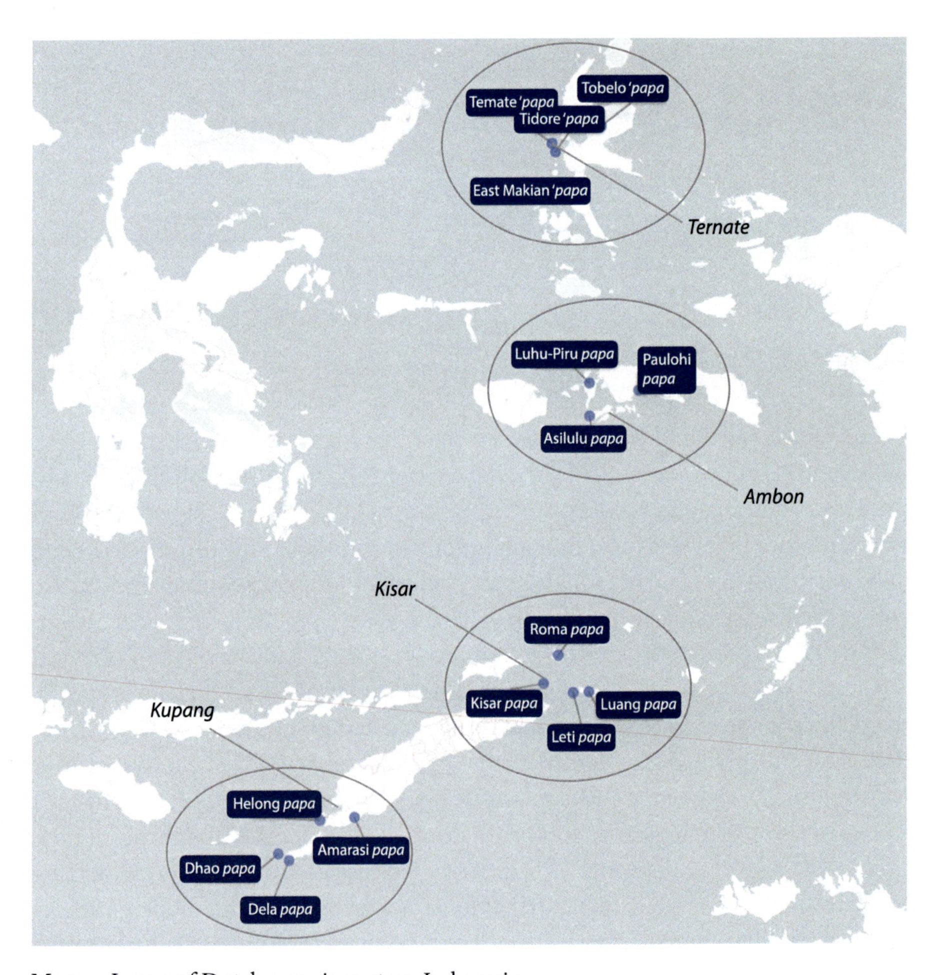

Map 3. Loans of Dutch *papa* in eastern Indonesia

loaning from Dutch was not simply through Malay varieties, but reflected numerous small-scale contact events and highly localised processes of diffusion, including spread between indigenous languages. In the following sections we show that influence from Ternate was an important mechanism for the dispersal of loanwords, including Dutch ones, throughout the Moluccas.

4. The Ternate language, its history and importance

The clove (*Syzygium aromaticum*) is a spice plant native to the island of Halmahera and its satellites whose highly aromatic flower buds were much sought after in the pre- and early modern period. The volcanic islands to Halmahera's west–Ternate, Tidore and Makian–became important centres for the cultivation, collection and trading of cloves from at least the 11th century (van Fraassen 1987: 30). The clove trade attracted ships to them, first from Majapahit Java, Arabia and China, and later in the 16th century from the naval powers of Europe (van Fraassen 1987: 28). Foremost amongst the centres of the spice-producing Moluccas was the island which came to be known as Ternate. Although situated on a tiny volcano at the fringe of the Spice Islands, the sultanate of Ternate exerted influence and power over a large swathe of people, controlling a small empire of tributaries that stretched, by some accounts, from southern Mindanao in today's southern Philippines and the eastern part of Sulawesi Island through the Raja Ampat Islands and the Ambon and Seram regions to Timor in the south (van Fraassen 1987: 333ff).

One of the spheres in which Ternate has had the most enduring influence is that of language. The Ternate language is a Papuan (or non-Austronesian language) closely related to the language of Tidore, another powerful sultanate located on the volcanic island of the same name to the south of Ternate. Both are part of the larger North Halmahera family whose members cover much of the northern half of the Halmahera archipelago. De Clercq (1890: 191) calls Ternate "de lingua franca van den Molukschen Archipel", elaborating:

> the original language of the actual Ternate people is understood by almost all subjects of the Sultan in beach settlements within the vast area of the sultanate; it is commonly used by traders when they come into contact with the population and is often preferred over their own language by *Alfurs* who have converted to Islam.[5]

5. Original: "de oorspronkelijke taal der echte Ternatanen wordt door bijna alle onderdanen des Sultans in de strandnegorijen van zijn uitgestrekt gebied verstaan, door handelaren bij aanraking met de bevolking algemeen gebezigd en door Alfoeren, die tot den Islam overgingen, dikwerf boven hun eigen taal verkozen."

The importance of Ternate as a language of general use in the Moluccas is evident from encounters of Dutch ships sailing westwards from New Guinea. Sailors could tell their position was in the vicinity of the Moluccas when they encountered the Ternate language. As the voyage of Jacob Le Maire and Willem van Schouten west across the Pacific neared its end in 1616, they remark that on the 3rd of August they had sailed past the end of New Guinea and already by the 5th they met a group with whom they could speak: "We could understand these people quite well, because they spoke some words of Ternate and one of them spoke Malay, a language which *Coopman* Aris Claesz had a good command of" (Schouten 1644: 49). Similarly, after having completed a voyage around Australia, New Zealand and New Guinea, an entry from Abel Tasman's journal in 1643 noted that a few days after they had left Cenderawasih Bay, they were approached by a small boat with six men and were asked in Ternate where they were heading; a crew member on board spoke Ternate and they were able to work out their position (Roeper & Wildeman 2006: 205). Although knowledge of Ternate was not always very deep, it was still more advanced than that of Malay: Dutch missionaries in Halmahera found that the local population hardly knew any Malay at all, while most at least "could speak Ternate to the extent that they were able to answer questions from the judge reasonably well" (Hueting 1930: 8).

Although of historical importance, the precise role of the Ternate language, both in contact with foreign trading powers and in the formation of unique varieties of Malay, has yet to be studied by linguists. Whilst it is beyond the scope of this chapter to provide such as treatment, a preliminary investigation of the role of the Ternate language in contact with Europeans and its impact on local Malays is presented in the following subsections.

4.1 Language use in European contact

Having uncovered the spice routes used by Asian and Middle Eastern traders for centuries, Europeans began arriving in the Moluccas in the 16th century: the Portuguese first in 1512, the Spanish in 1521, the English in 1579, and the Dutch in 1599. Over time and with fluctuating fortunes, these different European groups established forts, variously on the islands of Ternate, Tidore and Makian.

From the time of the earliest contacts with Europeans, it is clear from the historical sources that Malay was known by at least some people in the Moluccas. Letters written by the sultan of Ternate to the Portuguese king (1521, 1522) and to the English king (1605) are written in a literary Malay very close to the forms used in the Malay courts of the time, with little obvious local flavour (Litamahuputty 2012: 5–7, Gallop 2003: 413–418). Malay wordlists with some limited, but specifically Moluccan characteristics compiled in Ternate (1599, 1623) might be taken to indicate that a local Malay variety was already present in the Moluccas, but could just as well reflect Malay as used by their European compilers (Litamahuputty 2012: 8). The author of the *Treatise on the Moluccas* (c. 1544) describes the place as a Babel where the use of Malay was in "vogue":

> These peoples have many and different languages so that the islands represent a Babel; for not only does every one of them have its own, but there are also towns with different languages. Some speak from their throat in the Hebrew manner, others from the point of their tongue. So they resemble Latins, Germans, Englishmen, and Frenchmen. The [languages] are so many and so varied that neighbours scarcely understand each other, from which it seems to follow that the [islands] were populated by foreign crews. The kings, princes, and those who are familiar with them have a way of speaking not comprehensible to the others. At present the Malayan language has come into vogue; and most of them speak it and avail themselves of it throughout the whole region, where it is like Latin in Europe.
> (Jacobs 1971: 75)

From João de Barros' telling of Diego Lopez de Sequeira's experiences in the Moluccas, it is abundantly clear that in the early 16th century Malay was a language of elite communication with valued trading partners from the Malay courts to the west: "and if there is a language in which they are able to make themselves understood by one another, then it would be Malay, which the most prominent among them have begun to learn since the Moors started coming to get their cloves" (de Barros 1706: 131). Even in the second half of the 19th and first half of the 20th century, Malay was not widely in use in Halmahera. When the first Dutch missionaries arrived on Halmahera in the 1860s, the population in the interior of Halmahera did not speak Malay, while some people in coastal settlements were bilingual (Hueting 1930: 37). A similar situation was reported by Fortgens (1905: 23) about 40 years later, including the fact that not all Ternate officials on Halmahera could speak Malay.

Ternate appears to have been learned by Europeans.[6] In letters and reports written by Jesuit missionaries stationed in the Moluccas in the earliest period of contact with Europeans, knowledge of local language is mentioned on occasion: *sabia muito bem a lingoa daquela terra* [knew the language of that country very well] (Jacobs 1974: 702) or *sabem a lingoa da terra* [knew the local language] (Jacobs 1974: 702). Such statements are typically taken to refer to Malay (Jacobs 1974: 701). However, it is not at all clear that that is the only, let alone correct interpretation. Some sources explicitly name other languages. For instance, the Italian

6. We are very thankful to Betty Litamahuputty who identified most of the source passages referenced in this paragraph.

Lorenzo Masonio writing to a friend in Europe, apologises for his language errors, explaining that he never speaks Italian anymore, but only Spanish, Portuguese, Ternate, and Malay (Jacobs 1984: 332). In another document, it is observed that Antonio Fernandez, who had worked a few years in the Moluccas, "knew the Malay and Ternate languages" (Jacobs 1974: 355). Also the Dutch frequently used the Ternate language for administrative matters, with letters to and contracts with the Ternate court being written in Dutch and then translated into Ternate. Gijsbert van Lodensteyn, governor of the Moluccas (1629–1633), complains that translations of previously made contracts with the Ternate leaders were not very accurate, that not all parts of the Dutch-language contract were translated into Ternate, and that contracts were lost and new translations of older contracts had to be made (Tiele & Heeres 1890: 152). In his well-known *notitie* of 1670, Cornelius Speelman bemoans that the people being sent to him in Sulawesi did not have the requisite languages and would be better assigned elsewhere. He particularly observes that one Jan Jappan should be sent back to Ternate where his abilities in Ternate could be put to good use at court (Noorduyn 1983). Although such observations of language use in historical documents are typically quite limited, it is clear that knowledge of Ternate was also important for European trade in the Moluccas.

The major trading partners of the earliest Europeans also did not rely exclusively on communication in Malay, but in many cases learnt the languages of the new arrivals. According to the author of the *Treatise on the Moluccas*, Moluccan elites spoke Portuguese fluently and, on Tidore, Spanish. Later, a man captured from Tidore "knew Portuguese as well as if he had grown up in Lisbon" (Jacobs 1971: 239), while on Tidore "the chiefs of that island speak Portuguese and Castilian, sometimes mixing in Biscayan" (Jacobs 1971: 259). And Portuguese language skills persisted in Ternate long after the Portuguese were forced to relocate to Tidore in 1574. For instance, Kecil Gegogoe, the uncle of the sultan of Ternate, is noted to be fluent in Portuguese by the English during their 1605 visit to the Moluccas (Middleton 1855: 64–65). However, Dutch seems rarely to have been learnt by Moluccans. Only some Christianised elites are known to have learnt Dutch. For instance, a Prince of Siau, a small island near Manado, on Sulawesi, was noted in 1696 to be competent in Dutch (NA 1.04.02–8070), but no such observations exist for the Muslim groups of Ternate and Tidore. François Valentijn (1724, I-2:112) observed that a *kapitein* based in Ternate had taught Dutch to a Tidorese courtier in the early 18th century. This was regarded as a very dangerous, near traitorous action, as it was considered to give the local peoples an unwise insight into Dutch affairs.

4.2 Spheres of lexical influence

The 16th and 17th centuries in the Moluccas were times of enormous dynamism, not only politically but also linguistically. It is clear from the historical sources discussed above that Ternate was a melting pot in which multiple languages were in common use. Ternate and Malay seem to have intermingled freely. We see this, for instance, in the Malay-Dutch vocabulary published in 1623 where the Dutch missionaries Sebastiaan Danckaerts and Caspar Wiltens make note of important Ternate words commonly used in the Malay of the Moluccas. For instance, they list *monára* 'work' as one of the Ternate words commonly used in the Malay of their time. Map 4 shows that this Ternate word (a regular reflex of Proto-Core North Halmahera *monaram 'work, tool') is not only borrowed into regional Malays around Halmahera but also other languages on and around Halmahera. Because we know from historical observations that Malay had little role outside of urban centres in the early European contact period, it cannot be assumed that the dispersal of such words in the Moluccas was by means of Malay varieties. Rather Ternate lexemes spread outwards from Halmahera into surrounding languages independent from Malay, and as Malay use increased the most widely used Ternate words were also taken up into the local Malay varieties. Over time Ternate was gradually replaced as the language of intergroup communication and in its place rose a variety of Malays with a strong lexical imprint from Ternate. Yet, there has to date been no research into the extent and nature of Ternate lexical influence on these Malay varieties (Paauw 2009: 73).

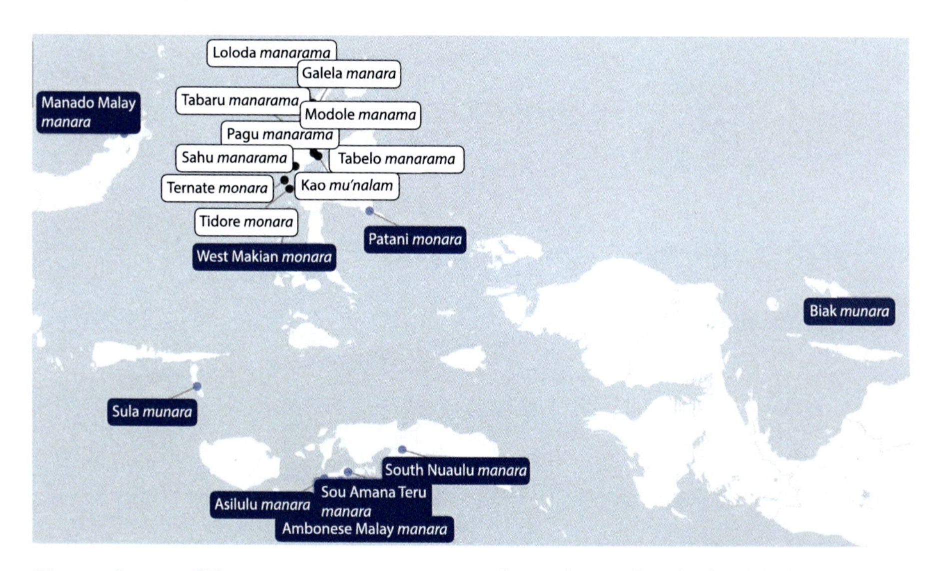

Map 4. Loans of Ternate *munara* ~ *monara* in the Moluccas (marked in blue)

In order to understand the vectors via which Dutch loans in Ternate came to be dispersed throughout eastern Indonesia, it is essential to have a picture of the lexical relationships that exist between the different vehicular varieties of Malay in eastern Indonesia. Map 5 sets out the geographical spheres of lexical influence that exist with respect to Malay varieties across eastern Indonesia. Whilst the map captures broad generalisations, dividing neighbouring islands into different Malay blocks is an idealisation which does not do justice to the complexities of Malay language use and how varieties shade into one another. As marked in the map, the defining lexical relationship that groups the Malays of the northern part of eastern Indonesia together is the presence of lexemes that ultimately go back to Ternate and the Papuan language of the same name as the island. Ternate lexemes have been borrowed into many indigenous languages of the North Moluccas and surrounds, but find their widest dispersals where they made their way into regional Malays as they developed into a web of interconnected lingua francas.

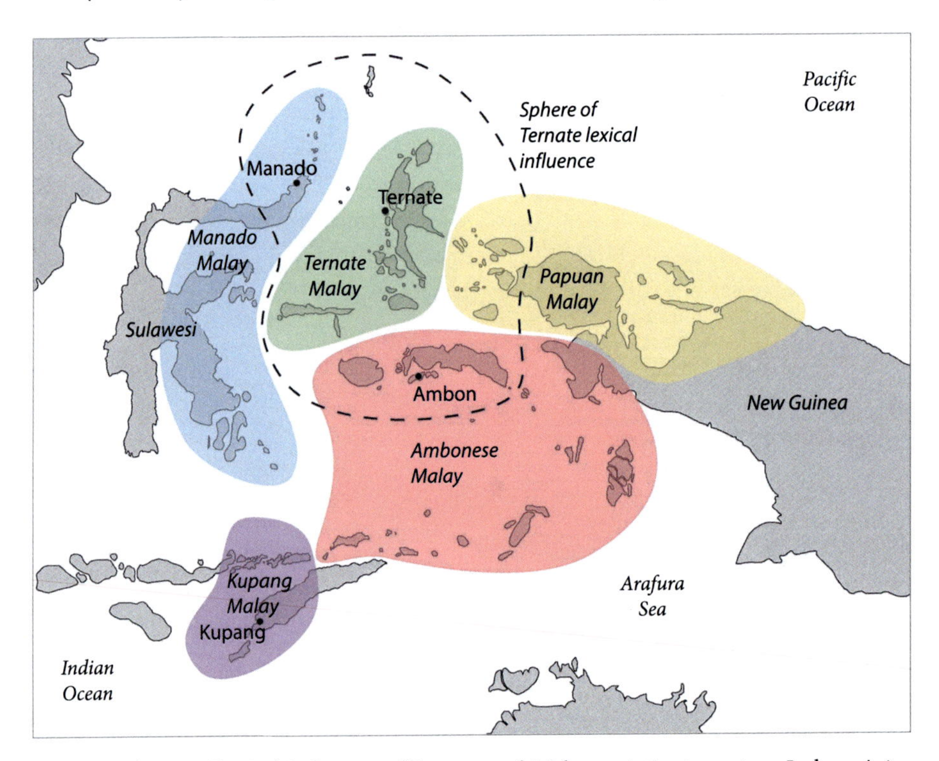

Map 5. Spheres of lexical influence of Ternate and Malay varieties in eastern Indonesia†

† "Papuan Malay" on this map is restricted to the northeast regions of the Bird's Head of New Guinea because this is where the materials which we use for this study are from. The label "Northwest coastal Papuan Malay" is perhaps a better descriptor of the variety that we deal with. In general, "Papuan Malay" is a problematic name as there are multiple varieties of Malay spoken in the western half of New Guinea (Donohue 2011).

Differences in the number and identity of Ternate loans in Malay varieties around Halmahera point to different historical forces at play, that is, different time-depths in the formation of the Malay varieties and different pathways by which Ternate lexemes entered the Malay varieties. For example, Ambonese Malay has numerous lexemes ultimately from Ternate, but these cannot all be understood as having been transferred via Moluccan Malay varieties such as Ternate Malay. Ambonese Malay *tatabuang* < Ternate *tatabuang* 'set of gongs' is not known in the existing documents on North Moluccan Malay, and was likely introduced into Ambonese Malay by another route. Ambonese Malay is thought to have initially begun its development following the establishment of the Portuguese settlement on the island in the late 16th century. The Portuguese had moved to Ambon after having been expelled from Ternate in 1575, and perhaps brought Ternate lexemes with them. Another route for the transmission of Ternate words into Ambonese Malay is via the many local languages of Ambon. Numerous Ambonese groups were aligned with the sultanate of Ternate and had long-standing trading relations with them (van Fraassen 1987: 275–281). This resulted in loans from Ternate into local Ambonese languages and then into Ambonese Malay. For instance, Ternate *gocefa* 'raft' is borrowed into Ambonese languages such as Asilulu *gusepa* and Larike *gusepa* 'raft' and from them into Ambonese Malay as *gusepa* 'raft'. This pathway is apparent from the phonological adaptions that have taken place: the indigenous languages of Ambon typically lack *c* and *p* and adapt those sounds as *s* and *f*; since Ambonese Malay has both *c* and *p*, the appearance of *s* and *f* in *gusepa* 'raft' is unexplained if we view the lexeme as a direct borrowing of Ternate *gocefa* without the mediation of other languages.

In short, very little work has been done to create a picture of historical language use in the parts of the Moluccas where Europeans collected and built forts, let alone the vast regions beyond them. The assumption that contact between the Ternate and Europeans was only facilitated by Malay and that Malay was the vehicle for transmission of loanwords is too simplistic and, crucially, does not fit with many of the known historical facts. Whilst a significant role for Malay cannot be denied, the historical sources from the earliest times suggest that Ternate was an important language in its own right. What is more, Ternate words can be shown to have spread both in indigenous languages and additionally in Malay varieties in different ways. In what follows, we show that among the many Ternate lexemes that were loaned into indigenous languages and regional Malay varieties are a body of lexemes that Ternate had itself loaned from Dutch. In this way, with Ternate as the vector of dispersal, Dutch loans can be seen to have achieved some wider dispersals in eastern Indonesia.

5. Out of the microcosm: Dutch borrowings in Ternate and beyond

As a major centre of both local and colonial power in the early modern period, Ternate occupies a special position with respect to the spread of Dutch loanwords in eastern Indonesia. The direct loans from Dutch that are found in Ternate, and the rationale for treating them as such, are set out in Section 5.1. As an important regional lingua franca, Ternate facilitated the spread of Dutch loanwords into other languages, discussed in Section 5.2. Section 5.3. deals with Dutch loanwords which spread via Ternate into eastern Malay varieties as well as local languages.

5.1 Dutch loans in Ternate

Table 1 sets out the 111 loans that we posit to be borrowed directly from Dutch into Ternate. We did not consider words to do with modern technologies (e.g., mechanised transport, telecommunications, etc.), a domain where Dutch loans abound. Instead, we focussed exclusively on loans that could plausibly go back to the early modern times, thus reflecting the period of significance for Dutch-Ternate contact. In compiling this list, in order to determine that a Ternate form was a direct borrowing from Dutch, we required either that there was no Malay loan of the Dutch word, or that the Ternate form showed phonological and/or semantic differences from the Malay loan such that it warranted treatment as an independent borrowing.[7]

Some systemic differences can be observed in the adaption of Dutch loans in Ternate and Malay.[8] For example, Dutch *eu* (/ø/) is adapted as *e* in Malay (and /i/ or /u/ before /r/), but as *o* in Ternate (e.g. *beul* 'executioner' > *bol* 'executioner'). Hence, Ternate *trosol* 'disturb, annoy' was likely directly borrowed from Dutch *treuzelen* 'dawdle'. In both Malay and Ternate, Dutch /ɛi/ (spelled <ij> or <ei>) is replaced by /ai/, /e/ or /i/, but in Ternate it is also sometimes reflected as /ei/ [ɛi] (e.g. Ternate *sandrei* 'celery' < Dutch *selderij* 'celery'). Hence, Ternate *rei* 'row' is likely directly from Dutch *rij* 'row'. The Dutch diphthong spelled <ui> (pronounced approximately /œy/ ~ /ʌy/) is adapted to /e/ or /i/ in both Malay and Ternate, but in Ternate replacements by /oi/ (e.g. Ternate *krois* < Dutch *kruis* 'cross') and /u/ (e.g. Ternate *perumpis* 'to chew tobacco, tobacco quid' < Dutch *pruimpjes* 'quid') are also found.

---

7. Throughout this section we use the term "Malay" to refer to western Malay varieties that were used as the basis for standard Indonesian. Where a specific variety of Malay in eastern Indonesia is meant, we always refer to it using its particular name, e.g., Ambonese Malay.

8. Phonetic adaptions in Malay based on de Vries (1988).

Table 1. Dutch words hypothesized to be loaned directly into Ternate

Dutch source	Ternate
aardappel 'potato'	*artape*
admiraal 'admiral'	*amral* 'pennant'
afrekenen 'pay'	*afreken*
akkoord 'agreed'	*akor*
arrest 'arrest'	*ares*
bal 'ball'	*bal*
balans 'balance'	*balas* 'state of equilibrium, balance'
benauwd 'stuffy, poorly ventilated'	*benau* 'sultry'
berekenen 'calculate'	*bereken*
beul 'executioner'	*bol*
bloes 'shirt, blouse'	*bilus*
borduren 'embroider'	*boldir, budur*
boot 'boat'	*bot*
brik 'kind of ship'	*brek* 'k.o. ship'
brood 'bread'	*brot*
burger 'citizen'	*borgo, borgor* 'freeman, citizen soldier'
commanderen 'command'	*komder* ~ *komter* 'command'[a]
controleur 'control'	*kontolor* 'inspector, supervisor, inspect, check'
dam 'checkers (game)'	*dam-dam* 'chequered'
deuntje 'tune'	*donci* 'tune'
dozijn 'dozen'	*dosin, disin*
dukaton 'k.o. coin'	*likitong* 'k.o. coin'[b]
epaulet 'epaulette'	*plet, pelet* 'shoulder badge of officers'
fiskaal 'officier of the VOC'	*fiskal* 'Dutch secretary'
flauwte 'sudden loss of consciousness'	*flaut* 'fainted'
fluit 'flute'	*filut, filutu*
gaanderij 'balcony'	*gandaria* 'verandah in front of house'
gebed 'prayer'	*gebet* 'church service'[c]
gek 'crazy, mad'	*hek-hek* 'a foolish person; windbag'
gouvernement 'colonial government'	*gufernement* 'colonial government'
gouverneur 'governor'	*gufernur* 'governor'
grap 'joke'	*garap*
gulden 'golden'	*golden* [d]

Table 1. *(continued)*

Dutch source	Ternate
kardoes 'package'	*gardus* 'cartridge'
kastje 'cabinet'	*kasi, kas* 'box, case'
klaag(je) 'complaint'	*kalak, kalaki* 'accusation, charge, accuse'
klaar 'finished'	*kalar*
kleur 'color'	*kler*
kapstok 'hatstand'	*kapstok* 'hatstand'
klamp 'clamp'	*klam* 'door-catch'
klarinet 'clarinet'	*klawarnet* 'clarinet'
komedie 'comedy'	*komedi* 'place under the balcony of the sultan's palace where music is performed, comedy, musical performance'
kop(je) 'cup'	*kopi* 'cup'
kroon 'crown'	*kron* 'crown'
kroontje 'crown'	*kronci* 'crown'
kruis 'cross'	*krois* 'cross'
kruisen 'to cruise'	*krois* 'to cruise'
kwart(je) 'quarter'	*kwari, kuari* 'string of coins worth 25 cents'
kwast 'tassel, brush'	*kuwas*
legger 'large barrel'	*leger* 'water channel'
lepel 'spoon'	*leper* 'spoon, ladle'
lever 'liver'	*lefer* 'k.o. disease'
lijfwacht 'bodyguard'	*liwaka* 'Dutch guard for the Sultan'
maak klaar 'get ready'	*makalar* 'get ready'
marcheren 'march'	*marsel* 'march'
mars 'march'	*maris*
metselen 'lay bricks, build'	*mesel* 'floor, cement, cement wall, cement floor'
mevrouw 'madam'	*mamfrou* 'Mrs'[e]
muzikant 'musician'	*mojikan, miskan* 'musician playing a drum with a skin on both ends, fastened to his waist'
officier 'officer'	*ofsir* 'officer'
oppas 'guard'	*upas* 'valet (court official of the lowest rank), sultan's attendant'
over 'over'	*ofor* 'over'
paar 'pair'	*par* 'pair'

Table 1. *(continued)*

Dutch source	Ternate
pijper 'piper'	*peper* 'piper, musical instrument'
plakkaat 'placard'	*palakat* 'public notice'
platte boontjes 'kind of bean'	*platboncis* 'kind of bean'
pluim 'plume'	*pelem* 'plume'
pond 'metric pound'	*pont* 'unit of measurement'
potje 'little pot'	*poci* 'oil lamp'
potje thee 'pot of tea'	*pocete* 'pot of tea'
prins(je) 'prince'	*prins, prinsi* 'title for the male descendants of the ruler'
pruimpjes 'quid'	*perumpis* 'to chew tobacco, tobacco quid'
raad 'council'	*rat* 'Council of the Indies'
raaien 'guess'	*rai-rai* 'approximately'
remedie 'remedy'	*ramedi* 'put a lot of effort into making up for something, putting things in order'
resident 'head of the Dutch administration'	*resident* 'head of the Dutch administration'
rij 'row'	*rei* 'row'
roffel 'drum'	*rofol* 'drum roll'
rustbank 'sofa'	*rosbang* 'sofa'
selderij 'celery'	*sandrei* 'celery'
schalmei 'shawm'	*iskilmai* 'clarinet-shaped wind instrument which plays the tune at the lego performances in the Sultan's palace'
schildwacht 'sentry'	*skilwak* ~ *silwak* 'sentry'
scherm 'screen'	*skerm* 'screen'
schoener 'k.o. boat'	*iskunyer* 'k.o. boat'
schuitje 'small boat'	*iskuci* 'rowing-boat'
schroef 'screw'	*iskruf* 'screw'
servet 'napkin'	*saraweta*
smeerlap 'nasty or disgusting person'	*smerlap* 'scoundrel'
Spaanse mat 'Spanish dollar'	*pasmat* 'Spanish dollar'
sterk 'strong'	*sterk, sterek* 'good, beautiful'
stinken 'to stink'	*stinken* 'sweet-smelling'
storing 'disturbance'	*istori* 'noise, uproar'[f]
strik 'tie, knot, bow knot'	*strik* 'bow (e.g. in ribbon)'
streep 'stripe'	*sterep* 'stripe, striped'

Table 1. *(continued)*

Dutch source	Ternate
te laat 'too late'	*talat* 'late'
tent(je) 'tent'	*tenti* 'canvas, canvas sunshade'
tolk 'interpreter'	*tolk*
treuzelen 'dawdle'	*trosol* 'disturb, annoy'
(uit)monstering 'outfitting'	*mantereng, mentereng* 'outfit, uniform'
vals 'false'	*falus* 'false (of weights)'
van doen (hebben) 'to require'	*fandun* 'need, involved'
veranderen 'to change'	*farandel* 'change'
verbannen 'banish'	*forban* 'to ban'
vergaderen 'to gather, assemble'	*fargader* 'to have a meeting'
verhemelte 'canopy'	*farhemel* 'tester (of a four-poster bed)'
verspieden 'spy'	*forspit* 'a scout (e.g. after an elopement the person who goes to sound out the parents of the girl about their attitude towards the affair), to scout'
vloer 'floor, ground'	*flur*
voorhuis 'front section of the house'	*fores, foris* 'living/reception room'
voorschot 'advance, down payment'	*forskot* 'advance payment, down payment'
vork 'fork'	*forok, fork*
weer 'weather'	*wer* 'weather'

a. Voorhoeve & van Fraassen (no date) *komder* and *komter* as variants for 'command', but they also assign an additional nominal meaning 'delegate' to *komder*. It is not clear at this time whether this a separate borrowing or not.
b. Comparative investigation of this item and the kind of coin it referred to, have made clear that this did indeed refer to the Dutch *dukaton*, a silver coin with a horse on it, often referred to as the *zilveren (rijder)* or the *vlaamsche rijder*. The adaption of initial Dutch *d* as *l* is unexplained. It is possible that various intermediates were involved, but further attestations of the form have not been identified at this time. Tidore is the most plausible source, as it evidences the change *d > *l* /_*i*, but the form is not attested there.
c. Ternate also had *kabeti* 'lead in prayer, lead a Christian service'. The difference in the initial consonant, the final vowel, and the meaning all suggest that this was likely the result of a distinct borrowing event.
d. This form is unexpected: Modern Dutch has *gouden*, but Middle Dutch *gulden*. It is conceivable that this is in fact a loan from English.
e. The nasal in the Ternate is unexpected and suggests that the source form was not *mevrouw*, but a (possibly dialectal) form *mən vrouw*. Such a source form with a nasal would adequately explain the appearance of the /mf/ cluster in Ternate, as clusters with nasals are always homorganic in Ternate.
f. Voorhoeve & van Fraassen (no date) suggest this is from *verstoring*, but the loss of the initial *ver-* would be unexpected.

Oftentimes differences between Dutch loans in Ternate and Malay are small, but where they are sufficiently distinctive and/or not part of a systematic difference between Malay and Ternate, we regard them as sufficient evidence of independent borrowing. For instance, Dutch *akkoord* is loaned into Malay as *akur* and Ternate as *akor*. There is no evidence for a pattern of adaption whereby Malay *u* becomes *o* in Ternate, and so Ternate *akor* is treated as a direct loan from Dutch. Similarly, loans of Dutch *schuitje* are found in Ternate as *iskuci* and Malay as *skoci*. The highly distinctive prosthetic *i* and the less distinctive, but still notable medial *u*, as opposed to the Malay *o*, both suggest that borrowing of *schuitje* took place independently in Ternate. However, we exclude Ternate *sloki* 'small drinking glass for gin' < Dutch *slokje* 'little sip', as there are no distinctive phonological differences to set it apart from Malay *səloki* 'shot glass'; epenthetic, unstressed central vowels are rendered very inconsistently in spoken and written speech in the eastern Indonesian region.

Semantic and morphological differences can be crucial for detecting direct loans in Ternate as opposed to scenarios where Malay acts as an intermediary. For instance, Dutch *potje* is loaned as *poci* into both Ternate and Malay, but with different semantics: Ternate *poci* 'oil lamp', but Malay *poci* 'earthenware receptacle for boiling coffee or tea; teapot; coffeepot'. The Ternate equivalent of the latter Malay term is *pocete* < Dutch *potje thee*. Malay *kas* 'crate, case, wardrobe' is loaned from Dutch *kast*, while Ternate *kasi* 'box, chest' is borrowed from Dutch *kastje*.[9] In both cases, the differences between the Ternate and Malay forms make clear that distinct borrowing events took place in each of the languages.

In numerous cases, it is difficult to decide whether a word was borrowed directly from Dutch or is part of wider spread via Malay. For example, Ternate *dam-dam* 'chequered' could be a direct borrowing from Dutch *dam* 'king (in checkers)' or an indirect borrowing of Malay *dam* 'checkers (game), checker (pattern)'. The innovative semantics 'checker (pattern)' suggests the latter possibility, while the reduplicated form of the Ternate word indicates an independent borrowing or an intermediate source other than Malay. Likewise, Ternate *palakat* 'public notice' could be directly from Dutch *plakkaat* 'placard' or via Malay *plakat* 'placard'. The innovative form in Ternate, which is also found in several other languages, and the epenthetic vowel /a/ suggests an independent borrowing. Nevertheless, it cannot be excluded that the word was first borrowed from Malay and then its semantics and phonological form was changed. Only cases where there is

9. From the sources it appears that there may be a lexical split underway in Ternate whereby *kasi* is becoming specialised as 'box, chest', while *kas* under Malay influence is 'cupboard'. Originally, these would have just been variants, as dropping final *i* is common in Ternate.

at least some evidence for direct borrowing from Dutch into Ternate have been included in our study.

Not included in our body of Dutch loanwords are a number of lexemes in Ternate whose loan sources are equivocal. For example, there are several Ternate words which do not fit the usual phonotactic rules of the language and "look Dutch", but for which no Dutch source word has been identified yet. For instance, *st* is not a cluster known in native Ternate words, but is recurrent in known Dutch borrowings. Items such *stager* 'belt' and *stingkam* 'kind of very fine cloth' are therefore suspected as loans from Dutch, though the source is not known. Another excluded item is Ternate *sitingki* 'k.o. fragrant mango, *Mangifera odorata*'. Whilst we suspect Dutch *stinkje* 'smelly one' to be the source, the semantic shift makes the connection too speculative at this stage.

Within the body of loans from Dutch in Ternate, there is evidence for different layers of loaning. This is seen most clearly in the application of different phonological adaptions in the process of loaning. We have identified two recurrent, differential processes of adaption that suggest loan may have taken place into Ternate at different times:

i. Prosthesis of *i*. Dutch words with initial *sch* /sx/ are typically loaned into Ternate with prosthetic *i* (e.g., *schoener* > Ternate *iskunyer*), but not always (e.g., *schildwacht* > Ternate *skilwak* ~ *silwak*).
ii. Variable *-er* and *-el*. Dutch verbs ending in *-eren* are often adapted with final *-er* (e.g., *vergaderen* > Ternate *fargader* 'to have a meeting'), but on occasions with final *-el* in Ternate (e.g., *veranderen* > *farandel* 'change').

A possible third process is worth mentioning. Some Dutch words loaned into Ternate appear with a final *i* that can often be dropped. There are two possible explanations for such forms. Firstly, they could represent the Dutch diminutive suffix *-je* adapted as final *(c)i* in Ternate (e.g., *kronci* 'crown' < *kroontje* 'little crown', *prinsi* ~ *prins* 'title for the male descendants of the ruler' < *prinsje* 'little prince'). Alternatively, final *i* in Ternate could be seen as paragogic (i.e., appended to the end of a word). Some North Halmahera languages require open syllables in word-final position and hence add a final vowel to consonant-final roots. This does appear to be the case with some loanwords from other languages in Ternate (e.g., Ternate *ahadi* ~ *ahad* 'Sunday' ultimately from Arabic *ʔaḥad*). Hayami-Allen (2001: 30–31) writes that the process of final vowel loss is ongoing in contemporary Ternate. This could be argued to mean that the final *i* on many Dutch loanwords is also paragogic. Because final *i* does not occur on Dutch loans in Ternate where Dutch *-je* would be impossible, we tentatively assume that Ternate final *i* on Dutch loans represents the Dutch diminutive, but recognise that this is not unproblematic.

The prolonged and intensive contact with speakers of Dutch led to the borrowing of words into Ternate from a wide range of semantic fields. Most common are loans that pertain to administration (e.g. *afreken* < *afrekenen* 'to pay'), justice (e.g. *forban* < *verbannen* 'to ban, banish', *bol* < *beul* 'executioner') and the military (e.g. *ofsir* < *officier* 'officier'). In other words: terms that were necessary for day-to-day Dutch-Ternate interactions in the political sphere. Loans from the field of technology (e.g. *leger* 'water channel' < *legger* 'water barrel') and cultural activities are also found (e.g. *komedi* 'place under the balcony of the sultan's palace where music is performed, comedy, musical performance' < *komedie* 'comedy'). Ternate also borrowed several expressions from Dutch as unanalysed chunks (e.g., *makalar* < *maak klaar* 'get ready', *talat* 'late' < *te laat* 'too late', *fandun* 'need, involved' < *van doen* 'have to').

Most loans in Ternate retained semantics broadly in line with their Dutch sources, but semantic shift does occur in some cases. Especially frequent are semantic narrowings where a semantically broad original became restricted to expressing a specific cultural artefact. For example, *mojikan, miskan* 'musician playing a drum with a skin on both ends, fastened to his waist' < *muzikant* 'musician' or *iskilmai* 'clarinet-shaped wind instrument which plays the tune at the *lego* [k.o. dance] performances in the Sultan's palace' < *schalmei* 'shawm'.

5.2 Dutch loans spread from Ternate to non-Malay languages

Of the Dutch loans borrowed into Ternate, several have spread further without also being borrowed into local Malay varieties. In some cases, the spread from Ternate is apparent because Malay varieties have a loan from a different source, e.g. Malay *bola* < Portuguese *bola* 'ball', while Ternate *bal* < Dutch *bal* 'ball'. In other cases, Malay and Ternate borrowed from the same language but separately; this is apparent due to different phonological forms, e.g. Malay *lusin* vs. Ternate *dosin, disin* < Dutch *dozijn* 'dozen'.

For the majority of Dutch loans of this type, the dispersal from Ternate into other languages is often quite limited, typically only one or two other languages. Ternate *sterk* ~ *sterek* 'good, beautiful' < Dutch *sterk* is only known to be borrowed into two languages to the south of Ternate, Tidore *sterk* and Taba *sterek*. That these represent Dutch loans via Ternate is indicated by the fact that they also have the figurative meaning 'good, beautiful' found in Ternate. Ambonese Malay also has the form *sterek* but has retained the original meaning 'strong in physique', pointing to an independent borrowing directly from Dutch. In other cases, however, it is unclear whether these Dutch loans of limited distribution represent borrowing via Ternate or independent borrowing events. For example, in the case of Tidore *artafe* 'potato' and Larike *wer* 'weather', it is unclear whether these are loans via Ternate *artape* 'potato' and *wer* 'weather' or independent borrowing event from Dutch. Both routes are possible given what is known about historical interactions in the area.

Dutch loanwords dispersed via Ternate extend maximally from the east coast of Sulawesi through to Cenderwasih Bay to the east of the Bird's Head of New Guinea, as well as south through the Central and Southern Moluccas. Map 6 illustrates this "maximal" distribution on the basis of loans reflecting Dutch *bal*. Not all of these can be attributed to circulation from Ternate with complete certainty. Indeed, even where dispersal is from Ternate multiple intermediate vector languages must be assumed. Additionally, the possibility of independent borrowing from Dutch must also be considered. But at least for some of the contact situations that are known about there is reason to exclude that scenario in this case. For instance, the contact between Dutch speakers and local groups on Kisar resulted in a body of loanwords directly from Dutch, as described in Section 3. However, direct borrowing is not supported by the data in the case of Dutch *bal*, because Dutch *b* is adapted as *p* in direct borrowings in Kisar and Leti. The fact that we have *b* in Kisar and Leti loans of *bal* suggests that the loans entered the languages by a different route, and likely at a later date once *b* had already entered the languages as a loan phoneme.[10]

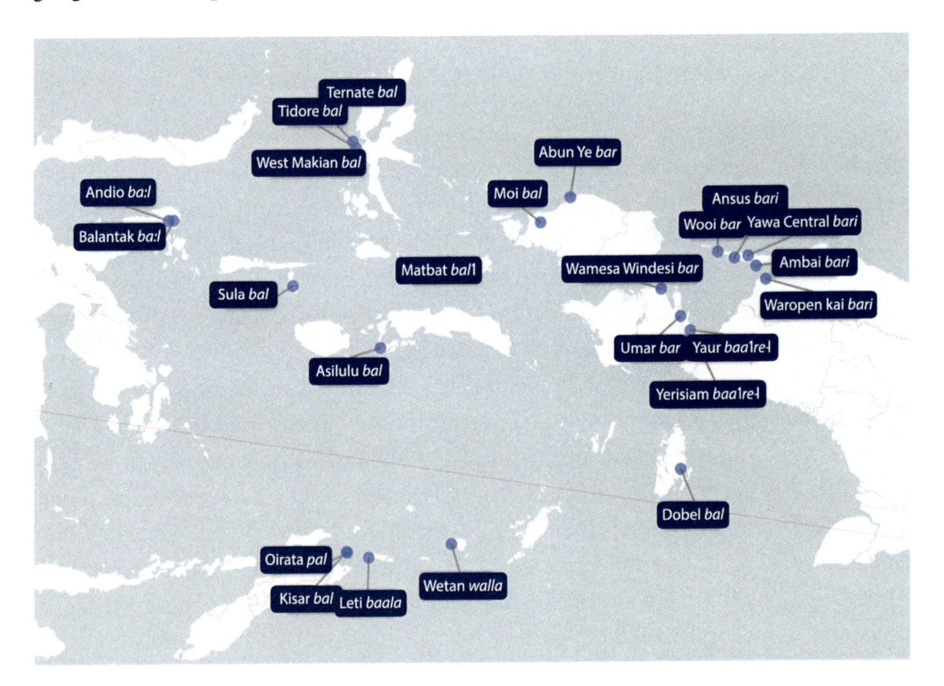

Map 6. Distribution of borrowings of Dutch *bal*

10. The phoneme /b/ is not part of the native inventory in these languages.

More typical for loanwords from Dutch via Ternate, but without the involvement of Malay, is a more limited distribution involving languages around Halmahera, but particularly extending east through the Raja Ampat islands. An example of this kind of distribution is seen with Ternate *fandun* 'need' < Dutch *van doen* 'have to' in Map 7. Unlike many other Dutch loans where borrowing can be seen to have taken place repeatedly across Indonesia, this loan stands out for its uniqueness to this part of Indonesia. Biak was key to this eastern dispersal as it was spoken throughout the Raja Ampat islands and on settlements on the north coast of the Bird's Head as a lingua franca (Schapper and van Schie forthcoming). Biak speakers were involved in the trade networks with the sultan of Tidore and are known to have regularly travelled to the east of Halmahera (Kamma 1972: 8). Some older lists state that loans of Dutch *van doen* are also present in some Moluccan Malay varieties (Ambonese Malay *van doen,* van Hoëvell 1876; Manado Malay *fandoeng,* de Clercq 1876), but it is not attested in modern-day descriptions of those languages. Given that the historical record makes clear that Malay was not used in the regions where *fandun* is found, dispersal via the local lingua francas, Ternate and then in turn Biak, represents a better historically grounded scenario for the spread of this loan.

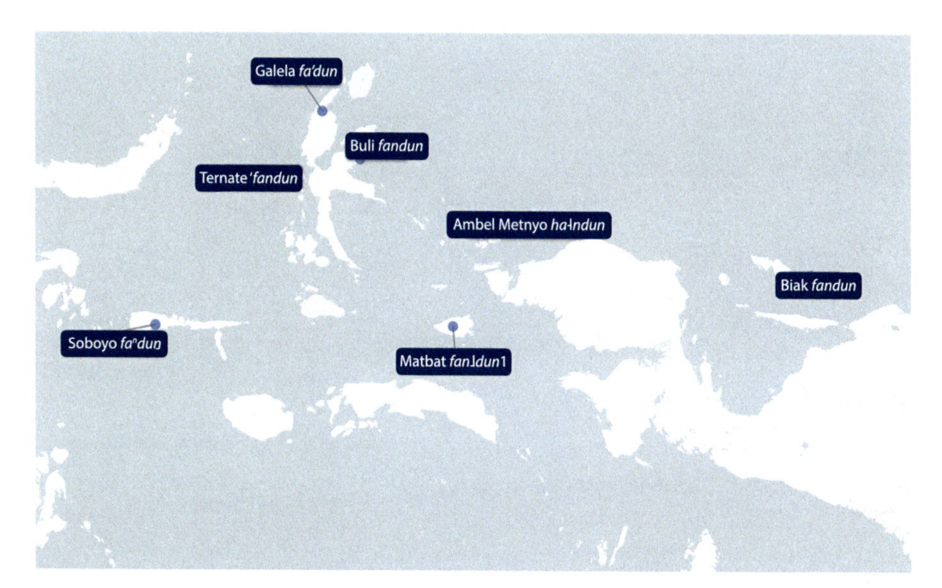

Map 7. Distribution of borrowings of Dutch *van doen*

5.3 Dutch loans spread from Ternate into Malay varieties

Numerous Dutch loans borrowed into Ternate have also entered local Malay varieties in the region, contributing to their distinct character. Of these, some have diffused only within Ternate, that is, from Ternate to Ternate Malay, but not further (e.g., Ternate Malay *benau* 'sultry' < Ternate *bernau* < Dutch *benauwd* 'stuffy, poorly ventilated'; Ternate Malay *flaut* 'faint' < Ternate *flaut* < Dutch *flauwte* 'sudden loss of consciousness'). In other cases, there is diffusion to a relatively small number of languages in the region, including local North Moluccan and Manado Malay (e.g., Ternate Malay, Manado Malay, Tobelo, Gane *leper* 'spoon' < Ternate *leper* < Dutch *lepel* 'spoon'). The directionality of borrowing from Ternate to Malay varieties here is suggested by particular loan adaptions typical of Ternate: (i) the loss of the final segment is common in Ternate, but not in Malay, and (ii) replacement of final Dutch *l* with *r* which is known to occur in Ternate in the environment of *e* (see fuller description in Section 5.1).

Map 8. Distribution of borrowings of Dutch *vork* (blue) versus *Portuguese garfo* (red)

For those items that have wider distributions, it is not at all apparent that local Malay varieties necessarily played a large role in dispersing the Dutch loans that had entered Ternate. For instance, take the dispersal of loans of Dutch *vork* 'fork' in Map 8. Whilst the precise languages which have the loan are variable, there is little difference in the overall extent of loan dispersal when compared to the loans of Dutch *bal* 'ball' in Map 3, where there was no known penetration into eastern Malay varieties. Also in the case of Dutch *vork*, loanwords spread following established trade and contact routes centred around Ternate. Particularly interesting here is that loans of Dutch *vork* seem to have largely displaced those of Portuguese *garfo* 'fork'. Given the Portuguese were present in the Moluccas almost a century before the Dutch, the Portuguese loans were likely earlier and the remaining forms represent this earlier loaning. The replacement with a later Dutch loan throughout much of the region speaks strongly to the influence flowing from Ternate where the Dutch were based.

Not all Dutch loans in Malay varieties in the Moluccas originate in a loan into Ternate. This is particularly apparent in cases where two borrowing trajectories are found, one via Ternate and one via varieties of Malay. Dutch *fluit* 'flute' was independently borrowed by Ternate and the Malay varieties (Map 9). Ternate simplified the onset as *filut* ~ *filutu* (blue in Map 9), while Malay varieties kept the consonant cluster: Ternate Malay *floit*, Ambonese Malay *floit*, Manado Malay *floit* (red in Map 9). Gamkonora, Sahu and Sula adopted the Ternate forms while other languages borrowed the form from a Malay variety. Additionally, there are Dutch loans that are found in local Malay varieties in the region that are not known in Ternate. These include: North Moluccan Malay *kakarlak*, Ambonese Malay *kakerlaak*, Manado Malay *kakerlak*, Papuan Malay *kakerlak* 'cockroach' < Dutch *kakkerlak*; North Moluccan Malay *lur*, Ambonese Malay *luur*, Papuan Malay *lur* 'spy on, peek at' < Dutch *loeren*. Such loans are further indications that Dutch loans did circulate through Malay varieties, but these tended to be different from those that originated in Ternate and probably part of a later period of Dutch influence after Ternate had lost much of its function as a lingua franca and where Malay had become established.

Map 9. Distribution of loans of Dutch *fluit* (blue – loaned via Ternate; red – loaned via Malay)

6. Concluding discussion

Speakers of Dutch were present in the Moluccas from the time of the late 16th century. The form of this presence was not that of an all-encompassing administrative or military system. Rather, it involved many small bases where Dutch speakers lived in close contact with indigenous peoples, speaking a range of different languages. Over the centuries of colonial rule, these contacts lead to numerous micro-dispersals of Dutch words, often only into one single language. When studying the broad sweep of Indonesian linguistic history, such small-scale contacts are easily overlooked. It has been the purpose of this chapter to draw attention to the existence of loanwords resulting from these contact events within the Moluccas.

Perhaps the most consequential contact with Dutch speakers that occurred in the Moluccas was on the island of Ternate. Here the Dutch mingled with the local people speaking Ternate and many unique loanwords made their way from Dutch into the Ternate language. We have argued that the role of Ternate in dispersing many Dutch words has been overlooked because of the subsequent dominance of Malay in the Moluccas. It is easy to assume that many of the distinctive Dutch loanwords found in the Moluccas were transmitted through local Malay varieties, but Ternate was an important lingua franca before Malay and many loanwords from it are found throughout the region. As the administrative language of the most powerful indigenous state in the region, Ternate was learned by the local population as well as incoming Europeans. Malay, on the other hand, was of lower importance as an inter-ethnic means of communication. Dutch loanwords were first adopted into Ternate and then spread by traders and officials into the local languages. This is similar to the way Ternate loans dispersed throughout the region.

In the context of both these microcosms of contact and the larger picture of loanword spreads via Ternate, it is useful to consider the concept of "imposition". In a situation where a higher status minority group learns the language of the lower status majority, the minority may impose features of their non-native variety of the majority language onto the majority (cf. Hickey 2010: 19). Dutch speakers, who as representatives of the colonial government formed such a high-status minority group, likely used Dutch words while speaking Ternate or other local languages, especially for new or Dutch-specific concepts. The local population picked up the Dutch words while communicating with Dutch speakers in a local language rather than while speaking Dutch. Dutch may have been learned by a few elites, but to a lesser extent than, for instance, Ternate was learned by speakers of Dutch. While it is possible that Dutch loans pertaining to the court of Ternate were introduced by Dutch speaking Ternate elites, loans pertaining to new foods, architecture, technology, or common exclamations were more likely spread through imposition. Imposition is also the most likely scenario in microcosms of contact where a very small group of Dutch speakers (sometimes only a missionary and his family) lived among the local population and used their language in daily life.

As lingua francas whose use and extent overlapped to a significant extent in the early modern period, Ternate and Malay in the Moluccas both took on loanwords from Dutch. While many loans are unique to one language or the other, oftentimes the same loanwords are found in Ternate and Moluccan varieties of Malay. This speaks to the importance and interplay of both Ternate and Malay as contact languages in the early period of the Dutch presence in the Moluccas, a fact that is easily overlooked given the subsequent dominance of Malay.

References

doi Adelaar, K.A., and D.J. Prentice. 1996. Malay: Its History, Role and Spread. In *Atlas of Languages of Intercultural Communication in the Pacific, Asia, and the Americas*, ed. by Stephen A. Wurm, Peter Mühlhäusler and Darrell T. Tryon, 673–693. Berlin: Mouton de Gruyter.

de Barros, João. 1706. *De doorlugtige scheeps-togten der Portugysen na Oost-Indiën, mitsgaders de voornaamste gedeeltens van Africa en de Roode-Zee … / Voor desen ten deele versameld en in 't Hoogduyts uytgegeven door den vermaarden heer Johan Lodewyk Gottfried … maar nu volkomen, gelijk deselve door Joan de Barros … uyt de egte handschriften der reysigers beschreven zijn … uytgevoerd … Alles onlangs uyt het Portugys in 't Nederlands getrouwelijk vertaalt.* Leyden: Pieter vander Aa.

Berg, René van den. 1995. Forestry, Injections and Cards: Dutch Loans in Muna. In *Tales from a concave world: Liber amicorum Bert Voorhoeve*, ed. by Connie Baak, Mary Bakker and Dick van der Meij. Leiden: Department of Languages and Cultures of South-East Asia and Oceania.

de Clercq, F. S. A. 1876. *Het Maleisch der Molukken: lijst der meest voorkomende vreemde en van het gewone Maleisch verschillende woorden, zooals die gebruikt worden in de residentieën Manado, Ternate, Ambon met Banda en Timor Koepang ; benevens eenige proeven van aldaar vervaardigde pantoens, prozastukken en gedichten.* Batavia: Bruining.

doi Clercq, Frederick S. A. de. 1890. *Bijdragen tot de kennis der residentie Ternate.* Leiden: Brill.

Collins, James T. 2003a. *Asilulu-English Dictionary.* Jakarta: Badan Penyelenggaraan Seri Nusa, Universitas Katolik Indonesia Atma Jaya.

doi Collins, James T. 2003b. Language Death in Maluku: The Impact of the VOC. *Bijdragen tot de Taal Land- en Volkenkunde van Nederlandsch-Indië* 159. 247–289.

doi Donohue, Mark. 1996. Notes on the Use of Geser as a Trade Language in Eastern Indonesia. In *Atlas of Languages of Intercultural Communication in the Pacific, Asia, and the Americas*, ed. by Stephen A. Wurm, Peter Mühlhäusler and Darrell T. Tryon, 717–718. Berlin: Mouton de Gruyter.

doi Donohue, Mark. 2011. Papuan Malay of New Guinea: Melanesian Influence on Verb and Clause Structure. In *Creoles, their Substrates, and Language Typology*, ed. by Claire Lefebvre, 413–435. Amsterdam: John Benjamins.

Ellen, Roy. 2003. *On the Edge of the Banda Zone.* Honolulu: Hawai'i University Press.

Engelenhoven, Aone van. 2016. The Dutch Enigma of Kisar Island: Buku Tembaga (Southwest Maluku, Indonesia). In *Vêrlander, Forgotten Children of the VOC*, ed. by G. Snoeijer and N. Peters, 60–91. Amsterdam: Vêrlander Publishing.

Florey, Margaret, and Michael C. Ewing. 2010. Political acts and language revitalisation: community and state in Maluku. *Endangered Austronesian and Australian Aboriginal language: essays on language documentation, archiving and revitalization*, ed. by Gunter Senft, 155–173. Canberra: Pacific Linguistics.

Fortgens, J. 1905. Vier weken onder de Tabaru en Waioli van Noord-West Halemahera. *Mededeelingen vanwege het Nederlandsch Zendelinggenootschap* 49(1). 1–53.

van Fraassen, Chris F. 1987. Ternate, de Molukken en de Indonesische Archipel. *Van soa-organisatie en vierdeling : een studie van traditionele samenleving en cultuur in Indonesië.* PhD thesis, Leiden University.

Gallop, A. T. 2003. Seventeenth-century Indonesian Letters in the Public Record Office. *Indonesia and Malay World* 31. 412–439.

Gil, David. 2023. Recent Contact Features in Northwest Papuan Malay. *NUSA: Linguistic studies of languages in and around Indonesia* 75. 53–116.

Gonda, Jan. 1952. *Sanskrit in Indonesia*. New Delhi: International Academy of Indian Culture.

Hägerdal, Hans. 2019. Wetar and Kisar in Indonesia, and East Timor: Colonial Encroachment, Migration, and Strategies of Survival in the 17th Century. *Indonesia and the Malay World* 47. 199–219.

Hayami-Allen, Rika. 2001. *A Descriptive Study of the Language of Ternate, the Northern Moluccas, Indonesia*. University of Pittsburgh: PhD dissertation.

Hickey, Raymond. 2010. Language Contact: Reconsideration and Reassessment. In *The Handbook of Language Contact* (Blackwell Handbooks in Linguistics), ed. by Raymond Hickey. 1–28. Chichester: Wiley-Blackwell.

van Hoëvell, G.W.W.C. 1876. *Vocabularium van vreemde woorden voorkomende in het Ambonsch-Maleisch benevens korte opmerkingen over dit locaal-Maleisch en verder enige Ambonsche spreekwoorden, eigenaardige uitdrukkingen en gezegden te Ambon gebruikelijk*. Dordrecht: Blusse en Van Braam.

Hueting, Anton. 1930. *Geschiedenis der zending op het eiland Halmahera*. Oegstgeest: Zendingsbureau.

Huizinga, Fré. 2004. *Merkusoord: Sources on the first Dutch establishment in New Guinea (1828–1836)*. Jakarta: Penerbitan Naskah Sumber Arsip Nasional Republik Indonesia.

Jacobs, Hubert (ed.). 1971. *A Treatise on the Moluccas (c. 1544): Probably the Preliminary Version of António Galváo 's Lost Historia Das Molucas*. (Sources and Studies for the History of the Jesuits, 3). Rome: Jesuit Historical Institute.

Jacobs, Hubert (ed.). 1974. *Documenta Malucensia. Vol. I (1542–1577)*, (Monumenta Historica Societatis Iesu, 109). Rome: Jesuit Historical Institute.

Jacobs, Hubert (ed.). 1984. *Documenta Malucensia. Vol. III (1606–1682)*, (Monumenta Historica Societatis Iesu, 126). Rome: Jesuit Historical Institute.

Jacob, June and Charles E. Grimes. 2003. *Kamus Pengantar Bahasa Kupang*. 2nd edn. Kupang: Centre for Regional Studies, Universitas Kristen Artha Wacana.

Jones, Russell (ed.). 2007. *Loan-words in Indonesian and Malay*. Leiden: KITLV Press.

Kamma, F. C. 1972. *Koreri: Messianic Movements in the Biak-Numfor Culture Area*. NY: Springer.

Litamahuputty, Betty. 2012. *Ternate Malay: Grammar and Texts*. Leiden University: PhD dissertation.

Locher-Scholten, Elsbeth. 1981. *Ethiek in fragmenten: Vijf studies over koloniaal denken en doen van Nederlanders in de Indonesische archipel, 1877–1942*. Utrecht: HES.

Loth, V. C. 1995. Pioneers and Perkeniers: The Banda Islands in the 18th Century. *Cakalele* 6: 13–35.

Middleton, Henry. 1855. *The Voyage of Sir Henry Middleton to Bantam and the Maluco Islands; Being the Second Voyage Set Forth by the Governor and Company of Merchants of London Trading into the East-Indies*. Edited by Bolton Corney. London: Hakluyt Society.

Nieuwenkamp, W. O. J. 1922. Drie weken op Alor. *Nederlands-Indië Oud en Nieuw* 7(3): 67–88.

Noorduyn, J. (ed.). (1983). *Nederlandse historische bronnen* 3. Amsterdam: Nederlands Historisch Genootschap. https://www.dbnl.org/tekst/_ned017198301_01/. (accessed: 19.11.2024)

Paauw, Scott H. 2009. *The Malay contact varieties of eastern Indonesia: A Typological Comparison.* State University of New York at Buffalo: PhD dissertation.

Rodemeier, Suzanne. 2006. *Tutu Kadire in Pandai – Munaseli. Erzählen und Erinnern auf der vergessenen Insel Pantar (Ostindonesien).* Passau: LIT Verlag.

Roeper, V. and D. Wildeman (eds). 2006. *Het journaal van Abel Tasman 1642–1643. Nationaal Archief. Den Haag.* Zwolle: Waanders Uitgevers.

Schapper, Antoinette & Anne van Schie. Forthcoming. Lingua francas of the SHWNG region: Untangling the historical dynamics of Biak and Wamesa loanwords. In *New perspectives on the history of SHWNG languages*, ed. by Laura Arnold and Antoinette Schapper.

Schouten, Willem Corneliszoon. 1644. *Iournael ofte beschryvinghe van de wonderlijcke reyse.* Amsterdam: Jan Janssen.

Sharma, M. Madhava. 1985. *Unsur-unsur bahasa Sanskerta dalam bahasa Indonesia* [*Elements of Sanskrit in Indonesian*]. Denpasar: Wyāsa Sanggraha.

Sijs, Nicoline van der. 2010. *Nederlandse woorden wereldwijd.* Den Haag: SDU.

Sneddon, James N. 2003. *The Indonesian Language: Its History and Role in Modern Society.* Sydney: UNSW Press.

Steinhauer, Hein. 1983. Notes on the Malay of Kupang (Timor). In *Studies in Malay dialects: Part II*, ed. by James T. Collins, 42–64. Jakarta: Universitas Atma Jaya.

Stokhof, W.A.L. 1975. *Preliminary Notes on the Alor and Pantar Languages (East Indonesia).* Canberra: Pacific Linguistics.

Tiele, P.A. and J.E. Heeres (eds.). 1890. *Bouwstoffen voor de geschiedenis der Nederlanders in den Maleischen Archipel, De opkomst van het Nederlandsch gezag in Oost-Indië, Tweede reeks (buitenbezittingen), vol. II.* 's-Gravenhage: Nijhoff.

Voorhoeve, C.L. and Chris F. van Fraassen. no date. A dictionary of Ternate. Unpublished manuscript.

Valentijn, François. 1724. *Oud en Nieuw Oost-Indiën, Vol. 1. Dordrecht*, Amsterdam: Joannes van Braam, Gerard onder de Linden.

de Vries, Lourens J. 1998. Schelden in Inanwatan. In *Mengelwerk van Muysken* (Publikaties van het Instituut voor Algemene Taalwetenschap, 72), ed. by A. Bruyn and J. Arends. 4–6. Universiteit van Amsterdam.

Voorhoeve, C.L. & Ch. F. van Fraassen. no date. Prelimaries to a Ternate-English dictionary. Unpublished manuscript.

doi Vries, J. W. de. 1988. Dutch loanwords in Indonesian. *International Journal of the Sociology of Language.* De Gruyter Mouton 1988(73). 121–136. .

CHAPTER 13

Newspapers as a window into language beliefs of the past

Language contact and conflict in Flemish-American press

Yasmin Crombez
Vrije Universiteit Brussel | Fonds Wetenschappelijk Onderzoek Vlaanderen

Within heritage language linguistics, a recent paradigm shift has emanated from the field of (historical) sociolinguistics, investigating (1) the influence of extra-linguistic factors and (2) heritage languages in the past (see Brown 2019). Drawing inspiration from these new directions, this chapter investigates the language beliefs of Flemish emigrants in the United States with particular attention to the pre- and post-migration sociolinguistic ecology. To achieve this, a discourse analysis was conducted using three Flemish-American newspapers dating from 1890 until 1959, specifically focusing on discourse surrounding the use of Dutch and English. Results show that, while Flemish emigrants hold favorable attitudes toward English, their stance regarding societal multilingualism differs in the New Country compared to the Old Country.

Keywords: heritage language linguistics, Heritage Belgian Dutch, historical sociolinguistics, language attitude research

1. Introduction

The field of heritage language linguistics, which, broadly speaking, studies minority languages that connect speakers to their roots (cf. Aalberse et al. 2019: 1), has undergone notable changes in the last decades. Where early studies mainly focused on describing dialectal patterns (e.g. Gilbert 1965), comparing different properties to the 'home variety' (e.g., Van Marle and Smits 1993), or creating glossaries (e.g., Correa-Zoli 1970), heritage research today also concentrates on language acquisition and processing (e.g., Polinsky 2008), maintenance and attrition

https://doi.org/10.1075/impact.55.13cro

(e.g., Schmid 2011), and on heritage language education (e.g., Kagan, Carreira, and Chik 2017). Most studies, however, tend to examine the *structural* and *formal* features of *contemporary* heritages languages. Less attention has been paid to (1) heritage languages of the past and (2) the influence that extra-linguistic factors, such as language attitudes and the environment before the migration, have in the heritage-language context. Even though these variables have been proven to play a sometimes highly significant role in language change and variation in other contexts (cf. Karatsareas 2018). As a result, several recent studies have started to tackle these lacunas, utilizing (historical) sociolinguistic methods (see for instance Litty 2019; Hoffman and Kytö 2019 for research on historical heritage languages; and, amongst others, Moro 2018; Sánchez et al. 2018 for research on linguistic attitudes toward contemporary heritage languages), thereby broadening the scope of heritage linguistics by offering new insights into historical and social dimensions. Nevertheless, there are still some gaps to be filled.

First, while numerous European languages have been explored extensively in heritage language linguistics, the study of Dutch as a heritage language has predominantly been confined to Netherlandic Dutch, with most studies taking a structural approach (e.g., Van Marle 2001, Noordegraaf 2008, Smits and Van Marle 2013). The language use of Flemish emigrants and the influence of sociolinguistic factors remain uncovered ground to a very large extent. Nonetheless, Belgian Dutch in heritage settings is an interesting case to examine due to its multifaceted sociolinguistic history, which differs greatly from the language history of Netherlandic Dutch. This is of crucial importance, because, as suggested by Brown & Bousquette (2018: 201), not only the environment after the migration can influence the development of a heritage language, but the pre-immigration context too can play a role in language change and variation. With respect to the language use of early Flemish emigrants, this hypothesis seems supported in a recent case study on French and English lexical influence (Crombez et al. 2024).

Second, heritage language research investigating language attitudes and ideologies in historical contexts – thus combining the above-mentioned new research trajectories – is notably scarce (though see Collet 2016; Moquin 2019). As mentioned earlier, it is necessary to move beyond a sole focus on language use and explore language attitudes and ideologies too, as well as adopt a diachronic perspective to fully understand the dynamics of heritage languages (cf. Kasstan et al. 2018; Brown 2019). Attitudes and ideologies are integral to social processes, serving not only as products of their socio-cultural environment but also as reflections of it. By investigating the beliefs surrounding language, researchers can uncover how majority and minority languages are evaluated, as well as the broader sociolinguistic context in which these evaluations take place.

In connection to the above, there are also methodological aspects that require further exploration. When looking at contemporary heritage language attitude research, most studies rely on interview techniques (e.g., Hietpas and Vanhecke 2022; Moquin and Wolf 2023) or experimental methods (e.g., Moro 2018; Lloyd-Smith et al. 2020). However, as argued by Walsh (2022: 19), societal treatments of language, such as discourse analysis, are equally valuable when it comes to discovering attitudes on language, especially regarding attitudes that are reflected and shaped by print media. In the heritage context, a source that would prove to be particularly fruitful is heritage community press: newspapers published by heritage communities, often on a local level, informing their readers about ongoing matters in the New Country, the Old Country, and their immediate living environment (cf. Park 1922). Yet, so far, with the above-mentioned exceptions of Collet (2016) and Moquin (2019), most research relying on heritage community newspapers addresses socio-historical issues (e.g., Olzak and West 1991), investigates their role in assimilation processes (e.g., Hickerson and Gustafson 2016), or concentrates on their contribution to identity construction (e.g., Viola and Verheul 2019).

As such, the objective of this study is twofold. On a theoretical level, I wish to add to the growing body of research on heritage languages from a historical sociolinguistic perspective by (1) investigating the language beliefs[1] present in Flemish-American communities, and by (2) paying explicit attention to the role of the pre-immigration context. On a methodological level, the goal is to demonstrate how heritage community newspapers can offer valuable insights when it comes to studying language beliefs present in immigrant communities. To achieve this, this chapter presents a case study which analyzes the discourse surrounding English and Belgian Dutch in three Flemish-American newspapers. I specifically highlight discourse indicating how Flemish-American immigrants and successive generations position themselves toward the learning and use of the English language, as well as the maintenance and preservation of Belgian Dutch as a community language. Through this analysis, the chapter aims to illuminate the sociolinguistic environment of Flemish-American communities in the late 19th, early 20th centuries.

The chapter starts with a brief overview of the Belgian language history which is necessary if the impact of the pre-immigration environment is to be investigated. In the following section, the historical context of the Flemish migration to North America is laid out. In the fourth section, the field of heritage language linguistics

1. 'Language beliefs' is used throughout this chapter as an overarching term for language ideologies and attitudes as they often interact and influence each other, making their boundaries difficult to define. This challenge is particularly pronounced in historical research due to methodological limitations (see Havinga & Krogull 2022).

is introduced more broadly and previous sociolinguistic research on historical heritage language beliefs is discussed more specifically. In Section 5, I introduce the material used in this study: Flemish-American newspapers. The methodology is demonstrated in the sixth section, while the results are presented in Section 7. The chapter ends with a conclusion in Section 8. Note that throughout this chapter 'Belgian Dutch' and 'Flemish' are used interchangeably to refer to the language use of Flemish emigrants. No distinction is made between more standardized or more dialectal language use based on these terms in what follows.[2]

2. The language history of Belgian Dutch

To comprehend the sociolinguistic dynamics in 19th-20th century Belgium, it is necessary to go back to the 16th century. More specifically to the Fall of Antwerp in 1585 which led to the political separation of the Low Countries: the northern part (covering much of the territory of the Netherlands today) became an independent nation called the Republic of the United Netherlands, while the southern part (corresponding to present-day Belgium) fell under Spanish (1585–1714), Austrian (1714–1794) and eventually French rule (1795–1814) (Van der Sijs 2004: 30–31; Janssens and Marynissen 2011: 102–4). This resulted in repercussions not only in economic and political domains, but also on a linguistic level as the focal point of Dutch standardization efforts shifted to the Northern Netherlands. In the Southern Netherlands, this process was more complicated (though not nonexistent, cf. Vosters et al. 2010; Rutten and Vosters 2011). The social elite and the ruling class used French as their language of communication and preferred it as the overt language of prestige. Hence, there was no support for Dutch from political organizations, exemplified by the lack of official recognition of Dutch language norms (Vandenbussche 2009: 256; Vosters et al. 2010; Janssens and Marynissen 2011: 137–40). This changed in the 18th century, when the 'rivalry' between French and Dutch stimulated standardization efforts in the southern part. These efforts evolved further between 1815 and 1830 when the Northern and Southern Netherlands were briefly reunited under Willem I. During this time Dutch was recognized as an official language, but lost that status in 1830 when Belgium became an independent nation (Van der Sijs and Willemyns 2009: 265–74). Nevertheless, the seed was planted and under the impetus of the Flemish Move-

2. In part because the standardization process was still ongoing during the period under investigation in this study, in part because many present-day Dutch-speaking Flemings refer to their own language as Flemish without implying dialectal language use (cf. Willemyns 2003).

ment[3] the northern standard language norms were adopted in the south at the end of the 19th century (Janssens and Marynissen 2011: 141–45; Vosters 2013).

Still, the position of Dutch in Belgium was far from stable before the late 20th century due to the presence and pressure of French. French has influenced the language use of Flemish speakers on multiple linguistic levels. This led to a 'language purification tradition' that started in the 19th century, when numerous intellectuals argued that Belgian Standard Dutch could attain the same societal prestige of French only if all French elements were eliminated, and persisted until the mid-20th century (Van Hoof and Jaspers 2012; Vosters 2013). Despite recent studies indicating that the extent of the 'Frenchification' of Dutch should not be exaggerated (e.g., Vanhecke and De Groof 2007; Verheyden 2023), this part of the Belgian language history has nonetheless had lasting impacts: many Flemish speakers harbor negative sentiments towards French (cf. Deprez and Geerts 1977), yet French has influenced the Belgian Dutch morphology (see e.g., Rutten et al. 2015), lexicon, and grammar (see e.g., Verheyden 2023).

3. Belgian transatlantic migration

During the 19th century, Belgium was not only struggling linguistically, but also economically. Almost all of Europe was plagued by food shortage caused by the potato famine and crop failures, land shortage because of the rapidly growing population, and high poverty rates due to industrialization. Numerous people faced unemployment as home industry was replaced by wage labor and mechanized industry, and those who had a job in the new factories were working for meager pay (Musschoot 2002; Cohn 2008). The standard of living decreased drastically during the 19th century, which became one of the major push-factors for Europeans to emigrate, alongside political or religious reasons (Cohn 2008). More specifically, between the 1830s and the 1930s approximately forty million people crossed the Atlantic Ocean to settle in the United States or Canada (Hatton and Williamson 1992). North America was after all an inviting destination: there was a favorable migration policy – especially toward Western Europeans – which included providing early emigrants with free agricultural land as enacted by the Homestead Act of 1862. Additionally, North America offered better employment opportunities and improved wages as its economy experienced rapid growth, particularly from the 1880s onward (Cohn 2008: 75; Caestecker 2014: 62). Besides these economic pull-

3. The Flemish Movement can be described as a group of intellectuals striving for the recognition of Dutch as an official language in Belgium, as well as for political and economic equality (for more details see Van der Sijs and Willemyns 2009: 277).

factors, European mass migration was further aided by the arrival of the steam engine around the mid-19th century, making travel easier and cheaper.

As such, an estimated hundred and fifty thousand Flemish emigrants decided to search for better living conditions in North America as well, encouraged by personal success stories from Flemings who had already undertaken the trip and by the Belgian government (Musschoot 2002; Nauwelaerts and Caestecker 2008). The latter saw migration as a solution to the socio-economic issues that were troubling Belgium in the first half of the 19th century, and thus actively promoted moving: the more people left for other countries, the fewer jobs, less space, and less food were needed (Feys 2004, 2014). When focusing on the profiles of the Flemish emigrants, research shows that before the turn of the 20th century it was predominantly young men in their twenties who resettled in North America to farm or work in factories. At the beginning of the 20th century, women and young couples started to cross the ocean as well, turning labor migration into settlement migration (Caestecker 2014: 64). In terms of settlement places, Flemings frequently joined distant or old acquaintances through chain migration (Caestecker 2014: 62). Settling in the same areas eased the transition from their old life and allowed them to form close-knit communities (Caestecker 2014: 63). These communities were mostly situated around the Great Lakes: Moline (Illinois), Rock Island (Illinois), Mishawaka (Indiana), South Bend (Indiana), De Pere (Wisconsin), Milwaukee (Wisconsin), Green Bay (Wisconsin) and Detroit (Michigan) were popular destinations, although some Flemings also went to other states or traveled to Canada. Due to the rise of nationalism and xenophobia in the New and Old World after World War I, European migration slowed drastically and virtually came to a complete halt following the stock market crash in 1929 (Nauwelaerts & Caestecker 2008). Nevertheless, because of this century-long mass migration, North America became the home of numerous heritage languages making for an incredibly diverse and interesting linguistic landscape.

4. Heritage language linguistics

Heritage languages can be broadly described as "minority languages that are learned in a bilingual or multilingual environment" (Montrul and Polinsky 2021: 1). A more detailed and popular definition is provided by Rothman (2009: 156): "a language spoken at home or otherwise readily available to young children, and crucially this language is not a dominant language of the larger (national) society". Furthermore, a heritage language creates a bond between its speakers and their cultural roots, and often exhibits signs of language shift resulting in language attrition or erosion because of the pressure of the dominant language

(Fishman 2001: 81). Alternatively, it has the potential to evolve into a distinct variety, as observed in the case of Jersey Dutch, discussed by Prince (1910).

In the last decade, the field of heritage language linguistics has undergone notable changes, including a shift from a predominantly structural, formal, and synchronic perspective to one encompassing sociolinguistic and diachronic points of view as argued for by, amongst others, Kasstan et al. (2018), Brown and Bousquette (2018), and Brown (2019). Recent studies have started to pay attention to the social settings in which heritage languages are spoken (e.g., Brown 2017), recognizing that linguistic outcomes are shaped by "specific socially determined language contact settings" (Aalberse et al. 2019: 44). This includes investigating the impact of social variables related to the speakers as an object of study. Kühl and Peterson's (2018) study on the transmission of Danish in Utah reveals that gender significantly influences language maintenance, with women preserving Danish longer than men. Similarly, Raña-Risso and Barrera-Tobón (2018) discovered differences in New York-Spanish subject placement depending on the generation of speakers.

Extending this line of inquiry, researchers started to explore how prestige, attitudes, and ideologies contribute to heritage language dynamics (cf. Milroy 1992; Nagy 2018). For instance, Karatsareas (2018) studied contemporary Greek Cypriot attitudes in London toward Standard Modern Greek and Cypriot Greek. The results mirrored the attitudes present in Cyprus, with positive views of Standard Modern Greek and more negative evaluations of Cypriot Greek. However, London Greek Cypriots also showed reluctance to accept Cypriot Greek in informal settings, which contrasts with the attitudes in Cyprus where the use of Cypriot Greek is generally approved of in informal settings. This implies two things: first, the standard ideology of the homeland affects the language attitudes of second-generation heritage speakers in the New Country, showing the influence of the pre-immigration environment (cf. Brown and Bousquette 2018: 201). Second, this effect led to a preference for the usage of Standard Modern Greek over Cypriot Greek, endangering the transmission and maintenance in London of Cypriot Greek as a heritage language (cf. Karatsareas 2018: 424). In a similar vein, but with opposite results, Arnbjörnsdóttir (2015: 76) found that linguistic purism prevalent in Iceland also surfaced in North American Icelandic communities. It was specifically present "in the form of loyalty to the old language", which could be witnessed from the plethora of texts the North American Icelanders published (Arnbjörnsdóttir 2015: 76). These studies demonstrate the necessity of considering the sociolinguistic setting not only after the migration, but also before when studying heritage language development.

4.1 Previous research: Attitudes toward heritage languages in the past

Language beliefs surrounding heritage languages in the past have begun to gain a modest level of interest as well (cf. Brown 2019). However, as Havinga and Krogull (2022: 297) point out, "researching language attitudes based on historical data seems, in many ways, quite different, and perhaps more challenging, too". The main challenge of investigating language beliefs of the past is methodological in nature: researchers cannot make use of standard sociolinguistic methods such as interviews (e.g., Nagy 2018) or experimental methods (e.g., Moro 2018). Instead, they must rely on other techniques and data to extract language attitudes and ideologies of the past. Discourse and content analysis, for instance, have proved to be highly beneficial for examining historical data (see e.g., Boemer 2016; Verheyden 2023). In historical heritage contexts, press media provide rich data that align well with these analytical methods. Many heritage communities had (and still have) a tradition of publishing their own newspapers (cf. Park 1922). As one of the "social mechanisms through which particular ideas or beliefs about language practices are produced, circulated and/or challenged", newspapers are indeed valuable for language attitude and ideology research (Johnson and Milani 2010: 4). After all, they do not only reflect, but also shape and influence the sociolinguistic ecology in which they appear, as well as the accompanying linguistic attitudes and standards (Bell 1991: 67–83; Rademann 1998: 49; Cotter 2003: 47; Percy 2012: 191).

Moquin (2019) investigated language ideologies held by Norwegian-Americans in the 19th and 20th centuries drawing on the heritage community newspaper *Reform* (1886–1941), published in Wisconsin. She discovered that as a strategy to prevent language loss and shift, the Norwegian-American newspaper linked language to morality. It did so by publishing articles that criticized the use of English within the Norwegian language and community by labelling English interference as a loss of religion and morality. This way they asserted that Norwegian was "the conduit to spirituality that must not be obstructed with impure speech" (Moquin 2019: 66). These kinds of claims aimed to safeguard Norwegian from internal community influences, but linking language and morality was also a strategy to protect the maintenance of Norwegian against 'external threats' (Moquin 2019: 68). Multiple articles were printed condemning 'English only'-laws (e.g., the Bennett Law of 1889[4], or the Babel Proclamation of

4. The Bennett Law of 1889 stated that all education in Wisconsin had to be taught in English if a school wanted to be recognized as legitimate. Specifically, in section five of the bill, the following declaration was found: "no school shall be regarded as a school unless there shall be taught therein, as part of the elementary education of children, reading, writing, arithmetic and United States history, in the English language" (cited in Kellogg 1918: 4). In 1890, the law was repealed, however, due to protests of the immigrant communities.

1918)[5], using the argument that if Norwegian could no longer be spoken in public life, all morality and religion would be lost. This reasoning is captured in the following statement printed in an edition from 1919: "If you want to see a godless Norwegian population here, then close the church door to them – the Norwegian church door [translated by Moquin (2019: 70)]" (Langback 1919).

Similarly, Collet (2016) analyzed the ideological leanings of the Flemish heritage newspaper the *Gazette van Detroit*. The goal was to uncover language attitudes toward Flemish within the Flemish-American community during the First World War by closely reading editions published between 1916 and 1918. Interestingly, her study showed that the language attitudes were clearly influenced by the nationalist and socialist ideologies the *Gazette* adhered to. For example, articles and readers' letters covering language rights in the Old Country primarily conveyed a political undertone: pleadings for equal rights and status for both Belgian Dutch and French functioned as a proxy for wanting political equality between the Flemish and the Walloons. In the New Country the linguistic interests were more socialist in nature. Flemings in North America often had a tough time on the job market due to their limited knowledge of English. Consequently, when the *Gazette* advocated for better working conditions for the Flemish people people, that included the demand "6 – That we be assigned Belgian Field Bosses, or people that understand our language" (Cobbaert, Baertsoen, and De Clercq 1916 as quoted in Collet 2016: 95). The socialist emphasis placed on Flemish language rights in North America should probably be contextualized within the socio-historical context of the Flemish-French language struggle, as the goal was achieving political, economic and social equality.

Collet's (2016) findings further corroborate the idea that the pre-immigration sociolinguistic context can exert an influence on the post-immigration environment (see also Arnbjörnsdóttir 2015; Karatsareas 2018). The negative sentiments toward French – and the social oppression it signifies – that existed in Belgium accompanied the Flemings to their new country, or at least resurfaced during the First World War. Questions that now arise are whether those beliefs were also present before and after the First World War, and whether they were replicated in or extended to English, especially considering that Dutch in North America was again occupying a low-prestige position and faced pressure from English as the dominant language. To answer these questions, further empirical research is needed. For this purpose, I examined Flemish heritage community newspapers

5. In 1918, in the aftermath of World War II, the governor of Iowa, William Harding, issued the 'Babel Proclamation' which "established a set of wartime rules that required, among other restrictions, that all conversations in public places, on trains, and over the telephone be held in English only" (Becker 2022: 69).

from the late 19th and early 20th centuries to shed light on the language beliefs that shaped the sociolinguistic environment of the Flemish-American community during the period when the Belgian language conflict was at its height.

5. Flemish-American heritage newspapers

The present study draws on three Flemish-American heritage newspapers to chart the language attitudes and ideologies of Flemings in North America over a longer period. In this section, I will discuss each newspaper's life cycle, ideological background, and audience. The papers were titled *De Volksstem* (the People's Voice), the *Gazette van Moline* (Gazette of Moline), and the *Gazette van Detroit* (Gazette of Detroit), respectively.

5.1 *De Volksstem*

De Volksstem ran weekly from 1890 until 1919 from the town of De Pere in Wisconsin. It was founded by John Heyrman – the president of the Democratic Party in De Pere – as a reaction against the Republican Bennett Law, which delegitimized schools where English was not the language of instruction (Stynen and Verdoodt 2015: 13). While the law was abolished a year later, *De Volksstem* did not disappear with it. As the only Flemish publication at the time, it quickly became the Flemish people's main source for information about the New and Old Country in terms of politics, economics, and culture, but it also printed more sensational articles and even what Stynen and Verdoodt (2015: 13) refer to as "gossip talks". Indeed, *De Volksstem*'s coverage exhibited a strong focus on local matters: from reporting on someone's drinking over the weekend to which visitors a particular family had received. On a more official note, however, *De Volksstem* not only covered standard news events or gave gossipy accounts, but also wished to unite the Roman Catholic Dutch-speaking community in North America by encouraging people to respect their Flemish identity and their 'old' way of living. In practice, this meant celebrating Belgian holidays, going to church, supporting the businesses of other Flemings, keeping up with news from Belgium, and, most importantly, preserving the Flemish language. To unite the Flemish readers that were scattered all over North America, *De Volksstem* covered news from almost every state by relying on local correspondents. This way, even though they could not meet in real life, the Flemish people were connected through the paper. The paper was distributed via local merchants as well as postal services given the presence of readers in the U.S.A., Canada and even in Belgium. After 29 years, *De Volksstem* ceased its activities and was absorbed by the *Gazette van Moline* in 1919.

5.2 *Gazette van Moline*

The *Gazette van Moline* was distributed weekly from the town of Moline in Illinois starting from 1907. The newspaper was founded by Edouard. Coryn and a priest called John Baptiste Ceulemans. The *Gazette van Moline*'s *raison d'être* is very much in line with that of *De Volksstem*: it was set on maintaining the Flemish identity and language, as well as the traditions and values. This sentiment was explicitly conveyed in their slogan, *Godsdienst – Eendracht – Vooruitgang* ('Religion – Unity – Progress'). Readers were urged to practice the Roman Catholic faith, build connections with fellow Flemings in North America, and support one another in adapting to their new way of life. The content of the *Gazette* was also similar to that of *De Volksstem*. It covered regional, national, and international events and shared updates about activities back in Belgium through correspondents based in both countries. They kept subscribers informed about significant news and upcoming events while helping them stay connected with fellow Flemish emigrants and those they knew in the homeland. Regarding its readership, the *Gazette van Moline* enjoyed considerable success, particularly during World War I: at the beginning of the war, it boasted approximately 3,500 subscribers, and by the war's end circulation had surged to 10,000 copies (Collet 2016: 86). By the start of World War II, however, its readership had dwindled significantly, leading to its acquisition by the *Gazette van Detroit* in 1940.

5.3 *Gazette van Detroit*

The last newspaper included in the analysis is called the *Gazette van Detroit*, founded by Camille Cools. With 104 years of publishing, from 1914 until 2018, it is the longest surviving Flemish-American newspaper. While *De Volksstem* and the *Gazette van Moline* had a clear religious background, the *Gazette van Detroit* exhibited a more humanistic and liberal stance as reflected in its slogan: *Het licht voor het volk – het recht voor het volk – Gelijkheid-Vrijheid-Ontwikkeling*, which translates to 'The light for the people – Justice for the people – Equality-Freedom-Development'. According to Collet (2016: 86) the three main motivators for the existence of the *Gazette van Detroit* were "the First World War, the living and working conditions of the Flemish immigrants and matters of language". Besides those topics, the *Gazette van Detroit*, like *De Volksstem* and the *Gazette van Moline*, covered international events, American politics, regional news provided by correspondents scattered across the country, as well as national and regional news from Belgium (Collet 2016: 86). As "the only Belgian newspaper in America", the new tagline from 1940 onward, the *Gazette van Detroit* reached its peak in terms of subscribers in the 1950s when over 10,000 copies were sold.

The significant increase in subscribers during that period likely resulted from the newspaper's decision to permit correspondents to write in English. This resulted in the *Gazette* becoming bilingual from the second half of the 20th century onward (Stynen and Verdoodt 2015: 71). However, in 2018 the newspaper was left with only 900 subscribers, forcing it to close its doors.

6. Methodology

To investigate the language beliefs in Flemish-American communities, I compiled a corpus consisting of the newspapers discussed above. Specifically, one random issue per year was selected for each newspaper. For *De Volksstem* this corresponded to an edition from the first week of March, for the *Gazette van Moline* and the *Gazette van Detroit* to editions from the last or final or penultimate week of November.[6] In total, 105 issues were analyzed using qualitative discourse analysis (cf. Hardy, Harley, and Phillips 2004). This method was selected because societal treatments of language are effective in uncovering ideologies and shedding light on attitudes, "in particular, the attitudes that are (re)produced in the printed press and other print media" (Walsh 2022: 19). As noted earlier, newspapers generate, disseminate and even challenge feelings and beliefs regarding language (cf. Johnson and Milani 2010). Moreover, Havinga and Krogull (2022: 304) highlight the often impractical and unnecessary distinction between language attitudes and ideologies in historical data analysis. This chapter adopts their view that "language attitudes should be studied within wider-held sets of beliefs and their socio-political context in order to understand their origins and impacts" (Havinga & Krogull 2022: 304). Applying qualitative discourse analytical methods aligns with this goal, as such methods aim "to reveal how [a text's linguistic, YC] features [are, YC] set up and replicate particular word views" (Griffin 2013: 99).

The analysis involved carefully reading each newspaper edition from front to back and extracting any text passages, including advertisements, that revealed overt or covert language attitudes and/or ideologies. Fragments explicitly stating a feeling or belief about Belgian Dutch or English, such as an article lamenting that a clergyman did not know Belgian Dutch (*De Volksstem*, 2 March 1904, page 4), were collected. Similarly, texts conveying implicit beliefs, such as an article mentioning that people born in the United States could attend Dutch classes (*Gazette van Detroit*, 27 November 1937, page 7), were also included.

6. If no edition was available in the first week of March or the last week of November, I selected the edition published closest to that period.

In addition to examining *what* was said – whether explicitly or implicitly – attention was given to *how* things were said, i.e. by using Belgian Dutch or English words, as this might provide further insights into the newspapers' positions toward both languages. Once collected, all relevant instances were categorized by theme or content and subjected to an additional close reading. This process aimed to formulate overarching statements that captured the underlying ideologies or attitudes.

It is important to acknowledge that discerning attitudes and ideologies from the past will always implicate some degree of speculation due to the inherent limitation of being unable to directly probe the thoughts, ideas and opinions of the individuals involved. Additionally, as this study draws on a single type of material, certain voices may be more represented than others. This calls for caution when considering the representativity of these findings for the entire Flemish-American community.

7. Language attitudes and ideologies surrounding Belgian Dutch and English

In this section, the discourse on Belgian Dutch and English across the three newspapers is examined in greater detail through several statements. The analysis begins with an exploration of how the Flemings positioned themselves toward Dutch, followed by a focus on their beliefs surrounding English. Each statement will be supported by examples that best encapsulate the expressed attitude or ideology. Note that the excerpts are exclusively presented through English translations within the main text for the sake of brevity and reader convenience.

7.1 Attitudes and ideologies surrounding Belgian Dutch

The analysis resulted in five overarching statements, each covering the most recurring themes in the newspapers. The statements encapsulate the predominant stances adopted by the Flemish-American community regarding (1) Belgian Dutch language maintenance; (2) the relation between the Flemish language and the Flemish identity; (3) culture as a means of Flemish language maintenance; (4) the use of Belgian Dutch for expressing emotions and practicing religion; (5) the Flemish language struggle. The statement on Belgian Dutch language maintenance is addressed first.

1. *Flemish must be maintained, no matter where in the world the Flemish people are*

When discussing the origins and backgrounds of the newspapers, it became clear that one of their primary goals was to help preserve Belgian Dutch in North America. This goal is at times explicitly articulated; for example, in the *Gazette van Moline*, the first excerpt (1) appeared in an article discussing the use of Flemish at home and the second (2) in an article about Flemish plays:

(1) It is our belief, a commendable practice, to use the Flemish language as much as possible in the household. It should not be that the Flemish language becomes extinct among Flemish-Americans! (22 November 1907, page 4)

(2) Not only in Flanders, Flemish! But also Flemish among all the Flemish, no matter where they reside. (20 November 1908, page 4)

The other two newspapers also echoed this sentiment repeatedly over time. In its first year, *De Volksstem* published an article titled 'The Protest of the Bishops' which contained a manifesto by Wisconsin Catholic bishops opposing the Bennett Law (cf. Supra). The manifesto argued that the law interfered with the upbringing of the church and the parents, deeming it most undesirable (22 March 1890, page 1). While the newspaper appears to simply summarize the manifesto without explicitly attaching a value judgment to it, the decision to publish it suggests that *De Volksstem* aligns with its message. If so, this implies that the immigrants believed their language was worth preserving, even in defiance of the law. Later, the Flemish community did seek to protect their language at an official level; in 1908, Camille Cools (cf. Supra) urged *Gazette van Moline* readers to sign a petition for the appointment of a Flemish-speaking consul in the United States, stating:

(3) It concerns our rights, the rights of the Flemish language; with your help, we hope to soon have consuls who speak Flemish; there are already thousands in the United States who have signed the petitions. C. Cools (20 November 1908, page 2)

The idea that Flemish deserves a legitimate place in America did not fade in the later decades of the 20th century. Despite the increasing presence of English within the Flemish-American community (cf. Infra), the importance of Flemish language skills, and the role that the newspapers play in this, continued to be emphasized:

(4) [...] there is a great danger that sooner or later the currently existing Flemish weekly newspapers in America will perish. This is something that absolutely should not happen. Thoughtful compatriots and friends of the Flemish people, the Flemish language, and the good old Flemish customs should immediately rally upon hearing such news to devise means for the preservation of our beloved Flemish press in America.

(Gazette van Moline, 23 November 1933, page 3)

Finally, the belief that preserving Belgian Dutch is important extends beyond the Flemish community in America to others as well. To illustrate this, the *Gazette van Moline* printed the following in an article about Flemish children who go to school in Paris:

(5) They do inhabit the French capital [...], yet they remain true and deeply attached to their own customs, their own art, and their own language. They know our proverb: "No richer crown than one's own!" It is delightful to hear how the students take pride in speaking our beautiful Flemish language and how three days a week they converse in "Civilized Dutch".[7]

(22 November 1917, page 2)

The *Gazette van Detroit* reported on a Flemish newspaper in Congo that aspired to preserve the Flemish language:

(6) Despite the numerous difficulties that made many doubt the viability of the publications, the director, Mr. G. Stampaert, persevered. He consistently encourages the Flemings in Congo to maintain their language.

(24 November 1950, page 2)

As the next statement will elaborate on, the emphasis on maintaining the Flemish language within the Flemish-American community should be seen in connection with a deeper desire to preserve a strong sense of Flemish identity. Identities can be, and often are, formed linguistically through the use of a language or certain linguistic features (Kroskrity 1999: 111). As a result, the loss of the language might then become associated with a loss of identity.

2. *Being able to speak Flemish makes you a Fleming*

This statement highlights the belief within the community that Flemish language skills and the Flemish identity are closely intertwined with each other. In fact, the discourse in the newspapers in the earlier decades suggests that speaking Belgian

7. Note that in this excerpt Flemish functions as a blanket term for the varieties spoken at home, ranging from dialects to regiolects, whereas 'Civilized Dutch' likely refers to a more standardized, supra-regional variety.

Dutch was a crucial prerequisite for identifying as Flemish. Consider the following excerpt from the *Gazette van Moline* in 1907:

(7) Our language, not foreign to us, is and remains the genuine confession of our essence. The language is like the blood of our tribe: our possession, the pledge, the inheritance of our fathers. The Fleming who doesn't know his mother tongue, who doesn't honor his mother tongue, is a maimed Fleming, but he isn't an English-American either! (22 November 1907, page 4)

The author makes it unmistakably clear that knowledge of the language is essential for a Flemish identity. Migrants who speak English can neither identify as Flemish nor as "English-American". The awareness and belief that identity and language are connected is also reflected in a quote from Victor Hugo printed in a piece in the *Gazette van Moline* about the German occupation during WWI. The Germans wrote they would conquer Belgium by banning the language and severing ties to the homeland. The response was:

(8) The renowned French writer, Victor Hugo, said: language is the people. Kill the language, and you kill the character, nature, and love of freedom of a people; only then can a people be enslaved. (26 October 1917, page 7)

Although the article and the quote address the oppression of the Flemish people in Belgium – and therefore do not directly relate to the experience of Flemish-Americans – they still offer insight into how Flemish-Americans viewed the role of language within their community.

The idea that speaking a certain language is essential to forming a specific identity can be traced back to the one nation-one language ideology prevalent in the 18th and 19th centuries (Horner and Weber 2012: 18). As Auer (2005: 405) explains, this ideology departs from the notion that "each collectivity (particularly a nation) expresses its own character (*Volksgeist*) in and through language." However, Auer (2005: 406) also notes that "seen from this perspective, migration unavoidably threatens identity. Migrants may switch (national) identity and become members of the receiving society, giving up their language of origin in the melting pot." As the later statements on English will illustrate, this shift began began to occur among Flemish-Americans from the second quarter of the 20th century onward, leading subsequent generations to connect with their Flemish heritage through means other than language (cf. Infra).

3. *Culture is an important medium to preserve Belgian Dutch*

To keep the Belgian Dutch language the newspapers appear to rely on the promotion of Flemish cultural heritage and typical Flemish activities. While much of this is achieved indirectly through advertisements for Flemish books (see Figure 1), reviews of Flemish plays, the publication of Flemish song lyrics and poems, and the inclusion of short stories by Flemish writers, there are also direct references to the role of culture in maintaining the language.

Figure 1. Advertisement for Flemish books, *Gazette van Moline*, 23 November 1922, page 7

An example of this was found in a 1924 edition of the *Gazette van Detroit*, which featured an article titled "Flemish Theater Life". In it, the author concludes that Flemish (and Netherlandic Dutch) theater companies "uphold the Flemish way of living in Detroit", supported by the *Gazette van Detroit*, as it informs readers about plays and meetings that "make you decide to put your mother tongue first in your family life" (*Gazette van Detroit*, 21 November 1924, page 4).

According to Pavlenko (2002: 169), musical and theater performances, along with the publication of serialized fiction, poetry and other literary works in heritage community press, were widely used for language maintenance purposes in immigrant communities. Pavlenko (2002: 174) attributes the ability of migrants to sustain a vibrant cultural life in the U.S. to 19th-century language ideologies that were tolerant of migrant languages. However, as will be discussed later, these ideologies began to shift around the turn of the century, driven by xenophobic sentiments fueled by the increasing number of migrants and the outbreak of the First World War.

4. *Flemish is the most suitable language for expressing religion and emotions*

As the vast majority of Flemish emigrants and their descendants were Roman Catholic, all three newspapers provided information on weekly church services. These announcements included the location, time, and the language in which the sermons would be delivered. While the neutral tone of the announcements seems to suggest that there was no clear preference for attending Mass in English or

Dutch, other articles stressed that Dutch was more suitable for expressing religious experiences or emotions. English, by contrast, was occasionally portrayed as a deceitful language and even associated with immorality. For example, in *De Volksstem* a journalist warned the readers about bad books which are a danger to one's faith by saying:

(9) A good choice at this point is of great importance; one finds, especially in English, a large supply of small, worthless books in which there is nothing that can nurture piety in the souls. (5 March 1902, page 1)

Similarly, a journalist in the *Gazette van Detroit* claimed that the Dutch language speaks closer to the soul:

(10) Enthusiasts of Dutch theater! That's where you should go! An evening of drama presented in the Dutch language speaks more directly and intimately to the soul than all the splendor of "jazz" and "stars". (29 November 1935, page 4)

In most instances, however, the tone is milder with the newspapers primarily highlighting the advantages of attending church services led by a Dutch-speaking priest:

(11) On Tuesday, 15 March, at 6 o'clock in the evening, Father DePoorter of Atkinson will travel to Victor, to give the Belgians the opportunity to express their Easter Message in their mother tongue. (De Volksstem, 2 March 1904, page 9)

These results are, to a certain extent, in line with those of Moquin's (2019) study on religion and morality in the Norwegian newspaper *Reform* (cf. Supra). She reported a strong connection between morality and language in the Norwegian-American community which instigated the ideology that only Norwegian could lead to righteousness and spirituality (Moquin 2019: 70). While the newspapers under investigation here do not seem to go as far as the Norwegian *Reform*, there are clear indications that Flemish heritage speakers favored their mother tongue for emotional and religious matters, which may have served as a strategy for language maintenance.

5. *Flemish language politics are transported to Flemish-American communities*

Finally, I examined discourse related to the Flemish language struggle which occurred in Belgium at the end of the 19th and the beginning of the 20th century. From as early as 1897 to as late as 1954, each newspaper published numerous articles discussing the roles of Dutch and French in Belgium in relation to culture, education, economics, and politics. The first mention of the language situation back home was found in a 1897 copy of *De Volksstem* (page 8) about the passing of the Coremans-De Vriendt bill – proposing that Flemish should be recognized as an official language in Belgium on par with French – and its nullification in essence by the addition of the Le Jeune amendment. In 1916, the *Gazette van Moline* printed a piece spanning half a page titled "The Language Struggle in Belgium" which revealed the journalist's stance on the matter:

(12) I myself was, am, and will remain one of the most convinced and fervent Flemish nationalists! I know as well as anyone that the Flemings were denied their most sacred rights. [...] I have testified with resentment, regret, and a bleeding heart about glaring injustices in linguistic matters.

The author continued to emphasize that the 'Flemishication' of higher education is of little use if Flemish is not also used as the language of instruction in primary and secondary education:

(13) The Flemishication of the University of Ghent is not desirable and cannot be fruitful nor sustainable until the future students of the institution are also adequately prepared through a sound Flemish primary and secondary education to successfully undertake the curriculum of the Flemishized university.

The journalist argues that the reason that this has not yet happened, or that the Flemish language has not gained an official position in general, is because the Flemings do not appreciate their own mother tongue enough:

(14) The first step that needs to be taken is to awaken the higher and middle classes of Flanders from their indifference in linguistic matters, instill in them a love and respect for, attachment to, and pride in their mother tongue, and imbue them with the conviction that their mother tongue – Flemish – is as honorable, noble, rich, elegant, dignified, powerful, and melodious as any other language in the world. (23 November 1916, page 4)

Thus, the newspapers not only reported on advancements or hindrances in the Flemish language struggle, but expressed their own opinions as well. In the *Gazette van Detroit*, I came across an article that insisted on informing the Flemish-Americans about the Flemish Movement, because:

(15) It is more or less a duty for every Flemish person to stay informed about everything happening in our homeland and to help and support our Flemish brothers across the ocean as much as possible. They are the ones fighting for the Flemish right, which is the right of us all. [...] Because yes! We need all Flemings to conquer the right that has been denied for so long, as the Flemish struggle is challenging, given the Francophile opposition. (24 November 1922, page 2)

In the subsequent decades of the period that I investigated the articles exhibit a less stringent tone as Belgian Dutch gains more rights in Belgium. Nevertheless, there are still writings addressing the position of Flemish in the home country:

(16) To encourage speaking "Flemish" in Brussels, a monthly magazine, "*De Brusselse Post*" has taken the initiative to advertise all merchants and agglomerations from Brussels who ensure that their billboards, advertisements, and employees will be bilingual. (Gazette van Detroit, 24 November 1950, page 2)

The above examples illustrate that, even though Flemish-Americans were no longer in Belgium and the language struggle did not impact them directly, they wanted to stay informed about it. Moreover, they appeared to support the ideas of the Flemish Movement, i.e. they advocated for Flemish to be officially recognized as one of Belgium's national languages. These attitudes and ideologies, however, extend beyond language itself. Language is a symptom of broader societal frictions and is thus easier focused on than the issues themselves. As Nelde (1998:290) articulates it: "Language problems in very different areas (politics, economics, administration, education) appear under the heading of language conflict." In this context, the minority position of Belgian Dutch in Belgium reflected the inequalities across political, economic, social, and cultural spheres, where French held the upper hand.

7.2 Attitudes and ideologies surrounding English

This section focuses on the attitudes and ideologies toward English within the Flemish-American community. Again, a critical reading led to five comprehensive statements outlining the beliefs of the Flemish-Americans regarding (1) knowledge of English; (2) the use of English; (3) the acceptance of English; (4) the dominance of English; (5) English and Flemish-American identities.

1. *Having knowledge of the English language is encouraged*

Based on the analysis of the discourse surrounding English, I argue that the newspapers have consistently encouraged their readers to learn the English language from the start of their publication. Implicitly this was done through printing advertisements for English classes; consider for instance the advertisement below on the right for a monthly magazine teaching 'correct' English (see Figure 2).

MARKTBERIGHTEN.

Zomertarwe	75 85
Wintertarwe	85-90
Gerst	50 60
Corn	75
Rogge	54 55
Haver, nieuwe	35-36
Boekweit	78
Erwten (Schotsche)	1 25
Geperst hooi	8 00-10 00
Los hooi	8 00
Boter	29
Eieren	24
Straight flour	2 60
Patent flour	2 70
Graham flour	2 60
Rogge flour	1 95
Grof meel, per ton met den zak	28 00
Fijn meel, " " " " "	29 00
Middlings, " " " " "	28 00
Bran " " " " "	27 00
Aardappelen	40 40
Uien, per bu	1 25

PATENTS

TRADE-MARKS and copyrights obtained or no fee. Send model, sketches or photos and brief description, for FREE SEARCH and report on patentability. [illegible] years experience.
Send [illegible]-cent stamp for NEW BOOKLET, full of patent information. It will help you to fortune.
READ PAGES 11 and [illegible] before applying for a patent. Write to-day.

D. SWIFT & CO.
PATENT LAWYERS,
303 Seventh St., Washington, D. C.

Correct English
How to use it,
Josephine Turck Baker, Editor.

A MONTHLY MAGAZINE

For Progressive Men and Women, Business and Professional, Club-Women, Teachers, Students, Ministers, Doctors, Lawyers, Stenographers, and for all who wish to Speak and Write Correct English.

Partial List of Contents.
Your Every-Day Vocabulary: How to Enlarge It.
Words, Their Meanings and Their Uses.
Pronunciations with Illustrative Sentences.
Helps For Speakers.
Helps For Writers.
Helps For Teachers.
Business English For The Business Man.
Correct English For The Beginner.
Correct English For The Advanced Pupil.
Correct English For The Foreigner.
Suggestions For the Teacher.
Correct English In the School.
Correct English In The Home.
Shall and Will; How to use them.
Should And Would; How to use them
Sample Copy 20c.
Subscription Price, $2 a year.
EVANSTON, ILLINOIS.
Please mention this paper.
Josephine Turck Baker's Standard Magazine and Books are recommend-

Uit Onzen Boekhandel

Boeken van 10c.
De Hel.

Het Nieuw Tooverboek.
Cartouche.

Figure 2. Advertisement for correct English in *De Volksstem*, 4 March 1914, page 5

At other times, there were advertisements for English language lessons in the form of an article. An example from the *Gazette van Detroit*:

(17) The evening schools are increasingly attended, and this year there is already a growth of 10% for the students in high schools and 24% for the students in elementary schools. Here, newcomers, without any cost, learn the language and customs of their second homeland and prepare themselves for obtaining their citizenship papers. (19 October 1923, page 5)

The *Gazette van Moline* went one step further and provided their readers with English lessons themselves (see Figure 3). In my random sample of 105 editions, this column appeared twice: in the editions of 1910 and 1922. Although it is not entirely clear for how long long or how frequently the *Gazette van Moline* published English lessons, a quick search in the digital archives of Rock Island County, which hosts the newspaper editions, yielded multiple results spanning several years.

Given the presence of numerous articles and advertisements containing information on English language classes, it appears that the Flemish-Americans were committed to integrating into American society, or at least on a structural level: proficiency in English was the first step in the naturalization process. However, the emphasis on learning English was probably also affected by what Pavlenko (2002: 165) terms the "English as the one and only language of American national identity"-ideology and Americanization efforts which gained prominence at the

HELPT U ZELF MET ENGELSCH LEEREN, wekelijksche Engelsche les der Gazette van Moline, in vorm van gesprekken—conversations . . . . . 4de Les . . .

Daar zult gij wel aan doen. Intusschen zijt gij nog niet uit uw bed.

Dat is waar. Kom, nu ben ik op. Ik zal mij terstond aankleeden.

IV.

HET NAAR BED GAAN.

Wel; zijt gij voldaan over den dag van heden?

Vrij wel; maar ik beken u, dat ik zeer moe ben. Ik zal mij dadelijk uitkleeden en naar bed gaan; binnen vijf minuten ben ik onder zeil.

Jan, geef mij een laarzeknecht, mijn pantoffels en mijn slaapmuts.

Daar zijn ze, mijnheer.

Hebt ge de vensterluiken gesloten?

You will do well. But meanwhile you are not yet out of bed.

In faith, it is true. Come, now I am up. I will dress myself immediately.

IV.

GOING TO BED.

Well, are you satisfied with your day?

Pretty well; but I confess that I am very tired. I am going to undress and get to bed directly; in five minutes I shall be dead to the world.

John, give me a bootjack, my slippers and my nicht cap.

There they are, sir.

Have you closed the shutters?

mijn onderbroek en mijn bovenbroek.

Hier zijn ze.

Ik vind mijn pantoffels niet.

Zij staan naast het nachttafeltje.

Geef mij wat warm water; ik ga mij scheren. Zijn mijn scheermessen goed scherp?

Zij zijn pas geslepen. Hier is de spiegel, de zeep en het kwastje.

Goed. Geef mij ook een handdoek en giet koud water in de kom.

Verlangt mijnheer, dat ik zijn haar in orde breng?

Maakt mij alleen de scheiding, ik zal mijzelven wel kammen. Waar is de grove kam, de fijne kam en de borstel?

drawers and pantaloons.

Here they are.

I do not find my slippers.

They are beside the night table.

Give me some warm water; I am going to shave. Are my razors sharpened?

They have just been set. Here is the looking glass, the soap and the shaving brush.

All right. Give me also a napkin and pour some cold water into the wash basin.

Do you wish that I should comb your hair, sir?

Part it for me only; I will comb it myself. Where is the large comb, the fine tooth comb and the brush?

Figure 3. Part of a column titled "HELP YOURSELF LEARN ENGLISH" in the *Gazette van Moline*, 23 November 1922, page 7

turn of the century, and even more so after WWI. Between 1917 and 1930 over 30 states implemented laws requiring non-English-speaking immigrants to enroll in public evening schools (Pavlenko 2002: 179).

2. *The English language is accepted within Flemish-American communities*

Even though the English language was to some extent imposed on the Flemish-Americans, they appeared to accept it willingly in most instances. The three newspapers contained multiple articles that reported on activities in either English or Dutch without placing any value judgment on the language. There were advertisements concurrently promoting Dutch and English books, the newspapers featured programs and reviews of plays performed in English, and they advertised the availability of printing services for post cards in Dutch and English. Furthermore, the language use in the newspapers themselves seems indicative of accepting attitudes toward English. The analysis revealed several occurrences of code-switching, sometimes in playful manner. In the translation, the code-switching is placed in italics:

(18) […] *Ant. Verhoeven deed Donderdag hetzelfde en bracht een nieuwen lezer voor de* DEMOCRAT. *Call again, gentlemen!*
[…] Ant. Verhoeven did the same on Thursday and brought a new reader for the DEMOCRAT. *Call again, gentlemen!* (*De Volksstem*, 4 March 1896, page 5)

(19) […] *Wij hopen dat ze alle drie een "pleasant holiday" zullen hebben. Niet te veel turkey Maurice, 't is niet goed voor uwe "waist-line".*
[…] We hope that all three of them will have a *"pleasant holiday"*. Don't eat too much *turkey* Maurice, it's not good for your *"waistline"*.
(*Gazette van Detroit*, 29 November 1946, page 6)

In addition, the newspapers occasionally included verbatim quotations in English in news stories, suggesting that the Flemings had a decent knowledge of English as well. An article reporting on a gas leak contained the following:

(20) *Bij velen stond het eten al op het gastoestel en hetzelve wilde maar niet aan de kook komen. Geen wonder, dat de huismoeders kwamen kijken "what was the matter," bemerkten zij weldra dat het vuur uit was.*
For many, the food was already on the gas stove, and it just wouldn't come to a boil. No wonder the housewives came to see *"what was the matter"* as soon as the fire was out. (*De Volksstem*, 14 March 1917, page 4)

3. *The knowledge or use of the English language is not always assured or wanted*

While most Flemish-Americans appeared to have acquired a certain level of English proficiency and generally held positive attitudes toward its use in many instances, there was also discourse present that indicated not all members of the community had this proficiency, and that the use of English was not always accepted. Clear examples are articles agreeing with the protests against the Bennett Law (cf. Supra) or depicting English as an unfit language for experiencing religion and emotions (cf. Supra). More subtly, the newspapers frequently included translations for English words and passages or marked English lexemes by placing them between quotation marks, especially during the 19th century and the first two decades of the 20th century. In the first edition of *De Volksstem* in the corpus, there was an article which contained a love letter written in English. The editors added the following remark: "We print the letter in both Dutch and English, as in the latter language alone, it would be entirely incomprehensible to most" (21 March 1890, page 3). Most of the time, however, the translations or markings were reserved for new concepts, as can be seen from Figure 4. The marked words "drug stores", "soda fountain" and "ice cream parlor" were probably novel to the immigrants.

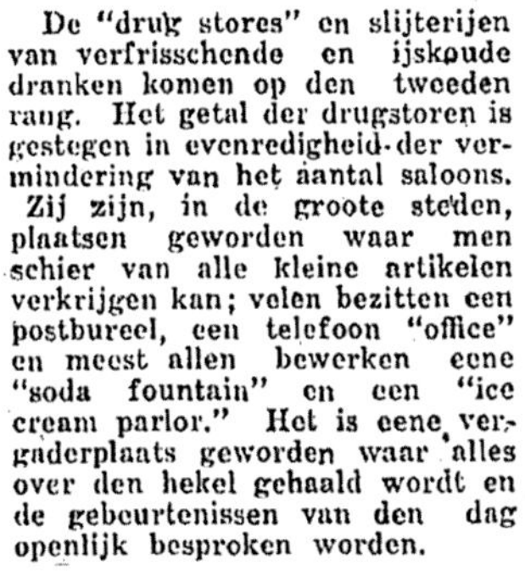

De "drug stores" en slijterijen van verfrisschende en ijskoude dranken komen op den tweeden rang. Het getal der drugstoren is gestegen in evenredigheid der vermindering van het aantal saloons. Zij zijn, in de groote steden, plaatsen geworden waar men schier van alle kleine artikelen verkrijgen kan; velen bezitten een postbureel, een telefoon "office" en meest allen bewerken eene "soda fountain" en een "ice cream parlor." Het is eene vergaderplaats geworden waar alles over den hekel gehaald wordt en de gebeurtenissen van den dag openlijk besproken worden.

Figure 4. Article in the *Gazette van Moline* containing marked English words, 23 November 1922, page 4

4. *The later in time, the more dominant English becomes*

Nevertheless, from the end of the 1920s onward, the presence of English became increasingly prominent – both in the language used by newspapers and in the lives of the Flemish-Americans. Emblematic is the following passage from an apology for typographical errors and printing mistakes in the *Gazette van Moline* in 1938:

(21) We need to have a bit of patience: the manager has explained to me that due to a shortage of Flemish typesetters, he must recruit boys from his family and teach them typesetting. These boys are, of course, raised in the English language. (23 November 1938, page 6)

The *Gazette van Moline* even listed the declining number of Flemish-Americans who understood Dutch as one of the main reasons for its bankruptcy in 1940:

(22) [...] due to the pressure and changing of times, the restriction on migration, the fading away of the older settlers, and the indifference of some toward the mother tongue and customs, the Gazette gradually lost its number of readers. (18 April 1940, page 1)

Indeed, the newspapers occasionally reported that second and third generation Flemish-Americans are often brought up in one language, viz. English. To this extent, consider the following advertisement (Figure 5), which addresses the parents in Dutch, but the children in English.

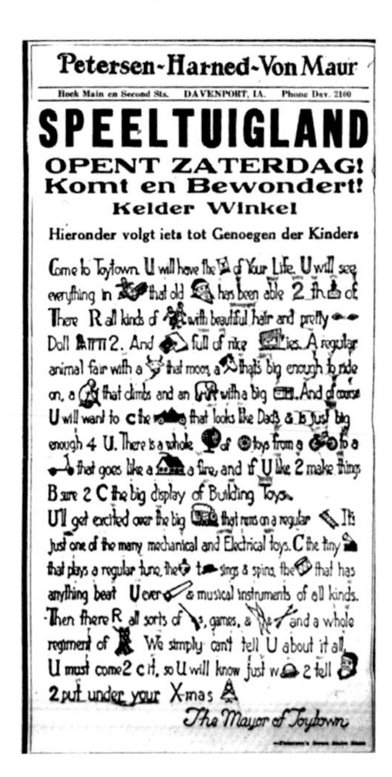

Figure 5. Bilingual advertisement for parents and children, *Gazette van Moline*, 22 November 1926, page 6

Regarding the language use in the newspapers, I observed that the marking of English words and phrases (cf. Supra) decreased, while the number of code-switches, and segments and advertisements fully written in English increased (see Figure 6). Moreover, whereas the *Gazette van Moline* and the *Gazette van Detroit* used to give the Dutch translation for an English lexeme, the opposite started to occur as well, indicating that some words might be more entrenched in English than in Dutch.

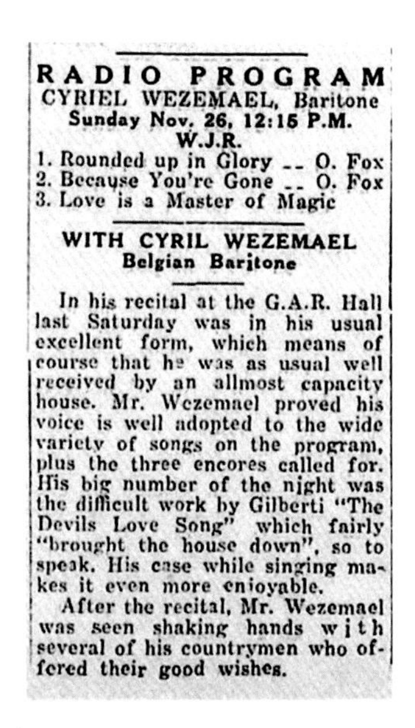

RADIO PROGRAM
CYRIEL WEZEMAEL, Baritone
Sunday Nov. 26, 12:15 P.M.
W.J.R.

1. Rounded up in Glory -- O. Fox
2. Because You're Gone -- O. Fox
3. Love is a Master of Magic

WITH CYRIL WEZEMAEL
Belgian Baritone

In his recital at the G.A.R. Hall last Saturday was in his usual excellent form, which means of course that he was as usual well received by an allmost capacity house. Mr. Wezemael proved his voice is well adopted to the wide variety of songs on the program, plus the three encores called for. His big number of the night was the difficult work by Gilberti "The Devils Love Song" which fairly "brought the house down", so to speak. His ease while singing makes it even more enioyable.

After the recital, Mr. Wezemael was seen shaking hands with several of his countrymen who offered their good wishes.

Figure 6. English article in the *Gazette van Detroit*, 24 November 1933, page 4

5. *Over time identities shift from Flemish to Flemish-American*

Finally, as English became more prominent from the 1920s and 1930s onward, a shift in identity construction became evident. As already briefly touched upon above, migration challenges one's identity (cf. Auer 2005: 406). As the years go by, the one nation-one language ideology is undermined by the expanding influence of English on functional, i.e. where English takes on functions of Dutch, and structural levels, i.e., where English affects Dutch phonologically, morphologically, syntactically, and lexically. Indeed, greater proficiency in English appears to correspond with greater integration into American society. One indication of this is the increasing number of announcements in the papers about Flemings receiving their American citizenship papers (see Figure 7).

Nieuwe Burgers
Martha Michelet, Emerence Leuntjes, Cyriel Van Dierendonck, Anna Van Dhuynslager,, Edward Welvaert, Willem De Winter, Prosper Ramon en Mrs. Emiel Smet bekwamen allen hunne volle Amerikaansche burgerspapieren. Proficiat!...

Figure 7. Article titled "New Citizens", *Gazette van Detroit,* 3 April 1942, page 6

This does not imply that the emigrants ignored their Flemish heritage; instead, they also adopted American traditions resulting in a more Flemish-American identity. A prime example of this is the following bulletin (see Figure 8) about Thanksgiving – for which the Flemish-Americans often use the loan translation *dankdag* – which states "that the United States is the best Country, even though we remain deeply attached to our small homeland with respect and love" (*Gazette van Detroit,* 19 November 1948, page 1). The longer the Flemish community existed in America, the more they embraced American customs and traditions, while still maintaining strong ties to their Flemish heritage.

THANKSGIVING

DANKDAG 25 NOVEMBER

Zooals de Pelgrims overtijd, hebben wij reden om Dankdag te vieren. Met enkel eens rond te zien naar de overige landen der wereld, zijn we overtuigd dat de Vereenigde Staten het beste Land is, al is het dat wij vol achting en liefde gehecht blijven aan ons kleine vaderland.

Figure 8. Bulletin about Thanksgiving, *Gazette van Detroit,* 19 November 1948, page 1

8. Conclusion

The present study sought to contribute to the growing body of research on historical heritage languages from a sociolinguistic point of view. By delving into the discourse surrounding English and Belgian Dutch in three Flemish-American newspapers that appeared between 1890 and 1959, I aimed to shed light on the linguistic attitudes and ideologies present in the Flemish-American community on the one hand, and to explore the value of heritage community newspapers in attitudinal research on the other.

The analysis revealed that Flemish-Americans in the late 19th and early 20th centuries held the belief that maintaining Belgian Dutch in North America was crucial. This ideology was at times explicitly expressed, with various editions featuring statements that emphasized that the Flemish language is and must remain an essential part of the Flemish community in America. More subtly, the motivation to preserve Dutch was evident in the publication of Flemish books and poetry, which encouraged the community to stay connected with the written language. Reports on activities such as Flemish plays, musicals, church meetings, and parties further highlighted the community's commitment to speaking and hearing Dutch beyond the family home.

In addition to their efforts to preserve Flemish in the New Country, the analysis also showed that Flemish-Americans were deeply concerned with the position of Flemish in Belgium. Numerous articles addressed the language struggle between French and Belgian Dutch in Belgium, often portraying the Flemish people as victims of injustice due to the presence and pressure of French.

The discourse surrounding Belgian Dutch in North America shares certain parallels with the discourse about Belgian Dutch in Belgium. This demonstrates that the beliefs and emotions tied to the Flemish language struggle traveled with the emigrants to North America, and confirms that the linguistic ecology before the migration can impact language attitudes and ideologies in heritage communities. Therefore, it is crucial to consider this factor in future studies to gain a full understanding of heritage language dynamics.

Furthermore, the loyalty to the Flemish language exposed the belief in an intrinsic link between language and identity which could be traced back to the one nation-one language ideology that was widespread at the time. Particularly in the first decades, the conviction was firmly held that possessing the ability to speak Flemish was an important precondition for identifying as Flemish. In the later decades, this ideology was challenged, however, as the English language took a more prominent place in the lives of the Flemings in America.

Indeed, this study found that the Flemish-American community accepted and encouraged English language acquisition. Early editions highlight the recognition of the practical benefits of English proficiency, especially for economic opportunities. Later editions express a broader cultural acceptance, as English proficiency became closely tied to social integration. Eventually, English became the primary language among Flemish-Americans and led to the construction of a Flemish-American identity. This transition reflects a common trajectory, where the heritage language – though still valued – gradually gives way to the dominant societal language, particularly among younger generations.

Finally, this chapter underscores the pivotal role of heritage community press in shaping and reflecting language beliefs. The newspapers proved instrumental in articulating and reinforcing the community's language ideologies and attitudes, serving as platforms for cultural expression and communal bonding. They were more than mere information carriers; they played a central part in the community's linguistic maintenance and were symbolic representations of the Flemish(-American) identity.

In conclusion, through an in-depth, qualitative discourse analysis of 105 heritage community newspaper editions, covering a period of 69 years, this study was able to paint a rich, longitudinal portrait of the Flemish-American immigrant community's language beliefs in the late 19th and early 20th centuries, reflecting a dynamic interplay between preservation and adaptation.

Acknowledgements

This research is part of a PhD project titled *Van het beloofde land: een historisch sociolinguïstisch onderzoek naar het Belgisch-Nederlands als heritage taal in Noord-Amerika* (1119924N) funded by Fonds Wetenschappelijk Onderzoek – Vlaanderen.
I am deeply grateful to Wim Vandenbussche and Rik Vosters for their valuable insights, help and support throughout this project, as well as to Rachyl Hietpas for her extremely thorough and helpful feedback on this paper.

References

doi Aalberse, Suzanne Pauline, Ad Backus, and Pieter Muysken. 2019. *Heritage Languages: A Language Contact Approach*. Amsterdam / Philadelphia: John Benjamins Publishing Company.

doi Arnbjörnsdóttir, Birna. 2015. "Reexamining Icelandic as a Heritage Language in North America." In *Germanic Heritage Languages in North America: Acquisition, attrition and change*, ed. by Janne Bondi Johannessen and Joseph Salmons, 72-93. Amsterdam / Philadelphia: John Benjamins Publishing Company.

doi Auer, Peter. 2005. "A Postscript: Code-Switching and Social Identity." *Journal of Pragmatics* 37 (3): 403–10.

doi Becker, Molly. 2022. "Talking American in the Midwest: Linguistic Diversity and Authenticity in the Twentieth-Century United States." *Journal of American Studies* 56 (1): 65–86.

Bell, Alan. 1991. *The Language of News Media*. Oxford: Blackwell.

Boemer, Magali. 2016. "Beliefs and Ideas about SLA in Newspaper Articles of the German-Speaking Community of Belgium (1919–1963)." In *Metalinguistic Perspectives on Germanic Languages: European Case Studies from Past to Present*, ed. by Gijsbert Rutten and Kristine Horner, 79–104. Historical Sociolinguistics 4. Oxford: Peter Lang.

doi Brown, Joshua R. 2017. "Language Maintenance among the Hutterites." *Yearbook of German-American Studies*, no. 52: 151–68.

doi Brown, Joshua R. 2019. "Historical heritage language ego-documents: from home, from away, and from below." *Journal of Historical Sociolinguistics* 5 (2): 1–10.

doi Brown, Joshua R., and Joshua Bousquette. 2018. "Heritage Languages in North America: Sociolinguistic Approaches." *Journal of Language Contact* 11 (2): 201–7.

Caestecker, Frank. 2014. "Hoe Het Meetjesland Amerika Vond." In *Boer Vindt Land: Vlaamse Migranten En Noord-Amerika*, ed. by Andreas Stynen, 58–66. Davidfonds.

Cobbaert, Frank, Gerard Baertsoen, and Omer De Clercq. 1916. "DE BEETWERKERS." *Gazette van Detroit*, April 14, 1916.

doi Cohn, Raymond L. 2008. *Mass Migration under Sail: European Immigration to the Antebellum United States*. Cambridge: Cambridge University Press.

doi Collet, Tanja. 2016. "Language Controversies in the Gazette van Detroit (1916–1918)." In *Discord and Consensus in the Low Countries*, 1700–2000, ed. by Jane Fenoulhet, Gerdi Quist, and Ulrich Tiedau, 1st ed., 1:81–101. UCL Press.

Correa-Zoli, Yole. 1970. *Lexical and Morphological Aspects of American Italian in San Francisco*. Stanford University.

doi Cotter, Colleen. 2003. "Prescription and Practice: Motivations behind Change in News Discourse." *Journal of Historical Pragmatics* 4 (1): 45–74.

doi Crombez, Yasmin, Wim Vandenbussche, and Rik Vosters. 2024. "Exploring Past and Present Layers of Multilingualism in Flemish-Emigrant Writing." In *Investigating West Germanic Languages: Studies in Honor of Robert B. Howell*, ed. by Jennifer Hendriks and B. Richard Page, 280–303. Studies in Germanic Linguistics. Amsterdam / Philadelphia : John Benjamins Publishing Company.

doi Deprez, Kas, and Guido Geerts. 1977. "Closure to French Influence in the Flemish Speech Community." *Lingua* 43 (2–3): 199–228.

Feys, Torsten. 2004. "Radeloosheid in Crisistijd: Pogingen van de Belgische Autoriteiten Om Een Deel van de Arme Bevolking Naar de Verenigde Staten Te Sturen 1847–1856." *Belgisch Tijdschrift Voor Nieuwste Geschiedenis*, 195–230.

Feys, Torsten. 2014. "De Grote Oversteek Tussen Twee Werelden: Van Het Meetjesland Tot Het Beloofde Land." In *Transatlantische Emigratie Uit Het Meetjesland Naar Het Beloofd Land*, ed. by Andreas Stynen, 84–105. ADVN.

doi Fishman, Joshua A. (ed.). 2001. *Can Threatened Languages Be Saved? Reversing Language Shift, Revisited: A 21st Century Perspective*. Clevedon / Buffalo: Multilingual Matters.

Gazette van Moline. 1907. "De Weerde van Het Onderwijs." *Gazette van Moline*, November 22, 1907.

Gilbert, Glenn G. 1965. "Dative vs. Accusative in the German Dialects of Central Texas." *Zeitschrift Für Mundartforschung*, 288–96.

doi Griffin, Gabriele. 2013. "6. Discourse Analysis." In *Research Methods for English studies*, ed. by Griffin Gabriele, 93-112. Edinburgh: Edinburgh University Press.

Hardy, Cynthia, Bill Harley, and Nelson Phillips. 2004. "Discourse Analysis and Content Analysis: Two Solitudes." *Qualitative Methods* 2 (1): 19–22.

doi Hatton, Timothy J., and Jeffrey G. Williamson. 1992. *What Drove the Mass Migrations from Europe in the Late Nineteenth Century?* National Bureau of Economic Research Cambridge, Mass., USA.

Havinga, Anna D., and Andreas Krogull. 2022. "Researching Language Attitudes Based on Historical Data." In *Research Methods in Language Attitudes*, ed. by Ruth Kircher and Lena Zipp 297–312. Cambridge University Press.

Hickerson, Andrea, and Kristin Gustafson. 2016. "Revisiting the Immigrant Press." *Journalism* 17 (8): 943–60.

doi Hietpas, Rachyl, and Charlotte Vanhecke. 2022. "Dutch and Flemish Language, Culture, and Identity in North America." *Bergen Language and Linguistics Studies* 12 (2): 6–18.

doi Hoffman, Angela, and Merja Kytö. 2019. "Varying Social Roles and Networks on a Family Farm: Evidence from Swedish Immigrant Letters, 1880s to 1930s." *Journal of Historical Sociolinguistics* 5 (2).

Janssens, Guy, and Ann Marynissen. 2011. *Het Nederlands Vroeger En Nu.* Leuven / Den Haag: Acco.

Johnson, Sally A., and Tommaso M. Milani, (eds). 2010. *Language Ideologies and Media Discourse: Texts, Practices, Politics.* Advances in Sociolinguistics. London; New York: Continuum.

doi Kagan, Olga, Maria M. Carreira, and Claire Hitchins Chik, (eds). 2017. *The Routledge Handbook of Heritage Language Education: From Innovation to Program Building.* New York: Routledge.

doi Karatsareas, Petros. 2018. "Attitudes towards Cypriot Greek and Standard Modern Greek in London's Greek Cypriot Community." *International Journal of Bilingualism* 22 (4): 412–28.

doi Kasstan, Jonathan R., Anita Auer, and Joseph Salmons. 2018. "Heritage-Language Speakers: Theoretical and Empirical Challenges on Sociolinguistic Attitudes and Prestige." *International Journal of Bilingualism* 22 (4): 387–94.

Kellogg, Louise Phelps. 1918. "The Bennett Law in Wisconsin." *The Wisconsin Magazine of History* 2 (1): 3–25.

doi Kroskrity, Paul V. 1999. Identify. *Journal of Linguistic Anthropology* 9 (1–2): 111–114.

doi Kühl, Karoline, and Elizabeth Peterson. 2018. "The Remains of the Danes: The Final Stages of Language Shift in Sanpete County, Utah." *Journal of Language Contact* 11 (2): 208–32.

Langback, Peder. 1919. *Reform*, April 3, 1919.

doi Litty, Samantha. 2019. "Letters Home: German-American Civil War Soldiers' Letters 1864–1865." *Journal of Historical Sociolinguistics* 5 (2).

doi Lloyd-Smith, Anika, Marieke Einfeldt, and Tanja Kupisch. 2020. "Italian-German Bilinguals: The Effects of Heritage Language Use on Accent in Early-Acquired Languages." *International Journal of Bilingualism* 24 (2): 289–304.

Marle, Jaap van (2001): American 'Leeg Duits' ('Low Dutch') – a neglected language. In Sture P Ureland (Hrsg.), *Global Eurolinguistics. European Languages in North America – Migration, Maintenance and Death*, 79–101. Tübingen: Niemeyer.

Milroy, James. 1992. "Social Network and Prestige Arguments in Sociolinguistics." In *Sociolinguistics Today. International Perspectives*, ed. by Kingsley Bolton and Helen Kwok, 146–62. London: Routledge.

doi Montrul, Silvina, and Maria Polinsky, (eds). 2021. *The Cambridge Handbook of Heritage Languages and Linguistics.* Cambridge: Cambridge University Press.

Moquin, Laura. 2019. "Language and Morality in Norwegian-American Newspapers: Reform in Eau Claire, WI." In *9th Workshop on Immigrant Languages in the Americas*, 64–71. Cascadilla Proceedings Project.

doi Moquin, Laura, and Kirsten Wolf. 2023. "Language and Identity: The Case of North American Icelandic." In *Icelandic Heritage in North America*, ed. by Birna Arnbjörnsdóttir, Höskuldur Thráinsson, and Úlfar Bragason, 271–91. Winnipeg, MB: University of Manitoba Press.

Moro, Francesca R. 2018. "Divergence in Heritage Ambon Malay in the Netherlands: The Role of Social-Psychological Factors." *International Journal of Bilingualism* 22 (4): 395–411.

Musschoot, Dirk. 2002. *Wij Gaan Naar Amerika: Vlaamse Landverhuizers Naar de Nieuwe Wereld* 1850–1930. Lannoo.

Noordegraaf, Jan (2008): Nederlands in Noord-Amerika. Over de studie van het Leeg Duits (Low Dutch).

Nagy, Naomi. 2018. "Linguistic Attitudes and Contact Effects in Toronto's Heritage Languages: A Variationist Sociolinguistic Investigation." *International Journal of Bilingualism* 22 (4): 429–46.

Nauwelaerts, Mandy, and Frank Caestecker. 2008. *Red Star Line: People on the Move*. Schoten: BAI.

Nelde, P. 1998. "Language Conflict." In *The Handbook of Sociolinguistics*, ed. by Florian Coulmas, 285–300. Malden (MA): Blackwell.

Olzak, Susan, and Elizabeth West. 1991. "Ethnic Conflict and the Rise and Fall of Ethnic Newspapers." *American Sociological Review* 56 (4): 458–74.

Park, Robert Ezra. 1922. *The Immigrant Press and Its Control*. Vol. 7. Harper & brothers.

Pavlenko, Aneta. 2002. "We Have Room for but One Language Here: Language and National Identity in the US at the Turn of the 20th Century." *Multilingua* 21 (2–3): 163–96.

Percy, Carol. 2012. "Early Advertising and Newspapers as Sources of Sociolinguistic Investigation." In *The Handbook of Historical Sociolinguistics*, ed. by Juan Manuel Hernandez Campoy and Juan Camilo Conde Silverstre, 68:191–210. Chichester: John Wiley & Sons, Inc.

Polinsky, Maria. 2008. "Gender under Incomplete Acquisition: Heritage Speakers' Knowledge of Noun Categorization." *Heritage Language Journal*. 6 (1): 40-71.

Prince, John, D. 1910. "The Jersey Dutch Dialect." *Dialect Notes*, no. 8: 459–84.

Rademann, Tobias. 1998. "Using Online Electronic Newspapers in Modern English-Language Press Corpora: Benefits and Pitfalls." *ICAME Journal* 22: 49–72.

Raña-Risso, Rocío, and Carolina Barrera-Tobón. 2018. "On the Relationship Between Subject Placement and Overt Pronouns in the Spanish of New York City Bilinguals." *Journal of Language Contact* 11 (2): 324–47.

Rothman, Jason. 2009. "Understanding the Nature and Outcomes of Early Bilingualism: Romance Languages as Heritage Languages." *International Journal of Bilingualism* 13 (2): 155–63.

Rutten, Gijsbert, and Rik Vosters. 2011. "As Many Norms as There Were Scribes? Language History, Norms and Usage in the Southern Netherlands in the Nineteenth Century." In *Language and History, Linguistics and Historiography. Interdisciplinary Approaches*, ed. by Nils Langer, Steffan Davies, and Wim Vandenbussche, 229–54. Oxford / Bern: Peter Lang.

Rutten, Gijsbert, Rik Vosters, and Marijke van der Wal. 2015. "Frenchification in Discourse and Practice: Loan Morphology in Dutch Private Letters of the Eighteenth and Nineteenth Centuries." In *Past, Present and Future of a Language Border: Germanic-Romance Encounters in the Low Countries*, ed. by Catharina Peersman, Gijsbert Rutten, and Rik Vosters, 143–69. Berlin/Boston: De Gruyter.

Sánchez, Liliana, Elisabeth Mayer, José Camacho, and Carolina Rodriguez Alzza. 2018. "Linguistic Attitudes toward Shipibo in Cantagallo: Reshaping Indigenous Language and Identity in an Urban Setting." *International Journal of Bilingualism* 22 (4): 466–87.

doi Schmid, Monika S. 2011. *Language Attrition*. Cambridge University Press.

Smits, Caroline & Jaap van Marle (2013): The Dutch Language in the USA. In *Language and space: an international handbook of linguistic variation Dutch*, ed. by Frans Hinskens, Johan Taeldeman, Jürgen Erich Schmidt, Gerold Ungeheuer & Herbert Ernst Wiegand, vol. 3, 821–840. Berlin: De Gruyter Mouton.

doi Stynen, Andreas, and Frans-Jos Verdoodt. 2015. "Vlaams-Amerikaanse Kranten En de Verschuiving van Identiteiten." *WT. Tijdschrift over de Geschiedenis van de Vlaamse Beweging* 74 (1).

Van der Sijs, Nicoline. 2004. *Taal Als Mensenwerk. Het Ontstaan van Het ABN*. Den Haag: Sdu.

Van der Sijs, Nicoline, and Roland Willemyns. 2009. *Het Verhaal van Het Nederlands. Een Geschiedenis van Twaalf Eeuwen*. Amsterdam: Bert Bakker.

Van Hoof, S., and J. Jaspers. 2012. "Hyperstandaardisering." *Tijdschrift Voor Nederlandse Taal- En Letterkunde* 128 (2): 97–125.

doi Van Marle, Jaap, and Caroline Smits. 1993. "The Inflectional Systems of Overseas Dutch." *AMSTERDAM STUDIES IN THE THEORY AND HISTORY OF LINGUISTIC SCIENCE SERIES* 4, 313–313.

Vandenbussche, Wim. 2009. "Historical Language Planning in Nineteenth-Century Flanders. Standardisation as a Means of Language Survival." In *Språknormering. I Tide Og Utide?*, ed. by Helge Omdal, 255–68. Oslo: Novus Forlag.

doi Vanhecke, Eline, and Jetje De Groof. 2007. "New Data on Language Policy and Language Choice in 19th-Century Flemish City Administrations." In *Germanic Language Histories from below (1700–2000)*, ed. by Stephan Elspaß, Nils Langer, Joachim Scharloth, and Wim Vandenbussche, 449–65. Berlin / New York: De Gruyter.

Verheyden, Charlotte. 2023. "'Ge moet zien dat gij uw vlaamsche taal niet vergeet': Een historisch-sociolinguïstisch onderzoek naar de invloed van het Frans op het Zuidelijk Nederlands." Doctoral dissertation, Brussel: Vrije Universiteit Brussel.

doi Viola, Lorella, and Jaap Verheul. 2019. "The Media Construction of Italian Identity: A Transatlantic, Digital Humanities Analysis of Italianità, Ethnicity, and Whiteness, 1867–1920." *Identity* 19 (4): 294–312.

Vosters, Rik. 2013. "Dutch, Flemish or Hollandic? Social and Ideological Aspects of Linguistic Convergence and Divergence during the United Kingdom of the Netherlands (1815–1830)." In *Ideological Conceptualisations of Language in Discourses of Linguistic Diversity*, ed. by Erzsébet Barát and Patrick Studer, Prague Papers on Language, Society and Interaction 3, 35–54. Frankfurt: Peter Lang.

Vosters, Rik, Gijsbert Rutten, and Marijke Van der Wal. 2010. "Mythes op de pijnbank. Naar een herwaardering van de taalsituatie in de Nederlanden in de achttiende en negentiende eeuw." *Verslagen en Mededelingen van de Koninklijke Academie voor Nederlandse Taal- en Letterkunde* 120 (1): 93–112.

doi Walsh, Olivia. 2022. "Discourse Analysis of Print Media." In *Research Methods in Language Attitudes*, ed. by Ruth Kircher and Lena Zipp, 19–34. Cambridge: Cambridge University Press.

Horner, Kristine, and Jean. Jacques Weber. (2012). *Introducing Multilingualism: A Social Approach*. London / New York: Routledge.

Willemyns, Roland. 2003. *Het Verhaal van Het Vlaams. De Geschiedenis van Het Nederlands in de Zuidelijke Nederlanden*. Antwerpen / Utrecht: Standaard / Spectrum.

CHAPTER 14

Grammatical discontinuity between Dutch and Skepi Dutch Creole

Bart Jacobs & Mikael Parkvall

Skepi Dutch Creole thrived during the 18th and 19th centuries as a lingua franca along the Essequibo River of what is now the Republic of Guyana. Drawing on both old and new data, this chapter aims to describe selected features from the Skepi noun and verb phrase and compare these features to the lexifier, Dutch, in order to assess the degree of grammatical (dis)continuity between the lexifier and the creole within the broader context of the debate on creole genesis.

Keywords: Skepi Dutch Creole, Essequibo, New Netherlands Dutch, broken transmission, pidgin-creole cycle

1. Introduction

1.1 Skepi

Skepi Dutch Creole[1] emerged in the mid-17th century in the Dutch colony along the Essequibo River of what is now the Republic of Guyana (Map 1). It thrived in the 18th and 19th centuries as a lingua franca between African slaves, European colonists, and local Amerindian traders and craftsmen. However, the language gradually fell into obsolescence following the English takeover of the colony in the early 19th century and the subsequent diffusion of English and English Creole in the region. It eventually became extinct toward the end of the 20th century.

Incidentally, the only other Dutch-lexified creoles in the world – Berbice Dutch Creole and Virgin Islands Dutch Creole – met similar fates, falling into disuse and becoming extinct during the 20th century, replaced by English and

1. The glossonym Skepi (a local pronunciation of "Essequibo") first surfaced in the work of Ian Robertson (1977, 1983, 1989), whose informants presumably referred to the language as such. In other (older) sources the language is always referred to as Dutch Creole or Creole Dutch, never as Skepi.

https://doi.org/10.1075/impact.55.14jac

English Creoles. Fortunately, Virgin Islands Dutch Creole is relatively well-documented, with a substantial body of literature (e.g. Stolz 1986, Van Rossem & Van der Voort 1996, Stein 1996, Bakker & Van der Voort 2008, Sabino 2008, Van Rossem 2017), including one of the earliest creole grammars ever written (Magens 1770). Likewise, Berbice Dutch was the subject of an excellent in-depth study by Kouwenberg (1994) following earlier documentation by Robertson (1976). In comparison, Skepi is by far the least well-documented of the three known Dutch-lexified creoles.

Map 1. Dutch colonies in the Guianas in the 17th and 18th century. The orange shaded area is where Skepi was spoken

Robertson (1977, 1983, 1989), who had previously introduced Berbice Dutch to a wider linguistic audience, was a pioneer in documenting Skepi. He published around 200 words and a dozen sentences. However, the data must be treated with caution due to the fact that his informants' command of the creole was already in an advanced stage of attrition. For several decades, Robertson's field data was the only source on Skepi. However, in 2013, Van der Wal discovered a late-18th-century sentence of about 30 words (Van der Wal 2013).[2]

More recently, Jacobs & Parkvall (2020, 2024) have unearthed two rich new sources for Skepi, dating to the 1790s and the 1830s. These discoveries have enabled a (re)assessment of the grammar and lexicon of the language as it was spoken between ca. 1750 and 1850, when it was still in its prime. The new sources include linguistic notes from the diary of reverend Thomas Youd (Youd 1833–1842; see Jacobs & Parkvall 2020) and in the academic work of Ernst Karl Rodschied, previously unknown to creolists (Rodschied 1792, 1794, 1796). The Youd data

2. Details about this discovery can be found here: https://www.universiteitleiden.nl/binaries/content/assets/geesteswetenschappen/onderzoeksprojecten/brieven-als-buit/brief-van-de-maand-december-2013.pdf

amounts to around 250 words and 50 sentences, including about a dozen complex ones. The Rodschied data consists of personal pronouns, four verbal paradigms, a 60-word text with translation, and ca. three dozen lexical items for flora and fauna. Our Skepi corpus, on which the analyses presented in this chapter are based, comprises all of the above-mentioned materials.

1.2 The creole genesis debate: Broken transmission versus gradual creolization

Scholarly interest in creole languages dates back to the 19th century, when researchers such as Van Name (1869), Coelho (1880–1886) and Schuchardt (1882) began to observe the ways in which creole grammars differ from those of their lexifiers.[3] Over a century and a half later, the field remains marked by intense debate about the nature of creolization and the origins of creole grammars.

The central question is whether creoles are genetic continuations of their lexifiers or whether they are in fact nativized pidgins that resist classification within the family tree model. The former position, often referred to as Uniformitarianism, argues for grammatical – and therefore genetic – continuity between the lexifier and the resulting creole. Proponents of this perspective typically posit that creolization is a gradual process, comparable in nature to the evolution of Romance languages from Latin (e.g. Chaudenson 1992 and elsewhere, Mufwene 2000 and elsewhere, DeGraff 2001 and elsewhere, Ansaldo and Matthews 2007, Aboh 2016). The pidgin-creole cycle, also known as Exceptionalism, on the other hand, asserts that creoles develop out of a pidgin. This model implies a negligible degree of grammatical continuity between lexifier and creole, portraying creolization as an abrupt rather than gradual process (McWhorter 1998, Parkvall 2008, Bakker et al. 2011, Daval-Markussen 2018, Jacobs 2023, Parkvall & Jacobs 2023). It should be no secret that we align with the pidgin-creole cycle.

3. The term 'lexifier' refers to the language from which a given creole drew most of its vocabulary. For instance, the lexifier of Jamaican Creole is English, that of Haitian Creole is French, and that of Cape Verdean Creole is Portuguese. On average, around 90 to 95% of a creole's vocabulary can be traced back to the lexifier. A handful of creoles appear to have more than one lexifier, at least synchronically: Berbice Dutch, for instance, is lexified by both Dutch and Eastern Ijo. Similarly, the vocabulary of Saramaccan shows a split between Portuguese- and English-derived lexical items.

1.3 Structure of the chapter

In the sections that follow, we discuss several key features of the noun phrase (Section 2) and verb phrase (Section 3), which are particularly illustrative of the grammatical discontinuity between Dutch and Skepi. It is important to note that the purpose of this chapter is not to provide comprehensive descriptions of the noun and verb phrases but rather to highlight features that indicate grammatical innovation, as opposed to inheritance from the lexifier. In Section 4, we present comparative data from a largely overlooked and now extinct colonial variety of Dutch once spoken in the New Netherlands colony on the east coast of the USA. This variety, like Skepi, developed in relative isolation from standard European Dutch. As we shall see, whereas Skepi exhibits clear evidence of a break in transmission, the New Netherlands dialect displays an unmistakable continuation of Dutch morphosyntax.

2. Noun phrase

2.1 Gender marking

Modern standard Dutch nouns are categorized into two grammatical genders: common gender and neuter.[4] These distinctions are primarily marked on determiners, but they appear marginally on adjectives as well. Thus, Dutch distinguishes the definite article *de* (common gender) from *het* (neuter), and demonstratives *deze* and *die* (common gender, proximal and distal) from their neuter counterparts *dit* and *dat*. (The indefinite article *een* is not marked for gender, and plural nouns always take the common gender determiners.) Adjectives display gender differentiation in indefinite noun phrases, with the suffix *-e* marking common gender.

---

4. Throughout the chapter, we shall use standard modern-day Dutch as a comparandum. It goes without saying, however, that the variety of Dutch spoken in 17th-century Essequibo must have displayed a number of archaic and dialectal traits vis-à-vis the modern standard in all areas of the grammar. Gender marking may have been one such area. According to Van der Sijs (2021:Chapter 8), the transition within Dutch from a three- to a two-gender system appears to have happened in the Renaissance period. However, the process was brought to completion only in the Northern and Central (Hollandic) Dutch dialects, whereas Flemish has in fact up to present retained a three-way grammatical gender system (despite simplifications in the case system) (cf. e.g. Devos & Vandekerckhoven 2005:70). As it happens, several lexical Skepi items give reason to suspect (West) Flemish / Zeelandic of having provided much (if not most) of the creole's Dutch lexifier input, but this remains to be investigated more thoroughly.

In the pronominal domain, there is a three-way gender distinction (masculine, feminine, neuter) for third-person singular subject and object pronouns, along with a two-way (masculine-feminine) distinction for third-person possessive pronouns. The latter distinction is governed by the gender of the possessor, not of the possessed.

As is typical of a basilectal creole, Skepi does not exhibit any of the Dutch gender distinctions. There is no trace in Skepi of the Dutch neuter determiners *het*, *dit* and *dat* (Table 1). Instead, Skepi features a proximal demonstrative *disə*, and we suspect that the definite article *di* doubled as a distal demonstrative. Adjectives in Skepi typically had one invariant form, most of which derived from the Dutch base form.[5] Furthermore, the creole lacked biological gender marking, all personal pronouns being gender neutral (Table 1).

Table 1. Lack of grammatical gender in Skepi

Skepi (normalized)[a]	Gloss	Translation	Dutch equivalent
di dop	DEF.ART baptism	'the baptism'	(Dutch ***de*** *doop*)
di plɛk	DEF.ART place	'the place'	(Dutch ***de*** *plek*)
di lant	DEF.ART land	'the land'	(Dutch ***het*** *land*)
di mɛsɛ	DEF.ART knife	'the knife'	(Dutch ***het*** *mes*)
disə snaps	DEM.PROX schnaps	'this schnaps'	(Dutch ***deze*** *schnaps*)
disə wɛrk	DEM.PROX work	'this work'	(Dutch ***dit*** *werk*)

a. Our reconstructed 'normalized' IPA rendering is based not only on our linguistic intuitions but also on our analysis of Youd's orthographic practices as well as on Rodschied's and Robertson's data. Note that the latter were already rendered in IPA.

It should be stressed that the absence of gender marking alone is not diagnostic of creolization, as many non-creole languages also lack gender marking. However, what matters here is that languages that do have gender marking very rarely lose it altogether (see for instance Priestly [1983] in the context of Indo-European). While English is sometimes put forth to counter that statement, English only eliminated *grammatical* gender marking while retaining *biological* gender marking in its personal pronouns. The fact that both forms of gender differentiation were lost in the transition from Dutch to Skepi is highly unusual and provides compelling evidence of a break in transmission.

5. In the Youd Papers we find, for example, <moi dak> 'a beautiful day' (≠ Dutch *mooie dag*), <ons father> 'our father' (≠ Dutch *onze vader*), <ander domine> 'another domine' (≠ Dutch *andere dominee*), but also <swarte domine> (cf. Dutch *zwarte dominee*).

2.2 Plural marking

Disregarding irregular forms, plural in Dutch is generally marked on nouns by means of the suffix *-en*. A smaller but still sizeable group of nouns, including non-integrated loanwords as well as all words with a schwa in the final syllable, receives a plural *-s*. Neither of the two pluralization strategies made their way into the creole. Instead, plural marking in Skepi seems to have been largely absent. For instance, plural is unmarked in Skepi *fɛjl janafu* (many-spirit) 'many spirits' (Youd), *4 blaba* (four-child) 'four children' (Van der Wal) and *mɔjə guto* nice-thing 'nice things' (Van der Wal).[6] However, evidence from the Youd corpus suggests that Skepi may have developed (or begun to develop) an innovative feature typical of quite a few Atlantic creoles, to wit: the use of the third-person plural pronoun as a nominal plural marker (1).[7]

(1) Qua Goodt oar[8]
kwat gɔt or
angry/evil God they/PL
'Angry Gods' (Youd); cf. Dutch: *kwade Goden*

2.3 Pronominal case distinctions

The Dutch paradigm of personal pronouns is characterized by a three-way case system, distinguishing subject from object and possessive pronouns. The 1sg and 3sg feminine, as well as the 1pl and 3pl pronouns have suppletive object and possessive forms: *ik* vs. *mij* vs. *mijn*, *zij* vs. *haar*, *wij* vs. *ons*, and *zij* vs. *hen* vs. *hun*.

6. In one case, Skepi appears to have borrowed the Dutch plural form wholesale: Skepi *kɛndrɛʃi* (← Dutch *kindertjes* 'children') vs. singular *kɛntɛ* 'child'. But note that the [ʃ] in *kɛndrɛʃi* (recorded by Robertson 1983) marks it as a potentially more recent loan, perhaps replacing the older word *blaba* 'child(ren)' found in Van der Wal (2013).

7. Homonymy between the third-person plural pronoun and the nominal plural marker is a phenomenon attested in around two dozen Atlantic creoles (Maurer 2013) including the Surinamese creoles, Guyanais French Creole and Virgin Islands Dutch Creole, as well as in some non-creoles (Parkvall 2000: 106). Berbice Dutch, unlike Skepi and Virgin Islands Dutch Creole, differentiates between the plural suffix and the 3pl pronoun.

8. The first line of our linguistic examples shows the spelling of the original source. The second line shows our reconstructed, 'normalized' phonological rendering (see footnote 7). We use the following abbreviations in our glossings: PL = plural, COP.LOC = locative copula, COP.EQ = equative copula, PST = past, FUT = future, IRR = irrealis, NEG = negator, IPFV = imperfective aspect marker, DEF.ART = definite article, 1SG/1PL etc. = first person singular/plural pronoun (all functions), POSS = possessive, SUBJ = subject.

Additionally, the pronouns *mij*, *jij* ~ *jou*, *zij*, *wij* and *jullie* all have unstressed forms: *me*, *je*, *ze*, *we* and *je* respectively.

These morphological distinctions were not carried over into the creole (see Table 2). Consistent with patterns observed in creoles around the world, Skepi eliminated case altogether.[9] A minor exception is the 3sg pronoun (*ɛm*), for which a dedicated possessive adjective in the shape of *ɛsə* appears to have existed.

The invariability of the Skepi personal pronouns can be illustrated by means of the 1sg *ɛk* (all examples from the Youd Papers):

- subject: <**ek** le lup> (1sg IPFV go) 'I'm going' (Dutch: *ik ga*)
- object: <gef **ek**> (give 1sg) 'give me' (Dutch: *geef mij*)
- possessive adjective: <**ek** son> (1sg son) 'my son' (Dutch: *mijn zoon*)
- prepositional object: <met **ek**> (with 1sg) 'with me' (Dutch: *met mij*)

This passepartout usage of *ek* in Skepi represents a clear instance of grammatical innovation rather than inheritance. We are not aware of any variety of Dutch that mirrors Skepi in this regard; even the semi-creole Afrikaans distinguishes between *ek* (subject) and *my* (object and possessive; Van Sluijs 2013b).

The following quote from Weerman & Evers-Vermeul (2002: 302) further underscores the significance of the loss of pronominal case:

> Apparently, the case distinction in personal pronouns is a rather stable phenomenon, since it can be witnessed in languages that underwent all kinds of deflection processes. As a matter of fact, all the Germanic cognates of English and Dutch have case distinctions [...] in their pronominal system. Even a highly deflected language like Afrikaans, sometimes described as semi-creole, has singular object pronouns that differ in form from pronouns appearing in subject position. (Weerman & Evers-Vermeul 2002: 302)

9. Several present-day creoles do of course show instances of pronominal case. However, the evidence suggests that such distinctions were gradually reintroduced into the creoles rather than being transmitted from the lexifier during creolization.

Table 2. Personal pronouns in the Skepi corpus

	Van der Wal	Rodschied	Youd	Robertson	Normalized	Dutch etymon
1SG	–	<ikke>	<ek>	*ɛk*	*ɛk* [a]	*ik* ~ *ikke* [b]
2SG	–	<joe>	<you>	*ju*	*ju*	dialectal *joe* [ju] [c]
3SG	<um> ~ <hom>	<em>	<em>; <asse> (POSS)	*ɛm*	*ɛm*; *ɛsə* (POSS)	*hem* [d]; *hem* + *ze* [e]
1PL	–	<ons> ~ <onso>	<ons>	*ɔns*	*ɔns*	*ons* [f]
2PL	–	<jinder>	<yender> ~ <ye>	*ɛndɛr*	*jɛndɛr* ~ *jɛ* [g]	2SG + *ander*? [h]
3PL	–	<or>	<oar>	–	*or*	*haar*(?) [i]

a. Our assumption that the 1sg was pronounced /ɛk(ɛ)/ is based on Robertson's field data. The <i> in Rodschied's <ikke> could be an artefact of his familiarity with Dutch, or it could point in the direction of internal variation.

b. The 1sg *ɛk(ɛ)* also characterized Berbice Dutch and sets the two Guianese Dutch creoles apart from Virgin Islands Dutch Creole, which had *mi* (from Dutch *mij*, but possibly influenced by Creole Portuguese *mi*).

c. The form *joe* [ju] is found dialectally both as a subject and as an object pronoun (standard Dutch *jij* and *jou*).

d. In standard Dutch, *hem* is the masculine 3SG object pronoun but dialectally also occurs as a subject pronoun.

e. We assume this form was patterned on constructions of the type *hem* '3SG.OBJ' + *ze* '3SG.POSS, informal, masculine)' which can occur informally in mainstream Dutch and appear conventionalized in a handful of Dutch dialects without specific geographical concentration. The standard Dutch 3sg possessive pronouns are *zijn* (masculine) and *haar* (feminine).

f. Like *hem*, Dutch *ons*, too, is an object pronoun in the standard but can occur in subject position dialectally.

g. It is not clear from the data how these two forms were functionally distributed.

h. The homophonous Virgin Island Dutch Creole 2PL *jender* has been the topic of some discussion. Van Name (1869: 161) assumed it was an internal innovation composed of the 2SG + Dutch *ander* 'other', mirroring the 2PL of numerous other languages. However, Hesseling (1905: 99) claimed a dialectal (West) Flemish origin. West Flemish 2PL forms such as *gander, ginder, giender, gender, gunder, junder* (Devos & Vandekerckhove 2005: 79, 81; Hinskens & Van Rossem 1995; De Vogelaer 2006: 140; Van Bakel 2001: 352, 355) indicate that West Flemish indeed has to be considered a possible, if not probable, source for *jender*.

i. We initially analyzed 3pl *or* as a reflex of a dialectal form of Dutch *ander* 'other', which is *aar* in Hollandic and *oar* in some Zeelandic dialects as well as in Frisian. However, it is more likely to be a cognate of Dutch *haar* 'her (3SG object, feminine)', pronounced [(h)o:r] in a number of Dutch dialects. Cognates of Dutch *haar* commonly had plural pronominal functions in older varieties of Dutch (see Van der Sijs 2010 under the keyword *haar*) and still do dialectally. Compare also German *ihr* 'her, their'.

2.3 Articles

In the context of grammatical discontinuity, the Skepi article system (Table 3) warrants closer examination. Our corpus reveals the presence of both a definite (*di*) and an indefinite (*en*) article. Although these two articles seem to have been functionally rather like their Dutch counterparts *de* ([də]) and *een* ([ən]), neither seems to derive directly from the lexifier forms. Rather, the phonological and orthographic evidence suggests that the Skepi indefinite article originates from the Dutch numeral *één* ([eːn]) 'one'. This can be inferred from the fact that Youd consistently spells it as <aen>, with <ae> consistently corresponding to an etymological /e/ rather than a schwa (e.g. <maester> 'master' ← Dutch *meester*, <gael> 'yellow' ← Dutch *geel*). Similarly, the definite article *di* seems more plausibly derived from the Dutch demonstrative *die* ([di]) than from the article *de* ([də]). (Indeed, in our corpus, the meaning of *di* seems to have varied between a definite article and a demonstrative pronoun.) These etymologies align with trends observed in other Atlantic creoles, many of which likewise derive their indefinite article from the lexifier numeral *one* instead of the indefinite article (Haspelmath 2013a) and their definite article from lexifier demonstratives rather than definite articles (Haspelmath 2013b). While such internal grammaticalization paths are not unexpected, they must be considered of major interest to creole studies in sofar as they provide compelling evidence that creole article systems are (re)built from scratch rather than inherited from the lexifier, thereby supporting the pidgin-creole cycle hypothesis.

Table 3. Articles in the Skepi corpus

	Van der Wal	Rodschied	Youd	Robertson	Normalized	Dutch etymon
definite article	<die>	<die>	<de>	*di*	*di*	*die* 'DEM.DIST'
indefinite article	–	–	<aen>	–	*en*	*één* 'one'

3. Verb phrase

3.1 Tense and aspect marking

The Dutch regular present tense features three different inflections: zero (1sg), *-t* (2sg, 3sg), and *-en* (all plural forms). Past tense is subdivided into the preterite, the perfect, and the pluperfect. Regular verbs exhibit four inflections in the preterite (singular *-te* or *-de*, and plural *-ten* or *-den*); the perfect is periphrastic (AUX + past participle) with either *hebben* 'to have' or *zijn* 'to be' in the AUX slot, and a past participle of the type *ge-* + stem + *-t* ~ *-d* (e.g. *maken* 'to make' → *gemaakt* 'made').

The pluperfect consists of the preterite of *hebben* 'to have' or *zijn* 'to be' + past participle. Other Dutch verbal intricacies include structures such as:

- the *aan* + *het* + V + *zijn* continuous construction;
- passivization of the type *worden* 'to become' ~ *zijn* 'to be' + past participle;
- the present participle in *-nd(e)*;
- separable verbs (roughly corresponding to English particle verbs, but with the possibility of prefixation to the host).

In addition, of course, Dutch is characterized by a sizeable class of irregular verbs displaying intricate vocalic as well as consonantal alternations in the formation of the preterite and past participle.

None of these inflectional or periphrastic structures were carried over into the creole, which instead, like most other creoles, makes exclusive use of invariable verb stems combined with preverbal tense and aspect markers. The sole creole verbal construction that bears any resemblance to Dutch is the future tense, realized as [*sa* + V] in the creole (with *sa* derived from Dutch *zal* ~ *zullen*) and as [*zullen* + V] in the lexifier. Table 4 summarizes the Skepi preverbal tense and aspect morphemes.

Table 4. Preverbal Tense/mood/aspect (TMA) markers in the Skepi corpus

TMA category	**Van der Wal**	**Rodschied**	**Youd**	**Robertson**	**Normalized**	**Dutch etymon**
Past	–	<weese>	<wes>	n.a.	*wes(ə)*	*geweest* [a]
Perfective	–	Ø	Ø	Ø	Ø	–
Imperfective	–	–	<le> ~ Ø	*di* ~ *da*	*lɛ*	*liggen* [b]
Future/Irrealis	<sel>	<sa> ~ <scha>	<sa>	*sa*	*sa*	*zal* [c]
Future-in-the-Past, Counterfactual	–	<sa weese>	–	–	*sa wes(ə)*	–

a. Dutch *geweest* is the past participle of *zijn* 'to be'.
b. Dutch *liggen* 'to lie' is pronounced [lɛxə] in several dialects.
c. Dutch *zal* is the singular form (all persons) of *zullen* 'shall'.

3.1.1 *Past (imperfective) tense (~ anterior)*

The preverbal past marker *wes* (2, 5) in all likelihood derives from Dutch *geweest* (the past participle of *zijn* 'to be').

(2) Here em wes set (Youd)
Hir ɛm wes sɛt
here 3SG PST COP.LOC
'Here s/he/it was'

3.1.2 *Future tense / irrealis*

As in Virgin Islands Dutch Creole and Berbice Dutch, the Skepi morpheme *sa* from Dutch *zal* 'shall (3sg)' encodes future events (3, 4). Common in (Atlantic) creoles is the combination of the future and the past tense marker to express conditionals. We found one such example in our Skepi corpus (5).

(3) Ons sa loup overland (Youd)
ɔns sa lop ofərland
1pl FUT/IRR go overland
'We shall go overland'

(4) As you ni passop you sa fall (Youd)
As ju ni pasop ju sa fal
If 2sg NEG watch.out 2sg FUT/IRR fall
'If you're not careful, you will fall'

(5) Ikke oko weese dinkie joe **sa** **weese** kos or
Ɛkɛ oko wesə dinki ju ***sa*** ***wesə*** *kɔs or*
1sg also PST think 2sg FUT/IRR PST kiss 3pl
'I thought you would have kissed them as well'
(Rodschied, our translation from the German original)

3.1.3 *Present tense / imperfective aspect*

Youd's data contain around ten unambiguous instances of the use of *lɛ* (from Dutch *liggen* or dialectal *leggen* 'to lie') as a preverbal imperfective aspect marker, which appears to have given dynamic verbs a present progressive reading (6, 7, 8, 9). The marker may have been inspired by Dutch continuous constructions of the type [*liggen* + *te* + V] 'to be V-ing'.[10]

(6) ek le sook em (Youd)
ɛk lɛ suk ɛm
1sg IPFV search 3sg
'I am looking for it'

10. Interestingly, in early Virgin Islands Dutch Creole texts the same IPFV marker *lɛ* appeared, before it was replaced by *lo*. Curiously, however, there is no trace of *lɛ* (or of any other imperfective aspect marker) in Rodschied's (1794) presentation of the Skepi verbal system. It is impossible to tell at this point whether *lɛ* had not yet grammaticalized or whether the marker had simply escaped Rodschied's attention. In Robertson's data we find *da* and *di* in the role of imperfective aspect marker, both of which, we assume, were borrowed into the language from Guyanese Creole somewhere in the course of the 20th century at the expense of *lɛ*.

(7) you le louphe? (Youd)
ju lɛ lofi
2sg IPFV go
'Are you going?'

(8) loor sailla le com (Youd)
lur sejla lɛ kom
look sailor IPFV come
'Look, the sailor(s) is/are coming'

(9) You le prat the whole[11] dak (Youd)
ju lɛ prat di hel dak
2sg IPFV talk DEF.ART whole day
'You're talking the entire day'

3.1.4 *Perfective past / the unmarked verb*

In most Atlantic creoles (and in particular those of the Eastern Caribbean and the Guianas), the inherent value of an unmarked dynamic verb is perfective. Indeed, the corpus data suggest this was the case in Skepi as well (10, 11, 12, 13, and 14).[12]

(10) weda gef you de makt (Youd)
wida gɛf ju di makt
who give 2sg DEF.ART power
'Who gave you the power?'

(11) you ni doon disa wark (Youd)
ju ni dun disə wɛrk
2sg NEG do this work
'You didn't do this job'

(12) *ju kika di braɪd?* (Robertson)
2sg see DEF.ART bride
'did you see the bride?'

11. Here, Youd's native tongue appears to have contaminated his Skepi output, as the actual Skepi word for 'whole' was *hel* (from Dutch *heel* 'whole').

12. For 10 and 11, the perfective past (as opposed to present-tense) reading is merely our own interpretation. But for 12, 13 and 14, it is the original translations that indicate a completive interpretation. And short sentences (amply found in Youd) such as *Ɛk fɛnt ɛm* (1sg find 3sg), for simple reasons of pragmatics, further support our analysis despite the lack of a translation. After all, an utterance meaning 'I found it' or 'I have found it' feels ever so slightly more natural than one meaning 'I am finding it' or 'I (habitually) find it'.

(13) *ɛndɛr ni lʌfɛ nʌg* (Robertson)
2pl NEG go still
'You haven't gone yet?'

(14) joe nie doen em nie (Rodschied, our translation from the German original)
ju ni dun ɛm ni
2sg NEG do 3sg NEG
'you didn't do it'

In sum, despite some uncertainties about the precise nature of tense and aspect marking in Skepi, we can confidently claim that the system outlined above was not modelled on standard Dutch or any Dutch dialect that we are familiar with. The typological discrepancy is simply too significant. Instead, the grammatical patterns observed in Skepi appear to have been constructed from the ground up, consistent with what one might expect from a language with pidgin ancestry. These patterns seem to be shaped by a combination of universal linguistic tendencies and influences from the substrate and adstrate languages.

3.2 Other innovative aspects of the Skepi verbal system

To conclude our discussion of the verb phrase, we briefly highlight three features that are suggestive of a break in grammatical transmission. First, the Skepi sentence negator *ni* (from Dutch *niet*) is placed preverbally (11), (13), (15), contrasting with its post-verbal placement in Dutch.[13] Second, the use of a zero equative copula suggests that adjectives in Skepi could function as stative verbs, as demonstrated in (16). Third, Skepi word order was strictly SVO. The Dutch verb-second rule for main clauses and verb-final rule for subordinate clauses did not apply to Skepi, as shown in (17).

(15) ek ne guet Godt (Youd)
ɛk ni wet Gɔt
1sg NEG know God
'I don't know God'

(16) ons father quat met ons
ɔns fadər Ø kwat mɛt
1pl father COP.EQ angry with

13. English- and French-lexicon creoles are likewise characterized by having abandoned the lexifier's postverbal negation patterns in favor of preverbal negation. Note also that the double negation in (14) is an exception in our corpus.

(17) As you com frag ek weran, ek ni sa gef you disa snaps (Youd)
As ju kom frag ɛk weran ɛk ni sa gɛf ju disə snaps
If 2sg come ask 1sg back 1sg NEG FUT give 2sg DEM.PROX schnapps
'If you come and ask me again, I won't give you the/this liquor'

We are unaware of the existence of any dialects of Dutch displaying any one of these features, let alone all three together.

4. Comparison with New Netherlands Dutch

To better contextualize the grammatical distance between Skepi and Dutch, New Netherlands Dutch – the Dutch colonial variety once spoken in the New Netherlands colony on the east coast of the present-day USA[14] – serves as a useful comparandum. The New Netherlands colony was formed roughly in the same period as the Dutch Essequibo colony. Furthermore, for both colonies, the turn of the 18th to the 19th century can be identified as the approximate cut-off point for their ties to the Netherlands.[15] From a linguistic standpoint, however, the two respective speech varieties are markedly different: unlike Skepi, New Netherlands Dutch, until its extinction, remained very much recognizable as a dialect of Dutch.

The first and arguably the only reliable field data for New Netherlands Dutch were published by Prince (1910, 1913),[16] though by that time the variety was already in an advanced state of attrition (Buccini 1995: 218; Noordegraaf 2014: 2). This attrition is relevant given that it can lead to the loss of key grammatical features. Nevertheless, in stark contrast with Skepi, New Netherlands Dutch retained several core elements of standard Dutch grammar. These include the regular plural endings in *-en* and *-s*, as well, a fairly run of the mill personal pronoun paradigm with case distinctions and tonic/atonic forms (see Table 5), and full verb inflections for person and number. Furthermore, the variety made standard

14. Alternatively known as Low Dutch, the colonial dialect was, up to the mid-20th century, spoken in a number of more rural places in the states of New York and New Jersey (Noordegraaf 2014: 12). See Van der Sijs (2009: 27–50) for an excellent overview of the rise and fall of the Dutch language on the American east coast.

15. According to Buccini (1995: 216), Dutch immigration to the colony came to a halt in the late 17th century, leaving the colony "largely isolated from the Netherlands" (1995: 231). However, Van der Sijs (2009: Chapter 1) notes that Dutch-speaking dominees continued to arrive to New Netherlands throughout the 18th century.

16. Other articles have appeared claiming to present fragments of New Netherlands Dutch, but serious doubts exist about their reliability and authenticity. For a good summary of the issue, see Noordegraaf (2008) and Van der Sijs (2009: 42–46).

use of all the Dutch tenses, including a preterite and a periphrastic perfect with past participles prefixed by *xje-* (standard Dutch *ge-*), hypotheticals with [*zāu* (Dutch *zou*) + V] as well as [*zou* + past participle + V], and separable verbs. Irregular verbs generally followed standard Dutch patterns (e.g. *sprêke, sprāk, xje-sprôke*[17] 'speak, spoke, spoken'; *dänke, dâxte, xjedâxt* 'think, thought, thought', Prince 1910: 481, 482).

In terms of syntax, sentence negation was postverbal (e.g. *äk wet nöt* 1sg know NEG 'I don't know'; Prince 1910: 477) and the variety adhered to the standard Dutch verb-second rule for main clauses (18) as well as to SOV word order in subordinate clauses (19).

(18) *Nāu zāle wāi en xûje dānkbâr tāit häbbe* (Prince 1913: 310)
now shall 1PL.SUBJ INDEF good thankful time have
'Now we shall have a good thankful time'

(19) *tut äk twäntix jâr āut wās* (Prince 1910: 467)
until 1SG twenty year old be.PST
'until I was 20 years old'

Some simplifications were observable, both in the noun phrase and in the verb phrase. For instance:

- New Netherlands Dutch only used a cognate of *hebben* in the role of perfect auxiliary, whereas standard Dutch uses *hebben* and *zijn*;
- the number of passive auxiliaries had likewise been reduced from two (*worden* and *zijn*) to one (only *zijn*);
- the present-tense paradigms of *zijn* and *hebben* had been regularized by discarding suppletive forms;
- Dutch grammatical gender distinctions had been dispensed with, the only remaining definite article being *de*.

But it should be clear that the extent and nature of these morphological reductions are fundamentally different from those seen in Skepi.[18] In fact, the data provided by Prince (1910, 1913) strongly indicate that these reductions were *gradually* entering the language, reflecting the effects of gradual language attrition

17. We have retained Prince's (1910, 1913) orthography.

18. Similar observations have been made by Buccini (1996), Deumert (2004: 140, 141) and Noordegraaf (2014) when comparing the nature and degree of grammatical reduction in New Netherlands Dutch to that in the semi-creole Afrikaans. Buccini (1996: 44), for instance, notes that "New Netherland Dutch (...), after two centuries of contact with English, remained indisputably a form of Dutch" whereas the reduction observable in Afrikaans is, according to Buccini (1996: 49), reminiscent of "the notions of pidginisation and creolisation".

rather than of an abrupt break in transmission. For example, although the articles *de* and *het* had merged into *de*, a number of relics of *het* are still visible in the Prince data.[19] Moreover, gender distinctions had been retained in the pronominal domain, specifically for the 3sg pronouns. Furthermore, although the present-tense paradigms of *hebben* and *zijn* had been regularized, Prince (1910) managed to elicit their original suppletive forms. Also, the past tenses and participles of these verbs had remained suppletive, showcasing a continuity that contrasts sharply with Skepi's near-total morphological overhaul.

In other words, whereas the Skepi data point to a rather abrupt and nearly complete disruption in the transmission of Dutch morphosyntactic patterns, New Netherlands Dutch appears to have experienced a much more gradual decline thereof, quite probably as a by-product of language attrition processes.

Table 5. New Netherlands Dutch pronouns, according to Prince (1910: 465)

	Subject	Object	Possessive	Atonic variants
1SG	*äk*	*māi*	*māin*	*mê* (object)
2SG	*jāi*	*jāu*	*jāu*	*je* (all functions)
3SG	*hāi* (masc.), *sāi* ~ *zāi* (fem.), *hät* (neuter)	*häm* (masc.); *hœr* (fem.); *hät* (neuter)	*häm* (masc.); *hœr* (fem.); *hät* (neuter)	*ze* ~ *se* (possessive masc.); *hê* (subject masc.); *se* ~ *ze* (subject fem.); *it* (subject neuter)
1PL	*wāi*	*ons*	*ons*	*wê* (subject)
2PL	*jœlli*	*jœlli*	*jœlli*	–
3PL	*hœlli*	*hœlli*	*hœlli*	*ze* ~ *se* (subject)[a]

a. These two atonic variants are not listed in Prince's personal pronoun table, but they appear on a few occasions in the glossary (Prince 1910: 468–484).

5. Final remarks

This chapter, drawing on existing as well as newly-emerged Skepi data, has highlighted a selection of key features from the noun and verb phrase. Within the noun phrase, the transition from Dutch (the lexifier) to Skepi (the creole) saw the complete elimination of gender marking, plural marking, and pronominal case distinctions. And although Skepi featured both a definite and indefinite article, these articles represent innovations rather than inheritance.

19. For instance, *het* was still the neuter 3sg pronoun, it had been preserved in *an't* + V + *wêzen* continuous constructions, and a handful of nouns appeared to have retained *het* as an article (Prince 1910: 465).

In the verbal domain, the discontinuity is equally pronounced. The complex inflectional morphology of Dutch was not transferred into the creole but was replaced by a system of invariable verb stems and preverbal tense and aspect markers. Preverbal negation provides further evidence of a break in transmission.

In sum, although Skepi's lexical inventory, including grammatical morphemes, was overwhelmingly derived from Dutch, its morphosyntactic framework underwent a complete overhaul. The grammatical matrix of the lexifier was not preserved in the creole. These findings are compatible with the view of creoles as nativized pidgins.

Acknowledgement

We wish to thank Peter Bakker, Cefas van Rossem and Marijke van der Wal for valuable discussion and commentary on Skepi-related issues.

References

Aboh, Enoch O. (2016): Creole distinctiveness: A dead end. *Journal of Pidgin and Creole Languages* 31.2: 400–418.

Ansaldo, Umberto & Stephen Matthews (2007): Deconstructing creole: The rationale. In: Umberto Ansaldo, Stephen Matthews & Lisa Lim (eds.): *Deconstructing Creole.* Amsterdam: Benjamins, 1–18.

Bakker, Peter & van der Voort, Hein (eds. & transl.) (2008): Grammar of the Creole language as used on the three Danish Islands of St. Croix, St. Thomas and St. John in America. Compiled and written by a native of St. Thomas. In: John Holm & Susanne Michaelis (eds.), *Contact languages, critical concepts in language studies*, 15–48. London/New York: Routledge.

Bakker, Peter, Aymeric Daval-Markussen, Mikael Parkvall & Ingo Plag (2011): Creoles are typologically distinct from non-creoles. *Journal of Pidgin and Creole languages* 26.1: 5–42.

Buccini, Anthony F. (1995): The Dialectical Origins of New Netherland Dutch. In: Thomas Shannon & Johan P. Snapper (eds.): *Dutch Linguistics in a Changing Europe. The Berkeley Conference on Dutch Linguistics.* Lanham: University Press of America, 211–263.

Buccini, Anthony F. (1996): New Netherland Dutch, Cape Dutch, Afrikaans. *Taal en Tongval* 9: 35–51.

Chaudenson, Robert (1992): *Des îles, des hommes, des langues: essai sur la créolisation linguistique et culturelle.* Paris: L'Harmattan.

Coelho, Adolpho (1880–1886): Os Dialectos Románicos ou Neo-Latinos na Africa, Asia, e América. In: Jorge Monais-Barbosa (ed.) (1967): *Estudos lingüísticos crioulos.* Lisbon: Academia Internacional de Cultura Portuguesa.

Daval-Markussen, Aymeric (2018): *Reconstructing Creole.* PhD thesis, University of Aarhus.

DeGraff, Michel (2001): On the origin of creoles: A Cartesian critique of neo-Darwinian linguistics. *Linguistic Typology* 5: 213–310.

Deumert, Ana (2004): *Language Standardization and Language Change. The dynamics of Cape Dutch.* Amsterdam & Philadelphia: Benjamins.

De Vogelaer, Gunther (2006): *Subjectsmarkering in de Nederlandse en Friese Dialecten.* PhD thesis, University of Gent.

Devos, Magda & Reinhild Vandekerckhove (2005): *West-Vlaams.* Tielt: Lannoo Uitgeverij.

Haspelmath, Martin (2013a): Indefinite articles. In: Michaelis, Susanne Maria & Maurer, Philippe & Haspelmath, Martin & Huber, Magnus (eds.) *The atlas of pidgin and creole language structures.* Oxford: Oxford University Press.

Haspelmath, Martin (2013b): Definite articles. In: Michaelis, Susanne Maria & Maurer, Philippe & Haspelmath, Martin & Huber, Magnus (eds.) *The atlas of pidgin and creole language structures.* Oxford: Oxford University Press.

Hesseling, Dirk Christiaan (1905): *Het Negerhollands der Deense Antillen. Bijdrage tot de Geschiednis der Nederlandse Taal in Amerika.* Leiden: A. W. Sijthoff.

Hinskens, Frans, and Cefas Van Rossem (1995): The Negerhollands word *sender* in eighteenth-century manuscripts. In: Arends, Jacques (ed.): *The early stages of creolization*, Amsterdam: Benjamins, pp. 63–88.

Jacobs, Bart (2023): Guyanais vs. Gardiol: Broken transmission vs. grammatical continuity. *Lingua* 296: 103625.

Jacobs, Bart & Mikael Parkvall (2020): Skepi Dutch Creole: The Youd Papers. *Journal of Pidgin and Creole Languages* 35.2: 360–380.

Jacobs, Bart & Mikael Parkvall (2024): Skepi Creole Dutch: The Rodschied papers. *Journal of Pidgin and Creole Languages* 39.2: 394–408.

Kouwenberg, Silvia (1994): *A grammar of Berbice Dutch creole.* Berlin: Mouton de Gruyter.

Magens, Jochum Melchior (1770): *Grammatica over det Creolske sprog, som bruges paa de trende Danske Eilande, St. Croix, St. Thomas og St. Jans i Amerika. Sammenskrevet og opsat af en paa St. Thomas indföd Mand.* Copenhagen: Gerhard Giese Salikath.

Maurer, Philippe (2013): Nominal plural marker and third-person-plural pronoun. In: Michaelis, Susanne Maria & Maurer, Philippe & Haspelmath, Martin & Huber, Magnus (eds.) *The atlas of pidgin and creole language structures.* Oxford: Oxford University Press.

McWhorter, John (1998): Identifying the Creole Prototype. Vindicating a typological class. *Language* 74.4: 788–818.

Mufwene, Salikoko (2000): Creolization is a social, not a structural, process. *Creole Language Library* 22: 65–84.

Noordegraaf, Jan (2008): Nederlands in Noord-Amerika. Over de studie van het Leeg Duits (Low Dutch). *Trefwoord*, 1–29.

Noordegraaf, Jan (2014): Koloniaal Nederlands in verandering. Afrikaans versus Amerikaans Leeg Duits. In: S. Predota & J. Karpinski (eds.), *Neerlandica Wratislaviensia.* Wroclaw: Wydawnictwo Uniwerstetu Wroclawskiego, 64–92. Online postprint version: https://research.vu.nl/ws/portalfiles/portal/1037568/Koloniaal+Nederlands+in+verandering.pdf (accessed: 03-04-2024)

Parkvall, Mikael (2000): *Out of Africa.* London: Battlebridge.

Parkvall, Mikael (2008): The simplicity of creoles in a cross-linguistic perspective. In: Matti Miestamo, Kaius Sinnemäki, and Fred Karlsson (eds.): *Language Complexity. Typology, Contact, Change*. Amsterdam: Benjamins, 265–285.

Parkvall, Mikael & Bart Jacobs (2023): Why Haitian is a creole, Michif an intertwiner, and Irish English neither: a reply to Mufwene. *Folia Linguistica* 57.1: 217–226.

Priestly, Tom (1983): On "drift" in Indo-European Gender Systems. *Journal of Indo-European Studies* 11.3/4: 339–363.

Prince, J. Dyneley (1910): The Jersey Dutch dialect. *Dialect Notes* 3: 459–484.

Prince, J. Dyneley (1913): A text in Jersey Dutch. *Tijdschrift voor Nederlandsche Taal- en Letterkunde* 32: 306–312.

Robertson, Ian. (1976): Dutch creole languages in Guayana. *Boletín de Estudios Latinoamericanos y del Caribe* 23: 61–67.

Robertson, Ian. (1977): *Berbice Dutch: A description*. PhD thesis, University of the West Indies, Trinidad.

Robertson, Ian. (1983): The Dutch linguistic legacy and the Guyana/Venezuela border question. *Boletín de Estudios Latinoamericanos y del Caribe* 34: 75–97.

Robertson, Ian. (1989): Berbice and Skepi Dutch: A Lexical Comparison. *Tijdschrift voor Nederlandse Taal- en Letterkunde* 105: 3–21.

Rodschied, Ernst Karl (1792): Reisebeschreibung nach Rio Essequebo in Guiana, und Nachrichten von den daßigen Krankheiten und der Naturgeschichte dieses Landes. *Medicinisches und physisches Journal* 28: 57–89.

Rodschied, Ernst Karl (1794): Fortsetzung seiner Naturhistorischen und Medicinischen Beobachtungen, aus Rio-Essequebo. *Neues Magazin für Aertzte* 16.2: 97–136.

Rodschied, Ernst Karl (1796): *Medizinische und chirurgische Bemerkungen über das Klima, die Lebensweise und Krankheiten der Einwohner der hollaendischen Kolonie Rio Essequebo*. Frankfurt: In Der Jaegerschen Buchhandlung.

Van Rossem, Cefas (2017): The Virgin Islands Dutch Creole Textual Heritage. *Philological Perspectives on Authenticity and Audience Design*. PhD Thesis. Nijmegen: Radboud University.

Sabino, Robin (2012): *Language contact in the Danish West Indies: giving Jack his jacket*. Leiden: Brill.

Schuchardt, Hugo (1882): Uber das Negerportugiesische von S. Thomé. *Sitzungsberichte der Wienische Akademie von Wissenschaften* 101.2: 889–917.

Stein, Peter (ed.) (1996): *Christian Georg Andreas Oldendorp: Criolisches Wörterbuch: Erster zu vermehrender und wo nöthig zu verbessernder Versuch, sowie das anonyme J.C. Kingo zugeschriebene Vestindisk Glossarium*. Tübingen: Niemeyer.

Stolz, Thomas (1986): *Gibt es das kreolische Sprachwandelmodell? Vergleichende Grammatik des Negerhölländischen*. Frankfurt am Main/Bern/New York: Peter Lang.

Van Bakel, J. (2001): Jullie-Een dialectgeografische oefening. *Handelingen van de Koninklijke Commissie voor Toponymie en Dialectologie* 73.1.

Van der Sijs, Nicoline (2009): *Cookies, coleslaw, and stoops: The influence of Dutch on the North American languages*. Amsterdam: Amsterdam University Press.

Van der Sijs, Nicoline (ed.) (2010): *Etymologiebank*, https://etymologiebank.nl/

Van der Sijs, Nicoline (2021): *Taalwetten maken en vinden: het ontstaan van het Standaardnederlands*. Gorredijk: Sterck & De Vreese.

Van der Wal, Marijke J. (2013): Contact met creooltaal: 18de-eeuws Skepi voor het thuisfront, brief van de maand December 2013. Downloaded from: https://www.universiteitleiden.nl/binaries/content/assets/geesteswetenschappen/onderzoeksprojecten/brieven-als-buit/brief-van-de-maand-december-2013.pdf (accessed: 26-02-2022)

Van Name, Addison (1869): Contributions to Creole Grammar. *Transactions of the American Philological Association* 1: 123–167.

doi Van Rossem, Cefas & van der Voort, Hein (eds.) (1996): *Die Creol Taal: 250 years of Negerhollands texts*. Amsterdam: Amsterdam University Press.

Van Sluijs, Robbert (2013a): Negerhollands. In: Michaelis, Susanne Maria & Maurer, Philippe & Haspelmath, Martin & Huber, Magnus (eds.), *The survey of pidgin and creole languages. Volume 1: English-based and Dutch-based Languages*. Oxford: Oxford University Press.

Van Sluijs, Robbert (2013b): Afrikaans. In: Michaelis, Susanne Maria & Maurer, Philippe & Haspelmath, Martin & Huber, Magnus (eds.), *The survey of pidgin and creole languages. Volume 1: English-based and Dutch-based Languages*. Oxford: Oxford University Press.

doi Weerman, F.P., & Evers-Vermeul, J. (2002): Pronouns and Case. *Lingua* 112: 301–338.

Youd, Thomas (1833–1842): *West Indies Mission: Original Papers: Letters and Papers of individual missionaries, catechists and others: Thomas B. Youd*, 1833–1842. Church Missionary Society Archive: West Indian Mission Records (1819–1861), CWO 100.

CHAPTER 15

Dutch names in a Mexican Mennonite Old Colony community?

Emma Hoebens

The Old Colony Mennonite residents of Salamanca, Mexico, are descendants of Anabaptists from the 16th-century Netherlands. Their everyday language is Plautdietsch, an East-Low German variety that exhibits notable Dutch influence, particularly in its lexicon. The Plautdietsch first names (call names) and corresponding hypocoristic forms in these communities suggest a Dutch linguistic legacy. The Mennonites' naming traditions – personal names, colony names, and street village names – serve as acts of memory preservation, reflecting their diasporic history from the Netherlands into the Americas. Language use and name-giving may be safeguarding continuity in the Old Colony archipelago. However, fieldwork from Chihuahua shows that increased exposure to modernity can significantly impact naming traditions. For now, the legacy embedded in the Plautdietsch call names of Salamanca's Mennonites remains a living testament to their Dutch history.

Keywords: Old Colony Mennonites, Plautdietsch and Dutch name-giving, sociolinguistics

1. Introduction

Heinrich introduces himself as *Heinrich* when spoken to in German, as *Enrique* when a Mexican comes to his workshop, and in his dealings with Creole-speaking Belizeans he calls himself *Henry*. But when his wife addresses him in Plautdietsch, she says *Hendrik*. It takes a while for the outsider to notice the name changes, but a longer stay in the Old Colony Mennonite community of Salamanca in Quintana Roo, Mexico, brings the awareness that a Dutch person can identify with this community not only because of the Mennonites' Northern European phenotype and their Dutch/Prussian/Ukrainian antecedents – but also in the field of first names or call names and their hypocoristic forms employed in this Plautdietsch speaking community. Talking among themselves,

https://doi.org/10.1075/impact.55.15hoe

the inhabitants of Salamanca only use their Plautdietsch call names, but they write their names in High German.[1]

This chapter starts with a short historical overview of the (Dutch) Mennonite diaspora, followed by a discussion of the relevant literature on Plautdietsch, call names, and Netherlandic input (sections 1.1 and 1.2). Next, I compare the Plautdietsch call names that I gathered during my field research in Salamanca, with Dutch and German versions, with historical data on Mennonite name-giving, and with present-day developments in other European Mennonite communities in Mexico (sections 2 and 3). In section 4, the Plautdietsch hypocoristic forms of the call names are subsequently compared with the diminutive suffixes used in the Dutch- and High/Low-German-speaking areas. These data are then used to evaluate whether the Plautdietsch call names and their hypocoristic forms are related to Dutch as opposed to other Low German or even High German varieties. In Section 5, I will discuss the relevance of name-giving for the Mennonite Old Colony and the fragility of survival as a Plautdietsch-speaking isolated community.

1.1 Salamanca and the wanderings of the Mennonite community

Before expanding on the Plautdietsch call names and their hypocoristic forms, I will first provide a brief overview of the origins of the Mennonite community of Salamanca (based on Sawatzky 1971, Epp 1993, Siemens 2012, Contreras Hernández 2018).

The *ejido*[2] Salamanca located in the southern state of Quintana Roo, Mexico, was established by Old Colony Mennonites. It is a subsidiary colony of the larger Old Colony community of Little Belize, situated near the Mexican border in Belize. Across Latin America, including Mexico and Belize, there are approximately 230 Mennonite settlements inhabited mostly by conservative Old Colony Mennonites of European descent (Le Polain de Waroux et al. 2021). These Mennonite communities, characterized by their traditional values, trace their lineage back to the Anabaptist movement that was founded in 1537 by the Frisian church reformer Menno Simons (1496–1561).

1. The term 'call names' refers to the names used in Plautdietsch in the Salamanca community. They are only used in speech. The term 'first names' will be used for the (High German versions of) names registered on, e.g., birth certificates.

2. *Ejido*: communally organized landownership, introduced in Mexico in 1936, based on indigenous community and agricultural traditions (Contreras Hernández 2018: 101)

Fleeing from fierce persecutions, many of these Anabaptists, later called Mennonites, were allowed to settle in Prussia in the Vistula delta around modern-day Gdańsk. Among the Prussian Low German-speaking inhabitants, the Anabaptist communities developed the local Low Prussian Low German into their own Mennonite Low German variety or Plautdietsch (Siemens 2012, Epp 1993). For two centuries the Dutch language from the Dutch Biestkens Bible (the first version of which appeared in 1560) remained their church and school language. In 1789, shortly after having adopted the High German Luther Bible and German as their church language and language of education (Thiessen 2003), a first group of Mennonites left an increasingly less hospitable Prussia for the newly conquered "New Russia" of Catherine the Great, part of what now is Ukraine. Some twenty years later, when another wave of Mennonite colonists built the Molochna colony near the Molochna River, the first group of Mennonites, who had formed the Khortytsya colony, northwest of Khortytsya Island in Ukraine,[3] became *Ooltkolonia*, i.e., residents of the old colony (Sawatzky 1971). Feeling pressured by the Russian government and threatened regarding their religious principles and education, in 1874, approximately 8,000 traditional Mennonites, mostly from the old colony, left for Canada, where they settled in Manitoba and Saskatchewan. In 1916, in Manitoba, Canada, English became the compulsory language of education. At the time, a majority of Old Colony Mennonites had formed a separate religious group and decided to leave Canada. After several negotiations about their demands as a religious community, they settled in the north of Mexico in 1922 (Sawatzky, 1971). In 1958, various groups of Old Colony and *Kleine Gemeinde* families (see below) abandoned Mexico and settled in Belize. In 2002, a group of descendants of Old Colony Mennonites in Little Belize formed the Salamanca Colony in the south of Mexico, due to a growing lack of land in Belize (Contreras Hernández, 2018). Nowadays the young settlement of Salamanca has approximately 1800 inhabitants, who speak Plautdietsch among themselves and who learn to read and write in their Luther Bible High German (Huachdietsch).

Over the centuries, Plautdietsch has become part of the (oral) identity of the Old Colony Mennonites as they continue to establish new colonies across the Americas. These new Old Colony communities are still located far away from modern worldly influences to ensure the preservation of their religious community. However, in some places, such as Chihuahua (Mexico), Blue Creek (Belize), and Paraguay, Old Colony Mennonite communities are also opening up to a more

3. The Molochna and Khortytsya colonies are located within the borders of Ukraine: Molochna and Khortytsya is a transcription of their names in Ukrainian and is used here to indicate the geographical sites. When referring to the Mennonite Low German varieties, the (German) terms most common in the literature, "Molotschna" and "Chortitza" are used.

modern and worldly way of life and schooling, which has begun to influence their language use. It is important to note that within the Old Colony Mennonite communities to this day Plautdietsch remains primarily an oral language and is not written and seldom read. Nevertheless, publications in Plautdietsch do exist in Canada and Germany, ranging from bibles and catechisms to novels and poetry, in varying orthographies.[4]

1.2 Dutch presence in the Plautdietsch language/community

In Salamanca, the Mennonite inhabitants speak Plautdietsch. It is based upon West Prussian Low German and incorporates influences from the Low German, Low Saxon, Low Franconian, and Frisian varieties of the Netherlands (Epp 1993, Siemens 2012, de Graaf & Nieuweboer 1993, 2001). In the literature, the original Ukrainian names Khortytsya and Molochna of the Ukrainian Mennonite settlements have served to indicate two main linguistic forms of Plautdietsch, in English known as the Chortitza and Molotschna varieties. In Latin America, the Chortitza (Old Colony) variety is dominant, because its speakers constituted the largest group of Mennonites to leave for America. The Molotschna variety is more common among the Mennonites who remained in Russia and, later in the 20th century, returned to Germany, or emigrated to Canada, Mexico, and Paraguay. In the Americas, the Molotschna variety was originally only spoken by a small group of so-called Mennonite *Kleine Gemeinde* families,[5] and then also by the Mennonites who arrived from Russia in the Americas in the 1930s and 1940s (Epp 1993, de Graaf & Nieuweboer 2001, Siemens 2012). These varieties of Plautdietsch exhibit lexical influence of the various languages with which the Mennonites interacted during their diaspora, mainly Russian, English, and Spanish.[6] The differences between the Chortitza and Molotschna varieties that are mentioned by the Salamanca Old Colony residents concern the pronunciation of verb infinitives and noun plurals (Chortitza variety: *-en* in both cases; Molotschna variety *-e* in both

4. In 1982, at the University of Winnipeg, a serious attempt was made to create an unambiguous spelling guide for Plautdietsch (Reimer 1982: 7). Nevertheless, later publications show that this attempt at standardization was not fully adopted, not even by the participating experts (including Rempel, Thiessen, Epp). The German magazine *Plautdietsch Freund* has its own spelling guide.

5. In 1812, in the Molochna Colony in Ucrania, a small group of Mennonites (Kleine Gemeinde) formed a separate, more conservative congregation. In 1874, they joined the Old Colony migration to Canada. Some families later also migrated to Mexico.

6. See Thiessen 1963 on Dutch and Low Prussian heritage and borrowings from other European languages; Siemens 2012 on Frisian, Baltic, and Slavic influences; Epp 1993 and Hovland 2020 on English and Spanish influences.

cases) and what they explain as 'the Old Colony say Kjoakj where the *Kleine Gemeinde* people say Tjoatj' (for church), which is identified as the palatalization of "k" (Chortitza variety: k > kj; Molotschna variety k > tj) (Epp 1993: 91). The speakers of any of these varieties have no problem in communicating in Plautdietsch (Moelleken 1972).

De Graaf and Nieuweboer, in their study of Plautdietsch, as spoken in the Siberian Altai area, have sought to determine features that would establish a genuine connection between Plautdietsch and the Netherlands. While they acknowledge the recognizability of the Plautdietsch language for native Dutch speakers, they temper the enthusiasm for considering it as an originally Dutch language: "The resemblances between Plautdiitsch and Dutch, or rather the Low Saxonian dialects of the Dutch language, sometimes taken as 'evidence' of the non-German origin of Plautdiitsch, are often exaggerated [...]"(De Graaf & Nieuweboer 2001: 32). They state that the resemblances found mainly indicate a relationship with Low German dialects in general. They do have an eye, or rather an ear, for the given names and family names used by the Mennonites, which, as they observe, still provide clues about the Mennonites' Dutch origin: "Here you can find people with names like Henritj, Klaus, Mariitje and family names like Friizen, Koop, Klaassen or Ditj." (De Graaf & Nieuweboer 2001: 27). But they do not address these features when analyzing the language itself. They pay no further attention to the call names, and neither does Nieuweboer in his work on the Altai Dialect of Plautdietsch (1999). Thiessen describes Plautdietsch (1963: 26) as a Low-Prussian variety with a Netherlandic inheritance and later (2003: x) observes that "Mennonite Low German retains a larger number of vocabulary of Dutch provenance than previously assumed".

2. Fieldwork: Assembling the corpus

To conduct this research on call names I began by compiling a list of names that were used within the Mennonite Old Colony community of Salamanca and names that I found mainly in Plautdietsch texts in 2021.[7] For comparison, I also conducted an additional smaller field study in Chihuahua-based Mennonite schools. The Salamanca corpus is primarily based on oral transmission, by asking the informants in Salamanca, since Plautdietsch is a spoken language. Because

7. Mennonite informants in Salamanca were crucial in checking my data on the Plautdietsch names and for the recordings. Due to privacy agreements, their names will not be mentioned. I communicated mainly in German, but often a mixture of Plautdietsch and Dutch proved to be more comprehensible.

High German is the only reading and writing language, the names are officially registered (on birth certificates and other documents) in High German, while with non-Mennonite Mexicans, the men tend to introduce themselves with the Spanish version of their name, and at home, among themselves, they use the Plautdietsch names.

The Salamanca corpus formation began by checking the list of Mennonite names based on the names that I heard in Salamanca and found in the Plautdietsch literature.[8] In the four families I was visiting in 2021, the list of Plautdietsch names that I had compiled was examined against the names they were using. There were a few names among them that they identified as part of the Plautdietsch usage, but that were not in use in Salamanca, and some names they even did not recognize. I compiled a list of all the Plautdietsch names they gave me.

To build a representative corpus, I asked the men and women in the various families I visited for their own names and their children's names. This resulted in a corpus of 51 women's and 45 men's first names in Plautdietsch, as they were in use in Salamanca in 2021 and 2022. I also reviewed a list of plot owners, consisting of male names, as only males are entitled to own land. This list, however, did not yield many new names.

I only registered the Plautdietsch names currently used in the colony. There were very few non-Plautdietsch names in the first draft list; in one family English versions were used for their children (*Henny, Willy*, and *Johnny*), and in another family, two girls were named *Nancy* and *Melissa*. These names were registered as such on their birth certificates, and since these did not have an oral Plautdietsch version they were excluded from the corpus. After having seen, heard, and checked the names of 279 men (plot owners, names given by my informants and names recollected in the families) and 51 women (names given by my informants, and recollected in the families), I identified only 15 distinct male names and 15 distinct female names. The list spans individuals aged 0 to 70 years.

These data of the 2021–2022 research were consistent with data from an ethnographic research project Carroll Janer conducted in the community of Salamanca in the years 2013–2017: when its inhabitants were asked by the Mexican municipal authorities to register their Belizean birth certificates, Carroll Janer collected the names, written in the German version, on their birth certificates (Carroll Janer 2017: 111). He also mentions the remarkable lack of variety in first names (and last names) which caused some problems with the Mexican authorities. His list of first names, although in the written German version, corresponds to the Plautdietsch corpus I collected in Salamanca, but in a slightly different order.

8. Literature consulted to find Plautdietsch names: Canadian Plautdietsch storybooks, online magazine *The Daily Bonnet*. In 2022, Glenn Penner (researcher at Mennonite Heritage Center, Winnipeg) was of great help; we exchanged and discussed our call name registers.

The Plautdietsch call names used in Salamanca and the German names of Carroll Janer are enumerated in Table 1. To the Plautdietsch names, I have added their equivalents in Dutch. The spelling of the Plautdietsch call names as shown in Table 1 is in the first place based on the *Huachdietsch-Plautdietsch Rejista* 2015 (Stoeckl 2018), and for the names not registered, I used the most frequently found written versions in several Plautdietsch texts (written and published in by Epp 1972 and Ens 2011). In a few cases (*Jeat, Bejmin*), where I could not find the name in writing, I based its spelling on the recorded sound. The name versions in Dutch conform with names registered in the *Nederlandse Voornamenbank* (Dutch first names databank) of the Meertens Institute,[9] and the name versions in German are copied from Carroll Janer's text based on the (Mexican and Belizean) birth certificates.

Table 1. Plautdietsch call names in Salamanca and German names on birth certificates

Call names in Salamanca 2022				**First names on birth certificates (Carroll Janer 2017: 111, 112)**	
Women		**Men**		**Women**	**Men**
Plautdietsch	**Dutch**	**Plautdietsch**	**Dutch**	**German**	**German**
Aun	An	Hendrikj	Hendrik	Anna	Heinrich
Truud	Truud	Obraum	Abram	Getruda	Abram
Ut	Oet	Bint	Bint	Agatha	Bernhardt
Trien	Trien	Wellm	Willem	Katharina	Wilhelm
Tina	Tina	Fraunz	Frans	Justina	Franz
Neet	Neeta	Jehaun	Johan	Aganetha	Johann
Lies	Lies	Peeta	Peter	Elisabeth	Peter
Leen	Leen	Klos	Klaas	Helena	Nicolas
Saush	Sara	Kjnals	Knelis	Sara, Sarah	Cornelius
Marie	Marie	Jap	Jaap	Maria	Jacob, Jakob
Sush	Suus	Jeat	Gert	Susanna	Gerhard
Iet	Iet	Dov	David	Judith	David
Ester	Esther	Iesak	Izaak	Esther	Isaac, Isaak
Eev	Eef	Bejmin	Benjamin	Eva	Benjamin
Jreet	Greet	Hermaun	Herman	Margaretha	Herman

9. The Meertens Institute is an Amsterdam-based Dutch research institute that studies and documents language and culture in the Netherlands, and Dutch language and culture throughout the world (cf. Meertens Institute website).

3. Call names: Analyzed and compared

3.1 Similarities and differences between the Plautdietsch and Dutch call names

The call names used in Salamanca are reminiscent of Dutch call names and most of them are based on Judaeo-Christian names. As such, they are a continuance of names that were in use in the 16th- and 17th-century Netherlands, i.e. from Flanders in the southwest to Groningen in the northeast. From the 12th- and 13th-centuries Germanic names in Germanic Northern Europe were increasingly replaced by Judaeo-Christian names (Van der Sijs 2000: 149–152, Kunze 2004: 32–42), and in Salamanca, alongside some names of Germanic origin (*Hendrik, Bint, Wellm, Jeat, Herman,* and *Truud*), we see call names based on names in the Old and New Testament and saints' names (*Obraum, Fraunz, Jehaun, Peeta, Klos, Kjnals, Jap, Dov, Isaak, Bejmin, Aun, Ut, Trien, Tina, Neet, Lies, Leen, Saush, Suss, Iet, Ester, Eev* and *Jreet*). According to the *Voornamenbank* of the Meertens Institute, in the Netherlands, even until 1947, *Maria, Anna, Catharina* (*Trien*), *Grietje*, and *Elisabeth* were among the ten most popular women's names, while among the ten most popular men's names, we find *Peter, Jacob (Jaap)* en *Johan*. Other Plautdietsch names (like *Ut, Leen, Kjnals* or *Bint*) now sound old-fashioned but recognizable to the modern Dutch ear.

The *Nederlandse Voornamenbank* of the Meertens Institute offers additional information about name-giving traditions. In the Netherlands in many cases the call name was not the name registered, but derived from the official name and was used 'in talk' (as elsewhere), so there is a difference between the registered name and the call name. But note that name registration only became obligatory in 1811; in 1795 in Flanders. Common call names were for instance *Trien, Leen*, and in Flanders *Niet*, for *Katrien, Magdalene*, and *Agneet* (Goemans, 1934: 292). This is also the case in Germany, where "Rufnamen lebten (und leben) in der gesprochenen Sprache: gelangten sie aufs Papier, wurden sie nicht selten auf ihre Ausgangsform [...] zurückgeführt [...]." (Kunze 2004: 35; translation: "Call names are (and were) part of spoken language: in writing, they were often copied back to their original form"). Regarding the conservatism in name-giving, until World War II, traditional Judaeo-Christian names dominated the spectrum, among Catholics and Protestants alike, and in most families (in the Netherlands and elsewhere) the custom was to name the newborns after family members. Often the grandparents came first and then the aunts and uncles of the child. According to Kunze (2004) and Gerritzen (2001), this practice is the reason why for centuries the stock of first names hardly renewed. Until today, among the Old Colony Mennonites in Salamanca, only occasional one-time innovations (see under section 2) are observed, but the name-giving is not specifically related to the existing names in the family. When I asked whether there was a tradition in naming the children or in choosing names for firstborns, people would shrug and deny this, and godparents do not exist among the Old Colony Mennonites.

Historical data from Mennonite registers seem to confirm the idea that the call names used in Salamanca were brought along from the Netherlands, as they largely correspond to those traditionally recorded in the Mennonite communities established in 17th and 18th century Prussia: according to Krahn (1957) the Mennonite communities in Prussia preserved Dutch-sounding first names and Dutch surnames, as witnessed by the baptismal register that was kept since 1695 in the Mennonite community of Alexanderwohl:

> This list contained only 40 different names, all the others being repeated. Heading the list of male members in frequency was Peter (90), followed by Jakob (74). Among the female names, Ancke (Anna) ranked highest (107) with Marike (Maria) following (79). The names still had a Dutch ending, indicating the cultural and linguistic adherence to their background. (Krahn 1957)

In itself, it is not surprising that the names mentioned by Krahn would still be written in Dutch because Dutch was the official school and church language for the Mennonites during that time. Therefore, the names were registered in Dutch and probably were Dutch. In the second half of the 18th century, when the High German Luther Bible was officially adopted, the registers of baptized church members switched to High German (Buchheit 1982, Thiessen 2003, Siemens 2012). Krahn does not elaborate on the "Dutch endings" mentioned by him.

Other population censuses of Mennonite congregations in Prussia are kept in the Mennonite Heritage Archives (Winnipeg), such as "The complete 1776 Census of Mennonites in West Prussia" (Penner 2017). This census mentions lists of inhabitants of plots in the villages, with the given name and surname of the owner, almost always a man, plus the number of (nameless) family members and their gender. If a woman (always a widow) turns out to be the owner, it says *Witwe* (widow) + the family name of the man, no first names of women are written. This 1776 census yields the following top 3 first names for men: 1. Jacob, 2. Heinrich, 3. Peter; 170 names were counted, 32 different names were found, half of which occurred only once or twice. Penner comments about the registration in German: "First names have also changed over the centuries. A few examples are: Goerth = Gerhard; Jonas = Hans = Johann; Harm = Hermann; Dirks = Dirk = Diedrich; Gils = Julius; Knels = Cornelius; Conert/Konert = Conrad." (Penner 2017). This may reflect the 18th-century change from registering first names in Dutch to registering first names in High German.

In the German language territory, *Johannes, Heinrich, Hermann, Konrad, Anna, Maria, Elisabeth,* and *Katharina* are among the most popular names around the 15th century (Kunze 2004). Their more common short forms, or call names, are *Hans, Heinz, Anni, Marie, Lisa,* and *Katrin*, and then-known hypocoristic forms (derived from Elisabeth, Margaretha, Heinrich, Fritz) are *Liseke, Greteke, Heinle,* and *Fritzeke*, although in the East-Frisian borderland between the Dutch province of Groningen and German Low Saxony, names like *Antje* and *Ancke* are registered (Kunze 2004: 37, 73); but overall, the Low German and German call names, and their hypocoristic forms, differ more from the Plautdietsch names in Salamanca than the Dutch versions.

In the following Figures 1 and 2 the frequency is displayed of the top popular given names mentioned in the Alexanderwohl registers of 1799 and 1875[10] (Krahn 1957), the Carroll Janer overview (2017), and the data I collected in Salamanca in 2021–2022. The two most popular names for women in the 18th century according to Krahn are *Ancke* and *Marike*, in Salamanca they are *Marie* and *Trien*, *Aun* comes third. Regarding men's names, the most popular in the 18th century were *Peter* and *Jakob*. About a hundred years later in Salamanca, we have *Jap (Jakob)* and *Jehaun (Johann), Peter* comes in fourth, and *Hendrik* fifth.

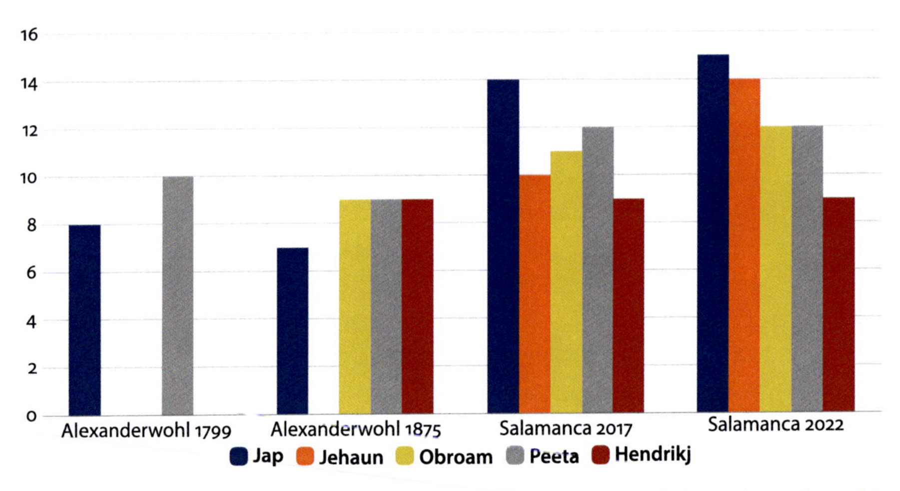

Figure 1. Most popular Mennonite men's names from 1799 to 2022 (%), in Alexanderwohl and Salamanca, based on Krahn (1957), Carroll Janer (2017), Hoebens (2023)

10. This Mennonite congregation has antecedents in the Netherlands, Prussia, and Ucrania from where it migrated in 1874 to Kansas, USA. Many of their community registers are well preserved (Krahn 1957).

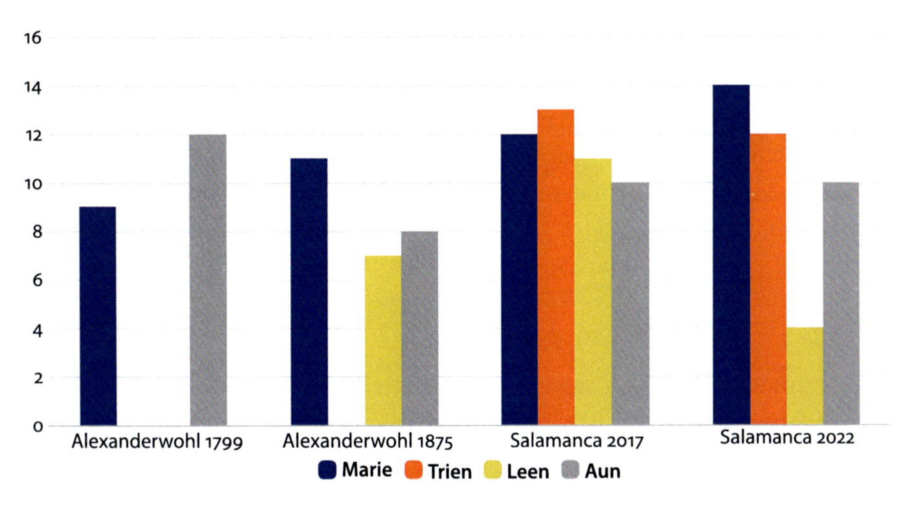

Figure 2. Most popular Mennonite women's names from 1799 to 2022 (%), in Alexanderwohl and Salamanca, based on Krahn (1957), Carroll Janer (2017), Hoebens (2023)

The data indicate little variation in the names over time and during the Mennonite diaspora. The names mentioned as the most frequent coincide with names popular in the 16th-century Netherlands. But until today, most of the Dutch name versions shown in Table 1, though not very popular, are still in use in the Netherlands, according to a 2017 survey on the Meertens Institute's *Voornamenbank*, and quite a few of them particularly in areas where the Protestant churches still have closed communities, the Dutch so-called Bible-belt. Among the present-day Salamanca Old Colony Mennonites, the popularity of certain names, and their names in general, have changed little since their ancestors left the Low Countries. Both Krahn (1957) and Penner (2017), while reviewing historic registers, remark on the lack of variety, or the sameness of the names. This is also, or perhaps even more so, a prominent feature of the name-giving in Salamanca. The name choices seem to have been reduced but are an intrinsic part of their centuries-old traditions. Hypocoristic forms, used only in children's names in Salamanca, will be further discussed in section 4.

The particularly limited variety in traditional Mennonite names is commented on by Andrew Unger, of Mennonite origin, in his online Canadian (Mennonite) satirical magazine *The Daily Bonnet* (April 13, 14 2017): "When Menno Simons received the Ten Commandments back in 1536, he was also provided with a list of holy and righteous Mennonite first names, ten for women and ten for men. [...] However, recently *The Daily Bonnet* has discovered the original list of Mennonite names as given to Menno Simons himself. If your own name is not on this list, you may have to question the moral character of your parents." Among the ten names for women (April 13, 2017) and for men (April 14, 2017), only three names are not in the list collected in Salamanca: *Arthur* and *Menno* for men, and *Edna* for women. All three names are recognized in Salamanca but were not in use, and except for *Arthur* (Plautdietsch *Aot*) were said to be known but very uncommon in their midst. As a tenth name for women, Unger states: "The 10th acceptable Mennonite woman's first name on the list is to simply add "Mrs." to your husband's name." Though this is mild satire, it may explain the absence of women's names among the plot owners, which is also observed in the Canadian stories in Plautdietsch.

3.2 Mennonite names in Salamanca compared to those in ethnic Mennonite communities in Chihuahua

The Old Colony Mennonites in Salamanca constitute one of the more secluded Mennonite communities in Mexico. In Chihuahua, the northern Mexican state where the first Mennonite settlers arrived in 1922, an expanding process of modernization[11] among traditional Mennonites is taking place, which seems to entail a change in name-giving. During a fieldwork stay in Chihuahua (in September 2021), I visited the following educational institutes, in (descending) order of degree of orthodoxy:

1. one exclusively Mennonite Old Colony school;
2. one halfway modernized exclusively Mennonite *Komitee* (Old Colony) schools;
3. two modern, exclusively Mennonite *Kleine Gemeinde* schools;
4. two modern *Konferensa* schools (*Conferencia Menonita de México*), where all religions are admitted.

In the traditional Old Colony schools, lessons are still taught in *Huachdietsch*, the Old Colony Mennonite ritual way of pronouncing their Bible High German. The children's given names resemble the names in Salamanca, with a little variation and a few names in a Spanish or English version. The *Komitee* schools offer a mixed German/Spanish curriculum. They are the product of collaboration, in an Old Colony committee, with USA Amish and Canadian Mennonite teachers. At the five more modern schools (2,3,4), Spanish and German are taught, and in two of them, English is taught as a third language. Their curricula comply with government regulations and offer a wider, more secular range of subjects, such as biology, physics, and geography. The children's given names project a more

11. Modernization includes for example: education according to Mexican standards, a generalized and personal use of modern technology, more Mennonite and non-Mennonite Mexicans living in proximity, and Mennonite Mexicans participating in local Mexican politics.

worldly stance. Spanish and English names are common, especially in the *Kleine Gemeinde* and the so-called *Konferensa* schools. The latter were the first modern schools among the Chihuahua Mennonites, founded in the early 1960s with the aid of USA- and Canada-based Mennonite Conference churches and now administered by the *Conferencia Menonita de México* (Carl-Klassen 2021). I have added some images taken of a names list from the Old Colony school (Figure 3), and of a names exercise from the *Kleine Gemeinde* School (Figure 4), with permission from the school administration.

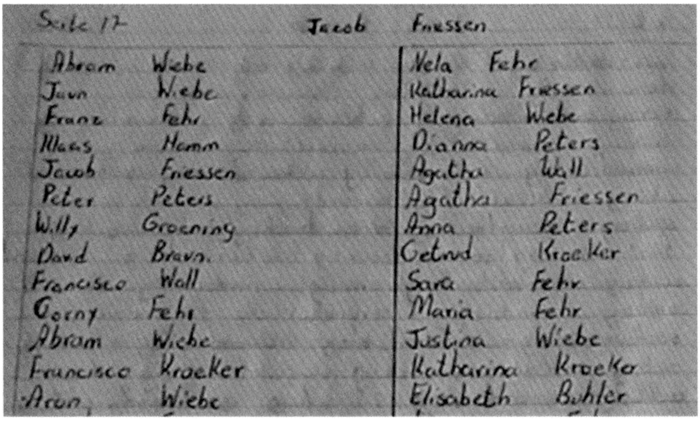

Figure 3. Students' names list, Waldheim Old Colony school, Manitoba Chihuahua Campo 23. Waldheim

The complete list of students in the Waldheim Old Colony school in *campo* 23 consists of 29 boys and 27 girls (56 persons). There are 15 different boys' names and 17 different girls' names. The traditional names are almost all written in their High German version. The boys' names show more non-traditional forms (*Francisco, Pancho, Johny, Willy, Corny*) than the girls' names (*Dianna, Susy*). The Spanish or English boys' names correspond to the traditional names (*Franz, Johann, Wilhelm, Cornelius*) and so does the name of *Susy* (*Susana*). Most frequent names: girls *Agatha* 4x, *Anna* and *Eva* 2x; boys *Abram* 6x, *Jacob* 4x. The Old Colony schools are open for six months each year, and it proved to be tough to find one functioning in September 2021. The two teachers said it was more difficult to find teachers for these schools. This school was attended by children from at least three Old Colony *campos* or *Darpa*.[12]

12. *Darp* in Plautdietsch, *campo* in Spanish Mexico, *street-village* in English, is the name for the approx. 1 mile-long street of about 11 plots on either side that form a village within a Mennonite Old Colony colony. Salamanca consists of 17 of these *Darpa* (cf. Dutch dorp – dorpen).

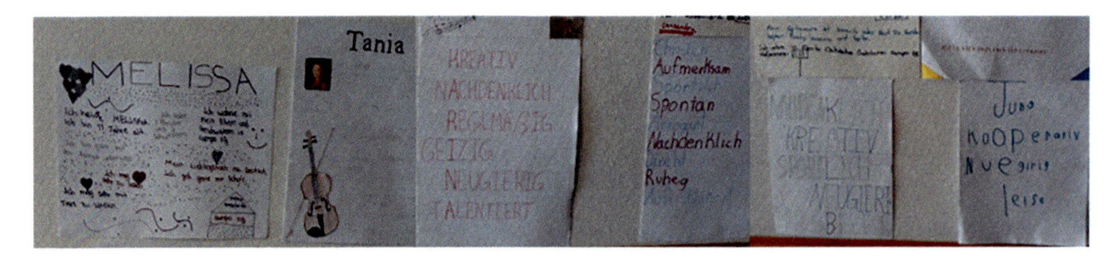

Figure 4. El Ancla *Kleine Gemeinde* school, *campo* 106 Swift Current Chihuahua
Schoolwork with first names at the *Kleine Gemeinde* school, *campo* 106

At the *Komitee* schools, of which I visited *Los Cienes* in *campo* 103, the learning is still rather traditional and the children who attend are mostly from Old Colony Mennonite families in several *campos*. They learn to read and write High German in Gothic letters, as they do in the Old Colony schools, but they follow the complete primary and secondary (junior high school) courses in Spanish. Their names show more variety and more Spanish (and English) influence than in the Waldheim Old Colony school: besides *Margaretha* and *Maria*, their workbooks had names on them such as *Anthony, Juan, Pablo, Alexander, Veronica*, and *Amanda*.

The names in the artworks of the students of the school *Centro Educativo Trilingüe El Ancla* (CETA) in Swift Current (Figure 4) show a clear difference from the name-giving in Salamanca. Here we see *Melissa, Tania, Karina, Cassandra, Kaleb, Joel*. At this school the names seemed much more English- and Spanish-oriented than Germanic. Other names registered included *Logan, Dimitri, Silvano, Pablo, Dorothea, Emma*, and *Veronica*. The *El Ancla* school is an exclusively ethnic Mennonite school with a modern curriculum that includes German, Spanish, and English. This school's 30th Anniversary Book 1976–2006, contained lists of all the students' first (and family) names from 1976 till 2006. A comparison of the first names in 1976 with those in 2006, evidenced how naming had changed since 1976. At that time, the names almost completely corresponded to the traditional names in Salamanca. The 2006 names list disclosed a clear shift towards non-traditional names, like the ones presented above. Table 2 compares the numbers of different and traditional first names registered in 1976 and 2006 respectively.

The more modern and worldly context at school and in the Chihuahua surroundings seems to encourage individuality, which is reflected, among other things, in name-giving.

At the *Konferensa* schools, students come from Mexican Mestizo, Rarámuri,[13] and mixed Mennonite/Mestizo or Mennonite/Rarámuri or all Mennonite families. The *Kleine Gemeinde* (eg. El Ancla) and *Konferensa* schools have a good rep-

13. Rarámuri, the largest indigenous group in Chihuahua who still speak their Uto-Aztec language with the same name.

Table 2. Comparison of 1976 and 2006 traditional Mennonite first name use at CETA

Numbers	1976		2006	
students (total)	74		173	
female/male	36 f	38 m	85 f	88 m
distinct names	16	16	63	58
traditional names	16	15	19	20
trad. names in %	31/32=99%		39/121=23%	

Source: CETA 30 Year Anniversary Book 1976 -2006 *Unterwegs mit Gott*

utation and offer education from pre-school to senior high school. Primary starts with education in contemporary standard German, but from the second year onwards the Mexican-Spanish curriculum is followed, German and later English being part of the school subjects.

Back in the Old Colony Salamanca community, at school in *campo* 3, Schönfeld, among 31 pupils, 15 girls and 16 boys, 15 different names were in use. The girls' names: *Leen, Maria, Truud, Sush, Eev*, and *Saush*; the boys' names: *Fraunz, Jehaun, Peeta, Kjnals, Isaak, Obraum, Dov, Jap, Hendrikj* (Fieldwork, December 2022).

In Chihuahua, even the Mennonite Old Colony communities are more in touch with the modern world around them than the residents of Salamanca in Quintana Roo. Back in 1996, Kelly Hedges, in her study of the Old Colony Mennonites in Chihuahua, already described the Old Colony Mennonites' (personal) use of cars, and radios, and their frequent contact with the Mexican way of life. Nowadays the use of cell phones and the internet adds up to even more contact and more communication outside the religious communities. A comparison of the increase of non-traditional first names among Mennonites in Chihuahua with the data of an increasing variety in name-giving in the Netherlands in the second half of the 20th century (Meertens Institute *Nederlandse Voornamenbank* and Bloothooft and Onland, 2019), shows that access to horizon-broadening means of communication (television, radio, internet) contributed to these developments. The approach to the non-Mennonite environment is also motivated by the growing lack of independent farming work for the young Mennonites in Chihuahua, who increasingly are taking jobs outside the Mennonite colonies. That is not the case in Salamanca, where farming is still the main source of work and income for all men. Moreover, the lack of variety in names not only implies conservatism but also should be considered from their religious perspective: within the Old Colony Mennonite rules, collectivism by far outweighs individuality (Warkentin 2010), whereas the use of given names may imply an aspect of unicity that stresses individuality (Gerritzen 2001). Contact with the modern world also undeniably involves exposure to and the following of worldly trends up to a certain extent. The lack of variety in the given names in the traditional Mennonite Old Colony communities, however, seems to emphasize a community sense over individuality.

4. Plautdietsch/Dutch call names with Dutch diminutive suffixes?[14]

Understandably, the hypocoristic forms of the Plautdietsch names with their "Dutch ending" (Krahn 1957) sound familiar to the Dutch listener. Table 3 gives a list of Plautdietsch call names in Salamanca. Dutch names in diminutive form normally have the suffix *-je* (*Truudje*) or *-tje* (*Auntje*). This ending originated from the older ending *-ke*, which was preserved in southern Dutch dialects, and which we still observe in some names, such as *Marieke* [məriəkə].

Table 3. Plautdietsch call names with hypocoristic forms as recorded in Salamanca in 2022[a]

Women's names + hypocoristic forms		**Men's names + hypocoristic forms**	
	pronunciation simplex and diminutive		pronunciation simplex and diminutive
Aun – Auntje	ɔ:n – ɑ:ncə	**Hendrik - Hendrikje**	hɛndrɪk – hɛndrɪksᵏjə
Truud – Truudje	trit – tricə	**Obraum – Obraumkje**	ubrɑm – ubrɑmᵏjə
Ut – Utje	u:t – u tjə	**Bint – Bintje**	bi:ənt – bi:ᵊncə
Trien – Trientje	tri:n – tri:ncə	**Wellm – Wellmtje**	ʋɑ:lm – ʋɑ:lmcə
Tiena - Tina	ti:na	**Fraunz – Fraunzke**	frɑ̱:ns – frɑnskʲə
Neet – Neetje	nɔit – nɔcə	**Jehaun – Jehauntje**	jəhɔ:n – jəhɑ̱ncə
Lies – Liesje	li: s – lisᵏjə	**Peeta – Peetatje**	pʰaitɐ – pʰaitʰɐkjə
Leen – Leentje	lɔin – lɔⁱncə	**Klos – Klosje**	klu:s – klusᵏjə
Saush – Saushkje	sɑ̱ʃ – sɑ̱ʃᵏje	**Kjnals – Kjnalsje**	ᵏʃnɑ:ls – ᵏʃnɑlsᵏjə
Marie – Marietje	məri – məricə	**Jap – Japa/Japakje**	jæp – jæpɐ – jæpɛkjə*
Sush – Sushkje	zy:ʃ – zyʃ ᵏjə	**Jeat – Jeata/Jetakje**	je:t – je:tɐ – je:tɐkjə*
Iet – Ietje	i:t – icə	**Dov – Dofje**	du:f – du:fᵏjə
Ester	ɛstəɹ	**Iesak - Iesakje**	izɑk – izɑkjə
Eev – Eefje	ɔif – ɔifjə	**Bejmin – Bejminke**	bɛimiŋ – bɛimiŋkʲə
Jreet – Jreetje	gᵊrɔit – grɔcə	**Hermaun – Hermauntje**	hɛɹmɔn – hɛɹmɔncə

*= deviation in diminutive suffixing: -ɐ / -ɐkjə

a. Spelling based on Stoeckl 2018, Epp 1972, Ens 2011. Names not found in writing follow the recorded sound. See section 2.

14. The hypocoristic forms in this case, expressing endearment, make use of a diminutive suffix.

4.1 Diminutive suffixes in Plautdietsch: (Low) German or Netherlandic?

Van der Sijs (2021) describes how as early as the 14th century in North Holland there was palatalization of *-kijn* if the stem ended in *-t* (2021: 404–415; see also Schönfeld 1970: 229). As a result, *hont-kijn* 'little dog' changed to *hon-tjen*. In Flanders, this development took place in the 15th century. In some Dutch areas, especially in Flemish Brabant, the change from *k* to *tj* did not take place. In several dialects in the east and south (of the Dutch language area) the suffix *-(e)ke* has been preserved to this day, e.g., compare Brabant *strateken, veldeken*.

At the end of the Middle Ages, the suffix *-kijn* was not only used in the Dutch areas but also in the German areas. In the High German area it changed according to the High German sound shift to *-chen*, e.g., compare *Mädchen*. In Low German, on the other hand, as in eastern areas of the modern-day Netherlands, the suffix *-ken* was preserved. (Van der Sijs (ed.) 2011: 66–67), see Figure 5.

In most Dutch and most Low German varieties, no umlaut is used in hypocoristic forms: in High German dialects, the diminutive was usually formed with an umlaut, e.g., compare *Baum* with the diminutive *Bäumchen*. In Standard Dutch the vowel *oo* is preserved in all forms: *boom, boomke* or *boompje*. However, in the Dutch Low Saxon and Limburgish dialects umlaut occurs, e.g., *boom – beumke, jong – jeungske* (Van der Sijs (ed.) 2011: 48–49). The map of Figure 6 offers a view of the isogloss of diminutive forms without/with umlaut in the Dutch language area.

The Plautdietsch hypocoristic forms of the call names display a frequent use of the diminutive suffixes *-je* and *-kje*, without the umlaut. The treatment of diminutives is not very extensive in the various Plautdietsch grammars, dictionaries, and orthography guides (Rempel 1995, Thiessen 2003, Zacharias 2009, Siemens 2012) but it coincides more or less with the following explanation: "Diminutives are formed by the addition of the suffix *kje* and are always neuter. If the noun ends in *t* or *k* then the diminutive is formed by adding the suffix *je*. Examples are: Schwienkje, Me'jalkje, Kautje, Krietje, Büakje." (Rempel 1995: vii). Zacharias adds that: "[...] If the word ends in 'kj', an 's' is added, followed by '-kje': Kjoakj, Kjoakjskje; Stoakj, Stoakjskje [church, little church, heifer, little heifer]. If the word ends in 't', only '-je' is added: Haunt, Hauntje; Kjint, Kjintje [hand, hand, child, child]. The words with this form are all neuter." (Zacharias 2009: xxi). The above examples in Plautdietsch confirm the absence of umlaut in nouns and names when a diminutive suffix is used. The resemblance with the Dutch diminutive suffix is noticeable.

Further research moreover reveals a remarkably high frequency of diminutives in the Dutch regions of the North Sea (the Netherlands with East Frisia) and those of the Baltic Sea, in what is now Poland, the area around Gdańsk (Schäfer

Figure 5. Diminutive suffixes in the Low German, and High German areas (Van der Sijs (ed.) 2011: 66–67)

2024: 74, based on Wenker Atlas data), where the Mennonites lived for 200 years. However, the present study is too small to determine that the diminutive form in Plautdietsch can be traced back to the influence of language varieties from the Low Countries.

4.2 Historical use of names with diminutives in 17th-century Dutch writing

Thieleman Janszoon van Braght's *The Martyrs Mirror*, well-known among Mennonites, was first published in 1660 (Westerbeke, ed., 2019). Several families in Salamanca have a beautifully-bound photocopy of the second edition (1685) with drawings by Jan Luyken. It contains many stories about Christian martyrdom, especially about the Anabaptist martyrdom in the Netherlands in the 16th century.

Figure 6. Isogloss between diminutive forms with or without umlaut in the Dutch-speaking areas (Map 1.8 from Van der Sijs (ed.) 2011: 48)

It also contains first names and different ways of writing the diminutive suffix. Besides the fact that this is a well-known book among Mennonites, comprising quite a few names that resemble the names used by Old Colony Mennonites, it also illustrates the period of transition in speech and spelling arrangements (see 4.1). Table 4 shows the variation in the diminutive suffixes used in some names in *The Martyrs Mirror* that correspond to names used in Salamanca.

Table 4. Spelling variation in some first names and hypocoristic forms in Van Braght's *The Martyrs Mirror* (1660–1685)

Women	*Men*
Anneke, Annetgen	Claes, Class, Claesken
Trijn, Trijnken, Trijntjen Trijntgen	Hendrick, Heijndrick, Hendrich, Hendrik
Mary, Mariken, Maritgen, Marritge	Jaap, Jaapje
Griet, Grietje	

The pronunciation of the hypocoristic forms in Salamanca points to a development similar to that of Dutch hypocoristic forms. Dutch was the writing-and-reading language until the second half of the 18th century (see section 1.1) and there has always been contact with the Dutch Anabaptists, who frequently visited Gdańsk; they were consulted and they also had a say in religious discussions. This contact lost frequency but did not disappear when the ancestors of the Salamanca Old Colony Mennonites settled in Ukraine (Urry 2010).

5. Conclusion

Plautdietsch name-giving among the Old Colony Mennonite residents of Salamanca is related to name-giving practices and call names commonly used in the Netherlands and Flanders at the times their ancestors left these regions (16th century), and which were still fairly popular until the second half of the 20th century. Contact with the Dutch language of the Bible and with fellow Mennonites from the Netherlands until far into the 18th century may have contributed to the conservation of the Dutch-sounding names and their hypocoristic forms. The Plautdietsch call names certainly suggest a Dutch legacy.

From the times of their settlement in Ukraine, the Salamanca Mennonites' forefathers kept geographical and social distance from surrounding non-Mennonite environments, due to a strong tradition of religious otherness, which also must have been adjuvant in upholding the century-old name-giving practice. Name-giving in general, not only in the first names, seems to be part of a geographic memory conservation act among the traditional Mennonites. The Mennonite diaspora is filled with names from their older and more recent past. From the Netherlands, these Anabaptists took with them the Dutch call names or first names to Prussia (16th century) and further on. It is interesting to note that throughout the diaspora, until this day, the names of their German-Prussian villages were and are used for the *Darpa* or street villages that constitute the colonies in Ukraine, Canada, Mexico, and the rest of America (such as – in Plautdietsch – *Scheental, Rennlaunt, Kjlienstaut, Greental, Scheenfelt, Blumental*, etc., some *Darpa* in Salamanca). The Canadian names of the Mennonite settlement areas, such as *Manitoba, The Hague*, and *Swift Current* (1874–1900), were used for the new colonies in the states of Chihuahua and Durango in Mexico (1922), and in Bolivia, Mennonites from Mexico formed colonies with the names of *Chihuahua, Durango* (1960), etc. Finally, in the last century, place names from the Netherlands were used in Brazil and Paraguay: there we find Mennonites in colonies called *Witmarsum* (1930), *Friesland* (1937), and *Volendam* (1947). The name-giving traditions concerning the names of colonies and street villages emphasize even more the conservative, archaic nature of the Mennonite Old Colony communities.

Today's Salamanca Old Colony Mennonites have maintained otherness in language and culture. Their refusal to accept or even allow modern technologies that are considered non-beneficial for their congregational life has kept the virtual influx of modern worldly tendencies and influences at bay. This seems to be important in the conservation of their name-giving tradition. The fieldwork data from Chihuahua show that worldly influences, or globalization, can have a considerable effect on the process of name-giving among the ethnic-religious Mennonites. For now, I have been able to register, live, a Dutch heritage in the Plautdietsch call names of the Mennonite Old Colony residents in Salamanca, Quintana Roo, Mexico.

Acknowledgement

The present text is part of an ethnolinguistic research project into the role of language use in Salamanca; more on this in the PhD dissertation by Emma Hoebens, *Taal als muur Een sociolinguïstisch onderzoek naar taal en cultuur van de mennonietengemeenschap Salamanca in Bacalar, Quintana Roo, Mexico*, 2025, Radboud University Nijmegen.

References

Bloothooft, Gerrit & David Onland. 2019 "Hoe populair is mijn voornaam sinds 1790?" Neerlandistiek, *Online tijdschrift voor taal- en letterkunde*. November 28, 2019.

Buchheit, R. H. 1982. "Language maintenance and shift among Mennonites in south-central Kansas." *Yearbook of German-American Studies*, 17, 111–122.

Carl-Klassen, A. 2021 "'Very Steady Steps Toward Education': 50 Years of Education Reform in Chihuahua's Southern Mennonite Colonies" *Anabaptist Historians*. Posted on April 29, 2021. https://anabaptisthistorians.org/2021/04/29/very-steady-steps-toward-education-50-years-of-education-reform-in-chihuahuas-southern-mennonite-colonies/

Carroll Janer, I.E. 2017. La gente que nos alimenta. Herencia, parentesco y sangre entre los menonitas de la vieja colonia en el ejido Salamanca al sur del estado de Quintana Roo, México. Ph.D. Thesis. Mexico. ENAH/INAH.

Contreras Hernández, Valeria. 2018. *Plautdietsche Arbeit. trabajo y organización social: el caso de los menonitas de Salamanca, Bacalar, Quintana Roo.* Tesis de licenciatura (Bachelor Thesis). Facultad de Ciencias Antropológicas. Mérida: Universidad Autónoma de Yucatán.

Ens, Gerhard. 2011. *Dee easchte Wienachten enn Kanada enn aundre Jeschijchten.* Edmonton. RTP Archive Press.

Epp, Reuben. 1996. *The Spelling of Low German & Plautdietsch: Towards An Official Plautdietsch Orthography.* The Reader's Press. Hillsboro. Kansas.

Epp, Reuben. 1993. *The Story of Low German & Plautdietsch: Tracing a Language Across the Globe.* The Reader's Press. Hillsboro. Kansas.

Epp, Reuben. 1972. *Plautdietsche Schreftsteckja.* Steinbach. Derksen Printers.

Gerritzen, Doreen. 2001. 'Voornamen: wat onderzoeken we en waarom?' Gramma 8, 249–266.

doi Goemans, L. 1934. "Westvlaamsch « leite » — Leuvensch « laat »", *Handelingen van de Koninklijke Commissie voor Toponymie en Dialectologie* 8(1), 261–266.

Graaf T. de & R. Nieuweboer. 1993. "De taal der Mennonieten in Siberië en hun relatie met Nederland". *Doopsgezinde Bijdragen* nieuwe reeks nr. 19. https://www.dhkonline.nl/publicaties/db_nr/nr_19_1993/175_aa_189-19_1993/

Graaf, T. de & Nieuweboer, R. 2001. The language of the Siberian Mennonites. In I. Rauch, & G.F. Carr (Eds.), *New insights in Germanic linguistics II* (pp. 21–34). P.I.E. — Peter Lang.

Hedges, Kelly L. 1996. *Plautdietsch and Huuchdietsch in Chihuahua: language, literacy, and identity among the Old Colony Mennonites in northern Mexico.* Ph.D. New Haven: Yale University.

doi Hovland, Fallon. 2020. "Plautdietsch in Contact: Influences of English and Spanish on Mennonite Plautdietsch Speakers in Seminole, Texas." *Journal of Amish and Plain Anabaptist Studies* 8(1): 43–58.

Krahn, Cornelius. 1957. "Names (Mennonite)". Global Anabaptist Mennonite Encyclopedia Online. Retrieved 29 October 2022, from https://gameo.org/index.php?title=Names_(Mennonite)&oldid=121349

Kunze, Konrad. 1998/2004. Namenkunde. Vor- und Familiennamen im deutsche Sprachgebiet. Dtv-Atlas. Deutscher Taschenbuch Verlag. München. 5. Auflage 2004.

Moelleken, Wolfgang Wilfried. (1972) *Niederdeutsch der Molotschna- und Chortitza-Mennoniten in British Columbia, Kanada.* Phonai. Band 10. Monographien 4.

Nederlandse Voornamenbank. Meertens Instituut (online) https://nvb.meertens.knaw.nl/

Nieuweboer, Rogier. 1999. *The Altai dialect of Plautdiitsch (West-Siberian Mennonite Low German)* Lincom Studies in Germanic Linguistics. Lincom Europa. München.

Penner, Glenn H. (2017) "The Complete 1776 Census of Mennonites in West Prussia, Version 7, September 2017." https://www.mennonitegenealogy.com/new.html

doi Le Polain de Waroux, Yann, Janice Neumann, Anna O'Driscoll and Kerstin Schreiber. 2021. "Pious pioneers: the expansion of Mennonite colonies in Latin America." *Journal of Land Use Science.* 16, no. 1 (2021): 1–17.

Reimer, Al (1982). "There is now an "official" way to write Low German". *Mennonite Mirror.* Vol.11. nr. 10. June 1982. Pp. 7, 8.

Rempel, Herman. (1995) *Kjenn jie noch Plautdietsch? A mennonite Low German Dictionary.* PrairieView Press. Gretna CA. Neche USA.

doi Sawatzky, Harry Leonard. (1971) *They Sought a Country: Mennonite Colonization in Mexico.* University of California Press. Berkeley. Los Angeles. London.

doi Schäfer, Lea. (2024). „Faktoren von Frequenz und Produktivität von Diminution in frühen Dialekterhebungen des Deutschen; Factors of frequency and productivity of diminution in early German dialect surveys". *Zeitschrift für Wortbildung / Journal of Word Formation.* 8.

Schönfeld, M. & A. Van Loey. (1970). *Schönfeld's historische grammatica van het Nederlands: klankleer, vormleer en woordvorming.* Zutphen, Thieme.

Siemens, Heinrich. (2012) *Plautdietsch. Grammatik, Geschichte, Perspektiven.* Tweeback, Bonn ISBN 978-3-9811978-5-3 (zugl. Dissertation, Universität Bonn 2011)

Sijs, Nicoline van der. (2021) *Taalwetten maken en vinden. Het ontstaan van het Standaardnederlands.* Sterck & De Vreese. Gorredijk.

Sijs, Nicoline van der. (ed.) (2011) *Dialectatlas van het Nederlands.* Bert Bakker.

Sijs, Nicoline van der & Jaap Engelsman. (2000) *Nota bene: De invloed van het Latijn en Grieks op het Nederlands.* Den Haag: SDU.

Stichting De Gihonbron. Middelburg. https://theologienet.nl/bestanden/braght-t-j-van-en-a-van-haamstede-martelaren-alle-doopsgezind-en-hervormd-in-nederland.pdf

Stoeckl, A. (2018) *Daut Groote Huachdietsch – Plautdietsch Rejista* 2015. Detmold. Plautdietsch Freunde.

Thiessen, J. (1963) *Studien zum Wortschatz der kanadischen Mennoniten.* Marburg: N.G. Elwert Verlag.

Thiessen, J. (2003) *Mennonite Low German Dictionary.* Max Kade Institute for German-American Studies. University of Wisconsin-Madison. Wisconsin.

Unger, Andrew. (2017) "Learn the Meaning Behind Your Common Mennonite First Name" (Women's List) and (Men's List). *The Daily Bonnet.* Satirical news by Andrew Unger. April 13,14, 2017. https://www.ungerreview.com/learn-meaning-behind-common-mennonite-first-name-womens-list/- en https://www.ungerreview.com/learn-meaning-behind-common-mennonite-first-name-mens-list/

Urry, J. (2010). "De beleving van rijkdom en armoede door Nederlandse en Russische doopsgezinden". In *Doopsgezinde Bijdragen nieuwe reeks* nr. 35/36 pp 23–58. 2010. Doopsgezinde Historische Kring. Uitgeverij Verloren. Hilversum.

Warkentin, Karen. (2010) *'So Ha' Wie Daut Emma Jedohne,' (That is How We Have Always Done It): The Collective Memory and Cultural Identity Of The Old Colony Mennonites in Bolivia.* MA Thesis. Department of History. University of Manitoba/University of Winnipeg.

Westerbeke, Willem. (2019) *Groot Martelaarsboek; al de bekende martelaren in Nederland.*

Zacharias, Ed H. (2009) *Ons Ieeschtet Wieedabuak.* Winkler, MB. Published by Author Ed H. Zacharias.

CHAPTER 16

Variation and stability in variants of heritage Dutch

Suzanne Aalberse & Robert A. Cloutier
University of Amsterdam

This chapter provides an overview of linguistic variation and stability of heritage Dutch in seven parts of the world. In the context of research on first and second language acquisition strategies in Dutch as well as on other heritage languages, we contextualize and interpret observations taken from existing research gathered using diverse methods such as the analysis of letters, recordings, and standardized tests. The chapter ends by discussing the implications of the results for the study of contact linguistics in general and for Dutch in particular and by identifying loose ends and directions for future research.

Keywords: heritage Dutch, variation, stability, cross-linguistic influence, reduced input

1. Introduction

The goal of this chapter is to give insight into linguistic change and stability in seven forms of heritage Dutch, particularly focusing on the following questions: which linguistic features are reported to change; which linguistic features are robust, and how can we understand areas of robustness and change in connection to the heritage scenario? Before diving into the linguistic characteristics of variants of heritage Dutch, we first define what we mean by heritage speakers in Section 2. We then provide some background information on the studies of varieties of heritage Dutch, from which our observations are drawn, in Section 3. Section 4 contains the heart of the chapter and discusses variation and stability in heritage Dutch in the domains of phonology, morphology, (morpho)syntax, and semantics. The reported forms of change and stability are connected on the one hand to change and stability in first and second language acquisition of Dutch and on the other to change and stability in heritage languages other than Dutch. Section 5 discusses how the circumstances of the language contact scenario affect

https://doi.org/10.1075/impact.55.16clo

the outcome observed in the heritage languages. The chapter ends by discussing the implications of the results for the study of contact linguistics in general and for heritage Dutch in particular and by identifying loose ends and directions for future research.

2. Defining heritage languages

Before discussing heritage languages, let us first define what is meant by the term. The first to use the label *heritage language* was the Canadian government, who coined the term *heritage languages* in the 1970s for minority languages that were non-indigenous, hence for immigrant languages. The term began to be used by American language policy makers in the 1990s (Cummins 2005: 585) and started to gain currency with theoretically-oriented linguists in the beginning of this century (Van Deusen-Scholl 2003: 212). The nice part about the term *heritage language* is that the label connects the language to something positive: it is a language related to the heritage of the speaker rather than focusing, for example, on the minoritized status of the language.

Authors who refer to heritage languages almost always use this term to refer to a language without an official status in the country where it is spoken. The term is often used for languages that are connected to the ancestry of the speaker. Fishman (2006: 12) writes "millions upon millions of refugees and immigrants have arrived on America's shores with strong hopes of maintaining the ethnolinguistic traditions that defined them to themselves, to their neighbors, and to their God." We follow the idea that heritage languages are part of what defines the identity of the speaker. Fishman (2006: 12) later states that heritage languages have a particular family relevance to learners. The family relevance is implicitly or explicitly assumed to be a part of what defines heritage languages, but this is not true for all authors who define heritage speakers. Rothman (2009), for example, includes all speakers who naturalistically learn languages that are not official languages of the country where they live as heritage language speakers. Following this definition, a child in the US who plays with Dutch-speaking children and acquires the language via play would also be a speaker of heritage Dutch, independent of the ancestry of this child. In this chapter, we assume that a heritage language is mainly spoken by people who learned this language as part of their identity and connection to the homeland of their ancestors; they may have learned the language naturalistically, but this does not have to be case.

Fishman (2006: 12) distinguishes three types of heritage languages: indigenous, colonial and immigrant. This expands the original Canadian definition, which only refers to the last type, namely immigrant languages, and explicitly excludes indigenous languages as types of heritage languages. In this chapter, we use the term *heritage languages* in a restricted sense, specifically for immigrant languages and not for indigenous languages or colonial languages such as for Surinamese Dutch or Berbice Dutch. Note, however, that the distinction between immigrants and colonizers is not always easy to make. In Fishman's framework, Dutch in the US would technically be a colonial language because it was one of the languages of the colonizers of the United States: Van der Sijs (2009: 29) reports that Dutch was the official language on the east coast of the United States from 1624 until 1664. We would not consider Dutch as a heritage community language in this period because the number of people who spoke the language because of their family background was outnumbered by second language speakers due to its official status. The type of Dutch that was spoken during this period could, however, have influenced later heritage Dutch in the US. We chose to restrict the term *heritage languages* to migrant languages because they serve specific identity purposes that affect use (Carreira 2004) and because the existence of a home language variety and possible contact with the homeland creates different dynamics than in indigenous minority languages.

Authors like Polinsky (2011) and Valdés (2000) only refer to a language as a heritage language when speakers shift dominance: the heritage language is the language that was a speaker's dominant language in early youth but that is no longer the dominant language due to exposure to the majority language in, for example, school. Many variants of heritage Dutch described in this overview fit with this idea of dominant language shift toward the majority language, but some language variaties were maintained for a long period of time and were also taught in school, and were used for newspapers and in church. This chapter does not consider dominant language shift from the heritage to the majority language as a fundamental part of being a heritage speaker. This is in line with Kupisch (2013), who presents heritage speakers who are schooled in their heritage language and are as proficient as monolingual speakers of the homeland language.

Some definitions of heritage languages also include early age of onset as a part of the definition for being a heritage speaker, for example, Rothman (2009). Most of the research presented in this chapter concerns speakers who acquired Dutch from birth, but this is not true for all speakers in the studies presented in this chapter. For example, Daan (1987) includes speakers who learned Frisian in the home environment and accessed Dutch via church and school. Because Dutch is used within the new immigrant community as a way to connect to the homeland, we do consider these to be speakers of heritage Dutch (as well as of heritage Frisian). Being a community language, however, is not central to the definition for heritage speakers. Individuals who use Dutch at home even though there is not a wider Dutch-speaking community are also considered heritage speakers in this chapter as is the case for the speaker of heritage Dutch in Indonesia presented in Giesbers (1997).

We considered including language islands in the definition of heritage languages because heritage languages and language islands are sometimes presented under the umbrella term of Dutch in the USA (for example, see van der Sijs 2009). Rosenberg (2005: 221) describes language islands as "internally structured settlements of a linguistic minority on a limited geographical area in the midst of a linguistically different majority." We, however, decided to exclude these contexts in the chapter because the main source of divergent language development in language islands is dialect convergence rather than contact with the majority language as there is often no contact with surrounding languages. Although dialect convergence is common in heritage languages communities, we consider contact with the larger majority language a crucial factor for heritage languages. The criterion of language contact is usually not explicitly expressed in the literature as being part of the features that define heritage languages, but phenomena discussed in relation to heritage languages such as language shift and crosslinguistic influence are only possible given contact with the more powerful and dominant majority language. Table 1 presents and compares features of heritage languages as defined in the literature. The symbol ✓ means that a criterion is explicitly mentioned by the author. The symbol (✓) means that the criterion is implicitly part of the author's definition. The symbol x means that the criterion is explicitly not part of the core definition (i.e., that it does not matter whether a speaker meets the criterion or not to be considered a heritage speaker), and a question mark means the status is not clear.

In short, we define heritage languages as immigrant languages that are connected to the place of origin of the ancestors of the immigrants and that are not the main and/or official language of the wider society where the immigrants moved. Language contact with the majority language is a crucial factor in being a heritage language. It is assumed that most speakers, but not necessarily all, acquire the heritage language naturalistically from birth; in addition, a few may also get some formal training in the heritage language, for instance, at a heritage language school, but this is not necessarily (and often not) the case. The heritage language may be a community language but does not have to be. This definition of heritage languages excludes some contact varieties of Dutch such as language islands and creoles, but it is still quite broad. The next section provides some brief information on the variants of heritage Dutch under discussion.

Table 1. Criteria for heritage language status

	Fishman (2006)	Valdés (2000)	Polinsky (2011); Polinsky and Kagan (2007)	Carreira (2004)	Rothman (2009)	Kupisch (2013)	Current chapter
No official status	✓	(✓)	(✓)	(✓)	✓	(✓)	✓
Personal and ethnic or ancestral ties to the language	✓	(✓)	(✓)	✓	x	?	✓
No access to the standard language	?	?	?	?	?	x	x
In contact with the majority language	(✓)	(✓)	(✓)	(✓)	(✓)	(✓)	✓
Dialect contact	?	?	?	?	?	?	x
Community language	?	✓	✓	?	?	?	x
Dominant language shift	(✓)	✓	✓	(✓)	(✓)	?	x
Early age of acquisition	?	✓	✓	(✓)	✓	✓	x

3. Background on selected variants of heritage Dutch

This chapter reports on previous work on variants of heritage Dutch spoken in the United States, Canada, New Zealand, Australia, South Africa and Indonesia. This selection was based on the availability of research and also largely reflects the areas that welcomed the most Dutch migrants. We are indebted to Klatter-Folmer and Kroon (1997) who inspired many of these studies and brought them together in an edited volume. In this section, we will provide the context of these studies by providing some information on the migration numbers and periods in Section 3.1, giving some details on the type of linguistic research presented in this chapter in 3.2 and by explaining how we use data from first and second language acquisition of Dutch and some information on heritage languages other than Dutch are used to make sense of the data presented and to provide avenues for future research.

3.1 Migration numbers

Between 1840 and 1940, about 250,000 people emigrated from the Netherlands (Broeze 1988 in Elferink and Smits 1997: 22). This number is quite low compared to emigrants from other European countries: the same period showed emigration of 18 million people from the British Isles and 10 million from Italy. Pre-war emigration from the Netherlands consisted mostly of rural farmers seeking cheap land (Swierenga 1993). After the Second World War, the emigration situation in the Netherlands changed briefly as there was a large desire to emigrate, which reached a peak in 1948 when over 30 percent of the Dutch population was found "favourable to emigration" (Elferink and Smits 1997: 22). In 1952, a new emigration law was passed, resulting in more than 300 emigration offices spread throughout the country and yielding an emigration peak in 1952, when more than 48,000 emigrants left the Netherlands (Elferink and Smits 1997: 25). In the period between 1950–1954, 180,350 emigrants left the Netherlands. Of these emigrants, 82,244 moved to Canada, 54,309 to Australia, 14,625 to South Africa, 13,330 to the USA, 11,608 to New Zealand, 1,961 to Brazil and 2,273 to other nations. This chapter includes information of the language situation of emigrants who moved to these popular emigration countries as well as one study on a Dutch emigrant in Indonesia to show how the range of variation in heritage Dutch may be affected by the language contact context. Many of the countries where Dutch emigrants moved were Anglophone countries. Among the studies that we present, Brazil and Indonesia are the only two countries where a language other than English is the dominant language of the country.

3.2 Type of research

The data provided in Section 4 are based on previously published works. In this subsection, we present some background on these studies.

Canada

The data presented on Canada are based on Vermeer (1997), who in 1991 administered the *Taaltoets allochtone kinderen* 'language test for non-Dutch children', a standardized oral proficiency test that includes auditory discrimination and the formation of plurals of nouns, to 15 children aged 5–12 in Ontario in Canada. The children he tested took part in a heritage Dutch class, but most children used mostly or only English at home; only two of the children he tested spoke Dutch at home. Eleven of the children were Canadian-born, and four arrived in Canada at a very young age. Seven children had two Dutch parents, and eight had one Dutch and one Canadian parent. The mean age of the children was 9.8 years old, and on average, they had been attending the heritage Dutch language school for two and a half years.

Australia

The data on heritage Dutch in Australia are based on Clyne (1977; 1991), Clyne and Pauwels (1997), de Bot and Clyne (1989), and Ammerlaan (1997). Clyne conducted and recorded interviews with 200 postwar Dutch-speaking migrants and their children in 1971–1972. His participants were asked to talk in Dutch about their impressions of Australia and/or their life in Australia as well as their language and reading habits and to describe pictures of a typically Dutch and a typically Australian scene. A short segment of speech was also recorded in English, including the description of a picture (Clyne 1977; de Bot and Clyne 1989). Ammerlaan performed a picture-naming and recognition experiment with 76 participants who were Dutch-Australian immigrants and who did not use Dutch and felt that they had lost their Dutch (Ammerlaan 1997: 75–79).

South Africa

The data on heritage Dutch in South Africa are based Raidt (1997), who sent out 1,300 questionnaires to Dutch migrants in Johannesburg and the PWV area (Pretoria, Witwatersrand, Vereeiniging) plus a request to write a short letter in Dutch about factors influencing their personal use of Dutch. She received 300 questionnaires, and 285 were accompanied by a letter. Of her respondents, 260 were born in the Netherlands, 32 migrated before the age of 12, and eight were born in South Africa. The informants lived in urban environments in both English- and Afrikaans-speaking suburbs and towns (219).

United States

The data on heritage Dutch in the United States are based on Daan (1987), van Marle and Smits (1997), and Smits and van Marle (2015). Daan gathered data on heritage Dutch in Pella, Iowa; Holland, Michigan, and Sheboygan (Reformed denomination) and Little Chute (Roman Catholics) in Wisconsin from August to October 1966. She recorded 285 informants over 122 sessions totaling 75 hours. The recordings included Dutch, Frisian and Dutch dialect data. Daan (1987: 238) noted personal information based on a questionnaire she had developed earlier. The respondents who were interviewed by Daan mostly belonged to the second immigration wave. They themselves or their (great) (grand) parents moved away from the Netherlands between 1830 and 1940. 157 participants belonged to the first generation and 128 to the second, third or fourth generation (Daan 1987: 107). Van Marle and Smits built on the corpus by Daan and added new interviews with some of the same participants from Pella, Iowa. Apart from recording spontaneous speech, van Marle and Smits also administered an accessibility judgement test of about 25 sentences to 14 informants, who together judged a total of 375 sentences.

New Zealand

The data on heritage Dutch in New Zealand are based on Klatter-Folmer (1997), who combined various research methods to investigate three generations of speakers of heritage Dutch. She had one informant for the first generation, five for the second generation, and two for the third generation. She conducted interviews on the personal linguistic history and on the language attitudes of all three generations of informants, and she analyzed letters in Dutch and language proficiency tests by the first two generations. Her corpus of letters consisted of a total of 45 letters: 40 written between 1973–1990 by the female subject of the first generation, four written between 1984–1990 by a participant of the second generation and one letter written in 1990 by another participant of the second generation.

Brazil

The data on heritage Dutch in Brazil are based on Schoenmakers-Klein Gunnewiek (1997). Her corpus consists of 176 letters written over the period 1974–1992 by two female participants in Brazil to their family in the Netherlands. The length per letter is 1–4 pages. The letters of one informant consist of a total of 55,600 words, and the letters of the other consist of 27,900 words (Schoenmakers-Klein Gunnewiek 1997: 104). Migration to Brazil consisted mainly of full family migration. Relatively homogenous groups of Dutch farmers went to new Dutch communities and continued working as they did in the Netherlands. For the first-generation Dutch speakers, contact with Brazilians was often limited to work where the boss was Dutch and some of the workers Brazilian. Going back to the Netherlands was not common before the 1970s (Schoenmakers-Klein Gunnewiek 1997: 100).

Indonesia

The data on heritage Dutch in Indonesia are based on work by Giesbers (1997). Giesbers described data from a 55-minute interview with one 45-year-old man who moved to Indonesia at the age of 13. There is no support for his Dutch in a wider Dutch-speaking community, but the informant comes into contact with Dutch via Dutch tourists who visit his hometown, reading Dutch newspapers, and writing letters in Dutch. The informant works in Malang in East Java, and he has a Dutch mother and an Indonesian father. The informant works in a restaurant and in the tourist office. Apart from the interview, he also completed a retelling task for a news item in a newspaper. During the interview, the informant talked about the history of his restaurant and the tourist office.

4. Variation and stability in heritage languages per linguistic domain

This section presents an overview of reported variation and stability in heritage Dutch for the domains of phonology (4.1), inflectional morphology on verbs and nouns (4.2), gender assignment and gender agreement (4.3), verb placement (4.4) and semantics (4.5). As shown above, there are many rich sources available on heritage Dutch ranging from a corpus of letters of two speakers of heritage Dutch in Brazil to the homeland over a timespan of sixteen years (see Schoenmakers-Klein Gunnewiek 1997) to linguistic experiments and tests to recordings of 285 participants in the United States. It would be advantageous if all these sources of data were available in one location (cf. van der Sijs 2014).

To make sense of the varied outcomes reported, it is useful to think about what might have caused these outcomes. Some changes are expected to be more generic than others. Important characteristics of the heritage scenario are that speakers often have little or no access to the norm, that they might not all be schooled or literate in the heritage language (Pires and Rothman 2009; Kupisch and Rothman 2018), that there might be less input, that speakers might be dominant in another language and that speakers might feel the urge to mark their heritage identity and sometimes exaggerate differences between their heritage and dominant languages for this purpose of identity marking (see Kühl and Braunmüller 2014). To contextualize the reported variation, we will briefly discuss what we know about the linguistic domain discussed in heritage languages in general and because order of acquisition plays a role in the robustness of a phenomenon, we will also sometimes link to studies on first and second language acquisition of Dutch. We provide a table for each linguistic subdomain in heritage Dutch: a ✓ indicates that a feature is reported for a particular variant; a ✗ indicates that a feature is reported as non-existent in a particular variant; a – indicates that no information is reported for a feature in a particular variant.

4.1 Phonology

Handbooks on heritage languages (see for example Montrul 2015; Polinsky 2018; Aalberse, Backus, and Muysken 2019) often report that heritage sound systems are relatively robust. This robustness is sometimes related to the very early acquisition of phonology; not arriving at certain acquisitional stages due to less input is not expected. Lloyd-Smith, Einfeldt, and Kupisch (2020: 290), however, shows that this stance on robustness is countered by "widely-reported instances of crosslinguistic influence (CLI) in child bilinguals and the fact that many heritage speakers end up sounding foreign in their native, heritage language." They carried out two accent-rating experiments in German-Italian bilinguals, comparing the bilingual speech samples to those of monolingual and second language (L2) control groups. The samples were rated by monolingual native German- and Italian-speaking judges for foreign accent (*yes* or *no*) and for degree of certainty (*certain*, *semi-certain*, or *uncertain*). Lloyd-Smith, Einfeldt, and Kupisch found that the heritage speakers score between first and second language speakers, which suggests there is variation in accent between heritage speakers and homeland speakers but less so than in second-language speakers. Daan (1997: 248) writes about her heritage Dutch informants that "there were very few exceptions to the general rule that the informants' articulation and intonation sufficed for the investigators to determine which region they or their ancestors came from in the Netherlands": this observation that regional background can be detected in their speech is in line with the idea that global[1] accents are relatively stable.

The studies on heritage Dutch that we present in this chapter do not all discuss phonology, which may be related to various factors including the interest of the researcher, the relative robustness of this domain, and/or the methods used. Differences in global accent, for example, cannot be examined in a corpus of letters or a grammaticality judgment task. Those studies that do mention phonology reported phonological variability in heritage Dutch involving the reduction of consonant clusters, loss of the distinction between long and short vowels and shifts in lexical stress.

Deletion of dentals in word-final consonant clusters is reported in heritage Dutch in Indonesia for words such as *dienst* 'service' and *maand* 'month' as well as in finite verbs where second/third person singular present is encoded with *-t* (Giesbers 1997: 146). The dental *-t* to encode second/third person singular present and on past participles is also left out by some speakers of heritage Dutch in South Africa in their Dutch letters (Raidt 1997: 226–227). Giesbers (1997: 166) also reports deviating stress patterns on the lexical level, mostly a stress shift to the first syllable, for example, pronouncing the word *ongeveer* 'approximately' with stress on the first rather than on the last syllable, and one instance of the reverse in the word *transit* 'transit' with stress on the final rather than the first syllable as found in homeland Dutch. Lastly, vowel length distinctions are reported as being variable in two studies: Vermeer (1997: 146) finds that speakers of heritage Dutch in Canada do not always perceive differences between lax and tense vowels, and Giesbers (1997: 167) reports the replacement of a lax for a tense vowel four times and the opposite twice in heritage Dutch in Indonesia. Table 2 summarizes the variability in phonology that is reported in the studies on heritage Dutch.

---

1. Llyod-Smith et al. use the term global accent to contrast it with specific aspects of an accent such as voice onset time. Global thus refers to overall accent in this context.

Table 2. Reported changes in heritage Dutch phonology

Land	USA	CAN	AUS	NZL	IDN	BRA	ZAF
Consonant cluster reduction	–	–	–	–	✓	–	✓
Loss of vowel length distinctions	–	✓	–	–	✓	–	–
Change in lexical stress	–	–	–	–	✓	–	–

4.2 Inflectional morphology on verbs and nouns

This subsection focuses on inflectional morphology of nouns and verbs in variants of heritage Dutch because this area of morphology is well described in the literature on heritage languages. Polinsky and Scontras (2020: 9) list various reasons why inflectional morphology is among the better described parts of heritage languages. Because many studies focus on variation rather than on stability, morphology is an interesting domain: it is very susceptible to change in language contact situations (Kusters 2003; Trudgill 2011) because "a significant component of morphology serves to encode dependency relations, where the features or position of one constituent determine the shape of another constituent. Such relations, established at a distance are vulnerable to change." Deflection in heritage languages may be a generic effect of language contact regardless of the morphological complexity of the dominant language or it may be an effect of crosslinguistic influence due to contact with a dominant language with less inflectional morphology than the homeland language. Many researched heritage languages, like most variants of heritage Dutch, are in contact with English, which has a modest amount of morphology, so it is likely that the two reinforce one another in heritage languages in Anglophone contexts.

Although inflectional morphology is described in much more detail in the literature, it would be interesting to investigate derivational morphology in heritage languages as well. Anecdotal evidence for the possibility of crosslinguistic influence on derivational morphology exists from student papers written by native Dutch speakers in the Netherlands who very frequently use English in their daily lives and whose Dutch derivational morphology is affected by their knowledge of English, especially via correspondence rules (Thomason 2001). For example, the Latin suffix *-tie* in Dutch often corresponds to its English counterpart *-tion*, for instance, in words like ***formatie*** 'forma**tion**', ***creatie*** 'crea**tion**', and ***irritatie*** 'irrita**tion**'. The correspondence between *-tie* and *-tion* is then overgeneralized to words like *abortus* 'abortion', where the innovation *abortie* has been created by some speakers using *-tie*, corresponding to the form *abortion* of the English word. In the studies we present, one example of a part of speech confusion is mentioned namely the use of the noun *calculatie* 'calculation' in a context where the verb *calculeren* 'to calculate' is intended Giesbers (1997: 168–169). Such confusions are more expected if heritage Dutch is in contact with languages that do not overtly encode differences between nouns and verbs. Whereas core grammar in first language acquisition tends to be in place around the age of four, the productive use and interpretation of derivational affixes is still in process of being acquired ate the age of 12 (Tyler & Nagy 1989). Following the idea that what is learned late in first language acquisition is vulnerable to loss in contact situations (Montrul 2008) we expect derivational morphology to be vulnerable. Because derivational morphology in children and adolescents acquiring homeland Dutch is an under-researched area, we will leave this area for future research and move to Dutch inflection, which has been investigated quite thoroughly.

In this section, we focus on person and number in verbs and number marking on nouns. Homeland Dutch finite singular verbs in the present tense encode first person with the bare stem and second and third persons with the suffix *-t*. Both the plural forms and the infinitive are encoded with the suffix *-en*.

If we consider language acquisition of verbal forms as a source of innovation, we see that both the bare stem and the *-t* form are potential candidates for over-generalization: the *-t* form is the most frequent finite form, and the bare form is phonologically the most attractive. In young children acquiring Dutch, both the bare and the *-t* forms are overgeneralized to all persons and to the plural, but the plural *-en* form is never overgeneralized to the singular (Polišenská 2010). Moreover, the bare stem overlaps with English and could thus also occur and perhaps be reinforced due to crosslinguistic influence in Anglophone contexts – this would also be the case for Afrikaans and Indonesian. Alternatively, speakers of heritage Dutch in Anglophone contexts could potentially overuse the *-t* and *-en* forms as a form of hypercorrection to emphasize differences between their heritage language and the majority language using a correspondence rule where an English bare verb stem corresponds to a heritage Dutch verb form with *-t* or *-en* (cf. Thomason 2001). If we look at Table 3, we can see that loss of *-t* on the finite verb is reported in four variants of heritage Dutch, namely in the US, New Zealand, Indonesia, and South Africa. The opposite, namely overgeneralizing the suffix *-t* to first person singular present, is reported in three variants: the US, Indonesia, and South Africa. Klatter-Folmer (1997: 206) describes a second-generation speaker in New Zealand who consistently uses bare forms rather than using the suffix *-t* for second and third persons. Absence of number marking on verbs is also reported in four variants of heritage Dutch: the US, Australia, Brazil, and South Africa. Schoenmakers-Klein Gunnewiek (1997: 113) also describes the use of plural marking in the singular. Absence of the suffix *-en* for infinitives is reported in two variants of heritage Dutch: Australia and South Africa.

Nouns in homeland Dutch encode the plural with either the suffix *-s* or the suffix *-en* primarily based on phonological properties of the noun. Using the bare form of nouns for plural is reported in two studies: Giesbers (1997: 168) for Indonesia and Smits and van Marle (2015: 393) for the US. Overgeneralization of the plural allomorph *-s* to contexts where the plural marker *-en* is expected is described for variants in the US, Australia, and South Africa. Overgeneralizing *-en* to contexts where the allomorph *-s* is expected is not reported. Clyne and Pauwels (1997: 45) describe the overgeneralization of *-s* and connect it to the similarity to the English plural morpheme *-s*, which we take to mean that they did not find instances of *-en* overgeneralization.

Table 3. Reported changes in heritage Dutch morphology

	USA	CAN	AUS	NZL	IDN	BRA	ZAF
Overgeneralization of bare form to 2/3S	✓	–	–	✓	✓	–	✓
Overgeneralization of suffix *-t* to 1S	✓	–	–	x	✓	–	✓
Weak verbs replace strong verbs	–	–	–	✓	–	–	✓
Loss of number marking on verbs	✓	–	✓	–	–	✓	✓
Loss of suffix in infinitive	–	–	✓	–	–	–	✓
Overgeneralization of plural marker *-s*	✓	–	✓	–	–	–	✓
Overgeneralization of plural marker *-en*	–	–	x	–	–	–	–

4.3 Gender assignment and gender agreement

Gender is a domain that is susceptible to variation. Blom, Polišenská, and Weerman (2008) show that gender assignment, that is knowing whether a noun is assigned to the common or neuter gender, takes until the age of seven for monolingual homeland Dutch children. Young children, both monolingual and bilingual, overgeneralize the forms associated with the more frequent common gender, such as the common gender definite article *de*. Gender agreement combines with definiteness with respect to attributive adjective inflection: in homeland Dutch, most attributive adjectives are inflected with the suffix *-e* (pronounced as schwa), for example, the adjective *mooi* 'beautiful' becomes *mooie* when modifying most nouns as in common gender *een mooie dag* 'a beautiful day', definite neuter gender *het mooie boek* 'the beautiful book', and plural *(de) mooie boeken* '(the) beautiful books'. The uninflected attribute adjective is restricted to only one context, namely if a neuter singular noun is used in an indefinite context as in *een mooi boek* 'a beautiful book'. This rule for the use of the uninflected form of attributive adjectives is not acquired by sequential bilinguals, thereby resulting in overgeneralization of the inflected form (Blom, Polišenská, and Weerman 2008). Based on these observations from child language acquisition, one would expect the neuter definite article *het* and the uninflected attributive adjective to be vulnerable to loss among speakers of heritage Dutch.

If we consider potential crosslinguistic influence from English, we can observe two possibilities. With respect to definite articles, the Dutch common gender *de* is phonetically (and functionally) similar to the English definite article *the* (Klatter-Folmer 1997: 206; Clyne and Pauwels 1997: 45); this similarity could reinforce the tendency of overgeneralizing common gender *de* observed in language acquisition among homeland Dutch children. With respect to attributive adjective inflection, English never inflects adjectives, so the uninflected attributive adjective, which is underused among homeland Dutch children, could receive a boost in Anglophone contexts, competing against the tendency of overgeneralizing the inflected attributive adjective observed in language acquisition among homeland Dutch children.

If we look at Table 4 below we see that the expected overgeneralization of the common gender *de* is borne out and is reported for heritage Dutch in Australia (Clyne and Pauwels 1997: 45), Indonesia (Giesbers 1997: 168), New Zealand (Klatter-Folmer 1997: 205), and South Africa (Raidt 1997: 228). Daan (1987: 55, 71) reports that older variants of Dutch spoken in the United States have lost the neuter gender though Smits and van Marle (2015), despite not explicitly mentioning gender assignment, observe more frequent use of uninflected attributive adjectives for neuter nouns, which suggests that the gender distinction has not completely been lost in heritage Dutch in the United States. The studies in Canada and Brazil do not report on article or attributive adjective use. Giesbers (1997: 168) explicitly mentions that he did not find overgeneralizations of the neuter article. Raidt (1997: 228) only observes overgeneralization of the common gender to the neuter and related this to interference from English and/or Afrikaans. Pauwels and Klein also only mention overgeneralization of the common gender to the neuter. Klatter-Folmer (1997: 205) observes the same pattern of unidirectional overgeneralization for first-generation participants but finds overgeneralization in both directions in second-generation speakers. Raidt does not observe overgeneralization of the neuter article (228); however, she does find overgeneralization of the demonstrative pronoun in both directions (229), so the common gender demonstrative pronoun is used in neuter context and vice versa. Possibly the formal similarity between the English demonstrative *this* and the Dutch neuter demonstrative *dit* stimulated the overgeneralization of the neuter form to common gender contexts. Raidt (1997: 329) only reports on the overgeneralization of the common gender demonstrative die in contexts where the neuter is expected and not vice versa.

Smits and van Marle (2015: 397) find overgeneralizations of both the inflected and uninflected forms of attributive adjectives in their spontaneous data: in the grammaticality judgment test, participants accepted both inflected and uninflected forms as correct. Raidt (1997: 230) reports on the overgeneralization of inflected adjectives in attributive position, and she does not report on overgeneralizations in the other directions explicitly; however, she gives examples of uninflected possessive personal pronouns instead of inflected ones, such as *ons kinderen* 'our children' instead of homeland Dutch *onze kinderen* (229), suggesting overgeneralization of the bare form, probably due to crosslinguistic influence from Afrikaans and English. Giesbers (1997: 168) reports on the overgeneralization of inflected attributive adjective forms only, finding no evidence for uninflected attributive adjectives. The other studies do not report on adjectival inflection.

Table 4. Reported adnominal gender assignment and agreement in heritage Dutch

Overgeneralization of	USA	CAN	AUS	NZL	IDN	BRA	ZAF
common gender definite article *de*	–	–	✓	✓	✓	–	✓
neuter gender definite article *het*	–	–	x	✓	x	–	x
common gender demonstratives *deze* and *die*	–	–	–	–	–	–	✓
neuter gender demonstrative *dit*	–	–	–	✓	–	–	–
inflected attributive adjective	✓	–	–	–	✓	–	✓
uninflected attributive adjective	✓	–	–	–	x	–	?

Most of the reported data are as expected: the common gender definite article *de* is overgeneralized, which can be related to a combination of the observed tendency among monolingual and bilingual acquisition of homeland Dutch as well as crosslinguistic influence from English *the*, and we find evidence for the overuse of the bare form, which can be related to crosslinguistic influence, because the majority languages English and Afrikaans do not inflect adjectives. There is also evidence for the overgeneralization of the inflected form, which is by far the most frequently used attributive adjective form in homeland Dutch, in Indonesia, where the majority language, like English and Afrikaans, does not inflect adjectives.

The most surprising result is the presence of *het*-overgeneralization in second generation speakers in New Zealand as described by Klatter-Folmer (1997: 206). How can we understand this pattern? On a somewhat related phenomenon, Doreleijers, Mourigh, and Swanenberg (2023) show that whereas Dutch ethnolects were first associated with the overgeneralization of common to neuter gender only, now ethnolectal speakers also overgeneralize the neuter gender to common gender nouns in order to create a more academic persona. Apart from this socially motivated hypercorrection, the overgeneralization of neuter gender could also have a language internal motivation. It could be the case that some speakers use semantic features to reorganize parts of the gender system. The role of semantics in the Dutch gender system was first described in pronominal reference in Audring (2009) and Kraaikamp (2017), who both show that high individuation/animacy is associated with common gender in pronominal reference and low individuation/animacy with neuter gender. Cornips et al. (2012) suggest that this association of low individuation with neuter gender not only plays a role in pronominal reference but also in the acquisition of nominal gender: they report that children acquire the gender of neuter mass nouns such as *gras* 'grass' faster than of neuter count nouns such as *boek* 'book'. The role of animacy in gender assignment is also evidenced in Hinskens et al. (2021: 92), who report that in the speech of Moroccan and Turkish Dutch speakers, "in nouns referring to animate entities, biological gender seems to outweigh grammatical gender (genus), as in e.g., *de meisje*; *de wijf*; *de jongetje*; *de dier* ('the girl', 'the woman', 'the boyDIM', 'the animal'); in standard Dutch these nouns have neuter gender (and thus select the definite article *het*)." Given these associations of the neuter gender with the feature mass, it is possible that semantics plays a role in the (non-)retention of neuter nouns in first-generation immigrants. One would expect retention of the neuter gender longest in mass nouns.

If it is indeed the case that mass nouns retain their neuter gender longer whereas common gender is more quickly overgeneralized to animate nouns, the semantic association of low individuation with neuter gender could become stronger in the input for second-generation speakers and hence become even stronger for a third generation. One would expect these cascade effects in scenarios where intergenerational transmission plays an important role. Socially motivated overgeneralizations are also expected during intergenerational transmission and are enhanced by the presence of normative comments either during teaching the heritage language or via the arrival of a new wave of immigrants commenting on overgeneralization of the common gender *de* in the previous generation.

For future research, it would also be interesting to see what happens when Dutch is in contact with a language that has neuter gender as a default gender. Egger, Hulk, and Tsimpli (2018) report on Greek-Dutch bilingual children who overgeneralize neuter gender in Dutch under the influence of the default status of neuter gender in Greek.

4.4 Word order and conjunctions

Dutch sentential word order can be characterized by the following two properties: object-verb (OV), meaning that all verbs apart from the finite verb in a main clause appear in sentence-final position following the object, and verb-second (V2), meaning the finite verb in a main clause always appears as the second constituent. We can observe OV word order in root infinitives as in (1), with respect to the main verb in complex predicates as in (2), and subordinate clauses as in (3).

(1) *Een boek* ***lezen***
A book read
'**to read** a book'

(2) *Ik wil een boek* ***lezen***
I want a book read
'I want **to read** a book'

(3) *Hij zegt dat ik een boek* ***wil lezen***
He says that I a book want read
'He says that I **want to read** a book'

The V2 property, which requires the finite verb in a main clause to be the second constituent in the clause, means that if a main clause starts with a constituent other than the subject, the subject will follow the finite verb, i.e., subject-verb inversion will take place, as shown in (4) (cf (2) above where the finite verb follows the subject).

(4) *Morgen* ***ga*** *ik een boek lezen*
Tomorrow go I a book read
'Tomorrow I **will** read a book'

With respect to the presence of conjunctions in subordinate clauses, uninflected subordinate clauses in Dutch appear without a conjunction as shown in (5) whereas finite subordinate clauses always begin with a conjunction as shown in (6). The required presence of subordinating conjunctions contrasts with English where the subordinating conjunction of the sentence in (6) can be left out.

(5) *Ik hoop hem te zien*
I hope him to see
'I hope to see him'

(6) *Ik hoop dat ik hem zal zien*
I hope that I him shall see
'I hope (that) I will see him'

If we look at the order of acquisition of word order, homeland Dutch children begin by producing root infinitives like in (1) above (Blom and de Korte 2011 and references therein). After a stage when only root infinitives are produced, monolingual and bilingual children of homeland Dutch either continue to produce root infinitives in sentence-final position, adhering to the OV word order in Dutch, or produce a finite verb in second position; this contrasts with adult learners of Dutch, showing that children have no problem with inversion contexts. Moreover, Blom and de Korte (2011) show that children overgeneralize the use of finite auxiliary and semantically empty verbs like *doen* and *maken* to fill the second position. These verbs, referred to as *dummies*, do not always have a semantic function but seem to fill the V2 position, further demonstrating the robustness of V2 syntax in the acquisition of homeland Dutch. If the effects of reduced input in heritage speakers are present, then one would expect the overuse of auxiliaries in second position to maintain the robustness of V2 word order. If we examine the differences and similarities between Dutch and the contact languages, we can observe that despite having underlying OV syntax, the most frequently used order in Dutch (cf. Clahsen and Muysken 1986) is SVO, and this matches the word order in the contact languages of the variants of heritage Dutch described here, though none of the contact languages except for Afrikaans have OV and V2 syntax to the extent found in homeland Dutch. The majority contact languages are also freer in their usage of conjunctions.

If we look at the descriptions of the heritage languages, none of the studies report on the overuse of auxiliaries, which could be either because it does not happen or because the overuse is not an obvious deviation from homeland Dutch. Overusing auxiliaries would still create grammatical sentences and hence not be an obvious form of variation, potentially disguising underlying changes. Backus, Doğruöz, and Heine (2011) refer to a change that fits within the existing grammar as a *system preserving change*. These types of changes can be detected by comparing frequencies of occurrence (see for example Bao 2010).

The omission of conjunctions is mentioned for heritage Dutch in New Zealand by Klatter-Folmer (1997: 206) as shown in (7). None of the other studies report on conjunction use.

(7) *En hoop bij jullie alles oké is*
(*en hoop dat bij jullie alles oké is*)
(and hope that with you everything okay is)
'And hope (that) everything is okay with you'

Clyne and Pauwels (1997: 46) show that V2 syntax is not always adhered to in heritage Dutch despite the fact that finite verbs always form the second constituent of a main clause in homeland Dutch, resulting in subject-verb inversion if the first constituent is not the subject of a sentence. They report, for example, the following:

(8) *Gisteren* *ik* ***ben*** *ziek geweest*
yesterday I am sick been
'Yesterday I **was** sick'

In homeland Dutch, the constituent *gisteren* 'yesterday' would be directly followed by the finite verb *ben* 'am' because of the V2 rule. Absence of subject-verb inversion is not reported for child acquisition of homeland Dutch though the lack of subject-verb inversion and OV orders are reported to occur in adult second language acquisition of Dutch (Blom and de Korte 2011). Schoenmakers-Klein Gunnewiek (1997: 113) does not explicitly report on subject-verb inversion but does present examples of utterances beginning with adverbials that are directly followed by a finite verb hence showing subject-verb inversion and implicitly suggesting stability – the robustness of this rule in the acquisition of homeland Dutch could have been reinforced by its application in Afrikaans. The other studies do not report on subject-verb inversion.

Clyne and Pauwels (1997: 46) and Klatter-Folmer (1997: 206) report on deviation from OV order. Clyne and Pauwels show the finite plural verb *praten* 'speak' preceding the specification *in het Hollands* 'in Dutch' in a subordinate clause in (9). Though prepositional phrases are more flexible in their word order (Koster 1974), homeland Dutch would have a preference for the constituent *in het Hollands* 'in Dutch' to precede the verb in this context. Additionally note the absence of subject-verb inversion between *ze* 'they' and *verstaan* 'understand' as well as the absence of an overt object with the verb *verstaan* 'understand', both of which would be required in homeland Dutch.

(9) *Maar als wij praten in het Hollands, ze verstaan drommels goed.*
but if we talk in the Dutch, they understand damn well
'But if we talk in Dutch, they understand damn well'
(Clyne and Pauwels 1997: 46)

Klatter-Folmer (1997: 206) provides examples of adverbs following the main verb whereas the verb is expected to follow the adverb in homeland Dutch, for example in (10).

(10) *totdat ik* ***ga*** *echt* (Klatter-Folmer 1997: 206)
Until I go really
'Until I really **go**'

Homeland Dutch would use the order *echt ga* 'really go'. Children acquiring homeland Dutch never use these orders. Although this order is not a direct translation from English, the verb being less sentence-final might be influenced by the majority language English. Table 5 summarizes the outcomes we found on changes in syntax in Dutch heritage languages. The reported changes are not many, leaving this domain open for future research.

Table 5. Reported changes in heritage Dutch syntax

	USA	CAN	AUS	NZL	IDN	BRA	ZAF
Conjunction omission	–	–	–	✓	–	–	–
No subject-verb inversion	–	–	✓	–	–	–	–
Complex predicate with multiple verbs preceding the object	–	–	–	–	–	–	–
Subordinate clause with verb-subject order	–	–	✓	–	–	–	–
Overuse of auxiliaries	–	–	–	–	–	–	–

4.5 Semantics

An expected generic effect of the heritage context is that subtle differences in meanings can be lost, especially if these subtle meanings are not reinforced by the majority language. Subtle meaning differences require frequent input, which is what heritage speakers often lack. Schoenmakers-Klein Gunnewiek (1997) hypothesizes that the conceptualization of events in the heritage language is affected by conceptualization in the majority language. For example, the Dutch verb *pakken* 'take' implies an intention by the subject and control over the situation so *de trein pakken* 'to take the train' is fine, but *een ziekte pakken* 'to contract/ catch an illness' (literally 'to take a disease') is ungrammatical since becoming ill is an unintentional process. Schoenmakers-Klein Gunnewiek (1997) reports that speakers of heritage Dutch in Brazil use the expression *een ziekte pakken* under influence of Brazilian-Portuguese *pegar* 'take', which is not sensitive to the features intention and control.

Flecken (2010) shows that conceptualization affects not only the lexicon but also grammatical features. Grammatical aspect marking, for example, is linked to particular perceptions of reality. The Conceptualization Hypothesis then predicts that those structures that are conceptualized differently in the heritage language and in the dominant language will be vulnerable to change.

A frequent loss of subtle meaning differences that is described in heritage Dutch is the collapse of the two auxiliaries that encode perfect tense, namely *zijn* 'to be' and *hebben* 'to have' (see Algemene Nederlandse Spraakkunst ('General Dutch grammar') | 2.3.2.8.iv.a Het gebruik van zijn: algemene regels (ivdnt.org)).

The verb *zijn* 'to be' is used with intransitive verbs that describe a change of state in the subject such as *groeien* 'to grow' and *sterven* 'to die' or when a direction with an (implied) endpoint is expressed. Variants of heritage Dutch sometimes show loss of the verb *zijn* 'to be' as a perfective marker. This is described for heritage Dutch in Anglophone contexts such as Australia (Clyne and Pauwels 1997: 44–45) and South Africa (Raidt 1997: 230) as well as in non-Anglophone Brazil (Schoenmakers-Klein Gunnewiek 1997: 104–105). We can interpret the loss of the auxiliary as the result of a generic effect of meaning loss but also as the result of conceptualization. The semantic difference governing perfective auxiliary selection in homeland Dutch is not conceptualized in the same way as the majority languages English, Afrikaans, and Portuguese.

Changes in semantics (e.g. extensions of meanings, expansion of uses to informal registers) can also be motivated by form similarities between a word from the heritage language and a word in the majority language. For example, Schoenmakers-Klein Gunnewiek (1997:112) finds the utterance *wat gepasseerd is* ('what happened') in the corpus of letters of Dutch Brazilians. This utterance is marked and the more neutral Dutch version would be *wat gebeurd is* ('What happened'). It could be the case that form similarity with Brazilian *passar* motivated the selection of the verb *passeren* rather than the verb *gebeuren*. Clyne and Pauwels (1997: 44) report the use of the Dutch word *smal* 'narrow' with the meaning of the phonetically similar English word *small*.

Meanings also get expanded via the route of calques. In a speaker of heritage Dutch in Indonesia, Giesbers (1997: 173) reports the use of the question word *waarom* 'why' to mean 'what's going on' based on Indonesian *kenapa* 'why', as well as the use of the word *al* 'already' in numerous contexts as a perfective marker, functioning similarly to Indonesian *sudah* 'already'. Both these semantic extensions can be directly traced back to Indonesian. Moro (2018) hypothesizes that heritage language speakers will find translational equivalents for grammatical categories that are obligatorily encoded in the majority language. Future research in heritage languages could look more deeply into obligatory markings in the majority languages and find out if there are proxies for these categories in the heritage language.

Another domain that is very open to cross-linguistic influence is collocations. Preposition use is very susceptible to contact-induced change. Klatter-Folmer (1997) shows how speakers of heritage Dutch in New Zealand select prepositions in collocations that seem motivated by the majority language English, for example, the use of the preposition *met* 'with' rather than the preposition *tegen* 'against' in the collocation *oneerlijk* ***met*** 'dishonest with' as opposed to homeland Dutch *oneerlijk* ***tegen***, or the use of the preposition *van* 'from' rather than *uit* 'out' when describing a person's origin, for instance, in the utterance *een meneer* ***van*** *Zwit-*

serland 'a man from Switzerland' as opposed to homeland Dutch *een meneer* ***uit*** *Zwitserland*. These uses match with a convergence scenario. Giesbers (1997: 173) reports similar forms of convergence in the speaker of heritage Dutch in Indonesia, who says *bang zijn* ***tegen*** 'being afraid against' rather than the homeland Dutch *bang zijn* ***voor*** 'being afraid for'.

Innovative use of prepositions is also observed in heritage Dutch in Brazil, where Schoenmakers-Klein Gunnewiek (1997: 108) reports the use of *denken* ***op*** rather than *denken* ***aan*** 'to think of' and the use of ***op*** *de eerste klas komen* rather than ***in*** *de eerste klas komen* 'to enter first grade'. The uses of *op* seem to be influenced by the Portuguese preposition *em* as the distinction between the Dutch prepositions *aan* and *op* (both translate to 'on' in English) is crosslinguistically rare. Table 6 summarizes the reported changes in semantics in heritage Dutch. Collocations are frequently imported into the heritage language and loss of the perfective auxiliary zijn ('to be') is observed in three contexts of heritage Dutch.

Table 6. Reported variation in semantics in heritage Dutch

	USA	CAN	AUS	NZL	IDN	BRA	ZAF
Loss of the perfective auxiliary *zijn* 'to be'	–	–	✓	–	–	✓	✓
Semantic extension based on form similarity	–	–	✓	–	–	✓	–
Calques	–	–	–	–	✓	–	–
Collocations	–	–	✓	✓	✓	✓	–

5. Heritage languages and the contact scenario

The previous section described what linguistic features were attested in a set of studies of variants of heritage Dutch. We saw that the majority language is a factor in the outcome of language contact, but even if the language contact pair are identical, language outcomes can differ depending on the contact situation. Muysken (2013: 270) argues that "languages do not interact in a single way, but rather in many different ways, depending on the social setting of the contact" (cf Thomason and Kaufman 1988; van Coetsem 1988) and continues: "In other words, it does not suffice to say: when two languages A and B come into contact, X happens, but we need to specify the circumstances" (710). This section describes some of the aspects of the situation of the heritage language which can be taken into account when looking at outcomes.

Investigating contact with more varied contact languages

Most of the reported variants of heritage Dutch have been in contact with English. Giesbers (1997) on heritage Dutch in Indonesia and Schoenmakers-Klein Gunnewiek (1997) on heritage Dutch in Brazil illustrate the potential effects of crosslinguistic influence in contact situations with languages other than English. For example, Giesbers shows that the adverb *al* 'already' fulfills more grammatical functions in heritage Dutch in Indonesia than in homeland Dutch. It would be interesting to see what Dutch words are selected to encode grammatical categories that are present in the majority language but not in homeland Dutch. Research on World Englishes shows that the use of the English word *already* as an aspect marker is prolific as a result of contact with a variety of Asian and African languages (Bao 2010; Siemund 2018). It would also be informative to investigate heritage Dutch in contact with a language such as Greek where neuter gender is the default gender. We know from language acquisition studies that Dutch-Greek bilingual children have a preference for the neuter gender (Egger, Hulk, and Tsimpli 2018), and we know from first language acquisition studies that semantic features play a role in the robustness of neuter gender.

Language usage patterns and levels of stability

The effect of language use patterns on the development of the heritage languages is described by Daan (1987: 103), among others, who writes about situations of triglossia where Frisian is spoken at home, Dutch in church and in the heritage community, and English in the wider community. The Dutch dialects have changed considerably due to use in the heritage community as a result of convergence with other dialects whereas Frisian, which is only used in the home context, is much more stable. Network ties also affect the language contact outcome.

Both Schmid (2011) and Moro (2018) show that the heritage language speakers in their respective samples who are most innovative, namely those who show the most contact-induced innovations, are speakers who use both the heritage and majority language in the same context(s) and with the same people. Under these circumstances, both languages are activated in the brain. By making the languages more similar to one another, the processing load of switching is reduced. It is also interesting to note that highly innovative speakers are often fluent speakers, as evidenced, for example, by their high rate of words per minute (Moro 2018). Unlike what is sometimes assumed in second language literature, deviations from the norm do not necessarily correlate with a lack in fluency. Frequent use makes speakers fluent; co-activation causes contact-induced innovations. Speakers who do not use their heritage language frequently tend to be closer to the homeland language norm but are sometimes also less fluent.

Longitudinal corpora and the lifespan perspective

Schoenmakers-Klein Gunnewiek (1997) and Klatter-Folmer (1997) have corpora of letters written over substantial timespans. These and possibly other letters can provide insight into the stability and change over a speaker's lifetime. Sanz-Sánchez (2024) shows the relevance of a lifespan perspective on contact-induced change. Longitudinal data can inform us about what parts of the language remain stable across the lifespan, what parts of the language fluctuate, and what parts of the language are stable with respect to an innovation once it has been introduced. Openness to innovation is also affected by the people we speak to, and different stages in life can yield a different network of speech partners among speakers of heritage languages. The younger we are, the more likely exchanges in the heritage language take place with (grand) parents and other people from older generations, and the older we get, the more likely it becomes that our speech partners are younger and more open to innovation. After retirement, exchanges with colleagues might decrease, and exchanges with family members, friends, and neighbors might increase.

Social networks, settlement patterns and horizontal versus vertical patterns of interaction

Of the studies we examined, some heritage speakers are part of a community of Dutch speakers whereas others do not have the support of a Dutch-speaking community. Language maintenance is more likely if a Dutch speech community exists, but even if the smaller community consists of many fellow heritage speakers, language maintenance is not a given. Brown and Salmons (2022: 18) propose the following hypothesis: "If communities give up horizontal patterns in favor of vertical ones, shift follows"; the notion of horizontal and vertical patterns comes from the sociologist Warren (1978), who distinguishes two key patterns of interactions within communities, namely horizontal interactions, which concern the relationships that local units share with each other on the local level, and vertical interactions, which concern the relationships through which local units are oriented to the larger society beyond the community. When heritage Dutch was still used in newspapers, schools and churches and when speakers all had jobs in their community, the possibilities for using Dutch were extensive. By upscaling the publication of newspapers to a larger public and by looking for jobs outside the community, the heritage language was less likely to be used. Less use means less activation of the language, potentially leading to retrieval problems and the loss of less frequently used patterns. Future research could investigate domains of use of the heritage languages from newspapers, jobs, church sermons, social activities like dancing and playing cards to social media. Note that van der Sijs and Doreleijers (2019) show that Dutch migrants in the 21st century maintain Dutch more than the Dutch migrants from the 20th century that we have presented. In an online survey among 7,000 Dutch migrants in 130 countries outside the Netherlands, they found that 97% of their participants speak Dutch weekly, and of those, 64.6% use the language more than eight hours a week, especially at home and on social media. Almost all participants (97%) also read Dutch newspapers online.

For the older Dutch heritage communities, both Daan (1987) and Crombez (forthcoming) show how usage patterns vary across different religious communities. Apart from the fact that communities attach a different value to home languages, communities also differ with regards to language behavior, for example, the acceptability of using loanwords or mixing languages. Crombez, Vandenbussche, and Vosters (2024) argue that not only the language ideology in the new country but also the ideology in the homeland is an important factor to consider. They investigate "the tumultuous Belgian language history and the crucial opposition between French and Dutch throughout the centuries" (284) and its effects on language choices and language use among Belgians in the USA, building on Kasstan, Auer, and Salmons (2018: 388), who "stress that the prestige of the (heritage) language variety as well as the role of the standard language ideology 'back home' are important to consider" as well as Arnbjörnsdóttir (2015), who finds effects of linguistic purism in the homeland on attitudes towards Icelandic as a heritage language. Crombez, Vandenbussche, and Vosters (2024) also show that language contact can occur before migration. For example, Flemish was already in contact with French in the homeland, and too they show evidence from a diary of a Flemish migrant in the United States who uses both English and French loanwords in his Dutch.

Literacy and schooling in the heritage language

Daan (1987: 132) reports on a participant who was educated as a minister in Grand Rapids in the Dutch language. His Dutch is characterized by Daan (1987: 133) as 'good' by which she means that he uses few loanwords and calques, has no/little grammatical interference and does not switch to another language without notifying the listener about the switch in language behavior. Another factor that shows some connection to language ideology is literacy. Literacy in the heritage language provides access to the norm; it affects how language is processed and in general halts change. Kupisch (2013) finds no significant differences between heritage language users and their monolingual native homeland peers if the heritage speakers are literate and schooled in the heritage language. Future research could investigate the role of literacy in heritage Dutch more systematically.

Length of contact and intergenerational transmission

Much research presented here is based on data produced by first- and second-generation speakers, but Klatter-Folmer (1997) includes interviews with the third generation, and Daan (1987) includes speech by the third and fourth generations. The type of change that occurs in heritage languages is greatly affected by the time depth of the heritage language situation. Intergenerational transmission creates the opportunity for reanalysis and the move from incipient to established change. Backus, Doğruöz, and Heine (2011) show how forms of contact-induced change such as the use of the numeral *one* as a proxy for an indefinite article in contact languages expands to more linguistic contexts over time. Weerman (2002) shows how the acquisitional patterns of one generation can feed new patterns in the next generation. The interaction of strategies of different types of learners across generations is referred to as a *cascade effect* by DeGraff (2009) and Aboh (2015), comparing stages in language transmission to a waterfall, where changes to the input enacted by one generation triggers changes in how that input is processed and acquired by younger learners. If the heritage community supports both horizontal (interacting in the heritage language with peers) and vertical transmission (interacting in the heritage language with different generations), the likelihood of crosslinguistic influence and divergence becomes higher.

Circles of homeland identification

Which individual is considered to share linguistic, cultural and geographic ancestry with another is situation dependent. Speakers who might not identify as having similar backgrounds in the home country might identify as having similar backgrounds in the land of migration because of more closeness to each other than to the people in the land of migration. Daan (1987) already shows that speakers from different dialect backgrounds formed new communities with a new heritage language variant that showed convergence between different dialects of Dutch. dentifying as being linguistically, culturally and geographically similar can also transcend national boundaries. Crombez (forthcoming) shows evidence for the rise of a merged low countries identity in Catholic Dutch and Flemish migrants in the Midwest of the United States. She describes the newspaper *De Volksstem* from DePere, Wisconsin, which had both Flemish and Dutch Catholics as its targeted readers. She shows that plays were held in Dutch for both Flemish and Dutch migrants in Chicago, and she adds that both groups of migrants refer to fellow migrants as *taalgenoten* 'language companions', suggesting a shared Low Countries identity among Flemish and Dutch migrants. We did not find evidence for convergence with languages related to Dutch such as (Low) German, but that linguistic boundaries can be fluid is exemplified by the way immigrants from different Scandinavian countries interact with each other (Kinn, Hjelde, and Lund Stokka, forthcoming), which has yielded a pan-Scandinavian heritage language use that transcends national borders. Kinn and Lund Stokka (personal communication) shared quotes from their transcribed corpus of heritage Norwegian in Argentina that illustrate language mixing beyond national boundaries. In (11), the speaker refers to his language as Svorsk, a blend of Swedish and Norwegian, and in (12), the participant refers to their language as 'home-baked Scandinivian'.

(11) *Men det ble til slutt en som jeg sier til mine arbeidskamerater det ble*
but it became to end a like I say to my colleagues it became
ikke norsk # det ble svorsk
not Norwegian # it became Svorsk
'But it became, in the end, like I say to my colleagues, it did not become Norwegian, it became Svorsk.'

(12) *jeg sier alltid at det var # et hjemmebakt skandinavisk språk for det var*
I say always that it was # a home-baked Scandinavian language for it was
jo mor med norsk og far med dansk
MOD.PART mother with Norwegian and father with Danish
'I always say that it was a home-baked Scandinavian language, because we had a mother who spoke Norwegian and a father who spoke Danish'

6. Conclusion

This chapter defined heritage languages as immigrant languages that are connected to the place of origin of the ancestors of the immigrants and that are not the main and/or official language of the wider community where the immigrants moved. It is assumed that most speakers acquire the language naturalistically at a young age, though this may not always be the case, and that heritage languages are used alongside the majority language of the new country. The two main effects of contact that we find are reduction due to lack of input and crosslinguistic influence from the majority language. Most speakers described are first- and second-generation speakers. Only Daan (1987) and Smits and van Marle (1997) include third- and fourth-generation speakers. Klatter-Folmer (1997) interviewed third-generation participants, but because of their young age, they were not able to complete the language tasks (letter writing and language tests). Other studies did not mention third- or fourth-generation speakers, but their absence is in line with the idea that Dutch speakers tend to shift to the majority language easily. If Dutch is maintained in speakers who migrated before the 21st century, this is often for religious reasons. Note, however, that van der Sijs and Doreleijers (2019) find more language maintenance in migrants from the 21st century, who read Dutch newspapers online and use social media. It would be interesting to see intergenerational transmission in these new migrants.

The study of heritage languages also offers ways to examine social practices and social contacts. In trilingual speakers, one can investigate the semantic domains a speaker borrows and from which language. We also reported on circles of identity: who belongs and does not belong to the in-group changes after migration. For example, we presented Daan (1987), who described people from different dialect backgrounds coming together and linguistically converging, and Crombez (forthcoming), who describes how Flemish and Dutch Catholics see themselves as one group.

The central question in this chapter was to identify the features of Dutch that are more stable and therefore more resistant to change and those that are more vulnerable to change as a result of the effects of reduced input and/or crosslinguistic influence. A feature that is quite robust, for example, is the common gender definite article *de*, which is retained in all variants of heritage Dutch, whereas the neuter definite article *het* seems more susceptible to loss. However, note that Klatter-Folmer (1997) reports on the overgeneralization of neuter *het* in second-generation speakers in addition to overgeneralization of common gender *de*. Raidt (1997) reports on the overgeneralization of the common article *de* as well as the neuter demonstrative *dit*. In Anglophone contexts, the overgeneralization of common gender *de* and of the neuter demonstrative *dit* could be influenced by the phonetic similarity to the English words *the* and *this*, respectively. Overgeneralization of the neuter *het*, on the other hand, could also be a form of hypercorrection – it would be interesting to see if such hypercorrections can be transmitted to a new generation and if so, how neuter gender is conditioned as one could imagine formal and semantic factors playing a role. Lastly, it would be interesting to observe heritage Dutch in a context where the majority language encodes gender very transparently, such as Greek; acquisition studies on bilingual children suggest a more robust use of gender in these situations.

If we look at stability and variation in the domain of word order, it seems like the subject-verb-object (SVO) order is robust: it is reported for all variants of heritage Dutch observed. Note, however, that this order is not only very frequent in Dutch but also the most frequent order in the majority languages, which could reinforce the robustness of this word order pattern, and it would be interesting to observe what happens with this order in contact with a majority language that does not itself exhibit this order. Subject-verb inversion and object-verb orders seem quite vulnerable word order patterns despite their robustness in homeland Dutch; language acquisition studies show that child learners of homeland Dutch start with root infinitives with OV order and later exhibit a period where they overgeneralize semantically empty verbs in second position. Though such overuse of dummy auxiliaries to maintain V2 order is grammatical, it would be interesting to test whether some heritage speakers make use of and maintain this strategy. If this were the case, one would expect their occurrence to be more frequent than in homeland Dutch. Such structure preservering changes are less noticeable and require larger amounts of data to be identified.

Within the domain of phonology, we looked at the reduction of word-final consonant clusters and a shift in stress patterns, which are reported more than loss of changes in vowel length. Only the speakers of heritage Dutch in Canada, who more often acquire Dutch in a heritage school than at home, and one speaker of heritage Dutch in Indonesia seem to be less sensitive to vowel length differences.

Inflectional morphology has received much attention in the study of heritage Dutch. The distinction between inflected and uninflected attributive adjectives is vulnerable in all variants. Overgeneralization of the second and third person singular *-t* marker to first person singular and overgeneralization of the first person bare form to second and third person are likewise observed relatively frequently. The plural and infinitival *-en* marker is less often dropped but still vulnerable. In nominal plural marking, instances of overgeneralizing the suffix *-s* to *-en* contexts have been reported. Information on derivational morphology is scarce and an interesting avenue for future research. The only reported difference between homeland and heritage Dutch comes from the speaker of heritage Dutch in Indonesia who had one instance of using a noun in the position of a verb.

In the domain of semantics, a vulnerable feature is the distinction between the perfective auxiliaries *hebben* 'to have' and *zijn* 'to be', the use of which is determined by the semantics of the lexical verb. Many variants of heritage Dutch show the loss of the perfect auxiliary *zijn* 'to be' at the expense of *hebben* 'to have'. This is in line with the English, Afrikaans, and Portuguese verbal systems, which could suggest crosslinguistic influence, but loss of subtle semantic distinctions is also expected in the case of reduced input. The overgeneralization of *hebben* 'to have' for the perfect reported for heritage Dutch in Indonesia, where this change cannot be attributed to the majority language, supports the hypothesis that reduced input is an important factor in the loss of this distinction. We also observed evidence for Schoenmakers-Klein Gunnewiek's (1997) conceptualization hypothesis, meaning that heritage speakers conceptualize an event via the majority language. We also saw that collocations are affected by the majority language and if a word from Dutch and the majority language are similar in form, the Dutch word can take on the meaning from the majority language.

This chapter focused on linguistic variation and stability and discussed generic effects versus the specific effects of crosslinguistic influence. Muysken (2013) shows that knowing which two languages are in contact is not enough to explain the outcome of language contact; factors such as the time depth of the contact situation and community norms also affect the outcome of the heritage scenario. We relied on existing studies, each of which had its own focus and used its own methods. Studying different variants of heritage Dutch with the same set of linguistic and sociolinguistic research methods would enhance our insights into what conditions affect the (non-)occurrence of a certain linguistic feature. Triangulation of methods would also help to gain a better insight in how types of outcomes relate to one another (cf van Osch et al. 2018).

Such an exercise would be greatly helped by a digitally available corpus of variants of heritage Dutch (cf van der Sijs 2014). We looked at factors affecting the scenario, and we hope the overview of factors in the scenario alongside the overview of linguistic features will open avenues to investigate stability and change in heritage Dutch.

References

doi Aalberse, Suzanne, Ad Backus, and Pieter Muysken. 2019. *Heritage Languages: A Language Contact Approach*. Amsterdam; Philadelphia: John Benjamins Publishing Company.

doi Aboh, Enoch Oladé. 2015. *The Emergence of Hybrid Grammars: Language Contact and Change*. Cambridge: Cambridge University Press.

Ammerlaan, Tom. 1997. "“Corrosion” or ‘Loss’ of Immigrant Dutch in Australia: An Experiment on First Language Attrition." In Klatter-Folmer and Kroon 1997, 69–97.

doi Arnbjörnsdóttir, Birna. 2015. "Reexamining Icelandic as a Heritage Language in North America." In *Germanic Heritage Languages in North America: Acquisition, Attrition and Change*, edited by Janne Bondi Johannessen and Joseph C. Salmons, 72–93. Amsterdam: John Benjamins Publishing Company.

Audring, Jenny. 2009. "Reinventing Pronoun Gender." PhD dissertation, Amsterdam: Vrije Universiteit Amsterdam. https://www.lotpublications.nl/reinventing-pronoun-gender-reinventing-pronoun-gender.

doi Backus, Ad, A. Seza Doğruöz, and Bernd Heine. 2011. "Salient Stages in Contact-Induced Grammatical Change: Evidence from Synchronic vs. Diachronic Contact Situations." *Language Sciences* 33 (5): 738–52.

doi Bao, Zhiming. 2010. "A Usage-Based Approach to Substratum Transfer: The Case of Four Unproductive Features in Singapore English." *Language* 86 (4): 792–820. https://www.jstor.org/stable/40961718.

doi Blom, Elma, and Siebe de Korte. 2011. "Dummy Auxiliaries in Child and Adult Second Language Acquisition of Dutch." *Lingua* 121 (5): 906–19.

doi Blom, Elma, Daniela Polišenská, and Fred Weerman. 2008. "Articles, Adjectives and Age of Onset: The Acquisition of Dutch Grammatical Gender." *Second Language Research* 24 (3): 297–331.

doi Bot, Kees de, and Michael Clyne. 1989. "Language Reversion Revisited." *Studies in Second Language Acquisition* 11 (2): 167–77.

Broeze, E. 1988. "The Condition of the Netherlands 1940–1979." In *The Australian People: An Encyclopedia of the Nation, Its People and Their Origins*, edited by James Jupp, 354. Angus & Robertson Publishers.

doi Brown, Joshua R., and Joseph Salmons. 2022. "A Verticalization Theory of Language Shift." In *The Verticalization Model of Language Shift: The Great Change in American Communities*, edited by Joshua R. Brown, 1–24. Oxford University Press.

doi Carreira, Maria. 2004. "Seeking Explanatory Adequacy: A Dual Approach to Understanding the Term Heritage Language Learner." *Heritage Language Journal* 2 (1): 1–25.

doi Clahsen, Harald, and Pieter Muysken. 1986. "The Availability of Universal Grammar to Adult and Child Learners – a Study of the Acquisition of German Word Order." *Interlanguage Studies Bulletin (Utrecht)* 2 (2): 93–119.

Clyne, Michael. 1977. "Nieuw Hollands or Double Dutch." *Dutch Studies* 3:1–30.

doi Clyne, Michael. 1991. *Community Languages: The Australian Experience.* Cambridge University Press.

Clyne, Michael, and Anne Pauwels. 1997. "Use, Maintenance, Structures and Future of Dutch in Australia." In Klatter-Folmer and Kroon 1997, 33–51.

doi Coetsem, Frans van. 1988. *Loan Phonology and the Two Transfer Types in Language Contact.* Dordrecht: Foris Publications.

Cornips, Leonie, Aafke Hulk, Claasje Reijers, and Paz Gonzalez. 2012. "When Semantics Meets Morpho-Syntax: The Role of Count/Mass Feature in Acquiring *Het* as Definite Determiner in Monolingual and Bilingual Dutch." *Estudios Lingüísticos/Linguistic Studies* 6/7:75–89.

Crombez, Yasmin. Forthcoming. "Van Het Beloofde Land: Een Historisch Sociolinguïstisch Onderzoek Naar Het Vlaams Als Heritage Taal." PhD dissertation, Brussel: Vrije Universiteit Brussel.

doi Crombez, Yasmin, Wim Vandenbussche, and Rik Vosters. 2024. "Exploring Past and Present Layers of Multilingualism in Flemish-Emigrant Writing." In *Investigating West Germanic Languages: Studies in Honor of Robert B. Howell*, edited by Jennifer Hendriks and B. Richard Page, 276–300. John Benjamins Publishing Company.

Cummins, Jim. 2005. "A Proposal for Action: Strategies for Recognizing Heritage Language Competence as a Learning Resource within the Mainstream Classroom." *The Modern Language Journal* 89 (4): 585–92. https://www.jstor.org/stable/3588628.

Daan, Jo. 1987. *Ik was te bissie... Nederlanders en hun taal in de Verenigde Staten.* Zutphen: De Walburg Pres.

Daan, Jo. 1997. "Dutch in the United States of America." In Klatter-Folmer and Kroon 1997, 283–302.

doi DeGraff, Michel. 2009. "Language Acquisition in Creolization and, Thus, Language Change: Some Cartesian- Uniformitarian Boundary Conditions." *Language and Linguistics Compass* 3 (4): 888–971.

doi Doreleijers, Kristel, Khalid Mourigh, and Jos Swanenberg. 2023. "Negotiating Local In-Group Norms in Times of Globalization. Adnominal Gender Variation in Two Urban Youth Varieties in the Netherlands." *Globe: A Journal of Language, Culture and Communication* 15 (October):117–43.

doi Egger, Evelyn, Aafke Hulk, and Ianthi Maria Tsimpli. 2018. "Crosslinguistic Influence in the Discovery of Gender: The Case of Greek – Dutch Bilingual Children." *Bilingualism: Language and Cognition* 21 (4): 694–709.

Elferink, Jan-Willem, and Mari Smits. 1997. "Post-War Migration from the Netherlands." In Klatter-Folmer and Kroon 1997, 25–36.

doi Fishman, Joshua A. 2006. "Three Hundred-Plus Years of Heritage Language Education in the United States." In *Developing Minority Language Resources: The Case of Spanish in California*, edited by Guadalupe Valdés, Joshua A. Fishman, Rebecca Chávez, and William Pérez, 12–23. Buffalo: Multilingual Matters.

Flecken, Monique. 2010. "Event Conceptualization in Language Production of Early Bilinguals." PhD dissertation, Nijmegen: Radboud Universiteit Nijmegen. https://www.lotpublications.nl/event-conceptualization-in-language-production-of-early-bilinguals-event-conceptualization-in-language-production-of-early-bilinguals.

Giesbers, Herman. 1997. "Dutch in Indonesia: Language Attrition or Language Contact?" In Klatter-Folmer and Kroon 1997, 163–80.

doi Hinskens, Frans, Roeland van Hout, Pieter Muysken, and Ariën van Wijngaarden. 2021. "Variation and Change in Grammatical Gender Marking: The Case of Dutch Ethnolects." *Linguistics* 59 (1): 75–100.

doi Kasstan, Jonathan R., Anita Auer, and Joseph Salmons. 2018. "Heritage-Language Speakers: Theoretical and Empirical Challenges on Sociolinguistic Attitudes and Prestige." *International Journal of Bilingualism* 22 (4): 387–94.

doi Kinn, Kari, Arnstein Hjelde, and Marie Lund Stokka. Forthcoming. "The Norwegian Language in Argentina: A First Look at Heritage Norwegian in a New Context." *Bergen Language and Linguistics Studies.*

Klatter-Folmer, Jetske. 1997. "Language Shift and Loss in a Three-Generation Dutch Family in New Zealand." In Klatter-Folmer and Kroon 1997, 195–214.

Klatter-Folmer, Jetske, and Sjaak Kroon, eds. 1997. *Dutch Overseas: Studies in Maintenance and Loss of Dutch as an Immigrant Language.* Tilburg: Tilburg University Press.

Koster, Jan. 1974. "Het Werkwoord Als Spiegelcentrum." *Spektator: Tijdschrift Voor Neerlandistiek* 3:601–18. papers2://publication/uuid/0663E10D-1ED8-447E-AF21-456E3CF197CF.

Kraaikamp, Margot. 2017. "Semantic versus Lexical Gender: Synchronic and Diachronic Variation in Germanic Gender Agreement." PhD dissertation, Amsterdam: Universiteit van Amsterdam. https://www.lotpublications.nl/semantic-versus-lexical-gender.

doi Kühl, Karoline, and Kurt Braunmüller. 2014. "Linguistic Stability and Divergence: An Extended Perspective on Language Contact." In *Stability and Divergence in Language Contact*, edited by Kurt Braunmüller, Steffen Höder, and Karoline Kühl, 13–38. John Benjamins Publishing Company. https://www.jbe-platform.com/content/books/9789027269553-silv.16.02kuh.

doi Kupisch, Tanja. 2013. "A New Term for a Better Distinction? A View from the Higher End of the Proficiency Scale." *Theoretical Linguistics* 39 (3–4): 203–14.

doi Kupisch, Tanja, and Jason Rothman. 2018. "Terminology Matters! Why Difference Is Not Incompleteness and How Early Child Bilinguals Are Heritage Speakers." *International Journal of Bilingualism* 22 (5): 564–82.

Kusters, Christiaan Wouter. 2003. "Linguistic Complexity: The Influence of Social Change on Verbal Inflection." PhD dissertation, Leiden: Universiteit Leiden. https://www.lotpublications.nl/linguistic-complexity-linguistic-complexity

doi Lloyd-Smith, Anika, Marieke Einfeldt, and Tanja Kupisch. 2020. "Italian-German Bilinguals: The Effects of Heritage Language Use on Accent in Early-Acquired Languages." *International Journal of Bilingualism* 24 (2): 289–304.

Marle, Jaap van, and Caroline Smits. 1997. "Deviant Patterns of Lexical Transfer: English-Origin Words in American Dutch." In Klatter-Folmer and Kroon 1997, 255–272.

doi Montrul, Silvina. 2015. *The Acquisition of Heritage Languages*. Cambridge: Cambridge University Press.

doi Moro, Francesca R. 2018. "Divergence in Heritage Ambon Malay in the Netherlands: The Role of Social-Psychological Factors." *International Journal of Bilingualism* 22 (4): 395–411.

doi Muysken, Pieter. 2013. "Language Contact Outcomes as the Result of Bilingual Optimization Strategies." *Bilingualism: Language and Cognition* 16 (4): 709–30.

doi Osch, Brechje van, Aafke Hulk, Suzanne Aalberse, and Petra Sleeman. 2018. "Implicit and Explicit Knowledge of a Multiple Interface Phenomenon: Differential Task Effects in Heritage Speakers and L2 Speakers of Spanish in The Netherlands." *Languages* 3 (3): 25.

doi Pires, Acrisio, and Jason Rothman. 2009. "Disentangling Sources of Incomplete Acquisition: An Explanation for Competence Divergence across Heritage Grammars." *International Journal of Bilingualism* 13 (2): 211–38.

doi Polinsky, Maria. 2011. "Reanalysis in Adult Heritage Language: New Evidence in Support of Attrition." *Studies in Second Language Acquisition* 33 (2): 305–28.

doi Polinsky, Maria. 2018. *Heritage Languages and Their Speakers*. Cambridge University Press.

doi Polinsky, Maria, and Olga Kagan. 2007. "Heritage Languages: In the 'Wild' and in the Classroom." *Language and Linguistics Compass* 1 (5): 368–95.

doi Polinsky, Maria, and Gregory Scontras. 2020. "Understanding Heritage Languages." *Bilingualism: Language and Cognition* 23 (1): 4–20.

Polišenská, Daniela. 2010. "Dutch Children's Acquisition of Verbal and Adjectival Inflection." PhD dissertation, Amsterdam: Universiteit van Amsterdam. https://www.lotpublications.nl/Documents/247_fulltext.pdf.

Raidt, Edith H. 1997. "Interference, Shift and Loss of Dutch in South Africa." In Klatter-Folmer and Kroon 1997, 99–119.

doi Rosenberg, Peter. 2005. "Dialect Convergence in the German Language Islands (*Sprachinseln*)." In *Dialect Change*, edited by Peter Auer, Frans Hinskens, and Paul Kerswill, 221–35. Cambridge: Cambridge University Press.

doi Rothman, Jason. 2009. "Understanding the Nature and Outcomes of Early Bilingualism: Romance Languages as Heritage Languages." *International Journal of Bilingualism* 13 (2): 155–63.

doi Sanz-Sánchez, Israel. 2024. "Language Acquisition across the Lifespan in Historical Sociolinguistics." In *Lifespan Acquisition and Language Change: Historical Sociolinguistic Perspectives*, edited by Israel Sanz-Sánchez, 2–42. Amsterdam: John Benjamins Publishing Company.

doi Schmid, Monika S. 2011. "Contact x Time: External Factors and Variability in L1 Attrition." In *Modeling Bilingualism: From Structure to Chaos. In Honor of Kees de Bot*, edited by Monika S. Schmid and Wander Lowie, 155–76. Amsterdam: John Benjamins Publishing Company.

Schoenmakers-Klein Gunnewiek, Marian. 1997. "Dutch Language Loss in Brazil and the Conceptual Hypothesis." In Klatter-Folmer and Kroon 1997, 99–119.

doi Siemund, Peter. 2018. "Modeling World Englishes from a Cross-Linguistic Perspective." In *Varieties of English Around the World*, edited by Sandra C. Deshors, 133–62. Amsterdam: John Benjamins Publishing Company.

doi Sijs, Nicoline van der. 2009. *Yankees, Cookies En Dollars: De Invloed van Het Nederlands Op de Noord-Amerikaanse Talen*. Amsterdam: Amsterdam University Press.

doi Sijs, Nicoline van der. 2014. "Systematisch onderzoek naar Nederlandse contactvariëteiten." *Taal en Tongval* 66 (2): 117–42.

Sijs, Nicoline van der, and Kristel Doreleijers. 2019. "Onderzoeksrapport vertrokken Nederlands: Pilotonderzoek naar de Nederlandse taal en cultuur in den vreemde." Koninklijke Nederlandse Akademie van Wetenschappen. https://pure.knaw.nl/ws/portalfiles/portal/12175008/Onderzoeksrapport_Vertrokken_Nederlands_complete_tekst.pdf.

doi Smits, Caroline, and Jaap van Marle. 2015. "On the Decrease of Language Norms in a Disintegrating Language." In *Germanic Heritage Languages in North America: Acquisition, Attrition and Change*, edited by Janne Bondi Johannessen and Joseph C. Salmons, 389–405. Amsterdam: John Benjamins Publishing Company.

Swierenga, Robert P. 1993. "The Delayed Transition from Folk to Labor Migration: The Netherlands, 1880–1920." *International Migration Review* 27 (2): 406–24. https://heinonline.org/HOL/P?h=hein.journals/imgratv27&i=788.

Thomason, Sarah Grey. 2001. *Language Contact: An Introduction*. Edinburgh: Edinburgh University Press.

doi Thomason, Sarah Grey, and Terrence Kaufman. 1988. *Language Contact, Creolization, and Genetic Linguistics*. Berkeley: University of California Press.

Trudgill, Peter. 2011. *Sociolinguistic Typology: Social Determinants of Linguistic Complexity*. Oxford: Oxford University Press.

doi Tyler, Andrea, and William Nagy. 1989. "The Acquisition of English Derivational Morphology." *Journal of Memory and Language* 28 (6): 649–67. https://www.proquest.com/scholarly-journals/acquisition-english-derivational-morphology/docview/1297341171/se-2?accountid=14615.

Valdés, Guadalupe. 2000. *Spanish for Native Speakers: AATSP Professional Development Series. Handbook for Teachers K-16 (Vol. 1)*. Fort Worth, TX: Harcourt College Publishers.

Van Deusen-Scholl, Nelleke. 2003. "Toward a Definition of Heritage Language: Sociopolitical and Pedagogical Considerations." *Journal of Language, Identity & Education* 2 (3): 211–30.

Vermeer, Anne. 1997. "Language Maintenance and the Dutch Heritage School in Ottawa." In Klatter-Folmer and Kroon 1997, 139–51.

Warren, Roland Leslie. 1978. *The Community in America*. 3 rev. Chicago: Rand McNally College Publishing Company.

Weerman, Fred. 2002. *Dynamiek in Taal En de Explosie van de Neerlandistiek*. Amsterdam: Vossiuspers UvA.

CHAPTER 17

"O this is Eden!"

Dutch overseas animal names

Nicoline van der Sijs
Institute for the Dutch Language, Leiden

When the Dutch migrated to continents outside of Europe in the 17th century, they encountered entirely new habitats. Confronted with the new flora and fauna, they faced the task of assigning names. They had three options: adopt the native name, coin a new Dutch name, or transfer an existing Dutch name of a similar animal or plant to the native species. This chapter aims to describe the Dutch names given to native animal species on overseas continents. The focus is on how the Dutch language was adapted and utilized in these new environments; therefore names borrowed from native languages are excluded. The objective of this chapter is to identify differences in naming practices and in the quantity of newly-coined Dutch names across continents, and to provide explanations for these variations. Despite differences between the continents, it turns out that in the past there existed a special variety of 'overseas Dutch'.[1]

Keywords: Dutch morphology, Dutch animal names, migration, historical sociolinguistics

1. Introduction

"O this is Eden!," wrote the Dutch poet Jacob Steendam in 1661 in his hymn *'t Lof van Nuw-Nederland* ("In Praise of New Netherland"). Steendam lived in New Amsterdam (current New York) from 1650 until 1661 and is considered to be the first American poet. He describes the new country as 'a land of milk and honey'. In a famous short poem in 1662 he adds:

> The birds obscure the sky, so numerous in their flight;
> The animals roam wild, and flatten down the ground;
> The fish swarm in the waters and exclude the light;

1. I would like to thank Gertjan Postma for his useful remarks.

https://doi.org/10.1075/impact.55.17van

> The oysters there, than which none better can be found;
> Are piled up, heap on heap, till islands they attain;
> And vegetation clothes the forest, mean and plain.[2]

Like Adam in paradise, the Dutch in America were faced with a natural environment for which they lacked words. At first, they tried to refer to animals and plants using words from their native tongue. In this way, Adriaen van der Donck described the American animals in his *Beschryvinge van Nieuvv-Nederlant* (Description of New Netherland), published in 1655. For instance, when he relates that the waters and rivers are rich in fish, he uses Dutch fish names for these, such as *steur, salm, carper, baers, snoeck, forellen, vooren, bot, ael* and *paling* (sturgeon, salmon, carp, perch, pike, trout, rock-bass, flounder, eel and elver).

However, with this approach, the Dutch could not distinguish between the European and American species. Therefore, after a while, they started assigning new names to the American species. The same happened on other continents, for instance in South Africa. Scholz (1974: 15) points out that Jodocus Hondius in his *Klare besgryving van Cabo De Bona Esperanca* ('Clear description of the Cape of Good Hope'), published in 1652, used the Dutch names *lepelaars, meerkoeten, rotganzen, scholvers, slobben* and *talingen* (spoonbills, coots, brent geese, cormorants, shovelers and teals) to describe the South African water birds. Most of these names were in time replaced by more distinctive names. How this was done is the subject of this chapter.

The Dutch voyages, settlements, and language contacts outside Europe have been described already in Chapter 1 of this book, together with an overview of the Dutch words adopted by other languages and vice versa. This chapter concerns the naming practices of the Dutch, concentrating on the animal world they encountered on the four continents, or parts of continents, where they settled: Indonesia, North America, South America and the Caribbean, and (South) Africa. In Section 2, I describe the language data collection process, detailing the relevant languages and sources from which material was obtained (2.1) and elucidating the methodology employed for data collection (2.2). In Section 3, I present the language data, and I bring forward an explanation for the differences in naming practices between the continents. Finally, in Section 4 I provide some concluding remarks.

---

2. In Dutch: "'t Gevoogelt doofd de lucht, wanneer se sich vervoeren. / Het wild-gedierte kneust, en plet de vaste grond, / De Visschen, krielen in de wat'ren: en beroeren / Diens klaerheyd: d'oesters (die men nergens beter vond) / Verheffen hoop op hoop, en maken menigh Eyland: / 't Gewas vercierd het bosch: en bou, en hoy, en Wey-land." See Funk 1992 for the text and for background information.

2. The language data

When the Dutch settled on overseas continents, they came into contact with new languages, and exchanged loanwords. Moreover, overseas Dutch developed separately from the Dutch of the Low Countries, and even gave rise to new creole languages based on Dutch. In Section 2.1, I provide background information on the language contacts and developments of the Dutch language on the overseas continents, along with the sources available to us. In Section 2.2, I explain how the overseas animal names were selected from the available sources.

2.1 The Dutch language on overseas continents

In 1596, the first Dutch ship arrived on Java, marking the beginning of Dutch expansion into the Indonesian Archipelago. The Dutch East India Company (VOC) was founded in 1602 for trade with Asia, especially Indonesia, where varieties of Malay were spoken. The VOC era lasted until about 1800, followed by the colonial period until 1949, when Indonesia gained independence. The Constitution Act established Malay under the name Bahasa Indonesia ('Indonesian language') as the national language of the Republic of Indonesia. During the colonial period, the number of Dutch settlers increased in Indonesia, leading to more intensive language contacts with the locals. This period saw the emergence of Indo-Dutch, a variety of Dutch influenced by Malay. The Indo-Dutch lexicon is described in Mingaars et al. 2005. For this chapter, I collected relevant animal names borrowed from Dutch by Malay (based on Van der Sijs 2010) and from Indo-Dutch (based on Mingaars et al. 2005 and Van Dale 2022).

In 1609, the first settlers from the Low Countries landed on the American east coast, where they founded a Dutch province they called New Netherland. By 1664, the colony was taken over by the English, and English became the main language. The Dutch settlement, however, retained the Dutch language well into the nineteenth century. Here, Dutch developed into a distinct variety known as *Laag Duits* or *Low Dutch* (described in Van der Sijs 2009). Unfortunately, concrete information about this variety is limited, and no Dutch names for native animal species have been passed down to us. Nevertheless, some original Dutch names have survived in American English (collected in Van der Sijs 2009), which are used in this chapter.

In 1634, the Dutch West India Company took control of the Dutch Antilles, including Aruba, Bonaire, Curaçao, Sint-Maarten, Sint Eustatius, and Saba. These islands had previously been conquered by Spain in 1499, giving rise to the creole language Papiamentu. In 1667, the Dutch also took over Suriname from the English, who had settled there before them. During English rule, the English-based creole language Sranan Tongo (literally 'Suriname tongue') had developed. Both the Dutch Antilles and Suriname became colonies of the Netherlands around 1800, with Dutch as the official language in administration and education. In Suriname and the Netherlands Antilles, Dutch evolved into separate varieties known as Surinamese Dutch and Antillean Dutch, respectively. Surinamese Dutch is well established and documented, while Antillean Dutch is less commonly used, as Papiamentu is the dominant language of the Dutch Antilles. For this chapter, I collected relevant animal names borrowed from Dutch into Sranan Tongo and Papiamentu (based on Van der Sijs 2010), as well as animal names in Surinamese Dutch (from Van Donselaar 1989, 1994, 1995–1999, 2000, 2013) and Antillean Dutch (from Joubert and Van der Sijs 2020).

Between 1591 and 1625, the Dutch established a colony in the Essequibo region (then called Iskepe), in modern-day Guyana. Here a Dutch creole language, Skepi Dutch, emerged as a lingua franca among Dutch, native peoples, and enslaved Africans. The colony was briefly taken over by the English in the seventeenth century. In 1627, another Dutch colony was founded along the Berbice River, giving rise to the creole language Berbice Dutch. In the eighteenth century, the Dutch also established plantations along the nearby Demerara River. In 1796, the British took control of Essequibo, Demerara, and Berbice, which were officially ceded to them in 1814 and merged into British Guyana in 1831. Both Berbice Dutch and Skepi Dutch have been considered extinct since circa 2000. For this chapter, I collected the Berbice and Skepi Dutch animal names (from Jacobs & Parkvall 2020, Kouwenberg 1993, Robertson 1983, 1989, 1994, and Van der Sijs 2010).

Another extinct Dutch creole developed on the US Virgin Islands, where Dutch and Flemish colonists settled around 1665. These islands were never Dutch. Between 1672 and 1733 they were taken over by the Danish West India Company. At that time, a few hundred Dutch, English and Danish planters already lived there; the number of enslaved people would not have been much more. When the Danes appropriated the islands, a rudimentary form of a Dutch-based creole was spoken, now called Virgin Islands Dutch Creole. Dutch planters and enslaved people probably brought the language with them from the island of Sint Eustatius, one of the Dutch Antilles. Until the end of the eighteenth century, Virgin Islands Dutch Creole was the most important language on the Virgin Islands. From 1730 onwards, Moravian (German) missionaries christianized the population of the islands, and translated numerous religious texts into Virgin Islands Dutch Creole. Consequently, from this language many more texts have been handed down to us than from Berbice Dutch and Skepi Dutch.[3] During the nineteenth century many switched from Virgin Islands Dutch Creole to the Eng-

3. Virgin Islands Dutch Creole texts are collected in Van Rossem & Van der Voort 1996.

lish creole language that had emerged on the islands: Virgin Islands Creole English (see Bøegh & Bakker 2021). In 1917, the Danes sold the islands to the United States. Virgin Islands Dutch Creole became extinct in 1987. For this chapter, I gathered the Virgin Islands Dutch Creole animal names from Van Rossem 2017, 2021, Van Sluijs 2017, and Van der Sijs 2010.

Lastly, on the African continent, the Dutch established a victualling station in South Africa in 1652, which developed into a permanent settlement. The Dutch Cape colony was occupied by the British in 1795 and ultimately passed into British hands in 1814. Until then, Dutch was the official language. Even after the British takeover, Dutch continued to be used. Under the influence of local languages, Dutch developed into *Afrikaans*, a daughter language of Dutch that was recognized as a distinct language by the South African government in 1925. Afrikaans and English were declared official languages in 1961, with nine Bantu languages added in 1994. In South African English, many words are borrowed from Afrikaans or Dutch. These were used for this chapter (based on Silva 1996; Van der Sijs 2010).[4]

To summarize, for North America and Africa I relied on Dutch animal names that were borrowed in the two English varieties spoken there, American English and South African English. For Indonesia, and South America and the Caribbean, two different sources were available: on the one hand Dutch loanwords in the main languages of the area (Malay, Sranan Tongo, and Papiamentu), and on the other hand animal names found in Dutch varieties (Indo-Dutch, Surinamese Dutch, Antillean Dutch, and the three creole languages based on Dutch: Virgin Islands Dutch Creole, Berbice Dutch, and Skepi Dutch). This means I was able to collect animal names from eleven languages on four continents.

2.2 Methodology of data collection

The aim of this chapter is to chart how the Dutch language adapted to new overseas habitats by exploring how names were assigned to unfamiliar animal species. Therefore, only names for animal species that do not occur in the Low Countries are relevant.

This criterion automatically excludes the names for animals that the Dutch brought with them to the overseas territories, often along with the animals themselves. Especially in the three Dutch-based creole languages a number of animal

4. Afrikaans is only included in this chapter through Dutch/Afrikaans loanwords found in South African English: since Dutch developed naturally into Afrikaans, the number of Dutch animal names in Afrikaans was too extensive to include them here. A historical overview of animal and plant names used in South Africa up to 1845 is provided in Scholtz 1974.

names occur that were ruled out because they denoted a species native to the Low Countries instead of an indigenous species new to the Dutch, such as *hond* (dog), *hoen* (chicken), *koe* (cow), *rat* (rat), *schaap* (sheep), and *varken* (pig). For the same reason, Dutch loanwords in Sranan Tongo, Papiamentu or Indonesian designating animal species that were imported by the Dutch, were excluded, such as *bok* (goat), *herder* (sheepdog), *kalkoen* (turkey), *konijn* (rabbit), *marmot*, *poes* (cat), and the names for fish, in salted or dried form, that the Dutch brought with them, such as *sardine* and *ansjovis* (anchovies). Finally, scientific animal names that Dutch contact varieties or regional languages borrowed from Dutch were left out, for instance *antilope, hyena, gorilla, leeuw* (lion), *kameel* (camel), *parkiet* (parakeet), *pelikaan* (pelican), and *salamander*. Most of these words are found in Malay.

If you apply these criteria, something interesting emerges. In some cases, a Dutch name refers in one area to an imported species, while in another area the same name is transferred to a species native to the area. This is the case with *haring* (herring), *konijntje* (rabbit), *kanarie* (canary bird), *kalkoen* (turkey), *kameel* (camel) and *parkiet* (parakeet). Taking the example of *konijn*: Indonesian *kelinci* indicates the species imported from the Low Countries (Oryctolagus cuniculus), while Sranan Tongo *kon(i)koni* and Surinamese Dutch *konijntje* refer to the aguti, and Papiamentu *konènchi* to the eastern cottontail (Sylvilagus floridanus). Virgin Islands Dutch Creole *kameel* and Papiamentu *kamel* refer, just as Dutch *kameel*, to the humpbacked mammal, while with South African English *kameel* or *camel* the giraffe is meant. In Indonesian and Papiamentu *haring* refer to the herring (as a delicacy), while in Suriname it is used for another, larger fish species.

The phenomenon occurs especially in bird names. Indonesian *kenari* and Papiamentu *kanari* refer to the well-known songbird, while Sranan Tongo *kanari* and Surinamese Dutch *kanarie* refer to an indigenous bird species (Tangara). Indonesian *parkit* refers to the parakeet in general, while Surinamese Dutch *parkiet* and Sranan Tongo *prakiki* refer to the brown-throated parakeet (Aratinga Pertinax). Finally, while in Indonesian, Papiamentu and Sranan Tongo the Dutch name *kalkoen* refers to the turkey, in Surinamese Dutch *kalkoen* indicates a black-green forest bird with red spots on the head (Marail), of course resembling a turkey.

At this point a caveat is in order. Sometimes the sources mention that the Dutch name is transferred overseas to a different species than that living in the Low Countries, but they do not mention which species is concerned. There are good reasons for this: the names were often assigned before the development of scientific nomenclature, and the name givers were not biologists and probably unaware of biological specifics of the species. However, this means we often cannot pinpoint what overseas species was meant. Even worse, in some cases the sources give no information on the species at all – this is especially the case for Dutch varieties that are by now extinct. In those cases, I presumed – possibly wrongly – that the name referred to the species of the Low Countries, and I left the name out.

3. Dutch animal names used across continents

In this section, I present the Dutch animal names used in the eleven languages outside Europe for new animal species. In Section 3.1 the data are classified into categories, according to language, wordtype, phyla and word origin, in Section 3.2 those names are listed that occur in multiple languages, and in Section 3.3. these are further analysed.

3.1 Categorization of the overseas Dutch animal names

Table 1 presents the number of Dutch animal names assigned to native animal species in eleven languages across four continents. This concerns a total of 595 names.

Table 1. Number of animal names in eleven languages across the four continents

Continent	Language	Number	Dutch variety	Number	Total
Africa	South African English	116			**116**
Indonesia	Bahasa Indonesia	2	Indo-Dutch	40	**42**
North America	American English	10			**10**
South America & Caribbean	Sranan Tongo	48	Surinamese Dutch	309	**357**
	Papiamentu	32	Antillean Dutch	8	**40**
			Virgin Islands Dutch Creole	20	**20**
			Berbice Dutch	7	**7**
			Skepi Dutch	3	**3**
Total general		**208**		**385**	**595**

The disparity in numbers among the continents and languages is notable; more on this in Section 3.3. It should be noted that this table and the following ones are based on accidentally preserved data, so the numbers would probably have been larger in reality. For instance, little is known about Skepi Dutch.

Some of the 595 names occur in multiple languages (these are given in Section 3.2). Out of these 595 names, 504 are unique, meaning they occur in only one language. Of these unique names, 251 are exclusively found in Surinamese Dutch.[5] This prevalence of Dutch animal names in Surinamese Dutch can be attributed to several factors. In Suriname, Dutch maintains a strong presence, serving as a lingua franca between the different population groups speaking various languages. Moreover (and as a result of this), the vocabulary of Surinamese Dutch has been described in much more detail than that of other Dutch varieties, and this has been done by a biologist (Van Donselaar) who has undoubtedly paid extra attention to the animal world. While this may introduce some bias, it cannot be remedied.

Table 2 categorizes the 504 unique animal names by phyla, with birds ranking highest, twice as much as mammals. Arthropods and fishes follow next, each with roughly equal representation. Apparently birds and mammals were the most noticeable for the Dutch. The Dutch were without doubt impressed by the brightly coloured birds in warmer regions, as witnessed by the fact that many bird names refer to a colour (as in Surinamese Dutch *witbuiklijster* 'white + belly + thrush', *witstaartgoudkeelkolibrie* 'white + tail + golden + troat + hummingbird', and *blauwvleugelvink* 'blue + wing + finch'). In general, names are assigned specifically to conspicuous, useful or harmful animals. This is exemplified by the general Dutch term *rups* (caterpillar), which in South African English specifically denotes a harmful caterpillar species.

5. All modern Sranan Tongo, English and scientific names of birds in Suriname are collected on the website https://www.surinamebirds.nl/php/listsranan.php. Here are mentioned some 60 names in Sranan Tongo that are loaned from Surinamese Dutch or Dutch. I have not included these names in this chapter, because they are recently attributed (from 1994 onwards) by biologists, even to new bird species that have only lately populated Suriname. It is thus not clear to what extent the names reflect the naming practices of the oldest Dutch settlers, and it is also uncertain if these names are actually used by the local population. Therefore, for this chapter only the Sranan Tongo bird names are included that are in general use, as shown by the fact that they are mentioned in Blanker & Dubbeldam 2005 and Stichting Volkslectuur Suriname 1995. Even with this restriction, the number of Dutch names used in Suriname far exceeds that of any other continent.

Table 2. Animal names classified by phylum

Phylum	Number
Birds (B)	216
Mammals (M)	105
Arthropods (A)	71
Fishes (F)	67
Reptiles (R)	36
Molluscs and amphibians (W)	9
Total	504

Table 3 classifies the animal names by word type: base words, compounds, and derivations. The compounds abound. More in Section 3.2.

Table 3. Animal names classified by word type

Word type	Number
Base words	59
Compounds	418
Derivations	27
Total	504

Table 4 classifies the animal names by etymological origin:[6] inherited words (words that are based on a Proto-Germanic word), loanwords, derivations from a proper name, and onomatopoeic words.

Table 4. Animal names classified by etymological origin

Etymological origin	Number
Inherited words	419
Loaned or partly loaned	67
Derived from a proper name	6
Onomatopoeic	6
Onomatopoeic and proper name	6
Total	504

Most animal names are based on an inherited word, such as the bird name *snip* 'snipe' (borrowed in Sranan Tongo and Papiamentu), the derivation *blazer*

6. Based on *Etymologiebank*.

'blower', designating the hog-nosed snake in American English, or the compound *bosmuis* 'bush + mouse', loaned in Sranantongo. Inherited base words are by definition old, and apparently new animal names are preferably derived from or composed with an inherited word. Loanwords are in the minority, and they mainly denote animals that are not native in the Low Countries, such as *flamingo*, used for the red ibis in Suriname. For examples see the following section.

3.2 Dutch animal names found in more than one overseas language

To illustrate which Dutch animal names are used on the four continents, Table 5 lists the 64 animal names found in multiple overseas languages, adding up to 154 overseas names. This selection out of the total 595 names represents all languages, phyla, word types, and origins.[7]

From Table 5, we can draw several conclusions. As to the ***phyla***, a Dutch overseas name always refers to the same phylum, with the exception of the name *roodbekje* ('red + beak'): in Papiamentu, this is the name for a fish, while in South African English, it refers to a bird.

In relation to the word types, combined with word origins, we observe the following. All ***base words*** consist of names that are used both in the Low Countries and overseas, albeit with a different meaning. This shows that these names are transferred to a new species abroad, mostly one that is in some way similar to the home species. For instance, *raaf* (raven) was transferred to a large parrot species (macaw) in Suriname, *vos* (fox) is used in the Caribbean for the forest fox, and *worm* is used in this area in the broad sense of 'invertebrate, caterpillar, maggot'. In the Low Countries, *snoek* (pike) refers to a freshwater fish, while in overseas areas a salt-water fish is denoted, which in South African English was originally called *seesnoek* 'sea pike' (Scholtz 1974: 16).[8]

Sometimes the differences are very striking, especially when it comes to the seven base words that are loanwords in Dutch. For instance, in Suriname *buffel* 'buffalo' (in Dutch a French loanword) is used for a 'tapir', and *flamingo* (in Dutch a Portuguese loanword) for a red ibis. In the Caribbean *baboen* 'baboon' refers to the howler monkey, and *tijger* 'tiger' to a jaguar or cougar. As already stated in 2.2, the names for *kanarie* 'canary' and *parkiet* 'parakeet' are transferred in Suriname to native bird species; in Indonesian and Papiamentu the names refer to the well-known cage birds, so these languages are not mentioned in Table 5.[9]

---

7. Researchers who are interested in all the data can contact me.

8. Interesting examples of transfer that only occur in one language and are therefore not included in Table 5, are European Dutch *kameel* (camel) and *eland* (moose): in South African English these names are used for the giraffe and eland antelope, respectively.

9. The same goes for *haring*, which is not a loaned name, see 2.2.

Table 5. List of the 64 Dutch animal names that are found in more than one overseas language

Dutch name	Word type[a]	Language	Name	Phylum[b]
aardvarken	'earth + pig'	Am English	*groundhog*	M
		SA English	*earth-hog, aardvark*	M
baars	base word	Surinamese Dutch	*baars*	F
		Papiamentu	*bèrs*	F
baboen [c]	base word, loanword	Sranan	*babun*	M
		Surinamese Dutch	*baboen*	M
		VIDC[d]	*babun*	M
blauwdas	'blue + necktie'	Sranan	*blawdas*	B
		Surinamese Dutch	*blauwdas*	B
blauwduif	'blue + dove'	VIDC	*blau difie*	B
		Papiamentu	*buladeifi*	B
blauwvink	'blue + finch'	Sranan	*blawfink*	B
		Surinamese Dutch	*blauwvink*	B
blauwvogeltje	'blue + bird'	Sranan	*blawforki*	B
		Surinamese Dutch	*blauwvogeltje*	B
boktor	'goat + beetle'	Papiamentu	*bakator*	A
		Indonesian	*boktor*	A
boneknaap	'bean + boy'	Papiamentu	*boneknap*	F
		Antillean Dutch	*boneknaap*	F
bosschildpad	'bush + tortoise'	Sranan	*bus'sekrepatu*	R
		Surinamese Dutch	*bosschildpad*	R
botervis	'butter + fish'	Surinamese Dutch	*botervis*	F
		Sranan	*botrofisi*	F
brandhoornvis	'fire + horn + fish'	Papiamentu	*branthorives*	F
		Antillean Dutch	*brandhoornvis*	F
brandvis	'fire + fish'	Papiamentu	*brantfes kòrá*	F
		Antillean Dutch	*brandvis*	F
buffel	base word, loanword	Sranan	*bofru*	M
		Surinamese Dutch	*buffel*	M
duif	base word	Surinamese Dutch	*duif*	B
		Sranan	*doifi*	B
		VIDC	*dufje, difi*	B

Table 5. *(continued)*

Dutch name	Word type[a]	Language	Name	Phylum[b]
duikelaar	derivation	Papiamentu	*dekla*	B
		Sranan	*doklari*	B
		Surinamese Dutch	*duikelaar*	B
duizendbeen	'thousand + leg'	Papiamentu	*lisinbein*	A
		Sranan	*lusunbe*	A
flamingo	base word, loanword	Sranan	*flamingo*	B
		Surinamese Dutch	*flamingo*	B
grassteeltje	'grass + stalk'	Papiamentu	*grastèlchi*	F
		Antillean Dutch	*grassteeltje*	F
grauwe monnik	'grey + monk'	Sranan	*granmorgu*	F
		Surinamese Dutch	*grauwmunnik*	F
grietjebie	'girl + child'	Surinamese Dutch	*grietjebie*	B
		Sranan	*grikibi*	B
haas	base word	Surinamese Dutch	*haas*	M
		SA English	*hasie*	M
harder	base word	Papiamentu	*(h)aldu*	F
		Sranan	*ardri*	F
		SA English	*harder*	F
haring	base word	Surinamese Dutch	*haring*	F
		Sranan	*elen*	F
hertenbeest	'deer + animal'	SA English	*hartebeest*	M
		Berbice Dutch	*hatibesi*	M
houtluis	'wood + louse'	Surinamese Dutch	*houtluis*	A
		VIDC	*houtulus*	A
		Papiamentu	*atalèis*	A
jakob-evertsen	derivation, name	VIDC	*Jacob Evert*	F
		SA English	*Jacob Evertsen*	F
kanarie	base word, loanword	Surinamese Dutch	*kanarie*	B
		Sranan	*kanari*	B
kemphaantje	'fight + rooster'	Surinamese Dutch	*kemphaantje*	B
		Sranan	*kepanki*	B
kinkhoorn	'kink + horn'	Antillean Dutch	*kinkhoorn*	W
		Papiamentu	*kenkon*	W

Table 5. *(continued)*

Dutch name	Word type[a]	Language	Name	Phylum[b]
konijntje	derivation, loanword	Surinamese Dutch	*konijntje*	M
		Sranan	*kon(i)koni*	M
		Papiamentu	*konènchi*	M
krab	base word	VIDC	*krabu*	A
		Sranan	*krabu*	A
		Berbice Dutch	*krabu*	A
		Skepi Dutch	*krabu*	A
kreeft	base word	SA English	*kreef*	A
		VIDC	*kreeft*	A
		Papiamentu	*kref*	A
		Sranan	*krefti*	A
likhand	'lick + hand'	Sranan	*likanu*	M
		Surinamese Dutch	*likan, likhand*	M
lomp	base word	Surinamese Dutch	*lomp*	F
		Sranan	*lompu*	F
makreel	base word, loanword	Papiamentu	*makré*	F
		Sranan	*makrere*	F
marsbanker	derivation, name	Am English	*mossbunker*	F
		SA English	*maasbanker*	F
		Papiamentu	*masbangu*	F
mierenfluiter	'ant + whistler'	Sranan	*mirafroiti*	M
		Surinamese Dutch	*mierenfluiter*	M
mijt	base word	Surinamese Dutch	*miet*	A
		Sranan	*miti*	A
nachtaap	'night + monkey'	SA English	*nagapie, night ape*	M
		Surinamese Dutch	*nachtaap*	M
negerkop	'negro + head'	Sranan	*nengrekopu*	B
		Surinamese Dutch	*negerkop*	B
parkiet	base word, loanword	Sranan	*prakiki*	B
		Surinamese Dutch	*parkiet*	B
raaf	base word	Sranan	*rafru*	B
		Surinamese Dutch	*raaf*	B
rijstvogel	'rice + bird'	Indo-Dutch	*rijstvogel*	B
		Surinamese Dutch	*rijstvogel*	B

Table 5. *(continued)*

Dutch name	Word type[a]	Language	Name	Phylum[b]
ronkertje	derivation	VIDC	*roenkertje*	B
		Sranan	*lonkriki*	B
roodbekje	'red + beak'	Papiamentu	*robèki*	F
		SA English	*rooibekkie*	B
schildpad	'shield + toad'	Am English	*skillpot*	R
		Berbice Dutch	*skelpata*	R
		VIDC	*skildpat*	R
		Sranan	*sekrepatu*	R
		Surinamese Dutch	*schildpad*	R
snip	base word	Papiamentu	*snepi*	B
		Sranan	*snepi*	B
		Surinamese Dutch	*snip(je)*	B
snoek	base word	SA English	*snoek*	F
		Indonesian	*senuk*	F
		Papiamentu	*snuk*	F
		Sranan	*snuku*	F
		Surinamese Dutch	*snoek*	F
soldaatje	derivation, loanword	Antillean Dutch	*soldaatje*	A
		Papiamentu	*soldachi*	A
Spaanse vrouw	'Spanish + woman'	Sranan	*spansfrow*	A
		Surinamese Dutch	*Spaanse vrouw*	A
spiering	base word	Am English	*spearing*	F
		SA English	*spiering*	F
spikkelkat	'speckle + cat'	Sranan	*spigrikati*	F
		Surinamese Dutch	*spikkelkat*	F
spinnenkop	'spider + head'	VIDC	*spinkop*	A
		Papiamentu	*spenekòk*	A
sprinkhaan	'jump + rooster'	VIDC	*springhaen*	A
		Berbice Dutch	*springhan*	A
		Sranan	*sp(r)inka*	A
		SA English	*sprinkaan*	A
steenduifje	'stone + dove'	VIDC	*stendifi*	B
		Sranan	*stondoifi*	B
		Surinamese Dutch	*steenduifje*	B

Table 5. *(continued)*

Dutch name	Word type[a]	Language	Name	Phylum[b]
tijger	base word, loanword	Berbice Dutch	*tigri*	M
		Sranan	*tigri*	M
		Surinamese Dutch	*tijger*	M
tijgerkat	'tiger + cat'	Sranan	*tigrikati*	M
		SA English	*tiger-cat*	M
		Surinamese Dutch	*tijgerkat*	M
trompetter	derivation, loanword	Surinamese Dutch	*trompetter*	F
		Papiamentu	*trompèt*	F
vos	base word	Surinamese Dutch	*vos*	M
		VIDC	*vos*	M
worm	base word	Surinamese Dutch	*worm*	A
		Berbice Dutch	*worum*	A
		VIDC	*worm*	A
		Sranan	*woron*	A
zeeduif	'sea + dove'	Sranan	*sedoifi*	B
		Surinamese Dutch	*zeeduif*	B
zeegans	'sea + goose'	Sranan	*segansi*	B
		Surinamese Dutch	*zeegans*	B
zeekat	'sea + cat'	SA English	*sea-cat*	W
		Papiamentu	*sekat*	W

a. For compounds, the meaning of each word part is translated into English.
b. Abbreviations used for the phyla are: A (Arthropod), B (Bird), F (Fish), M (Mammal), R (Reptile), and W (Mollusk or amphibian).
c. *Baboen* is in Dutch a variant of *baviaan* 'baboon' (a loanword from French), in overseas Dutch especially referring to howler monkeys. Therefore, Van Donselaar (1989) concludes that the Surinamese Dutch and Sranan names are based on Dutch *baboen* and not on English *baboon.*
d. Abbreviation for Virgin Islands Dutch Creole.

While for the base words it is clear that they are transferred from the Low Countries to other continents, this does not seem to be the case for derivations and compounds, since most of these are only found overseas and not in the Low Countries.[10] Apparently, they were deliberately coined to designate new animal species. Of course, these Dutch derivations and compounds can easily have been formed or used in the Low Countries too, but they received their special meaning abroad.

---

10. The South African case is discussed in Scholtz 1974: 21–26, with numerous examples. He states that the older a name is, the more likely it has been transferred from the Low Countries to South Africa.

Of the 27 ***derivations***, twelve have the diminutive suffix *-(t)je* (three are mentioned in Table 5: *konijntje, ronkertje, steenduifje*). This suffix is used to distinguish the name of the species in the Low Countries (without diminutive suffix) from that abroad. In this way *konijn* 'rabbit' is distinguished from *konijntje* 'aguti' in the Caribbean, and *gans* 'goose' from *gansje*, in Papiamentu indicating the brown pelican or heron (not in the table). *Streepje* 'little stripe' in South African English refers to a striped fish, while Surinamese Dutch *blauwtje* 'little blue' and *kortje* 'little short one' refer to a blue and a small bird, respectively. A last example is *geitje* 'little goat', which in South African English refers to a venomous lizard, likely a case of folk etymology based on a homophonic Khoi word.

Other derivations end with the suffixes *-er* or *-aar*, which in Dutch is used to derive nouns from verbs.[11] In Table 5 we find the bird name *duikelaar* (from *duiken* 'to duck'), and the fish name *trompetter* (from *trompetten* 'to trumpet').

In some cases animal names are derived from ***proper names***. This is the case with the fish *marsbanker* ('type of horse mackerel'). This was named after the shoals in Marsdiep, a channel between Den Helder and Texel in northern Holland, where the fish used to be abundant. When the Dutch moved to the American East Coast, they saw what is currently called the 'Atlantic menhaden,' which, like the Dutch horse mackerel, swam in shoals, which is why they called the fish *marsbanker*. The Dutchman Jacob Steendam, mentioned in the introduction, was the first to use the word *marsbanker* to refer to an American fish species.

Another interesting example is the fish name *jakob-evertsen*, used in South African English and Virgin Islands Dutch Creole. This is derived from the name of the seventeenth-century skipper Jacob Evertsen, known for his red-spotted face, resembling the fish's skin. Some proper names are attributed to birds whose calls resemble Dutch names, such as *grietjebie* in Surinamese Dutch (based on the woman's name *Grietje*), and, not in Table 5, *piet-van-vliet* in Indo-Dutch, and *Jan Frederik* and *piet-my-vrouw* in South African English. These names are ***onomatopoeic***, similar to the derivation *ronkertje* ('little hummer'), referring to a hummingbird in Virgin Islands Dutch Creole and Sranan Tongo.

The vast majority of overseas animal names are however ***compound*** words, and these seem mostly to have been newly coined overseas. The formations are quite predictable. The second part is often a general or specific name of an animal: *aap* (monkey), *beest* (animal), *duif* (pigeon), *gans* (goose), *haan* (rooster), *kat* (cat), *luis* (louse), *pad* (toad), *tor* (beetle), *varken* (pig), *vis* (fish), *vink* (finch), *vogel* (bird). This name is not always to be taken literally but metaphorically: a *zeegans* ('sea + goose') is not a species of goose but a flamingo. Compounds

11. The origin of *harder* 'gray mullet' is uncertain, so this is counted as base word, just as *haring* and *spiering*: the suffix *-ing* is no longer productive in the formation of fish names.

with *kat* (‘cat’) denote different species: *tijgerkat* is a mammal (ocelot or serval), *spikkelkat* is a fish, and *zeekat* is a mollusc (octopus). All these species probably reminded the name givers in some way of a cat.

The first part of the compounds often provides a specification, such as a color (*blauw, grauw, rood, spikkel* – ‘blue, gray, red, speckled’), habitat (*aarde, bos, gras, hout, rijst, steen, zee* – ‘earth, forest, grass, wood, rice, stone, sea’), or a characteristic (*brand* ‘fire’ used for ‘poisonous’, *nacht* ‘night’ for ‘nocturnal’, and *spring* for a jumping animal).

The entire name can be an ultra-short description of the animal, such as *aardvarken* ‘earth + pig’ for an animal that roots around in the ground like a pig, *blauwdas* ‘blue + necktie’ and *blauwvogeltje* ‘blue + bird’ for a blue-striped or blue bird, *boktor* ‘goat + beetle’ for a beetle whose head resembles that of a goat, *grassteeltje* ‘grass + stalk’ for a long thin fish, *likhand* ‘lick + hand’ (originally named *likkie-han*) for an anteater which in captivity licks its paws when hungry, *roodbekje* ‘red + beak’ for a fish with a red beak, and *Spaanse vrouw* ‘Spanish + woman’ for a praying mantis whose movements and posture resemble those of a noble Spanish lady. From the examples *grassteeltje* and *blauwvogeltje* it is clear that sometimes the diminutive suffix *-tje* is added to the compound, indicating a small and harmless species.

Some compounds incorporate words borrowed from local languages, often describing the habitat of the new animal, so they are half borrowings. Instances are Indo-Dutch *sawaslang* (‘paddy field + snake’), and Surinamese Dutch *krontoblauwtje* (‘coconut tree + blue’) and *mangrokanarie* (‘mangrove + canary’). Since these names refer to a specific landscape, they are only found in one continent and region, so they are not mentioned in Table 5.

As to word types, word origins, naming motifs and phyla, the naming practices in the overseas continents are identical. But how about the overseas ***diffusion*** of the Dutch names? Are names restricted to a particular continent or region, or are they used more widely?

From Table 5 it appears that 17 out of the 64 names are used on multiple continents. No name is found on all four continents, but two names occur on three continents, namely *marsbanker* (America, Africa, Caribbean),[12] and *snoek* (Africa, Caribbean, Indonesia). The remaining fifteen are mostly found in Africa and Caribbean: *haas, harder, hertenbeest, jakob-evertsen, kreeft, nachtaap, roodbekje, sprinkhaan, tijgerkat* and *zeekat*. America and Africa share *aardvarken, schildpad* and *spiering*, while Indonesia and Caribbean share *boktor* and *rijstvogel*. An interesting case is Dutch *aardvarken*. It is used for two very different species and in different forms: South African English *aardvark* (also translated as

12. Caribbean is used as abbreviation for the wide region of South-America and the Caribbean.

earth-hog) refers to the 'ant-bear', while the American English translation *groundhog* refers to the 'woodchuck'.

It is important to note here that Caribbean (more precisely South America and Caribbean) encompasses four very widely separated regions: Suriname, the Dutch Antilles, US Virgin Islands and Guyana, where seven different languages were spoken. Twenty Dutch names are used in two of these four regions, and six even in three, namely *schildpad, sprinkhaan, worm* (found in Suriname, US Virgin Islands, Guyana), *houtluis, kreeft* (in Suriname, the Dutch Antilles, US Virgin Islands), and *krab* (in Suriname, the Dutch Antilles, Guyana).

3.3. Analysis of the data

From the wide diffusion of Dutch animal names across continents and regions, noted in the previous section, we can safely conclude that in the past there existed a special variety of 'overseas Dutch' or non-European Dutch, consisting of Dutch words with new meanings and newly coined words. This variety was not geographically restricted, but was transported across the oceans from one continent or region to another by Dutch traversing the seas.

Be this as it may, the disparity in numbers of Dutch animal names among the continents and languages, as noted in Table 1, is striking. By far, the majority of Dutch names are found in South America and the Caribbean, particularly in Surinamese Dutch. This underlines the strong position that Dutch had and still has in Suriname: much stronger than on the Dutch Antilles. In American English, the least Dutch animal names were found, but this can be accounted for by the fact that the Dutch transferred authority over the New Netherland colony to the English after only about fifty years, and from that point on, English became the dominant language. While Dutch remained in use as a spoken language for a long time on the East Coast of America, it is conceivable that communication about the surrounding flora and fauna mainly took place using English terms. In any case, we know very little about what Dutch looked like in North America before the 19th century, so it is not surprising that few Dutch animal names from this area were found. South Africa occupies a middle position, but the tables would of course be turned if we took into consideration the animal names in Afrikaans instead of only those borrowed by South African English.

What is surprising, however, is the small number of animal names in Indonesia, compared to those on other continents. In Indonesia, I found only 42 Dutch animal names: two in Indonesian (*boktor* and *snoek*), and 40 in Indo-Dutch. The contrast with the 357 neologisms in Suriname is striking. How can we explain this?

The explanation must lie in the position of Dutch. In Suriname, Dutch was historically the language of administration and education, and it served as a lingua franca for the multicultural and multilingual population of Suriname. Dutch language policy was aimed at educating the multicultural population in Dutch. As early as 1876–24 years earlier than in the Netherlands! – compulsory education was introduced in Suriname for all children from the age of seven to twelve, with Dutch as the only language of instruction.

In Indonesia, the situation was quite different. When the Dutch settled in the Indonesian archipelago, two lingua francas were already in use, namely Malay and Portuguese. The Dutch adopted those lingua francas in their interactions with the local population and did not introduce Dutch as a language of communication, although it was used as a language of administration.[13] Only in the 1850s did a debate arise about whether the indigenous population should be provided with Dutch education, but it was decided not to do so. Dutch was considered 'the path to the West,' the path to development and Western knowledge. The Dutch feared that if the indigenous population gained access to that Western knowledge, it could potentially give rise to ideas about autonomy. Therefore, Dutch education in Indonesia was reserved for an small elite (Groeneboer 1993, 1998, Ostler 2005, Swaan 2002, Van der Sijs 2022). As a result, only a very small percentage of the Indonesian population spoke Dutch, while the Dutch often used Malay. The result of this is that Dutch did not become the language of communication in Indonesia (as English did in India or Portuguese in Brazil). Moreover, the Dutch apparently did not coin new Dutch words to designate the Indonesian fauna, but rather adopted the Malay names.[14]

Thus, the quantity of Dutch animal names reflect the former Dutch language attitude and language policies on the different continents, which in the so-called West (Caribbean) greatly differed from those in the East (Indonesia). The overseas animal names show that the Dutch were easily able to provide foreign fauna with new Dutch names. Whether they actually did so depended on their attitude towards Dutch and the local languages they had contact with.

13. The Dutch did introduce a large number of words for Dutch or Western European concepts that were unknown in Indonesian society, concerning education, religion, governance, science, fashion, art, and foodstuff: as was shown in Chapter 1, Indonesian has borrowed by far the most Dutch loanwords of all languages.

14. Older Dutch travel reports about Indonesia do contain such names as *stinkdas* 'stink + badger' and *slanghalsvogel* 'snake-necked + bird' (both also found in Afrikaans), but these have not been preserved in Indonesian or Indo-Dutch and may never have been used outside of travel descriptions.

4. Concluding remarks

In this chapter, I described the Dutch names given to native animal species on four continents in eleven languages. I found 595 names, of which 504 were unique, meaning they occurred only in one language. In naming practices, no differences could be found between the continents: most names concerned birds and mammals, and most were newly coined compounds describing the main characteristics (colour, habitat) of the animal in question. Less often, an existing Dutch basic name was transferred to an overseas species.

However, there was a significant difference in the quantity of Dutch names across continents. Surinamese Dutch contained by far the most words, while American English had the least. Most remarkable, though, was the small number of names in Indonesia. I explained this by the lack of a Dutch language policy in the Indonesian Archipelago in the past. Finally, the wide diffusion of Dutch animal names across continents and regions adds weight to the idea that there was a special variety of 'overseas Dutch'.

This study is only a first step. I can think of various follow-up studies. For instance, it would be enlightening to compare the Dutch data with the nomenclature in overseas territories where English, Portuguese, Spanish or French was dominant: especially since the languages mentioned have often remained the language of communication or the official language in those territories to this day, unlike Dutch in Indonesia. It would also be interesting to investigate the distribution of Dutch words in other word fields, such as plant names and specific local customs.

References

Blanker, J.C.M. & J. Dubbeldam. 2005. *Prisma woordenboek Sranantongo, Prisma wortubuku fu Sranantongo*. Utrecht: Prisma.

Bøegh, Kristoffer Friis & Peter Bakker. 2021. "Words from Dutch Creole in Virgin Islands Creole English." *Trefwoord*: https://ivdnt.org/actueel/tijdschrift-trefwoord/.

Etymologiebank: https://etymologiebank.nl/.

Funk, Elisabeth Paling. 1992. "De literatuur van Nieuw-Nederland." *De Nieuwe Taalgids* 85: 383–396.

Groeneboer, Kees. 1993. *Weg tot het Westen. Het Nederlands voor Indië* 1600–1950. Leiden: KITLV Uitgeverij.

Groeneboer, Kees. 1998. *Westerse koloniale taalpolitiek in Azië: het Nederlands, Portugees, Spaans, Engels en Frans in vergelijkend perspectief*. Amsterdam: KNAW.

doi Jacobs, Bart, and Mikael Parkvall. 2020. "Skepi Dutch Creole: The Youd Papers." *Journal of Pidgin and Creole Languages* 35 (2): 360–380.

Joubert, Sidney, and Nicoline van der Sijs. 2020. "Antilliaans-Nederlandse woorden en hun herkomst." *Trefwoord*, https://ivdnt.org/actueel/tijdschrift-trefwoord/.

Kouwenberg, Silvia. 1993. *A grammar of Berbice Dutch Creole*. Berlin/New York: Mouton de Gruyter.

doi Mingaars, Peter, Jaap Heij, Maudy Smith, and Pim Posthumus. 2005. *Indisch Lexicon. Indische woorden in de Nederlandse literatuur*. Houten: Hes & De Graaf.

Ostler, Nicholas. 2005. *Empires of the Word: A Language History of the World*. New York: HarperCollins Publishers.

Robertson, Ian E. 1983. "The Dutch linguistic legacy and the Guyana/Venezuela border question." *Boletín de Estudios Latinoamericanos y del Caribe* 34: 75–97.

Robertson, Ian E. 1989. "Berbice and Skepi Dutch." *Tijdschrift voor Nederlandsche Taal- en Letterkunde* 105: 3–21.

Robertson, Ian E. 1994. "Berbiciaansche woorde". *Amsterdam Creole Studies* XI, 67–74, I–II.

Scholtz, J. du P. 1974. *Naamgewing aan plante en diere in Afrikaans*. Kaapstad: Nassou, second edition.

Silva, Penny (ed.). 1996. *A Dictionary of South African English on Historical Principles*. Oxford: OUP.

Stichting Volkslectuur Suriname. 1995. *Woordenlijst Sranan-Nederlands, Nederlands-Sranan, English-Sranan*. Paramaribo.

Swaan, Abraham de. 2002. *Woorden van de wereld. Het mondiale talenstelsel*. Amsterdam: Bert Bakker.

Van Dale = *Van Dale Groot woordenboek van de Nederlandse taal*. 2022. ed. by Ton den Boon and Ruud Hendrickx. Utrecht/Antwerpen: Van Dale Lexicografie, 16th edition.

doi Van der Sijs, Nicoline. 2009. *Cookies, coleslaw and stoops. The influence of Dutch on the North-American languages*. Amsterdam/Chicago: AUP.

Van der Sijs, Nicoline. 2010. *Nederlandse woorden wereldwijd*. The Hague: SDU.

Van der Sijs, Nicoline. 2022. "1602. De Nederlandse taal gaat overzee." In: *Nog meer Wereldgeschiedenis van Nederland*, ed. by L. Heerma van Voss e.a., pp. 183–188. Amsterdam: Ambo/Anthos.

Van Donselaar, J. 1989. *Woordenboek van het Surinaams-Nederlands*. Muiderberg: Coutinho.

Van Donselaar, J. 1994. "Oude Nederlandse woorden in het hedendaagse Sranantongo." *Trefwoord* 9, 63–67.

Van Donselaar, J. 1995–1999. "Vroegere dateringen van dierennamen in bronnen over Zuid-Amerika." *Trefwoord* 10: 84–90, 12: 182–186, 13: 197–204.

Van Donselaar, J. 2000. "Planten- en dierennamen uit Suriname in de Grote Van Dale." *Trefwoord*: https://ivdnt.org/actueel/tijdschrift-trefwoord/.

Van Donselaar, J. 2013. *Woordenboek van het Nederlands in Suriname van 1667 tot 1876*, ed. by Nicoline van der Sijs. Amsterdam.

doi Van Rossem, Cefas, and Hein van der Voort (eds). 1996. *Die Creol Taal. 250 years of Negerhollands texts*. Amsterdam: AUP.

Van Rossem, Cefas. 2017. *The Virgin Islands Dutch Creole Textual Heritage: Philological Perspectives on Authenticity and Audience Design*. Utrecht: LOT.

Van Rossem, Cefas. 2021. "Drie keer Nederlands Creools." In: *Wat gebeurt er in het Nederlands?! Over taal, frequentie en variatie*, ed. by N. van der Sijs, L. Fonteyn, and M. van der Meulen, 307–313. Gorredijk: Sterck & De Vreese.

Van Sluijs, Robbert. 2017. *Variation and change in Virgin Islands Dutch Creole*. Utrecht: LOT.

CHAPTER 18

Language contact in online spaces

Multiple sources of non-finite causal constructions in Dutch

Martin Konvička
Freie Universität Berlin

In this chapter, I analyse the two Dutch non-finite causal constructions *want* X 'because X' and *omdat* X 'because X' from historical and comparative perspectives. I particularly focus on the relationship between language-internal and language-external factors in their development. To that end, I show how these constructions have developed in Dutch from causal clauses while also discussing their use in the multilingual context of computer-mediated communication. Against this backdrop, I conclude that they cannot be explained solely as resulting from processes within Dutch nor as merely structural borrowings from other languages, such as English. Instead, these constructions should be analysed as multiple-source constructions. In other words, language contact as a factor cannot be ignored and must always be considered.

Keywords: non-finite causal constructions, because, want, omdat, because X, want X, omdat X, computer-mediated communication, multiple-source constructions

1. Introduction

When considering processes of language change, there are typically two possible explanations: the language-internal or endogenous one, which accounts for a particular development as a change from within, and the contact-induced or exogenous one, which explains a specific development as arising under the influence of another language. Although distinct in principle, it is often challenging to distinguish between these two possibilities.

When faced with this sort of dilemma, some linguists, such as Lass (1997: 209), prefer the language-internal explanation "because endogenous change must occur in any case, whereas borrowing is never necessary" (but see, e.g. Filppula

https://doi.org/10.1075/impact.55.18kon

2003). Lass' view stands in a longer tradition of treating language contact as a peripheral phenomenon and thus not the primary explanation for language change (see, e.g. Heine & Kuteva 2020: 94; Milroy 2003). Following this principle, language contact as an explanation is dismissed unless there is overwhelming evidence to the contrary. When language contact and language-internal development represent equally plausible explanations, language contact is disregarded because it is deemed not "necessary".

However, this principal methodological preference for language-internal explanations is as arbitrary a decision as the hypothetical dis-preference of language-internal factors. To avoid this arbitrariness, I adopt a different approach in this chapter and follow Joseph (2015: 205) in arguing that "a multiplicity of explanations generally needs to be considered."

In particular, I will focus on the development of the non-finite causal constructions *want* X (1a) and *omdat* X (1b) in Dutch (see, e.g. Konvička & Stöcker 2022: 335) and argue that they represent classic examples of so-called multiple-source constructions (Van de Velde, De Smet & Ghesquière 2015).

(1) a. De Leidsebuurt telt de hele dag scooters, vooral van en naar: Weteringschans, Marnixstraat, Max Euweplein. Nadruk op spitsuren in de ochtend en in de hele avond, **want uitgaansgebied.** (Twitter, 2019)
'The Leidsebuurt has lots of scooters the whole day. Mainly to and from: Weteringschans, Marnixstraat, Max Euweplein. Emphasis on rush hours in the morning and the whole evening because nightlife area.'

b. Wat doet hij? Obama bashen. Alles wat Obama heeft gedaan moet anders **omdat Obama.** (Twitter, 2019)
'What does he do? Bashes Obama. Everything that Obama has done must change because Obama.'

As neither language-internal developments nor language-external factors can be solely held responsible for the development and spread of these constructions in Dutch, an explanation that integrates both perspectives is called for.

Figure 1 (taken from Konvička 2024b: 176) illustrates one such account by visualising the complex network of constructional lineages influencing the Dutch non-finite causal constructions. On the one hand, *want* X and *omdat* X constructions represent the language-internal continuations of causal clauses with the conjunctions *want* and *omdat*, respectively. On the other hand, these constructions are also shaped endogenously by language contact with other languages, predominantly English, in online spaces.

The necessity for a broader perspective that combines endogenous and exogenous factors is not exclusive to the non-finite causal constructions above. The Dutch 'time'-*weg* construction (2a) is also difficult to explain as either a purely

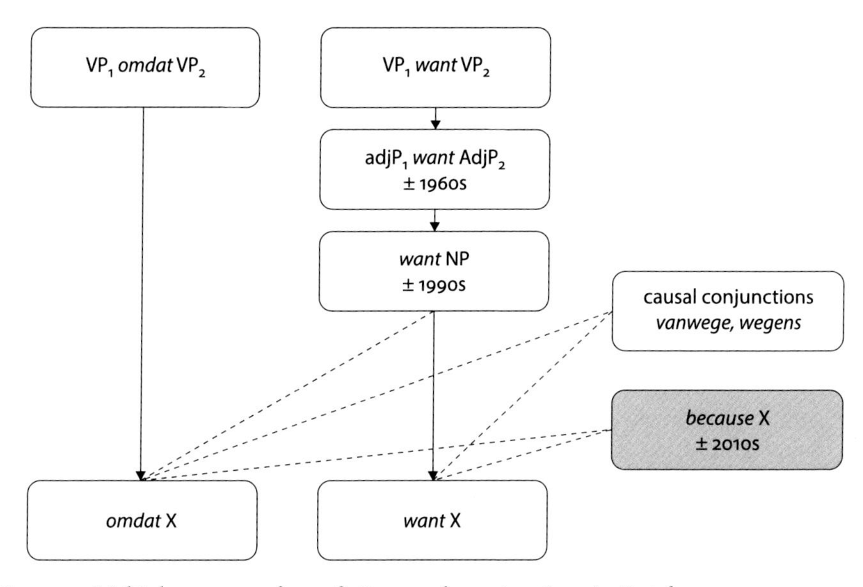

Figure 1. Multiple sources of non-finite causal constructions in Dutch

language-internal development or a purely contact-induced phenomenon arising from the influence of the English 'time'-*away* construction (2b) (Colleman 2016).

(2) a. *Vanavond zappen we de avond weg. Lekker hersenloos.* (Colleman 2016: 99)
'This evening, we will channel surf the evening. Nicely brainless.
b. *When the cat's away....the mice will facebook, online shop and twitter the day away.* (Colleman 2016: 95)

Although language contact is the most likely explanation for the emergence of (2a), unlike in the case of non-finite causal constructions, the question remains whether the Dutch construction is an instance of direct constructional borrowing or rather a combination of constructional borrowing and language-internal development. These difficulties, however, arise only if one is forced to choose between an endogenous and an exogenous explanation. Although such a choice is sometimes necessary, it is not always necessarily helpful.

Against this backdrop, I will use the Dutch non-finite causal constructions to discuss in my contribution the interplay of language contact and language-internal developments in language change. I will argue that these constructions are best described as multiple-source constructions (Van de Velde, De Smet & Ghesquière 2015). This means that they do not originate from a single older construction in Dutch or in another language. On the one hand, non-finite causal constructions represent a continuation of older language-internal patterns. On the other hand, they have also been formed by contact with other languages, predominantly English. This language contact, which I will examine later, occurs particularly in the context of translocal online spaces such as social media.

To show that the Dutch non-finite causal constructions result from a combination of internal processes within Dutch and external influences from other languages, I first offer a general description of their formal and functional aspects (Section 2) before examining their endogenous development (Section 3). Next, I address the exogenous factors in their development within the context of computer-mediated communication (Section 4). Finally, I conclude my contribution with a summary and concluding remarks (Section 5).

2. Non-finite causal constructions in Dutch

2.1 Form

Non-finite causal constructions follow a matrix clause and formally consist of two slots that can be filled lexically with varying degrees of flexibility. The first slot contains the connector, while the second contains its complement. In Dutch, the connector slot is typically filled by *want* 'because' (3a) or by *omdat* 'because' (3b).

(3) a. *nee* ***want lowlands*** [1] (Twitter, 2013) (Konvička 2019: 162)
'no, because Lowlands (=annual music festival in the Netherlands, MK)'

b. *Op zaterdag!!! Met extra mensen* ***omdat lowlands!!!*** (Twitter, 2018) (Konvička 2019: 162)
'On Saturday!!! With extra people because Lowlands!!!'

Canonically, the causal connectors *want* and *omdat* are used as conjunctions to introduce main (4a) or subordinate clauses (4b) that express cause or reason.

(4) a. *Trouwens Loek, je hebt geluk gehad* ***want Lowlands is nu uitverkocht!*** (Konvička 2019: 162)
'By the way Loek, you were lucky because Lowlands is sold out now'

b. *Wat ik aan het doen ben? Huilen in een hoekje* ***omdat lowlands nu echt helemaal is uitverkocht.*** (Konvička 2019: 162)
'What am I doing? I'm crying in the corner because Lowlands is now really completely sold out.'

Unlike causal connectors in causal clauses, however, causal connectors in non-finite causal constructions, as the term suggests, are not complemented by finite

1. It should be noted that all examples taken from social media are left in their original form. The non-standard use of punction marks, capitalisation, and typographical errors reflect the authentic language use.

verb forms. Beyond this limitation, the complement slot can be filled by a wide variety of elements, including noun phrases (5a), proper names as a subcategory of noun phrases (5b), adjectival phrases (5c), pronouns (5d), non-finite verb forms (5e), adverbial phrases (5f), interjections (5g), and emojis (5h).

(5) a. *Aantoonbaar slechte wetgeving voeren we gewoon in* ***want regeerakkkoord.*** (Twitter, 2019)
'We simply introduce demonstrably bad legislation because coalition agreement'

b. *Natuurlijk snappen ze wat de intenties zijn. Dit mag echter niet naar buiten komen,* ***want Wilders.*** (Twitter, 2017)
'They naturally understand what the intentions are. However, this cannot come out because Wilders (=Geert Wilders, the leader of the Dutch Party for Freedom/Partij voor de Vrijheid, MK).'

c. *Of medewerkers plaatsen er zeer positieve reacties op. Alles kan* ***want lekker anoniem.*** (Twitter, 2017)
'Or co-workers publish very positive reactions. Everything is allowed because nicely anonymous.'

d. *Maar het is vast hierbij gebleven.* ***Want IK!*** *IK! IK!* (Twitter, 2019)
'But it has remained like this. Because ME! ME! ME!'

e. *Nú al een productieve zondag* ***want hardgelopen*** (Twitter, 2014)
'Already having a productive Sunday because jogged'

f. *Goedemorgen en sorry,* ***want te laat.*** (Twitter, 2017)
'Good morning and sorry, because too late.'

g. *Snapchat in de gaten houden voor uitgaan filmpje van Sophie, Monica en Steve* ***want yeah...*** (Twitter, 2015)
'Checking Snapchat for a new video by Sophie, Monica and Steve because yeah...'

h. *realistisch kijken of je het jezelf kan veroorloven ... zo ja doen!* ***Want*** 😍 (Twitter, 2016)
'Realistically consider whether you can afford it...if yes, do it! Because 😍'

The fact that the causal connector can be combined with such diverse elements has led to a discussion of word class membership of the connectors in these constructions. While earlier proposals in this discussion tried to formulate a uniform categorisation for all uses of the connector in these constructions (Konvička 2018), the recent proposals take a more fine-grained approach (Konvička 2023).

Based on the complement type, three possible word class categorisations of the connector can be established (Konvička 2023). First, causal connectors complemented by elliptical phrases, such as (6a), are considered to be conjunctions, just as if full clauses complemented them. Second, causal connectors complemented by noun phrases, such as (6b), are considered to be prepositions. Third, in combination with emojis, interjections, or any other elements not compatible with the two previous categorisations, as given in (6c), the connector is analysed as a member of a third category, corresponding neither to conjunctions nor prepositions.

(6) a. *Dit is minder bekend,* ***want minder algemeen.*** (Geerts et al. 1984: 1161)
'This is less known because less general.'

b. *net speciaal naar andere kant van campus gelopen voor soja melk in koffie, nu geen soja melk in koffie hebben* ***want verkeerde automaat.*** *hoe is jullie dag?* (Twitter, 2019)
'Just walked to the other side of the campus only to get soy milk for my coffee, now I have no soy milk in coffee because wrong vending machine. How's your day?'

c. *Alles leuk en aardig met dat nieuwe seizoen Twin Peaks, maar waar kan ik het oude weer zien? M'n dvd-speler de deur uitgedaan,* ***want 2017*** (Twitter, 2017)
'All is well and good with the new season of Twin Peaks, but where can I watch the old one again? Thrown away my DVD player because 2017'

Finally, one last point to mention about the structure of *want* X constructions is the apparent restriction regarding their position in relation to the matrix clause. As all the examples discussed so far suggest, non-finite causal constructions always follow their matrix clauses and never precede them (Bailey & Seyerle 2019; Konvička & Stöcker 2022; but see Kanetani 2019: 151).

2.2 Function

The primary function of non-finite causal constructions such as *want* X is expressing causality between the matrix clause and the element in the X slot. This causal link can be divided into three prototypes: real-world causality, epistemic causality, and speech act causality (Sweetser 1990: 76–77). However, as Pander Maat and Sanders (2000) show, these three categories are not discreet but rather form a continuum based on the importance of the speaker's volition for the causal link.

In (7a), an example of real-world causality, the lack of housing serves as the physical reason why children nowadays stay at home. In (7b), a case of epistemic causality, the lack of tan causes the speaker/writer not to *want* to wear shorts even though there is no physical causation, as was the case in (7a). Lastly, the example in (7c) demonstrates speech act causality. The fact that the speaker/writer is too late is the reason why they say *sorry*.

(7) a. *Babyboomers: Voor mijn dertigste kwam ik niet in aanmerking voor een huurwoning. Nu blijven de kinderen tot 35 jaar thuis,* ***want geen woning.*** (Twitter, 2019)
'Baby boomers: I was not eligible for a rented home until I was thirty. Nowadays, children stay at home until they are 35 because no home.'
b. *Wij zijn spierwit, dus geen korte broeken ed* ***want witten benen.*** (Twitter, 2019)
'We are as white as a sheet so no shorts, Ed, because white legs.'
c. *Goedemorgen en sorry,* ***want te laat.*** (Twitter, 2017)
'Good morning and sorry, because too late.'

Furthermore, *want* X constructions also exist as so-called *pseudo-causal constructions* (Konvička 2019:162; Konvička 2024a:324–326). These constructions formally follow the pattern of regular causal constructions, such as those discussed in (7), but do not, in fact, functionally express any cause or reason at all. Instead of conveying reason or cause, the expression in the complement slot of the construction contains a semantically vacuous expression, such as *redenen* 'reasons' in (8).

(8) a. *Ik heb weer een hoop blurays besteld* ***want redenen.*** (Twitter, 2016)
'I have once again ordered a bunch of Blue-rays because reasons'
b. *ff* (=eventjes, MK) *rond me kamer dansen* ***omdat redenen*** (Twitter, 2016)
'dance around the room for a moment because reasons'

Another type of pseudo-causal construction is given in (9). Here, the expression that is supposed to convey the cause or reason is, in fact, an exact copy of a preceding expression and, therefore, cannot convey cause or reason.

(9) a. *Chocola met koffiestukjes bij de* ***koffie want koffie.*** *KOFFIE.* (Twitter, 2017)
'Chocolate with bits of coffee with (a cup of) coffee because coffee. COFFEE.'
b. *TERROR* ***OMDAT TERROR!*** (Twitter, 2019)
'Terror because terror!'

The pseudo-causal constructions, particularly their pleonastic variants in (9), are comparable with the so-called *pseudo-conditionals* (Declerck & Reed 2001:359). As illustrated in (10), they formally also resemble conditional constructions, from which they deviate functionally.

(10) *I need to do this on my own. If I fail, I fail. If I pass, I pass.* (Sommerer 2023:353)

Although pseudo-causal constructions fail to express causality semantically, they do have a pragmatic function, namely that the speaker/writer shows that the reasons are so obvious that they should already be known to the addressee or that the addressee does not need to know the exact reasons (see Konvička 2024a).

2.3 Data

Empirically, the present study is based on a corpus of posts collected on the social media platform Twitter, which was renamed to X in July 2023.[2] This type of data has been chosen because Twitter has been characterised as particularly "tolerant towards deviations from the norms of [standard language]" (Bohmann 2016: 170). Consequently, tweets can be seen as representing *conceptually spoken language* (Koch & Oesterreicher 1985; Landert & Jucker 2011; Burger & Luginbühl 2014: 173–200). They obviously represent written language, but they are structurally closer to spoken language in certain important aspects. This is especially important when studying non-standard constructions such as *want* X or *omdat* X. Moreover, online communication platforms have been frequently associated with the emergence and spread of non-finite causal constructions (e.g. Bailey 2012; Whitman 2014; McCulloch 2014; van Oostendorp 2014; Stefanowitsch 2014).

The complete corpus consists of Twitter posts in Dutch, German, and English, which were collected in November 2019 (Konvička & Stöcker 2020). For the Dutch subset of the corpus, a total of 10,000 tweets containing the connectors *want* and *omdat* were collected first. Subsequently, only those tweets that lacked a finite verb form between the causal connector and the final next punctuation mark, such as a full stop, an exclamation mark, or a question mark, were singled out. In the final step, the results were manually checked for false positives (see Konvička & Stöcker 2022: 339–342).

This selection process yielded a final collection of 185 instances of *want* X and 10 instances of *omdat* X. This means an overall frequency of 1.85% for non-finite causal constructions with *want* and 0.01% for those with *omdat* as the connector in this sample. The difference in the frequency of the two variants of non-finite causal construction in Dutch can be explained in two ways.

Firstly, non-finite constructions with *want* are older than *omdat* X and have been modelled analogously at a later stage (see Konvička 2018: 21, but also Section 3.3). Secondly, it has been noted that causal constructions with *want* show a higher degree of subjectivity than those with *omdat* (Degand 1998; Pit, Pander Maat & Sanders 1997). This disparity can also account for the higher frequency of *want* X constructions because subjectivity plays a crucial role in the semantics and pragmatics of the *because* X constructions (Bergs 2018: 54).

---

2. I adhere to the original terminology, such as *Twitter*, *Twitter users* or *tweets*, because all data discussed in this study were collected prior to the rebranding.

3. Development of non-finite causal constructions in Dutch

In the previous section, I outlined the formal and functional properties of Dutch non-finite causal constructions, along with the empirical basis of the present study. Now, I will proceed to discuss the language-internal factors that influence their development. Firstly, I examine the development of *want* X (3.1), then I analyse the meta-linguistic discourse surrounding it (3.2), and finally, I address the development of *omdat* X (3.3).

3.1 Language-internal development of *want* X

In this section, I outline the language-internal developmental pathway of the *want* X construction, which begins with non-elliptical causal clauses, advances through elliptical non-finite causal constructions, and ultimately results in novel non-elliptical non-finite causal constructions. This trajectory is supported by the following three observations. Firstly, all early examples of non-finite causal constructions are textual ellipses. This holds not only in Dutch but also in other languages (Rehn 2015; Bergs 2018: 45; Konvička 2020: 255; Konvička & Stöcker 2022: 346). Secondly, non-elliptical non-finite causal constructions are relatively recent innovations across languages. Finally, the gradual shift of non-ellipses via elliptical constructions towards novel non-ellipses is by no means limited to the development of non-finite causal constructions. A similar scenario can be observed in cases such as (11), where an erstwhile dependent modifier, the adjective *Hamburger* (11a), becomes, over time, independent as a noun (11c) (see, e.g. van Bree 1996: 167; Hüning 2000: 125).

(11) a. *Hamburger* NP
b. *Hamburger (steak)*
c. *hamburger*
d. *cheeseburger, veggieburger, fishburger...*

The combination of the adjective *Hamburger* modifying a noun phrase in (11a) does obviously not constitute an ellipsis. However, in certain situations, the modified noun phrase can be omitted if the reference is clear from the context. A case in point is the culinary context of (11b) in which *Hamburger* remains an adjective, but the noun *steak* can be elided. If used frequently enough, this elliptical structure can gradually cease to be perceived as elliptical. An expression that began as an adjective can eventually be reanalysed as a noun and used independently. The final evidence of the new non-elliptical status is provided by the fact that *Hamburger*, originally a modifying adjective, can itself be modified (11d). Similar examples of German demonymic adjectives that, over time, develop into independent nouns, such as in (12), are no exceptions.

(13) a. *Pilsen*$_{N}$ > *Pilsner*$_{ADJ}$ NP > *Pilsner*$_{ADJ}$ (*Bier*$_{N}$) > *Pilsner*$_{N}$ > *pils*$_{N}$
b. *Budweis*$_{N}$ > *Budweiser*$_{ADJ}$ NP > *Budweiser*$_{ADJ}$ (*Bier*$_{N}$) > *Budweiser*$_{N}$ > *bud*$_{N}$

In summary, the language-internal development of causal *want* X constructions should be seen in the context of a broader type of language change, in which elliptical constructions serve as a midpoint between two non-elliptical endpoints. However, this process should not be understood teleologically, as if elliptical constructions must inevitably lead to non-elliptical in the end. However, the key point is that elliptical constructions *can* give rise to non-elliptical ones, as exemplified by the Dutch non-finite causal construction *want* X.

Three types of *want* X constructions can be distinguished based on their ellipticity (Konvička & Stöcker 2022: 345). Firstly, some *want* X constructions can be analysed as textual ellipses (13a). Secondly, some *want* X constructions can be analysed as contextual ellipses (13b). Finally, some *want* X constructions cannot be analysed as ellipses at all (13c).

(13) a. *Kees is afgevoerd* ***want altijd dronken*** (Kuitenbrouwer 1987: 14)
'Kees is fired because always drunk'
b. *Geen Nederlandse tv-presentator spreekt zo goed Engels als de amper twintigjarige Linda de Mol (Adam Curry telt niet mee* ***want Amerikaanse pa****)* (Kuitenbrouwer 1987: 43)
'No Dutch TV anchor speaks such good English as the barely twenty years old Linda de Mol (Adam Curry does not count because American dad)'
c. *Het is koud, alles is statisch en mijn huid is een stuk perkament ondanks alle vaseline, dus ik heb net een luchtbevochtiger gekocht. natuurlijk in de vorm van een kikker,* ***want yeah.*** (Twitter, 2018)
'It's cold, everything's still and my skin is a piece of parchment despite all of the Vaseline, so I have just bought a humidifier. Naturally in the form of a frog because yeah'

Elliptical constructions can be classified based on the cues needed for the recovery of the elided material. In some cases, such as (13a), the linguistic context, sometimes termed *co-text*, is sufficient, while in other cases, such as (13b), the broader, non-linguistic context of the utterance is needed. Finally, in cases like (13c), no recovery is possible because these constructions are not elliptical at all.

The utterance in (13a) is an example of a textual ellipsis. The elided part of the structure can be recovered by means of its co-text. The matrix clause of the *want* X construction in (13a) contains a copula verb followed by an adjective phrase, while the *want* X construction itself consists of the connector *want* followed by an adjective phrase. This allows for a (relatively) precise recovery of the copula verb and the subject, as indicated by the square brackets in (14).

(14) *Kees is afgevoerd* ***want*** [Kees/hij is] ***altijd dronken***
'Kees is fired because [Kees/he is] always drunk'

The utterance in (13b) is an example of contextual ellipsis. The elided part of the construction can be inferred from the non-linguistic context. Unlike in (14), there is no parallel structure in the co-text on which a recovery could be based. However, world knowledge can be used instead. In the concrete case of (13b), this pertains to the understanding that having an American father can explain one's proficiency in English. Nevertheless, contrary to textual ellipses, the recovery is less precise, as illustrated by the fact that both (15a) and (15b) are viable interpretations.

(15) a. *Adam Curry telt niet mee* ***want*** [?hij heeft een] ***Amerikaanse pa***
'Adam Curry does not count because [?he has an] American dad'
b. *Adam Curry telt niet mee* ***want*** [?hij had een] ***Amerikaanse pa***
'Adam Curry does not count because [?he had an] American dad'

Finally, the utterance in (13c) is an example of a non-elliptical *want* X structure. Neither its co-text nor its non-linguistic context can be used as a basis for the recovery of elided material because the construction does not contain anything that was elided and could, therefore, be recovered. Constructions of this type, such as (16), are as non-elliptical as regular causal clauses introduced by *want* (17).

(16) *natuurlijk in de vorm van een kikker,* ***want*** [???] ***yeah.***
'naturally in the form of a frog because [???] yeah'

(17) *natuurlijk in de vorm van een kikker, want dat willen we zien.*
'naturally in the form of a frog because that is what we want to see'

However, the boundaries between the three types of *want* X constructions discussed above are not always clear-cut. It can be particularly challenging to distinguish between *want* X as a contextual ellipsis and non-ellipsis.

Above, I have discussed the example repeated here as (18) as a case of contextual ellipsis. However, the question is how do we know that we are supposed to look for contextual clues to recover any elided material in the first place? The reason for this is the fact that we know, based on our linguistic knowledge, that causal connectors such as *want* are usually followed by a finite clause. If we find anything less than a full clause in the complement of *want*, we automatically assume that something must have been omitted and start looking for clues, be they co-textual or contextual, that will allow us to recover the elided material.

(18) *Adam Curry telt niet mee* ***want Amerikaanse pa***
'Adam Curry does not count because American dad'

Consequently, the structure consisting of a causal connector followed by a noun phrase in (18) can be considered to be a contextual ellipsis. In contrast, a similar structure, differing only in the choice of the causal connector, such as the examples in (19), will not be considered elliptical at all.

(19) a. *Adam Curry telt niet mee* ***wegens Amerikaanse pa***
'Adam Curry does not count because of American dad'
b. *Adam Curry telt niet mee* ***vanwege Amerikaanse pa***
'Adam Curry does not count due to American dad'

The hypothetical structures in (19), therefore, illustrate that it is not solely the structure but rather our knowledge of it that leads us to consider it as a case of ellipsis. Scholars studying ellipses from conversational (e.g. Selting 1997: 118) or semiotic perspectives (e.g. Knobloch 2013) are, therefore, sometimes sceptical of the concept of ellipsis itself. As Knobloch (2013) shows, all utterances are underspecified in various ways, and we always rely on diverse textual or contextual clues for their interpretation. Thus, elliptical constructions do not radically differ from non-ellipses in their form; rather, they vary in their degree of context dependence.

After discussing the mechanism behind the language-internal process responsible for the rise of *want* X, I address a different aspect of the construction in the next section: the fact that even relatively old developments are sometimes perceived as recent.

3.2 Non-finite causal constructions and the recency illusion

In the previous section, I described the development of the Dutch non-finite causal construction *want* X. In this section, I will focus on the meta-linguistic discourse around it. Not all linguistic innovations are noticed right at the time of their emergence. Sometimes, it can take time until the speech community recognises the existence of a novel structure. When this finally happens, the time of the discovery tends to be equated with the time of the emergence of the innovation, which leads to the phenomenon known as the *recency illusion* (Zwicky 2005). One such example is the Dutch non-finite causal constructions.

For Dutch, these constructions were discussed by Marc van Oostendorp (2014) shortly after *because* as part of the English non-finite causal construction *because* X had been chosen as the Word of the Year 2013 (American Dialect Society 2014). However, constructions of this type were already discussed two decades ago and already back then described as "nieuwere" or 'recent' (van der Horst 2004: 18) (20).

(20) *Volgende week is het weer feest, **want 2 december*** (1999) (van der Horst 2004: 18)
'There's a holiday again next week because 2 December.'

Van der Horst was, however, not the first person to notice the unusual way that the Dutch connector *want* was being used. Lemmens (1991), more than a decade earlier, points to a number of examples from the 1980s, among other things, to the fascinating observation by Jan Kuitenbrouwer in *Turbotaal* (1987). In a journalistic, non-academic, and entertaining manner, he portrays the way young people in Amsterdam and other Dutch cities used to speak during the 1980s. Among the many features of the Dutch "yuppie talk" discussed by Kuitenbrouwer is also the by-now familiar construction in (21).

(21) *Kees is afgevoerd, **want altijd dronken.*** (Kuitenbrouwer 1987: 14)
'Kees is fired because always drunk.'

Although Kuitenbrouwer's jocular report can give the impression that it describes a new way of speaking, this is not quite the case. As de Vries (1971), for example, demonstrates, comparable constructions were already in use in the 1970s and even in the 1960s.

The authoritative grammar of Dutch, *Algemene Nederlandse Spraakkunst* (Geerts et al. 1984: 1161), also identifies constructions of the type $AdjP_1$ *want* $AdjP_2$ (22), although it notes that they are not unanimously accepted.

(22) *Dit is minder bekend, **want minder algemeen.***
'This is less well-known because less general.'

This assessment is also further supported by an opinion piece by P. C. Uit den Boogaart (1986). In response to a letter from a concerned reader, he indicates that similar constructions were used twenty years earlier, in the 1960s. This claim is also backed, for instance, by Bos (1964: 232), who briefly discusses constructions such as (23).

(23) *een onevenwichtig – **want gepassioneerd** – mens* (Bos 1964: 232)
'an unbalanced – because passionate – person'

Whether the Dutch *want* X construction really developed in the 1960s, however, remains an open question. While this is possible, there are also reasons to stay cautious. First, all the later claims from the 1970s, 1980s, and 2000s concerning the recency of the construction were eventually disproven. Furthermore, the text discussing the construction in the 1960s does not mention its novelty, which could indicate that it was not perceived as a new phenomenon. Second, the closely related and structurally similar languages exhibit equivalent constructions documented much earlier: in the 19th century for German (Konvička & Stöcker 2022) and the 16th century for English (Bergs 2021).

Regardless of when it emerged, the Dutch case illustrates how easily speakers fall for the idea that a certain construction is an innovation, even though it has been part of their language for decades.

3.3 *Omdat* follows *want*

In addition to the more common non-finite causal construction with *want* (24a), Dutch also has a functionally equivalent, albeit much less frequent, construction with *omdat* (24b) (Konvička 2019: 165; Konvička & Stöcker 2022: 342). The main reason for this difference in frequency is the fact that the latter construction has emerged only later, in analogy with the former.

(24) a. *Wie dat in vraag stelt moet vervolgd worden want klimaatontkenner.* (Twitter, 2019)
'Whoever questions that must be persecuted because climate change denier.'
b. *Op zaterdag!!! Met extra mensen omdat lowlands!!!* (Twitter, 2018)
'On Saturday!!! With extra people because lowlands!!!'

Although *want* X constructions, such as (24a), were reported as early as the 1960s (e.g. Bos 1964: 232), it was not until much later that similar constructions with *omdat* (24b) emerged. The grammaticality of such constructions as $AdjP_1$ *omdat* $AdjP_2$ (25) was even explicitly rejected (e.g. Heijden 1998). Meanwhile, constructions of the type $AdjP_1$ *want* $AdjP_2$ were considered grammatical, even though not generally accepted (Haeseryn et al. 1997: 1559; Broekhuis & Corver 2019: 207).

(25) **goede omdat dure sigaretten* (Heijden 1998: 38)
'good because expensive cigars'

The observation that non-finite causal constructions with *omdat* have emerged later than those with *want* makes it plausible to conclude that the *omdat* constructions have developed in analogy to the *want* constructions. Thus, the *omdat* X construction exemplifies a multiple-source construction. It combines the lineage of subordinating *omdat* clauses with the lineage of non-finite causal constructions with *want* in the connector slot (see Figure 1).

On the one hand, *omdat* X constructions represent a further development of *omdat* clauses, just as *want* X constructions are the continuation of *want* clauses. On the other hand, though, the wider variety of complements of *omdat* in *omdat* X must also have been influenced by the existence of functionally equivalent constructions like *want* X. Moreover, *want* X constructions themselves are also linked to other Dutch causal constructions. In particular, the combinations of *want* and noun phrases are connected both in their form and function to prepositional causal constructions with *vanwege* 'because of/due to', *wegens* 'because of/due to' and other prepositions. Against this backdrop, I will explore language contact, particularly language contact in online spaces, as an additional factor in the development of Dutch non-finite causal constructions in the next section.

4. Language contact in online spaces

In Sections 2 and 3, I have discussed the non-finite causal constructions *want* X and *omdat* X from a purely Dutch-centric perspective. One of the intriguing aspects of these non-finite causal constructions is, however, that formally and functionally equivalent constructions are attested in a wide range of languages, including English (26a), German (26b), Danish (26c), Czech (26d), Slovak (26e), French (26f), and Finnish (26g) (see, e.g. Bohmann 2016; Bergs 2018; Wessman 2017; Konvička 2020; 2024b; Wolfer, Müller-Spitzer & Ribeiro Silveira 2020; Konvička & Stöcker 2022).

(26) a. *Maybe I'll take dog and see if I can locate source... also peeing* ***because aging small dog bladder.*** (Twitter, 2019)

b. *Bin am überlegen mir The Quarry zu holen weil ich Until Dawn schon mega gefeiert hab, aber ich bin unsicher* ***weil Geld und so*** (Twitter, 2022)
'I'm thinking about buying The Quarry because I've really enjoyed Until Dawn, but I'm unsure because money and stuff'

c. *En fan med blognavnet Amen Fashion har mistet titlen,* ***fordi Lady Gaga*** (Twitter, 2011)
'A fan with the blog name Amen Fashion has lost the name because Lady Gaga.'

d. *Neboli hlasujte pro naše krajské kandidáty,* ***protože vláda, protože Babiš, protože Sobotka.*** (Konvička 2020: 244)
'In other words, vote for our regional candidates, because government, because Babiš, because Sobotka.'

e. *Prečo Mizík nie je Kotlebovej strany zmizík?* ***Lebo Fico*** (Twitter, 2017)
'Why is Mizík not the end of Kotleba's party? Because Fico'

f. *Je cours* ***parce que la pizza*** (Twitter, 2015)
'I run because pizza'

g. *Osta auto,* ***koska nopea, koska kaunis*** (Niemi 2015)
'Buy the car because fast, because nice.'

This list of languages featuring non-finite causal constructions is, however, not intended to be exhaustive. It merely illustrates their distribution. Although the constructions, as discussed in Sections 3.1 and 3.2, predate the rise of social media or the internet, online contexts play a significant role in their usage.

Constructions like *want* X are cross-linguistically more acceptable and frequently used in contexts of computer-mediated communication, including Twitter, other social media platforms, and WhatsApp messages. In these contexts, English plays a particularly significant role. In 2013, approximately 22% of all Twitter users originated from the United States, with about 51% of all tweets written in English. Similarly, in 2020, nearly a decade later, English remains the most commonly used language online, with a share of 25.9% (Johnson 2022). Although the nature of the present study does not permit us to draw any conclusions about the multilingualism of individual speakers/writers, based on data for Twitter in general, we can draw the following three concrete conclusions about language contact on the platform.

First, looking at the most used languages on Twitter, English is the language used in more than 51% of all tweets. This is at least based on a study of language use in tweets that identified 104 individual languages in a sample of 62 million tweets (Hong, Convertino & Chi 2011: 519).

Second, studies have shown that approximately 10% of all Twitter users are multilingual (see, e.g. Hale 2014). Not only do these users communicate in more than one language, but they are also more active than monolingual users, playing a crucial role as bridges between the language communities with which they interact. This suggests that the various languages used online do not represent separate and isolated languages but, at least to some degree, overlapping categories.

Third, we must also consider the global role of English as a lingua franca, a role that English also – or perhaps even more so – plays in digitally connected, translocal spaces such as social media (see, e.g. Pennycook 2007; Blommaert 2010; Pimienta, Prado & Blanco 2010).

Against this backdrop, it is probable that the non-finite causal constructions of the type *want* X in all the various languages listed in (26) arise not only from language-internal processes but also from language contact among them. Furthermore, this language contact occurs in online spaces rather than in the traditional sense of border regions characterised by a high degree of multilingualism.

This form of language contact taking place in online contexts can be described by the concept of *networked multilingualism* (Androutsopoulos 2015). Complementing traditional studies on language contact in physical contexts, this concept describes those

> multilingual practices that are shaped by two interrelated processes: being *networked*, i.e. digitally connected to other individuals and groups, and being *in the network*, i.e. embedded in the global digital mediascape of the web.
>
> (Androutsopoulos 2015: 187–188, original italics)

Alongside language-internal factors, as discussed in Section 3.1, networked multilingualism and, consequently, language contact through computer-mediated communication should be regarded as contributing factors in the emergence and spread of non-finite causal constructions in Dutch and other languages.

One of the central questions underlying all considerations of the influence of language contact is how we ascertain that contact with other languages really does play a role. As I showed in Section 3.1, the *want* X construction could also be partially explained in language-internal terms. Conversely, the existence of cross-linguistic equivalents of *want* X in many different languages and the use of these constructions within the context of networked multilingualism makes it difficult to rule out language contact as a factor completely. Therefore, the account of the development of Dutch non-finite causal constructions such as *want* X and *omdat* X should not side with either the language-internal or contact-induced explanation but should instead aim to integrate both.

5. Summary and concluding remarks

In this chapter, I have focused on the emergence and spread of the Dutch non-finite causal construction *want* X and its less frequent variant *omdat* X. The main question in this regard has been how much weight to put on language-external factors in contrast to language-internal ones. In this context, I have adopted an integrative approach that considers linguistic structures as generally having not just a single source but multiple ones: not only multiple sources within a single language, Dutch in the case of *want* X, but also multiple sources in more than one language.

To advocate for the integration of both language-internal and external sources in the development of Dutch non-finite causal constructions, I first outlined their historical context within Dutch and then the potential influences from other languages. Language-internally, I demonstrated that the foundation for the Present-Day *want* X constructions must be seen in causal clauses introduced by *want*. In certain contexts, these clauses can become textual ellipses, whereby the finite verb, typically a copula verb, is elided if this verb has already appeared in the matrix clause. These elliptical non-finite constructions can ultimately lead to non-elliptical causal constructions of the type *want* X. This scenario is not only supported by synchronic data on *want* X but is also backed by other processes that transition from non-elliptical constructions to novel non-ellipses through an intermediary stage of textual or contextual ellipses.

Besides *want* X, speakers of Dutch also have the variant *omdat* X at their disposal. Based on, among other things, meta-linguistic comments, I was able to show in Section 3.3 that *omdat* X must have emerged in analogy to *want* X and, therefore, also later. Currently, however, *omdat* X and *want* X are formally and functionally equivalent.

However, the Dutch non-finite causal constructions do not exist in isolation. Such constructions have been identified across a wide range of different languages. Most importantly for the present discussion, they are attested in English as well as in French, German, Czech, and Finnish. In all these languages, the non-finite causal constructions are particularly frequent in language used on social media. Consequently, a question arises as to whether the spread of this construction is due to parallel developments in all of them or whether the construction is a case of structural borrowing.

As we cannot dismiss either of these options, I propose treating *want* X and *omdat* X constructions as the outcomes of an interplay between both language-internal developments and language contact. Language contact in online spaces plays a particularly important role due to the frequent use of non-finite causal constructions on social media.

The role of language contact in the development of one specific construction in Dutch, which might be considered peripheral, also holds more general implications. The whole discussion about the importance of language-internal factors over language contact is based on the presupposition of the existence of individual, separable, and countable languages.

The need to decide whether to focus on language-internal developments or language contact phenomena arises only when we accept individual languages as the boundaries within which we conduct our considerations. Instead of thinking about constructions as belonging to languages, we might also think about constructions as belonging to communities (see, e.g. Höder 2012; 2018).

Languages are abstractions and, to a large degree, social constructs that can be made and unmade (see Krämer, Vogl & Kolehmainen 2022). The same applies to dialects and regional varieties so that eventually, the only reliable subject of analysis becomes the idiolect. At that point, however, the distinction between language-internal developments, i.e. idiolect-internal developments, and language contact, i.e. contact among individual idiolects, becomes baseless. To paraphrase a famous quote, it would be language contact all the way down.

What follows from this realisation is that language (or idiolect) contact should not be understood as a factor that "is never necessary" (Lass 1997: 209). On the contrary, endogenous factors should feature prominently in our analyses of the emergence of linguistic structures. One way to achieve this, as I have tried to show in this text, is to look not merely for a single origin of a construction but rather always to consider multiple sources.

References

American Dialect Society. 2014. "Because" is the 2013 Word of the Year. *American Dialect Society*. https://www.americandialect.org/because-is-the-2013-word-of-the-year. (9 November, 2018).

doi Androutsopoulos, Jannis. 2015. Networked multilingualism: Some language practices on Facebook and their implications. *International Journal of Bilingualism* 19(2). 185–205.

Bailey, Laura. 2012. Because reasons. *linguistlaura*. https://linguistlaura.blogspot.com/2012/07/because-reasons.html. (16 August, 2022).

Bailey, Laura R. & Olivia Seyerle. 2019. I didn't write this talk because syntax. European Dialect Syntax IX. Glasgow. https://kar.kent.ac.uk/93558/. (16 August, 2022).

doi Bergs, Alexander. 2018. Because science! Notes on a variable conjunction. In Elena Seoane, Carlos Acuña-Fariña & Ignacio Palacios-Martínez (eds.), *Subordination in English*, 43–60. Berlin: De Gruyter.

Bergs, Alexander. 2021. Because older than you think: tracing the diachrony of a 'new' causal conjunction. Presented at the International Conference on English Historical Linguistics (ICEHL-21), Leiden.

doi Blommaert, Jan. 2010. *The Sociolinguistics of Globalization*. Cambridge: Cambridge University Press.

doi Bohmann, Axel. 2016. Language change because Twitter? Factors motivating innovative uses of because across the English-speaking Twittersphere. In Lauren Squires (ed.), *English in computer-mediated communication. Variation, representation, and change*, 149–178. Berlin: De Gruyter.

Bos, Gijsbertha F. 1964. *Het probleem van de samengestelde zin*. The Hague: Mouton & Co.

Bree, Cor van. 1996. *Historische taalkunde*. Leuven: Acco.

Broekhuis, Hans & Norbert Corver. 2019. *Syntax of Dutch. Coordination and ellipsis*. Amsterdam: Amsterdam University Press.

doi Burger, Harald & Martin Luginbühl. 2014. Mündlichkeit und Schriftlichkeit. In *Mediensprache. Eine Einführung in Sprache und Kommunikationsformen der Massenmedien*, 173–200. 4th edn. Berlin: De Gruyter.

doi Colleman, Timothy. 2016. A reflection on constructionalization and constructional borrowing, inspired by an emerging Dutch replica of the 'time'-away construction. *Belgian Journal of Linguistics* 30. 91–113.

doi Declerck, Renaat & Susan Reed. 2001. *Conditionals: a comprehensive empirical analysis*. Berlin: Mouton de Gruyter.

Degand, Liesbeth. 1998. Het ideationele gebruik van want en omdat: Een geval van vrije variatie? *Nederlandse Taalkunde* 3. 309–326.

doi Filppula, Markku. 2003. The quest for the most "parsimonious" explanations: Endogeny vs. contact revisited. In Raymond Hickey (ed.), *Motives for language change*, 161–173. Cambridge: Cambridge University Press.

Geerts, G., W. Haeseryn, J. de Rooij & MC van den Toorn. 1984. *Algemene Nederlandse Spraakkunst*. Groningen: Wolters-Noordhoff.

Haeseryn, Walter, Kirsten Romijn, Guido Geerts, Jaap de Rooij & Maarten C. van den Toorn. 1997. *Algemene Nederlandse spraakkunst*. 2nd edn. Groningen: Nijhoff.

Hale, Scott A. 2014. Global connectivity and multilinguals in the Twitter network. In *Proceedings of the SIGCHI Conference on Human Factors in Computing Systems*, 833–842. Toronto Ontario Canada: ACM.

Heijden, Emmeken van der. 1998. Volgorderestricties en andere karakteristieke eigenschappen: principiële verschillen tussen nevenschikking en onderschikking. *Neerlandica extra muros* (36). 36–47.

Heine, Bernd & Tania Kuteva. 2020. Contact and Grammaticalization. In Raymond Hickey (ed.), *The Handbook of Language Contact*, 93–112. 2nd edn. Hoboken, NJ: Wiley.

Höder, Steffen. 2012. Multilingual constructions: A diasystematic approach to common structures. In Kurt Braunmüller & Christoph Gabriel (eds.), *Hamburg Studies on Multilingualism*, 241–258. Amsterdam: John Benjamins.

Höder, Steffen. 2018. Background and basic concepts of Diasystematic Construction Grammar. In Hans C. Boas & Steffen Höder (eds.), *Constructions in Contact: Constructional perspectives on contact phenomena in Germanic languages*, 37–70. Amsterdam: John Benjamins.

Hong, Lichan, Gregorio Convertino & Ed H. Chi. 2011. Language Matters in Twitter: A Large Scale Study. In *Proceedings of the Fifth International AAAI Conference on Weblogs and Social Media*, 518–521. https://www.aaai.org/ocs/index.php/ICWSM/ICWSM11/paper/view/2856/3250. (10 July, 2019).

Horst, Joop van der. 2004. Want en wegens. In Saskia Daalder, Theo A.J.M. Janssen & Jan Noordegraaf (eds.), *Taal in verandering. Artikelen aangeboden aan Arjan van Leuvensteijn bij zijn afscheid van de opleiding Nederlandse Taal en Cultuur aan de Vrije Universiteit Amsterdam*, 17–22. Münster: Stichting Neerlandistiek VU, Nodus Publikationen.

Hüning, Matthias. 2000. Het ontstaan van een morfologisch procédé. *Nederlandse Taalkunde* 5(2). 121–132.

Johnson, Joseph. 2022. Most common languages used on the internet as of January 2020, by share of internet users. https://www.statista.com/statistics/262946/share-of-the-most-common-languages-on-the-internet/. (22 February, 2022).

Joseph, Brian D. 2015. Multiple sources and multiple causes multiply explored. In Hendrik De Smet, Lobke Ghesquière & Freek Van de Velde (eds.), *On multiple source constructions in language change*, 205–221. Amsterdam: John Benjamins.

Kanetani, Masaru. 2019. *Causation and Reasoning Constructions*. Amsterdam: John Benjamins.

Knobloch, Clemens. 2013. „Ein Teil, das fehlt, geht nie kaputt" – Ellipsen in Grammatik und Kommunikation. In Mathilde Hennig (ed.), *Die Ellipse. Neue Perspektiven auf ein altes Phänomen*, 19–38. Berlin: De Gruyter.

Koch, Peter & Wulf Oesterreicher. 1985. Sprache der Nähe – Sprache der Distanz. Mündlichkeit und Schriftlichkeit im Spannungsfeld von Sprachtheorie und Sprachgeschichte. In Olaf Deutschmann, Hans Flasche, Bernhard König, Margot Kruse, Walter Pabst & Wolf-Dieter Stempel (eds.), *Romanistisches Jahrbuch*, 15–43. Berlin: Walter de Gruyter.

Konvička, Martin. 2018. Want/omdat X en de vaagheid van de linguïstische categorieën. *Neerlandica Wratislaviensia* 28. 17–31.

Konvička, Martin. 2019. De verborgen complexiteit van want/omdat X. *Internationale Neerlandistiek* 57(2). 161–183.

Konvička, Martin. 2020. Protože změna: K české kauzální konstrukci protože X. *Naše řeč* 103(3). 243–263.

Konvička, Martin. 2023. Category membership and category potential: The case of vague because. *Lexis. Journal in English lexicology* (22).

Konvička, Martin. 2024a. Cause and comment. Two functions of non-finite causal constructions. *Pragmatics & Cognition* 31(2). 318–338.

Konvička, Martin. 2024b. *Because reasons. Non-finite causal constructions in English, German, Dutch, and Czech.* PhD thesis. Berlin: Freie Universität Berlin.

Konvička, Martin & Kristin Stöcker. 2020. Because X in Dutch, English, and German. Corpus. GitHub. https://github.com/kwossi/becauseX. (18 February, 2022).

Konvička, Martin & Kristin Stöcker. 2022. (Non-)Ellipses in Dutch, English, and German: The case of because X. *Nederlandse Taalkunde* 27(3). 333–367.

Krämer, Philipp, Ulrike Vogl & Leena Kolehmainen. 2022. What is "Language Making"? *International Journal of the Sociology of Language* 2022(274). 1–27.

Kuitenbrouwer, Jan. 1987. *Turbotaal. Van socio-babble tot yuppie-speak.* Amsterdam: Aramith.

Landert, Daniela & Andreas H. Jucker. 2011. Private and public in mass media communication: From letters to the editor to online commentaries. *Journal of Pragmatics* 43(5). 1422–1434.

Lass, Roger. 1997. *Historical Linguistics and Language Change.* Cambridge: Cambridge University Press.

Lemmens, Marcel. 1991. Want-zinnen. Mag het ietsje minder zijn? *Onze Taal* 59. 14–15.

Pander Maat, Henk & Ted Sanders. 2000. Domains of use or subjectivity? The distribution of three Dutch causal connectives explained. In Elizabeth Couper-Kuhlen & Bernd Kortmann (eds.), *Cause – Condition – Concession – Contrast*, 57–82. Berlin: De Gruyter.

McCulloch, Gretchen. 2014. Where "because noun" probably came from. *All things linguistic.* http://allthingslinguistic.com/post/67507311833/where-because-noun-probably-came-from. (16 August, 2022).

Milroy, James. 2003. On the role of the speaker in language change. In Raymond Hickey (ed.), *Motives for language change*, 143–157. Cambridge: Cambridge University Press.

Niemi, Laura. 2015. Kokonainen lause ei mahdu, koska merkkimäärä. *Kotus-blogi – kaikkea kielestä.* Kotimaisten kielten keskus. https://web.archive.org/save/https://www.kotus.fi/nyt/kotus-blogi/blogiarkisto/laura_niemi/kokonainen_lause_ei_mahdu_koska_merkkimaara.14771.blog. (9 February, 2022).

Oostendorp, Marc van. 2014. Want boos/verdrietig/bekaf. https://neerlandistiek.nl/2014/01/want-boosverdrietigbekaf/. (8 February, 2022).

Pennycook, Alastair. 2007. *Global Englishes and Transcultural Flows.* London: Routledge.

Pimienta, Daniel, Daniel Prado & Álvaro Blanco. 2010. *Twelve years of measuring linguistic diversity in the Internet: balance and perspectives.* Paris: UNESCO.

Pit, Mirna, Henk Pander Maat & Ted Sanders. 1997. 'Doordat', 'omdat' en 'want'. Perspectieven op hun gebruik. *Taalbeheersing* 19(3). 238–251.

Rehn, Anneliise. 2015. Because Meaning: Language Change through Iconicity in Internet Speak. In *Summer Undergraduate Research Fellowship Conference Proceedings.* Berkeley, CA: University of California. https://escholarship.org/uc/item/0r44d2bh. (16 July, 2019).

doi Selting, Margret. 1997. Sogenannte ‚Ellipsen' als interaktiv relevante Konstruktionen? Ein neuer Versuch über die Reichweite und Grenzen des Ellipsenbegriffs für die Analyse gesprochener Sprache in der konversationellen Interaktion. In Peter Schlobinski (ed.), *Syntax des gesprochenen Deutsch*, 117–155. Opladen: Westdeutscher Verlag.

doi Sommerer, Lotte. 2023. If that's what she said, then that's what she said: a usage-based, constructional analysis of pleonastic conditionals in English. *Corpus Pragmatics* (7). 345–376.

Stefanowitsch, Anatol. 2014. Weil ist faszinierend, weil Sprachwandel. *Sprachlog*. http://www.sprachlog.de/2014/01/10/weil-ist-faszinierend-weil-sprachwandel/. (8 February, 2022).

doi Sweetser, Eve E. 1990. *From etymology to pragmatics. Metaphorical and cultural aspects of semantic structure*. Cambridge: Cambridge University Press.

Uit den Boogaart, P.C. 1986. PCUdB. *Onze Taal* (55). 108.

doi Van de Velde, Freek, Hendrik De Smet & Lobke Ghesquière. 2015. On multiple source constructions in language change. In Hendrik De Smet, Lobke Ghesquière & Freek Van de Velde (eds.), *On multiple source constructions in language change*, vol. 79, 1–17. Amsterdam: John Benjamins.

Vries, J.W. de. 1971. Want en omdat. *De nieuwe taalgids* 64(4). 414–420.

Wessman, Kukka-Maaria. 2017. Rating the acceptability of non-standard language. How Finnish language users rate variants of the verbless koska X 'because X' internet meme construction? Poster presented at the 14th International Cognitive Linguistics Conference, Tartu, Estonia.

Whitman, Neal. 2014. Why is the Word of the Year "because"? Because… *Visual Thesaurus*. web.archive.org/web/20160618092427/https://www.visualthesaurus.com/cm/dictionary/why-is-the-word-of-the-year-because-because/.

doi Wolfer, Sascha, Carolin Müller-Spitzer & Maria Ribeiro Silveira. 2020. Mit der Fähre nach Island, weil Flugangst. Textsortenspezifische Angemessenheit von weil mit Verbletztstellung, weil mit Verbzweitstellung und in elliptischen Konstruktionen empirisch untersucht. *Deutsche Sprache* (2). 174–192.

Zwicky, Arnold M. 2005. Just between Dr. Language and I. *Language Log*. http://itre.cis.upenn.edu/~myl/languagelog/archives/002386.html. (22 February, 2022).

Index of languages and language varieties

Dialects and languages within groups (such as Cantonese) can be found under the relevant standard language or language group (Chinese), but creole varieties such as Berbice Dutch or Creole English are given a separate entry, because of their hybrid nature.